NETWORKS

Timothy Ramteke

Prentice Hall Career and Technology
Englewood Cliffs, New Jersey 07632

Library of Congress Cataloging-in-Publication Data

Ramteke, Tiimothy.
  Networks / Timothy Ramteke.
     p.   cm.
  Includes bibliographical references and index.
  ISBN 0-13-958059-X
  1. Telecommunication. Computer networks. I. Title.
TK5101.R36 1994   93-41893
004.6--dc20   CIP

Acquisitions Editor: **Holly Hodder**
Editorial Assistant: **Melissa Steffens**
Marketing Manager: **Ramona Baran**
Managing Editors/production: **Mary Carnis and Patrick Walsh**
Director of Production Services: **David Riccardi**
Production Coordinator: **Ilene Levy Sanford**
Cover Design: **Laura Ierardi**
Cover Photo: courtesy of **Charles Becker** ©1992

© 1994 by Prentice Hall Career and Technology
Prentice-Hall, Inc.
A Paramount Communications Company
Englewood Cliffs, New Jersey 07632

Although, tediously, every effort was made to ensure the integrity of this text, the publisher assumes no responsibility for errors, or for damages incurred from using its information.

Printed in the United States of America
10 9 8 7 6 5 4 3 2 1

ISBN 0-13-958059-X

Prentice-Hall International (UK) Limited, London
Prentice-Hall of Australia Pty. Limited, Sydney
Prentice-Hall Canada Inc., Toronto
Prentice-Hall Hispanoamericana, S.A., Mexico
Prentice-Hall of India Private Limited, New Delhi
Prentice-Hall of Japan, Inc., Tokyo
Simon & Schuster Asia Pte. Ltd., Singapore
Editora Prentice-Hall do Brasil, Ltda., Rio de Janeiro

. . . in honor of Father and Mother,
who with love, worked hard for others.

Overview

Contents

PART II: VOICE NETWORKING

PART III: WIDE AREA NETWORKS

9/28/93

Preface

The network of wire cables of a suspension bridge provides support for vehicular traffic. Likewise, protocols used in telecommunications support information traffic between end-system applications. These protocols have recently become quite sophisticated as more enhancements are introduced. Nonetheless, network protocols have become crucial to almost all businesses, especially as they become international. Just as bridges are necessary to move goods and materials between separated land masses, so must telecommunication networks provide a smooth transfer of information of all kinds.

The task of presenting the complex and changing field of networks is impossible for one person to handle. Thus, the skills of many were pooled together to create this text. Each expert in his/her field made the information presented in these pages relevant and current. Despite their very busy schedules, these experts were willing to provide extensive professional assistance. Their names are listed as footnotes on the chapter title pages. A special thought of gratitute is extended to those whose names did not get mentioned, for one reason or another. I am grateful and indebted to each of them for their thoughful contributions.

The text will be most useful to those who have had a course in data communications. However, the fundamentals necessary for the understanding of networks are reviewed in the first part of the text: Chapters 1 through 4. The second part, Chapters 5 through 11, covers voice networks in detail. The third part covers WANs (Wide Area Networks) in Chapters 12 through 15. The remaining four chapters cover LANs (Local Area Networks) and how they are integrated with WANs. These divisions are idealistic, since these categories tend to overlap one other throughout the text.

Four sequences of topics have been depicted in Figure A. They are digital transmissions, voice networks, WANs, and LANs. Each of these sequences may represent an independent course, taken in junior or senior years of college or in a graduate level course. This book then can be used for courses which concentrate on each of these sequences. Each sequence depends on the topics covered in the first four chapters.

Every section of each chapter is important. However, due to lack of time one may need to limit coverage of every section. As a suggestion, the most important sections of each chapter are indicated. One may decide to select different sets of sections, depending on what will be emphasized. The chapters that are not prerequisites for others are shown off to a side. However, the text should be used sequentially, whenever possible.

Reader comments, questions, and especially suggestions for improvements are welcome. Please feel free to write to me at 47 Duke St, New Brunswick, NJ, 08901 or on the internet at ramteke@pilot.njin.net

Many thanks to Holly Hodder, Melissa Steffens, Mary Carnis, Pat Walsh, and others at Prentice Hall. Also, thanks to Steve Jobs and many others for giving us the Macintosh, along with MacDraw and PageMaker, use of which made creating this text fun. Additionally, I would like to thank my wife, Beth Binde, for teaching me Unix. Together with her, my thanks to Mom, Daniel, Sarah, and Jonathan for helping around the house. Lastly, with due respect to all faiths, allow me to praise and glorify my Lord Jesus Christ for saving me from sin.

Keep on networking!

Tim

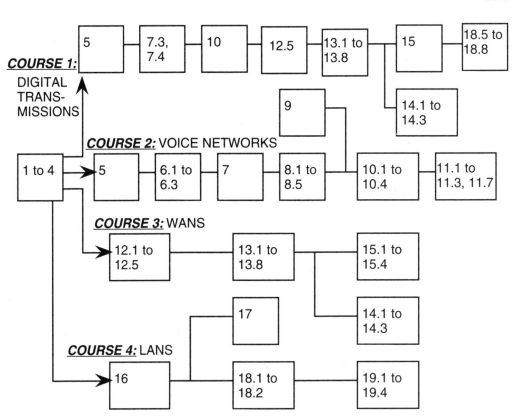

Figure A The four courses which this text can support and their respective sequence of chapters/sections.

Chapter 1

Welcome to Telecommunications

Telecommunications is a very dynamic and changing field. There are always new technologies being developed and adopted on all fronts, which makes it an exciting field to be in. These first four chapters take the view that the reader is new to the field and so sets the groundwork that is needed for the chapters which follow. This chapter, in particular, provides a historical perspective which give reasons as to why things are the way they are today. It also provides fundamental concepts of how a simple telephone call is made and gives an introduction to the various standard organizations.

1.1 HISTORICAL SURVEY

1.1.1 The 1800s

Telecommunications means communications at a distance just as telescope refers to a device which enables one to see objects at a distance. As we know today, telecommunications started with the telegraph. It was invented by a physicist name Henry in 1831. However, Samuel Morse made its use practical by inventing the repeater, which allowed transmissions for longer distances.

In 1845, the Western Union Telegraph Co. was formed and by 1861, the first telegraph lines spanning the continent were installed. The first Trans-Atlantic cable was installed in 1865 and the world was on its way to interconnecting itself with networks.

It was as early as 1854 when Philip Reise was able to send sound over wires. Many consider him to be the inventor of the telephone. However, it wasn't until 1876 that Alexander Bell obtained the patent for it. On the same day that Bell invented the telephone, Eliza Gray also invented the telephone, independently.

Bell tried to sell his invention to Western Union, but was laughed at and was turned down. This was similar to when the inventors of the first digital computer, John

---

Chapters 1 through 4 and 6 have been augmented by Wally Bartus of AT&T, the most dynamic teacher in the field.

Atanasoff and Clifford Berry, approached IBM and were told that IBM would never be interested in electronic computers. Bell formed his own company in June of 1877 and called it the Bell Telephone Company. In 1879, he bought out Western Electric and in 1885, Bell incorporated AT&T (American Telephone & Telegraph).

1.1.2 The Independents

When, in 1893 the telephone patent ran out, many independent telephone companies were formed. They were mostly interested in serving the rural areas which AT&T didn't find profitable. Soon the independents were also bringing their services into the cities. It became necessary for a home to have several phones if access to all surrounding areas was needed, one for each telephone company. This was necessary, because the Bell system didn't interconnect with them and so the network services had to be duplicated, at least in urban areas.

Soon AT&T was buying up the independents. The Department of Justice insisted that AT&T violated the Sherman Anti-Trust Act. In response, Nathan Kingsbury, a vice president of AT&T, issued a unilateral letter, rather than a consent decree, called the Kingsbury Commitment in 1913. It ensured that AT&T would not buy out any more independents and would allow the independent networks to be interconnected with its own and would dispose of its Western Union stock. This meant that now homes only needed one telephone and that today we still have the existence of these independents. Currently, there are approximately 1400 independents.

Realizing the monopolizing nature of AT&T, Congress signed the Communications Act of 1934. From this the FCC (Federal Communications Commission) was created to protect the public from high prices and poor service.

Today, the FCC regulates interstate and international communications. "Inter" means between places while "intra" means within a place. For instance an interstate highway exists between states and an intrastate highway exists within a state. The PUCs (Public Utility Commissions), which come under the jurisdiction of each state, control and regulate intra-state communications.

1.1.3 The Road to Divestiture

Moving quickly to 1968, the Carterfone Decision allowed private devices to be connected to the telephone network. In this decision, the FCC decreed that AT&T could not prohibit connections, but could establish standards that must be met by connecting devices. This stimulated companies to buy PBXs from companies other than the local telephone companies.

In the same year, William McGowan met Jack Goeken. McGowan was a Harvard Business School graduate. He found out that Goeken's company called MCI (Microwave Communications, Inc.) was not permitted to build a microwave link for truckers operating between Chicago and St. Louis. MCI was opposed by AT&T, General Telephone, Illinois Bell, Southwestern Bell, and Western Union.

Everyone who was in the telecommunications industry believed that it was nonsense to try to fight the FCC and AT&T. However, McGowan knew nothing about telecommunications. He set up his office close to the FCC in Washington, D.C. and within three years was able to provide this service to not only the truckers but also to other businesses. Needless to say, soon other cities were being served and other carriers were being established. In 1974 McGowan filed a lawsuit against AT&T for antitrust violations and in 1975, the Department of Justice did the same which eventually led to the divestiture of the Bell System in 1984. Divestiture means creating separate independent companies out of one. Even Robert Allen of AT&T said that McGowan, more than anyone else, reshaped the monopolistic industry to be a highly competitive one.

Going back to 1949, the Justice Department tried to break up the Bell System by making Western Electric independent. However, in 1956 a Consent Decree was signed that allowed Western Electric to be part of AT&T as long as it only furnished common carrier communication services.

As a modification to this decree, the MFJ (Modified Final Judgment) was approved by Judge Harold Green in 1983 and took effect on January 1, 1984. It created eight independent companies out of the Bell system. These were AT&T and seven RBOCs (Regional Bell Operating Companies).

At that time there were 23 local BOCs (Bell Operating Companies), out of which SNET (Southern New England Telephone) and Cincinnati Bell remained with AT&T while the other 21 BOCs were divided among the RBOCs. The RBOCs are Ameritech, Bell Atlantic, Bell South, Nynex (NY and New England eXchange), Pacific Telesis, Southwestern Bell, and US West. Bellcore (Bell Communications Research) was created for all the RBOCs and the Bell Labs remained with AT&T. They serve as research and development facilities.

1.2 HANDLING OF CALLS

1.2.1 LATAs, IXCs, and LECs

At the time of divestiture, the country was divided into 184 LATAs. (Local Access and Transport Areas). These areas were divided so as to define the share of the business between the BOCs and the long distance companies. In 1993, there were 189 LATAs, out of which 161 were Bell LATAs and 28 were independent LATAs.

LATA boundaries are determined by community of interest and usually don't change. Although LATA boundaries follow state boundaries and area code boundaries in many cases, they don't have to. Consider Figure 1.1 where the LATAs are shown for the state of California. Here, the area code for Pasadena and Los Angeles are different, but they are in the same LATA, whereas the area code for Stockton and Fresno are the same but are in different LATAs. When most phone numbers available in an area code become assigned, it becomes necessary to split it into two area codes, thereby doubling the number of available phone numbers. Americans today are using more phone numbers than they did before, because of the proliferation of modems, cellular phones, and fax machines.

The term telco (telephone company) is used to refer to the operating company in the local area, whether it be a BOC or an independent. The telco is also called the LEC (Local Exchange Carrier). Here, the term "exchange" refers to a LATA and not the 3-digit number which comes after an area code in a phone number. Most telecommunications traffic within a LATA is handled by the telco, with increasing inroads made by cellular carriers.

Long distance carriers such as AT&T, MCI and Sprint, which haul traffic between LATAs are called IECs or IXCs (InterEXchange Carriers). In the last figure, 11 LATAs are shown out of which 10 are Bell LATAs served by Pacific Bell. The one independent LATA is served by GTE. There are many independent companies operating within these LATAs. However, regardless of who the telcos are, if the call is being made within a LATA, it is usually handled by the LECs. Calls which cross a LATA boundary must be handled by an IXC. In this case, there may be more than two carriers which handle the call: the LEC which connects the caller to the IXC, the IXC itself, and the LEC which connects the IXC to the person being called.

For example, in Figure 1.1, we see that Santa Cruz and Crescent City although far from each other and having separate area codes are part of the same LATA, and calls between them are handled by the LECs. This call doesn't require the services of an IXC, because the call is within the same LATA.

However, if a person in Santa Cruz makes a call close by to Monterey, using the same area code does require the services of an IXC. This is because the call is an inter-LATA call.

Originally, the RBOCs were not allowed to compete in the long distance services, manufacturing and information services. In 1991, the ban on information services was removed and at the time of this writing, there is activity to remove the ban on long distance services and open the competition within the LATAs.

1.2.2 Defining Terms and Call Routing

Let us first define some terms using Figure 1.2 which are necessary in order to examine how calls are routed.

A line is a link which connects a terminal (such as a telephone) to a network. A switch is typically an electronic device which provides a connection between two lines or trunks. A trunk is a connection between two switches and a trunk group is a collection of trunks between one pair of switches.

A CO (Central Office) is a building where the telco terminates all telephone lines from the local area and connects these lines to the switches which are inside the CO. A PBX (Private Branch eXchange) is a switch which provides switching between extensions in one facility such as a building. A CO is for the use of the public but a PBX is primarily for the use of the building occupants. Chapters 7 and 8 discuss COs and PBXs further.

Figure 1.2 shows an example of how these items may be interconnected. Let us see how various types of calls are handled. When phones which are attached to the same CO connect, it is called an intra-office call. The term "office" here refers to a CO. For example, a call between 356-2512 and 356-9199 is an intra-office call while a call between 356-2512 and 718-1212 is an inter-office call.

The phones in the building are considered to be phones in a private network, while all the remaining ones are considered to be part of the public network. The formal name for the public network is the PSTN (Public Switched Telephone Network). The PSTN is also referred to as the DDD (Direct Distance Dialing) cloud. DDD implies that the network can allow a person to make long distance calls without the assistance of operators. IDDD (International DDD) refers to the PSTN which extends around the globe.

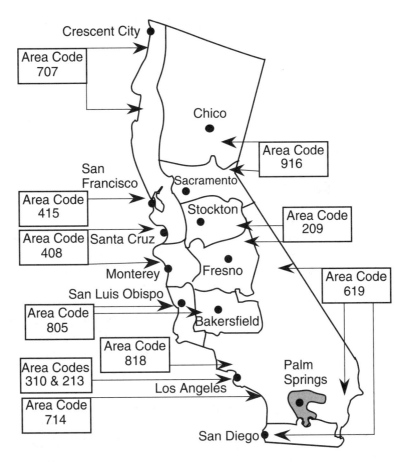

Figure 1.1 This map shows the ten LATAs of California, which are called service areas by Pacific Bell. The LATA shown as shaded is entirely served by GTE and not by Pac-Bell. Notice that an area code such as 916 may span two LATAs, and one LATA, such as the San Francisco LATA, may have several area codes.

When a phone from the PSTN calls the main number of the building, the attendant (previously referred to as the switchboard operator) may answer the call and transfer it to an extension in the building.

Private telephones in the building simply dial an extension to reach someone else in the building. To reach someone in the PSTN, the person at an extension must first get a dial tone from the PBX. Then he/she must dial a special digit called an access code such as 9, and then receive a dial tone from the CO. Now the person may dial anywhere he/she wishes in the public network, depending on the privileges granted by the PBX.

As we have said, IXCs must handle inter-LATA calls. They use POPs (Point Of Presence) to interface their networks with those of the telcos. For an IXC to have coverage in all parts of the country, it must have at least one POP in every LATA. When a CO hands off a call from a customer to an IXC, it usually has predefined that

Welcome to Telecommunications

customer's primary IXC. This is called presubscription. It can be changed from call to call by dialing special digits.

Now, if extension 4816 dials 389-1167 over the public network, the telco's network knows which POP to hand the call over to. If the call is presubscribed to Sprint, then the Sprint POP on the egress side (receiving side) will hand the call over to the CO belonging to the local telco, which then connects the call to 389-1167.

Hence, intra-facility calls are typically handled by a PBX and intra-LATA calls by the COs. Finally, inter-LATA calls are handled by two or more COs, POPs, and possibly PBXs.

1.3 STANDARDS

1.3.1 Open Systems

Traditionally, computer and communications companies tried to commit their customers to their own specific product line. Because of the investment made in the vendors' products, the customers were locked in. If the customer received poor service, the vendor wasn't much concerned, because the chance that the customer would scrap his/her investment and switch to another vendor was slim. Also, from the customer's perspective if the new vendor might prove to be the same way or even worse.

Today, vendors are still trying to keep customers using proprietary solutions, but customers are starting to look for open systems. An open system, although difficult to

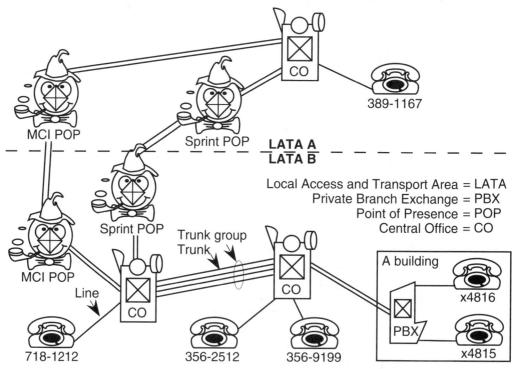

Figure 1.2 Calls can be handled in various ways.

define, means that the customer can use his existing product on any computer or network. Also, open system products can be purchased from several vendors—the customer is not locked in with one vendor.

Lets look now at some examples of proprietary and open products. The Intel 586 microprocessor is a relatively proprietary product, whereas the SPARC (Scalable Processor ARChitecture) chip is an open solution or a standard. Other vendors can manufacture it freely. Similarly, mainframe computers and their operating systems such as IBM's MVS are proprietary solutions, while the IBM's PC and Unix are standards or open systems.

The PC is open, since many companies are allowed to make it. This is because initially, IBM didn't expect it to sell as well as it did. On the other hand, the Macintosh is a proprietary product. In the networking arena, OSI (Open Systems Interconnection) is an open network architecture. An application which is written to operate on OSI can run on any hardware, operating system, or network as long as it is OSI based. On the other hand, IBM's SNA (Systems Network Architecture) is not completely open nor completely proprietary.

There are many reasons why customers are choosing open system products, the most important one being the protection of their investment. If the system is open and the customer doesn't like the vendor he/she can switch vendors and still protect his investment. When there is competition, service from all vendors improves and prices go down, even when the vendor with which a customer is dealing provides good service. It is easier to hire skilled personnel. Many vendors claim that their product is open, but one should be careful that they are not misled into a proprietary system, although there may be reasons to go that route.

1.3.2 Organizations

Figure 1.3 shows many of the standard organizations. The hierarchical structure relating the various organizations does not hold true that rigidly. They all interface with one another to some degree.

In the UN (United Nations), there is the ITU (International Telecommunications Union) which is based in Geneva. It consists of CCITT (Consultative Committee for International Telegraph and Telephone) and CCIR (Consultative Committee for International Radio). CCIR assigns radio frequencies that effect international boundaries similar to what the FCC does domestically.

CCITT receives its input from various organizations. PTTs (Post, Telegraph, and Telephones) are government monopolies similar to our postal system in America. Most countries in the world have their own PTTs which provide their telecommunications services. The only voting members of CCITT are the PTTs and the US Department of State.

ANSI (American National Standards Institute) is probably the next most important organization for us. It is the dominant one in setting American standards.

The ISO (International Standards Organization) sets standards for nuts, bolts, film type, etc. In telecommunications it is noted for setting the OSI reference model.

IEEE (Institute of Electrical and Electronic Engineers) is a professional society. It is responsible for setting many of the LAN standards covered in Chapter 16.

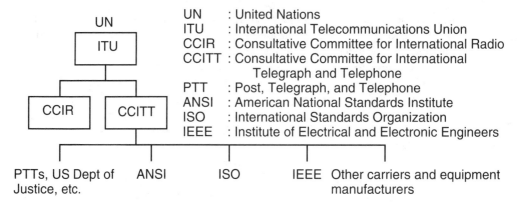

Figure 1.3 Some important standards organizations.

Aside from these organizations, there are many carriers and equipment manufacturers which are represented in the CCITT.

Bellcore also has been very active in recommending standards such as SONET (chapter 15) and SMDS (chapter 18). SONET (Synchronous Optical NETwork) is a standard used to transport digital signals over fiber and SMDS (Switched Multimegabit Data Services) is used to interconnect LANs over a wide geographical region.

Since standards take a relatively long time to become established, many vendors and users are creating forums which help a new technology get off its feet quickly. The frame relay forum is a good example of such a forum. It was able to move a concept to reality in a matter of two years. Currently, the ATM forum is very active.

One last comment should be made about de facto standards. They are standards not because any agency has approved them, but they are standards solely on the fact that they exist and are used. Sometimes official standards are first approved then the engineers try to make them work. On the other hand, de facto standards are not accepted by the industry until they are proved to work. An example of such a standard is TCP/IP (Transmission Control Protocol/Internet Protocol) which is only documented in a large number of RFCs (Request For Comments). Although no standards body originally approved this set of internetworking protocols, it became more popular than OSI simply because it works.

Exercises

1. Who received the patent for the telephone?
   a. Reise   b. Morse
   c. Bell   d. Gray

2. What prefix means between places?
   a. inter   b. intra
   c. intro   d. pre

3. Who was probably the most responsible for breaking up the Bell System?
   a. Judge Green
   b. McGowan
   c. Robert Allen
   d. FCC

4. Which system provides intra-facility switching?
   a. CO
   b. POP
   c. PBX
   d. trunk group

5. Who were some of the inventors of the telephone?

6. To protect the public interest from AT&T's monopoly, what did Congress do?

7. What was the MFJ modifying?

8. Within what area may an LEC handle the entire call?

9. When more phone numbers need to be made available, what is done?

10. What is the opposite of an open system?

11. Describe the Kingsbury Commitment and its effects.

12. What historical event was similar to when Western Union showed no interest in Bell's telephone?

13. List some key events and their dates that led to the breakup of the Bell System.

14. What are some advantages that one can give about the Bell breakup? Disadvantages?

15. Describe how an inter-LATA call is made and what points the call goes through.

16. Describe the advantages from a user point of view of having an open system and a proprietary system.

Chapter 2

Network Architectures and OSI

2.1 WHAT IS A NETWORK?

In the early days when computers came into existence, most businesses only had one large computer to do their processing. Because of the expense, processing was even sent off to other computer facilities and the charges were based on CPU time and other items. The computer was located in one room where workers brought their computer jobs, coded in stacks of punched cards. These were then read by a card reader.

Today, although we still have data centers, much of the processing is being off-loaded to smaller computers, many times located on desktops. So instead of depending on one computer to do all the work, we have many smaller computers at our disposal. And instead of us having to walk down the hall to submit our jobs to the computer, the computer has come to the workers and their desktops.

Furthermore, since the combined power of many small systems (or computers) is greater than the power of one large system, these smaller systems are tied together using data communication links. These interconnections of computers, which are self-governing and not controlled by one another, are called networks. An internet is a network of networks.

Currently, just as it is necessary for a computer to be properly powered, so has it become necessary for a computer to be connected in a network to be useful. Hence, we have a "marriage" of communications and computers. Data communications is not possible without computers and computers are almost useless without data communications.

So anyway, what is a network? A network can simply be definded as the interconnection of two or more independent computers or switches. A "good network" should be a network that doesn't look like a network to the end user. The end user should not have to specify the route through which data is acquired; that should be the concern of the networking software.

There are primarily two types of networks; LANs (Local Area Networks) typically provide networking capabilities within a facility (or a building). However, they can extend to adjacent facilities in a campus environment and can span distances of two or three miles. WANs (Wide Area Networks) span much greater distances and even go around the globe. There are also MANs (Metropolitan Area Networks), which are difficult to define as either WANs or LANs. Since the characteristics of WANs and LANs differ substantially, the last half of the text is divided into these two sections.

2.2 WHY NETWORK?

One reason to network is that the sharing of resources can be done easily. Resources are application programs (such as word processing packages), data, printers, modems, etc. In a LAN environment, instead of needing to install a word processing package on each and every station, we only need to install it on a file server. Of course, we must have the necessary licence. This makes the package available to all. Similarly, instead of buying each computer a low-cost printer, we can buy a few high speed, high quality printers which are accessible to all.

Networks also provide reliability. In the 1960s, if the central computer was down, then no one could process any jobs. But today, with multiple computers available, if one goes down, we still have many others to fall back on.

It is true that one large mainframe (computer) has maybe ten times the processing power of that of a high-end microcomputer. However, the mainframe costs at least 1000 times as much. So for the same money spent on a mainframe, we could buy 1000 microcomputers and after networking them, could have 100 times as much processing power than a mainframe.

Networks also allow us to be mobile. If we have an account on a computer in Dallas, and happen to be in San Francisco one week, we can still log on to the computer in Dallas from San Francisco, if the two sites are part of a network. We are not forced to be in the same place where our computing facility happens to be.

In a LAN environment, we don't have to depend on every worker to back up their work each day. From one central computer, an operator can back up everyone's work on a regular basis. Basically, networking makes administration of the computer systems more manageable.

2.3 NETWORK ARCHITECTURES

2.3.1 What is a Network Architecture?

The remainder of this chapter explains the concepts of network architectures, which, although not that complicated, are difficult for the beginner to grasp. Since every single chapter on WANs and LANs is based on this one, it is imperative that the reader gain a good understanding of this material. To reinforce the concepts and ideas presented, there is a liberal use of analogies.

When building a house, although it is possible for one person to do so alone, a contractor will usually have teams of workers specializing in their fields do their part of the job. The excavators dig the ground, the masons lay the foundation, the carpenters put up the frame, etc. Each team does its own part of the job. This way the functions of building a house have been divided into distinct components.

Similarly, when designing a network, since this is also a complex task, it is designed using distinct components called layers. Each layer serves a certain function or purpose in the entire networking scheme. These functions could be, for instance, to check for errors in transmission or to encrypt (scramble) data, or a number of other things.

By designing a network into layers, we can isolate such networking functions into modules, which individually become easier to design than if the entire network were designed as one whole piece. In the previous analogy, that would represent having one person build the entire house.

By separating a network into layers, we can also make the network more flexible to implement changes in the future. That is, if a new method of performing the services of a layer is invented, we can swap it with the old method used in that layer. Then we can see if the network performance improves. If it does, good; if not, we can revert back to the old method easily. The set of methods and rules used in a particular layer is called that layer's protocol.

For example, if the protocol used by the excavators was to use picks and shovels, and now we want to change that protocol to using a steam shovel, or later, a backhoe, then we can try changing it and see if it works better. To the masons, it doesn't matter how the excavators dig the hole. The excavators provide their services to the masons who continue the job from there. The services provided by a layer to the upper adjacent layer is called an interface.

Figure 2.1 shows a computer called Host A transmitting data to Host B, made by different manufacturers. Of course, communication may also occur in the opposite direction. This network is shown as using only three layers. The definitions of the layers and the interfaces between them is called a network architecture. A network architecture differs from our builders in the sense that the builders are always going up the layers, i.e., from the excavators to the roofers. In data communication, it is called a simplex transmission or data only goes one way, as to a printer.

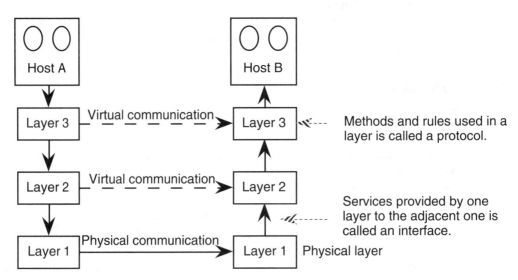

Figure 2.1 Transmission of data from Host A to Host B over a network is shown in solid arrows. There is no direct communication between peer layers except at the physical layer.

A network architecture should be able to handle transmission in both directions, either using half-duplex or full-duplex methods. Half-duplex is the transmission of data in one direction at a time and full duplex is the simultaneous transmission in both directions. In the figure, Host A sends data, it is processed by layer 3 and sent to layer 2. The protocol at layer 2 processes what layer 3 has forwarded to it and sends the data to layer 1.

Layer 1 then sends the data over a physical communication link to layer 1 of Host B. This same process is done in reverse, until the data reaches Host B. Layer 1 is always called the physical layer, because over this layer, the actual data is sent and received. Hence, the communication between layer 1s is called physical communication and between the upper layers is called virtual communication. The protocol for all the layers except for the first one is implemented in software. We can think of layer 1 as a modem for now.

2.3.2 Examples of Network Architectures

There are many network architectures that are defined. Some are proprietary used by one particular vendor and some are standards used by more than one vendor.

SNA (Systems Network Architecture) is the architecture defined by IBM. Originally, it used only one host or mainframe. See Figure 2.2. This was locally connected by a FEP (Front End Processor) which handled all the communications related processing for the host. The FEP was then connected to cluster controllers, possibly in many different cities using communication links. The cluster controllers were then connected to dumb (or without a CPU) terminals.

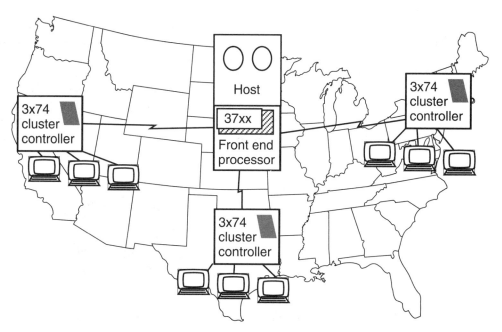

Figure 2.2 An example of an SNA network.

The cluster controllers received all the data for the terminals and properly distributed it. SNA was run on such networks, but today it has evolved into a much more sophisticated network called APPN (Advanced Peer to Peer Networking). There are others such as DECnet and AppleTalk that are proprietary architectures. DECnet is evolving into a network architecture called OSI.

OSI (Open Systems Interconnection) Reference Model is an international standard set forth by ISO (International Standards Organization). It allows for networking between hosts made by any vendor.

The family of LAN architectures, which is a subset of OSI, include IEEE 802.3 and IEEE 802.5. These architectures are run on Ethernet and TRN (Token Ring Network) networks, respectively. Figure 2.3(a) shows an Ethernet where stations are connected to one cable called a bus and Figure 2.3(b) shows a TRN where stations are connected in a ring.

2.3.3 Another Analogy

Let us review the basic concepts underlying network architectures as explained using Figure 2.1 before we go into more detail.

In Figure 2.4, we have two users, A and B representing the two hosts in Figure 2.1. However, here we have only two layers shown instead of three. User A is in Germany and user B is in India. They want to communicate with each other using morse code. We don't have translators between German and Marathi (an Indian language), but we do have English translators to each language. So when a person in Germany says in German that I want to go home, the protocol used in the second layer translates it into English. This message is then forwarded to the telegraph operator who converts it to morse code.

The telegraph operator who is part of the physical layer in India receives the message and forwards it to its second layer, which translates it for the person in India.

If we change the protocol used in the first layer from a telegraph system to a telephone system or a postal system, all we need to do is to replace that one protocol. This does not effect the second layer. The services the second layer receives is the same. Likewise, network architectures provide specific networking services between their layers. The protocol used in a specific layer is a concern for that layer and does not concern any other, although the overall performance of the network is dependent on the protocols used at each layer.

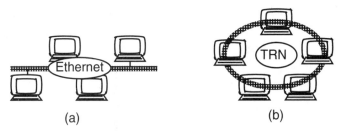

(a)   (b)

Figure 2.3 (a) An Ethernet LAN. (b) A Token Ring Network.

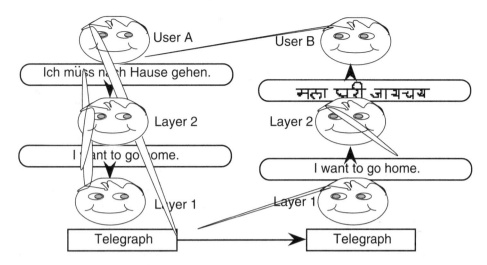

Figure 2.4 An analogy of a network architecture is a person in Germany communicating with a person in India, which requires the message to be transformed in various ways.

2.4 OSI

In the previous analogy, the entire message at each layer was transformed. However, in network architectures, although this can happen, headers and trailers can also be added by the protocol at each layer. Let us now look at the layers of OSI, the architecture that other architectures are compared against in data networking.

2.4.1 Overview of OSI

Figure 2.5 shows the seven layers of the OSI reference model. They are physical, data link, network, transport, session, presentation, and application. Each layer serves its own set of functions which we will outline later on, but for now let us see how these layers are interrelated.

When a host transmits data over the network, it is first handed over to the protocol used in the application layer. The application layer will process this data and may add some control information in a field called the header. This header is intended for the application layer on the receive end and forms the means for the two peer application layers to communicate virtually. The data, along with the application header, is called an APDU or an application PDU (Protocol Data Unit).

This APDU then is forwarded by the application layer to the presentation layer in the transmitting host. The APDU, including the application header, becomes the data portion for the PDU at the presentation layer. This is called the PPDU (Presentation PDU). The presentation header is the means for this presentation layer to communicate with its peer presentation layer at the receive end. The PPDU is handed over to the session layer.

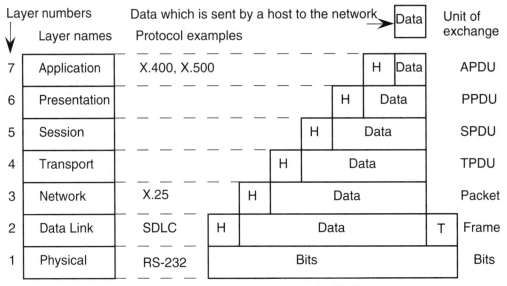

PDU : Protocol Data Unit,   H : Header,   T : Trailer

Figure 2.5 The OSI reference model. Layers 1, 2, and 3 make up the communications subnet.

This process is repeated for each layer, until at the data link layer, a trailer is added as well. Finally, the physical layer transmits the second layer's frame using a bit stream.

On the receive side, this process is done in reverse. The first layer receives the bits and hands over a frame to its second layer protocol. It then strips off the header and trailer, processes whatever is encoded in them, such as check for data errors, and hands off the data portion of the frame to the third layer.

The third layer considers the data portion of the frame as a packet, strips off the header and processes it. The data portion of the packet is then handed over to the fourth layer. This is repeated until the application layer forwards its data to its user for whom the data is intended. And if all the protocols are implemented properly, the receiving host can interpret the transmitting host's message. This is done despite the differences that exist between the hosts, regardless of their vendors, operating speeds, sizes, and so on. The obvious inherent tradeoff is a large increase in overhead for the flexibility of communicating with diverse systems.

2.4.2 The Communication Subnet

The reader may want to study Section 2.4.3 at this time that describes an analogy for what is covered in this section.

The lower three layers of the model serve a set of functions that differ from those served by the upper four layers. The components of the lower three layers are part of what is called the communications subnet. These three layers are concerned about getting the data to the correct node in the network using the available communication links and packet switches. A packet switch is a generic term used for processors which route packets to the correct network node using these three layers. It can also be thought of as a router. A bridge, on the other hand, forwards frames using only the lower two layers of the OSI model.

The upper four layers are processed by the host and pertain to how the end users are using their applications. Although all seven layers can be implemented in a host, the function of the lower three layers is to route packets to the correct node.

For example, we have three hosts (also called end systems) which are connected to each other using three communication links as shown in Figure 2.6. Each of the three hosts are concurrently processing several jobs or applications. In order for them to communicate with one another they must use the three layers of the subnet.

Here, Host A is sending data to Host C. The 3rd layer in Host A encodes its packet with a DA (Destination Address) of Host C. However, although the communication link labeled Link 1 would be more direct, let us say that there is other traffic on it from other applications and is therefore getting congested. Hence, the network layer chooses to send the packet via link 2. The 2nd layer encodes the DA of Host B in its frame and sends it over the first layer.

Host B's second layer strips off the header and hands over the packet to layer 3. Layer 3 looks at the DA of Host C and doesn't hand over the data portion of the packet to its layer 4, but instead reconstructs the packet and sends it back down to layer 2. This layer encodes a DA of Host C and sends the frame over link 3.

The network layer at host C detects its own DA and doesn't reroute the packet like Host B did. Instead, the packet's data is sent to Host C's 4th layer whose data then reaches the user there. Host B has acted as a packet switch, also called an intermediate system. On the other hand, Hosts A and C have behaved as end systems.

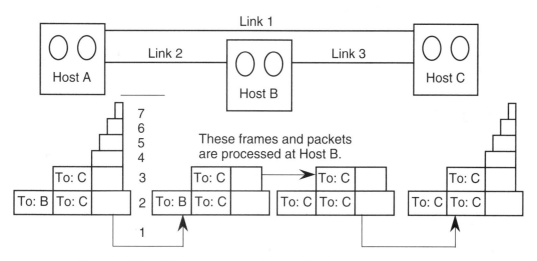

Figure 2.6 Host B is acting as a packet switch as Host A sends a message to Host C. The arrows show how the data is moved.

2.4.3 An Analogy for a Subnetwork

Considering another analogy depicted in Figure 2.7, a person who lives in San Diego is sending a birthday card to her cousin in Chicago. The postal distribution center, acting as the fourth layer in this example, sends it off into in a bag labeled for Chicago.

The postal workers at the airport performing layer 3 services decide the bag must go via Denver. The workers performing layer 2 services place this bag in an aircraft container headed for Denver. The airplane, our physical layer transportation system, gets the container to the Denver airport. Here, the layer 2 personnel take the bags out of the container and give them to the layer 3 personnel to sort them out.

The layer 3 personnel sort out these bags. The ones that go to the distribution center in Denver are sent there. The one with the birthday card in it is sent to Chicago. Others that are going to other cities are properly routed by these 3rd layer personnel. The 2nd layer personnel then place our bag in a container headed for Chicago.

This mechanism is repeated at Chicago and the 3rd layer personnel there send the bag to its distribution office and the card reaches its destination.

2.4.4 Description of the Layers

Follow Figure 2.5 as we start describing the layers from 1 to 7 in the OSI model. All layers except the physical layer are implemented in software.

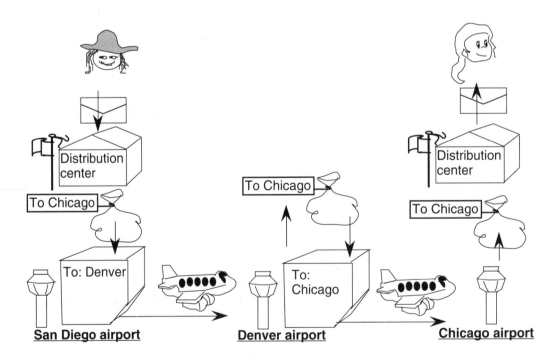

Figure 2.7 In this analogy of routing mail for Chicago, the facilities in Denver are acting as a layer 3 packet switch.

Network Architectures and OSI

The Physical Layer: The physical layer primarily concerns moving bits from one node to the next over a physical link, whether it be a copper wire, satellite, microwave, etc. How many volts are a logical 1 and how many are a logical 0, what is the clock rate, is the transmission full duplex or half duplex—all are issues that concern this layer. Variations of RS-232 are examples of protocols which are used here. In essence, the mechanical, electrical, functional, and procedural characteristics are addressed here.

The Data Link Layer: The data link layer takes the bits that are received by the physical layer and detects errors. For transmission where errors have occurred, the data link layer will request its peer entity to retransmit the data until it is received error-free. Error detection and correction is simply called an error control. If the acknowledgment sent by the receiver gets lost, transmission of data may be duplicated. This is also part of error control.

Besides error control, the data link layer also provides logical synchronization, flow control, and addressing of network nodes. After a receiver synchronizes its clock with the incoming data stream, it must establish where a data frame starts, where it ends, and so on. This is called logical synchronization or framing.

Data flow control is the process by which a receiving node controls the transmitter by making sure it does not send more data than it can receive. Sometimes, flow control is achieved by the receiver not sending an acknowledgment to the transmitter, thereby forcing the transmitter to wait before sending the next transmission. However, a core objective of this layer is reliable information transfer.

The Network Layer: When the data link layer forwards data packets to the network layer, the network layer doesn't have to be concerned about errors in the data. As was covered in the Section 2.4.2, this layer performs routing.

Referring again to Figure 2.6, when the third layer in Host A is sending a packet to Host C, via Host B, the data link layers between each host pair detect errors and retransmit frames if necessary. The network layer has no knowledge if any frames had to be retransmitted over any links or not. However, the network layer at Host B determines if the packet goes to Host C or if it goes to the application at Host B.

In addition to routing, this layer is also responsible for establishing and maintaining connection, while controlling congestion in a network and creating billing information where necessary. Chapter 13 details X.25, a protocol used in this layer.

Transport Layer: As seen in Figure 2.6, the transport layer is not invoked for data passing through a node, such as Host B. Only a data source node (Host A) or a destination node (Host C) uses this layer. All the upper layers from 4 to 7 are called end-to-end layers.

This layer divides up a transmitting message into packets and reassembles them at the receiving end. It can send packets via multiple connections to Host B, enabling it to achieve a high bandwidth, without concerning the session layer. When a connection is established, this layer can request a quality of service that specifies the acceptable rate of errors, the amount of delay, security, and so on. It can also provide data flow control while performing this function on an end to end basis.

In Figure 2.7, San Diego's postal distribution center places letters going from many people to Chicago into one bag. The transport layer can send data from many terminal dialogues over one channel. The process of placing many messages using one channel is called multiplexing.

The Session Layer: The session layer manages logging in and logging off procedures. It manages dialogues between two users/applications. If a certain operation is allowed to be performed by only one user at a time, the protocol in this layer manages such operations, for example, preventing two users from updating the same set of data in a data base simultaneously.

Suppose a user is transferring 100 dollars from data base A to data base B over a network. If the 100 dollars were deducted from data base A but the transaction to add the 100 dollars to data base B was lost, it would be the session layer's responsibility to either roll back data base A to what it was and send an "unsuccessful transfer" message to the user or, otherwise, attempt to complete the transfer again.

Presentation Layer: The sixth layer is responsible for converting file record formats. It performs conversions between ASCII and EBCDIC character codes, does data compression, and encrypts data if necessary. It can also do terminal type conversion.

What is an Application? A software application for a PC is the software which determines how the user is using the PC. If one says that he wants to buy a pickup truck so he can do odd jobs and make some money on the side, then doing odd jobs for others is the application for which the truck is being purchased.

Similarly, a network application is the reason to use the network in the first place, whether it is to transmit a video conference, send a medical image, or to simply send voice. All these are examples of network applications

The Application Layer: In OSI, which addresses data networks, the protocol used in the application layer determines how the user is using the data network.

This could be X.400 which provides Email (Electronic Mail) or it could be X.500 which provides directory services for directories which are distributed over a network. The application in this layer may also perform problem partitioning, which requires the task of one large job to be performed by several hosts. It could manage distributed data bases. Basically, the application layer allows the user to use the network for whatever purpose he/she needs it for.

Exercises

1. Which of the following is NOT a reason to network?
   a. easy access to resources   b. increased reliability
   c. better security   d. mobility of personnel

2. The services provided by adjacent layers is called what?
   a. interface   b. protocol
   c. virtual communication   d. network architecture

3. Which of the following in NOT an example of a network architecture?
   a. SNA
   b. DECnet
   c. FEP
   d. APPN

4. Which layer is responsible for dividing a message into packets?
   a. network
   b. transport
   c. session
   d. presentation

5. Which layer is responsible for correcting errors and establishing framing?
   a. data link
   b. network
   c. transport
   d. session

6. Which layer uses a frame for its PDU?
   a. data link
   b. network
   c. transport
   d. physical

7. A set of rules used in a layer is called what?

8. What is the unit of transfer used in the network layer?

9. X.400 is an example of a protocol used in which layer?

10. As data is being sent down from the application layer into the physical network, do the PDUs become larger or smaller?

11. What is the name for the network which uses only the lower three layers in the OSI model?

12. How something is being used is said to be the _____ .

13. Define a network in your own words.

14. How are networks categorized? Describe the categories.

15. Designing networks using layers must be important, because all networks are designed that way. Why?

16. Describe the process as data moves up and down the OSI layers and virtual communication occurs horizontally, between the peer layers.

17. Describe the communications subnet.

18. List the functions which are the responsibility of the data link layer.

Chapter 3

Analog and Digital Signals

3.1 DC CIRCUITS

3.1.1 Ohm's Law

During a given time span, a DC (Direct Current) voltage provides a constant voltage source, as seen in Figure 3.1(a). Here, regardless of the value of time, the voltage stays the same. What we see is a display of an oscilloscope after its leads are placed across a DC voltage source. The horizontal axis shows time and the vertical one shows voltage. See Figure 3.1(b). Batteries of flashlights and cars are examples of DC voltage sources.

On the contrary, Figure 3.1(c) shows an AC (Alternating Current) voltage supply. This voltage varies from +10V to –10V. For example, at t = 0.5 sec., the voltage is +10V, at t = 1.0 sec. it is 0V and at t = 1.5 sec. it swings to –10V. The range of an AC source goes between positive voltages and negative voltages. The household

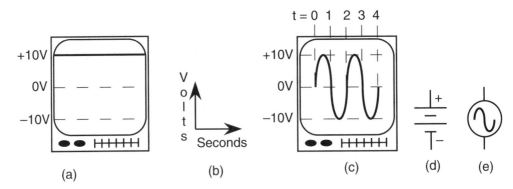

Figure 3.1 (a) DC voltage display. (b) Labels for an oscilloscope axes. (c) AC voltage display. (d) DC voltage symbol. (e) AC voltage symbol.

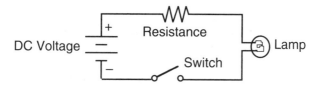

Figure 3.2 When the switch closes, current flows and the lamp lights.

voltage source is an example of AC voltages and is rated at 120V. The schematic symbols for DC and AC sources are shown in Figures 3.1(d) and (e), respectively.

Figure 3.2 shows schematically an electrical circuit where a DC source is connected to a lamp. Resistance represents the amount of hindrance to the flow of current. Resistance can be introduced in the circuit intentionally. However, the connecting wires, lamp, and even the battery inherently provide some resistance to current. Resistance is measured in ohms.

If the switch is open, then no current will flow and if it is closed, then it will. This is noticed by the lamp lighting when the switch is turned on and off. If the amount of resistance is increased, then less current will flow. The amount is determined by Ohm's law:

$$V = IR$$

where V is the voltage, I is the current, and R is the resistance. They are measured in volts, amperes (amps), and ohms, respectively. For example, if the source is 10V and R is 20 ohms, then the current would equal 0.5 amps.

In Figure 3.3(a), we see that a 10 VDC source is applied across two resistors. If they are 20 and 30 ohms, then the total resistance the source experiences is 50 ohms.

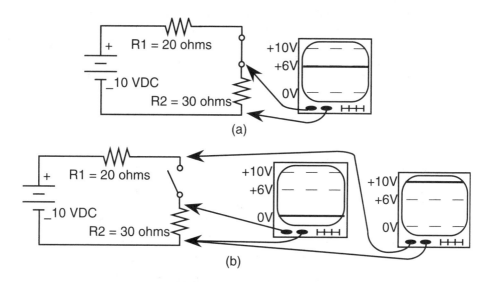

Figure 3.3 (a) When current flows, R2 has 6V. (b) When no current flows, R2 has 0V and the open has 10V.

Using Ohm's law, we get a current of 0.2 amps which must flow through all the components of this circuit. If we multiply this current by each of the resistors, then the voltage on the two resistors would equal 4V and 6V. The 6V across R2 measured with an oscilloscope is shown in the figure.

Now, if we open the switch as is done in Figure 3.3(b), then no current will flow. Since the resistors need a current to have voltages applied across them, neither would have a voltage. Note that across R2, the voltage reading is 0V. However the voltage across the open switch is 10V, since it actually measures the voltage across the source, even if no current is flowing.

3.1.2 Digital Signals

If we look at the oscilloscope the instant the switch is closed, the voltage on R2 will jump from 0V to 6V. This is shown in Figure 3.4(a). Similarly, the display will look like Figure 3.4(b) the instant the switch is turned off after being on. For the state when the switch is turned on (6V), we will call it a binary 1 level and when it is turned off (0V), we will call it a binary 0 level. Binary levels are also called logical levels and have only two states – 0 and 1.

A signal with two voltage levels is called a digital signal while one with continuously varying values is called an analog signal. The signal shown back in Figure 3.1(c) is an example of an analog signal.

If we turn the switch on and off repetitiously, we would get the display as shown in Figure 3.4(c) and if we increase the rate at which the switch is changing states, then we get the display shown in Figure 3.4(d). The waveform of Figure 3.4(d) has a higher frequency than the one in Figure 3.4(c).

A clock on a computer is an example of a digital signal. A clock's rate of change is even or periodic as shown in Figures 3.4(c) and (d). It provides no transfer of information, but only marks time in even increments, so as to keep all computer components in synchronization. Think of it as the computer's heartbeat.

Contrary to the clock, Figure 3.4(e) shows a digital signal where the intervals between the 1s and the 0s are not even or periodic. The uneven intervals can be used to encode information so that voice, data, video, images, etc., can be transmitted digitally.

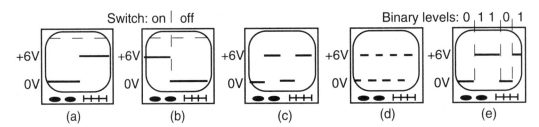

Figure 3.4 (a) Switch going on. (b) Switch going off. (c) A clock signal.
(d) Increasing the clock frequency. (e) A digital signal.

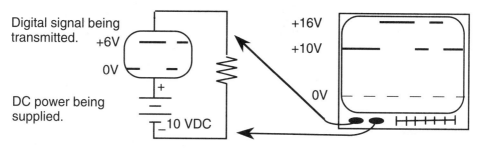

Figure 3.5 Phantoming power.

3.1.3 Phantoming Power

Many digital transmission lines need a device called a repeater. The purpose of a repeater is to "clean" a poor digital signal and retransmit a good one. To power such a device, which is usually installed in a remote place, one can send a voltage over the same line as the one being used to transmit the digital signal. This is called phantoming power.

Figure 3.5 shows such a circuit. The voltage source is added to the digital signal which is being transmitted. From the oscilloscope display, we see that there is at least 10V available at all times to be used as a power source. Above this 10V, the digital signal is "riding" which transfers the intended information.

3.2 ANALOG SIGNALS

Figure 3.6(a) shows an analog signal and its three characteristics. The amplitude is the strength of the signal and is measured in volts. Figure 3.6(b) shows the strength of the signal being reduced. An example of this is when we turn down the volume on a radio.

Period is another characteristic and is just the reciprocal of frequency. In Figure 3.6(a), the period is shown to be 0.5 seconds. It is measured over the time it takes a waveform to repeat itself. To find the frequency, we simply divide 0.5 sec into 1 and get 2 cycles per second. Figure 3.6(c) shows the period being cut in half to .25 sec and hence the frequency is being doubled to 4 cycles per second. Hz (Hertz) is the unit to

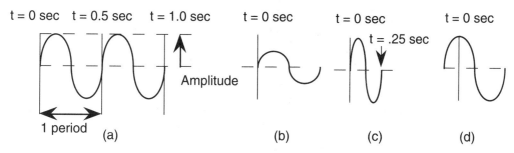

Figure 3.6 Varying the three characteristics of an analog signal.

Analog and Digital Signals

measure cycles per second. An example of doubling the frequency is when we play a note one octave higher than the last. Frequency determines the tone of a signal.

The timing of a signal is given by the phase. It is measured in degrees. The phase angle of a signal doesn't make any sense unless it is compared to a reference. Figure 3.6(d) shows the signal starting earlier than the one starting in Figure 3.6(a) and so has a positive angle phase shift.

3.2.2 Modulation

When a low frequency information signal is encoded over a higher frequency signal, it is called modulation. The encoding can be done by varying one or more characteristics we have just described. For instance, an audio signal (one which is audible to the human ear) can be used to modify an RF (Radio Frequency) carrier. When the amplitude of the radio frequency is varied in accordance to the changes in the audio signal, it is called AM (Amplitude Modulation), and when the frequency is varied, it is called FM (Frequency Modulation). See Figure 3.7(a). These are the methods used by the two kinds of broadcast stations.

In Figure 3.7(b) we are amplitude and frequency modulating a digital signal. Variations of these modulating methods are common with modems (MOdulator/ DEModulator) that are used to transmit digital signals over an analog line. Here, the carrier frequency has to be audio, and not RF, to be able to send it over a voice grade line.

3.2.3 Capacitors and Inductors

A capacitor is nothing more than two conductors that are close together but are not touching each other. It stores energy in an electric field and is measured in farads. It passes AC signals but blocks DC signals.

Unwanted capacitance between two pairs of telephone wires can cause the conversation from one pair to be heard on the other pair. This is called crosstalk. It

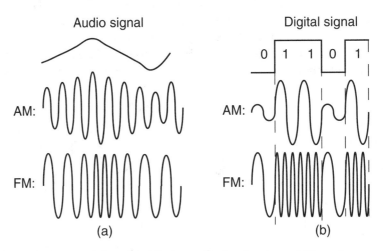

Figure 3.7 (a) Modulating an audio signal over RF carriers. (b) Modulating a digital signal over audio carriers.

occurs because the wires are conductors separated from each other by an insulator introducing capacitance. Voice is an analog signal which the capacitance of the wires are able to pass and so we have crosstalk.

To compensate for this capacitive effect, wires are twisted around themselves introducing what is called an inductive effect. Inductors of course also produce an inductive effect and inherently are opposite of capacitors. Physically, inductors are made by coiling up a wire and are increased in value by forming the coil around a magnet. Hence, they are also called coils. Their unit of measure is Henry, they store energy in magnetic fields, block AC signals and pass DC signals.

When a telephone wire pair becomes longer than 3 miles, it becomes necessary to add inductors to further compensate the capacitive effect. These inductors are called loading coils. When digital signals are transmitted over lines which were once used for voice, these loading coils must be removed. Although digital signals have only two states, the transition of voltage between these states is quick and represents a significant AC signal for those instances more so than normal voice signals. However, inductors block AC so they are not suited for digital signals which have sharp rises and drops of voltage. Therefore, loading coils are removed for digital transmissions and instead repeaters are installed.

3.2.4 Low-Pass Filter

In Figure 3.8(a) we have a circuit with a capacitor. Its frequency response curve is shown in Figure 3.8(b). How does such a curve differ from an oscilloscope display? While the oscilloscope uses time or seconds for its horizontal axis, the response curve uses frequency. The voltages on this curve are plotted by changing the frequency of the AC source. The oscilloscope measurements are shown at three points along the curve. Near the displays, the equivalent circuits are shown for low and high frequencies. The circuit in Figure 3.8(a) resembles these equivalent circuits at those extreme frequencies.

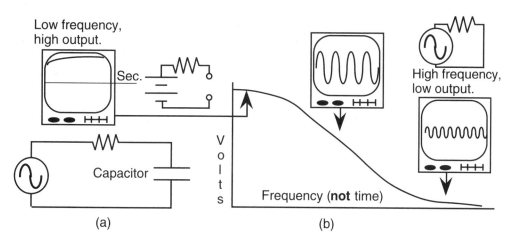

Figure 3.8 (a) A low-pass filter. (b) Its frequency response curve. Oscilloscope displays are shown for several points along the curve.

When frequency is close to zero, the source appears as a DC source, since a DC source provides a constant voltage source. As seen by the low-frequency equivalent circuit, the capacitor blocks DC and opens the circuit, which makes it similar to Figure 3.3(b), and so all the voltage appears across the open.

When the frequency is high, the source appears more as an AC source and as we said before, capacitors pass AC making the capacitor appear as a short. This is shown by the equivalent circuit for the high frequencies. Since the voltage across a short is zero, there is no voltage on the capacitor at the high frequencies.

We have seen why this circuit provides an output voltage for low frequencies and hardly any for high frequencies; thus it is called a low-pass filter. Such a filter passes low frequencies and shorts out the high ones.

3.2.5 Bandwidth

To Figure 3.8(a), we have added an inductor to give us Figure 3.9(a). This circuit is called a bandpass filter, since it passes a band of frequencies and blocks the rest. This is shown by its frequency response curve in Figure 3.9(b).

When engineers design an amplifier or a speaker, they attempt to make the response flat; that is, they try to let all frequencies for a range pass through uniformly, instead of amplifying one set of frequencies more than another. However, with an equalizer, a user has the facility to do that.

The range of frequencies that a device or a transmission medium passes is called the bandwidth. The bandwidth for HI-FI equipment is around 20 kHz while for a voice grade transmission line it is only about 3 kHz. This difference in bandwidth is evident between the voice qualities of a disc jockey and a listener who calls into a radio station over a telephone line. The term bandwidth when used with digital transmissions refers to the number of bits per second or the amount of transmission capacity available.

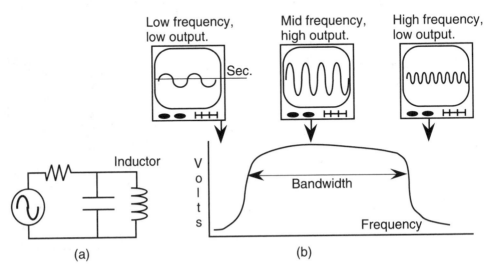

Figure 3.9 (a) A bandpass filter. (b) Its frequency response curve.

3.3 MULTIPLEXING

The process of sending several communication channels (or conversations) simultaneously over one link is called multiplexing. The process of separating them on the receiving end is called demultiplexing. Multiplexing and demultiplexing are done by a multiplexer, also referred to as a mux. FDM (Frequency Division Multiplexing) and TDM (Time Division Multiplexing) will be outlined here.

3.3.1 FDM

Figure 3.10 shows an FDM multiplexer. This mux is receiving 12 voice channels on its inputs and is combining them for transmission over one communication link. Each channel uses a bandwidth of 3 kHz. However, so that one channel doesn't interfere with another, the channels are separated from each other and are allocated 4 kHz each.

Each channel is offset on the output frequency spectrum so as to assign each channel its share of the available bandwidth. This way many voice channels can be transmitted over the same link.

3.3.2 TDM

Instead of dividing the available frequencies between all channels, one can divide the available time between them. This is called TDM. Figure 3.11 shows two channels carrying digital signals into a TDM mux. Using its clock, the mux transmits the data from the first input over every odd time slot and transmits the data from the second input over every even one. This way, the data from both inputs are transmitted over one output.

For example, at t = 3 and t = 4, the first input is transmitting a binary 1 and the second one is transmitting a binary 0. The first input's binary 1 is transmitted at t = 3

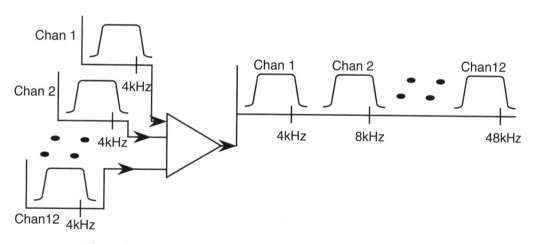

Figure 3.10 FDM (Frequency Division Multiplexing) transmits many analog channels over one link by allocating each channel a portion of the available bandwidth.

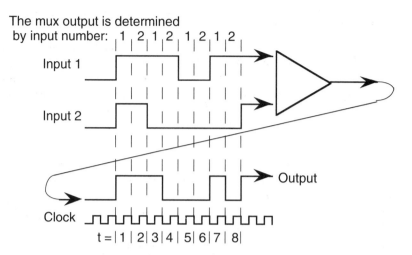

The mux output is determined
by input number: 1 2 1 2 1 2 1 2

Input 1

Input 2

Output

Clock

t = | 1 | 2 | 3 | 4 | 5 | 6 | 7 | 8 |

Figure 3.11 TDM (Time Division Multiplexing) transmits digital channels over one link by allocating each channel a portion of the available time.

and the second input's binary 0 is transmitted at t = 4. This way, the mux alternates between the inputs. Of course, on the receiver's side, the TDM mux must be synchronized so that it forwards the proper bits to each recipient.

Figure 3.11 illustrates bit interleaving, since the mux changes the channel after every bit. On the other hand, if 8 bits from each channel are sent together, then the mux would be using what is called byte interleaving multiplexing.

Often terminals are idle and with TDM they are still assigned a time slot on the output data stream. Those time slots would, in fact, be wasted. A statistical multiplexer, however, would make use of those idle times and would be more efficient. Stat-muxes allow the sum of the input speeds to exceed the output speed, because it assumes that not all inputs are transmitting simultaneously.

One can easily see how TDM can be extended to more channels. However, the link speed must be greater than the sum of the input speeds in the same way that the output bandwidth for a FDM mux must be greater than the sum of the input bandwidths. Yet, with TDM not much extra time is required for overhead, but with FDM, we had to separate the channels from each other forcing us to use more bandwidth than what was actually being used. Hence, FDM is said to be less efficient than TDM.

3.4 POWER

3.4.1 P = VI

Similar to Ohm's law, (V = IR) is the power equation which defines power as:

$$P = VI$$

where P is power in watts, while V and I are the familiar variables used in Ohm's law.

Back in Figure 3.3(a), we had obtained 0.2 amps of current through the circuit with 4V on R1 and 6V on R2. To calculate the power dissipated in R1, we simply multiply its voltage by the current, giving us 0.8 watts (4V times 0.2 amps). Similarly, we get 1.2 watts (6V times 0.2 amps) on R2. Since these two components are dissipating a total of 2.0 watts of power, the power source must be supplying that amount.

Suppose there is a hair dryer rated at 1200 watts and the usual residential voltage applied is 120 VAC, then the hair dryer must use 10 amps of current. This is found by substituting the known variables in the power equation and solving for I.

3.4.2 Decibels

Alexander Graham Bell, besides inventing the telephone, also worked to help those who had hearing disabilities. He noticed that the human ear detected changes in sound which depended on logarithms, from which he defined the unit called a decibel. In telecommunications, this unit is used when working with power levels. Let us first discuss logarithms; then we will go on to decibels.

Logs: Logs (logarithms) complement powers of ten in a similar manner as square roots complement squares. When we write:

$$10^X = 1000$$

we are saying 10 must be multiplied by itself how many times to give us a 1000? The answer (or X) is 3. We can get this same answer by taking a log of both sides.

$$\log (10^X) = \log (1000)$$

And just as a square root of a square of a number reduces the expression to just that number, so the log of 10 to the power of X is simply X. Our problem thus reduces to:

$$X = \log(1000)$$

Here, using a calculator one can find that the log of 1000 is indeed 3.

Dbs: Dbs (or Decibels) specify the difference between two power levels. It does not specify the absolute power. It is defined as:

$$db = 10 \log (P2/P1)$$

where P1 and P2 are the power in watts which are being compared. Figure 3.12 shows a 4-stage device which consists of 3 amplifiers and one filter. The power at each point is also shown. By using a calculator to find the logs, let us find the gain for the first 3 stages.

Using the Formula: For stage 1, P1 is 1 mW (milliwatts) and P2 is 2 mW. Substituting these into the equation, we get:

$$db = 10 \log (2/1) = 10 \log 2 = 10 (0.3) = 3 \ db$$

Analog and Digital Signals   **31**

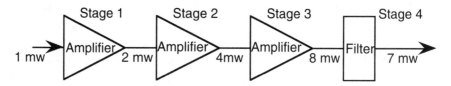

Figure 3.12 A 4-stage amplifier showing the various power levels.

For the second stage,

$$db = 10 \log(4/2) = 10 \log 2 = 10 \ (0.3) = 3 \ db$$

From these two results, we see that as long as the power is doubled, the gain of the stage is 3 dbs. So the gain of the third stage must also be 3 dbs.

Adding dbs: Now, let us find the gains for several stages together. For instance, for stages 1 and 2 the gain is:

$$db = 10 \log (4/1) = 10 \log (4) = 10 \ (.6) = 6 \ dbs$$

where P2 is 4 mW taken at the output of stages 1 and 2 and P1 is 1 mW taken at the input of stages 1 and 2. These two stages are grouped together for this calculation. Similarly, the gain for the first three stages is:

$$db = 10 \log (8/1) = 10 \log 8 = 10 \ (.9) = 9 \ dbs$$

From these calculations, it is evident that if we know the gains of the individual stages, we can add them up to find their composite gain.

Negative dbs: When the output power decreases as it does for stage 4, the gain in dbs becomes negative. This can be confirmed by calculating the gain for stage 4.

$$db = 10 \log (7/8) = 10 \ (- 0.06) = - 0.6 \ dbs$$

Dbms: While the unit of db specifies the ratio of powers, the unit of dbm specifies the actual power. This is done by referencing the input power to 1 mW, as shown below:

$$dbm = 10 \log (P2/1mW)$$

Hence, the power level for the input of stage 1 is:

$$dbm = 10 \log (1mW/1mW) = 10 \log (1) = 10 \ (0) = 0 \ dbm$$

and for the output of stage 1 is:

$$dbm = 10 \log (2mW/1mW) = 10 \log (2) = 10 \ (.3) = 3 \ dbm$$

Pattern used to communicate	Communication protocol A	Communication protocol B
00	It is sunny.	I want to go home.
01	It is raining.	I am going home.
10	It is snowing.	I am almost home.
11	It is doing none of the above.	I am home.

Figure 3.13 The actual meaning of given bit patterns is predetermined by the communication protocol in use.

3.5 CODING AND ADDRESSING

In digital systems, the smallest unit of information one can retrieve is a bit. Two bits are called a dibit, 4 are called a nibble and 8 are called an octet. Generally, an octet is also called a byte, although, in some cases, a byte may not be 8 bits.

If only one bit of information is being sent, then only one piece out of a possible two pieces of information can be sent. For example, the two end points which are communicating may agree that if a binary 1 is being sent, then that would represent that it is sunny and if a 0 is being sent then it would mean that it is not sunny.

If the two end points would like to communicate with each other using more pieces of information, then more bits are needed to encode those pieces of information. Using two bits allows one to communicate with four possible codes. Figure 3.13 shows two examples of coding methods. Whatever method of coding is used by the transmitter, the complementary method of decoding must be used by the receiver. Encoding and decoding methods are part of the communications protocol that is in use.

If we increase the number of bits used to transmit information to 3, then we have the possibility of encoding up to 8 different combinations. The number of combinations for 3 and 4 bits are shown in Figures 3.14(a) and (b). From these examples, we can see that, given the number of bits, one can calculate the number of possible codes available by this formula:

$$\text{Number of possible combinations} = 2^{\text{(The number of available bits)}}$$

Let us look at two examples of how to apply this formula. If a computer has only 128 octets of data, for the CPU to access any one of these octets, it must use 7 bits to

000	100
001	101
010	110
011	111

(a)

0000	0100	1000	1100
0001	0101	1001	1101
0010	0110	1010	1110
0011	0111	1011	1111

(b)

Figure 3.14 (a) The number of possible combinations using 3 bits. (b) The number of possible combinations using 4 bits.

address the proper octet, because with 7 bits, there are 128 (or 2^7) possible combinations, where each combination can be used to identify each of the 128 octets. However, each octet itself can store one out of a possible of 256 (or 2^8) combinations of data.

Suppose a network has 30 computers and the transmitting computer must code the address of the receiving computer with every data frame which it sends. In this case, how many bits must be used to encode the address? The answer is 5, since with 5 bits, we have 32 combinations available out of which 30 can be used to assign addresses for existing computers, leaving us with 2 spare addresses for future additions.

3.6 SYNCHRONIZATION

3.6.1 Three Kinds of Synchronizations

When a device receives a data stream, it must determine precisely where each bit begins. This is called bit synchronization. Once it determines where each bit begins and ends, it must know how to group them into octets, or which bit is the first one out of a group of eight. This is called character synchronization. Once it determines the octets, it must be able to determine which octets form the address field, or data field, and so on. This is called logical synchronization (or framing) and is usually handled by OSI's second layer, although, as is done with T1s, this is established by the hardware.

3.6.2 Asynchronous Communication

Bit and character synchronization can be established by either asynchronous or synchronous communications. Asynchronous communication is depicted in Figure 3.15(a). When no data is being sent, the line is idle and when a character is being sent, it is preceded by a start bit. The sudden change in voltage in the start bit signals the receiver that a character is being sent and after the data bits are sent, then a stop bit is sent. The receiver's internal clock uses the edge of the start bit to get itself in sync with the timing of the received signal.

Asynchronous transmission allows characters to be sent randomly and one at a time, since synchronizing information is carried with each character.

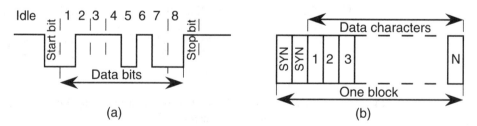

Figure 3.15 (a) Asynchronous communication. (b) Synchronous communication.

Analog and Digital Signals

3.6.3 Synchronous Communication

Synchronous communication, as shown in Figure 3.15(b), is more efficient. Instead of transmitting one character at a time, it transmits one block of data at a time and places special SYN characters at the beginning of the block to provide synchronization. Since characters are sent in groups, larger buffers are needed than are needed with asynchronous transmission.

In synchronous transmission, the voltage level transitions which normally occur in the data are used to maintain the synchronization of the receiver clock. If too many consecutive bits have the same value (either all 0s or all 1s), then the clock might slip. Accommodations have to be made so that the clock stays in sync.

Asynchronous terminals typically operate from 300 bps to 19,200 bps, while synchronous terminals typically operate from 19.2 kbps to above 1 Mbps.

3.6.4 STM vs. ATM

Having nothing to do with synchronous and asynchronous transmissions as we have discussed so far, are the terms STM (Synchronous Transmission Mode) and ATM (Asynchronous Transmission Mode). Figure 3.11 showed how the TDM preassigns every input channel its slice of the available time. This is also called STM. A receiving terminal at the demux knows that every other bit of data belongs to it. With ATM, this is not so. At one point in time, a receiving terminal may get many bits of data contiguously and at another time, it may have to wait. ATM is covered in Chapter 18.

Part of ATM's design is to accommodate isochronous traffic. Isochronous traffic means traffic that is sensitive to any latency or delay. If a response from a host to a terminal is slow in being received, one can live with that. It is data and is not isochronous. However, if a voice conversation is being chopped into digital packets, then they must arrive at the listener's end within a given amount of time, or else the conversation would become unnatural. Voice and video are examples of isochronous traffic.

3.6.5 Clocking

As digital signals are transmitted at higher and higher rates, the problem of clocking becomes much more critical than it ever was with analog signals. Jitter is a problem associated with digital signals which can't stay in sync. There are four types of clocks which have been defined, based on their accuracies. A stratum level 4 clock is the least accurate type of clock and a stratum level 1, which is based on atomic clocks, is the most accurate. Private networks can be synchronized by using their carrier's network clocks. But they can also be synchronized by using LORAN-C (LOng RAnge Navigation-C), Navstar GPS (Global Positioning System), or other independent clocking sources.

Many times a network is operated using two or more clocks. Even if they are stratum level 1 clocks, they can go out of sync after a while. A network which accommodates for such timing differences is said to be operating under plesiochronous operation. SONET (Chapter 15) allows traffic from one carrier to be transformed to another carrier at high speeds. It also makes allowances for plesiochronous operation, since different carriers use their own network clocks and may not be totally in sync with each other.

3.7 INFORMATION ENCODING

3.7.1 Methods of Transmitting Information

Information as was discussed in Section 3.5 is what the user wants to communicate. Examples of information are voice, data, video, fax, medical image, etc. Signaling determines how a connection is going to be made to the recipient so that he or she is ready to receive the information. Information can be transmitted using analog lines or digital lines. The type of line is determined not just by looking at it physically, but is determined by the type of equipment that is connected to it on the other side.

For example, COs place analog equipment on the typical phone lines coming from residences. Hence a typical phone line is an analog line. If a CO were to attach digital equipment on that line, then it would be a digital line. ISDN (Integrated Services Digital Network) requires that the existing analog lines be converted to digital ones by having the COs and customers replace the end equipment.

Figure 3.16(a) shows that to send voice over an analog line, a simple telephone provides all the circuitry necessary to do that. It also shows that the device to convert voice to a digital signal requires the introduction of a codec (COder and DECoder). A codec converts voice to digital, while a video codec converts a video signal to a digital one.

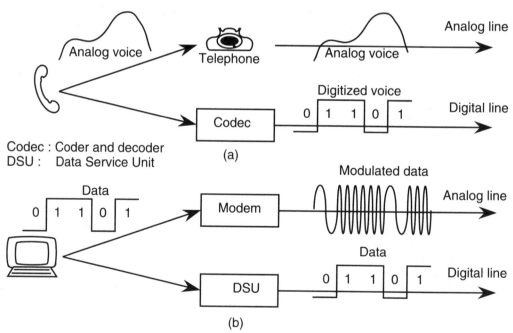

Figure 3.16 (a) Sending voice over analog and digital lines.
(b) Doing the same with data.

Analog and Digital Signals

To transmit data over an analog line, one needs a modem as seen in Figure 3.16(b) and to send it over a digital line, one needs a DSU (Data Service Unit, also called Digital Service Unit). A DSU provides the necessary interface for data to be sent and received over a digital line.

3.7.2 Advantages of Converting Voice to Digital

Let us discuss why most voice transmissions are being converted into a digital format. One reason is that a digital signal is less affected by noise. In Figure 3.17(a), an analog signal is being transmitted over a transmission medium. When it arrives at the first line amplifier, the signal has become weak and has picked up noise and interference. To boost the weak signal, a line amp has been added. Unfortunately, it ends up amplifying the noise as well. If amplification is needed over several segments of a transmission path, the signal would become poor and not be suitable to be called "toll-quality".

If a digital signal on the other hand, as seen in Figure 3.17(b), is transmitted over the same medium, the repeater at the other end can recreate the signal. Any "fuzziness" in the signal is eliminated, because the signal should be either a 1 or a 0 and nothing in between. The line amp can not as easily eliminate the fuzziness in analog signals, because it can't distinguish noise from signal as well.

Even as late as the 70s, one could tell when a call was being made across the continent or in the same town. Today, with digital transmissions, one has difficulty noticing any variations in voice qualities. The maximum number of line amps for analog signals is limited, but the maximum number of repeaters for a digital signal is virtually limitless. The circuitry used for digital equipment is easy to design (if it hasn't been designed already to be used for computing devices). FDM used with analog channels is inefficient and expensive. TDM used with digital channels is more efficient, uses less overhead, and is less expensive.

However, because the bandwidth required for one voice channel (64 kbps) was significantly higher than the usual data channel (300 bps), many ruled out the possi-

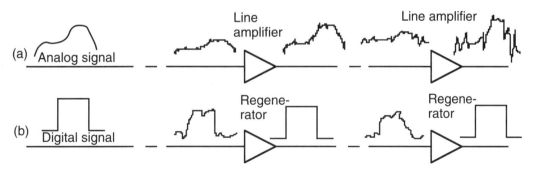

Figure 3.17 (a) The degradation of analog signals after being transmitted over a distance. (b) The regeneration of a digital signal after being transmitted over a distance.

bility of digitizing voice to ever become popular. Since then, more bandwidth is becoming available on network links and the required bandwidth for a toll-quality voice channel is dropping as research and development continues in this field. For instance, in 1978, a video conference required 6 Mbps of bandwidth and by employing sophisticated compression algorithm methods, in 1993 it only required 0.08 Mbps to provide the same quality signal.

3.7.3 PCM

A simple method of converting voice is shown in Figure 3.18. The voice signal is placed on an imaginary grid, where discrete voltage levels are assigned digital codes. Then the voice signal is sampled at an even rate and the voltage of the voice in digital form is transmitted. For example, at sample 1, the voice signal is close to a digital value of 01 and at sample 2, it is close to a level of 10, and so on. Then these bits are transmitted and the receiver constructs a signal from them. The difference between the actual voice signal and the reconstructed signal is called quantizing noise, and it becomes an issue only if the voice is converted between analog and digital forms several times. Repeaters do not perform such conversions; only codecs do.

If we want to represent voice into digital form more accurately, we will need to increase the sampling rate as well as increase the number of levels. Hence, increase the number of rectangles and reduce their sizes on the grid. It is said in order to accurately code voice into a digital form, the sampling rate must be at least twice the highest frequency of the analog voice channel. This is called the Nyquist's theorem.

Hence an encoding method called PCM (Pulse Code Modulation) uses 8000 samples per second, corresponding to about two times the analog channel's bandwidth (or 2 times 4 kHz). It uses 8 bits to encode the levels for each sample providing a total of 2^8 or 256 levels. However, a level of 0 is not used, since it would present too many 0s in a sequence (actually 8 zeros) for a clock to maintain synchronization.

Therefore, with 8000 samples per second and 8 bits per sample, the rate for one voice channel using PCM is 64 kbps. The method of performing PCM in North America and Japan is called the mu-law and the one used in Europe is called the A-law.

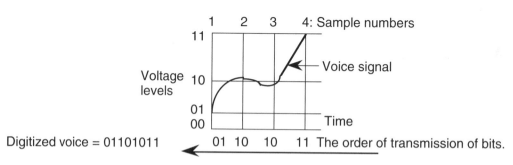

Figure 3.18 A simple example of converting voice into a digital signal.

Another popular method of digitizing voice is called ADPCM (Adaptive Differential PCM). It uses only 4 bits per sample, but only codes the differences between the extrapolated level and the actual level. So it doesn't need as many bits per sample as PCM does. Its bandwidth of 32 kbps provides a quality of voice that is indistinguishable from PCM.

To store the amount of voice generated by a conversation for 1 minute would require about 0.5 Mbytes of memory using PCM. This is because 1 minute equals 60 seconds and each second generates 64,000 bits. This amounts to 3,840,000 bits or dividing by 8 yields 480,000 bytes. Of course, using voice compression techniques would greatly improve and reduce this number.

CDs (Compact Discs) compared to PCM require much more bandwidth since they provides HI-FI quality. An analog bandwidth of 20 kHz necessitates the sampling rate to be 44.1 kbps, which is about double the amount. Each sample is coded with 16 bits instead of 8 bits which are used in PCM. Multiplying 44.1 kbps, 16, and 2 for each of the two stereo channels, yields a rate of 1.4112 Mbps. This is considerably greater than PCM's 64 kbps rate. However, by the time error correction codes, synchronization bits, and other processing is added, the actual rate for a CD becomes 4.3218 Mbps.

3.7.4 Video Compression

Unlike an audio signal encoded on a CD, digitizing video depends on complex compression algorithms. Notice that with CDs compression was not used. Without compression, a broadcast video signal would require 4.7 Mbps of bandwidth for color. HDTV (High Definition TV) would require 100 Mbps. But with compression, these rates can be reduced by as much as a factor of 100 with little apparent loss in quality. Medical images, such as X-rays, can be reduced by a factor of 3 but not much more than that without losing resolution.

There are two types of compression used with video—intra-frame and inter-frame. Intra-frame compression reduces the amount of data needed to send one frame. Inter-frame compression depends on the fact that two adjacent frames are usually similar to each other and only require the transmission of the differences between them. Both techniques make use of the characteristics of the human eye to make the picture appear good without having to transmit all of its details.

For example, since the human eye is more sensitive to brightness than it is to color, more bits per frame are used to encode the former than the latter. Also, the eye is less sensitive to abrupt changes than it is to gradual changes; hence, less bits are used to encode abrupt changes in signal than to gradual ones. That is, less information is transmitted with small changes, because most current applications are for meetings ("talking heads") which have fewer changes than, say, a juggling act would have.

Briefly, video compression techniques typically divide a picture into blocks of 8 pixels by 8 pixels as shown in Figure 3.19. Depending on its color, brightness, and other characteristics, each pixel is assigned a value. See the middle grid of Figure 3.19(a). After this block is averaged and detailed information is removed, a much simpler grid is constructed as shown toward the bottom of the figure. This summarizes intra-frame compression.

Intra-frame compression | Inter-frame compression

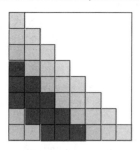

5	0	0	0	0	0	0	0
7	5	0	0	0	0	0	0
10	7	5	0	0	0	0	0
15	10	7	5	0	0	0	0
15	15	10	7	5	0	0	0
15	15	15	10	7	5	0	0
10	15	15	15	10	7	5	0
10	10	15	15	15	10	7	5

9	-5	2	1	0	0	0	0
-5	2	1	0	0	0	0	0
1	1	1	0	0	0	0	0
0	0	0	0	0	0	0	0
0	0	0	0	0	0	0	0
0	0	0	0	0	0	0	0
0	0	0	0	0	0	0	0
0	0	0	0	0	0	0	0

(a)

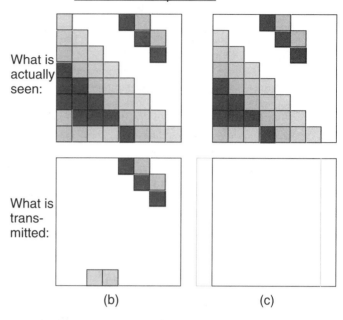

What is actually seen:

What is transmitted:

(b)　　　　　　(c)

Figure 3.19 (a) With intra-frame compression, an 8 by 8 pixel block is digitized by marking each pixel with a set of values. These are then further simplified by compressing the data and losing some of the information. The number on the upper left corner gives the average characteristic of the block. (b) In time the frame in figure (a) changes to what is shown. According to the lower figure, only the changes since the last frame are transmitted. (c) If the object has simply moved, then only the amount and direction of the shift is transmitted.

In Figure 3.19(b), a few changes are added to the frame. Instead of transmitting the entire frame, only the changes shown on the bottom of the figure are transmitted. Similarly, if the object in the block moves, then only the information concerning the shift is transmitted. See Figure 3.19(c).

Exercises

1. How many voltage levels does an analog signal have?
   a. 1　　　　　　　　　　　　　　b. 2
   c. 3　　　　　　　　　　　　　　d. many

2. When a DC voltage is added to a digital signal to transmit power, what is the process called?
   a. multiplexing　　　　　　　　　b. filtering
   c. phantoming　　　　　　　　　d. amplifying

3. In Figure 3.9, the high frequencies are being shorted by which device?
   a. battery
   b. resistor
   c. capacitor
   d. inductor

4. When converting an analog line to a digital one, which devices must be removed?
   a. batteries
   b. resistances
   c. capacitors
   d. loading coils

5. Which device converts voice into digital form?
   a. modem
   b. multiplexer
   c. codec
   d. DSU

6. Besides for the characteristics which are used to modify an analog signal in Figure 3.7, what other characteristic could be modified as well?

7. If R2 in Figure 3.3 were 20 ohms, then what would be its voltage and power?

8. In Figure 3.12, if the output of stage 3 were 12 mW, then what would be its gain in dbs?

9. Many times with asynchronous transmission, a parity bit is used with each character to allow for error correction. In that case, how many bits are needed to send each character?

10. A voice digitizing method doesn't use compression. If it transmits at 16 kbps and has a sampling rate of 4000 samples per second, how many voltage levels can it encode?

11. How many 300 baud terminals can be attached to a 2400 baud line using a TDM multiplexer?

12. How do capacitors and inductors differ?

13. Draw a high-pass filter circuit and explain its operation.

14. Draw an amplitude modulated signal which modulates this data: 10010.

15. Describe the difference between synchronous and asynchronous transmissions.

16. What do asynchronous transmission and ATM have in common?

17. Describe, in your own words, how video is digitized and how it is similar to and different from digitizing voice, say using PCM?

Chapter 4

Transmission Systems

4.1 INTRODUCTION

When fiber was beginning to be introduced in the late 1970s, many wondered if it would replace other transmissions media and would become the dominant choice in the telecommunications industry. Although fiber is being deployed at a rapid rate on long-haul point-to-point runs, other technologies play a significant role in connecting many widely separated remote sites together, while yet others concentrate on cutting down costs. Even the inexpensive twisted pair is being developed so that it could transmit rates of 100 Mbps.

The first part of this chapter will present the transmission media which are used close to the ground, then will cover the ones that go over the ground, and then those which include space. The latter part will discuss systems which are generally associated with voice transmissions and PBXs.

4.2 TWISTED PAIR

4.2.1 Voice-Grade Lines

As seen in the last chapter, telephone wires inherently provide a capacitive effect which is compensated for by having the pairs twisted around themselves introducing an inductive effect. This prevents crosstalk or having the conversations from one pair interfere with an adjacent one.

Typically, the size of telephone lines range from 22 AWG (American Wire Gauge) to 26 AWG. The diameter of a 22 AWG wire is 0.025 inches and that of a 26 gauge wire is 0.016 inches. As the AWG number decreases, the wider the wire and the lesser its resistance becomes. Also, its bandwidth rating increases.

POTS (Plain Old Telephone Service) is commonly provided by the COs to residences using twisted pair wires. Since their bandwidth is rated at 3 khz, they are also called voice-grade lines. Category 3 cabling or Voice-grade UTP (Unshielded

42

Figure 4.1 (a) Category 3 UTP (voice-grade UTP). (b) Category 4 UTP. (c) STP. (d) Category 5 UTP (data-grade UTP).

Twisted Pair) lines are terms also used for them. They have no protective metal shielding around them and ANSI approves it for data rates of up to 10 Mbps.

4.2.2 Other Types

For its TRNs (Token Ring Networks), IBM first introduced the Type 1 cabling, also called STP (Shielded Twisted Pair). There are two pairs (or 4 wires) in this cabling. Each pair is wrapped around in a conductive shielding or a wire braided mesh. Then both of these groups are shielded again before being enclosed in a plastic covering. See Figure 4.1. This shielding protects the data being transmitted from interference such as power lines. It is the thickest and the most expensive of all twisted pair cables.

While Category 3 UTP was primarily meant for voice transmissions, Category 4 UTP (as STP) is designed primarily for data transmission. It is certified for rates of up to 20 Mbps. This is achieved by twisting the pairs tighter than they are for Category 3 UTP.

Probably the most promising of all twisted pair cables is the Category 5 UTP, which is also called data-grade UTP. It is recommended by ANSI to operate at 100 Mbps. EIA/TIA (Electronic Industries Association/Telecommunications Industries Association) has also approved its use in its 568 Commercial Building Wiring Standard.

Category 5 UTP, like STP, comes with 2 pairs. It is only slightly more expensive than Category 3 UTP. Yet it can send data 10 times as fast. Although STP can also be used for transmission at rates of 100 Mbps, it is almost half an inch thick, whereas Category 5 UTP is only 0.25 inches thick. This makes it easy to install around bends and inside ducts. However, since it is unshielded, care must be taken that it is not installed near elevators, copying machines, or other sources of interference.

4.3 COAX

When many telephone transmissions were required to be placed on one medium, the twisted pair didn't provide the needed bandwidth. Coaxial cable (or just coax) was introduced which carried frequencies of up to 10 GHz. Coax has an inner conductor which is surrounded by a braided mesh, as seen in Figure 4.2(a). Both conductors share a common center axial, hence the term "co-axial." Coax comes in two types—broadband and baseband—and are distinguished by how they are used.

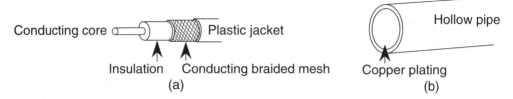

Figure 4.2 (a) Coaxial cable. (b) Waveguide.

4.3.1 Baseband Coax

Baseband coax is widely used in Ethernet. It carries only one channel; that is, only one data transmission can exist on the cable at any time. The data is placed on the medium in digital form and rates of 10 Mbps are easily achieved. Data can travel in both directions. They have an impedance of 50 ohms. Impedance is like "AC resistance" due to capacitive and inductive effects and, in this case, specifies the electrical characteristics of the cable.

4.3.2 Broadband Coax

Broadband coax with an impedance of 75 is commonly used with cable TV. It transmits analog signals in only one direction. To transmit in both directions, a dual cable system must be implemented. However, because of its large bandwidth of 300 Mhz to 450 Mhz, it can carry many channels simultaneously. Using FDM, one can send video, audio, and data. However, since this is an analog system, modems are required for transmission of data.

For broadband coaxial systems, sophisticated devices such as amplifiers and splitters are necessary, as well as services of skilled engineers to install and maintain them.

4.3.3 Waveguides

Waveguides are not a kind of coax. However, as transmitting frequencies are increased in a coax, they tend to travel in space, requiring no conductors. To guide such signals along a transmission path, they are placed in a hollow metal pipe called a waveguide. See Figure 4.2(b). However, most waveguides in use are rectangular in cross section, with a two to one ratio of the two dimensions. They can transmit microwave signals with frequencies ranging over 100 GHz.

4.4 FIBER

4.4.1 Overview

Just as microwaves are propagated and guided by confining them in a waveguide, optical signals or light can also be handled in a similar manner by sending them through an optical fiber. Work with such signals was done as far back as 1880 when Alexander Graham Bell received a patent for a photophone. This device transmitted voice using daylight rays for a distance of up to 200 meters.

However, it was not until 1971 when Kapron, Keck, and Maurer at Corning Glass Works were able to send signals for a few hundred meters with losses of 20 db per km. Currently, it is possible to send optical signals for distances greater than 70 miles without requiring repeaters and with losses which are less than 0.1 db/km.

Sending information by using lightwaves prevents interference from electrical source, radio waves, lightning and so on. This enables error rates which are in excess of 10^{-9}. This number is equal to having only one error in every billion bits. Fiber not only provides impressive low error rates but also provides a very high data transfer rate. On customer premises, it can operate above 100 Mbps, while long distance carriers pass over 1 Gbps through these thin strands.

Fiber is not susceptible to corrosion as is copper cabling. It is difficult to tap, providing excellent security. Also, it is immune to crosstalk. Lastly, fiber is not bulky but easy to handle. However, because it is expensive and difficult to work with, other media still compete with it.

4.4.2 Construction

Many fibers are constructed similarly to what is shown in Figure 4.3. The core and cladding are constructed using glass. Light energy travels through these two sections. Surrounding them is a protective coating to prevent moisture from entering. The layer of Kevlar and other materials are added to give it its strength, so the fiber is not easily snapped. Finally, a polyurethane coating completes its construction. Since fiber can't carry electrical power to remote repeaters, such as the ones in trans-oceanic cables, copper cables must also be added if they are needed to deliver power.

The core and the cladding have different indices of refraction which force light at some angles to stay within the core while enabling others to escape. See Figure 4.4. When light enters the fiber, either from an LED (Light Emitting Diode) or an ILD (Injection Laser Diode), it travels through it due to total internal reflection.

4.4.3 Types of Fiber

When the core diameter is large, there are more rays with varying angles of index which are accepted into the fiber than when the diameter is small. The mode of propagation of a light ray, which depends on its angle of incidence, is simply called a mode. So as the diameter of the core increases, the number of propagation modes increase, and the fiber is called a multimode fiber. In such a case, more rays arrive at the distant end out of phase from each other and can destructively interfere with each

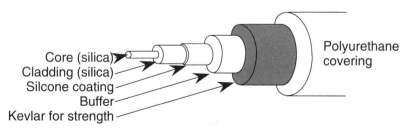

Figure 4.3 Typical fiber construction.

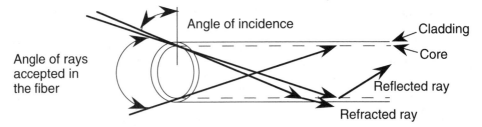

Figure 4.4 The angles of rays accepted in a fiber depends on the diameter of the core.

other. However, in a single mode fiber, only one mode of propagation exists and there is no interference from other modes.

Based on the construction of the core and the cladding, there are primarily three types of fiber—multimode step index, multimode graded index, and single mode step index. The typical diameters of their cores and claddings are shown in Figure 4.5. The index profiles show the index of refraction across the cross section of the fiber. Notice that there are only two values of index of refraction for the step index fibers. For these fibers the index of refraction doesn't change within the core or the cladding. However, for the graded index fiber, the core is made up of concentric layers of material which have a slightly different index of refraction.

The modes (or rays) in a multimode step index fiber can destructively interfere with each other. So its bandwidth is limited to around 10 MHz for distances of 1 km. Most of the power in a multimode fiber travels in the core and it is the easiest to manufacture.

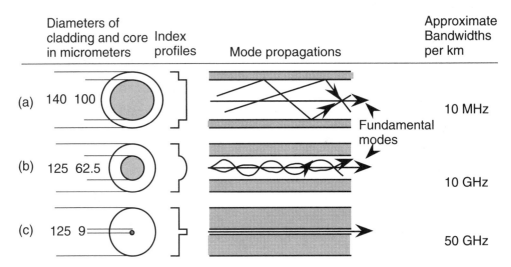

Figure 4.5 (a) Step index multimode fiber. (b) Graded index multimode fiber. (c) Step index single mode fiber.

In a graded index multimode fiber, because of the varying amounts of refractive indices of the core material, the modes do not sharply reflect, but are gradually refracted into the core as seen in Figure 4.5(b). It provides a bandwidth of about 10 GHz.

Single mode fiber propagates only one mode effectively. Up to 50 percent of the energy may be transferred through the cladding and the rest through the core. Since there is no intermodal interference, the bandwidth is in the order of 50 GHz. This type of fiber is typically used for long distances, but due to its small size, it is difficult to work with.

4.5 SHORT-HAUL SOLUTIONS

4.5.1 Microwave Radios

Laying of fiber over long distances is usually an expensive project. It requires obtaining rights of access where many times it is almost impossible to get one. Even after the fiber is finally laid, if some backhoe operator gets too excited, the cable can be cut losing large amounts of communications. If a catalog sales outfit loses its incoming calls for too long, it can soon go into bankruptcy.

Instead, it is much easier to set up two towers and have a pair of microwave systems provide the needed communications link. These systems operate from 2 GHz to 23 GHz and provide a beam width between 1 to 5 degrees. They provide a line-of-sight solution that can span a distance of 60 miles. This limitation is determined by the heights of the towers and the curvature of the earth. Digital radios can provide a data rate of up to 44 Mbps.

These systems can be set up and made operational in a day. Their installation cost is much less than that for installing copper or fiber for the same distances. They have an expected life time of 20 years. Furthermore, one can initially buy a low-cost system and then be able to increase its capacity as the usage grows.

Many use microwave systems for backup. For instance, a site can use fiber going to one CO and have a standby microwave connected to an alternate CO, eliminating possible points of failures. Many times, these systems are also used to bypass the LEC (and its charges) to gain direct access to a POP.

The main disadvantage of microwave is obtaining an FCC license for its operation; although, in emergencies, temporary licenses can be obtained. If a high rise building is built obstructing the transmission path, then alternate routes have to be investigated.

4.5.2 Infrared

Lasers and infrared are also used on a limited basis to obtain short haul links. Infrared is a light signal while microwave is a radio signal. Both, actually are electromagnetic waves which can be located on an electromagnetic spectrum. See Figure 4.6. Although weather conditions such as fog and rain attenuate (or reduce the strength of) microwave signals, they attenuate infrared signals even more. Infrared systems are usually limited to a range of only about a mile.

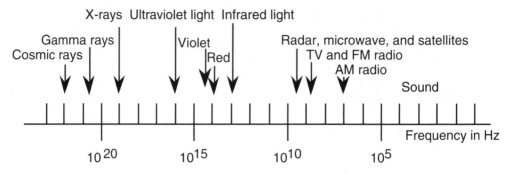

Figure 4.6 The electromagnetic spectrum. Visible light exists at around 10^{14} Hz.

Infrared systems can also reach speeds of 44 Mbps and are as inexpensive and easy to install as microwave systems are. Their beam width is even narrower than that of microwaves. They can also be used to connect LAN stations in house. One of the biggest costs of setting up a LAN is its installation. LAN stations are difficult to move around once they are installed. Using infrared or other wireless means provide LANs with this flexibility. As with microwave, line of sight is necessary, but an important advantage is that there is no licensing fee required.

4.6 SATELLITES

4.6.1 An Overview

While one-hop short-haul systems allow the bypassing of the local telephone carrier, satellites allow one to bypass the entire PSTN. These "birds" are placed 22,300 miles above the equator so that they rotate at the same rate as the earth does (once a day). This is called a geosynchronous orbit. They carry anywhere from 10 to 46 transponders. These transponders are microwave repeaters which receive uplink signals at one frequency, amplify them, and retransmit them at a different frequency.

The area of the earth where the transmitted signal can be received is called the footprint. The delay for signals that take this round trip journey in space is about 300 msec, which is substantially more than terrestrial transmission delays and therefore limits their usability to remote data entry.

Satellites are broadcast systems, where any station in the footprint of the down link signal can receive the transmission at the same time as other receivers. For instance a newspaper which is printed at various locations in America, can get the transmission in less time than if the transmission were to occur over point-to-point links. Yet, the advantage of broadcasting also presents a problem of privacy. In order to control piracy, the signal can be encrypted.

Table 4.1 shows three bands of frequencies where satellites can operate. The C band, referred to also as the 6/4 GHz band, is one of the oldest and the one most widely in use. Its capacity is being exhausted and the Ku band is becoming as widely used. The signals in the C band are weak and require larger earth stations compared to those which use the Ku band. They are more susceptible to interference from microwave

Table 4.1 Satellite Bands				
Band Names	Other Names	Uplink Frequencies	Downlink Frequencies	Available Bandwidths
C	6/4	5.925 - 6.425 GHz	3.700 - 4.200 GHz	500 MHz
Ku	14/12	14.00 - 14.50 GHz	11.70 - 12.20 GHz	500 MHz
Ka	30/20	27.50 - 30.00 GHz	17.70 - 20.20 GHz	2500 MHz

radios than the Ku band frequencies. However, the Ku band is more susceptible to interference from rain and other weather conditions than the C band is.

When satellites were first being deployed, they used a method called FDMA (Frequency Division Multiple Access) to divide up the satellite resources among the users. Currently, TDMA (Time Division Multiple Access) is more common. Figure 4.7 shows how 3 stations can use the same satellite simultaneously using either of these two methods.

With FDMA, all stations can transmit simultaneously but each one is only allocated a portion of the available bandwidth. With TDMA each station takes turns transmitting, but when their turn comes up they can use the entire bandwidth.

4.6.2 VSATs

Although geosynchronous satellites were launched in the late 1960s, they were only cost effective for large businesses. It was not until 1984, when the VSATs (Very Small Aperture Terminals) were first introduced, that satellites became more commonly used. These satellite systems are named after the small antenna dishes which they use, which are between 1.2 and 2.4 meters. Although VSATs can operate in the C-band, they are mostly used in the Ku-band region.

These systems are widely used for low-speed applications such as credit card authorization, inventory control, and production monitoring. So some of the biggest users of these systems are the automotive, retail, and financial industries. Until the end of the 1980s VSATs were deployed as a star network as depicted in Figure 4.8. Currently, they are deployed in either star or mesh configurations.

The idea behind the star configuration is that having one hub with a large antenna allows for stations to be smaller in the many remote locations. The large antenna at the

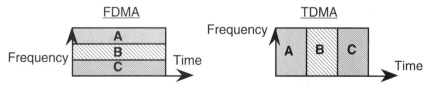

Figure 4.7 In FDMA, stations divide up the frequencies and transmit simultaneously. In TDMA, they divide up the time and wait their turns.

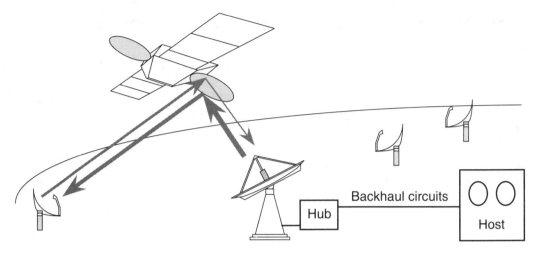

Figure 4.8 A star-configured VSAT network. The widths of the arrows indicate the relative strengths of the transmitted signals.

hub is big enough to send strong signals which the smaller VSAT dishes can pick up. Also, the large hub is sensitive enough to pick up the weak signals sent by the VSATs. However, this arrangement requires that all traffic must use the central hub. So if two remote sites need to communicate, the transmission must be relayed via the hub. Since the cost of a hub can be high, it is commonly leased from a satellite service provider where it is shared between many users.

VSATs do provide several advantages. They are easily and quickly deployed in remote areas. The cost is not primarily based on the distances between the stations, unlike terrestrial transmission methods, but is based on the number of VSAT stations. Furthermore, if necessary, they can be easily moved to different locations, increasing the flexibility of the network map. They are also reliable, providing availability that is better than 99.5 percent. Their error rates are in the order of 10^{-7} compared to 10^{-5} for copper lines.

4.6.3 Hub-Less VSATs

By increasing the size of the antennas to about 5 meters, transmissions can exist between the VSATs directly, without requiring the "double hop" via the hub. This places less demand on the satellite, and since it now requires no hub, it is either called a hub-less or a mesh-configured network. With the elimination of the hub, a common point of failure, the network inherently becomes more reliable. With larger sized VSATs, it is possible to break the typical 56 kbps barrier associated with star networks and achieve speeds of up to 2 Mbps.

This makes the network suitable to carry two-way video and LAN traffic. The network can be configured in real-time, allowing one to adjust bandwidths between sites or even add and delete sites as needed. This can be done without losing any data. However, unlike star-based networks which can accommodate hundreds of VSATs, these are more practical when used with less than 100 or so stations, partly because the bigger VSAT dishes are more expensive than those used with the star-based ones.

Transmission Systems

4.7 PREMISES DISTRIBUTION

For the remainder of this chapter, transmission systems which were originally introduced for voice networks will be discussed. This section will start this set of topics by covering typical wiring schemes for customers' premises.

When a telephone in a building is connected to a PBX, it is not connected by running one continuous line to the PBX. Instead, the installation is done systematically by first connecting the telephone to an IDF (Intermediate Distribution Frame) located on the same floor. Then using multi-pair cables, called the risers, the IDFs from each floor are connected to one MDF (Main Distribution Frame) which is then tied to the PBX. See Figure 4.9. Besides for the IDFs, risers, and the MDF, a premises distribution system is also categorized into the wiring needed at the telephone and the horizontal subsystem.

This method of distributing the wiring provides for better management. Faulty lines can be tested at the distribution frames easily. Lines can be added and deleted easily. Nonetheless, documents and labels specifying which wire goes where is important for such systems.

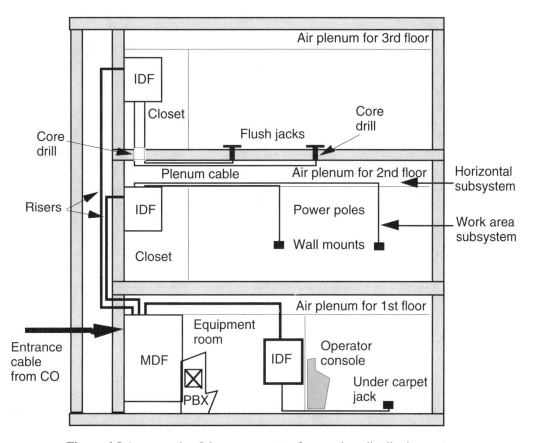

Figure 4.9 An example of the components of a premises distribution system.
(Adopted from Robert Brunson.)

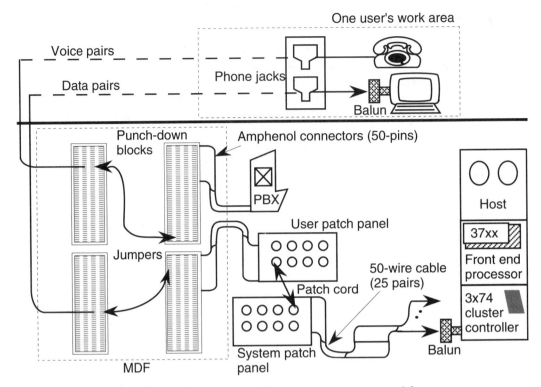

Figure 4.10 Details of one set of lines as they are connected from one work area through an MDF to a PBX and a host. (Adapted from Dick Manzo.)

As seen in Figure 4.10, all the lines coming from the PBX are connected to a group of punch-down blocks in the MDF. Similarly, the pairs from the riser cables are terminated on another group of punch-down blocks. Then the pins from each set of these blocks are cross connected with jumpers. Hence, the distribution frames are also called cross-connect systems.

Changes can now be accomplished by simply changing the jumpers. The figure shows how telephone wiring can be used for the transmission of data as well. Here, old coax systems are interfaced with the twisted pairs using devices called baluns (BALanced/UNbalanced).

4.8 TRUNK TYPES

Usually customer premises require connections to the PSTN through the local telco. The part of the distribution system where the customer's wiring and the telco's wiring interfaces is called the demarcation point or, simply, the demarc. There are many types of trunks which provide communications between the private switching system (or the PBX) and the PSTN. Following are some of these systems.

4.8.1 CO Trunks

Not every telephone connected to a PBX may simultaneously need to communicate with an outside line. Instead of having separate outside lines for every telephone, most installations have a much smaller number of trunks going to the local CO. By having the phones share these trunks, it cuts down on the cost while still providing access to the PSTN for every telephone.

Figure 4.11 shows some types of trunks which may be connected to a PBX. A CO (Central Office) trunk is a popular trunk used between a CO and a PBX. A person in the public network can dial into the PBX over a CO trunk. Similarly, a private system phone can use the CO trunk to dial out. Hence it is called a two-way trunk.

4.8.2 DID Trunks

A DID (Direct Inward Dialing) trunk is a one-way trunk used only to call into a private system. While a call coming into the PBX over a CO trunk generally requires an operator to transfer the call to the appropriate station, a DID trunk, working with the PBX, sends the incoming call to the appropriate station directly.

The customer is assigned a set of telephone numbers which may or may not be listed in the public telephone directory. This does not require extra digits for an extension. When a person in the public network dials a DID number, the CO signals the PBX that a call is coming over a particular DID trunk. When the PBX is ready, the CO sends the last 4 or so digits so that the PBX can complete the connection. At another time, the same trunk can be used to connect a different PBX phone.

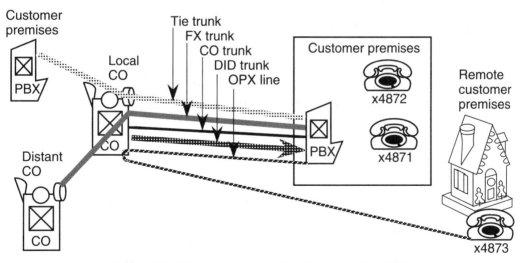

Figure 4.11 The various types of trunks used with a PBX.

4.8.3 FX Trunks

Similar to the CO trunk, is the FX (Foreign eXchange) trunk. It is used when a customer premise does a lot of calling to a distant location or even a distant state. If the call crosses LATA boundaries, then of course an IXC and its POPs are involved in providing the trunk. With the FX, the customer makes local calls at the distant location for a flat monthly rate for the trunk and for any local charges which apply. Also, if the customer has many users who call in from that distant location into the PBX, they can make the calls as if they were local calls to them.

4.8.4 Tie Trunks

Another type of trunk is a tie trunk. It is also referred to as tie line, leased line, or a dedicated line. These trunks can be used to tie two PBXs together or to send data between computer related devices. If the amount of traffic is not sufficient, then dial-up lines or POTS lines are used instead. Tie trunks do not go through switches but only go through line conditioning equipment. So they transmit data with less errors than POTS or switched lines. They are paid on a 24 hour basis and the charges are not reduced, even if the usage becomes low.

4.8.5 OPX Lines

The last type of trunk is not really a trunk but a line, because it doesn't go to a switch but to a telephone. The OPX (Off-Premise eXtension) line typically connects a PBX to a remote customer site. If the main customer site and a remote customer site are, say, divided by a highway, then the customer is not allowed to string his own telephone line over the public area. The telco is allowed to do that for the customer by offering an OPX line.

4.9 DIGITAL CARRIER SYSTEMS

Many times digital signals are sent over copper wires over a limited distance. They are also sent over coax, fiber, and other media, of course. A common method of sending digital signals over a pair of wires is called the T1 carrier system.

A T1 carrier system carries 24 voice channels which are encoded using the PCM technique. Some of the voice bits which are digitized are pre-empted to send signaling bits. So the 64 kbps used for one voice channel doesn't only have the voice bits but also contain signaling bits. Signaling is the information which sends off-hook conditions, dial tones, dialing digits, etc., and is covered in Chapter 5.

The 24 channels times the 64 kbps rate gives a rate of 1.536 Mbps. However, for synchronization purposes (called framing), another 8 kbps is added to give the total rate of 1.544 Mbps. The term "T1" is typically meant for using twisted wire pairs to send this signal. However, this signal in general is called a DS-1 (Digital Signal level 1), which can be sent over any medium.

European countries use a different system called the CEPT (Conférence Européenne des Postes et Télécommunications) system. It designates rates starting at the E1 levels. An E1 level is derived by using PCM coding on 30 channels. However, this PCM coding doesn't pass the signaling needed for the channels. Signaling takes a full 64 kbps and so does framing. It requires another 64 kbps channel. Together, there are a total of 32 channels with a rate of 64 kbps. This provides a final rate of 2.048 Mbps. Other signal levels derived from T1s and E1s are shown in Table 4.2.

4.10 LONG DISTANCE SERVICES

4.10.1 WATS Services

For a long time, basic long distance service allowed a customer to directly dial throughout the nation or internationally. The charges were then included in the monthly bill. This type of service at that time was called MTS (Message Telecommunications Service). It is still used by individuals and firms that have low calling volumes.

MTS was augmented by WATS (Wide Area Telecommunications Service). It handles both incoming (or 800 service) and outgoing calls. WATS is basically a billing method rather than a method of setting up physical circuits. It sets up pricing structures based on the concept of bands.

For example, a subscription to WATS band 0 allows for calling anywhere within the customer's state. Band 1 allows calling anywhere to the adjacent states, band 2 to their neighboring states, and so on. It was a difficult process to determine how many lines for each of the bands would be required, especially if the patterns of calling changed significantly from month to month.

Due to competition in the industry, the banded WATS service has become extinct, since the billing is complex and hard to understand. Today, WATS is used on a limited basis and is being replaced by virtual networks, which is the topic of Chapter 11. There are, however, many varied plans using distance and volume sensitive rate structures.

Table 4.2 Digital Hierarchies							
Used in Australia, Canada, Japan, and USA				Used in CCITT Countries and Europe			
Signal Level	Carrier System	Rate in Mbps	No. of Channels	Signal Level	Carrier System	Rate in Mbps	No. of Channels
DS0	-	000.064	1	CEPT0	-	000.064	1
DS1	T1	001.544	24	CEPT1	E1	002.048	30
DS1C	T1C	003.152	48	CEPT2	E2	008.448	120
DS2	T2	006.312	96	CEPT3	E3	034.368	480
DS3	T3	044.736	672	CEPT4	E4	139.264	1920
DS4	T4	274.176	4032	CEPT5	E5	565.148	7680

4.10.2 800 Services

In 1967, AT&T introduced 800 services which allow callers to call free to the 800 number. The owner of the 800 number pays for the incoming calls based on the volume of calls. Currently, 800 toll-free service is an 8 billion dollar business and it is often tied in with virtual networks.

Until 1993, when a CO would receive a dialed 800 number to connect, it would send the call to the proper IXC's POP by scanning the 3 digits following the 800 number. These three digits are called the NXX digits. AT&T had more NXXs allocated to them than the other carriers.

If a customer wanted to change carriers, he would have to change his 800 number as well, because the NXXs of the 800 numbers belonged to the carriers. This was something which businesses avoided, because to advertise the new number and make the public aware of the change would take time. Currently using SS7 (Signaling System 7) networks, customers can change carriers and take their 800 number with them. This is called 800 number portability. SS7 is covered in Chapters 5, 7, and 14.

800 numbers allow stores to close their doors and do all their selling over the phone. More people are making purchases using these numbers. Companies have the ability to provide outstanding service by using an 800 number. Customers are more willing to buy products if they have an 800 number to call. Many of the features of this service will also be covered in Chapter 11.

They also have their drawbacks. If an 800 service is out, it is difficult for a customer to detect it, especially if the activity on the 800 number is typically low anyway. Also, if someone calls a wrong 800 number, the company has to pay for that call. And what if one company advertises someone else's 800 number incorrectly? The company not at fault still has to pay for those calls and, worse yet, it loses business because of busy lines.

Exercises

1. Which of the following kinds of twisted pair wires is typically used with telephone connections?
   - a. STP
   - b. Category 3
   - c. Category 4
   - d. Category 5

2. Which section of a fiber is nested inside all the others?
   - a. core
   - b. polyurethane coverings
   - c. cladding
   - d. kevlar

3. Which type of access method shares the available bandwidth among the various users in a satellite system?
   - a. CDMA
   - b. DAMA
   - c. FDMA
   - c. TDMA

4. Which of the following is an advantage of VSAT systems over fiber?
   - a. quickly installed
   - b. higher bit rates
   - c. less prone to error
   - d. better management capabilities

5. Which of the following connects PBX trunk types to a distant CO?
   a. CO   b. DID
   c. tie   d. FX

6. Why is 64kbps added for signaling when calculating the 2.048 Mbps rate for E1 and nothing for T1?
   a. T1 doesn't support signaling
   b. Signaling bits are sent as part of the framing bits
   c. Signaling bits are sent as part of the voice channel bits
   d. T1 requires an extra channel dedicated for signaling, so actually it supports only 23 voice channels

7. Which types of rays stay within the fiber and which ones escape?

8. Which short-haul solution provides less attenuation due to weather conditions?

9. Transmission in which satellite band provides less interference from weather conditions and more interference from microwave signals?

10. What type of orbit are satellites placed in?

11. What is another name for a distribution frame?

12. Which service is replacing WATS?

13. Discuss some reasons why Category 5 UTP is becoming popular.

14. What are some reasons why baseband coax has dominated broadband coax in the LAN arena?

15. Name the three major types of fiber and discuss how they differ from each other.

16. When are star-based VSATs a better choice than mesh-based VSATS?

17. Discuss the five categories of a premises distribution system and explain their purpose.

18. What are the pros and cons of using tie trunks versus POTs lines?

Chapter 5

Signaling

5.1 WHAT IS SIGNALING?

Imagine if we were made with all of the parts of the body, but didn't have our nervous system. Then we would not be able to tell our feet to walk or to perform even the simplest actions. We would be paralyzed. Similarly, in a much simpler sense, a telephone network with sophisticated digital switches all interconnected would be useless if there were no method of communication defined between them. Therefore, signaling is said to be the nervous system of a network. It is the exchange of control information between two points in a network that establishes, maintains, and removes a connection.

5.2 STEPS TAKEN IN PLACING A CALL

5.2.1 Call Origination

We will use Figure 5.1 to outline the steps taken to complete an interoffice call. Here office means the CO (Central Office). In the telephone industry, the term EO (End Office) is used to refer to the switching equipment connected to a telephone which processes calls. I'll simply refer to it as the CO.

First, the calling party takes his or her phone off the hook, which completes an electrical circuit through the pair of wires. Current starts to flow and the equipment at the CO notices this current. Then the CO connects a register to the line to store the subscriber's dialed digits, and then it provides a dial tone, signaling him that the dialing can begin.

When a phone is on-hook, it draws no current from the CO and is said to be in the idle state. Conversely, when it is off-hook, it draws current and is said to be in the active state or is said to seize the line.

Eric Harvie of NJ Bell has been instrumental in helping me put this chapter together.

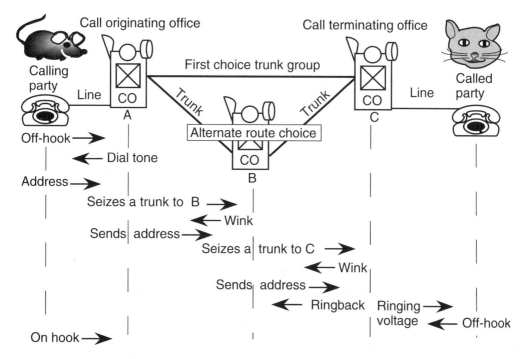

Figure 5.1 Exchange of signals over interoffice trunks.

5.2.2 Call Routing

The switch at CO-A searches its routing guide, and finds that the calling party is located at CO-C. The guide indicates that the direct trunk to CO-C is the first choice in routing the call. However, since all of the trunks to C are active, CO-A consults the routing guide again and finds an alternate route choice as the trunk group to CO-B.

CO-A finds and seizes an idle trunk connected to CO-B. CO-B connects a register to the circuit and sends a "wink" which is an off-hook condition followed by an on-hook condition. Sensing that CO-B is ready, CO-A sends the digits of the calling party.

From the received digits, noticing that the called party is not directly connected to it, CO-B obtains a connection to CO-C in the same manner that CO-A obtained one to CO-B. CO-C then realizes that the called party is connected to it and not to another CO, so it provides a ringing voltage to the phone, given that the phone is idle. A ringback, which is also called an audible ringing tone, is transmitted by CO-C back to the calling party's phone.

5.2.3 Answer Supervision

When the called party picks up the phone, the ringing voltage and the ringback tone are removed by CO-C. An off-hook signal, which is called an answer supervision signal, is transmitted to CO-A, and CO-A now knows that the called party has answered the phone. If necessary, a record for billing can begin and the call is connected.

5.2.4 Disconnect and Call Clean-Up

Figure 5.1 shows that the calling party has hung up first. However, the calling party may hang up first instead. This is called the disconnect phase. The call clean-up phase restores all the trunks to their idle conditions, and CO-A will stop the billing recording at this time.

5.3 TYPES OF SIGNALING FORMATS

Signaling which has only two states, such as on-hook or off-hook, presence of current or no current, application of a frequency or the absence of it, is said to provide a supervisory function.

Address signaling function is provided where a phone number is present in the signaling.

Information signaling is provided by tones and recorded announcements such as ". . . this number has been disconnected."

A dial tone is a combination of 350 Hz and 440 Hz signals. A ringback tone consists of 440 Hz and 480 Hz. A busyback signal or line busy tone uses combinations of 480 Hz and 620 Hz tones interrupted every second. A reorder tone or all trunks busy tone is the same as a busy tone but is pulsed twice as fast as a busy tone.

An alerting function is provided by ringing, flashing, and receiver off-hook tones. The ringing voltage of 90 VAC at 20 Hz activates the ringer on a phone. It typically is on for 2 seconds and off for 4 seconds.

Flashing is done by the subscriber after being connected. The subscriber momentarily goes on-hook and immediately goes off-hook again. Since the on-hook condition is for a short duration, the switch doesn't mistake it for a disconnect. Flashing allows an operator to get back on the line to signal a PBX that a special function code is to follow or to place a call on hold.

5.4 SIGNALING DELAYS AND INTEROFFICE SIGNALING

There are three types of delays present when processing a call over a network: dialing delay, answer delay, and post dialing delay. Dialing delay is the amount of time taken from getting a dial tone until the last digit of the phone number is dialed. The use of tone dialing over rotary pulse dialing has helped to reduce this kind of signaling delay. Answer delay is the time taken for the called party to pick up the phone from the time the first ring was heard.

Lastly, post dialing or ringing delay is the time between these two delays. It is the time taken between when the caller dials the last digit and until the time it takes for the phone to start ringing at the distant end.

5.4.1 Per-Trunk Signaling

Notice back in Figure 5.1 that if a direct trunk were available from CO-A to CO-C, this delay would have been shorter. Conversely, if a call had to go through many switches, then this delay would increase. This is because all of the switches which lie in the path of a call would do their switch processing one at a time. For example, in

Figure 5.1, CO-C could not start its switching process until CO-B received the phone address from CO-A.

The signaling described in Figure 5.1 is an example of per-trunk signaling, also known as CAS (Channel Associated Signaling). This means that all of the signaling (supervisory, addressing, information, and alerting type) is sent over the same physical path as the voice.

5.4.2 Common Channel Interoffice Signaling

Today the telephone carriers are using CCIS (Common Channel Interoffice Signaling), which is quite different in nature from per-trunk signaling. The idea behind CCIS is why use expensive voice grade trunks to send signaling. Instead separate the signaling from the voice path, and use an entirely different network just for signaling. Furthermore, since signaling information is basically data, that is on-hook, off-hook conditions, addressing, etc., make the signaling network a packet data network.

Figure 5.2 shows how the three switches are connected to each other using CCIS. Here, the voice paths are separated from the signaling paths. STPs (Signaling Transfer Points) are used in the signaling network to properly route packets of signaling. So when CO-A finds no trunks available to CO-C to make a call, it notices free trunks to CO-B. Then CO-A sends the address of the destination phone it wishes to connect to, to an STP. After the STP network has found out that the destination phone is idle and available to take a call, all involved switches are directed and simultaneously notified to complete the voice path to CO-C. After making a continuity check of the path, the ringing is activated.

Since the STPs are critical for network operations, they are deployed in pairs. So if one fails the other one can take all of the signaling traffic. SS7 (Signaling System 7), which is the current implementation of CCIS, is the topic of Chapter 14. SS7 is a type of packet switching network so it is left for discussion after Chapter 13.

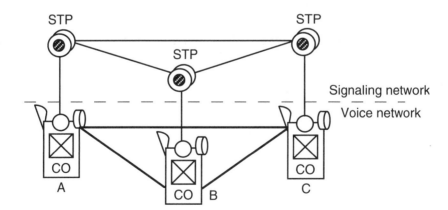

Figure 5.2 CCIS uses a data packet network that is separated from the voice network. STPs (Signaling Transfer Points) are the packet switches which comprise the signaling network.

5.4.3 The Advantages of CCIS

The advantages of CCIS are many. First, the post dialing delay is reduced drastically. Within a LATA, a connection is made as soon as the last digit is dialed. For a coast to coast call the typical delay is 4 seconds compared to 20 seconds as experienced with per-trunk signaling.

Furthermore, not as many voice trunks are as necessary as before, because the voice trunks only handle voice, and each call uses the voice trunks for less time. With per-trunk signaling, the called switch provides the busyback signal over the voice trunk. With CCIS, in such a case, the voice trunks are not used at all. Information that the distant phone is busy is relayed to the calling switch over the signaling network, and the calling switch provides the busyback signal to the phone.

One of the early reasons why CCIS was introduced was to provide 800 number service. Since then CCIS has become the vehicle to provide calling card, virtual network, ISDN, and many new sophisticated services.

The signaling network, a packet switched network, is very efficient in transporting data. The signaling for all of the circuits is handled over a common link from the switch to the STP, and every voice circuit doesn't need its own separate link.

This is the reason why it is called common channel signaling. The signaling for all of the calls is sent over this common channel. With per-trunk signaling, the signaling for each call between a pair of switches travels on a separate channel, which is unlike CCIS.

5.5 KINDS OF ADDRESS SIGNALING

5.5.1 Dial Pulsing

Rotary dial pulses have been the traditional method of signaling an address (or a phone number). Once a phone goes off hook and it receives a dial tone, it can start sending the first digit. In Figure 5.3, the digits being sent are 4 and 2. The number of times the line is made to go on-hook determines the digit that is being dialed. Since the duration of the break is relatively small, about 60 milliseconds, the switch does not inadvertently disconnect the phone. The percent break of dial pulsing is defined to be the ratio of break duration to the pulse period. This is usually kept at 60%.

Although the waveform of dial pulsing looks digital, it is slow and the dialing delay depends on the digits dialed. A zero requires 10 pulses and since each pulse period is 100 milliseconds long, it takes one second just to dial the number zero.

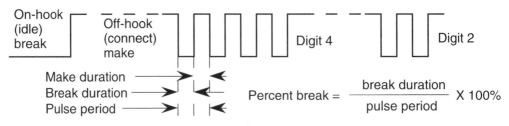

Figure 5.3 Typical train of rotary dial pulses.

5.5.2 DTMF Signaling

With tone signaling or DTMF (Dual-Tone MultiFrequency) signaling, all digits are transmitted with the same small delay, around 120 milliseconds. The digits are placed in a matrix as shown in Figure 5.4. Here dialing a number activates two different signal generators: one determined by the row the digit is in and one determined by its column. For instance, when a "1" is dialed, a 1209 Hz and 697 Hz tone are superimposed and transmitted.

DTMF provides a "*" and a "#," characters not found on rotary dials. However, the letters "q" and "z" are still missing. The four positions available from the right column are not currently used, but could be used for special purposes.

It seems as if the assignment of these frequencies was made randomly. To minimize false signaling due to harmonic interference and the human voice, these frequencies were chosen. False signaling is the misinterpretation of control signals due to unintended causes.

DTMF reduces dialing delay especially if a prerecorded number is dialed. It uses solid state equipment which reduces the equipment needed at the switches. It is also compatible with modern electronic switches and provides end-to-end signaling.

End-to-end signaling allows a phone to interact with a computer on the dialed end of the circuit. Voice processing applications, covered in Chapter 9, would not be as advanced as they are today without DTMF. In essence DTMF allows an ordinary telephone to have the functionality of a computer terminal.

5.5.3 MF Signaling

DTMF signaling is used for subscriber lines and MF (MultiFrequency) signaling is used between switches or for interoffice trunks. MF signaling, which came before DTMF and is now being phased out by SS7, uses combinations of two frequencies out of a possible six. See Table 5.1 for how these frequencies are used. In MF signaling, the human voice could possibly simulate one of these control signals (false signaling),

	ABC	DEF		
1	2	3	11	697 Hz
GHI	JKL	MNO		
4	5	6	12	770 Hz
PRS	TUV	WXY		
7	8	9	13	852 Hz
	OPER			
*	0	#	14	941 Hz
1209	1336	1477	1633 Hz	

Figure 5.4 DTMF uses a grid made out of row frequencies and column frequencies to assign frequency pairs to the digits. 11 through 14 are currently not used.

Table 5.1 MF Frequency Pair Assignments			
Frequencies (in Hz)	Digit	Frequencies (in Hz)	Purpose
900 + 700	1	1700 + 700*	Ringback from coin control
1100 + 700	2	1700 + 900*	Delay operator
1100 + 900	3	1700 + 1100*	Start of address
1300 + 700	4	1700 + 1300	Transit code
1300 + 900	5	1700 + 1500	End of address
1300 + 1100	6		.
1500 + 700	7		* These frequency
1500 + 900	8		combinations have other
1500 + 1100	9		functions as well
1500 + 1300	0 or 10		

so the duration of the tones was increased. Also, before the digits were transmitted a start-of-address frequency pair was sent and afterwards the end-of-address frequency was sent.

5.6 SIGNALING TYPES PROVIDING SUPERVISION

5.6.1 SF Signaling

Unlike the addressing signaling methods which were just described, SF signaling is used to exchange on and off conditions or provide supervisory signaling. With SF (Single Frequency), when a customer line is idle a continuous tone is transmitted and when the tone goes off, the CO knows that the customer is seizing the line. See Table 5.2. If the CO provides a tone, that is interpreted as a ringing condition, and if the tone is absent, it is interpreted as an idle condition. SF can also provide addressing, if the tone is turned on and off as with dial pulsing.

DTMF, MF, and SF signaling are considered as facility independent signaling formats. This means that these tones can be sent over twisted pair, coax, microwave, fiber, or any other transmission facility. Dial pulsing is an example of facility dependent signaling, in that it can only be used on a twisted pair with a – 48 VDC power source. Dial pulsing is also categorized as DC signaling, in that it requires DC voltage and current to operate. The signaling types which are being described next, loop start and ground start, are also types of DC signaling.

5.6.2 Loop Start Signaling

In analyzing circuits with DC loop currents, keep in mind that AC signals can still ride on top of DC voltages. Dial tones, DTMF signals, and voice are examples of such AC signals. If a path is open for DC current, using a capacitor, it can short AC signals.

Table 5.2 SF (Single Frequency) Operation		
	From customer line to CO	From CO to customer line
Tone ON Tone OFF	idle seizure	ringing idle and busy

The purpose of these descriptions is to study DC loop currents and not the AC voltages that are also typically present.

Loop start signaling is commonly used on residential or subscriber loops, and it requires only one pair of wires. One lead of the pair is called the tip and the other is called the ring.

Figure 5.5(a) shows the phone being on hook. Notice that the contact is open in the phone at that time, allowing no current to flow in any direction. No current yields 0 Volts across all three resistors. That is, since voltage is equal to current times resistance, and current is zero, voltages across all the resistances are zero. Furthermore, the voltage on the tip side of the pair is 0V, and from the ring it is − 48 VDC.

Figure 5.5(b) shows when the phone goes off-hook the contact is closed, the circuit is completed, and current may flow through the loop. At the CO about 20 Volts is dropped both on the tip lead and on the ring lead, leaving only 8 VDC across the telephone. The presence of DC current is detected at the CO which then attaches a dial tone generator and a digit receiver to the circuit. All AC signals ride on top of the DC voltage.

When a call comes in, and an incoming 90 VAC ringing voltage arrives, it rides on the DC voltage and activates the ringer.

5.6.3 Advantages of Ground Start Signaling

Ground start signaling uses DC loop currents and one twisted pair as does loop start signaling. However, ground start signaling is used primarily with PBXs and not on subscriber loops. Using loop start signaling with PBXs introduces several of the following problems which are not present in ground start signaling. First, let me clarify a definition. A ground start line between a CO and a PBX is referred to as a trunk on the PBX side and is referred to as a line on the end office side.

Suppose a PBX which is not equipped to detect dial tones sends an off-hook condition over a loop start line. Then it must wait a pre-specified amount of time before sending out its dialing digits, expecting that enough time has passed to receive the dial tone. By chance if the CO hasn't sent the dial tone yet and isn't ready to receive the digits at that time, then the dialing digits will get lost. With ground start this problem is eliminated.

If on a line, a ring is received which begins with the 4-second quiet period, instead of the 2-second ringing period, and at the same time, the PBX seizes that line

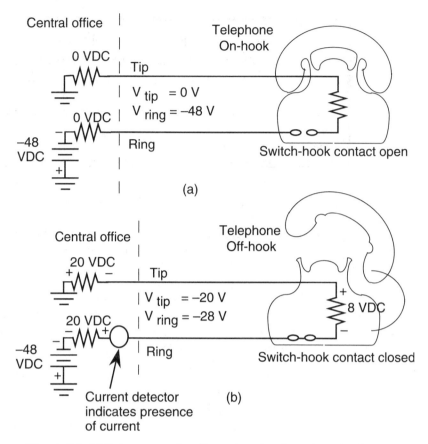

Figure 5.5 (a) In loop start signaling, when the phone is on-hook, no current is present and the voltage across the ring is – 48 Volts. (b) When the phone goes off-hook, current flows and this voltage becomes – 28 Volts. The current detected in the loop is noticed by the CO and it connects a digit receiving register and sends a dial tone.

to make a call, then the two calling parties are surprisingly connected. This is called glare and is more common on home phones which use loop start signaling. In a business environment, however, this phenomena is undesirable. With ground start, the CO provides a positive trunk seizure.

The last advantage ground start signaling poses over loop start is that the former provides answer supervision. This means that if the distant end hangs up while the PBX has that party on hold, then the CO can signal the PBX that the trunk has become free and is made available to initiate other calls.

5.6.4 Operation of Ground Start Signaling

Figure 5.6(a) shows the idle condition for ground start signaling, the following two diagrams show how an outgoing call is made, and the last two diagrams show how an incoming call is received. Notice that in loop start, one two-position switch is used, and here two three-position switches are used.

In the idle condition, neither batteries draw current, since both switches are in open condition. In Figure 5.6(b), the PBX is initiating a call by grounding its ring lead. This causes current to flow in the ring lead which is detected by the CO. The CO realizes that the PBX has gone "off-hook," and it attaches a digit receiver, sends a dial tone, and grounds its tip. The current in the tip lead is now detected by the PBX and

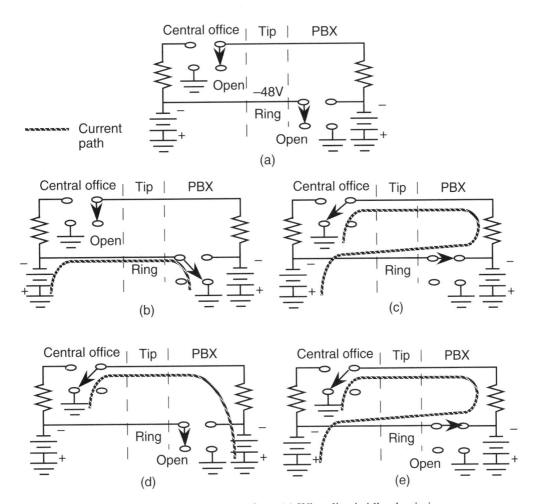

Figure 5.6 Ground start operation. (a) When line is idle, the tip is open at the CO and the ring is open at the customer end. (b) In an outgoing call, the customer grounds the ring. (c) Which the CO notices and grounds the tip, then the customer completes the loop. (d) In an incoming call, the CO grounds the tip first. (e) Then the customer completes the loop.

it knows that the CO is ready to receive digits. It does this by first closing the loop on the ring lead. Now a loop is established and dialing can commence.

Let us now look at how an incoming call is received by the PBX after the line has been idle as in Figure 5.6(a). Figure 5.6(d) shows that the CO will ground its tip lead to signal the PBX that it has an incoming call.

The PBX notices the current in the tip lead and restricts that trunk from being used for outgoing calls. After the PBX detects the ringing voltage, the PBX places a loop closure across the tip and ring leads as seen in Figure 5.6(e).

The CO detects the loop closure, terminates the ringing, and provides a voice path to the PBX. If the distant party hangs up first, the CO will open the tip lead which the PBX detects and the PBX will open the ring lead.

On the other hand, the PBX can terminate the call by opening the ring, causing the loop current to stop. This is noticed by the CO which, in turn, opens up the tip lead, returning the line to the idle state as shown in Figure 5.6(a).

5.7 DIGITAL CARRIER SYSTEMS

Signaling is inherently data and it becomes natural to encode it using bits. We have seen how a presence of current or frequency can carry one meaning and the absence the opposite. Similarly, in digital carriers, such as the common T1, any of the signaling functions can be implemented by setting certain bits as either a one or a zero. The bits which carry such information are called signaling bits, and the collection of them for one voice channel is called a signaling channel.

5.7.1 Robbed Bit vs. Clear Channel Signaling

As seen in the next to the last entry of Table 5.3, there exists no separate signaling channel for the T1, while one exists for the European E1 system. This is because with a T1, the signaling bits preempt or take possession of one voice bit out of every 48 voice bits, on any given voice channel. The loss of these occasional voice bits are not detected by the human ear. So the T1's 64 kbps voice channel not only includes the voice bits, but also the signaling bits. This is called robbed bit signaling, because the signaling bits in effect have "robbed" some of the voice bits.

On the other hand notice, with the E1 transmission format, that there is a separate channel just for signaling. This is because E1 does not rob voice bits to place signaling bits on instead, but transmits only voice on the 64 kbps voice channels.

The signaling for all of the 30 voice channels are combined into a separate 64 kbps signaling channel. The fact that no signaling appears in a voice channel is said to make the channel clear and so the E1 provides clear channel signaling. Both domestically and internationally, ISDN calls for clear channel signaling.

5.7.2 Common Channel Signaling

Common channel signaling has two meanings. Common channel interoffice signaling as depicted in Figure 5.2 provides a signaling network that is separate from the voice network. A link from a switch to the corresponding STP pair is a common link to carry signaling for all of the voice circuits associated with the given switch.

Table 5.3 Comparison of T1 and E1 Formats		
(BW = Bandwidth in bits per second)	T1	E1
BW of one voice channel	64 k	64 k
Total number of voice channels	24	30
BW taken by all voice channels	1536 k	1920 k
BW taken for framing	8 k	64 k
BW taken for a separate signaling channel	—	64 k
Total BW of the carrier system	1544 k	2048 k

Here, in the E1 system, we have seen what may be called common channel digital signaling. The 30 signaling channels that were separated from their respective voice channels are combined into one common signaling channel. As we'll see in Chapter 10, another T1 formatting scheme called the M44 format also uses clear channel and common channel digital signaling techniques.

5.7.3 In-Band vs. Out-of-Band Signaling Methods

Robbed bit signaling is also said to be in-band signaling, because the bits used for signaling occupy the same (in-band) bits that were originally intended for voice. Likewise, if the signaling bits don't use the voice bits for transmission, the signaling bits are said to be "out-of-band" from the voice bits. So out-of-band signaling is the same as clear channel signaling.

Sometimes a digital network management channel is sent along with the voice channels, to get error statistics and so forth. In this case, the management channel is also said to be in-band, contrary to having a management channel that is sent over a different facility than the voice channels. There will be more on this in Chapter 10.

What I have just described here is in-band and out-of-band digital signaling. This should not be confused with in-band and out-of-band analog signaling methods.

In a typical voice grade line, 300 Hz to 3300 Hz of bandwidth is available to transmit voice. Any signaling which uses frequencies within this range is called in-band (analog) signaling. MF, DTMF, and SF signaling use frequencies within this range, and so they are considered to be in-band analog signaling methods. An outdated N1 carrier system used a 3700 Hz signal which fell out of the voice bandwidth, and is an example of out-of-band analog signaling.

5.8 SIGNALING INTERFACES

As we have seen so far, signaling information can be sent over a variety of transmission facilities. On the local loop a metallic or a copper wire is used for sending DC loop currents. On the other hand between offices, MF signaling has been widely used, and if microwave or fiber is connected between them, one can't send DC currents, but only analog or digital signals.

In order to convert one signaling system to another kind, one needs to use an interface between them. In other words, an interface is a piece of equipment which uses a technique to interconnect two dissimilar transmission facilities or signaling methods.

5.8.1 4-Wire Termination Set

At the CO, subscriber lines which are 2-wire lines are interfaced with 4-wire metallic facilities using 4WTSs (4-Wire Termination Sets). See Figure 5.7. The 2-wire circuit for the local loop is economical and is used over short distances. 4-wire circuits require two pairs of wire, one for transmit (the T and R leads) and one to receive (the T1 and R1 leads). 4-wires provide a better quality of transmission and are used for longer distances. Unlike on the local loop, the direction of transmission is separated on long distance facilities, so 4WTSs are used for interfacing at this point. This is also called a hybrid circuit and it simply interfaces a 2-wire circuit to a 4-wire circuit.

5.8.2 E&M Signaling Interface

A very common interface used between metallic facilities and analog facilities is called the E&M interface. This interface is used for conversion between DC loop currents and in-band analog signaling. It is used on tie trunks between PBXs. The "e" lead stands for the "e" in rEceive (or Ear) and the "m" lead stands for the "m" in transMit (or Mouth). Also, SB and SG stand for Signal Battery and Signal Ground, respectively.

Figure 5.8 shows a 4-wire tie trunk between two PBXs. The tie trunk is considered as an analog facility in this case. Typically, there is an E&M interface at each PBX. This interface consists of a MFT (Metallic Facility Terminal) and an AFT (Analog Facility Terminal). The figure shows the condition of the interfaces during the idle condition. No current flows in any of the leads and there is no SF tone placed over the tie trunk.

If the calling PBX has to initiate a call for one of its users and has stored the dialed digits in a register, it requires a tie trunk to place a call. The seizure of the trunk is accomplished in the following manner, and is explained using the step numbers shown in the diagram.

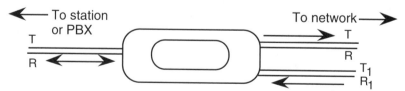

Figure 5.7 A 4WTS or a hybrid circuit converts a 1-pair line to a 2-pair one. On the 1-pair line, the receive and the transmit share the same pair, but on the 2-pair side of the hybrid the transmit and receive signals are kept separated.

In step 1, the 2-wire to 4-wire conversion is done, and in step 2 the MFT provides a loop closure across its M and SB leads. The presence of current in this loop is detected at the AFT, which in turn applies an SF signal over the tie trunk. Remember that DC currents can't travel very well over long distances, so the SF signal is used over this analog facility. This is step 3.

Step 4 requires the called PBX's AFT to notice an SF tone, and so in step 5 it closes the loop on its E and SG leads. The presence of current here is noticed by the MFT and causes the PBX to connect a register to receive the dialed digits. When it is ready, it then closes the M and SB leads. This is step 6.

The AFT notices the current, and sends an SF tone in step 7. The SF tone is noticed by the calling PBX's AFT and closes the E lead loop, causing current to flow here. Finally, in step 8, when the MFT notices the current, the calling PBX transmits the dialed digits stored in the register over its T and R leads. The digits are received on the called end over the T1 and R1 leads.

Once the connection is made by the distant PBX to the appropriate phone, conversation can take place over the T, R, T1, and R1 leads, and the connection phase of the signaling is complete.

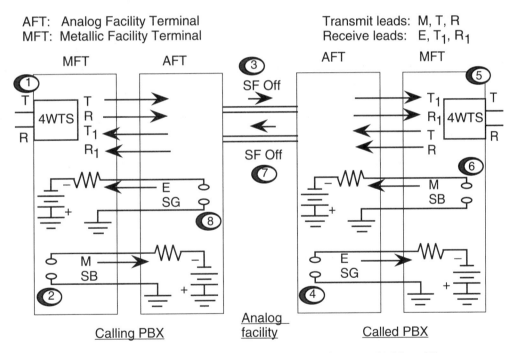

Figure 5.8 Conditions of E&M signaling interfaces used with an idle 4-wire tie line. (1) PBX finds a free trunk to make a call. (2) M lead is closed, current flows. (3) SF signal goes on. (4) E lead is closed for current to flow. (5) Called PBX is ready for the call. (6) It closes the M lead. (7) SF signal is turned on by the AFT. (8) The E lead is closed, and now the tie line is seized to pass the dialing digits.

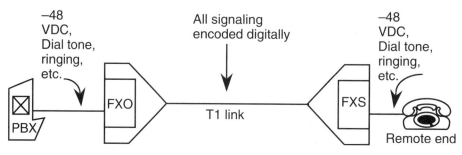

Figure 5.9 One circuit is shown here on a digital carrier such as a T1, where all analog signaling is converted to specific patterns of 1s and 0s.

5.8.3 Digital Signaling Interfaces

Figure 5.9 shows an example of how conventional analog signaling interfaces with digital signaling of a T1. Here, a T1 private line connects the PBX to a remote location making the phones at the remote end look as if they are part of the PBX system. The channel bank on the PBX side receives up to 24 voice channels from the PBX, multiplexes them over the digital T1 carrier and the channel bank at the remote end reverses this process.

FXO (Foreign eXchange, Office) forms the analog to digital interface at the PBX side, while FXS (Foreign eXchange, Subscriber) is the interface at the remote end.

When the phone is idle, the line card at the PBX provides the – 48 VDC to its channel bank, and the FXO converts that to 1s and 0s for that voice channel over the T1. At the remote end, the FXS recognizing this pattern of the received 1s and 0s, provides a – 48 VDC for the remote phone. This way the PBX thinks it has a phone attached to it, while the phone thinks it has a PBX line card attached to it, even though the signaling is converted to digital form between them over the T1.

So now, if the remote phone goes off-hook, the FXS interface notices it and transmits a certain pattern of 1s and 0s over the T1 for that circuit. This pattern, interpreted by the FXO, simulates a loop closure for the PBX just as if the phone had done so directly. The PBX now provides a dial tone, which the FXO converts to a different digital pattern, which the FXS then, in turn, converts back to an audible dial tone that is heard on the phone.

In this fashion, the FXO and FXS interfaces perform conversions between analog signaling for the end points and digital signaling for the T1 carrier which exists in-between them. In the E&M interface discussed earlier, one can easily see how a digital transmission medium can substitute a digital 1 for an SF tone and a digital 0 for the absence of the SF tone. Thus digital signaling interfaces are easily incorporated in place of many types of analog signaling forms.

Exercises

1. When a calling phone goes off-hook, it is said to
   a. provide answer supervision
   b. seize the line
   c. go in a post dialing mode
   d. initiate call routing

2. An off-hook condition immediately followed by an on-hook condition, is called what?
   a. a digit
   b. a disconnect
   c. supervision
   d. a wink

3. Which of the following signaling functions were NOT covered in the text?
   a. supervision
   b. information
   c. testing
   d. alerting

4. Which of the following is a facility independent signaling format?
   a. loop start
   b. DTMF
   c. E&M signaling
   d. ground start

5. What device is used to convert 2-wire to 4-wire signaling?
   a. E lead of E&M signaling
   b. M lead of E&M signaling
   c. a plain telephone
   d. 4WTS

6. When the CO lets the PBX connected to it know that the distance party has hung up, what is that called?

7. A loud pulsing tone heard on a phone when it stays off-hook too long is an example of what kind of a signaling function?

8. The time between the dialing delay and the answer delay is called what?

9. How is the time between the dialing and the answer delays reduced by the carriers?

10. What is the total number of frequency pairs possible with MF signaling? How many of them are used?

11. Give two names for the type of signaling which makes signaling bits use some voice bits for transmission.

12. Explain how an interoffice call would take place if a trunk between CO-A and CO-C were available.

13. What are the different types of signaling functions, and what do they mean?

14. Explain the benefits of CCIS over per-trunk signaling.

15. If you were given the choice to pick four characters for the last column of frequency pairs available in Figure 5.4, what would you choose and why?

16. What are some reasons why ground start signaling is better than loop start signaling?

Chapter 6

Switching

6.1 BASIC SWITCHING

6.1.1 Why Switch?

If four homes needed access to each other without switching, they would have to be connected as shown in Figure 6.1(a). Every location would need a separate phone for each of the other three locations, as well as separate lines for them. Imagine an entire city being wired this way. Every time a home needed to call a new location, the telco would have to install another line between them and connect another pair of phones. It would be a big task just to label each phone, specifying where each one is connected.

Without switches, each location needs n–1 phones and the network needs n(n–1)/2 phone lines to gain full access to the network. Here, n is the number of locations in the network. So a town with only 1000 customers would require the installation of half a million lines.

Fortunately, our telephone networks are connected using switches housed in COs. See Figure 6.1(b). In this case, each location only needs one phone and one line. However, now the entire network depends on the reliability of the CO. So, the COs are built so that they are not as effected by floods, earthquakes, or other calamities.

Another disadvantage of introducing switches is that we need a method of communication between the switches and the end users. This is necessary for a caller to be properly connected to his destination. As seen from the last chapter, this is called signaling. Signaling (also spelled signalling) transfers information between a user and a switch or between two switches.

As the number of COs which need to be interconnected increase, the problem of requiring more and more cross links reoccurs, but this time between the COs. To alleviate this problem, tandem switches are installed. See Figure 6.1(c). A tandem switch is a switch for switches, and serves the same basic purpose as the switch in Figure 6.1(a) does for telephones.

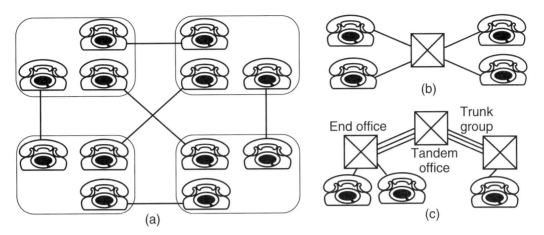

Figure 6.1 (a) Connecting four locations without a switch. (b) Here, with a switch. (c) A tandem switch connects switches.

6.1.2 Parts of a Switch

A switch is made up of two basic parts: the switching fabric or the switching network and its control. The fabric is where the individual lines or trunks are connected to complete the communications paths and the control mechanism signals the elements in the fabric when and how to make the connections.

Even the earliest type of a switch, the switchboard and its operator, exhibits these two properties. The operator himself or herself is the controlling mechanism who determines which patch cord should be connected to which jack. The physical switch board with its plugs, cords, jacks, and lamps is the switching fabric where the communication path is completed.

6.1.3 Space vs. Time Division Switching

Two approaches to building a switch are called space division and time division switching. Figure 6.2 shows examples of each. In each case, the inputs A, B, and C are connected to outputs E, F, and D, respectively. In these diagrams only the switching fabrics are shown; the control mechanisms needed to determine the overall states of the switches are not shown.

In Figure 6.2(a), the three switches on the left are performing what is called concentration, since each one reduces many inputs to one path. They select one of the input terminals. The switches on the right are performing expansion, since they select the proper outputs for the connections.

Here, the switches are set and don't change for the duration of the call. Also, two simultaneous connections can be established over different physical paths. Since the physical paths are separated within the space occupied by the switch, this approach is called space division switching.

Contrast this with time division switching depicted in Figure 6.2(b). Here, one switch is shown at three different times. During the first time interval the connection

Switching

for A is made, during the second interval the connection for B is made, and so on. This process is repeated and the information between the input and output terminals is passed, each connection taking its turn. Since the three connections must share the one physical path, they have to take turns sharing that path in a round robin fashion.

Notice, the connections don't divide up the physical space taken by the switch between themselves, but divide up the available time instead. Hence, this approach is called time division switching. It is very similar to time division multiplexing as was depicted in Figure 3.11. The only difference between them is with TDM, the connections between input terminals and output terminals are pretty much fixed. That is, input 1 connects to output 1, input 2 connects to output 2, etc., whereas, with time division switching, a given input can connect to any of the other outputs determined by the control mechanism in real time.

Figure 6.2(c) shows a matrix or a coordinate switch. Does this use space division or time division switching? Notice, it has three inputs on the left and three outputs on top. To provide a full set of connections between them, there are a total of 9 switches. Since each connection uses a different physical path, the switch is considered to use space division switching, although it has more switches than the one in Figure 6.2(a). There are only 2-position switches while the one in Figure 6.2(a) uses 3-position switches. Currently, switching in a matrix fabric is accomplished by using semiconductor technology such as VLSI (Very Large Scale Integration) which condense many transistors on one chip.

6.1.4 Blocking Factors

The two space division switches in Figures 6.2(a) and (c) are considered to be fully non-blocking. That is, all inputs can be provided with a connection to the outputs which are idle. A blocking switch is one that is designed with the idea that not all

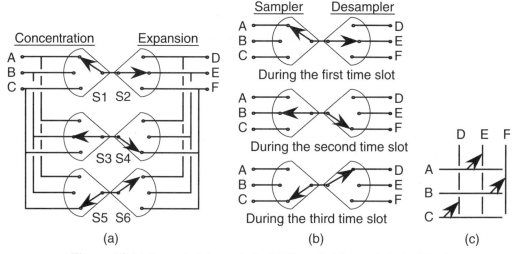

Figure 6.2 (a) Space division switch. (b) Time division switch. (c) Matrix switch. Each example connects A to E, B to F, and C to D.

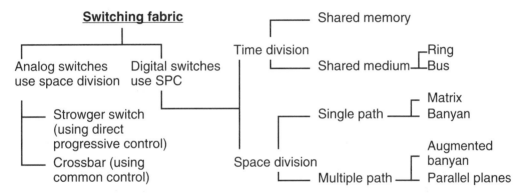

Figure 6.3 Categories of switching fabrics.

terminals will require simultaneous connections, so why build larger and expensive switching fabrics?

A blocking switch can be visioned by eliminating switches S5 and S6 in Figure 6.2(a). In that case, any two of the three inputs can get a connection, but if the third one requires one, it will get a busy signal. This would then be classified as a 33% blocking or a 67% non-blocking switch, since a third of the inputs are blocked or two-thirds are not blocked when the switch reaches its full capacity.

6.1.5 Further Categorizing of Switches

Besides for space division and time division switching, switches can be further categorized as shown in Figure 6.3. The first switch was manual, i.e., the cordboard. The early generation of switches which followed were primarily electromechanical, meaning that they used relays which were activated by electrical currents. These switches will be covered in the next section and typically employ space division techniques.

After the electromechanical switches came the digital switches which may use either time division or space division switching. Each of these switching categories are controlled by a technique that is unique to them. The Strowger switch uses a controlling technique called direct progressive control. The crossbar uses a method called common control and most of the digital switches use a method called SPC (Stored Program Control). First, let us discuss these controlling techniques. Then eventually we will outline the operation of the other switch types shown in Figure 6.3.

6.2 METHODS OF CONTROL

6.2.1 Direct Progressive Control

In 1892, the Strowger or the step-by-step switching system was invented by Almon B. Strowger and was first installed in independent telco COs. Interestingly, the Bell system didn't install these automated systems until about 25 years later. The step-by-step switch uses the direct progressive control mechanism to determine the switch states and provide the connections. The dialed pulses from the user's telephone directly selects and controls the switch position, from one switch to the next. The path selected by the dialed pulses is the same path through which the voice travels.

Figure 6.4 shows how an interoffice call is made using step-by-step switches. Here, the telephone on the left is calling the one on the right by dialing 427-5587. The three stages of these switches are line finders, selectors and connectors. When the telephone on the left picks up the phone to make a call, the line finder connects that phone line to the first selector.

This selector provides the dial tone. After receiving the first dialed digit, 4 in this case, it selects the 4th bank or position on the switch. Then it looks for an idle line to the next selector. Similarly, selectors 2 and 3 switch in accordance with the 2nd and 3rd dialed digits. In this example, these three digits designate an exchange that is located in a different CO. So these are hard wired using trunks to the 427 exchange. The calling phone continues to control the switches in this exchange as well, until the connector switch completes the connection using the last two digits.

6.2.2 Common Control

Another method of controlling the switching fabric is called common control. This type of controlling mechanism has been typically found with the crossbar switch. The crossbar switch was invented by L. M. Ericsson in Sweden only ten years after the step-by-step switch was invented. It played a dominant role until digital switches became widely available.

A basic block diagram of a crossbar switch is shown in Figure 6.5. The line link frame is a matrix switch as is the trunk link frame. The former connects lines while the latter connects trunks to the switch. Wires called junctors are used to tie these two switching frames together.

When a telephone goes off line, a register supplies a dial tone and stores its dialed address. Using this stored number, a logic circuit called a marker reserves an idle trunk

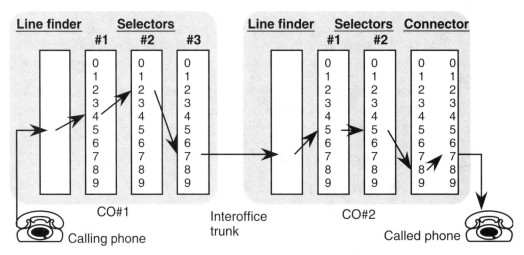

Figure 6.4 An interoffice call to 427-5587 being switched through step-by-step switches.

and sends individual commands to the switches to connect the path. Translators aid the marker in converting the dialed number into specific switch settings.

After the connection is made, which only takes less than a second, the services of the marker and other common control devices are not needed and can be used to establish another call while the connected one is still in progress. Since its equipment is shared between many calls, it is called a common control switch. A major advantage of this type of switch, besides not needing as much equipment, is alternate routing. In that, if one path through the switch is occupied by another call, then anther path can be investigated. This was not possible with the step-by-step switch.

6.2.3 Stored Program Control

Both of the previous generation switches were hard wired and inflexible. If a new telephone service (services are such features as call waiting, call conference, etc.) was to be made available, the switches had to be redesigned and then had to be individually rewired. With SPC (Stored Program Control), the switch operates under the direction of a CPU (Central Processing Unit) and the software running it. If a new service is required, then generally only the software has to be rewritten and tested. Then simply by distributing and installing the copies of the software upgrades on each switch, the new service becomes available. Also, there is less expertise required at each switch. AT&T's 4ESS (Electronic Switching System), for instance, although introduced in 1976, is still AT&T's primary switch used because the software running them has been upgraded many times since.

Figure 6.6 outlines the functions of an SPC system. At the heart of this switch is a special purpose CPU. It is designed for real time processing of logic and input and output operations, rather than for arithmetic processing. It has access to two types of memory, one where the software program is loaded and a data base of customer configurations are kept. The other is where information on call progress is kept. The memory where the program is stored is protected from being inadvertently written over and doesn't change until a new release of the generic software is installed or an end user subscribes to a new service or alters it.

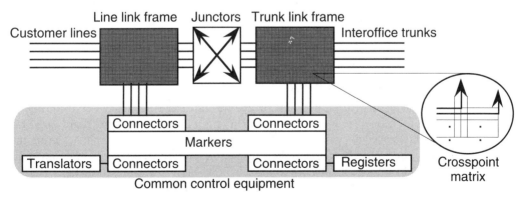

Figure 6.5 A functional block diagram of a typical common control switch.

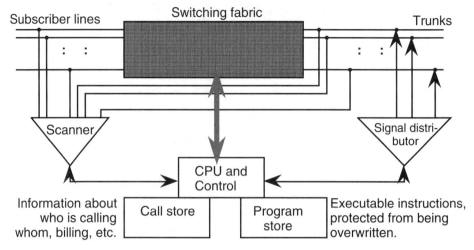

Figure 6.6 A simplified block diagram of a stored program control switch.

The call store memory is used to keep the digits of the calling party as they are received, the status of the lines and trunks, etc. The lines and trunks are constantly scanned at a high rate by the scanner to see which have changed their states. For example, if a line has gone off hook, then the CPU will provide a dial tone and while the subscriber is dialing the first digit, it will scan and serve other lines. When an incoming call from a trunk is received, the scanner detects it. The program instructs the control circuitry as to what to do in each situation. It specifies how paths are to be set up for calls in the switching fabric, when to provide a ringing signal or a busy signal, and so on. The distributor circuitry sends signals over the trunks to the next CO when attempting an interoffice call.

6.3 DIGITAL SWITCHING

So far we have considered switches which were initially used to handle voice switching in analog form. The 4ESS is a digital switch, but the trunks connecting to it were originally analog which were then converted to digital. Now, let us consider digital switches which are used to perform switching of voice, data, fax, etc., in signals which are in digital form.

6.3.1 Time Division Ring

To understand the operation of a time division ring, let us first consider an analogy of a train shown in Figure 6.7. This train has 4 cars (which represent 4 time slots) and it is used to switch calls for up to 8 telephones. These telephones bring their voice bits (or digitized voice) to their respective platforms, labeled A through H, at a rate of 64 kbps. Since the data from the telephones arrive at a rate of 64 kbps, the train itself must rotate at 64,000 rotations per second. Additionally, since the train has 4 time slots (or cars), there are a total of 256,000 time slots rotating per second.

Let us say that the engineer of this train is the control mechanism of the switch. As phone G requests from the engineer a connection to phone A, the engineer notifies both A and G that the car W has been assigned for this connection. So as G sees the train passing by, it dumps the next bit in car W which A then removes.

Similarly, if A needs to communicate back to G, the engineer may assign another car, say car Z, to do that transfer of voice bits. So, for a connection, 2 cars or 2 time slots are used—one for each direction. For this example, what is the non-blocking factor? How can the non-blocking factor be increased?

Since there are 8 telephones and only 4 time slots, the non-blocking factor is 50%. Since only 4 telephones can be active at any time. The non-blocking factor can be increased to 75% by adding two more cars (or time slots) and the switch can be made fully non-blocking by making it an 8-car train. To handle conversations (or 8 digital transfers) the speed of the ring must be 8 times 64,000 rotations per second or, simply, 512 kbps. As can be seen, this analogy fits the actual operation of the time division ring very gracefully.

6.3.2 Time Division Bus

Basically, if the time division ring is pulled at opposite points and straightened, then we have what is called a time division bus. Here again, 2 time slots need to be assigned for each conversation. Sometimes time division busses are referred to as time slot interchanges or loops.

As an example, let us calculate the minimum speed it takes a time division bus to be able to provide non-blocking switching capacity to 200 voice terminals.

200 voice terminals translate into 100 conversations and require 200 time slots. Assuming PCM coded voice at 64 kbps, we need a bus speed of 12.8 Mbps or 200 times 64 kbps.

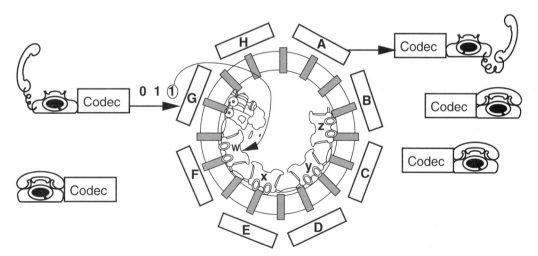

Figure 6.7 This time division ring based switch can support up to 4 conversations or 8 phones with no blocking.

6.3.3 Time-Space-Time Switching

Time-space-time is a common technique used in PBXs and telco switches. It allows many time division switched busses to be interconnected with no blocking. In Figure 6.8, there are 4 such busses shown existing in devices called modules A through D. These busses are connected to each other via a matrix switch providing a fully non-blocking capacity.

An intramodule call, or a call between two phones which are connected to the same module, doesn't get switched through the matrix. An intermodule call must be first switched in the time domain on the caller's module, then be switched in the space domain in the matrix, and finally be switched again in the time domain in the called party's module. Hence, the term "time-space-time" is used for this type of a switch.

Figure 6.8 shows two bits on the bus in A module which are to be switched to the B and C modules. First, the connection is made for B and then the one for C. This way, the bits are properly routed to their destination. The clock of the matrix switch must be 4 times that of the clocks of the time busses, so that it can accommodate the switching required for all 4 modules within a bus's one time frame. Bits for an intramodule call are simply redirected to the originating module. It is evident that the control elements for such a switch are quite complex, because they must be able to direct the various components of the switch in strict synchronization.

As an example, let us say that each of the modules provides a non-blocking capacity of 256 calls at 64 kbps. Each call requires 2 time slots so we need 512 time slots at 64 kbps. This results in a bus speed of 32.768 Mbps (or 64 kbps times 512). Suppose the maximum number of such modules which can be connected to the space switch is 10, then the switching speed of the matrix must be 327.68 Mbps.

6.3.4 Matrix Switches

When a data center has many hosts communicating to many locations via tie lines, the interconnections of in-house equipment can be difficult to manage. If a

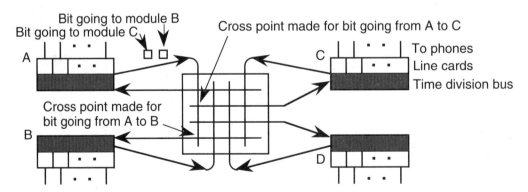

Figure 6.8 A time-space-time switch. Two bits are shown coming from module A going to B and C. Between the times that these two bits are switched, the matrix switches a bit for each of the other modules.

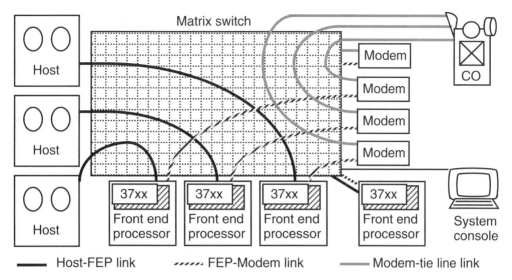

Figure 6.9 A device called a matrix switch (this term doesn't refer to the matrix switching fabric) provides excellent network management.

modem fails, for instance, the network operations personnel are under pressure to switch to the spare modem quickly. Being in a hurry may result in bringing a working circuit down, maybe because a good modem on a working line was replaced by a defective one by mixing up the cables and patch cords.

By using a matrix switch, managers can plan for reliable recovery and provide correct switching between devices. The term "matrix switch" here does not refer to the type of switching fabric as has been described up to this point, but to the type of device.

Figure 6.9 shows hosts, FEPs, modems, and tie lines connected via a matrix switch. Spare equipment and a system console are also connected to it. Now, a working modem can be swapped with a failed one, by simply clicking on an icon on the system console. Through the system console, the switch can be programmed so the cutover is done automatically instead. It can also provide monitoring and line statistics of all the interconnections.

6.4 ADVANCED SWITCHING CONCEPTS

ATM (Asynchronous Transmission Mode) is covered in Chapter 18. Here we will only look at switching techniques which are commonly used with ATM. Since the topics are complex and changing, only a survey of these concepts will be presented. The switches discussed in this section assume information to be parcelled into fixed sized bundles called cells. Cells are 53 bytes long and contain 48 bytes of data and a 5-byte header. The information in the header is used to switch the cell to the correct output.

6.4.1 Time Division vs. Space Division Revisited

Flipping back to Figure 6.3, we recall the two types of switches used with digital signals—time division and space division. We also have seen the operation of the ring, bus, and matrix switches. Now, let us consider the operation of the remaining ones.

Time Division Switching: A shared memory time division switch can be viewed in Figure 6.10. As the samples are received in the switch, they are entered in the buffer. The output from the buffer is selected in the order that the switching is to take place.

Time division switching fabrics are efficient for multicasting (transmissions from one source to many destinations) or broadcasting (transmissions from one source to all destinations). This is because the transmitted bits are going past all the outputs. Instead of only one port being signaled to copy the bits, more than one port can be signaled to copy them. This is analogous to ports other than A reading the bits from car W in Figure 6.7. Additionally, with time division switching, instead of all ports operating at the same speed, bandwidth on demand can be accessed dynamically by the ports allowing for variable input rates.

Space Division Switching: While in time division one transmission path is shared by all ports, in space division, many transmission paths are available at any given time. Hence, for one-to-many transmissions, such as broadcasts, time division is preferred, and for many-to-many transmissions space division is suitable. The capacity of a space division switch is determined by multiplying the port speeds by the average number of concurrent paths that are available in the switch.

In Figure 6.3, space division switching is divided into single path and multiple path categories. This means that with the former, there is only one physical path for a given input-output port pair, whereas with multipath space division switching, data arriving from a specific input port to a specific output port may travel different paths each time. In either case, multiple transmissions may occur simultaneously in the switching fabric.

Typically, cells of data use a routing tag in the header which enable the switching elements in the fabric to provide fast switching, by inspecting the tag. This is called self-routing. In other cases, label-routing schemes are used which rely on table lookup. Label routing provides efficient multicast switching, but requires maintenance of these tables.

6.4.2 Single Path Fabrics

One of the disadvantages of a matrix switch, shown in Figure 6.2(c), is that the number of crosspoint switches required for it is the product of the number of input and output ports. So if there are 8 inputs and 8 outputs, the fabric requires 64 switches.

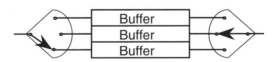

Figure 6.10 A shared memory switch.

In a Banyan switching fabric, shown in Figure 6.11, switching between 8 inputs and 8 outputs is provided using only 24 switching elements. Although the switches are twice as complex as the ones used in a matrix, the saving is still substantial. Additionally, much of the control is distributed in the fabric itself.

The Banyan switch is made up of binary switching elements which switch the call to one of two paths determined by one of the address bits. In Figure 6.11, the 8 inputs are connected to the left column of 4 switches. Any of these cells arriving at these 8 inputs can be switched very quickly to any of the 8 outputs shown on the right. As a cell arrives at any of the binary switching elements, the switch routes it to either the binary 0 or 1 output.

As an example, a path is shown for a cell arriving at input number 4 with a destination address of output 011 in its header. The MSB (Most Significant Bit) of the address, which is 0, routes the cell to the 0 output of the first switching element. The lower middle switching element switches the cell to its binary output 1 and so does the last switch.

Since all cells arriving at input destined for 011 follow this path, this fabric is considered to have a single path. However, other transmissions are possible at the same time, such as a cell headed from input 1 to output 000.

If two cells are contending for the same output, only one can be switched at that point. So unlike the matrix switch, the Banyan switch is a blocking switch.

When the switching elements of a Banyan switch are converted to, say, 4 inputs and 4 outputs (instead of 2 inputs and 2 outputs), then we have what is called a delta network. The delta fabric switches cells on 2 or more address bits rather on just 1 bit as is done in Banyan switches.

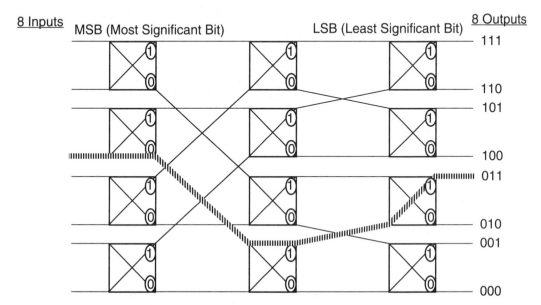

Figure 6.11 A Banyan switch fabric with a path to output 011.

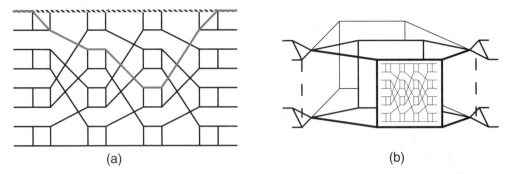

Figure 6.12 Two multipath fabrics: (a) Augmented Banyan. Here two paths between a port pair are highlighted. (b) Parallel planes.

6.4.3 Multipath Fabrics

Figure 6.12(a) has added another column of switches to the basic Banyan switch, making it what is called an augmented Banyan switch. It provides more than one path between a set of input-output ports, as can be seen from the two paths shown in the figure. Hence, this is called a multipath fabric. For every column of switches that are added, (or stages of switches that are added), the number of available paths double.

Another example of a multipath fabric is shown in Figure 6.12(b). It is called switching planes in parallel. It provides better reliability and performance, because a failure of one plane still maintains switching capacity.

6.4.4 Buffering and Contention Resolution

Regardless of the type of switch fabric that is used, there may be a need to do buffering. In a switching element, two cells may contend for the same output. If buffering is used external to the fabric, whether at the input or output ports, then a mechanism is required for contention resolution inside the fabric.

One mechanism that is used is to simply discard one cell. Another one is to deflect the cell in the wrong direction within the fabric. If enough stages are left within the fabric, a path to the correct output is possible. Otherwise, the cell may have to be recirculated back to the input ports. Cells may also be routed, based on their priority. Another method which is possible is reservation of output ports by the input ports. Much research and development in such switching architectures is well under way.

Exercises

1. Which of the following is NOT a space division switch?
   a. step-by-step   b. crossbar
   c. shared memory   d. matrix

2. Which of the following parts is NOT part of the crossbar switch?
   a. markers   b. registers
   c. connectors   d. selectors

3. A method of switching which requires the switching elements to route cells based on the information in their headers is called what?
   a. label routing   b. self routing
   c. direct routing   d. header routing

4. Which of the following is an advantage of time division switching?
   a. multicasting   b. multipath switching
   c. less number of cross points is needed   d. less maintenance on switching tables is required

5. Which part of a stored program control switch first notices when a line goes off-hook?
   a. distributor   b. CPU
   c. fabric   d. scanner

6. If another stage of switching elements is added to Figure 6.12(a), the augmented Banyan switch, how many paths will be available between every input-output pair?
   a. 2   b. 3
   c. 4   d. 6

7. Find the bus speed of a recently announced ATM-based LAN switch which supports up to sixteen 155 Mbps ports.

8. What are the maximum and minimum number of concurrent paths possible in Figure 6.11?

9. What type of switch interconnects other switches?

10. What kind of switch preceded the step-by-step switch?

11. In Figure 6.2(a) if the three switches on the left connected 5 inputs and the three switches on the right connected 5 outputs, what would be the non-blocking factor?

12. Suppose the modules in Figure 6.8 each connect 512 telephones. They are all using ADPCM or digitized voice at 32 kbps. If each module has a non-blocking factor of 40%, what is the bus speed for the modules?

13. Explain the two parts of a switch.

14. How can one tell if a switch is a time division switch or a space division switch? Can you design a switch that is based on frequency division?

15. List the three types of control methods and explain them. Give the advantages of the latter two over the previous ones.

16. How are analog switches differentiated from digital ones?

17. Try to draw a Banyan switch which has four inputs and four outputs.

18. With high capacity switching systems, what advantage does space division have over time division?

Chapter 7

The Public Switched Telephone Network

In this chapter the development of the PSTN (Public Switched Telephone Network) will be explored. This is also referred to as the DDD (Direct Distance Dialing) cloud. The network originally was built to carry telephone traffic, but today it is evolving into an information network that carries more than just voice. For this reason, it may be more appropriate to refer to it as the Public Switched Information Network.

7.1 BACKGROUND

Until recently, calls were routed in the PSTN using a method known as hierarchical routing. This is illustrated in Figure 7.1. All switching centers in the country were categorized as regional, sectional, primary, toll, or end offices. When a lower level office could not complete a call directly to the distant office, it required the services of the upper level offices.

Each lower class office was directly subject to upper class offices and the trunk group between such offices were called a final trunk group. For offices in two different areas that had a heavy usage between them, a high usage trunk was installed. So when a call could be completed using this type of a trunk, the upper final trunk groups and their offices were avoided, and the call was completed using less number of nodes.

Consider Figure 7.1. Whenever phone1 called phone2, then only the local office which connects the two phones handled the call completely. If phone1 made a local call to phone3, then the call would go through the tandem switch, but if a direct trunk were available between the two end offices then that would be used instead. If calls were made across a wider geographical region, as when phone1 called phone4, then the call would have to go through the two respective toll offices.

In preparing this chapter, special thanks go to Joseph Mastriani of NJ Bell, David Drosdick of Comcast, Dan Lawler of AT&T, Ronald Mitchell of MCI, and Robert Przybysz of Sprint.

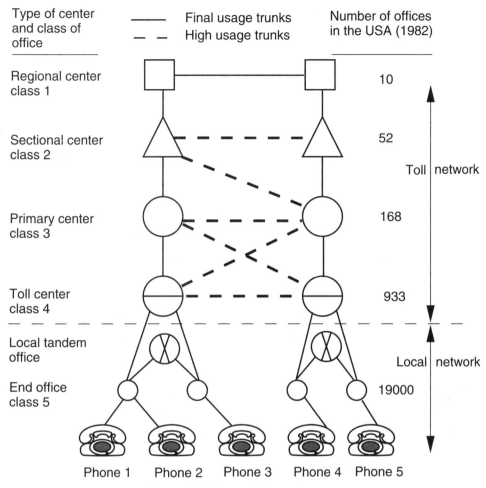

Figure 7.1 Hierarchical routing.

In such a case, if a high usage trunk existed between the two toll centers, then it would be used; otherwise, free trunks to upper class offices would be searched in order to complete the call. In extreme cases, a call would have to be switched through all the upper class offices and all the final trunk groups before it would find a path to its destination. Using many switches added noise, interference, and connection delay time to the voice call.

Completing a coast to coast call in this manner may have taken up to 20 seconds, with noise and interference added by the many switches. Today, IXCs complete calls using digitized voice in six seconds and use only 2 or 3 switches. This is because current networks are not hierarchical (where each switch has a primary path to only one other switch up the ladder), but each switch has direct links to all other switches. This is architecturally called a flat network. The remainder of the chapter will cover the operation of current networks.

7.2 THE LOCAL TELEPHONE NETWORK

7.2.1 The Distribution Plant

In Figure 7.2, the wiring for the POTS (Plain Old Telephone Service) connection is shown from a residence to the central office.

The wiring inside the residence is called IW (Inside Wiring), and since divestiture, time and material for this inside wiring has to be paid and maintained by the subscriber. He/she may have the telco provide this service or may do it him/herself. This wiring is connected to the NID (Network Interface Device), at which point the telco's responsibility begins. The NID is the demarc for the home and is non-existent for older lines. It is equipped with a termination block and protection against power surges.

A SNID (Smart NID) is also sometimes used, which provides remote loopback from the CO This allows the telco to test the continuity of the wire pair directly from the CO without having to send a technician to the house. This is accomplished by the CO sending a special signal to the SNID which places itself in the loopback mode.

From the NID, a connection is made to the telephone pole using a drop wire. In some developments, if the cable is buried, then the connection is made to a pedestal. The distribution of the subscriber lines from the SAC (Serving Area interface Concept) to the home is called the wire feeding plant or simply the distribution plant.

The SAC is a distribution frame safely placed on a lot away from hazards. This marks the boundary between the feeder and the distribution plants. Just as an IDF (Intermediate Distribution Frame) typically serves one floor or an area within a building, so does the SAC distribute the wiring to one serving area or distribution area for the telco.

From the SAC there are two ways to get to the CO via the feeder plant. One method simply sends the analog voice over a cable consisting of many wire pairs. Another method involves using a T1 multiplexer which is commonly called the SLC-96 (Subscriber Line Carrier), pronounced "slick 96." It is an AT&T trademark and its

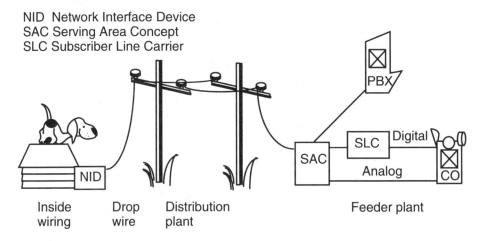

NID Network Interface Device
SAC Serving Area Concept
SLC Subscriber Line Carrier

Figure 7.2 Local facilities network from the home to the CO.

generic name is DLC (Digital Line Carrier). This multiplexer allows four groups of 24 voice circuits to be multiplexed onto 10 pairs of wire. With T1, one pair is used to transmit, and one is used to receive. Hence, 8 pairs are needed for four groups of T1s. And an extra two pairs are used to automatically backup an active pair, in case it fails. Fiber can also be used here instead of copper. The DLC system is more economical, serves more customers with far fewer wire pairs, is easy to maintain, and is more compatible with interoffice digital trunks.

7.2.2 Inside the CO

For the central office to activate a phone for a subscriber, it must have its TN (telephone number), CP (Cable Pair number), and OE (Office Equipment designation).

TN is the phone number assigned as it appears in the phone book. CP indicates the pair number at the CO which is connected to the NID at the customer's home. Finally, the OE specifies the actual line circuit that is dedicated on the CO's switch. When a phone number is changed, CP and OE designations remain the same; however, in electronic switching systems, the TN for the existing OE is changed through software, that is, through a terminal.

The cables from all the exchange areas that are served by the CO enter the cable vault or the cable entrance facility which is usually located in its basement. This can amount up to 200,000 pairs of wire. From here the cable pairs are cut down on termination blocks on the VMDF (Vertical side of the Main Distribution Frame). The heat coils and carbon blocks are located here for protection purposes. See Figure 7.3.

From the VMDF all pairs are cross connected over to the HMDF and from there the dial-up circuits are sent to the switches and the tie lines are sent to the toll equipment. In other words, the lines from the street come to the VMDF whereas the connections for switch and toll equipment come to the HMDF and the jumpers between these two sides of the MDF cross connect the lines to the appropriate equipment.

The lines from the switching equipment are connected to the HMDF (Horizontal MDF). Depending on which subscriber, specified by its CP, needs to be connected to which OE, a cross connect jumper is punched down between these two points.

Lines to the HMDF also come from the toll equipment. Toll equipment allows the CO to condition leased lines so that the signal levels are correct going out of the CO. In Figure 7.3, pair numbers 1001 thru 1004 go to the switch and pair 1005 comes to the toll equipment, gets conditioned and goes back out on pair 1006 to a different destination than from where it came.

There are basically four types of trunks leaving a CO. Interoffice trunks going to other COs are one kind; others are trunks going to PBXs, IXC trunks going to POPs, and trunks to cellular MTSOs (Mobile Telephone Switching Offices).

7.2.3 Interoffice Signaling Using SS7

The network in the North Jersey LATA is going to be used as an example in explaining interoffice signaling. This will allow us to refer to real names and a real network. Remember that SS7 (Signaling System #7) network is a packet switched network, and that all information passed on this network is done using data packets.

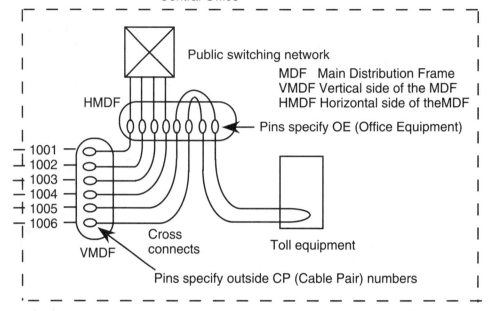

Figure 7.3 Dial-up lines coming into the CO go to the switching network, while dedicated lines get conditioned in the toll equipment and are routed out to other locations.

New Jersey Bell has approximately 130 COs in this area. There are 4 sector tandems and 2 equal access tandems. A sector tandem, shown in Figure 7.1, is used when no direct trunk is found between two COs. A maximum of two sector tandems may be needed to complete a call within this area. Equal access tandems allow IXCs to gain access to the local network.

This North Jersey LATA, illustrated in Figure 7.4, has one STP (Signal Transfer Point) pair, one STP in Newark and one in New Brunswick about 30 miles away. The STPs are of type #2A and are made by AT&T. All the COs which are part of the signaling system 7 network have direct 56 kbps signaling channels to both STPs. The STPs share their workload and continuously monitor each other's performance. If one STP fails, then the other will force all the signaling traffic on itself and send out alarms indicating that the other STP has malfunctioned.

It is acceptable for an LEC to place an STP pair in two different LATAs, as long as only the signaling crosses the LATA boundaries and not the traffic itself. The STPs shown in the figure also have links to the STPs in the adjacent LATAs, so that privileged calls can be made near the LATA boundaries. Privileged calls are local calls that are handled by an LEC near and across a LATA border.

The STP's rack has a circuit pack for each CO, where a DSU (Digital Service Unit) exists for each signaling channel. A DSU simply interfaces equipment with a digital line. The circuit packs for each CO communicate signaling data with each other using a CNI (Common Network Interface) ring. The CNI ring uses the same mechanism used in token ring networks, which will be discussed in Chapter 16.

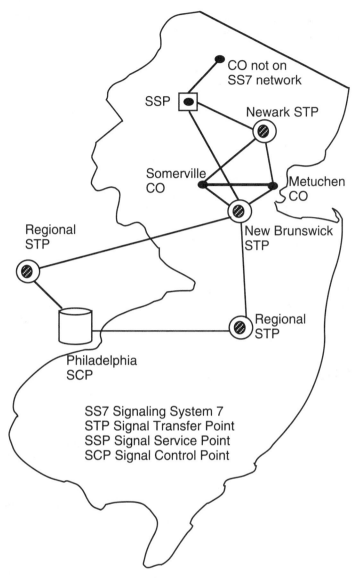

Figure 7.4 Bell Atlantic's North New Jersey SS7 network. For the sake of clarity, the links from the regional STPs to the Newark STP are not shown.

The COs which don't have direct access to the STP pair, can become part of the intelligent network by connecting to an SSP (Signal Service Point). MF signaling is used between such a CO and the SSP. The SSP then converts the older MF signaling to SS7 signaling over the links to the STP pair.

Let us now consider how a call is connected over the local network. Suppose a caller in Somerville dials 555-6789 in Metuchen. The CO in Somerville will realize that the exchange 555 is not in Somerville, and will request the STP in New Brunswick over the signaling network that it wants to place the call to 555-6789. If the 555 exchange was located in Somerville, then the STPs would not be utilized, and Somerville CO would complete the call itself.

The New Brunswick STP realizes that 555 is a Metuchen exchange and asks the Metuchen CO if circuit 6789 is idle. If phone 555-6789 is idle, then the STP is notified, and the STP sends packets to both the Somerville and the New Brunswick COs, giving instructions to connect the call on the trunk. Then the two COs make a continuity check over that trunk which is reserved for that call and the phone rings in Metuchen. The ringback signal for the caller in Somerville is provided by the Somerville CO.

Conversely, if 555-6789 were busy, then the Metuchen CO would notify the STP which in turn would notify the Somerville CO. Now the busyback signal is provided by the Somerville office to the caller in Somerville. Notice that a trunk between the COs is not utilized to provide this busyback signal as it would have been used in older signaling methods.

Finally, if anyone wants to make a call using Bell Atlantic's credit card, then authorization is obtained from a data base called the SCP (Signal Control Point), located in Philadelphia. The SCP is also used when an STP needs a Bell Atlantic 800 number to be converted to a POTS number. All 800 numbers have to be converted to their POTS equivalent before the call can be routed to its destination. Access to an SCP is provided via a regional STP over the SS7 network.

7.3 CELLULAR MOBILE TELEPHONE SYSTEM

7.3.1 Overview

The formal name for the modern cellular phone system is AMPS (Advanced Mobile Phone Service). EAMPS (Extended AMPS) is used to refer to the newer set of frequencies allocated to cellular service that provides a total of 832 channels instead of 666 allocated for AMPS.

The basic concept behind AMPS (or EAMPS) is simple, but the design and implementation is complex. A geographical region is divided into circular areas, called cells, that are between 2 to 12 miles in radius. For design purposes, they are shown as hexagonal areas. In Figure 7.5, each cell is served by a cell site which has a transmitter, a receiver, antenna, and related equipment. Cell sites are directly tied to an MTSO (Mobile Telephone Switching Office) which is tied to a tandem or the class 5 offices (or COs) in the local telephone network. The local telephone company is also referred to as the wire-line company which may be a BOC. The MTSO is like the CO for the cellular system. In a given region, half of the available cellular service is provided by the resident wire-line company and half by the competition.

All calls originating from the local telephone network are switched to the proper cell site where the mobilephone has the best reception. And likewise, all calls originating from the mobilephones are sent to the MTSO by the cell site with the best signal. The MTSO then forwards the call to the CO.

Depending on which cell site has the best signal level, a mobile unit latches on to that cell site at any given time, and all communication occurs with that one cell site.

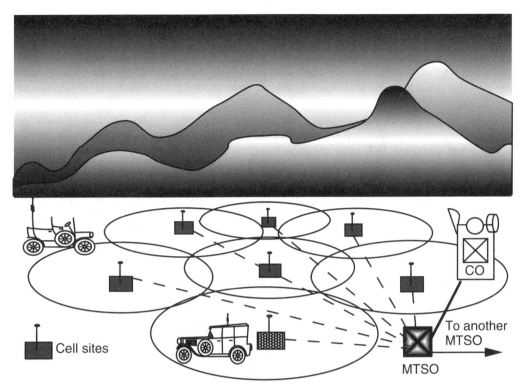

Figure 7.5 A cellular telephone system layout.

As the vehicle travels out of one area and into another, the cell site, noticing the drop in signal level, hands off the communication to another cell site with the MTSO's assistance. This is called handoff.

7.3.2 Advantages of AMPS

IMTS (Improved Mobile Telephone Service), which preceded AMPS, used large coverage areas, typically, 20 miles in radius. This required that transmitters had to have output power of up to 250 watts. Also, the same radio frequency could not be used in two areas that were closer than 75 miles; otherwise there would be interference in a channel also used by the other station.

This limited the number of channels available for mobilephones. In mid 1970s for instance, New York City had only 12 channels serving about 550 customers with almost 4,000 customers on a waiting list. There was no way of expanding the service dynamically if the demand in the region increased.

AMPS, developed by the Bell system, on the other hand, used many cells in a serving area. Since the cells were smaller than before, the transmitted output was reduced to 100 watts for a cell transmitter, 3 watts for a mobile transmitter and 0.6 watts for a portable unit. And since the output power was low, two cells could be as close as two miles (one cell apart) and still use the same set of frequencies. Interference from nearby cells using the same channels is called co-channel interference. As long as C/I (Carrier-to-Interference) ratio is at least 17 dbs, co-channel interference is negligible. This means that two cells using the same set of channels will not cause interference if the selected cell's signal strength is at least 17 dbs greater than the interfering cell's signal strength.

All this provided more channels per given amount of bandwidth. And if demand for service grew in one area, then cells could be split into smaller cells yet, where cells would reduce their effective power output. The net effect of this then was to increase the number of channels available in a given area. Of course, the design and planning of splitting cells became a complex procedure, but now at least it was feasible.

The technique of sectoring cells also improves the utilization of the frequency spectrum, or the available bandwidth. Sectoring involves dividing the cell into usually three pie-piece shape sectors. Now instead of transmitting all available channels in a cell in all directions (using an omnidirectional antenna), three directional antennas are used that transmit one third of the available channels in each of the three sectors. Sectoring allows placing cells closer together by facing the sectors which use the same channels in opposite directions. This increases the channel capacity of the system.

7.3.3 Reasons for Irregular Cell Shapes

Usually, cells are depicted as having hexagonal shapes, which are used for designing purposes, but realistically, antennas send off signals in circular patterns. However, circular radiation patterns are also not what is eventually achieved, as shown in Figure 7.6.

The initial deployment of the cellular system may have simply placed cells in regions where there was a high concentration of population and vehicular traffic, instead of placing them in a honeycomb-like grid. Also, if the center of a cell happened to fall in a river or off to a spot where a convenient tower or building stood, then the area covered by the cell would be moved somewhat. Sometimes a directional antenna would have to be used to avoid interference with other systems. Some communities don't allow a tower, so again a directional antenna tilting downwards would be placed outside the town. The terrain of the area covered by the cell, such as tall buildings, mountains, valleys, etc., changes the desired shape of area covered by cells. All of these factors change the desired symmetric cells to cells that are irregular in shape.

7.3.4 Distribution of Cell Channels

The FCC (Federal Communications Commission) has allocated 824 to 851Mhz and 869 to 896 Mhz for cellular service as shown in Table 7.1. This makes 25 Mhz of bandwidth available for transmitting and 25 Mhz for receiving. Since each one-way channel requires 0.03 Mhz, dividing .03 Mhz into the available 25 Mhz provides a total of 832 channels for the cellular system.

832 channels are divided into two equal groups of 416 channels called block A and block B. Channels in one block are for use by the wire-line company and channels in the other block are for use by the non-wire-line company. In any case, each mobile's

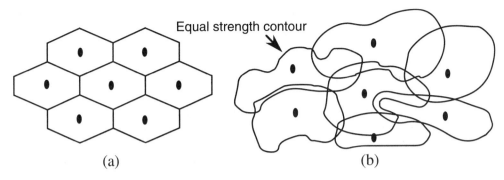

Equal strength contour

(a)   (b)

Figure 7.6 (a) Hexagonal shapes used in designing cellular networks.
(b) Actual shape of the cells is seldom uniform.

receive channel frequency is 45 Mhz above its transmit channel frequency. For instance, channel number 333 transmits at 835Mhz and receives at 880Mhz from the mobile.

7.3.5 Frequency Reuse

Considering only one block, or one cellular company's bandwidth allocation in a region, there are 416 available channels, 21 of which are used for signaling. This leaves 395 channels for voice traffic. Each cell site requires only one signaling channel to communicate signaling information with all of the mobiles in its area. So every twenty-first cell in a cell pattern uses the same signaling channel.

If every cell communicated using all of the available 395 channels, then channels from adjacent cells would interfere with each other. Hence, to reduce the amount of co-channel interference, cells are grouped together so that the channels allocated to one cell are unique in that group of cells . The number of cells in such a group is called the frequency reuse pattern or simply k. That is, the 395 channels are partitioned into k number of channel groups. This way, two cells which use the same set of channels are not adjacent to each other but are separated.

Table 7.1 ALLOCATION OF CHANNELS		
	Mobile Transmit	**Mobile Receive**
Bandwidth per channel	.03 Mhz	.03 Mhz
Frequency range for blocks A & B	824 - 849 Mhz	869 - 894 Mhz
Total spectrum allocated including unused portion	824 - 851 Mhz	869 - 896 Mhz
Number of channels for block A	416	416
Number of channels for block B	416	416
Total number of channels	832	832

For example, consider the cellular system shown in Figure 7.7 where k is 12. Here approximately 32 (or 395/12) voice channels are available to each cell. Two cells which are labeled with the same number use the same group of 32 channels. However, the co-channel interference, that is, the interference between two such cells, is neglible because they are sufficiently far apart. The value of k is typically 7 but may range from 4 to 21. As k is decreased, more channels become available per cell, but the chance of co-channel interference increases. To further reduce the amount of co-channel interference, cells are typically divided into 3 sectors where the available number of channels are further divided into three groups, each group supporting communications in one-third of the cell area. In Figure 7.7, this would mean that each sector would have 10 or 11 (32/3) channels per sector.

7.3.6 Operation

When a mobile unit is turned on and no calls are being made or received, it is said to be in the idle condition. When in idle condition the unit scans all 21 signaling channels and latches on to the cell site which has the strongest signal; usually that means the closest cell site. Now the mobile unit is capable of receiving and making calls since it has a radio link established with a cell site. See Figure 7.8. This is called self-location. The cell isn't aware of which mobile units are listening to it. After about a minute or so, the mobile unit rescans the 21 channels and may lock (or monitor the signaling channel) to different cell sites each time.

In some cellular systems, a mobile will notify the cell site when it locks on to it. This is called registration. This information is helpful for the MTSO when it needs to know its location to complete a call made to it.

When the mobile unit wants to place a call, it transmits the called digits over the signaling channel to the selected cell site. The cell site forwards the phone number to the MTSO, which then connects the cell to the wire-line CO. At the same time, the

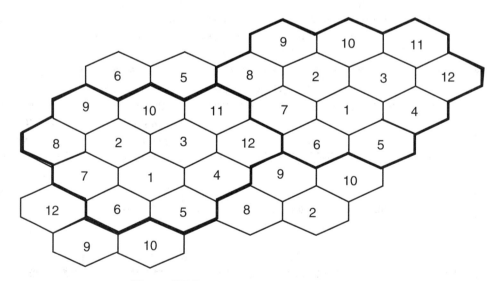

Figure 7.7 Frequency reuse pattern with k = 12.

The Public Switched Telephone Network

MTSO assigns a free full-duplex voice channel from the selected cell site to the mobile unit. The cell site tells the mobile unit which channel has been assigned for this call over the signaling channel, and it will then tune its transmitter and receiver to that voice channel. Finally, as the phone rings at the destination, it will be heard over the cellular phone.

When a call originates from the wire-line network, the CO detects that the phone number falls in the range of numbers assigned to a particular cellular company. The CO then forwards the phone number to the corresponding cellular company's MTSO. Since the MTSO doesn't know where the mobile unit is (unless registration is used), it sends the phone number to all the cell sites and to other MTSOs and their respective cell sites. Then all cell sites page the phone number on their respective signaling channels, hoping the mobile unit is on and is in the vicinity of one of the cell sites. When the mobile phone detects its own phone number being paged, it will answer the cell by retransmitting its own phone number and the ESN (Electronic Serial Number) of its mobile unit over the signaling channel to the cell site. ESN confirms the proper identity of the mobile unit so that the correct party is charged for the phone call. (The ESN is also transmitted when a mobile is making a call.) The MTSO checks the ESN and the phone number for a match, and will assign a full-duplex voice channel between the cell site and the mobile unit, and the call processing is complete.

Regardless of who initiated the call, once the mobile unit turns off the transmitter, a special signal is sent over the signaling channel and the MTSO frees the voice channel for another call.

7.3.7 Handoff

The mobile unit which is communicating via a cell site may eventually travel into another cell. The original cell site then notices that the signal strength from that unit

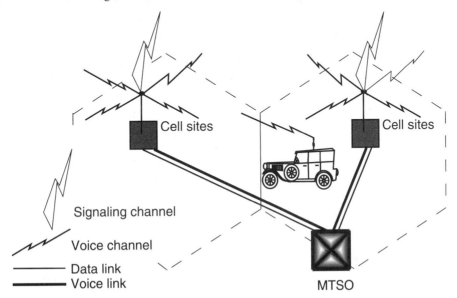

Figure 7.8 Operation of system between two cells.

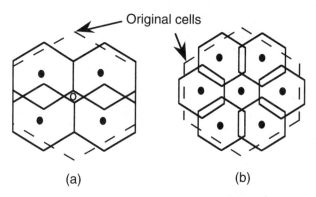

Figure 7.9 Two methods of splitting a cell: (a) The original cell is eliminated. (b) The original cell reduces its effective coverage.

is decreasing. It will then request the MTSO that another cell site be assigned to communicate with that unit. The MTSO then asks the other cells nearby to check the signal strength on the voice channel that is being used. The cell site which has the best reception with that mobile unit is told to communicate with the mobile unit, but this time, it would be on a different channel: a new voice channel that is free and is one of the channels that is allocated for that cell site. The handoff process disrupts communication for up to 200 milliseconds which doesn't effect voice calls as much as it does data transmissions.

7.3.8 Cell Splitting

One of the advantages of the cellular telecommunications systems is that if the traffic increases for a given cell so that it reaches its load capacity, then the cell can be split into several cells, thereby increasing the number of channels in the area.

Two ways in which a cell can be split are shown in Figure 7.9. The first method doesn't use the original cell site but divides the cell into four parts, creating 4 new cells. The other method, which is more common, shows that the original cell size decreases, but surrounding it, six new cells are created.

If we suppose the original cell site had 70 channels, and is split into 6 new ones, then the new cell sites will each initially use 10 channels. However, each of these cells could eventually increase their capacity to 70 channels, which would increase the available channels in the region. This is all easier said than done. Engineers have to be very careful when splitting cells that the rest of the system works without interference or interruption.

7.4 DIGITAL WIRELESS SYSTEMS

7.4.1 PCS

At the time of this writing, we communicate over the PSTN by dialing a location. With PCS (Personal Communications System), we'll be able to dial a person regardless of his/her location. It will be the concern of the signaling system to locate the called

The Public Switched Telephone Network

person and provide the connection. No longer will people need to provide a home number, work number, a mobile phone number, and their daily schedule. We only need to know that individual's number to reach them on the phone.

An individual needs to carry only one low-power pocket phone and if he/she is in their home then this phone acts like a cordless phone, communicating with the home's base station. If they are in a car, it acts like a cellular system. If they are in a shopping center, then it communicates with a microcell base and if they are in their work place it communicates over their wireless PBX system. Each time, the least expensive method of wireless communication is selected.

To make PCS successful, its cost to the public will have to be less than a cellular phone. Additionally, making it work so that many individuals can be on the system will require digital transmission techniques. This section describes four types of digital transmission techniques, which, although now used with cellular systems, may be used with PCS one day.

7.4.2 Europe's GSM

In 1982, a digital cellular standard that was uniform throughout Europe was established. This was unlike the non-uniform dialing plans in the PSTNs and the incompatible analog mobile cellular systems which existed at that time. It came to be known as GSM (Global System for Mobile Communication).

GSM uses TDMA (Time Division Multiple Access), as well as FDMA, to provide cellular access to its users. Voice is digitized at a rate of 13 kbps using a technique called LPC-RPE (Linear Predictive Encoding with Regular Pulse Excitation). The basic "building block" for GSM is called a time slot which has a duration of 0.577 milliseconds. One time slot transmits 156.25 bits as seen in Figure 7.10. A

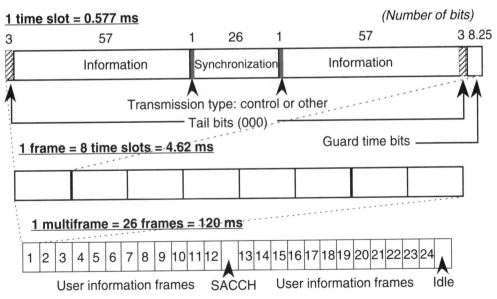

Figure 7.10 Slot and frame formatting used in GSM.

time slot begins and ends with 3 tail bits which are always 0s. During the guard time, which occupies 8.25 bits, no transmission occurs to accommodate for RF (Radio Frequency) rise and fall delays.

Two groups of 57 bits are used to transmit user information. The single bit adjacent to a group of information bits is used to designate whether control information is being sent, interrupting a speech or data channel. Lastly, 26 bits are used to keep the digital transmission in sync. Each mobile terminal is assigned its own time slot.

8 of these time slots comprise a frame and 26 frames comprise a multiframe. Out of these 26 frames, two frames are used for other purposes. One is called SACCH (Slow Associated Control CHannel) and is used for sending low bandwidth control information; the other is left idle.

7.4.3 North America's IS-54

Unlike Europe, which had 5 different analog cellular standards, Canada and the USA have only one—AMPS. However, Europe was allocated a new frequency block for its GSM system, whereas North America was restricted to evolve a digital system out of its existing analog frequency band. Hence, this system is called a dual-mode system. It is called EIA's IS-54 (Electronics Industry Association's Interim Standard 54).

IS-54 digitizes speech at a rate of 13 kbps using a technique called VSELP (Vector Sum Excited Linear Prediction). The structure of its time slot is different depending on whether the mobile is transmitting or receiving. See Figure 7.11. A frame consists of 1,944 bits and takes 40 milliseconds to transmit. A frame is divided into 6 time slots. A time interval of 6 bits is used to turn off the transmission and the same amount of time is used to bring the power back up to the operating level. These are called the guard and ramp times, respectively. A total of 260 bits is used for either

Mobile unit transmit

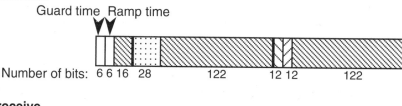

Mobile unit receive

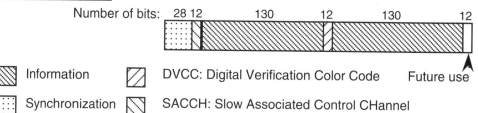

Figure 7.11 IS-54's time slots. 6 time slots make up a frame.

The Public Switched Telephone Network

transmitting or receiving. The 28-bit pattern used for synchronization is determined by the position of the slot in the frame.

The DVCC (Digital Verification Color Code) prevents a mobilephone from communicating with an interferring digital cell site. Replacing the "blank and burst" signaling used in AMPS, the SACCH (Slow Associated Control CHannel) provides transfer of messages between the cell site and the mobile set. By interrupting user data fields, a FACCH (Fast Associated Control CHannel) is also available to send messages which are urgent.

7.4.4 Europe's DECT

DECT (Digital European Cordless Telecommunications) is a European standard much different from GSM or IS-54. It uses microcells which are overlayed with GSM cells. Since, DECT is a low-power system, it can't hand over calls when an automobile is traveling at highway speeds. However, via GSM interworking, it can be used as a cellular phone and in a business environment, and it can communicate with a wireless PBX fixed port. It can be used as a residential cordless phone, to replace the local loop to the CO, to provide wireless LANs, to function with a telepoint, and to support other applications. Telepoint is a wireless public pay telephone.

Some applications such as cordless PBXs and wireless LANs are closed environments. That is, only one vendor may supply all equipment for the system. Standards for such systems are not fully specified, freeing the manufacturer to design their systems the way they want to, as long as their system can co-exist with other DECT systems. However, other applications are required to conform to a set of specifications called the PAP (Public Access Profile) which ensure that one manufacturer's base station can operate with other manufacturers' mobile sets.

Briefly, DECT uses 10 RF carriers which are each 1.728 MHz wide. Each carrier supports a frame that has 12 full duplex channels using 24 time slots. A frame is a 10 milliseconds long timeslot and a timeslot consists of 480 bits. 16 bits are used for a preamble, 16 for synchronization, 64 for a control channel, 320 for user information, and 64 bits for guard time. Other characteristics of DECT, as well as GSM and IS-54, are summarized in Table 7.2.

7.4.5 Qualcomm's CDMA

Spread Spectrum Communication: Spread spectrum technology has been used by the military since WWII to prevent the enemy from jamming communication signals. During the 1980s most of the engineering community was arguing that this technology would not work with digital cellular systems, because it was too complex and would be prohibitively expensive. Fortunately, a few "Einsteins" of our day at a company called Qualcomm proved otherwise and developed CDMA.

With spread spectrum communication, everyone is given a unique code from which they can interpret their transmission. It provides little interference to other users. In a military operation, jamming of a signal is possible once the enemy detects activity in a given frequency band. The presence of spread spectrum signals are difficult to detect. These transmissions do not occur over a narrow band but occur over a very large bandwidth so that the transmitted power is distributed over the bandwidth of the signal.

The Public Switched Telephone Network

Table 7.2 Summary of TDMA Cellular Systems

	GSM	IS-54	DECT
Mobile transmit frequency in MHz	890 - 915	824 - 849	1880 - 1900
Mobile receive frequency in MHz	935 - 960	869 - 894	1880 - 1900
Spectrum used by system in MHz	50	50	20
Bandwidth occupied per carrier in MHz	0.200	0.030	1.728
Number of frequency channels	125	832	10
Number of users supported per carrier	8	3	12
Total number of user channels	1000	2496	120
Modulation data rate of channel in kbps	271	48.6	1152
Rate of digitized voice in kbps	13	8	32
Rate of voice including error control (kbps)	22.8	13	32
Method of speech encoding	LPC-RPE	VSELP	ADPCM
Type of modulation used	GMSK	DQPSK	GFSK
Name of one of the control channels	SACCH	SACCH	C
Mobile output power in milliwatts	3.7 - 20,000	2.2 - 6,000	250

ADPCM: Adaptive Differential PCM
C: Control information channel
DECT: Digital European Cordless
    Telecommmunication
DQPSK: Differential Quadrature Phase
    Shift Keying
GMSK: Gaussian Minimum Shift Keying

GSM: Global System for Mobile
    Communication
IS-54: Interim Standard-54
LPC-RPE: Linear Predictive Encoding
    with Regular Pulse Excitation
SACCH: Slow Associated Control Channel
VSELP: Vector Sum Excited Linear
    Prediction

The effect of this is that an enemy "hears" only noise. Furthermore, these signals can be easily made secure using encryption algorithms.

Basically, there are two types of spread spectrum signals: direct sequence and frequency hopping. CDMA uses the direct sequence type where each transmission is given its own code. Frequency hopping has to do with changing the frequency of the carrier periodically. In both cases, synchronization is a very important requirement in order for the receiver to interpret the intended signal correctly.

Basics of CDMA: CDMA uses a PN (Pseudorandom Noise) code and a 64-chip Walsh code. The PN code is so named because although to the other users the transmission appears as random noise, it is interpreted as a clear channel to the receiver. It is a long code which allows CDMA to assign over 4 trillion codes to provide each person privacy. The Walsh codes enable a cell to operate with 61 conversational channels, three being used by the system itself. These channels are said to be orthogonal to each other. That is to say, the communication of any given channel goes undetected by the others. In geometry the x, y, and z axes are said to be orthogonal, since each axis can be varied independently from the others.

The Public Switched Telephone Network

Figure 7.12 attempts to illustrate how CDMA works. However, it is much more complex than shown here. Here, user 1 is given a Walsh code of "+ + – –" and whenever user 1 transmits a binary 1, it transmits "+ + – –" and whenever it transmits a binary 0 it transmits 0. Similarly, user 2 is assigned a code of "+ – + –" so that when it sends a binary 1 it sends that sequence and for a binary 0 it sends just a 0. These are symbols and they are made up of chips, 4 in this example. User 3's code is "+ – – +."

Now as Figure 7.12 shows, let us see what happens as user 1 transmits a bit sequence of "110," user 2 transmits "101," and user 3 transmits "010." Each of these bits get converted into 4 chips using the above encoding method. So user 1 transmits "+ + – – + + – – 0 0 0 0," user 2 transmits "+ – + – 0 0 0 0 + – + –," and user 3 transmits "0 0 0 0 + – – + 0 0 0 0." Now if we add the corresponding chips vertically, for each user, we end up with " 2 0 0 –2 2 0 –2 0 +1 –1 +1 –1." For example, for the very first chip, user 1's +1, user 2's +1, and user 3's 0 gives a +2 and so on.

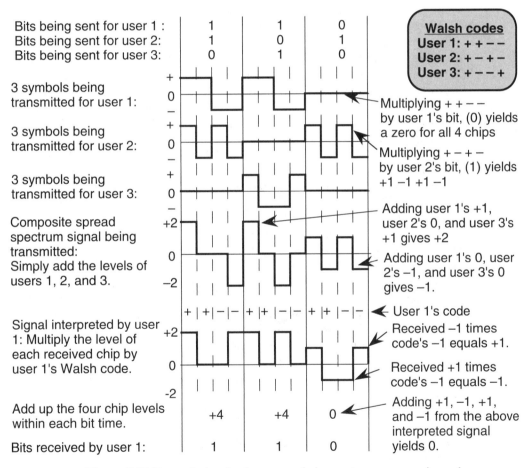

Figure 7.12 Transmission for three users being sent over one carrier and how user 1 interprets its transmission to be "110." The codes for each user are shown in the shaded inset.

Now, all users receive the same sequence of 0, +1, −1, +2, and −2. How do they interpret the bits intended for them? Let us only consider user 1. User 1 will multiply each chip that it receives with the chip of its code, that is "+ + − −." So for the first chip, +1 times +2 yields +2. For the second chip, +1 times 0 yields 0, and so on. So the first four chips equal "2 0 0 2." Then these values are added, giving 4. Following the figure, user 1 gets 4 for the next four chip-times and gets a 0 for the next four chip-times. If the 4 is interpreted as a binary 1 and 0 is interpreted as a binary 0, user 1 will receive its intended "110" bits from the composite signal. Using the same decoding method for users 2 and 3, we can arrive at "101" bits intended for user 2 and "010" intended for user 3.

The reason why this works is because the codes for the users are orthogonal. Notice if the corresponding chips for user 1's code (+ + − −) are multiplied by user 2's code (+ − + −), we get "+ − − +." If we add these, we get a 0. Similarly, if user 1's code is multiplied by user 3's code, the sum becomes a 0. However, if we do the same operation on a user's code with itself, such as "+ + − −" times "+ + − −," we get a sum of 4. Hence, these codes are said to be orthogonal.

Operation of CDMA: AMPS uses FDMA to carry one channel on each 30 kHz wide carrier. IS-54 uses FDMA and TDMA to place three channels on each 30 kHz wide carrier, thereby tripling the capacity of AMPS. CDMA divides the spectrum into 1.25 MHz bands. For every bit that is transmitted, the number of chips are many; therefore, the bandwidth of the carrier must be greater than what would have been necessary to transmit only the bits.

CDMA uses a k of 1. That is, every cell can use all of the available frequencies. The codes of the transmissions from adjacent cells are all different, so their transmissions appear as noise and there is no co-channel interference. Hence, the capacity of CDMA is from 10 to 30 times that of AMPS. The actual capacity depends on the acceptable level of error rate and voice quality.

Not only does CDMA provide greater capacity but since k is 1, the amount of network planning and placement of cells is greatly simplified. During the handoff process, the cell site from which the mobile unit is leaving, as well as the site to which the unit is entering, maintain contact with the unit. There is no sudden switch over between the cell sites, as is the case with AMPS. This is called soft handoff between the cells and works well, especially when transmitting data. Hard handoff occurs only when a unit changes its operating frequency from one 1.25 MHz band to another. Voice is encoded at rates of 1.2 kbps, 2.4 kbps, 4.8 kbps, and 9.6 kbps, depending on the level of activity of the transmitted signal.

AMPS and TDMA are susceptible to interference caused by multipath fading. This occurs when a transmitted signal bounces off mountains or buildings interfering with the primary received signal. CDMA turns the multipath signals into an advantage. By using a rake receiver, up to three different signals which have traveled different paths are combined into one strong coherent signal, making the reception clear even in typically difficult places.

One of the obstacles which CDMA had to resolve was the near-far problem. This occurs when a mobile unit close to the base station is received with more effective power than a unit further away. Power is controlled using various means. Open loop power control adjusts the transmit power based on the level of receive power. A base station controls the amount of power from the mobile units so that the power from a nearby unit doesn't drown out the power from a unit far away. This is called closed loop power control. Outer loop power control maintains a specified error rate from each of the mobile units. The overall effect is that the mobile units require minimum power to operate.

When there is a traffic jam in an area, many people use their mobile phones, loading down the system. CDMA provides a sophisticated method of load balancing, where the capacity of a geographical region is temporarily increased by distributing the increase in traffic to adjacent cells.

7.5 THE AT&T NETWORK

7.5.1 Overview

Let us now turn our attention to inter-LATA communication Networks. AT&T is the dominant communications provider for calls between LATAs and calls to foreign countries. On a typical day 140 million calls are processed, and the most number of calls ever recorded on one day was 177 million calls on Monday, June 1st, 1992.

For management purposes, AT&T divides its network into four components: transmission facilities, international network, North American network, and network services. The network control center is located in Bedminster, N.J., and regional control centers are in Atlanta and Denver. NEMOS (NEtwork Management Operation support System) is a very sophisticated management system that automates the surveillance and the management of the network.

All transmission is done digitally using fiber, satellite, microwave, and coax. The total network transmission facilities are over 2 billion circuit miles, that is about 8000 times around the world if it were wrapped continuously. AT&T belongs to a consortium of owners of TAT8, TAT9, and TPC cables. These are trans-atlantic and trans-pacific fiber cables, each of which can support up to 40,000 to 80,000 conversations.

The fastest growing component of the network, and for that matter many other networks, is the international network. IDDD (International Direct Distance Dialing) can be done to more than 200 nations. This means that without the caller needing operator assistance, AT&T can deliver the call to those countries. The network can reach a total of 270 countries and only a handful cannot be reached due to political restrictions.

7.5.2 North American Network

Domestically, AT&T has more than 120 4ESSs (Electronic Switching Systems), out of which 12 are used for international gateways. The 4ESS is a toll and tandem switch, that is, no telephone lines can be connected to it but only trunks from other switches. It can process 700,000 calls in an hour compared to the 5ESS which can handle 200,000 calls per hour. In regions where demand is low, 5ESSs are used, but the backbone of the American network consists of the 4ESSs.

The 4ESSs are configured in virtually a fully connected mesh network. There is a direct trunk from every 4ESS to virtually every other 4ESS. These trunks may go through intermediate 4ESS sites but they are not switched there. As shown in Figure 7.13 most switches have direct links to each other, but these links are shared or multiplexed over a common physical media.

The trunks between the 4ESSs carry only voice, data, or image traffic; signaling is transported over a separate network called the signaling network. Physically, the signaling network may share the transmission facilities of the 4ESS network, but logically these two networks are kept separate.

The signaling network consists of 12 mated pairs of STPs, which are connected in a fully meshed network. That is, every STP pair has a direct link to every other pair. For reliability purposes, a given STP pair may be hundreds of miles apart and the workload between them is shared. Each STP handles 50% of the traffic and if necessary is capable of handling all of the calls of the pair. All signaling links run at 56 kbps and each 4ESS is "homed" or linked to only one STP pair as shown in Figure 7.14.

7.5.3 Call Processing Over the Signaling Network

In Figure 7.14 if a call originates at 4ESS#1 and it needs a channel to 4ESS#2, then it will send a packet to STP#1 asking for the channel. STP#1 will interrogate 4ESS#2, providing the called party's phone number, if a path exists to the destination where the call is going. If 4ESS#2 can't complete the call, it will tell the STP and the STP will notify 4ESS#1. The 4ESS#1 will then provide the busyback signal to the caller and no trunks between the 4ESSs will be utilized.

However, if 4ESS#2 can complete the call to its destination, then the STP will give the go-ahead to the switches to switch simultaneously to the trunk specified by 4ESS#1's original request. Then a continuity and quality check is made on that trunk and the call is completed. Now the services of the STP are not required.

If a call is to be completed between two 4ESSs not homed to the same STP pair, such as a call between 4ESS#1 and 4ESS#3, the same procedure is followed, but now the two STPs must communicate with each other in deciding which trunk to use.

If no free trunks are available between two switches, then a third intermediate switch must be used to route the call. And if all three switches are homed to three

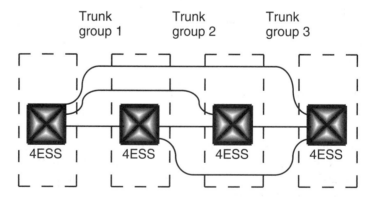

Figure 7.13 Switches in four cities located in a straight line can be fully connected using only three trunk groups by multiplexing the links.

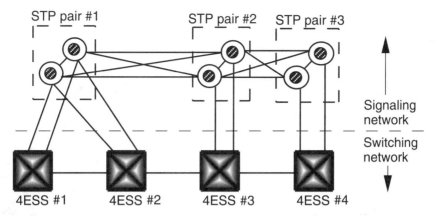

Figure 7.14 A segment of AT&T's SS7 network. Not all links are shown between the STP pairs and between the 4ESSs.

different STPs then all three STPs are required to process the call. For example, if in Figure 7.14 4ESS#1 needs to make a call to 4ESS#3 and no free capacity is available on the direct link between the two switches, then the call may be routed via 4ESS#4. In such a case the three switches are connected to three different STP pairs and all of those STPs must then send packets to complete the call.

7.5.4 RTNR (Real Time Network Routing)

In no case are two intermediate 4ESS switches used for call completion, but only one intermediate switch is ever needed to complete the call. However, since most switches are all fully connected to each other and there are over 120 of those, there are that many alternate routes possible.

RTNR dynamically calculates more than 120 possible routes to complete the call using one other 4ESS. By restricting to only one additional switch, the signal quality is kept high and calls can be completed in 4 to 6 seconds compared with over 20 seconds using the older hierarchical routing.

Prior to RTNR, AT&T used DNHR (Dynamic Non-Hierarchical Routing), which was not really a dynamic method of routing. It allowed for 14 alternate routes for every call between every 4ESS pair. These routes were preprogrammed in the 4ESSs for ten different time blocks during the day.

RTNR allows a 4ESS to calculate the most efficient route on a call by call basis. If a direct trunk is unavailable to the distant 4ESS, it will interrogate it via the signaling network for the status and capacity of the trunks connected to it. Then comparing the traffic of the trunks connected to itself and the trunks connected to the distant 4ESS, the calling 4ESS will decide which other 4ESS to use as an intermediate switch. Then through the signaling network the appropriate connections are made. In Figure 7.15, the calling 4ESS has received the traffic loads of the distant 4ESS to 120 other switches. From this data, the calling switch decides to use the intermediate switch with the lightest load on both trunk groups.

The Public Switched Telephone Network **109**

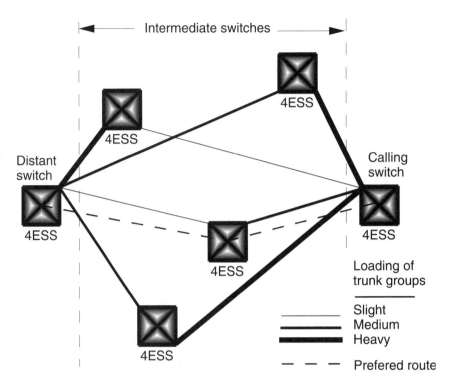

Figure 7.15 RTNR dynamically decides the best intermediate switch to complete a call by assessing the various trunk group usages.

7.5.5 NCPs (Network Control Points)

The last component of the AT&T communications network is network services. These services include SDN (Software Defined Network), its virtual network, 800 & 900 services, and calling card. They are provided by many databases called NCPs which are part of the signaling network and are connected to STPs as shown in Figure 7.16. These are AT&T's equivalent of NJ Bell's SCPs described in the local telephone network section of this chapter. The NCPs form a distributed database, storing data pertaining to 800 numbers, SDN customers, and so on.

For example, when an STP has to route an 800 number, it knows which NCP has the POTS (Plain Old Telephone Service) number conversion for it. Through the NCP the 800 number is translated into a POTS number and the STP can then complete the call. For instance, 1-800-544-3498 may be converted to 408-345-3277 in San Jose. Advanced 800 numbers provide geographic or time of day routing, which means that the call is directed to a different POTS number depending on the caller's area or on the time of day the call is made,

Authorization for a calling card is done through the NCPs. Also, SDN customers virtual network databases are stored here. All data in the NCPs is duplicated in at least one other site, and the STPs know which NCP has the data for the given customer or the number being called. NCPs and STPs are both 3B20 minicomputers which have long been characterized by their dependability.

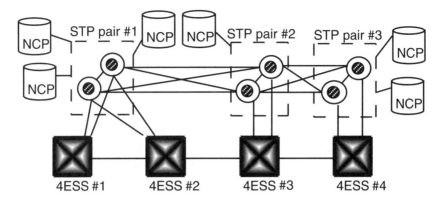

Figure 7.16 NCPs (Network Control Point) connected to the STPs provide advanced network services.

7.6 THE MCI NETWORK

Figure 7.17 shows the network architecture of MCI. It is divided into three layers: the administrative, logical, and physical layers. Let us first discuss the physical layer.

7.6.1 The Physical Layer

In this layer, the transmission network is 100% digital, though the media types are not all alike. Within this network, there is a subnetwork dedicated to transport data only, called DDN (Digital Data Network). DDN is used to carry only digital data signals, both those below 64kbps and those above 64kbps. Having this specialized network allows data to be transmitted with added accuracy and reliability.

This network is then tied to a software controlled distribution frame called DACS (Digital Access and Cross connect System). These devices are covered in Chapter 10. They add flexibility to the transmission network by being able to be reconfigured by the push of a few buttons. Customers can reconfigure their networks easily using the interfaces shown in the administrative layer.

A signal then travels from the transmission network, through the DACS to the switch. MCI has approximately 90 switches, some of which are NT's DMS-250s and others of which are DSC's DEX6000Es. Each switch has an AP (Adjunct Processor) to relieve it of its non-switching processing load. This allows the switches to function more swiftly and efficiently. APs provide CDR (Call Detail Recording) for each call to help expedite billing and provide up front fraud detection to prevent unauthorized users to gain access to private networks. It also provides protocol conversions between the MCI switches and other computer systems in the MCI network.

Each switch is homed to only one STP pair, of which there are five pairs. The STP network utilizes ANSI's version of signaling system 7 called TR-TSY-950. As in the AT&T network, an ordinary POTS type of phone call uses only the physical network resources.

The Public Switched Telephone Network
111

7.6.2 The Logical Layer

800 number conversions, credit card authorization, and virtual networks use the DAPs (Data Access Points), similar to the NCPs that are used in the AT&T network. Notice a major difference here is that the DAPs are connected directly to the switches. The DAPs are VAX 8700 minicomputers made by DEC. All 90 switches have a direct link to each of the three DAPs. So even if two links fail, a third DAP link exists. X.25 protocol is used in these links.

The data in all three DAPs is kept synchronized, meaning that the data is kept the same. This is done by the SCM (Service Control Manager). The SCM is an IBM 3090 mainframe which continuously downloads data from the NETCAP (NETwork CAPabilities manager).

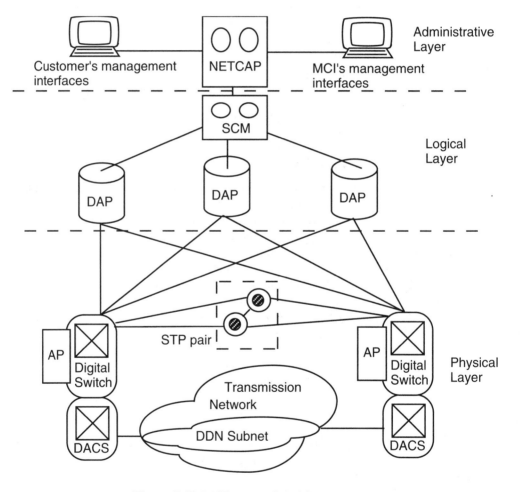

Figure 7.17 MCI's network architecture.

7.6.3 The Administrative Layer

The NETCAP is also a mainframe and it provides an interface between the management systems and the rest of the network. When a customer or MCI configures or reconfigures a customer specific network, the NETCAP provides the necessary security checking. It then screens the customer's inquiries and commands to make sure that they are of the proper format and prevents the customer from inadvertently misconfiguring his network. NETCAP then notifies the network elements and the appropriate billing computers. Management systems are discussed later in Chapter 11 on virtual networks.

7.7 THE SPRINT NETWORK

The backbone of Sprint's network consists of 46 DMS-250 switches made by Northern Telecom. This is also a fully connected mesh network where every switch has direct access to every other. The trunk between two switches is called an IMT (Inter-Machine Trunk). The entire network uses 23,000 miles of single mode fiber. The bandwidth of the fiber varies from 565 Mbps to 1.7 Gbps depending on the traffic requirement on the IMTs. In the future the bandwidth is expected to approach 10 Gbps by implementing wave division multiplexing.

The fiber network consists of 3 east-west routes, 5 north-south routes, and a total of 23 loops, which add survivability to the network in the event of failure. RDPS (Reverse Direction Protection Switching) allows switched traffic to automatically be rerouted in case there is a failure in the transmission path. Figure 7.18 shows how a fiber is terminated at a switch. First, the optical signal is converted into an electrical signal and demultiplexed into a number of DS-3 signal levels using an FOT (Fiber Optic Terminal). Then a bank of M13 multiplexers separates the DS-3 channels into DS-1 channels and the switch will separate the DS-1 channels into DS-0 channels as necessary.

Sprint has more than 325 POPs, some of which are owned and some of which are co-located in the COs.

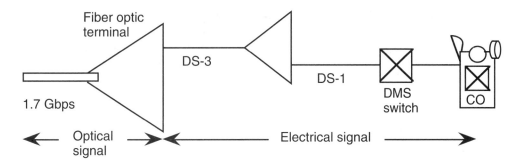

Figure 7.18 The optical signal coming off the fiber is demultiplexed into DS-3 levels which are further demultiplexed into DS-1 levels. DS-1 is the signal level that is received by the Sprint switch.

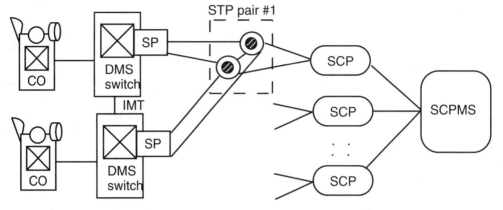

SP   : Signaling Point   SCP: Service Control Point
SCPMS : SCP Management System   IMT : InterMachine Trunk

Figure 7.19 Sprint's network architecture.

The fiber backbone network is the physical network that is used to carry traffic from the following seven networks: Circuit switching network is what is used for dialing a call. The SS7 network carries the signaling for the switches. Private leased lines are for businesses which need fixed amounts of bandwidth from point to point. SprintNet, formerly Telenet, is the world's largest x.25 network and frame relay; all share the bandwidth on the fiber network. Also, Sprint's ISDN and the Meeting Channel are on this network. The Meeting Channel is the world's largest videoconferencing network which allows the public to go to any of the 900 conference rooms and dial each other for a videoconference.

Sprint made a change to SS7 in December of 1988. Figure 7.19 shows that the DMS switches have SPs (Signaling Points) associated with them. These SPs assist the STPs and the DMS switches to perform call processing more efficiently.

Sprint has four pairs of STPs and is expecting to install the fifth pair at the time of this writing. These are connected to SCPs (Service Control Points). The SCPs act like the NCPs in the AT&T network. That is, they provide the "database dips" needed for 800 number conversions, credit card handling, and virtual network routing.

Unlike AT&T's distributed NCP network, there is a centrally located SCPMS (SCP Management System) which controls the SCPs. Sprint performs routing decisions in a distributed manner, closer to the switches. However, call processing decisions which require database lookups are done centrally in the SCPs.

7.8 COMPETITIVE ACCESS PROVIDERS (CAPs)

Lastly, this chapter can't be concluded without saying a word or two about Competitive Access Providers (CAPs). They have also been referred to as local bypass carriers. To high-volume users they provide specialized local services for which they require minimal regulatory approval. William Telecommunications, on the other hand, provides private line and other services to large customers on a nation-wide network.

Many miles of WilTel's 11,000 mile fiber optic network runs through unused gasoline pipelines, making it virtually indestructible against the backhoe.

CAPs compete with the local operating telephone companies by providing transmission facilities directly to the IXC's POPs in large metropolitan areas, thereby bypassing the local telco services. Customers who use bypass carriers then don't have the charges from the local telephone company. CAPs generally provide services over fiber optic networks with duplicate routes between network locations to provide superior service quality and security compared to the local telephone company. They also price themselves competitively with the phone companies to attract large volume users away from the telco. The cities of Chicago, Los Angeles, San Francisco, and Boston each have at least 4 CAPs. MFS (Metropolitan Fiber Systems) and Teleport Communications Group are examples of such CAPs, MFS being the largest with networks in 12 major metropolitan areas nationwide.

In many cases, the bypass carriers' networks cross LATA boundaries, because in most states they are not regulated and a customer may be able not only to bypass the LECs in both LATAs but also bypass the IXCs as well.

Of course, the BOCs don't like to lose large volume customers to these carriers. They have estimated an annual loss of revenues amounting up to three billion dollars while the CAPs claim to have revenues amounting to only 150 million dollars. Some BOCs are also refraining from buying AT&T 5ESS switches and equipment, because AT&T, like other carriers, allows their customers to bypass the LEC.

The BOCs must file for approval with the PUC for providing specialized and innovative services. Whereas the bypasses are not so regulated in most states, in some cases, they have laid miles of fiber to one location just to win one customer over. This type of catering to customers is not customary of the LECs.

CAPs provide not only access to the POPs, but also LAN interconnections and ISDN services over most fiber backbone networks. Digital microwave is also used by them. Some have centrex switches and provide centrex services to customers. Centrex is covered in Chapter 8. Others provide E1 conversion from DS-1 signals for overseas connections. Some provide speeds typical of LAN speeds such as 10, 16, and 100 MBPs which are meant for LAN interconnectivity. Others provide video pipes running at 384 and 768 kBPs.

One of the most attractive reasons why managers like CAPs is the added reliability they provide to their network. This is done by the alternate routes provided by these carriers, and in case a disaster strikes the established local carrier network, alternate routing is possible. The CAPs also provide network management functions such as rerouting and remote testing of circuits. Circuits can be rerouted to different COs. Similarly, if disaster strikes a POP, circuits can be switched not only to another POP of the same IXC but also to another POP of a different IXC.

In conclusion, CAPs not only provide a means to access IXCs directly, but now they are providing high quality services, greater reliability for access networks, and competitive pricing for their customers. This has forced the LECs to also improve their services and relationships with customers. LECs in major cities can't afford to tell customers " . . . too bad, take it or leave it," because now there is competition. Hence both the local exchanges and the competitive carriers improve. The result of competition between the carriers is high quality services to the end users and robust networks.

Exercises

1. In 1982, the telephone network was divided into how many sections? See Figure 7.1.

   a. 10

   b. 40

   c. 52

   d. 100

2. What device interfaces a residential home wiring with the local telephone network?

   a. SAC

   b. NID

   c. SLC

   d. IW

3. When a person moves from one house to another house within the same area, and wishes to keep the same phone number, what must be changed for that customer?

   a. TN

   b. OE

   c. CP

   d. HMDF

4. What type of signal is sent over the voice path between two COs in an SS7 environment?

   a. busyback

   b. ringback

   c. dial tone

   d. DTMF tones

5. If the bandwidth per channel for cellular system were .025MHz instead of .03 Mhz, how many channels would have been available in each block?

   a. 500

   b. 832

   c. 1000

   d. 1200

6. When k = 12, how many simultaneous conversations are possible per cell?

   a. 12

   b. 18

   c. 26

   d. 32

7. If AT&T has 117 4ESS switches, how many alternate routes are possible between two switches that use one other intermediate switch?

   a. 100

   b. 115

   c. 116

   d. 117

8. Which of the following is not a layer in the MCI network?

   a. application

   b. logical

   c. administration

   d. physical

9. What type of an office connects two COs together in the local network?

10. Which device multiplexes 96 subscriber lines to the CO using 10 pairs of wire?

11. Name the SS7 type of office which allows a CO, not on the SS7 network, to be part of that network?

12. When a cellular radio locks to the strongest signaling channel while idle, what is this condition called?

13. When a mobile radio leaves the territory of one cell and goes into another cell, what operation is performed by the cell sites?

14. What is the name of the AT&T network management system?

15. Which AT&T routing technique utilizes the instantaneous loading capacities of the intermachine trunks?

16. What are the names of the SCPs as referred to by AT&T, MCI, and Sprint?

17. Give reasons why the old hierarchical routing of telephone calls took longer than the current methods?

18. Explain how switched lines and dedicated lines are routed in a CO using Figure 7.2.

19. Using Figure 7.4, describe the steps of how a call from Metuchen to a Bell Atlantic 800 number located in Somerville occurs.

20. Describe the reasons why the current cellular telephone system is better than the previous systems.

21. Draw a frequency reuse pattern for k = 4.

22. Describe how a "wire-line" phone completes a call to a mobile phone.

23. Describe how an AT&T credit card call is made.

24. What are the advantages provided by CAPs?

Chapter 8

Private Switching Networks

8.1 BACKGROUND

This chapter will primarily discuss PBX concepts, and it can be thought of as a chapter on voice-based LANs. When PBXs are mentioned, modern, sophisticated equipment comes to mind. However, it is interesting to note that PBXs existed even in the early 1900s. These were called manual PBXs and they were actually a switchboard with an operator making connections using cords and jacks. Then in the 1920s, automatic PBXs utilizing step-by-step switching equipment were introduced. And in the 1950s, they were sporting the crossbar switches.

Today PBXs and associated equipment can perform a wide variety of functions, many of which will be covered in Chapter 9. These devices/switches allow both voice and data communications.

Yet PBXs in this country were owned by the telephone companies and were leased to their business customers. In 1968, the FCC ruled in the Carterfone Decision that customer provided equipment may be directly connected to the public telephone network as long as a carrier-provided protective coupling device was used. This was the birth of the interconnect industry and it prompted manufacturers, many from Japan and Europe, to sell voice based products. All the excitement in competition stimulated the further development of new products.

8.2 CENTREX

8.2.1 What is Centrex?

Centrex, which is a contraction of the words central and exchange, began in 1965. Centrex involves leasing a "PBX" at the central office, instead of owning one on the customer premises. Since all the voice switching is done at the CO, all the telephones must have their own pairs of wire going to the CO. Leasing these pairs to the CO then

---

Much of the information from this chapter has been kindly taught to me by Peter DePrima of Trecom Business Systems, Inc.

becomes one of the most costly items when considering the feasibility of making the Centrex decision.

Consider Figure 8.1 where both a simplified diagram of a PBX and Centrex installation is shown. Notice in the PBX system, phone 101 could ring phone 203 and only the inside wiring would be used because the switching would be done locally. However, in the Centrex system, when the same call is placed, the connection is made at the CO on their Centrex switch. Here two "street" pairs to the CO are utilized to make a connection between two phones within a building.

NT's (Northern Telecom's) S/DMS supernode, DMS-100, and AT&T's 5ESS are examples of common Centrex switches.

8.2.2 Centrex Advantages

Even though the requirement of many lines from the customer's premises to the CO typically makes Centrex more costly than acquiring one's own PBX, there are a number of reasons why Centrex is more attractive than PBX to many telecommunication managers.

Centrex service rates are constantly being restructured, and depending on what the telcos are allowed to offer by the regulatory agencies, the tariffs for Centrex are in many places more attractive than the cost of using a PBX. And if the customer's premises are in the vicinity of the local CO, the mileage charges for the Centrex lines are inherently lower.

To preserve a company's cash flow, Centrex is an attractive alternative. The incentive to purchase a PBX for tax advantages varies from year to year, and it should be investigated. If a company is unsure of how or if it is growing or decreasing in size,

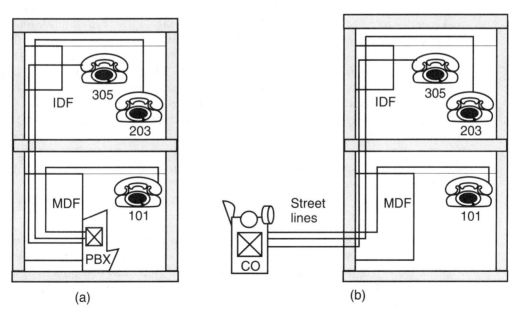

Figure 8.1 (a) PBX does the on-premise switching. (b) Centrex service does on-premise switching at the CO over leased lines.

no commitment has to be made on the capacity of the voice switching system. In fact, some PBXs have a limit to their capacity, while Centrex has no such limit.

Installing a city-wide network using a PBX requires lines and trunks from many locations all to be brought to a PBX via the CO. Since the lines may have to come through the CO anyway, it's more natural to switch them there, rather than bringing them to another location to be switched and then route them through the CO again to their destination. See Figure 8.2.

Centrex allows a network to expand to the outer reaches of a city by adding remote modules at the remote locations. This is called on-premise Centrex and is also shown in Figure 8.2(b). This eliminates much of the street wiring.

Centrex also allows a uniform dialing plan for an organization. If people move from one location in a city to another one outside the city, they can keep the same phone number if the two locations are part of one Centrex plan. Also, in such an arrangement, only one operator is needed to handle calls. Every site doesn't need its own operator.

Furthermore, with Centrex no maintenance is required on the user's part. All repairs on the switch are done by the telco. SMDR (Station Message Detail Recording), which gives exhaustive data reports on who called whom, for how long, and at what cost, etc., used to be mailed by the CO on a magnetic tape every month. Now a Centrex customer can retrieve these reports as often as it is needed from a terminal using a modem.

Similarly, when one person moved from one location to another and wanted to keep the same phone number, the "move" had to be done by the Centrex technician. Now customers have their own terminal from which they can not only do moves but also change phone station features, and add new phones and so on. This type of activity is called doing moves-adds-and-changes or MACs to software translations.

Probably the most important reason to chose Centrex over PBX is that Centrex is generally more reliable than PBX systems, although PBXs can be made just as reliable. Centrex, when located at the CO, is well protected against earthquakes, fires, and sabotage. Technicians trained on the equipment are at the location 24 hours a day. No time is lost in transporting technicians and parts to PBX sites. Of course, many large PBXs have a trained technician on site during business hours, but with Centrex, even small customers can have fast service around the clock.

Other advantages include no PBX room is needed that has to be kept cooled. No insurance is needed on the equipment and not as much staff is required to administer Centrex. However, Centrex is more closely regulated by the FCC and the state agencies. Its services are not homogeneous through all the LATAs and the SMDR information available may have some limitations.

8.2.3 CO-LANs

Centrex has always been lagging behind PBX in providing features and function-ality until the mid 1980s. Since then, this gap is closing. One reason why Centrex is "catching up" with PBXs is the service of CO-LAN which was first offered by Bell Atlantic in 1985. This allows customers to send and switch data over their voice network, which is a form of voice/data integration.

The first method of accomplishing this was using DOV modems (Data Over Voice). This device is required at both the CO and the customer premises as shown in

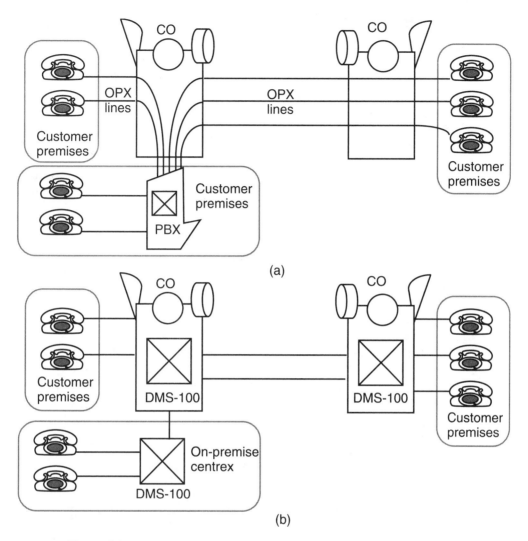

Figure 8.2 (a) Networking scattered sites in a metropolitan area requires leasing of many lines. (b) Centrex networking is a more natural solution for a metropolitan area network.

Figure 8.3(a). The DOV modem allows the transmission of both voice and data (up to 9600 bps) over a single pair of wires. So with the same wiring as for voice networks, customers receive data networking with only a nominal increase in charges.

The transmission of simultaneous data over the voice pair is done by modulating the data into an analog signal at around 100 kHz. This analog signal which carries the data information is then frequency multiplexed into the output. Since the voice is being carried at around 3 kHz and the modulated data at 100 kHz, using filters it is easy to separate the data signal from the voice signal at the CO. See Figure 8.3(b)

IVDT: Integrated Voice/Data Terminal FDM: Frequency Division Multiplexer
IVDM: Integrated Voice/Data Multiplexer TDM: Time Division Multiplexer
DOV: Data Over Voice

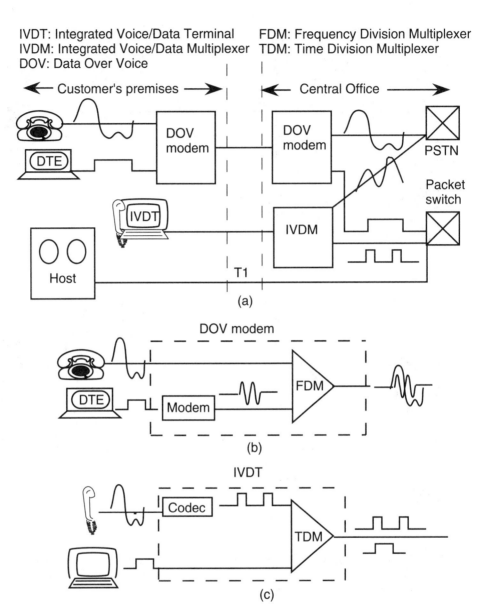

Figure 8.3 (a) Operation of CO-LAN showing the analog version using a DOV modem and the digital version using an IVDT. (b) A DOV modem combines voice and data into analog form. (c) An IVDT combines voice and data into digital form.

The problem is that, typically on a voice line, loading coils are needed every 3 miles, and these coils prevent transmission in the low end and the high end of the 4 kHz voice band. DOV modems multiplex the modulated data in this area of the bandwidth, so loading coils can't be used with them. Therefore, this limits the range of CO-LANs using DOV modems to 3 miles.

DOV modems at the CO do the same thing but in reverse. The demultiplexed voice goes to the voice switch and the data is directed to a packet switch. The voice and the data can be switched back to the customer's premises or can be routed to distant locations over the PSTN and packet networks. As shown in the diagram, data can also be switched back to the customer's site using a T1 link, typically to a host.

With the introduction of ISDN, a more sophisticated and expensive alternative exists using IVDTs (Integrated Voice/Data Terminals). This is also depicted in Figure 8.3(c). It allows for transmission of data at speeds up to 64 kbps. Signalwise, it is just the reciprocal of a DOV modem. Instead of modulating the data, it digitizes the voice and instead of frequency division multiplexing the analog signals, it time division multiplexes the digital ones. However, to the end user, the effect of either method is practically the same.

8.3 KEY SYSTEMS

8.3.1 The 1A2 System

Key systems were first introduced in 1953 when Bell Telephone came out with the 1A1 system. Ten years later, the 1A2 which followed it was a very popular product for a long time. Key systems allow a small business having 50 telephones or less to subscribe to fewer lines than the number of keysets (or phones) it has. This is possible, because the outside lines are shared among the keysets.

In Figure 8.4, a simple 1A2 system with a 3 x 5 configuration is shown. The 3 stands for the number of lines coming from the CO and the 5 is the number of keysets which are connected. These phone lines are being subscribed from the CO and the phone numbers, using any combination, can be terminated at any of the keyphones during installation. When the number 238-1001 is called from the outside, all the stations with that number on it will ring and any of them can pick up that line. When someone does pick up a line, that number will light up at the other phones indicating that it is in use. For calling out, the keysets would get their dial tone from the CO.

The 1A2 key system was called a "fat cable" key system, because no matter how many phone numbers were assigned to a keyphone (maximum being five in most sets), a 25-pair cable had to be snaked to the set. This was because each of the 5 possible phone numbers needed 3 pairs. Installing this fat cable around facilities was very costly and bulky.

The 1A2 keyset was more complex as compared to a PBX phone set which used "skinny" wire. The emphasis on calling with the 1A2 was with the outside world where, with a PBX one must first dial an access code, typically a "9," to get to an outside line. In a PBX system, usually an attendant, a person or an automated system handled the incoming calls, but with the 1A2, incoming calls were handled by anyone who had the number terminating to their keyset. Another difference between the 1A2 and the PBX is that the 1A2 simply passed the CO's dial tone, whereas the PBX provides its own. The 1A2 was also limited in that no SMDR (Station Message Detail Recording) was available. No tie trunks or DID (Direct Inward Dialing) trunks were supported by these key systems. It did not contain any switching intelligence. The collection of the users selecting the various buttons on the keyphones was the switching intelligence of the system.

8.3.2 EKS (Electronic Key Systems)

In 1983, twenty years after the introduction of the 1A2, a number of vendors started coming out with EKSs. Unlike the 1A2 sets, the sets of these systems use only a two- or three-pair wire, so these key systems are called "skinny-wire" systems. The KSUs are much smaller than before; they use microchips instead of electromechanical parts and are much easier to install. They can have tie lines, DID trunks, and the incoming calls can be taken by a receptionist, similar to the PBX. In fact today almost all of the features available on PBXs are available on EKSs, and this makes it hard to distinguish EKSs from small PBXs.

Northern Telecom's Norstar is one example of an EKS. It has an open architecture interface which allows third party vendors to write special purpose software for it. The Norstar can be programmed from a PC, and this stimulates writing of applications for the system by creative minds other than the NT engineers. Traditionally, this was unheard of in the PBX marketplace; PBX makers did not share their system software internals with others, so only they could enhance the feature set of their PBXs.

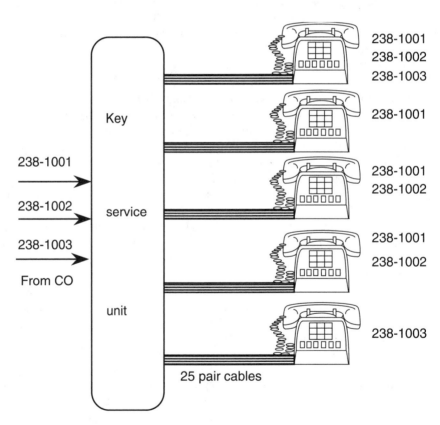

Figure 8.4 An atypical, 3 by 5 configuration of a 1A2 key system. Typically, the three incoming numbers would terminate at all of the key sets.

This makes EKSs in some ways superior to PBXs. For instance with a PBX, if a person changes his office location and wants to keep the same phone number, a technician must code this change on the PBX. However with the Norstar, a person only needs to take the phone along to the new office and plug it in there and the KSU will detect the move. No one has to program the change. This is done by a physical address hard coded in the keyphone sets at the factory. Such benefits are not yet widely available on PBXs.

Key systems can also be also used behind a PBX or Centrex. The term "behind" means on the customers side of the switch, and "in front" means on the public network side of the switch. In Figure 8.5, a KSU is shown to be connected behind the PBX using OPX lines. Although OPX lines would typically go through one or more COs, logically they make the key system appear to be part of the CO.

Without the key system, four telephones at a remote site would normally require leasing four OPX (Off Premise Extensions) lines from the telco. However, with the EKS located at the remote site, only two OPX lines may prove to be sufficient. In this configuration, if two remote phones are using the OPX lines to call out, then a third remote phone could not call anyone outside of its own facility.

Incidentally, in this example, if a caller from the PBX gets transferred by a remote site keyphone to a third person at the PBX, it is possible for the keyphone to signal the PBX and not the KSU to do the transfer. If the transfer is done through the KSU, then both OPX lines are tied up unnecessarily.

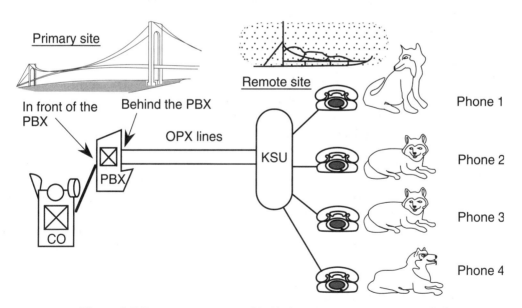

Figure 8.5 Key system connected behind a PBX or centrex can maximize its utilization.

8.4 OTHER SMALL VOICE SYSTEMS

8.4.1 Hybrid Systems

A hybrid system is similar to a key system, except, on a key system a caller chooses the line to make a call, but on a hybrid system the caller simply picks up the phone and the KSU-like device chooses the line that is free to make the call. So the hybrid system has a pool of lines to pick from to make a call while on a key system if all the lines designated for a set are busy, then that set can't make an outside call even though there may be other lines available. The tariffs for key system lines are less than those for hybrid lines. Companies who want less blocking of calls don't mind paying more for the hybrid system lines. The difference between these two systems from a given vendor many times is just in the software that comes with the unit.

8.4.2 KSU-less Systems

Lastly, the KSU-less system is ideal for telephone systems that have less than ten phones. They are less expensive than a key system, don't require a KSU, and are very easy to install.

8.5 EXAMPLES OF PBX FEATURES

The remainder of this chapter is devoted to PBXs. Features for PBXs are usually categorized into three groups: features for the stations (phones), features for the attendant console (traditionally thought of as the switch board), and features for the system in general. A sample of a few features will be presented here, just so the capabilities of the PBX can be illustrated. Most PBXs can be acquired with over a hundred features.

8.5.1 Station Features

Two common station features are call-transfer and call-forward. Call-transfer allows the called party to hand over the call to a third party, so that the third party and the original calling party may communicate.

Call-forward on the other hand, allows a person to go for lunch or to be absent and have someone else answer their calls for them from their own phone.

Call-park is another station feature. It is more commonly used in hospitals. For example, if an outside caller dials the hospital for Dr. Doctor, the attendant would tell the caller to stay on hold. The attendant would park the call on a phantom number, that is an extension that doesn't have a phone connected to it, and would page over the loudspeaker for the doctor, asking her to call that extension. Dr. Doctor can then call from any phone in the hospital, dial an access code and that extension would be connected to the caller. No ringback tone would be heard by the caller.

8.5.2 Attendant Feature

An example of a PBX attendant feature is called intercept. This feature prevents the attendant (operator) having to say, "not a valid phone number, please consult your directory." Also, this prevents the phone system from being congested with ring-no-answer conditions.

Automatic recall allows a party in a conversation to get the attendant back on the line.

8.5.3 System Features

Classes of service is an important system feature. This is a priority rating given to voice terminals (telephones). 64 different priorities can be assigned. Priority of 1 is given to the most important phone sets and 64 is usually assigned for the least important phone, such as in the cafeteria. However, usually only 8 different classes of service are assigned for simplicity. A telephone with a high class of service will have more station features activated on it, it will be allowed to make toll calls, and be given other privileges. The services associated with each class are programmed by the telecom manager.

SMDR (Station Message Detail Recording), already referred to in the section on Centrex, provides reports of which extensions were called by whom, at what time, for how long and at what cost. This type of information helps to manage telecommunications costs, bill departments on their utilization, and have control on phone abuse. CDR (Call Detail Recording) is another name used for it.

8.6 THE AT&T DEFINITY

As an example of a PBX system, the AT&T DEFINITY Generic 3 is being introduced. This is not an attempt to sell the product, but to explain a PBX in specific rather than general terms.

8.6.1 Telephone Instruments

As with other PBXs, the Generic 3 supports 2500 type sets. These are analog type desk or wall phones commonly used in homes. They come with two pairs of wire, out of which only one pair is used. These are analog type phones, because the spoken voice is sent out of the phone over one pair in analog form and the line card of the switch, where the pair terminates, has the codec to convert the voice to digital form.

AT&T's 7406 Plus is an example of a digital phone. A digital phone converts voice into the digital form before being sent out on the wire pair. The line card in the PBX then doesn't have to digitize the voice. The digitizing takes place in the handset. The 7406 is also an example of a feature phone. With an ordinary 2500 set, station features can be accessed by inputting dial access codes to activate and deactivate features. However, a feature phone allows the user to activate a feature simply by pressing a preprogrammed button instead of the keys of the keypad. This is also an example of a vendor-specific phone; that is, it will work only with one vendor's equipment.

Integrated voice/data workstations include a digital telephone and a PC running PC/ISDN Platform software. An interface card plugs into an eight-bit expansion slot in the PC which is connected to a voice terminal (phone) using a standard phone jack. With the workstation connected to the DEFINITY system, a person can communicate to a host or other PCs, while talking to a person in another location. The PC/ISDN Platform provides an open software interface for which customers and independent developers can create their own applications. Currently applications are available for advance message centers, terminal emulations, attendant workstations, etc.

8.6.2 Station Links

The connection from the voice terminal to the Generic 3 is done over four pairs of wire. One pair carries the digitized voice at 64 kbps, another carries data at 64 kbps, a third carries signaling at 8 kbps, and the fourth carries DC power from the wiring closet to the workstation. The two 64 kbps channels, called information channels, together with 8 kbps of signaling and 24 kbps of control and framing bits form AT&T's proprietary DCP (Data Communications Protocol), running at 160 kbps.

The voice and data channels go to the same line card, but since they each occupy a different time slot on the bus, they don't interfere with each other. Since the capacity of the data speed is 64 kbps, a communication speed of anything less wastes the bandwidth of the bus. The 32 kbps channel doesn't go to a line card, but to signaling control equipment.

Other vendors provide the same capabilities but with fewer pairs. Northern Telecom uses three pairs and Rolm uses only one pair. Rolm does this by multiplexing voice, data and signaling together, and then phantoming the DC power over the same pair. Phantoming means transmitting both the digital signal and the DC voltage over the same line. Other vendors can also phantom power if necessary.

8.6.3 DEFINITY Block Diagram Overview

In Figure 8.6, a simplified overview of the DEFINTIY Generic 3 is shown. The Generic 3 comes in four models. In this chapter we'll only consider the G3i and the G3r models. One G3i can support up to 2800 ports, both lines and trunks, while the G3r can support up to 29,000 ports. Many more lines can be supported if they are networked with other systems either locally or over a wider area.

The AT&T 3B20 minicomputers aid the Generic 3 by performing non-switching types of applications, such as: word processing, terminal emulations, message center processing, call detail recording, call management systems for ACD environments, and UNIX and local area networking. Audix is AT&T's voice mail system.

The PPN (Processor Port Network) is the master controller for the DEFINITY system, and may have up to 800 terminals connected to it directly. As more terminals are required, EPNs (Expansion Port Networks) are attached to the PPN until the limit is reached for adding terminals and EPNs, at which time other DEFINITY systems can be networked by adding more PPNs and starting the expansion process over again. In Figure 8.6, two G3s are shown as being networked. Previous models of AT&T PBXs, System/75, System/85, Generic 1 and 2, may also be networked with the G3s.

The EPNs may be co-located with their respective PPN or may be placed up to 5 miles away using a fiber connection. EPNs may be placed even up to 100 miles away by using a T1 link. Each T1 provides up to 24 terminals and with a maximum of four T1s, 94 information channels can be supported. Two channels out of the 96 channels

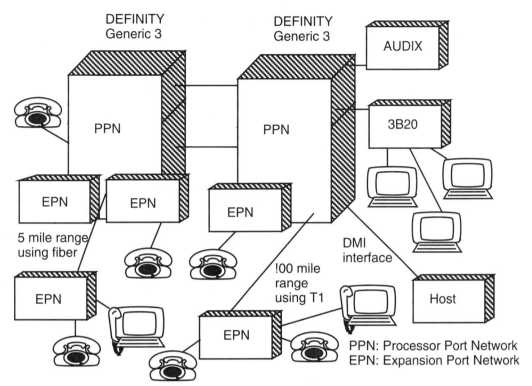

Figure 8.6 An overview of an AT&T DEFINITY communications system.

are required by the system. Terminals connected to any of these EPNs using fiber or T1 links appear as being part of the same DEFINITY system.

Using a T1 link, the DEFINITY can be connected to a host using the DMI (Digital Multiplexed Interface). This interface more closely resembles PRI of ISDN in that it carries 23 clear 64 kbps channels plus one 64 kbps signaling channel. The purpose of this interface is to replace many low speed connections to a host by one high speed connection which results in much lower costs. NT (Northern Telecom) along with DEC (Digital Equipment Corp.) developed the CPI (Computer to PBX Interface) which utilizes twenty-four 56 kbps channels. Both of these interfaces are migrating to ISDN compatible standards.

8.6.4 Additional Data Capabilities of the DEFINITY System

Some representative ways of interfacing data equipment with the DEFINITY system are shown in Figure 8.7. One should keep in mind that other vendors' PBXs are also capable of providing similar capabilities. These devices will be introduced in order starting from the top of the diagram. Remember that the native mode of operation for the DEFINITY uses the DCP format. This is 64 kbps for voice, 64 kbps for data, and 32 kbps for signaling and framing.

First, the ADM (Asynchronous Data Module) connected under a 7500 series BRI voice terminal allows data to be transmitted at a rate of 19.2 kbps.

The DTDM (Digital Terminal Data Module) connects to a digital voice terminal and allows communication of data at speeds of up to 64 kbps. It uses an RS-232C interface.

A MPDM (Modular Processor Data Module) is a multi-purpose data module. It can be used to connect an asynchronous host, an asynchronous terminal, or a synchronous terminal to the DEFINITY. It also supports data speeds of up to 64 kbps, and is available with RS-232C, RS-449, and V.35 interfaces. It can be used on a desktop or can be rack mounted with 7 others.

The 7400A allows the DEFINITY users to dial out to gain off-premise computer connections. Likewise, it allows off-premise users to dial into the computers which are connected with the DEFINITY. Access to the outside world over analog lines is done by using data sets (modems) and over digital lines by using DSUs (Digital Service Units). It supports speeds of up to 19.2 kbps. Typically, these are used in modem pools, which eliminates the need for a dedicated modem for every terminal, and the resource of modems is shared among the multiple users.

An ADU (Asynchronous Data Unit) allows an RS-232 connection to extend its range from 50 feet to 40,000 feet. This allows digital devices to be located far from the switch.

IBM's SNA (Systems Network Architecture), which is covered in Chapter 13, is the most widely used data network. Usually it includes a central host computer, which has an FEP (Front End Processor) connected to it. Then cluster controllers each supporting up to thirty-two 3270 type synchronous terminals are connected to the FEP, either directly or by using modems over tie-lines. The standard connection between the 3270s and the cluster controller uses an RG-93 type coax, running at 2.358 Mbps. AT&T, through the DEFINITY and its peripherals, provides a common twisted pair solution for wiring IBM's SNA network.

A 3270 data module converts a 3270 terminal interface to the DCP interface. Since the terminal transmits at 2.34 Mbps, the data module must buffer or store data, so it could release it on the twisted pair side at 64 kbps. The reverse is true; data coming from the DCP interfaces at 64 kbps and is collected until a block of data can be sent out at 2.34 Mbps. This process is called speed conversion. But there is also protocol conversion being done here, which changes the format of the data from one interface to the other. The 3270 data module also interfaces the switch with a PC running 3270 emulation.

A controller data module is a similar device which interfaces the cluster controller with the DEFINITY. Now both the PC and the 3270 terminal can access the host through the data modules and the DEFINITY communications system.

These two types of data modules enhance the SNA network in a number of ways. The 3270s are not tied to a particular host any more, but now have access to asynchronous computers and outside dial-up services. There is now a need for fewer cluster controllers, since not every terminal needs a dedicated connection to its respective controller. The connection into the cluster controller is switched, so that that resource is now shared.

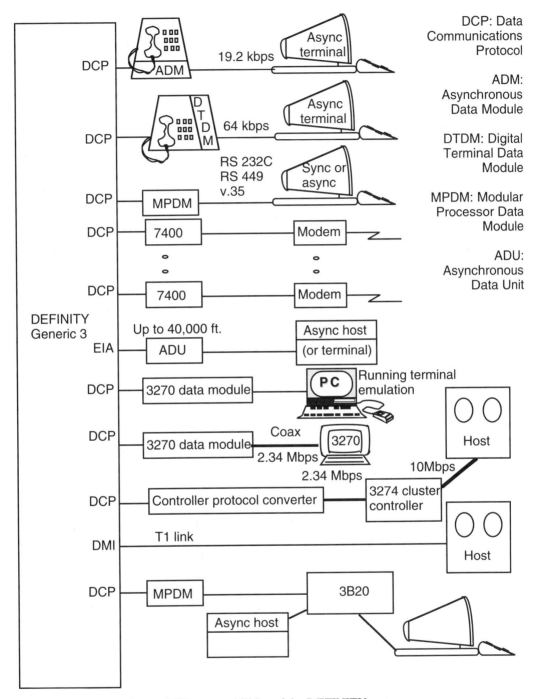

Figure 8.7 Data capabilities of the DEFINITY system.

As already mentioned there is no need to run expensive bulky coax around the building, so moves and changes are easier. The distance from the cluster controller to the terminal via the DEFINITY can be almost two miles, extending the distances the SNA network can be installed using twisted pair.

The last two connections shown in Figure 8.7 show a DMI connection to a host providing 23 data channels and one signaling channel. Also a connection to a 3B20 type of minicomputer is shown as providing office operation related applications.

8.6.5 DEFINITY Architecture

Figure 8.8(a) shows that only one PPN is sufficient to have a complete PBX system with 800 ports or less. As more lines and trunks need to be added two EPNs can be interconnected as shown in Figure 8.8(b). Both of these figures represent the G3i configuration of the DEFINITY system. When a third EPN has to be added then one must migrate to the G3r configuration, which can accommodate up to 25,000 stations using 21 EPNs as shown in Figure 8.8(c). In the G3r configuration, one must add extra carriers or circuitry called the CSS (Center-Stage Switch) in either the PPN cabinet or the EPN cabinets.

Figure 8.8(d) shows the block diagram of the G3r. This is comprised of the PPN, EPN, and the CSS blocks. At the heart of the PPN is a RISC (Reduced Instruction Set Computer) R3000A CPU made by MIPS. RISC architecture allows computer instructions to run faster because the CPU only has to look through a smaller table of instructions. It uses a 33 MHz clock and utilizes a 32 bit address and 32 bit data busses.

The PPN can come with up to 64 Mbytes of RAM. Call-processing, system programs, and administrative procedures are handled through here. Mass storage systems provide connectivity with SCSI-based tape and disk storage devices. System access and maintenance provides an interface to the DEFINITY management terminal. This terminal allows one to monitor line conditions, and to manage the entire system from one central location.

The Generic 3 introduces a new packet bus which provides efficient communication for the system between the various modules. The packet bus is extended through the EPNs. Along with the packet bus, a TDM bus which carries actual information runs in parallel with it. The final module shown in the PPN is the expansion interface. It provides a uniform method of interconnecting the various modules: PPNs, EPNs, and CSSs with each other. Typically, these modules are connected with each other using fiber links.

The CSS provides a fully non-blocking connection between all the port networks. This is accomplished through the space-division switch which has fan-out, fan-in, and multiplexer circuits that provide the necessary cross-point connections between the time-slots of the port network busses. Therefore, when the CSS is used in a system, the PBX is said to be "switched connected," or else it is said to be "directly connected" as in the G3i version.

Each EPN, similar to the traditional module of the System/85 or the universal modules of the Generic 2, contains an Intel processor, a time slot interchanger, a TDM (Time Division Multiplexed) bus, a packet bus, and the port circuits. The processor in the EPN communicates with the R3000A chip over the packet bus. It scans the ports

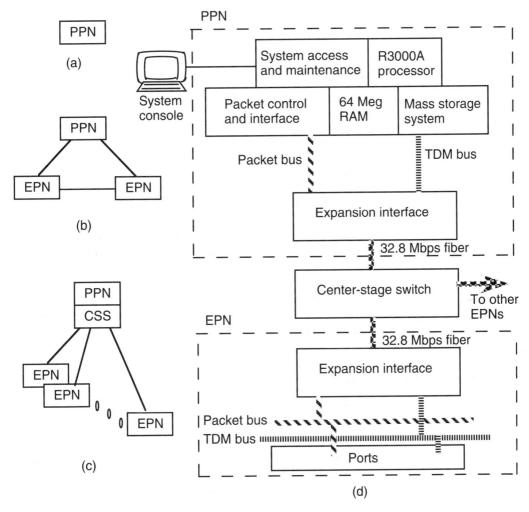

Figure 8.8 (a) For under 800 stations, one PPN is sufficient. (b) For under 2000 stations, 1 PPN and 2 EPNs can be configured. These two set ups are called the 3Gi configuration. (c) With the 3Gr configuration, a PPN, a CSS and up to 21 EPNs can be utilized. (d) An overview of the 3Gr architecture.

and provides a dial tone to anyone who is off-hook. It does intra-module switching as well as other real-time intensive processing.

The EPN processor takes the information (voice, data, etc.) bits off the TDM bus which need to communicate with other EPNs and places them appropriately on the time-multiplexed channel to the CSS. The CSS then switches these bits to their respective EPNs. So the EPN basically transfers the bits between the local TDM bus and the fiber optic channel connecting the CSS. An intra-module call is handled by one EPN and doesn't require the CSS, but inter-module calls are switched first over the

Private Switching Networks

TDM bus on the calling EPN then are space-division switched through the CSS and finally time-division switched on the called EPN. This is called time-space-time architecture and is commonly used in all PBXs.

8.7 TANDEM TIE-LINE NETWORKS

In Figure 8.9 an example of a PBX network of the 1960's using immediate start tie lines is shown. Here if phone1 wants to call phone2, it would simply get its PBX's dial tone and dial phone2's extension, because they are both part of one PBX system. However, if phone1 in Miami wanted to call phone4 in Houston, then phone1 would first listen to Miami PBX's dial tone and would dial trunk group access code 3. Then it would listen to Atlanta PBX's dial tone and would dial 5 to get Houston PBX's dial tone. Now phone1 can dial phone4's extension to make the connection.

Notice in this network, the caller does all the switching between the nodes manually. If the trunk group from Atlanta to Houston is busy, the caller would have to try again until all the links to the destination are available. The caller would have to know the trunk group access codes and how the network was configured in order to make a network call. Also, the extension number for two phones could be the same, and to uniquely identify a phone in the network knowing the phone number was not sufficient, one also had to know its location. If the caller had lost track of which PBX's dial tone was being heard, then the caller would be lost in the network and would have to start again.

8.8 PRIVATE NETWORKS

NT calls its PBX network scheme ESN (Electronic Switched Network) and AT&T calls its PBX network schemes ETN (Electronic Tandem Network) and DCS (Distributed Communication System), and others call theirs by yet other names. We will call all such networks, regardless of the vendor, private networks. One key difference between ESN and ETN is that ESN uses a central management center called the CMC (Communications Management Center) which has data links to all the switches. All network operations are performed and monitored from this central point. The advantages of private networks become apparent after having considered tandem tie-line networks in the last section.

8.8.1 Private Network Features

Private networks perform a number of networking features which earlier networks didn't provide. One such feature is the uniform dialing plan. This permits each terminal set to have its own unique identity (phone number) in a corporate-wide network. Typically, each PBX would have a unique 3-digit code similar to a CO's exchange, and each terminal would have a 4-digit extension number. This is called a 7-digit private dialing plan. Now the phone in Miami simply has to listen for one dial tone and dial the 7-digit number of phone 4 in Houston. Then the PBX in Miami

Private Switching Networks

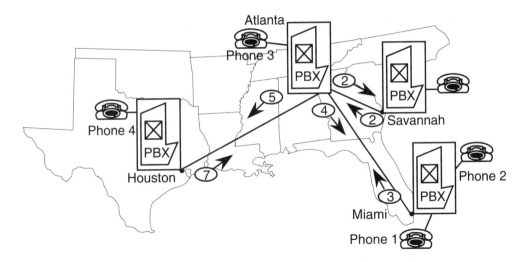

Figure 8.9 A tandem tie line network, showing the necessary codes to gain access for the specified PBX.

detecting the first 3 digits forwards the call to the Atlanta PBX and it does the same by forwarding the call to the Houston PBX.

Then the Houston PBX recognizes its own first 3 digits and completes the call using the last 4 digits. Here the switching between the PBXs is done automatically and not by the caller. Furthermore, regardless of from where the call is made, the dialed digits are the same. This allows one directory for all locations. With the tandem tie-line network, the set of access codes to reach phone 4 depends on where the caller is located.

CAS (Centralized Attendant Service) allows one location to handle attendant (or switch-board operator) services for all PBX locations. So there is no need to staff an attendant at every location, as there is if the PBXs are not networked.

Feature transparency provides the same features and PBX resemblance to all users, regardless of their location. To the user it looks like one large PBX rather than a network of PBXs.

DISA (Direct Inward System Access) is a nightmare for some companies. It allows an authorized employee of the corporation to dial into a PBX, provide an authorization code, and then have access to any of the PBX network resources. This allows the user to dial anywhere else on the private network or dial off onto the public network without using an attendant. Some DISA numbers with authorization codes have been sold on the black market allowing people to make international calls to their friends at the expense of the private network owners. Security measures should be taken within the PBX if DISA is to be utilized.

There are two methods of completing a call if alternate paths to the destination exist. One method is called AAR (Automatic Alternate Routing) which provides the best path to route a call over the dedicated tie-line network. The other method uses the PSTN to complete a call and it is called ARS (Automatic Route Selection).

8.9 ARS (AUTOMATIC ROUTE SELECTION)

8.9.1 The Decision-Making Process of ARS

ARS software determines the most inexpensive way to complete a toll call over the public network. LCR (Least Cost Routing) is similar to ARS except it decides the best route to take based on the time-of-day discounts. Many times the two terms are used interchangeably.

ARS is a table driven option that can be obtained with the purchase of a PBX. It can block 900 numbers, dial-the-weather, and other unnecessary calls based on the area code, exchange, or even the terminal phone number.

When a long distance call is made, say from Atlanta to Dallas as in Figure 8.9, it will monitor the tie trunk available to Houston and try using it to complete the call. From Houston, DDD service then can be used.

If the tie trunks are busy, then a WATS line can be used to reach Dallas directly. If neither a tie trunk or a WATS line is available, the PBX will wait typically for 10 seconds to see if one of them becomes free. If not, then it will give a 5 second warning tone providing a chance for the caller to hang up and try later. Finally, if the caller does want to try immediately and doesn't hang up, the PBX will dial over the DDD network to Dallas.

This is an example of the decision process that must be done by the PBX to complete a call using ARS. Typically, it's good to have at least 50% of the calls use tie trunks, to control long distance costs. The cost per call-minute is lowest for them. Usually 35% of the calls go over WATS lines and approximately 15% use DDD services.

8.9.2 A Case Problem

A Kansas City firm has extensive calling requirements to San Francisco, which has an area code of 415. Therefore, it has an FX trunk going there. Also the company has a WATS service area 3 to call customers on the west coast. See Figure 8.10.

Workers in group A need to call only numbers in 415 that have an exchange of 247, that is 415-247-xxxx numbers. They must use the FX trunk group as a primary choice and the WATS service as a secondary choice. They are restricted from using DDD services.

Workers in group B are required to call all numbers in area code 415 regardless of the exchange. Group C workers are allowed to call any west coast state. Both group B and C workers are to use FX and WATS services only. Group D workers are also allowed to call any west coast state, but they may utilize DDD services as well.

Finally, group E workers are allowed to call anywhere west of the Mississippi River, and if necessary to use DDD services. Of course, when group E calls Nebraska, the FX trunk and WATS service is not usable. Describe the calling patterns and FRL (Facilities Restriction Levels) needed to program the PBX. Each trunk group to a geographical region is assigned a number, called an FRL. If a trunk's FRL is high, then that trunk group has more calling restrictions, etc. When a caller calls over a trunk group, the PBX checks to see if the FRL allowed for the caller is greater than the FRL assigned to that trunk group, before letting the call go through.

Solution: First define the routing patterns that are required. The first pattern, called pattern 02, provides calls only to 415-247-xxxx. Pattern 03 provides calls to 415 except the 247 exchange. Pattern 04 includes all California, Oregon, and Washington area codes, except 415. Lastly, pattern 05 includes all area codes west of the Mississippi except for the west coast area codes. These are the areas the PBX is allowed to call. Notice routing patterns don't overlap one another.

Next, we must find the FRLs (Facility Restriction Level) that are needed. We start with the group that has the most calling restrictions (group A) and proceed with the groups which are given increasing calling privileges. Group A may call via FX or WATS trunks only to routing pattern 02. So they get the lowest FRL of 1. See Table 8.1. Then for the next group that has less restrictions, we give a FRL of 2. Two is then filled in the boxes corresponding to pattern 03 with FX and WATS as the transmission facilities. When a call is to be made by a phone which has an FRL of 2 to 415-247-xxxx (pattern 02), it falls in the first row of Table 8.1. Since 1 from the table is less than the 2 of the FRL of the caller, the call is allowed to connect, first by using FX and then by using WATS trunks. In general, if the FRL is equal to or greater than the FRL of the trunk group, then the call will be allowed to be carried by that trunk group.

Similarly, since workers of group C require added privileges, we have to create a new FRL that is greater than the previous ones, which is 3. Now group C workers with FRL of 3 may call patterns 02, 03, and 04 without being able to utilize DDD services since a higher numbered FRL has authorization to use lower numbered FRLs. Then group D workers need added privileges to use DDD services; an FRL of 4 is assigned

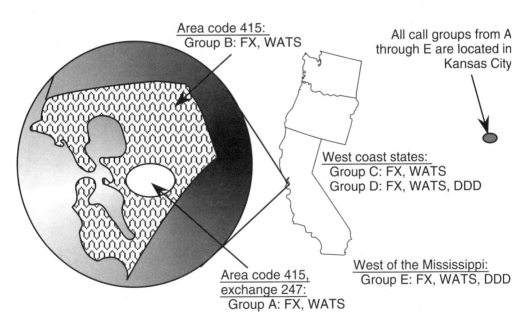

Figure 8.10 ARS restrictions placed on various groups of workers located in Kansas City in the case problem.

Private Switching Networks

137

Table 8.1 Facility Restriction Levels			
Patterns	FX	WATS	DDD
02	1	1	4
03	2	2	4
04	3	3	4
05	5	5	5

to them. Lastly, since group E workers may call more areas yet, they are given an FRL of 5.

In summary, when an outside call is made, first the pattern is selected (row in the table), then the facilities are checked (columns in the table) from left to right to see which one is available to use. If the number in the cell, specified by the row and the column, is less than or equal to the FRL of the caller, then the call is allowed to go through. Otherwise, a busy signal is sent. If trunk queuing is available on the system, the caller will be called back when a trunk is available with his/her FRL.

8.10 NETWORK ROUTING

Suppose our corporation has just acquired a western firm and it interconnects two networks using high capacity trunks between Atlanta and Las Vegas. See Figure 8.11. These two primary sites are called nodes and they would require a special software upgrade to handle network routing as it is being described.

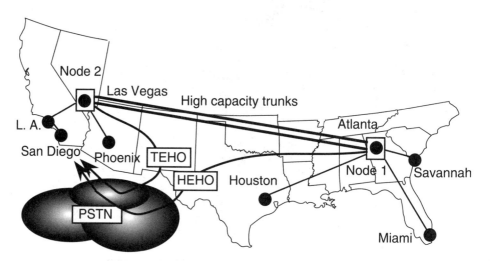

Figure 8.11 Two methods of hopping off a private tie line network over the public network.

Private Switching Networks

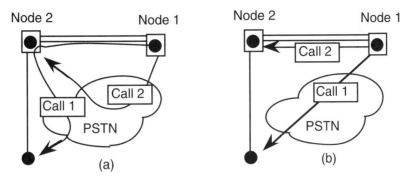

Figure 8.12 The tradeoffs of using two types of hop offs.

Let us suppose Miami's phone1 is calling a phone in San Diego. The preferred path of course is through the Las Vegas node, LA PBX and then to San Diego. If the trunk from Las Vegas to LA is busy, then the node at Las Vegas has two options in order to complete the call.

One, it can convert the private 7-digit phone number to the public 10-digit phone number. Maybe to even more digits, if an extension is also needed. Then dial the terminal in San Diego over the public network. This is called TEHO (Tail-End Hop-Off).

The alternative is to backhaul the traffic to Atlanta. Let Atlanta do the phone number conversion and have Atlanta use the DDD network to reach San Diego. This is called HEHO (Head-End Hop-Off).

It becomes tricky deciding where to hop off the private network into the public domain. As in Figure 8.12(a), if node 2 is close to the destination, it may be better to hop off there and to incur less DDD charges than doing a hop off from node1. However, this uses a circuit between the nodes and if it is the last available one, the next call from node 1 to node 2 would also have to use the DDD network.

It might have been better as shown in Figure 8.12(b) to have done a HEHO for call 1 and let call 2 go over the private network, rather than have both calls be routed over the public network.

Doing cost estimates, traffic engineering studies, trunk usage analysis, and various such tasks on private networks can be very tedious. Virtual networks are quickly replacing these private tie-line networks. Virtual networks eliminate the tie trunks and use the DDD network for all of the calls and allow the intelligence in the carrier's network to decide how to route the call. This is the topic of chapter 11.

Exercises

1. What is one of the advantages of owning a PBX over having Centrex?
   a. Reliability
   b. Fast service
   c. High data rates
   d. Easy to expand

2. What device is used to provide LANs in a Centrex setting?
   a. modem
   b. DOV modem
   c. EKS
   d. ISDN

3. Which of the following is NOT a characteristic of the 1A2 key system?
   a. It uses 2-pair wires to the voice terminals.
   b. Typically, one doesn't have to dial an access code to get an outside line.
   c. It does not allow tie trunks to be connected to it.
   d. Incoming calls are not generally handled by attendants.

4. Which PBX feature allows an operator to connect an incoming call to a person who is not by their phone set?
   a. Call-transfer   b. Call-park
   c. Call-intercept   d. Class of service

5. Which type of voice system uses a "pool" of outside lines, rather than have outside lines be assigned to specific stations?
   a. KSU-less system   b. EKS
   c. 1A2 system   d. Hybrid system

6. What unit is used to extend the range of an RS-232C connection?
   a. ADU   b. ADM
   c. MPDM   d. DTDM

7. What is the name of the host-switch interface used by Northern Telecom?
   a. DMI   b. CPI
   c. DCP   d. BRI

8. Which type of network requires the caller to know the trunk access codes to various locations when making a call?
   a. Tandem tie-line   b. Distributed Communications System
   c. Electronic Switched Network   d. Electronic Tandem Network

9. What type of voice switching system uses the CO to do the on-premise switching?

10. An IVDT converts voice to digital or data to analog? What type of multiplexing does it incorporate?

11. A set of OPX lines from a PBX to a remote location can be reduced by using what device behind the PBX?

12. The higher the class of service, does the phone terminal have more or less privileges?

13. What is the nomenclature of an ordinary residential phone set?

14. AT&T's DCP uses what speed for voice, data and signaling?

15. Name the advantage of private networks over tandem tie-line networks which provides the features of the network to resemble the features of a PBX.

16. When backhauling is done, what type of hop off is performed?

17. Describe the pros and cons of using Centrex over owning a PBX.

18. Give the reasons for owning a PBX over owning an EKS system.

19. How does a DOV modem work and how is it used?

20. Explain the functions of the various blocks as shown in Figure 8.5.

21. How does the switching in a CSS differ from the switching done in an EPN?

22. Explain the difference between the packet bus and the TDM bus.

23. Explain the reasons for using TEHO versus the reasons for using HEHO.

24. Describe the patterns and facilities restriction levels required for the following ARS problem. Draw a table.

A Boston firm has an FX trunk to New York and one to Detroit. Group A workers can call anywhere in the states using DDD service. (All international calls are blocked automatically.) Group B workers can call to New York using FX first, then WATS, and then DDD, but they can call Detroit using FX only. Group C workers have just the opposite privileges: they can call Detroit using any of the three transmission services, but can call New York using FX only.

Chapter 9

Voice Processing
and Call Distribution

9.1 INTRODUCTION

A voice processing system attempts to complete incoming and outgoing calls automatically, without requiring any personnel to handle the calls. It processes telephone-based transactions automatically. The incoming calls may require a connection to a specific extension, an access to some information, a facility to store a voice message in the event the called party is not available, or a number of such services. Traditionally, these services were provided by an operator or a secretary of some sort. The current technological advances are automating many of these tasks, which are mundane and routine for human beings. If designed and implemented with care, these systems can save considerable amounts of money and provide better services for callers. Computers interfacing with phone calls can't get tired, can't lose their temper, can't resign their jobs, don't need to be trained, can work without needing breaks, can handle many calls simultaneously, and can work around the clock.

The first part of this chapter covers the many kinds of voice processing systems; then it ends with ACD (Automatic Call Distribution) and IVR (Interactive Voice Response) systems. An ACD is a voice switch similar to a PBX, but it is designed to be used with a group of agents, any of whom can answer incoming calls or make outgoing calls. For instance, when an airplane reservation is to be made, the caller can be served by any agent and chances are that such a call goes through an ACD. The ACD places calls in a "queue" to route them to agents in some order. More on that later. Let us now consider the various kinds of voice processing systems.

Most of these voice processing systems can come as stand-alone units or they can be integrated with a PC, a host, or with a PBX. The PC-based products can serve a dual purpose of serving as a PC station and as a voice processing system. PC-based products offer open architecture with a choice of many components to provide a wide range of

Terry Henry of Dialogic Corp. and Al Hukle of Rockwell International have graciously provided their expertise in making this chapter outstanding.

142

technologies. They have the flexibility to be networked in a LAN configuration or to be integrated in a large scale system design.

9.2 METHODS OF PROVIDING SPEECH

9.2.1 Recorded Speech

The first voice processing system was introduced in 1931 by the Audichron Company in Atlanta. This system located in a CO was provided by Coca-Cola. Callers would call this number and before hearing a short advertisement, they would get the current time and temperature played back on two 78 rpm records. This is an example of audiotext, a kind of voice processing system.

The information audiotext or a voice processing system provides is generally prerecorded from someone talking into a microphone as shown in the top of Figure 9.1(a). Today this can be done using digitized speech. The natural analog voice is converted into digital form using techniques similar to PCM (Pulse Code Modulation), but compression techniques are also used to better utilize the memory space available. Remember from Chapter 3, one minute of voice takes .48 Mbytes of storage space using PCM. However, ADPCM and other more efficient voice encoding methods are commonly used, since they take less space.

The voice data in PCM form is not inteded for printing. Voice is meant to be heard on a speaker and not seen on a terminal. Similarly, text typed on a keyboard is meant to be seen on a screen and not be heard on a telephone. So protocols such as PCM are used for telephones to communicate with each other and protocols such as ASCII are used between terminals.

9.2.2 Text-to-Speech Conversion

Currently, most of the information in voice processing systems is stored as digitized speech. However, text-to-speech or synthetic speech technology is under development by many vendors. Here a new announcement can be recorded without having someone talk into a microphone, but by simply typing the message on a keyboard as in the bottom portion of Figure 9.1(a). The benefit assumed by a message stored in text is that it takes much less memory than a similar message stored by speech digitization. It is also easy to compose and edit. TTS is now starting to be implemented in applications that require playback of information stored on a database in large amounts and with information that is subject to frequent change.

Text-to-speech technology is still in its infant stage of development, because there are many rules in the English language. A word ending with "ough" may have any one of the seven pronunciations, such as in "dough," "rough," "through," "cough," etc. Also, there are about a hundred words that are pronounced differently depending on their context. For example ". . . did you read what I read about the present which was presented . . ." Another example is the simple word "the" which can be pronounced as "thee" or "thuh" depending on its usage. Many such rules of language make text-to-speech technology difficult to engineer, yet a lot of progress has been done for even large vocabularies.

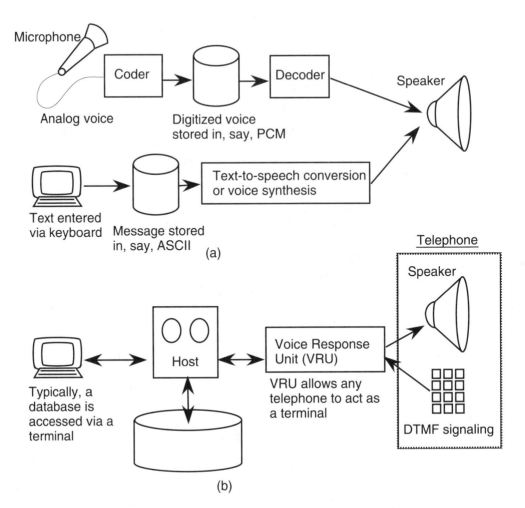

Figure 9.1 (a) Audiotext or digital announcers store messages that are accessed by anyone calling in. Messages are simply played back either from digitized speech or through voice synthesis. (b) A VRU allows information that is generally private to be accessible via a telephone. Here the data my be updated as well through the use of DTMF.

9.3 AUDIOTEXT INFORMATION SYSTEMS/PROGRAMS

Audiotext systems, also called information center mailboxes and voice bulletin boards, are more sophisticated than the original audichron system and provide the caller with the option to choose the information he or she desires. They can be used to access stock quotes, theater performance times, train schedules, store locations, and so on. The information is provided by the caller choosing selections from audio menus. For example, "If you want the sports score of today's game, enter 1, or if you want the sports score of yesterday's game, enter 2."

Digital announcers, also called passive intercept devices, are similar to bulletin boards, but they usually provide a single canned announcement, such as a change in the phone number, hours of operation, skiing conditions, and so forth.

Fax is used to augment many types of voice processing systems. The kinds of fax processing applications are fax-on-demand, fax mail, and fax broadcasting. Facsimile-on-demand is also similar to voice bulletin boards, but instead of a message being played back to the listener, information is faxed back to the caller. Fax mail digitally stores the fax at the receiving end, and is printed when the recipient is ready for it. Fax broadcasting transmits an image to a number of destinations, where the destinations are predefined in a distribution list.

Systems like the ones shown in Figure 9.1(b) which have a lot of data must store it in a computerized database. Here, the data is generally entered from a terminal keyboard and not through a microphone. To convert this type of data into spoken words TTS (Text-To-Speech) may be used or the information can be faxed out, for example, in a bank-by-phone application. The system that provides the capability of transferring electronic data into spoken language and DTMF signals into data is called an HIVR (Host Interactive Voice Response) system. The term IVR is very broad in its context and is used synonymously with voice processing systems. Unlike with the other systems mentioned above, HIVR doesn't only playback information, but also allows callers to "interact" with the system, through a telephone's DTMF input to enter or change data in a database.

Another difference between these systems is that the systems in Figure 9.1(a) generally provide information that is meant for the public, while an IVR can perform security checks before providing information that is personal to the caller. More on HIVRs later.

9.4 VOICE RECOGNITION

DTMF signaling was developed in 1958 by AT&T, and though we take it for granted these days, it was crucial in facilitating the advance of voice processing technologies. Yet, about a third of the phones in the USA and even more overseas, in some cases over 90%, do not have touch tone capability. Here, the spoken voice is the only method of accessing and controlling a voice processing device. Instead of pressing the keys on a keypad, the user commands the system by giving commands audibly. The user may just have to answer "yes" or "no" or provide a number from "0" to "9" to the questions, and the system will decipher what was said in the mouthpiece. Currently, these systems are being developed with a much larger vocabulary.

VR (Voice Recognition) is also referred to as speech recognition or ASR (Automated Speech Recognition) and it has two forms. One is SIVR (Speech Independent VR) which detects certain words that are being spoken independent of the speaker and speaker verification is another form where the speaker who is talking is identified by his or her voice.

Basically SIVR devices perform the "recognition" from the utterance of spoken English instead of identifying DTMF signals. This is done using the following four steps as depicted in Figure 9.2. The first step involves extracting special features of the voice from the input waveforms in order to reduce the amount of data that needs to be processed. This is done using DSP (Digital Signal Processing) chips. The second step matches the features of the given word with a possible correct model. Speech models, also called word patterns or templates, are stored in a collection beforehand. The third step, called DTW (Dynamic Time Warping) adjusts the chosen vocabulary template with the rate at which the word is being spoken by the individual, since every person voices their words at varying speeds. Lastly, an event detector circuit, many times using HMM (Hidden Markov Modeling), decides if the word being spoken is close enough to the template or should it tag the word as not being in the vocabulary. HMM has proven to be accurate for speaker independent and continuous speech, where no pauses are required between the spoken words. Artificial intelligence is playing a greater role in the development of this technology.

Speaker dependent voice recognition allows one to identify the caller. Sprint has introduced a "voice" credit card; where instead of dialing the credit card number to place calls, the callers identify themselves by their voices. This is more secure than a password which can be broken into. Furthermore, a caller needs only to say "CALL HUSBAND" to dial the user's husband at work. There's a lot of potential in applying this type of technology in the future.

A point often under-emphasized is that voice recognition also allows a more natural interface to a computer. One doesn't have to drag a keyboard around in a warehouse for instance; a portable phone which interfaces with a voice recognition system is sufficient. It also allows a person to enter data at a typical speed of 200 words per minute instead of the typical 30 wpm for typed in data. Voice recognition is a more accurate form of data entry than typed in data. In a working environment where hands are busy and eyes are busy, voice recognition provides a means to keep the mouth busy as well. (This is usually listed as one of its advantages!)

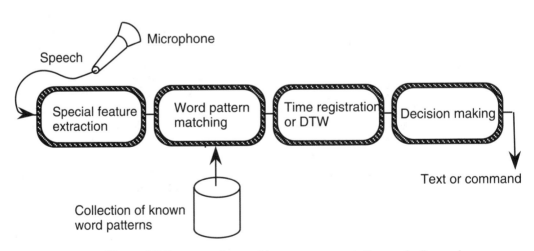

Figure 9.2 Four steps in matching an utterance to "recognize" speech as command input.

9.5 VOICE MAIL

In 1979, Gordon Matthews of VMX Inc. received a patent and installed the first voice mail system. VM (Voice Mail) allows a caller to leave a message after hearing a prerecorded greeting if the called party is unavailable or busy. VM, also called voice messaging, is an integrated system for all users or extensions, and with many more features than an answering machine. It also allows users to retrieve their messages from any location and not necessarily only from their own phone.

9.5.1 Why Voice Mail?

Sometimes missing an incoming call can mean a loss of a sale, service, or more importantly, one's own credibility. If customers can't reach you, because you are not by your phone, they're going to go elsewhere. Conversely, you can't stay by your phone continuously, because there are other responsibilities you may have to attend to. Secretaries may use the pink "While you were out" slips to let you know who called, but even those can be lost in the shuffle of a busy desktop. The slips are prone to human error. Important information, otherwise felt as trivial by the secretary, may be left out completely.

A message center can be used instead, where a human interface is necessary for projecting a caring and personal image. Here the message center operator types in the name, number, and the message of the caller for the person who is unavailable. When that person calls in the message center, the operator reads off any messages waiting for him. But again, with a message center it is hard to emphasize certain points, and leave a more personal message to the caller with all the inflections commonly heard in normal conversations. Messages from the message center are only available when someone is attending it. VM messages can be retrieved even at night.

To take down a message either on a slip or on a terminal requires an extra person. Even if a human touch is desired for important incoming calls, a tired or aggravated operator will not sound as nice as a pleasantly recorded VM greeting.

Preventing "telephone tag" is another reason for using VM. This occurs when two parties call each other at a time when the called party is not available to pick up his/her phone. With VM, the called party can leave a thorough and detailed message, such as, "I tried the "modify routine" command which you had recommended and I got error number 000512, what should I do next?" This may not be as efficient as talking to the person directly, but at least some progress has been made in reaching a solution. In this example, the service technician would have time to look up solutions or to ask the co-workers for assistance, before calling back.

Now that corporations and even small companies are competing in the international arena, telephone tag becomes more common when the caller is at work and the called party is at home sleeping. VM becomes attractive when workers are in different time zones.

With VM, people don't chitchat as much as they do in a real-live conversation, usually only business matters are discussed. It also offers more confidentiality and privacy than a message taken by a person. If a manager needs to call a department meeting, she may have to type a memo, make copies, and distribute it to her department members and hope they get it. With VM, a message is recorded once and the system, already knowing the people in the department, sends a copy of the message to each person's voice mail box. Not only that, but VM can tell the sender who listened to the message and at what time. VM is also useful for service technicians to keep in touch with their managers and to find out what customer to service next.

9.5.2 Size of The VM System

A VM port provides access to the VM system from the PBX, one user at a time. So if we want up to 10 users to simultaneously access the VM system, then we must have 10 ports available. The proposed VM unit should have one voice port for every 40 users. However, once data becomes available after the system is in place, the number of ports can be adjusted. 40 users per port is a quite conservative ratio. For light users 100 users per port will suffice. At any given time, one port allows only one user to access the VM.

A rule of thumb for the amount of memory, is to have 6 minutes of storage space per user. Again, this number can be drastically different depending on how the users utilize the system. So for example, a system for 1000 users should have at least 1000/40 or 25 ports and have a storage capacity of 1000 times 6 minutes or 100 hours.

Sometimes VM can be rented for a year or leased from a CO, and after getting the statistics, a meaningful RFP (Request for Proposal) can be written and a new system can be purchased.

9.6 AUTOMATED ATTENDANTS (AAs)

Dytel Corp. in 1984 introduced the first automated attendant system. AAs attempt to replace attendant console operators, formerly thought of as switchboard operators. When a caller dials into an office a recording is heard, such as, ". . . if you have a touch tone phone and know your party's extension, you may dial it now, if you need a sales representative, you may dial 1 now, etc. . ." Typically, such systems use AAs which many times are integrated with voice mail systems and other voice processing devices.

9.6.1 The Case For AAs

With a typical private voice switching system, such as with a PBX, centrex, or key system, there are many trunks coming in from the CO (central office) and many lines going to the phones or the extensions. This method of answering incoming calls creates the well known "hour-glass" effect as shown in Figure 9.3. Many trunks are coming into the operator and many lines are going out from the operator. Just like all the sand must pass through a narrow hole in an hour-glass, so must all incoming calls must pass through the operator. Using DID (Direct Inward Dialing) trunks and DISA (Direct Inward System Access) features is an attempt to correct this bottlenecking problem, but that isn't sufficient.

The console operator along with the outside caller has three problems to contend with:

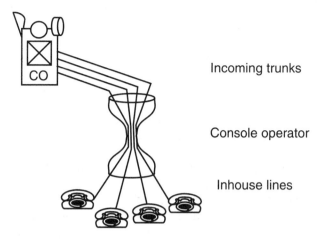

Figure 9.3 The "hour-glass effect" occurring due to a single console operator.

1. The calling party is on hold
2. The called party is not available (keeps ringing)
3. The called party is busy

In fact, one study shows that only 25% of all calls are successful on the first try. For this reason, the console operator has to handle call-attempts a number of times in order to successfully complete a call. The amount of frustration, on the operator's part, increases even more during the busy hours, which typically occurs during 10 AM - 11 AM and 2 PM - 3 PM.

One solution is to add another attendant console ($2,000), but that requires hiring an extra person. Another solution is to add more DID trunks, but not only are their costs going up, but also, they are useless for callers who need to get an extension number first.

9.6.2 Advantages of AA

A console operator can handle only one call at a time, but an AA can handle 10, 20, or 50 calls at one time. The console operator is forced to let incoming calls keep ringing, because the operator can't handle multiple calls simultaneously. If an over-worked operator does answer an incoming call before the caller hangs up, the operator isn't going to necessarily sound pleasant. The operator's job is boring and tedious. With an AA, the incoming calls are answered in one ring, and the voice announcement they hear is courteous and cheerful, because the AA doesn't get tired.

So even if a live operator is preferred by upper management, the operator can also be a reason for losing sales. An operator is more prone to human errors, directing the incoming calls to the wrong destination, and so frustrating the caller.

If an outside caller needs to relay some information to a person in house after hours and after the operator has gone off duty, the outsider cannot call in, but the insider must call out instead. AA allows outsiders to directly call into a facility, without an operator. And outsiders can dial directly to an extension, even if DID trunks are not available. It also allows one to access VM from outside after hours.

With AA, outside callers have quick access to workers inside a facility. Especially, if the callers know what extension they want, the connections are made quickly. AA does the routine job at a low price. A reasonable PC based AA can cost around $10,000. That is much lower than one has to pay an operator; besides the AA is working 24 hours a day.

How calls are being handled, how many callers drop off and for what reason, should more trunks be added or should their number be reduced, the answers to all such questions would normally come from interviewing the console operators. Now the AA can obtain statistics, to provide call management data. This data is accurate, it doesn't depend on anyone's memory, and can be used to streamline the operation.

Lastly, a small company's manager may have to work as an operator while doing other tasks. Now, AA provides both big and small companies to project a professional image to outside callers. Panel 9.1 summarizes the advantages of AAs.

9.6.3 AA Features

Operator Anywhere: This feature prevents dead-end calls. No matter which voiced menu the caller is in, the caller can reach a live operator simply by dialing "0."

Call Sequencing: If many callers are on hold, this feature will put them on a queue as they call in so that the first to go on hold will be the first who gets answered. A message may come up at regular intervals keeping the caller posted on how many calls are ahead of them.

Call Screening: The caller is prompted for his or her name, which is recorded. Then the system calls the intended extension and plays back the name saying "Mr/Ms. So N. So is on the line." If the called party wants to be connected, one key on the keypad is pressed, otherwise, a different key is pressed. In that case, the called party may hear something like this "Mr. No Not Yet is unavailable right now, but if you care to speak to his backup assistance, Mr. Back Jack, please press 1 now..." etc. This feature should be used with great care, since people are more used to being screened by a live secretary rather than a machine. The machine can't be diplomatic about it.

Screened Transfer: Suppose, in the previous example, "Mr/Ms. So N. So" pressed "1" and was transferred to Mr. Back Jack. If this were a screened transfer, the system, already having the caller's name, would ask Mr. Back Jack if he cared to talk to him or her, before giving her a choice of being transferred to yet another party, to the VM box, or to a live operator.

Monitored Transfer: Suppose "Mr/Ms. So N. So" had pressed 1 as before, but now the AA will make sure that the call is completed and Mr. Back Jack did answer

```
┌─────────────────────────────────────────────┐
│  Panel 9.1  Advantages of Automated Attendants │
├─────────────────────────────────────────────┤
│  1.  Handles multiple calls simultaneously.    │
│  2.  Isn't irritated by incoming calls.        │
│  3.  Caller can control his/her call routing.  │
│  4.  Available 24 hours/day.                   │
│  5.  Fast response time.                       │
│  6.  Provides call management data.            │
│  7.  Less expensive than hiring operators.     │
└─────────────────────────────────────────────┘
```

the phone before dropping off. This prevents the caller from getting a busy or a ringback tone and being "jailed" in the call path.

Directory Assistance: VM also supports this feature. AA can provide the caller with the extension just by having the caller provide the first few letters of the last name. This is all done by using the telephone keypad. For example, let us suppose that a person needs to find the extension of "Smith." That person would dial 7 (for "S") and 6 (for "m"). However on a keypad, a 7 represents letters "p", "r", and "s," and a 6 represents letters "m", "n", and "o." So the AA has to explore all the two-letter possible combinations generated by the 7 and the 6, namely:

```
pm pn po
rm rn ro
sm sn so
```

If "Smith" is the only person whose name begins with any of the above combinations, then the extension number will be given. Otherwise, the caller will be prompted to provide additional letters of the name until it finds the match in the directory. All these functions are being automated. The tasks which normally required console operators or switchboard operators are being done by CPU driven devices. What the vendors will come up with next only depends on their imagination and their insights into how tedious jobs can be automated.

9.7 INTRODUCTION TO CALL DISTRIBUTION SYSTEMS

9.7.1 How Are ACDs Used

"Please stay on hold, all of our agents are currently busy, one will be with you shortly . . ." We are all too familiar with this line which is an example of where ACDs are used. Catalog sales, nationwide hotel chains, car rental agencies, and a host of other applications use ACDs to distribute their incoming calls to agents. In an ACD environment, all agents are equally capable of handling the calls. When a caller simply wants anyone to take an order, or to make a reservation or to provide a service, and isn't interested in getting through to a particular person, then chances are the call is being routed through an ACD.

ACDs can be bought as stand-alone units or PBXs can be configured to function as ACDs with the proper software. The stand-alone units have a higher traffic volume capacity and provide better reporting capabilities than their PBX counterparts. Currently, there is a big push by the BOCs to provide CO based ACD service. It is very attractive for call centers to hire well qualified agents who may be handicapped or for some other reason prefer to work from home. Since this service is leased, no initial capital investment is needed. Basically, most advantages outlined for centrex in Chapter 8 also apply to CO-based ACD service.

9.7.2 Comparisons of UCDs and ACDs

UCDs (Uniform Call Distributors), which are not capable of handling a high volume of traffic, provide an alternative to ACDs. They always route the incoming calls always to the same set of agents. In Figure 9.4, the ACD will typically send the first call to the first agent, the second call to the second agent and so on in rotation, even if in the meantime agent 1 becomes free. So the next incoming call is automatically routed to the agent who has been idle the longest.

However, if the ACD unit in the figure was configured as a UCD, then four incoming calls would be routed in sequence to agent 1, agent 2, agent 3 and back to agent 1 if agent 1 has become idle. This way, agent 6 would have to take a call only if the other five agents were busy. The distribution of calls is done in the same manner as it is done in a hunt group with a PBX system. With the UCD, order is present, but with an ACD the workload is distributed evenly amongst the agents. The UCD system works well in a smaller office where a few workers are dedicated to handling incoming calls. When the call volume is low, the rest of the workers can concentrate on other work, but during peak hours they are available to relieve some of the traffic load.

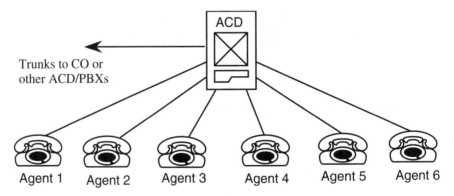

Figure 9.4 An ACD distributes workload for inbound or outbound calls evenly.

9.7.3 Call Sequencers

A more simple device than a UCD is what's called a call sequencer or an ACS (Automatic Call Sequencer). Using a call sequencer, there are lamps and buttons for every line that is connected to an agent's station. When a caller goes on hold, the lamp for that line flashes and as the caller continues to stay on hold, the rate at which its lamp flashes increases. When an agent becomes free to answer a call, he/she will select the line for which the lamp is flashing the fastest. The line for which the lamp is flashing the fastest signals the call that has been on hold the longest.

Here, the switching intelligence collectively is the group of agents deciding on which button to press or whose call to answer next, whereas with an ACD (or a UCD), the device provides the switching intelligence.

9.7.4 Call Centers

ACDs are only part of a bigger picture called call centers. In a call center, there are trunks coming from the CO into the ACD, which distributes the calls to the agents. Similarly, access to the data in a host is provided by a terminal for each agent. See Figure 9.5. Also, the call center managers can oversee the entire operation and provide assistance as needed. ACDs are used for inbound (incoming) calls or outbound (outgoing) calls. Telemarketing is an example of ACDs being used as outbound devices.

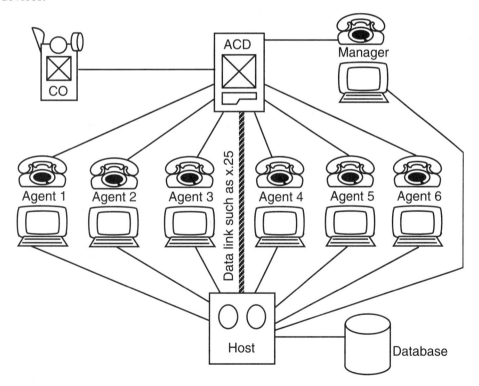

Figure 9.5 An ACD is only part of a bigger picture called a call center.

ACDs were first introduced by Collins Radio in 1973, when Continental Airline's reservation office in New York City needed a high capacity, special purpose switch to handle a high volume of incoming calls. Later, Collins was bought out by Rockwell International and today Rockwell owns almost 50% of the stand-alone ACD market. Its Galaxy model GVS-3000 is capable of supporting 1200 agents.

9.8 OUTBOUND TELEMARKETING

ACDs not only provide a means of distributing incoming calls to available agents, but also provide outbound calling which is used in telemarketing today. Telemarketing is a type of business where agents call customers to try to sell a product or service over the telephone.

Speed dialing is the most rudimentary type of telemarketing. When an agent is done with a call the "next-call" key is pressed. Then the autodialer dials the next phone number from a data base and the agent hears the call progress tones until someone answers or until the agent hangs up.

The next step up from speed dialing in sophistication is power dialing. A power dialer contains a database of names and numbers, and the rate at which to dial these numbers automatically is preset. Since typically, out of every four dialed numbers, only one number is contacted, power dialers dial many more calls than there are agents, and calls are directed to the next available agent only if the call is answered on the receive end. The rate of dialing is preset and fixed. So if more contacts are being made than expected, calls would have to be abandoned by the system. Furthermore, in these situations, more switch and trunking capacity is dedicated than what the agents can accommodate.

In contrast to these methods, predictive dialing uses sophisticated mathematical algorithms as well as real-time statistics to adjust the rate at which calls are being dialed. Here also, a computer with a database of names and numbers is connected to the ACD via a data link. A pacing algorithm residing in the host instructs the ACD when to dial the next number. It decides how fast to send the numbers to the ACD for dialing out by comparing the agent statistics sent to it by the ACD.

The ACD can detect the differences between ringing, no answer, busy, and a live person answering at the distant end. The ringing, no answer, and busy conditions are sent back to the host for further action on it's part. These phone numbers are stored and are automatically rescheduled for calling back. However, a live person answering the call causes the ACD to connect the call to an agent and supply this information to the host. The host then can update the agent's screen with the called person's data. In effect, predictive dialing systems use less resources to help a business make more sales than the other systems.

9.9 WHY ACDs?

Unlike PBXs, ACDs are money making devices and are indispensable for companies that use them. Many stores have closed their doors and are using a call center and an 800 number to conduct their business. ACDs play such an important role in call centers, that they have stringent reliability requirements and users don't mind paying up to 15 million dollars for one of these devices.

Usually, to get new customers for a product or service, a business has to create, promote, and pay for an advertisement giving a phone number to call. 95% of the cost to win a new customer goes into such efforts while only 5% of this cost goes into the call center itself including trunks, staff, and equipment. The cost of the ACD is typically less than 1 percent of the total cost, and to mismanage the call center and to have an inadequate ACD system is foolish. The call center can either take advantage of all the previous efforts or nullify it.

The call center provides the first impression of the company to prospective customers, and since it is more costly to gain new customers through advertising than to keep the current ones, businesses are providing excellent service with 800 numbers to keep the current customer base satisfied. Typically, this is done through the use of ACDs.

The purpose of an ACD is to give better service to customers by handling their calls faster with shorter call-holding times. As the time to answer calls decreases, less of an opportunity is given to customers to take their business elsewhere. Also, reports provided by the ACD are invaluable to management in achieving this objective.

9.10 GATES

Many times, agents are divided into functional groups called gates or splits, and incoming calls are routed to the appropriate gate. Functional groups are categories such as, sales agents, support agents, etc. As calls are received by the ACD, they are put in a queue or a waiting list. The calls are placed in this queue in the order they are received, just as customers in a bank lobby may form a line (or a queue) as they wait for a teller to serve them. The call waiting the longest in a queue is the first one to be connected to the next available agent.

Each gate in an ACD has its own queue of calls and if a queue in one gate gets too large or callers have to wait too long to be served, calls may overflow to other gates with shorter queues. Sometimes, calls from certain trunk groups may have a higher priority than the other calls, in which case, these calls may "cut in line" ahead of the calls already in queue. This is especially the case where overflow calls are redirected to other gates, since they have already waited on queue at the original gate. To handle overflow calls from other gates, agents should be trained to serve customers from gates other than their own.

This is analogous to a bridge which has separate lanes for cars and trucks. If there are too many trucks and only a few cars on the bridge, then the lanes with the trucks become congested even though the car lanes are half empty. However, if cars and trucks were all allowed to share the lanes together, then chances of traffic congestion become less. Likewise, cross-training agents to handle calls from different gates prevents callers from having to wait on "eternity hold."

Overflowing of calls to other gates can be done manually by the call center manager or it can be done automatically. Automatic overflow is accomplished by programming the overflow threshold in two ways. One is based on the length of time a call is on hold, while the other is based on the number of calls that are on hold. Overflowing of calls from the primary gate to other gates within one ACD is called intra-system overflow. Overflowing calls from one ACD to other ACDs is called inter-system overflow. Queue lengths can also be reduced by providing the caller with an option to leave a voice message, ask for a fax, etc.

9.11 THE TIME LINE

9.11.1 Network Setup

Figure 9.6 shows a timeline for an incoming call. Depending on the type of trunk being terminated at the ACD, time is required for setting up a connection.

Call centers may use WATS trunks to receive incoming calls, for which billing begins as soon as the ACD answers the call. If there are callers in the queue then it is not necessary for the ACD to answer the call on the first ring, because the caller will be placed on hold anyway. By allowing the phone to ring a few times before placing it on hold, trunk costs can be reduced.

9.11.2 Queuing

Queue time is an important part of the timeline. For every caller who hangs up because of being placed on hold too long, less revenue is received by the company. Most people will wait on hold for 40 seconds without music and 60 seconds with music. Typically, systems are configured so that callers wouldn't have to wait for over 20 seconds on hold.

Of course, as more agents are added (more trunks also have to be added) the smaller the queue length becomes and fewer calls are on hold. This is desirable during the busy hours, however, for most part of the day when the call center is not busy, more agents and trunks will be idle. Therefore, the call center manager must juggle these items so that calls are not lost due to inadequate resources (trunks and agents), and expenses are not wasted due to insufficient call volume. Queuing helps to make efficient use of agents and trunks, and ACD reports provide the data for management to adjust these numbers.

Many call centers keep historical data for months and years to help predict the number of agents required for special times when business may be heavy.

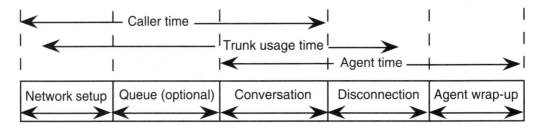

Figure 9.6 The time line of an incoming call showing the components of the call process.

If the ACD is integrated with the host, and ANI (Automatic Number Identification) is available, then the ANI service provides a means for the host to know the complete phone number of the caller, regardless of where the caller is located in the country. The host then can look up the phone number in its data base and identify the caller and search for the caller's record, if the caller is a previous customer. So while the customer is in queue and on hold, the host is actually doing work and getting the record.

Now when the call is forwarded to an agent, the data record from the host is also forwarded to the agent's screen. This simplifies the agent's work, gives faster service to the customer and frees up the trunk sooner. This is an example of switch to host integration. If ANI is not available, a VRU can prompt the caller to enter his/her identification number while on hold, to provide the same record look-up service.

9.11.3 Conversation

If the average call duration is two minutes, which is typical, then the trunk to agent ratio should be about 1.2 : 1. For applications where the call duration is only .5 seconds, such as credit card verification, this ratio can be as high as 3.0 : 1. That is, for every agent that is present, there are 3 trunks that are available.

9.11.4 Disconnection and Wrap-up Time

After the conversation is over, the ACD can signal the CO to disconnect the call as soon as the agent hangs up instead of waiting for the caller to hang up. This frees up the trunk sooner for a new call. The agent can press a special key to make him or herself unavailable for calls while finishing up with paperwork associated with the previous call.

9.12 ACD FEATURES

Out of more than 130 features available on ACDs, only a very small sampling of ACD features are listed here; first some call handling features are given then some management information features are given.

9.12.1 Call Handling Features

Direct Outward Dialing: Without the assistance of an operator, agents can make outside calls.

Incoming Call Identification: A message either in the headset or on the agent console or terminal identifies the caller's city or the trunk group. This helps the agent to know some information about the caller before the conversation begins.

Prioritization of Trunk Groups: This enables preferred customers or certain trunk groups to have shorter holding times than other callers.

Call Forcing: This allows the ACD to route the next incoming call to an agent as soon as he or she hangs up. Without this, after an agent completes a call, a button is pressed to signal the ACD that he is ready for the next call.

9.12.2 Management Information Features

Management information reports: are just as important to call centers as call processing features. There are all types of reporting available with ACDs: ones that are standard and ones that are customer specific, ones that are generated at any time interval (from real-time data and hourly reports to annual reports), to those that are generated by every split, every trunk, every agent, or every system.

Agent-level reports: provide the number of calls handled, average conversation length, average time spent in wrapping up calls, amount of breaks taken, and any such imaginable items. Any way, an agent who handles more calls doesn't necessarily make more sales, but may provide better, personalized service to the customers.

Queued Call Reports: specify the number of calls on hold per gate in increments of say 5 minutes. These reports also provide the average time a caller waits before the call is answered or before the caller abandons the call (hangs up).

Trunk activity reports: indicate when all trunks in a trunk group are busy, or how many trunks were out and at what times, and so on.

9.13 ACD NETWORKING

Figure 9.7 shows a network of ACDs linked together with tie-lines. A network control center which Rockwell calls a RMC (Resource Management Center) is a minicomputer where the activities of the ACDs are monitored and controlled by the network manager. The RMC is connected to all of the ACDs with x.25 type data links. These networks can comprise from 2 to about 20 linked ACDs, and usually, each switch serves one area of the country.

9.13.1 Advantages

The foremost reason for networking ACDs is the ability to generate one comprehensive report to include the activities of all of the switches. ACDs that are isolated from each other would generate a number of separate reports, making it necessary for someone to sort out the data manually. This could take days or weeks. Having one single report to present to upper management is much more desirable. This provides the network managers with up to the minute reports and enables them to make wise decisions that will impact the health of the entire call center system.

Overflow and diversion are the next important reasons to network ACDs. Overflow means that if one call center is being swamped with calls, maybe because of some product promotion in that area, then calls can automatically be directed to other centers with a lighter load. Managers can set up service level thresholds. A 100%

service level indicates that all of the calls are being answered and none are being abandoned. Typically, a service load of 85% is chosen. In this case, if the service level is approaching this amount, then calls are switched automatically to other centers. Diversion means that all calls to a gate or an ACD are directed to another ACD.

As the analogy of sharing lanes by trucks and cars was applied to overflowing calls from one split to another, so can it be applied here where calls can be overflowed from one system to another. If there are 500 agents on each of the 10 isolated ACDs, then each ACD has a maximum of 500 agents available even if agents on other ACDs may be idle. With networking the ten ACDs, however, resources are shared and we have one large system with 5000 agents available.

Networking allows workload to be distributed between call centers. If one area has a number of agents absent due to a flu of some kind, other centers can relieve such a center. Networking also adds reliability to the system, in that, if one center is down then calls from that center can be diverted to other locations.

Another advantage is that it is easier to staff the centers to provide 24 hour service to callers. With isolated ACDs, every center must be manned 24 hours a day to provide round the clock service. However, when networking, such as in Figure 9.5, the agents on the east coast can start going home at 5 PM because on the west coast it

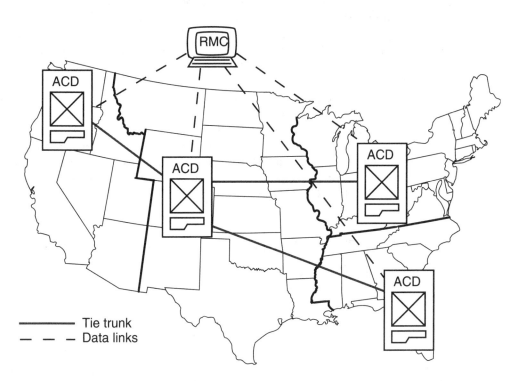

Figure 9.7 A well-planned ACD network should look like one ACD, rather than separate ones.

is only 2 PM, and agents there are available to handle the east coast calls. Similarly, as the east coast agents are available at 9 AM, they can handle the 6 AM west coast calls. Although international ACD networks are a rarity, they could provide much easier round the clock service than domestic networks.

9.13.2 ACD Network Links

About half of the networks use T1 tie-lines for inter-switch links, though they are costly and not as flexible as DDD service. ACDs provide direct T1 interfaces and analog trunks are not as desirable to provide access to ACDs, because they are subject to electrical noise and excessive signal level loss.

Other ACD networks use DDD services to distribute the calls between the various ACD sites. This is done via a terminal such as AT&T's Routing Control Service terminal. If one ACD center is flooded with calls while the others are not, the terminal allows the network manager to redirect 800 number calls from one ACD to another within five minutes from when the change was made. The change actually affects the SCP (Signal Control Point) of the IXC where the customer's networking data is stored.

At one time, different areas of the country had their corresponding 800 number to dial and if an ACD needed the capacity to accept calls from other areas it would need a separate trunk group for every such area. DNIS (Dialed Number Identification Service) avoids having to use separate trunk groups for every 800 number, because each 800 number can have it's own 4-digit DNIS number. Now only one trunk group is necessary as the carrier transmits the four DNIS digits to the ACD before each incoming call.

DNIS typically consists of four digits, but the public network is capable of sending up to seven. It can also be used to identify an area code or groups of area codes that a call originated from. Now when a call comes into an ACD, the DNIS signals the ACD where the call is coming from and this information can be provided to the agent's headset or on his or her data terminal. Knowing where the call is coming from allows the agent to be properly oriented and to serve the customer better. This information is also collected by the ACD MIS system or the host database and used for market research.

9.14 HOST INTERACTIVE VOICE RESPONSE (HIVR) SYSTEMS

As seen in the last section, call centers employ agents who take calls through an ACD and fulfill the requests or transactions through a host. This section introduces the technology which sets forth to automate this process of interfacing callers to hosts, without requiring any call center agents.

So back in Figure 9.5, think of the six agents and their related equipment being replaced by one HIVR unit. With a call center, the agents act as the translator between the voice of the caller and the data residing in a database, while the agents communicate with the computer using a data terminal. An HIVR system inserted between the trunks and the host allows the callers to directly interact with the database. An HIVR allows

Voice Processing and Call Distribution

the caller's touch tone phone to be used as a data terminal and the HIVR does the translation between the voice (which includes the DTMF pulses) of the caller and the data of a host. With a call center, the agents interact with a host and interpret what they see on their monitors. An HIVR using synthesized voice can "read off" what would normally be seen on an agent's screen. If the caller doesn't have a DTMF phone, the HIVR can use voice recognition to interpret the caller's audible response. Pulse-to-tone converters can also be used to convert the dial pulsing to digits on a limited basis.

Many more people have access to a telephone than those who have access to a data terminal. So as expected, HIVR is the fastest growing sector of the voice processing industry. HIVR benefits both those who call and those who are called. It provides better and faster service to customers (less time being on hold), and greater savings to companies who incorporate them.

However, an HIVR is capable of providing more functions than being a substitute to a call center. It can incorporate all of the voice processing technologies as covered in this chapter into one unit. It can be programmed using the C programming language which can be time consuming, or it can be programmed using an application generation package. An application generation package uses prewritten macros (units of programming code) and menus to help the user create a set of instructions for the HIVR, so that when a customer calls in, he or she is properly served. These instructions can be commands for a host, doing credit card verification, updating a database, or any such activities.

Most HIVR systems are based using IBM PCs or clones, and to the host they appear as an IBM cluster controller or a 3278 terminal. To access IBM's minicomputers: s/36, s/38 or AS/400, they can emulate an IBM 5251 cluster controller or a 5250 terminal. VT-100 or VT-200 terminal emulation is also available to interface with DEC's VAX minicomputers. This emulation capability allows the HIVR to make a telephone appear as a terminal to the host, and the host to appear as an agent to the caller. Some HIVR systems provide simultaneous access to two different types of hosts, which are required for certain applications

Initial attempts of automating call centers involves a simple technique called transaction processing. With transaction processing one talks into the phone to provide information that is given by an audio menu. The caller's responses are recorded as with a tape recorder and retrieved at a later time at the convenience of the called office.

HIVR is distinguished from audiotext in that audiotext retrieves information, with no interaction involved with a host. HIVR, on the other hand, attempts to make the telephone as a computer terminal, providing and updating information when required in an interactive manner. Both audiotext and HIVR can transfer information selected from large databases.

However, HIVR is interactive, which means "act upon each other." So as well as retrieving information through a host, HIVR allows the user to command the host in return and is able to transfer money or to make payments to preauthorized vendors or to place orders and perform other transactions.

HIVR systems allow college applicants to track their entrance applications or allows customers to get a status of an order or shipment. North Carolina is testing out

IBM's DirectTalk/2 system for the unemployed to file their claims over the phone rather than having to come in person and to wait on line each week.

Integrated HIVR (IHIVR) integrates the various voice processing technologies with an HIVR to allow a person to perform more than one task during a phone call. This can be such functions as leaving a voice message, altering an order if it hasn't been shipped, etc.

Exercises

For questions 1 through 4, match the description with the correct voice processing system.

A. Voice Mail   B. Automated Attendant
C. Audiotext   D. Voice Response Unit
E. Interactive Voice Response Unit   F. Transaction Processing
G. Voice Recognition

1. By use of a keypad, certain stocks owned by a user are sold.

2. By dialing the user hears a prerecorded weather forecast for the day.

3. By use of the keypad, data is selected and retrieved from a data base.

4. Messages of the caller are stored here if the called party is unavailable.

5. What is call processing?
   a. It is NOT the same as voice processing
   b. It is the same as call accounting where statistics are kept of who called whom, at what time, and for how long.
   c. It is a type of automated system, which completes calls coming in without human assistance.
   d. It is the technology which processes voice in analog form into digital form.

6.What type of call distribution system always forwards the incoming calls to a certain set of agents?
   a. ACD   b. UCD
   c. Call sequencer   d. IVR

7. Which of the following phases of the ACD time line does not include the agent's time?
   a. Disconnection   b. Wrap-up
   c. Queue   d. Conversation

8. Which of the following ACD features describes the maximum time a caller was placed on hold during the day?
   a. Incoming call identification   b. Queued call reports
   c. Trunk activity reports   d. Agent-level reports

9. Functionally, what is the opposite of speech synthesis?

10. Give two examples of information providers.

11. What is the name of the effect which is caused by the many incoming calls being switched by a few attendants?

12. For 400 users, how many hours of memory and how many ports are typically needed?

13. Which automated attendant feature will record the name of the caller and ask the called party if he or she wants to answer the call?

14. ACDs were first used in which industry?

15. One reason to network ACDs is to direct calls to other centers when the primary center is being flooded with calls. What is this feature called?

16. What type of telemarketing system simply dials more numbers than there are agents available, without relying on the current activity of the center?

17. Why are voice messages stored on DASDs (Direct Access Storage Devices) ?

18. Give reasons to network VM.

19. Explain reasons for networking ACDs.

20. Explain the differences and similarities between ANI and DNIS.

21. What is gating? and how does that improve the operation of a call center?

22. Why do you think HIVR systems are on the rise, while VM systems have plateaued out?

23. What is the difference between ACDs, UCDs, and ACSs?

24. Explain the components of a typical VM system.

Chapter 10

T1 Networking

10.1 BACKGROUND

One of the first times T1 was deployed for other than a phone company's use was in 1977. Two buildings in New York City were connected with a 600-pair copper cable which had reached its capacity. No additional pairs were available to accommodate new circuits. To lay another cable would mean digging up the streets without disrupting all sorts of other cables and pipes that were buried. Instead, channel banks were installed on both sides of the cable. And using only 2 pairs of the existing cable, a total of 24 voice channels were made available as illustrated in Figure 10.1.

This type of T1 multiplexing has been done by the phone companies since the 1960s and even before that using FDM (Frequency Division Multiplexing). However, the Tariffs for T1s were purposely overpriced, because the installation of T1s would result in savings for users and a loss of revenue for the phone companies. After divestiture, prices for T1s became realistic and there was a big rush to convert voice grade tie lines to T1s. Today even in Europe, Canada, and other countries, T1s are overpriced.

However, domestically, as fiber is being installed, bandwidth is becoming cheaper and so are T1s. Voice-grade lines are facing stiff competition, since one T1 may cost as much as six voice-grade lines.

10.2 ADVANTAGES

10.2.1 Savings in Operating Costs

Savings in operating costs is only one reason why companies have converted to T1s. T1 multiplexers and bandwidth managers can cost up to $100,000 per location; still, within one year the savings in phone bills can pay for this investment.

This chapter and chapter 13 were greatly enchanced by Michael Zboray of The Gartner Group. His efforts are very much appreciated.

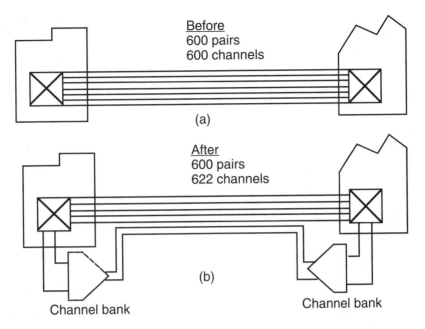

Before
600 pairs
600 channels

(a)

After
600 pairs
622 channels

(b)

Channel bank

Channel bank

Figure 10.1 (a) Before installing a T1 between two buildings in New York City, a 600 pair cable carried 600 voice channels. (b) After installing a pair of channel banks using two of the existing pairs, an additional 22 voice channels were made available.

10.2.2 Simplification

T1 circuits allow networks to be simplified. In Figure 10.2(a), Seattle and Minneapolis locations are linked together using separate lines. The two PBXs require 12 voice circuits, four CAD (Computer Aided Design) circuits run at 56 kbps, some synchronous terminals need a number of 9600 bps lines, and a group IV fax circuit requires another 56 kbps line.

Figure 10.2(b) shows how the same applications can be integrated by using only one T1. This one circuit is much more easily managed, monitored, and controlled than many discrete circuits. In this example, the 12 voice grade circuits occupy 12 DS-0 (Digital Signal level 0) channels, the five 56 kbps channels occupy 5 DS-0s, and the three 9.6 kbps channels can be subrate multiplexed into one DS-0 channel. This makes a total of 18 (12 + 5 + 1) DS-0 channels. Multiplexing these on one T1 link, which provides 24 DS-0s, provides 6 spare DS-0 channels for future expansion. This assumes standard T1 formatting. If proprietary formatting is used, even more capacity can be gained in one T1 circuit.

Here we have simplified only a two-point network. Imagine the simplification achieved by converting a 15 or even a 100 node network to all T1s. This advantage, gained by simplifying the network, introduces yet other T1 advantages.

T1 Networking

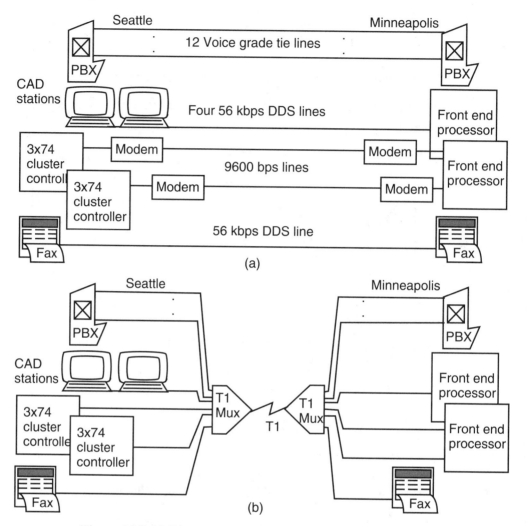

Figure 10.2 (a) Discrete lines for each application make a two-point network difficult to manage. (b) Consolidating all applications on a single T1 simplifies the network substantially.

10.2.3 Reliability

Managers all agree that reliability is far more important than cost savings for most networks. When a network goes down, it reflects upon the manager's competence. Revenue is lost every minute the network is down, and can very easily exceed the savings achieved by converting to T1s.

One may think that a loss of one circuit in Figure 10.2(a) is not as serious as the loss of the T1 in Figure 10.2(b). However, to introduce redundancy in Figure 10.2(a), all circuits would need redundant circuits, whereas with a T1, only one redundant circuit is needed. However, in a T1 network, there are several routes available between any two nodes, so that if the primary route fails, an alternate route can be selected automatically.

IXCs provide inherent redundancy when purchasing a T1. Now if the IXC's portion of the T1 link fails, within a second the link is automatically rerouted. Normally, the access portion of a link is the weakest, and spare circuits should be leased or alternate routes should be explored through the use of CAPs (Competitive Access Providers) or other methods. Remember, if a cable is cut that houses both the active and the spare pair, then probably both will get cut. Similarly, if both the LEC's and the CAP's cables go over the same bridge or an area, then at that point a catastrophe may knock out both access networks. In other words, ordering extra lines even from different carriers doesn't necessarily prevent a failure.

In Figure 10.3, if the link from A to D fails, then the T1 multiplexers can be programmed to route traffic through points B and C automatically. If not enough capacity is available on the alternate path, then less important circuits can be "bumped off" the network to make room for the important A to D circuits. Priorities of the circuits, of course, have to be determined and preprogrammed.

The control cards, data switching components, power supplies, and all critical components of the T1 muxes should be duplicated. Port cards are not duplicated unless the equipment they are connected to is also protected from failure or if they support many channels. Components which are duplicated, if not continuously tested, may fail when needed.

10.2.4 Network Control

T1 networks are not engraved in stone. They are flexible and can be changed as necessary. This gives the network user more control over the network. Certain circuits can be temporarily disconnected to create bandwidth for a videoconference channel. Once the conference is over, normal traffic can be restored on the network. Similarly,

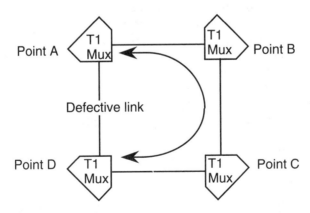

Figure 10.3 With alternate paths available in a network, traffic between two points can be automatically rerouted when a link fails. Here traffic between points A and D is routed through points B and C.

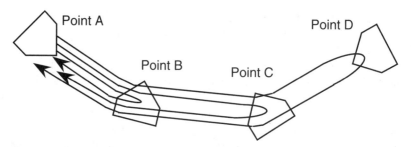

Figure 10.4 Remote loopback tests initiated from point A can help to isolate a faulty link. A loopback test usually sees if the transmitted signal pattern is received on the receive side. In this example, if the loopbacks are good to points B and C, but not to D, then a fault lies in the link between C and D.

at night during a certain time frame, a large chunk of the bandwidth can be automatically allocated for backing up a data center. To see if productivity at branch centers can be increased by increasing the terminal data transfer rates, then it can be easily tried. If no improvement is noticed, then the transfer rates can be configured back to what they were.

A major advantage in controlling a T1 network is achieved by having a control management center. No longer are network operators depending on personnel at remote sites to physically place a jumper on the right pins to provide a loopback test on a circuit or to physically rewire a circuit to reroute it on a different leg of the network. Instead, the operator using a management console at the central site can signal the T1 equipment to provide loopbacks, reroute channels, obtain line quality statistics, and so on.

Figure 10.4 shows how remote loopback tests can be performed from point A to points B, C, and D. By knowing the loop-codes for the T1 devices in the path, devices can be forced into a loopback mode one at a time, and tested to see if a transmitted test pattern matches the received one. If the tests are good to B and C but not to D, then the problem is determined to be between C and D. Proper parties can be notified without much finger-pointing going on between the vendors and the carriers.

Back in the setup of Figure 10.2(b), there is more than 6 DS-0's worth of bandwidth available. So if new circuits are to be installed, the capacity is already there and one doesn't have to wait for the carriers to get around to installing the circuits.

10.3 T1 SIGNAL TRANSMISSION

10.3.1 DS-1 over Various Media

Originally, T1 circuits used two pairs of copper wire to send 1.544 Mbps in each direction. This was done by removing loading coils and inserting repeaters every mile, which is the typical distance between manholes in city streets. These DS-1 signal rates can be sent over other mediums as well. Coaxial cable repeaters are needed every 40 miles. Fiber repeaters are used every 30 to 100 miles. DS-1s can also be transmitted using microwave or satellites. However, transmission of DS-1 rates over any of these mediums is currently called T1.

10.3.2 The Bipolar Format

The maximum distance T1s could be transmitted over copper was doubled to 1 mile by sending the signals in a bipolar format as shown in Figure 10.5(a). This was due to improved synchronization. The bipolar method alternates the voltage for every mark between +3V and –3V. It is also called AMI (Alternate Mark Inversion). This provides a built in error detection scheme. If a bit is lost due to an error, that is, if a 1 is misinterpreted as a 0 or vice versa, then two consecutive pulses of the same polarity is detected and it is flagged as an error. This event is called a bipolar violation (BPV), since it violates the rule of alternating the polarity of marks.

For example, in Figure 10.5(a), if the first –3 Volt pulse is lost, then a bipolar violation occurs at the second +3 Volt pulse, as shown in Figure 10.5(b). Also, if the third 0 is lost and becomes a 1 then a bipolar violation is detected at the fourth +3 Volt pulse.

From Figure 10.5(b), notice that every mark provides one transition between plus or minus 3V and 0V. These transitions aid the receiver to keep its clock synchronized with that of the transmitter. So T1s use a rule that is called the "ones density rule" to ensure that the receiver stays synchronized. This rule requires that on the average, at least 1 out of every 8 bits should be a mark or a minimum of 12.5% of the bits should be marks.

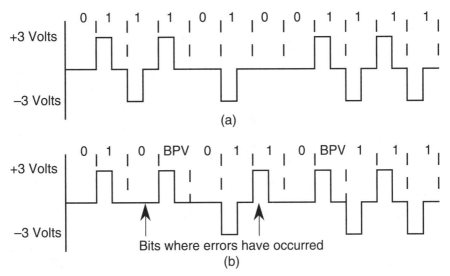

Figure 10.5 (a) The bipolar format of a T1 signal enforces the polarity of every logical 1 to be opposite that of the previous logical 1. A logical 0 is always represented by 0 Volts. (b) Due to errors on the line, if the second 1 in (a) is misinterpreted as an 0 or if the third 0 in (a) is misinterpreted as a 1, then in either case the bipolar rule is violated. This is called a bipolar violation or a BPV for short.

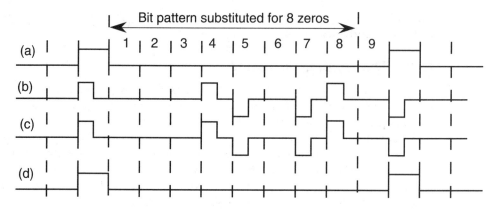

Figure 10.6 (a) Data with 8 or more consecutive zeros being sent to a T1 mux. (b) Signal being sent over the T1 span, where BPVs are inserted at the 4th and the 7th zeros to signal a stream of zeros. (c) The transmitted signal being received at the distant mux. (d) It determines the BPVs at the 4th and 7th positions as a signal for consecutive zeros and provides the original data stream to the terminal equipment.

10.3.3 The B8ZS Technique

Figure 10.6(a) shows that nine consecutive zeros are to be transmitted in the data stream. They will provide no voltage level transitions. With so many zeros, the receiving clock may drift and interpret them as being either 8 or 10 zeros instead. What the signal needs here is some marks to keep the receiver synchronized so as to maintain the ones density rule.

Digitized voice according to the encoding scheme doesn't allow 8 successive zeros. However, with data a long string of zeros is quite possible. As we'll see later, 56 kbps DDS (Digital Data Service) channels use only 7 bits out of every 8 possible bits to send data so that a mark can be forced at every 8th position to accommodate the ones density rule.

Another method of enforcing the ones rule is shown in Figure 10.6(b). With this method, the transmitter, when noticing 8 successive zeros, will induce BPVs at the 4th and 7th zero and AMI compatible marks at the 5th and the 8th zero. This is a code that signals the receiver that the BPVs are not really data errors but that this pattern replaces a string of zeros in the data instead. So the receiver will convert this pattern back to 8 zeros before forwarding the data to the terminal device. See Figure 10.6(d). This technique is called B8ZS (Binary 8 Zero Substitution) and it enables T1 to transmit consecutive zeros while still keeping the T1 equipment synchronized.

10.4 FRAMING TYPES

As covered in Chapters 2 and 3 and as outlined in Figure 10.7, a T1 channel bank receives 24 voice channels. Each channel is sampled 8000 times a second and 8 bits are used to encode the voltage level at each sample yielding a 64 kbps rate per channel, using PCM. The 24 voice circuits with 64 kbps each require a total of 1.544 Mbps of bandwidth. This rate is obtained by multiplying 64 kbps by 24 and adding 8 kbps for framing purposes. Let us now look at how these bits are organized or framed. Framing allows the receiving equipment to know which bits belong to which channel, and so on.

10.4.1 The D4 Frame

Figure 10.7 shows how one D4 frame is constructed. It combines one sample or 8 bits from each of the 24 channels, yielding a total of 192 bits. One bit is used for framing so that the receiver knows where a frame starts and ends. So one D4 frame occupies a total of 193 bits. A time slot is considered to be one sample or 8 bits.

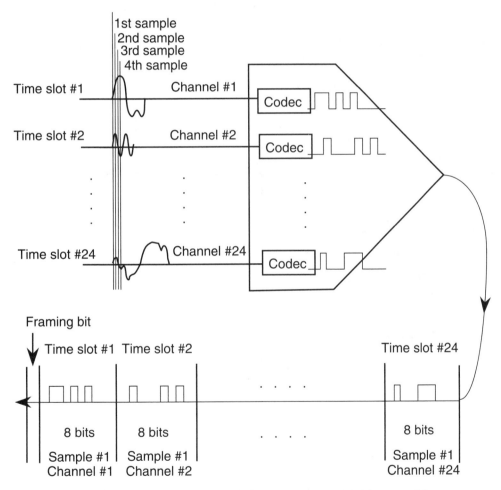

Figure 10.7 The codecs in the I/O ports of a T1 mux digitize up to 24 voice channels. In D4 framing, the corresponding 8-bit sample from each of the 24 channels are multiplexed using byte-interleaving. Together with one framing bit, the D4 frame requires 193 bits.

Notice also that the data stream is byte interleaved and not bit interleaved. This means that the first byte from channel 1 is placed first then the first byte from channel 2 and so on. A frame which is bit interleaved places all the first bits from the 24 channels first, then all the second bits, and so on.

10.4.2 The Superframe (SF)

A SF (SuperFrame), shown in Figure 10.8, is composed of twelve of these D4 frames. So a superframe consists of 12 voice samples from each of the 24 voice channels. With 12 framing bits, this makes a SF 2,316 bits long. The framing bits which are always "100011011100," allow the receiver to know where the frame starts and where it ends. Notice that the 1s and 0s come in groups of 1s, 2s, and 3s. The framing bits allow the receiver to block off frames and maintain logical synchronization.

The least significant bit of every 6th D4 frame is used for signaling that channel. This one bit that originally came from a voice sample is lost and signaling information is placed here instead. As mentioned in Chapter 5, this is called robbed bit signaling.

	F	Channel #1 1 2 3 4 5 6 7 8	Channel #2 1 2 3 4 5 6 7 8	. . . .	1 2 3 4 5 6 7 8 (Channel #24)
D4 frame # 1	1				
D4 frame # 2	0				
D4 frame # 3	0				
D4 frame # 4	0				
D4 frame # 5	1				
D4 frame # 6	1	A	A	. . . . . .	A
D4 frame # 7	0				
D4 frame # 8	1				
D4 frame # 9	1				
D4 frame # 10	1				
D4 frame # 11	0				
D4 frame # 12	0	B	B	. . . . .	B

Figure 10.8 A SF (Super Frame) combines 12 D4 frames as depicted in Figure 10.7. An SF contains 12 voice samples from each of the 24 voice channels with framing bits as shown. Also, the 8th voice bit in every 6th sample is pre-empted to place a signaling bit instead. This is called robbed bit signaling.

With voice (or video), if a bit is lost in every 6th byte, the ear (or the eye) cannot notice it; however, when data is integrated with voice in a T1 multiplexer, one cannot afford to lose any data bits. Because an error in data can mean the wrong character is displayed on a monitor, a check is drawn on the wrong amount, or any of such abnormalities.

So in order to send data through a T1 link, only the first 7 bits of each time slot are used and the 8th bit is forced to a 1. This prevents data from using the signaling bits. Therefore, the highest data rate through one DS-0 channel is not 64 kbps but 7/8th of that which is 56 kbps. This restriction applies only to signals being processed by classical channel banks only and not by proprietary T1 muxes.

10.4.3 Extended SuperFrame (ESF)

Figure 10.9 shows an extended superframe (ESF) which is twice as large as a SF. Here, instead of 2 signaling bits per frame per channel, there are four, labeled A through D. Also, there are 24 framing bits instead of the 12 with SF.

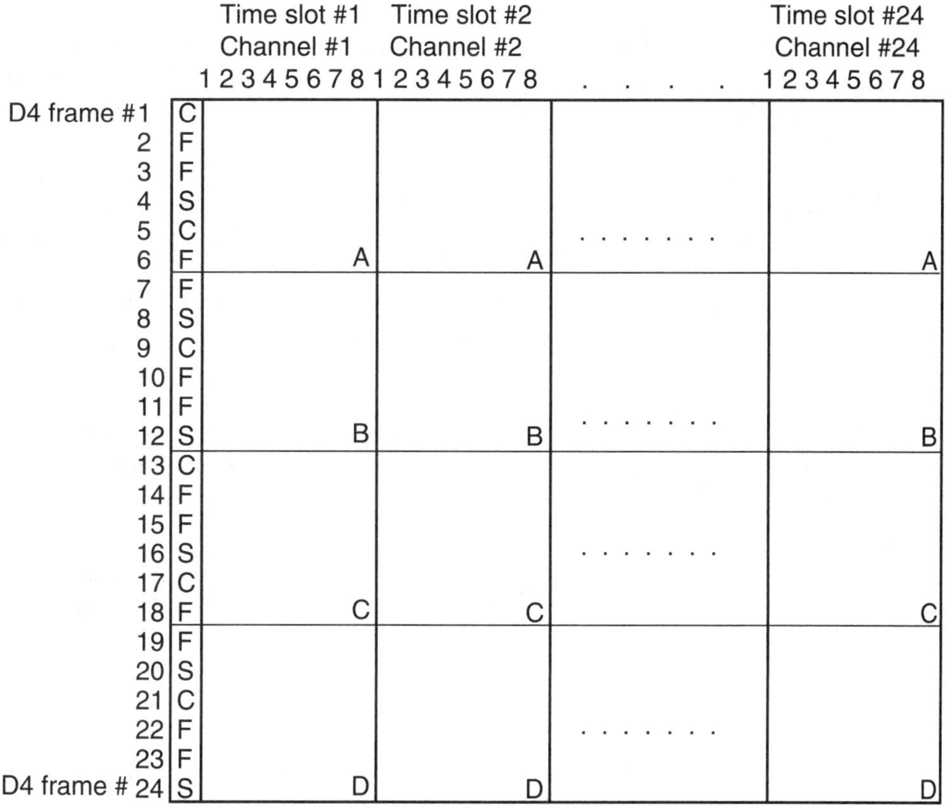

D4 frame	F bit	Time slot #1 Channel #1 1 2 3 4 5 6 7 8	Time slot #2 Channel #2 1 2 3 4 5 6 7 8	. . . .	Time slot #24 Channel #24 1 2 3 4 5 6 7 8
#1	C				
2	F				
3	F				
4	S				
5	C				
6	F	A	A		A
7	F				
8	S				
9	C				
10	F				
11	F				
12	S	B	B		B
13	C				
14	F				
15	F				
16	S				
17	C				
18	F	C	C		C
19	F				
20	S				
21	C				
22	F				
23	F				
# 24	S	D	D		D

Figure 10.9 ESF uses only six "S" bits for synchronization and they are "001011." "C" bits are used for error detection and the "F" bits are used for the FDL (Facilities Data Link) channel.

Out of these 24 bits, only 6 are used for logical synchronization, where the SF used all of its 12. This provides 18 bits per frame for other purposes. This includes 6 bits for error checking using the CRC (Cyclic Redundancy Check) method.

The remainder of the 12 bits are used to implement a T1 management channel called FDL (Facilities Data Link). Depending how the bits are set on this channel, line quality statistics can be obtained while live traffic is being sent over the T1. Sending a loop-up code over the FDL, distant equipment can be signaled into a loopback mode. Similarly, sending a loop-down code over the FDL can signal it back into normal service. These features make the ESF format a preferred method of transmitting T1s.

10.4.4 Other Framing Formats

When the DS-0s of a T1 circuit are switched in the public network, it is necessary that it conforms to D4, SF, ESF framing. However, if it is a dedicated T1 link, then any format can be implemented by the user to gain more bandwidth efficiency. This is as long as the end equipment is compatible and the T1 is framed. For the end equipment to be compatible usually means that it is provided by the same vendor. A *framed* T1 means that every 193rd bit is a framing bit; how the data is organized in the other 192 bits is left up to the user. A *formatted* T1, also called channelized T1 or DS-1, means that the T1 is bundled into 24 DS-0s and is mostly used for voice. However, a framed T1 can be used to send signals of any rate, such as 256 kbps or 768 kbps, as long as they fit in a DS-1. Because of fewer restrictions, a framed T1 can be easily used for many applications, including CAD or video.

A common inter-office voice formatting technique is called the M44 format. This format, intended for voice, compresses 44 voice clear channels on one T1. See Figure 10.10. There is also an M48 format which uses robbed-bit signaling to place 48 voice channels on one T1.

The M44 format divides T1s 24 DS-0 (64 kbps) channels into half, creating 48 32 kbps channels. These 48 channels are grouped in 4 bundles of 12 channels. Each

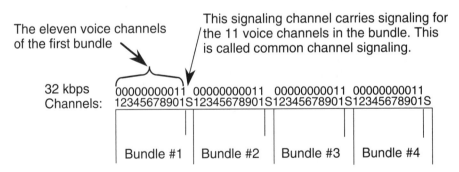

Figure 10.10 In the M44 format using ADPCM, each voice chanel requires only 32 kbps of bandwidth. In one T1, there can 48 of these channels, each running at 32 kbps. These 48 channels are divided into four bundles of 12 channels each. And in each bundle, there are 11 voice channels and one signaling channel.

bundle contains 11 voice channels using 32 kbps ADPCM coding, and one 32 kbps channel which contains the signaling for the other 11 channels. Since the voice bits are not robbed for signaling purposes, the voice channels are said to be clear. To send a 56 kbps data channel, one needs two of these 32 kbps channels.

The M44 format uses common channel signaling, which means that one common channel carries the signaling for the 11 voice channels in the bundle. Because the signaling is separated from the voice, channels cannot be switched at DS-0 levels. With M44, an entire bundle must be kept together while switching. If switching has to be done at DS-0 levels, the M44 format is changed to other formats which include the signaling with the voice.

10.5 NETWORK INTERFACING

10.5.1 At the Customer's End

A DSU (Data Service Unit) interfaces CPE to a digital line for DDS (Digital Data Service) speeds, that is, for speeds less than or equal to 56 kbps. For higher speeds, CSUs (Channel Service Units) are used to interface with digital lines. The purpose for using either a DSU or a CSU with a digital line is to provide network protection in the event the CPE inadvertently places unwanted signals. They also allow one to do loopback tests.

Figure 10.11 shows how a T1 line is brought to a customer's premises from the CO. At one time, the demarcation point was between the T1 mux or channel bank and the CSU. Then the CO would send power over the T1 line to power up the CSU. This allowed the CO to perform a loopback even if there was a power failure at the customer's site. Since then the FCC has allowed the customer to own the CSU, as long

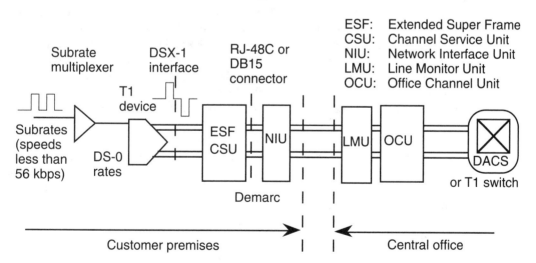

Figure 10.11 A T1 circuit requires only 2 pairs of copper wire, one to transmit and one to receive. Here, all of the T1 signal processing units are shown, both in the customer's premises and in the CO.

as it meets FCC specifications. Therefore, today the demarc has moved to the network side of the CSU.

Now that the customer is powering the CSU, some telcos are installing a NIU (Network Interface Unit) or a smart jack at the customer's side to enable them to perform loopback tests even if the customer is without power.

One of the functions of the CSU is to keep the T1 "alive" in the event of a CPE failure. The keep alive signal tells the CO that the CPE has failed, and it isn't the telco's concern. A keep alive signal could be a loopback noticed by the CO, or it could be a continuous stream of ones either framed or unframed.

The CSU is also usually responsible for enforcing the ones density rule, either by the B8ZS method or some other method. It is also the last place where the incoming signal is regenerated and alarm conditions are indicated.

10.5.2 At the Telco's End

OCU (Office Channel Unit) is similar to a CSU, except it is located at the CO. Using a LMU (Line Monitor Unit), the CO can do a loopback test between the CSU and OSU. Of course, the T1 link has to come down for this test, if it isn't down already. While the line is active, the LMU can command the CSU using the FDL channel of the ESF to provide line quality statistics as needed.

10.6 T1 SWITCHING

10.6.1 Channel Banks, Muxes, and Switches

Initially, devices which combined 24 analog voice channels into a DS-1 rate were called channel banks. Channel banks were not able to multiplex data, because they were primarily a device for voice circuits. T1 multiplexers, on the other hand, generally accepted voice or data circuits. They also performed subrate multiplexing which multiplexed a number of data channels at slow speeds (2.4 kbps, 4.8 kbps, etc.) on to one DS-0 channel. One standard for this is called SRDM (SubRate Data Multiplexing). T1 multiplexers can be managed and controlled via a terminal where a channel bank, used for more stable networks, is controlled by setting DIP switches. Today, the definition of channel banks and T1 multiplexers is becoming more blurred. Typically, a channel bank is inexpensive and a mux is more sophisticated. Bandwidth managers is also a term dubbed for high end T1 multiplexers.

The "common" T1 multiplexers are also called M24 multiplexers for the number of voice channels they multiplex. The difference between a mux and a switch is that a mux will separate the incoming T1 into 24 DS-0 channels where each channel communicates with the corresponding channel on the far end. A T1 switch, on the other hand, is able to divert the channels with a rate that is less than or equal to 64 kbps in any order so that any channel on the transmitting end can connect with any channel on the receiving end.

10.6.2 Intermediate Node Switching

If two T1 circuits are connecting Denver, Omaha, and St. Louis as shown in Figure 10.12, then we'll call the site at Omaha the intermediate node. Denver has some

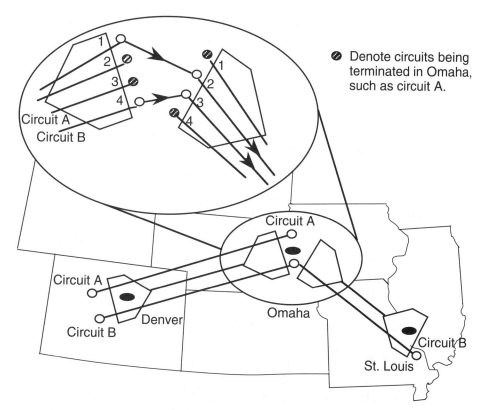

Figure 10.12 Circuit A simply goes from Denver to Omaha, while circuit B is first "dropped" in Omaha on channel 4 and then "inserted" in the link to St. Louis on channel 3.

channels which terminate at Omaha such as channel A, and some which continue on to St. Louis such as channel B. Similarly, St. Louis has channels going to the other two destinations. The node at Omaha is then responsible for sorting out channels from both ends and either "dropping" them off at Omaha or passing them through over the "other" link.

10.6.3 D/I (Drop and Insert) Using Single-Link Muxes

Figure 10.12 shows the "drop and insert" method of routing circuits using two single-link muxes. At Omaha only four channels are shown per T1 in the inset for convenience. In this arrangement, all circuits are demultiplexed down to the baseband level, which is the DS-0 level for channel banks and subrate channel level for muxes. These channels can be directed to their proper destinations from the I/O (Input/Output) ports on the muxes. The circuits which terminate in Omaha can simply be dropped there and the ones that need to continue over the next hop must be first dropped and then inserted. As an example, the B circuit in the diagram is dropped at channel 4 and then inserted in the second mux in channel 3.

This is the simplest switching method possible at an intermediate node, and it has some drawbacks. Namely, the number of I/O ports for all of the channels becomes expensive, but more important is the "spaghetti tangle" that is created by the cables interconnecting the two multiplexers. It is also mandatory that all T1s are maintained in common synchronization, as well as needing bit buffers.

Managing the circuits at this node can be difficult, especially if there are more than two T1 links to maintain. If one I/O port fails, someone may have to physically pull out the right cord and re-insert it in the proper jack. The job could have been easy and could have been done remotely from one central site, if the patch cords between the muxes were software controllable.

Another problem with this configuration is the introduction of quantizing noise in the voice channels. When voice is digitized, there is a slight amount of error introduced at each sample, and as the number of voice to digital conversions increase, this quantizing noise becomes significant. Our voice circuit B from Figure 10.12 will go through two voice to digital conversions (once at Denver and once at Omaha) and go through two digital to voice conversions (once at Omaha and once at St. Louis). This is also called D/A/D (Digital to Analog to Digital) conversion. Usually, a voice channel can go through three to five of these drop and insert nodes without experiencing any degradation. This is assuming that PCM is used. As the data rate of the voice channels are decreased below 64 kbps, the degradation becomes more acute.

10.6.4 Add and Drop

An add and drop device is also called a D/I multiplexer and it is shown in Figure 10.13 at Omaha. This configuration is logically similar to that of Figure 10.12, except instead of having two multiplexers back to back, each with a single T1 link, here there is a single multiplexer with two T1 links.

Our single channel B from Denver goes through this equipment without being demultiplexed and multiplexed again in Omaha. Therefore, no I/O ports are needed for channels that are passed. Furthermore, since data bits are transmitted as they enter the node, no quantizing noise is introduced.

10.6.5 DACS (Digital Access and Cross-connect System)

With traditional private leased-line circuits, the end points are fixed. Figure 10.14 shows such a voice grade tie-line from Denver to St. Louis going through distribution frames at the COs and POPs at the three cities. If that circuit had to be rerouted so it goes from St. Louis to Minneapolis instead, then the technicians at the necessary POPs and the COs would have to change jumper wires through their distribution frames to install the new path. This can take days to complete.

With T1s, the distribution frames and the "jungle of jumpers" at the COs and POPs are replaced with software controlled distribution frames called DACS (also abbreviated as DCS). Now, as long as the Minneapolis site has access to its CO, carrier operators using a terminal can almost instantaneously signal the DACS in Omaha to switch the T1 to go from St. Louis to Minneapolis. Users truly appreciate the flexibility gained in private T1 networks by the use of these "electronic patch panels." Also,

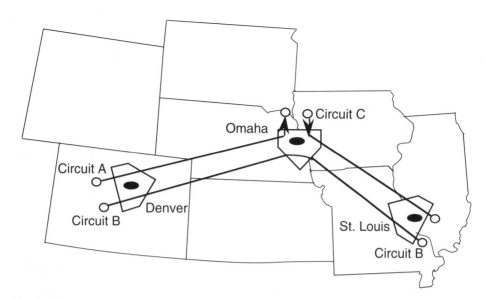

Figure 10.13 Omaha now has an add and drop type of multiplexer. Circuit B which originates at Denver is simply passed through to St. Louis without being demultiplexed. Circuit A is dropped in Omaha while circuit C is added there. (These are really two-way circuits.)

planning for disaster recovery is easily done through the use of DACS, since bandwidth-on-demand is available through DACS.

DACS does not only switch circuits at DS-1 levels, but also at DS-0 levels. So if a user has many remote locations within a LATA, each with one DS-0 channel requirement, then without a DACS one would have to bring all these DS-0 channels to a customer premise, where they would be multiplexed and they would then transmit the group of these channels to their destination as seen in Figure 10.15(a). However, with a DACS, the DS-0 channels can come directly to the POP where all the channels can be concentrated and then transmitted without the customer having to buy T1 gear. See Figure 10.15(b).

Because of DACS, private networks, instead of being "pinned up" for long durations of time, can now evolve into a "cloud" or into switched networks.

10.6.6 Proprietary Switching vs. DACS

However, DACS do have a few disadvantages. In-band signaling over the FDL channel cannot control the DACS. In fact, the DACS destroys the FDL bits for its own use making it useless for the end user. A separate signaling network to the DACS controller is needed so that the centralized management system can monitor and control it. When network maps are entered or changed they must be done by a technician through the use of a DACS controlling system. Unlike the way in which an in-band signaling channel can direct a T1 mux to change its configuration, the DACS needs separate links to control it by the end user.

DACS also cannot switch at rates below 64 kbps. So if one M44 T1 with 32 kbps voice channels must pass through a DACS, then that T1 must be converted into two 24 channel T1s. Of course, only a total of 44 channels can be distributed between the two T1s. This type of conversion is done by BCMs (Bit Compression Multiplexers).

Switching through a DACS can be done either by a transparent connection or on a channel by channel basis. In a transparent connection, the D4 frames in one superframe don't necessarily stay in order, but the superframes are reassembled using a different order of D4 frames. This keeps the delay through the DACS to two byte-times. The channel by channel DACS connection preserves the content of each superframe, but that forces the delay through the DACS to be up to 48 byte-times.

DACS are primarily used by carriers and most of the limitations associated with them are not present in private networks which use proprietary channel switching muxes. For instance, Timeplex's Link100 can switch channels at 400 bps granularity.

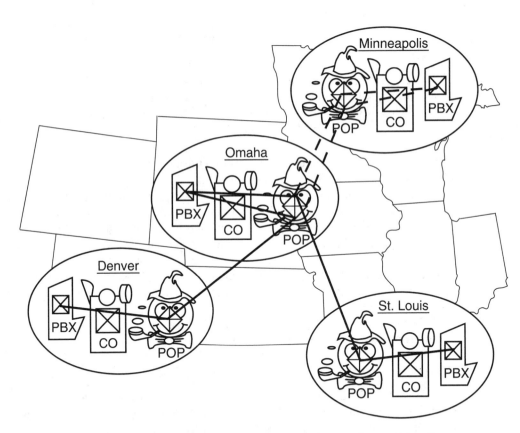

Figure 10.14 The solid line shows that installing a voice-grade tie-line from Denver to St.Louis via Omaha would have to utilize the distribution frames at all the POPs, COs, and customer locations. If this circuit had to be routed to Minneapolis instead of St.Louis, then the dotted line shows that jumpers at distribution frames would have to be installed at the POP in Omaha and at all three places in Minneapolis.

This means that, while a DACS can switch channels in 64 kbps increments, the Link100 can switch them at 0.4 kbps increments. And while the DACS doesn't allow in-band signaling, proprietary muxes provide such capabilities.

10.6.7 CCR

AT&T has a computer located in Freehold, NJ, which controls all of its DACS nationwide. Other carriers also have similar setups. Using several levels of security, users can either dial up or have a direct access into this computer to change their own networks. The customer using a terminal located at his or her own premises can reconfigure the network as needed without having to wait for the carrier to do it. AT&T calls this service CCR (Customer Controlled Reconfiguration). MCI calls it Digital Reconfiguration Service.

A more sophisticated and expensive service by AT&T is called BMS-E (Band-width Management Service-Extended). It reconfigures even faster than CCR and also

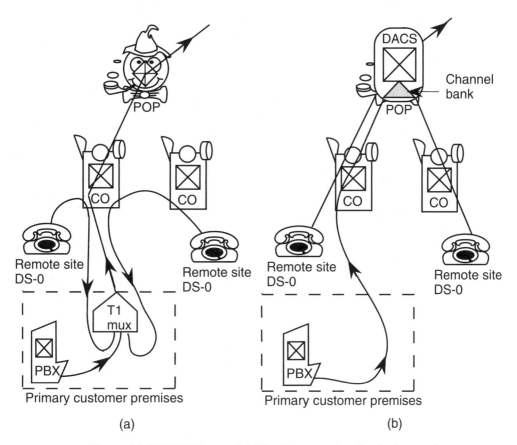

Figure 10.15 (a) Without a DACS, all remote site circuits have to be brought to the customer's premises, in order to multiplex them on a T1 circuit. (b) With a DACS and a channel bank located at a POP, it doesn't become necessary.

provides AAR (Automatic Alternate Routing), performance monitoring, traffic measurements, and self-initiated testing for the customer.

All carriers are developing management systems which allow customers to gain greater access to their facilities. On one hand it provides added control for private networks while creating a concern over the security and stability of the public network infrastructure.

10.7 NETWORK DESIGN CASE STUDY

10.7.1 Stating the Problem

Let us look now at a simple case study involving the design of a T1 backbone network.

On page 184, Figure 10.16 shows the corporate office and the main data center in Kansas City for a certain retail store chain. Besides Kansas City there are 6 remote locations. There are four other regional distribution centers around the country with the corresponding number of stores or remote locations as shown. Atlanta, besides being a regional center, is also a backup data center where data is backed up from the main data center, in case Kansas City experiences failure.

The traffic engineering department has done extensive traffic analysis and has given us the requirements as shown in Tables 10.1 and 10.2. The first row in Table 10.1 shows that we need seven 56 kbps channels from Kansas City to Atlanta, 3 to Seattle, 3 to Dallas, and 3 to New York. From Kansas City to Atlanta no 9.6 kbps channels are needed, but to Seattle, Dallas, and New York we need five 9.6 kbps each. Similarly, on the links from Atlanta to Seattle, Atlanta to Dallas, and Atlanta to New York we need three 56 kbps and five 9.6 kbps lines each.

The data requirements are for every store to have the following 9.6 kbps lines: two to Kansas City, two to Atlanta's data center, and five to its own regional distribution center. This is not given in a table, but all these data requirements are summarized graphically in Figure 10.17 on page 184.

Table 10.2 shows the voice channel requirements. From Atlanta to Kansas City there are 40 needed. From New York to Kansas City and Atlanta there are 20 and 25 required respectively, and so on. There are no entries in half of the table because these numbers are already provided in the other cells of the table. The remote stores don't have any voice tie line requirements.

10.7.2 The Analysis

Table 10.3 shows the 9.6 kbps data requirements from each of the New York stores to its regional center and to Atlanta and Kansas City using the requirements given above. For example, from each of the four stores for New York (labeled NY1 through NY4), there are 5 going to the New York regional center and two each going to Atlanta and Kansas City. Refer to Figure 10.17.

Table 10.4 shows three rows for Seattle stores, since there are 3 stores in that region. Similarly, Table 10.5 for Dallas has 2 rows since only 2 stores are located in the Dallas region.

Notice that Table 10.6 for Atlanta, though it has 4 rows for each of the 4 stores, has only 2 columns: one for Atlanta regional and one to Kansas City corporate offices. From each store in the Atlanta region, we need five 9.6 kbps lines for the regional center and two 9.6 kbps lines for the backup center. Since the regional and the backup center are the same for Atlanta, a total of 7 of these lines are needed.

For the same reason, the stores in Kansas City as shown in Table 10.7 also only have 2 columns: one for lines to Atlanta and one for Kansas City.

Now let us reduce all traffic requirements in multiples of DS-0 levels, in order to design the backbone network. To do this, we'll assume PCM coding which will require 64 kbps for each voice channel. For 56 kbps channels, we also need to dedicate an entire DS-0. Lastly, since a DS0 typically carries a maximum of 56 kbps of data, it can't support six 9.6 channels, which require 57.6 kbps (9.6 kbps times 6). So each DS-0 can only carry five 9.6 kbps channels.

Table 10.8 summarizes the total data requirements in terms of DS-0s between the cities. First let us look at how this requirement is 11 between Kansas City and Atlanta. From Table 10.1, there are seven 56 kbps channels required. Also, from Table 10.6, we need eight 9.6 kbps from each of the stores in Atlanta to Kansas City and from Table 10.7, we need twelve 9.6 kbps from each of the stores in Kansas City to Atlanta. The total number of 9.6 kbps between these cities is 20, which reduces the requirements to 4 DS-0s, given that each DS-0 supports only five 9.6 kbps channels. So the 7 DS-0s due to the 7 56 kbps lines and the 4 DS-0s due to the 20 9.6 kbps lines requires a total of 11 DS-0s between the two cities.

Let us consider the requirements between New York and Atlanta which is 6 in Table 10.8. From rows 3 and 4 of Table 10.1, we need three 56 kbps lines and five 9.6 kbps lines. This gives a total of 4 DS-0s for the New York regional center requirements.

Looking at Table 10.3, there are eight 9.6 kbps lines going from the stores to Atlanta which is an additional 2 DS-0s; together with the first 4 DS-0s from Table 10.1, the total requirement is 6 DS-0s as seen in Table 10.8.

Other numbers in Table 10.8 are calculated similarly. Notice that between New York, Seattle, and Dallas no requirements are given, so there are no DS-0s. Also, notice that the last column in Table 10.3, which is a column of 5s, does not get included in Table 10.8. This last column of 5s is the amount of bandwidth needed going to the New York center and does not go over the backbone network to the other cities, whereas the first two columns of 2s does go over the backbone network and gets included.

Finally, Table 10.9 shows the total voice and data DS-0 requirements. This is obtained by adding the corresponding cells between Table 10.2 (the total voice requirements) and Table 10.8 (the total data requirements). For example, between Atlanta and Kansas City we need 40 DS-0s for voice from Table 10.2 and 11 DS-0s from Table 10.8 for data needed, giving a total of 51 DS-0s.

10.7.3 Design

The next phase of this case problem is to design the map of the network, realizing there are 24 DS-0s in each T1. Table 10.9 is used for this entire process. First we'll start off by placing a T1 link for the larger numbers in the table. So between Atlanta and

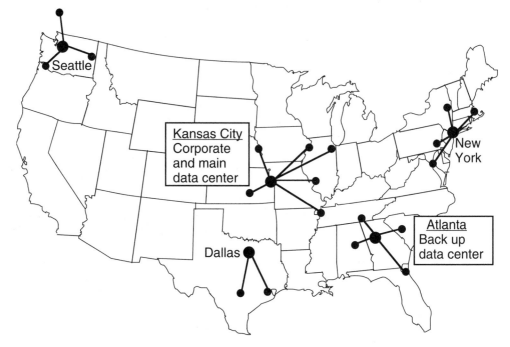

Figure 10.16 Traffic from the outlying locations is being concentrated at the four regional centers and at one corporate center in Kansas City. The data center is located in Kansas City and its backup is located in Atlanta. We are about to create a T1 backbone network to support these access networks.

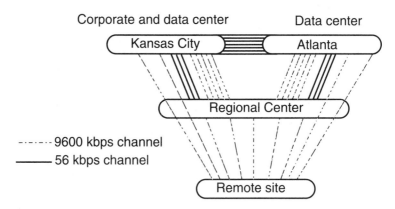

Figure 10.17 This summarizes the requirements for the case problem. From each remote site, there are two 9600 lines to each of the two data centers and five 9600 lines to the corresponding regional center. From each of the 3 regional centers, there are five 9600 bps and three 56 kbps lines to the two data centers.

Table 10.1 Regional's Data Requirements

From/To	AT	SE	DA	NY
KC 56k	7	3	3	3
KC 9.6k	0	5	5	5
ATL 56k	0	3	3	3
ATL 9.6k	0	5	5	5

Table 10.2 Regional's Voice Requirements

From/To	KC	AT	NY	SE
Atlanta	40	-	-	-
New York	20	25	-	-
Seattle	5	3	2	-
Dallas	11	9	7	1

Table 10.3 New York's 9.6k Requirements

From/To	AT	KC	NY
NY 1	2	2	5
NY 2	2	2	5
NY 3	2	2	5
NY 4	2	2	5

Table 10.4 Seattle's 9.6k Requirements

From/To	AT	KC	SE
SE 1	2	2	5
SE 2	2	2	5
SE 3	2	2	5

Table 10.5 Dallas' 9.6k Requirements

From/To	AT	KC	DAL
DAL 1	2	2	5
DAL 2	2	2	5

Table 10.6 Atlanta's 9.6ks

From/To	AT	KC
AT 1	7	2
AT 2	7	2
AT 3	7	2
AT 4	7	2

Table 10.7 KC's 9.6ks

From/To	AT	KC
KC 1	2	7
KC 2	2	7
KC 3	2	7
KC 4	2	7
KC 5	2	7
KC 6	2	7

Kansas City we need 2 T1s to start to accommodate the 51 DS-0s. There are 3 DS-0s (51 − 24 times 2 links) that still need to be routed, so let's place a 3 with this link. See the Kansas City-Atlanta connection in Figure 10.18(a). Similarly, satisfying the large number requirements first, the rest of the links are introduced in Figure 10.18(a), where a positive number over a link is the additional number of DS-0s that still have to be routed and a negative number over a link specifies the number of spare DS-0s available.

For example, when placing T1 between Kansas City and Dallas for its 16 DS-0s, 8 spare DS-0s are still available so a − 8 is placed over that link. Rates to Seattle may be higher than to other cities, so we want to limit the number of links there.

After satisfying the links shown in Figure 10.18(a), the entries, 9, 2, 7, and 1 of Table 10.9 remain to be accounted for in our network. The next largest number that needs to be taken care of is the 9 DS-0s between Atlanta and Seattle.

Let us place a third T1 link as shown in Figure 10.18(b) between Kansas City and Atlanta. Now the 3 between them shown in Figure 10.18(a) and the additional 9 going to Seattle take up 12 of the DS-0s over this new third T1 link. This leaves another 12 spare. For the Kansas City to Seattle link, the 9 channels from Atlanta need to be forwarded to Seattle. So now the number of spares from Kansas City to Seattle reduces to 4 from 13.

Figure 10.18(c) shows that the addition of 7 DS-0s between New York and Dallas is satisfied by adding another link from New York to Atlanta and then routing the 7 to Dallas from there. This reduces the number of spare DS-0s to 3 between Dallas and Atlanta. Furthermore, adding the 7 between New York and Atlanta that still needed routing in Figure 10.18(b) with the 7 going to Dallas take up 14 DS-0s on the new T1 link, leaving 10 spares. This is shown in Figure 10.18(c).

Figure 10.18(d) shows the number of spares left after routing the 2 DS-0s from Figure 10.18(c) between New York and Kansas City via Atlanta. Figure 10.18(e) shows the map after adding 2 DS-0s required according to Table 10.9 from New York to Seattle via Atlanta and Kansas City. Finally, Figure 10.18(f) shows the network after adding the one DS-0 from Table 10.9 from Dallas to Seattle via Kansas City.

10.7.4 Additional Design Issues

The final network achieved here is not necessarily the best solution. There are other solutions that may be better; after experience one can approach optimizing the solution. However, there are a few important concepts that should be emphasized here.

Table 10.8 DS-0 Data Requirements					Table 10.9 Total DS-0 Requirements				
From/To	KC	AT	NY	SE	From/To	KC	AT	NY	SE
Atlanta	11	-	-	-	Atlanta	51	-	-	-
New York	6	6	-	-	New York	26	31	-	-
Seattle	6	6	0	-	Seattle	11	9	2	-
Dallas	5	5	0	0	Dallas	16	14	7	1

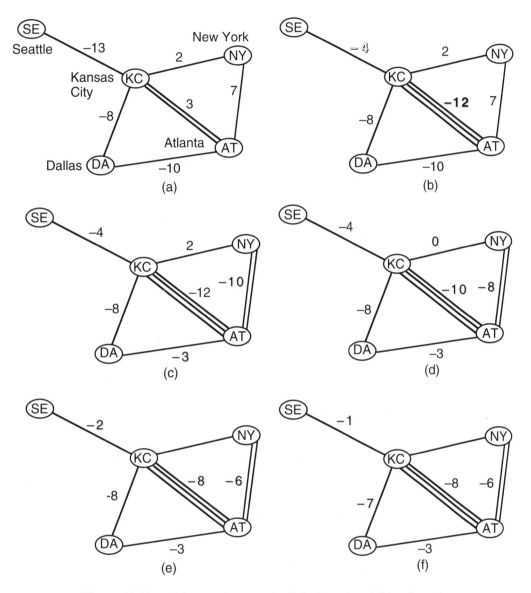

Figure 10.18 Positive numbers on the link show the additional number of DS-0s that still need to be satisfied, and the negative numbers show the spare number of DS-0s. The new values from the previous figure on each link are shown in bold. (a) The initial setup. (b) Add 9 channels from Seattle to Atlanta. Notice another T1 is added. (c) Add 7 channels from Dallas to New York by adding another T1. (d) Reroute the 2 channels needed between New York and Kansas City. (e) Add 2 from New York to Seattle. (f) Finally, add 1 from Seattle to Dallas.

T1 Networking

One is that no T1 tariffs were taken into account. These would have to be obtained before designing such a network. The link between New York and Kansas City is packed, while there is ample capacity via Atlanta. Traffic should be balanced across links and a couple of DS-0s should be routed via Atlanta for this purpose.

If ADPCM or some other voice compression technique is used instead of PCM, the entire design would have to be redone and would yield considerable savings. We have also assumed that the T1s were formatted or channelized. If they were simply framed, then we would not have to design the network in bundles of DS-0s, such as, requiring five 9.6 kbps channels per DS-0.

Lastly, installing fractional T1s connecting more city pairs than shown in our final network of Figure 10.18(f) would give a network that is reliable and resilient to failure. This is because the network would have more paths to route channels and the loss of a FT1 would be less catastrophic than the loss of a full T1.

Exercises

1. How many pairs of twisted copper are used to pass T1 signals?
   a. 1   b. 2
   c. 4   d. none; ordinary wire cannot be
                                       used for T1s.

2. "Only one circuit is needed rather than many different kinds" refers to which of the following advantages:
   a. lower costs   b. simplification
   c. reliability   d. network control

3. What is the bipolar format?
   a. Two voltage levels are used: +3V and 0V.
   b. Every mark is encoded with the opposite voltage polarity (+3V or –3V) as the previous mark.
   c. All spaces are encoded with a –3V and all marks are encoded with +3V.
   d. All spaces are encoded with 0V and all marks are encoded with +3V.

4. A D4 frame contains how many 8-bit voice samples per channel? For how many voice channels?
   a. It contains 24 samples for one voice channel.
   b. It contains 1 sample for one voice channel.
   c. It contains 12 samples for each of the 12 voice channels.
   d. It contains 1 sample for each of the 24 voice channels.

5. Which T1 interfacing device does unipolar to bipolar conversion?
   a. NIU   b. DSU
   c. CSU   d. LMU

6. What is a multi-link multiplexer?
   a. A multiplexer with many outputs.
   b. A multiplexer with many ports.
   c. A multiplexer used with many DACS.
   d. A DACS with many multiplexers connected to it.

7. What device converts a 44 channel T1 into two 22 channel T1s?
   a. DACS   b. BCM
   c. Inverse multiplexer   d. CCR

8. Which of the following is NOT a disadvantage of DACS?
   a. Transparent switching requires the T1 signal to be delayed by 48 bytes.
   b. Customer cannot control it using in-band digital signaling.
   c. It can not switch at rates below 64 kbps.
   d. One cannot keep the order of the D4 frames the same and still maintain a minimum delay.

9. Being able to change the bandwidth of a T1 by dropping a few channels for a videoconference temporarily explains which T1 advantage?

10. Which segment of a typical T1 has the weakest link as far as reliability is concerned?

11. If data to be sent is "11000100000000000100111," where the first "1" is +3V, what are the voltages of the bits as they are converted to output the signal? (There is a string of 12 zeros in there.)

12. What percent of an SF frame carries frame synchronizing bits? Answer the same question for an ESF frame.

13. What unit is being used by the telcos to gain loopback tests in case the customer's power fails?

14. What type of a mux will pass voice channels from one link to another link without doing D/A/D conversions?

15. What device is useful to combine DS-0 channels from many remote locations at a POP?

16. In Table 10.8, explain how 5 was calculated to be the number of DS-0s between Kansas City and Dallas?

17. Out of the advantages listed for T1, which do you consider to be the most important? Why?

18. What is the purpose of the bipolar format? How is that achieved?

19. Explain the purpose of the FDL channel? Where is it found? What are some functions not discussed in the text that you would like to see supported on this channel?

20. In Figure 10.11, explain the purpose of the various interfaces.

21. List the disadvantages of using drop and insert using single-link muxes over the other options.

22. List the advantages of DACS and CCR.

T1 Networking   **189**

23. What are the functions provided by a CSU?

24. Design the following T1 network using the same techniques discussed in the text: Los Angeles is the corporate office in this exercise, and Portland, Salt Lake City, and Denver are district offices. Denver and Los Angeles are the two data centers. All four cities each have three sales offices or remote sites off of them, making a total of 12 sales offices.

   The data requirements are as follows: From each sales office to LA office are two 9.6 kbps lines. From every district office to LA there are ten 9.6 kbps lines. From every district office to both data centers there is one 56 kbps. Between data centers there are four 56 kbps lines.

   The voice requirements are as follows: From Denver to LA there are 23 voice channels. From Portland to LA and Denver there are 7 and 3 voice channels, respectively. From Salt Lake City to LA, Denver, and Portland there are 15, 6, and 2 voice channels, respectively.

   Draw the traffic matrixes and design the network as shown in the example. Draw the final map with the amount of spare DS-0s on each link. Correct solutions may not be necessarily identical.

Chapter 11

Virtual Networks

11.1 INTRODUCTION

11.1.1 Purpose of VNs (Virtual Networks)

Recall from Chapter 8 the problem of designing and maintaining a private network based on tie-lines. The private network designer must decide whether and how a call should hop off the private network to gain access to the public network. Users have to constantly monitor the traffic patterns in deciding whether to add more trunks on some links or to remove trunks on others. Cost analysis has to be done at regular intervals to see how the network can be optimized. Also, pricing plans from the various carriers serving the different sites have to be constantly evaluated. Sorting out data from stacks of bills each month from the carriers can also be very tedious. Furthermore, as more sites are added to the private network, the problems of managing it become overwhelming.

Virtual networks, first introduced in 1984 by ISACOMM (which later became part of Sprint), take away the burden of managing a private network by having the carrier's signaling network take care of it. Since much of the traffic originated on a private network is sent over public facilities anyway, such as WATS and DDD service, why divide up the traffic so some of it goes over tie lines and the rest of it goes over the PSTN? Let the PSTN carry all of the traffic over its switched facilities and end up providing the customer with savings and advanced networking features.

In Figure 11.1(a), a private network is shown. Remote offices don't carry enough traffic to warrant a tie-line, so to reach them from the corporate private network, one must dial a 10-digit public number. This gives the remote office a sense of not belonging to the company. Yet in Figure 11.1(b), using a virtual network, all of the sites are part of the private virtual network. This does not require that the sites meet a minimum size requirement or generate a certain amount of traffic. People who are on

---

Among the many contributors, Gary Morgenstern and Rick Wallerstein of AT&T have been the most prominant ones in the writing of this chapter.

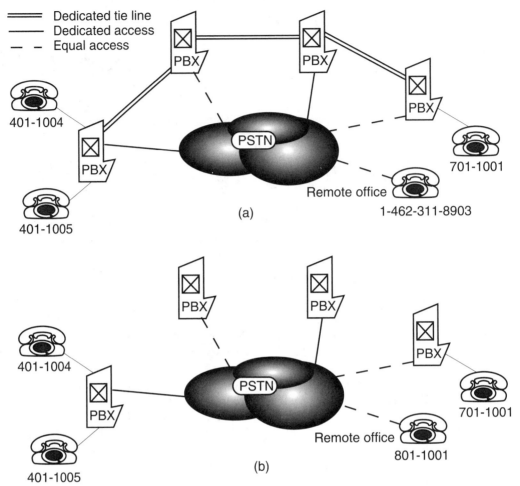

Figure 11.1 (a) Shows a private tie line network where all PBX sites are part of a 7-digit uniform dialing plan. The remote office is accessed via the 10-digit public numbering plan. (b) A virtual network equivalent, where all sites are part of a 7-digit private numbering plan. Notice the absence of point-to-point tie-lines.

the move, who may be at home, or at a public phone, or even using a cellular telephone can be part of the private virtual network. All of the traffic generated flows through the PSTN. In other words, a virtual network provides the desirable features of a private network while its calls traverse public switched network facilities.

The manner in which the calls are processed and routed is specified by the customer who provides parameters to the carrier's intelligent signaling network. Think of virtual networks as being similar to long distance centrex services. With centrex the local carrier does the switching for one location. Similarly, with a virtual network, the IXC does the switching for a private network. (However, BOCs also provide virtual network services.)

Many corporations use a private tie-line network in combination with a virtual network. A combination of both types of networks is called a hybrid network. It is used when traffic between two or more nodes is so heavy that use of interconnecting tie-lines between those nodes produces significant cost savings over use of the PSTN.

11.1.2 Operation of Virtual Networks

When a call originates from a phone, it enters the carrier's POP through one of the VN (Virtual Network) access methods (to be described shortly). The carrier's switch will detect which VN customer is calling and forwards the customer number, the calling party's number, and the called party's number to the SCP (Signal Control Point) through the STP (Signal Transfer Point). Recall from Chapter 7 that the SCP is a general name for AT&T's NCP and MCI's DAP. Sprint calls it an SCP. The SCP provides the translation for the 7-digit private phone number to the corresponding 10-digit public phone number or the POTS number. The entire call can be completed within 4 to 6 seconds.

Virtual network is not a new technology, but a new form of packaging advanced technology. To the user it is just another form of low cost bulk long distance service. The advanced technology that VNs rely on is in the carrier's SS#7 network. The intelligence of the signaling networks makes virtual networking powerful. Unlike older signaling techniques, SS#7 is software controlled, and to add a new feature to a VN offering, the carrier only needs to modify the software and update the change to all the installations.

VN service can be thought of as having four elements. One element is the method of accessing the POP from each customer location. A second is the transport and switching mechanism of the carrier's network. Third is the customer's VN description stored in the carrier's signaling databases. And last is the network management component which performs network monitoring, reconfiguration, and traffic analysis.

11.2 ADVANTAGES OF VN

11.2.1 Ease of Management

Probably the greatest advantage of VNs as already mentioned is not having to constantly optimize the network as a private tie-line network needs to be. Since all the traffic goes through the PSTN, managing the network becomes easy. Expensive tie-lines are replaced by low cost access lines to the associated POPs.

11.2.2 Corporate-wide Dialing Plan

Typically, the traditional tie-line networks of Figure 11.1(a), use a private 7-digit dialing plan to call any phone in the private network, and use the 10-digit public dialing plan to call anywhere in the public domain of phone numbers. So a user who is on the private network would dial a 7-digit number to dial another user on the private network or a 10-digit number to dial a user off the private network. An off-net user would have to dial 10 digits to call anyone, regardless of whether the destination is on or off the network.

When a VN is installed, the dialing plans for any of these phones can stay the same as before. Users don't have to be made aware of the VN installation; it is transparent to them. 7-digit dialers can continue dialing the same 7 digit numbers, and 10-digit dialers can continue dialing the same 10 digit numbers. Users don't have to be retrained in dialing on or off the network. The PSTN does the necessary number conversions. 7-digit private network plans and 10-digit public network plans can co-exist and yet be all on the same VN. If the customer chooses, he/she can instead use a 7-digit dialing plan for all locations.

11.2.3 Better Cost-to-Performance Ratio

Provisioning is the process by which a VN is installed and made to work. It involves more than just the installation of lines and software. When a new node is installed in a VN by a carrier, this change is transparent to the existing users. Getting such a service started is called provisioning the network.

At one time, it took 10 to 45 days to provision virtual network changes. Now, it is more adaptable to satisfying new networking needs quickly, and providing maximum performance for a network. Customers can do some of the provisioning themselves.

There is no capital investment necessary. When VNs were first introduced, only large companies could afford to pay for their high initial set up charges, but due to promotions that waive tariff charges, it now is possible to avoid this charge. In some instances, companies have saved over a million dollars annually by converting to the use of VNs. In short, VN users have all the benefits of private networks without having to bear their problems and costs.

There is no need to have trained personnel at all sites to maintain the network. In a private tie-line network, if reliability was a concern between two cities, then a redundant tie-line was usually installed between them, adding to the cost of the network. However, with a VN, the carrier's network itself inherently has redundant paths between many locations, making failure of an entire VN unlikely. In fact, VNs boast of providing 99.8% or better availability; that is, the failure can be less than two hours annually!

11.2.4 Other Advantages

Other advantages of virtual networks include the concepts of virtual offices and virtual companies. Now a worker's office doesn't have to be located physically in a given place. The office may be wherever the worker happens to be: at home, in a car, or at a public place.

Many times different companies depend on each other to provide a seamless service to their customers, such as the businesses used by an advertising agency. A virtual company is created by interconnecting the networks of such physically different but related organizations into one virtual network. This creates a sense of community among them and helps them to work better to yield better overall services.

Yet other advantages include flexibility that is gained by being able to change the network as demands change. There is a single point of contact when problems arise. The rates are reduced as the usage increases. This saves the customer from having to do extensive traffic studies each month. Finally, virtual network calls can be given priority over regular switched calls. Emergency calls have a higher priority. This is advantageous especially if there is a catastrophe in one part of the country, such as an earthquake, when everyone is trying to call their friends to see if they are fine.

There is no need to have PBXs from the same manufacturer at each node, as is the case in a private network. One doesn't have to replace the PBXs when a VN is installed. Furthermore, you can give calling card users the cost benefits of a VN, even though calls are originated from off-net sites. With a private network, only one call can traverse a trunk at a time. So if the traffic demands more calls between two points, then more trunks are needed. However, with VNs, the user isn't concerned about having enough trunks—the PSTN supports the long-haul traffic.

11.3 TYPES OF ACCESS

Another advantage of VNs over private tie-line networks is the number of access methods VNs provide their customers besides the traditional dedicated access line. Customers use their local trunks to provide switched access into the VN, and then as traffic volume increases, more local trunks may be added or may even be replaced with dedicated access facilities. The access methods outlined here don't only apply to VNs but also to other long distance services.

11.3.1 Switched Access

In Figure 11.2, the PBX has a switched access to a POP through a CO. A call from the PBX to the POP can go by either of the two paths shown. If the direct path is busy, then the call is switched over the alternate path. Similarly, residential phones calling long distance through a POP also employ switched access to the POP.

When the trunk between the CO and the POP is shared between many users, a customer's line to that CO trunk, though used only by that customer, is called a switched access line.

There are four categories of obtaining switched access to a POP and they are called "feature groups." Figure 11.3 illustrates these four types of feature groups. On the left, the PBX has a local trunk to the nearest CO or the end office. This CO can then provide switched access to an AT&T POP using feature group C, or to the other IXCs' POPs using feature groups A, B, or D via other COs. Let us now discuss these feature groups.

Feature group A type of switched access was made available after divestiture to reach a non-AT&T POP. One had to use DTMF signaling and not rotary dial telephone to reach the "alternate carriers." So to call long distance using a non-AT&T carrier, one had to dial a local phone number, after which the caller heard a second dial tone from the POP.

The connection to the POP was provided over the "line" side rather than the "trunk" side of the telco's switch. Though this was a low cost connection, it used only one pair of wires for both transmit and receive voice paths. Trunk side connections of a switch, on the other hand, use 4-wire connections to keep the transmit and receive paths separate in order to provide high quality voice transmission.

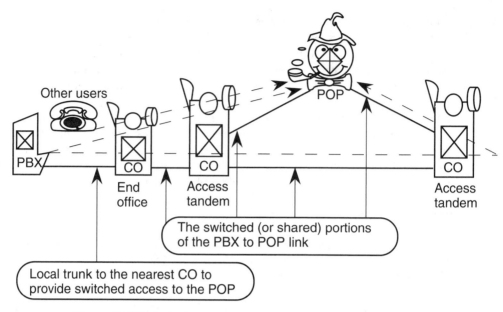

Other users

PBX

CO
End office

CO
Access tandem

POP

CO
Access tandem

The switched (or shared) portions of the PBX to POP link

Local trunk to the nearest CO to provide switched access to the POP

Figure 11.2 Switched access to an IXC's point of presence provides no predetermined path to it. Also the path is shared with other users, and it can go through either of the tandem switches.

Feature group A makes the POP look like an ordinary phone number, and this type of access is not necessarily routed through a tandem. So this type of access is becoming less and less common.

Feature group B is a predivestiture local access method. This type of access is obtained by dialing toll-free 950-0xxx or 950-1xxx. As an example, to obtain access to MCI, one must dial 950-1022 and for Sprint, 950-1033. This is a common nation-wide number.

After hearing a tone or an announcement, the user must dial the extra digits. This type of access is provided by two pair of wires and has better transmission quality on the trunk side of a telco switch. This switch now could reside either in an end office or an access tandem office. The tandem office switch must be upgraded to an electronic switching system for it to provide feature group B access. Since an authorization code still has to be entered in order to use this type of access, feature group B is also becoming less common in accessing IXCs.

Recently, however, large nation-wide companies such as pizza chains are using this access as an inexpensive way to obtain 800 number capabilities. Instead of dialing 11 digits typically associated with 800 number dialing, pizza customers can dial one 950 number anywhere in the country, and be connected to a pizza chain's nationwide network. In this case, the POP at feature group B in Figure 11.3 would then represent the pizza chain's network node switch. This switch would be in the same LATA as the serving CO. With 950-1xxx designation for this type of access, only 1,000 numbers are possible, but the NANPA (North American Numbering Plan Administration) is working with the BOCs to add another 9,000. Not only does this access provide a high quality 4-wire connection, but it also provides ANI (Automatic Number Identification) and answer supervision. Using feature group B instead of an 800 number requires that the user have its own network in place to interconnect private nodes between LATAs. Because of this overhead associated with 950 access, most companies find 800 service more suitable.

Feature group C access can only be provided by AT&T. A user need only dial a 1 to access the AT&T POP. This access offers 4-wire connections and automatic number identification. This type of access provides a very short call setup time, because due to predivestiture conditions, these lines are sent directly to the AT&T POP. See Figure 11.3.

Feature group D circuits are also 4-wire trunk side connections, and provide even a higher level of quality than feature groups A and B. This high quality is maintained

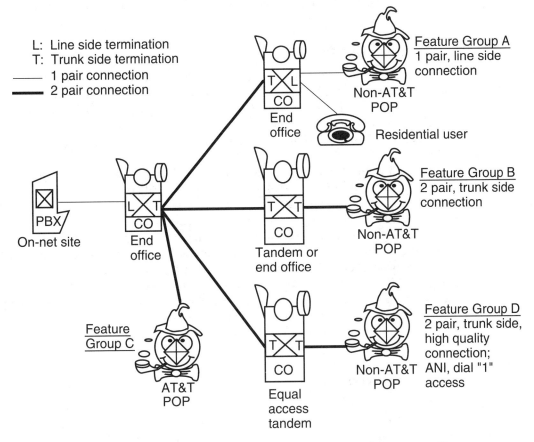

Figure 11.3 The four groups of switched access, where feature group D provides the highest quality connection to non-AT&T POPs. However, switched access to AT&T is faster than the access to the other carriers due to the existence of predivestiture connections.

by the federal courts, requirement of allowing a maximum of one tandem office for these circuits and the tandems have to be fully electronic. Instead of dialing a 7-digit number to access the POP, one needs to only dial 1.

According to MFJ, accessing any IXC should be just as easy as accessing AT&T; hence these are also called equal access circuits. Since the LEC provides the POP with ANI (Automatic Number Identification) with the call, rotary pulse dialing telephones can also be used.

A customer can access a POP two ways using equal access. Presubscription or primary access requires the customer to simply dial a 1, area code, and then the 7 digits, whereas non-presubscription or secondary access requires the customer to dial 10xxx, area code, and then the 7 digits. These are also known as "casual callers."

Accessing a VN using any of these switched access feature groups is simply called switched access. A location which uses a switched access to access a VN is called an on-net location, since the location presubscribes to the IXC and all calls are connected to the POP. This type of access is ideal for small locations which don't have the traffic volume to necessitate a dedicated line.

11.3.2 Dedicated Access

DAL (Dedicated Access Line) or special access line is used to provide dedicated access to the VN. The line is strictly for the use of one user and it is not shared. Instead of paying on a per call basis, the user pays one flat monthly charge. The circuit doesn't go through a switch at the CO, but is hard wired there to be routed to the POP. Of course, only high volume customers find it economical to install a DAL. These are usually T1s today.

A DAL differs from a WAL (WATS Access Line) in that a DAL provides a dedicated link up to the POP whereas the WAL provides a dedicated link only up to the equal access point. From there it is switched, as seen in Figure 11.4. Also, a WAL, cannot be used for placing local calls or for receiving any calls.

A DAL could be a single channel analog line or it could be carried over a high capacity digital line, such as a T1 or a T3. Oftentimes, as few as six single-line DALs might equal the cost of a T1 dedicated access line in which case the customer gains 18 channels (24 minus 6) for little or no additional cost. Whether the break-even point is as few as 6 or as high as 14 DALs is simply a financial question and is determined by costs of the single-line DALs as opposed to the cost of the T1. These costs are determined by the distance between the user's site and the POP and by the tariff rate for each.

11.3.3 Remote Access

A person can use an 800 number to access the VN while he/she is traveling and has no access to a company phone. This is called remote or 800 number access and is considered an off-net call. There are various forms of remote access.

Basically, the user dials an 800 number, possibly an authorization code, and the called number. He/she thereby has access to any VN location (on-net location) or any DDD call (off-net location). However, as with private tie-line networks, the caller may be restricted from calling certain areas.

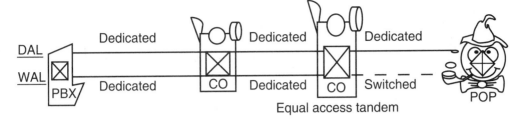

Figure 11.4 The top link shows a DAL (Dedicated Access Link) providing a dedicated channel up to the POP. And the bottom link shows a WAL (WATS Access Link) which provides a dedicated channel up to the equal access tandem. WALs cannot be used to place local calls or for receiving calls.

AT&T's version of remote access is called NRA (Network Remote Access). Soon the BOCs will be providing 800 number portability, and a customer will be able to keep the same 800 number and still be able to switch its IXC.

Lastly, an on-net location is any location that is defined in the customer's VN description, which resides in the carrier's database. The location could be served by switched or dedicated access. It could even be an employer's residence, as long as it is defined in the database. Conversely, any location not defined in the customer's database is referred to as an off-net location.

Compared to private networks, VNs offer a broad range of accessing methods which bring the advantages of a private network to the smallest customer sites and even to the customer's transient employees.

11.4 TYPES OF CALLS

11.4.1 Calls as Defined by AT&T

AT&T calls its virtual network offering SDN (Software Defined Network), MCI calls its network Vnet, and Sprint calls its network VPN (Virtual Private Network).

In Figure 11.5, a VN with the three general types of access methods is shown: special access or dedicated access, LESA (Local Exchange Switched Access) or equal access, and remote access. For billing purposes, AT&T's SDN defines eight types of calls. The eight types of calls are specified by combining the three types of access with the three types of egress.

The first type of call is from special access to special access and is labeled as number 1. The type of call which is labeled as 2 is from special access to LESA. In the same manner the other six types of calls for billing purposes are shown in the figure. Notice that there are three types of calls originating from special access (labeled 1, 2, 3), two from LESA (labeled 4, 5), and three from remote access (labeled 6, 7, 8).

11.4.2 Calls as Defined by Sprint

To determine the cost of the call, Sprint simply defines only four types of calls based on on-net and off-net locations. As with AT&T, it classifies equal access

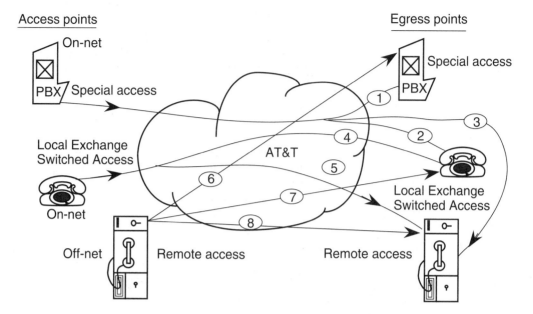

Figure 11.5 AT&T's method of classifying eight types of virtual network calls.

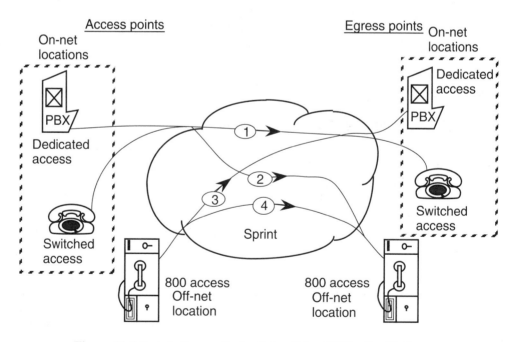

Figure 11.6 Sprint's four methods of classifying VPN calls. (1) On-net to on-net, (2) On-net to off-net, (3) Off-net to on-net, (4) Off-net to off-net.

locations as on-net locations. Any phone, even a cellular phone, if it is in the data base description for that customer's VN, is said to be an on-net location. As illustrated in Figure 11.6, there are four types of calls possible. The ones originating from on-net locations are labeled 1 and 2 and are destined for on-net and off-net egress locations, respectively. Similarly, calls labeled 3 and 4 are off-net to on-net and off-net to off-net, respectively.

11.4.3 Calls as Defined by MCI

MCI uses a completely different approach to pricing. It does not base the cost on the type of call, but on the type of access (how the call comes on the network), the transmission of the call, and the type of egress (how the call gets off the network).

11.5 FEATURES

One of the most appealing benefits of VNs is the richness of features they provide. Basically, whatever can be done on a private network can be duplicated on a VN. All major carriers use some form of SS#7 in their public network. So to incorporate a change or to add a new feature only the software has to be changed and updated at all locations. This should make duplications of features offered easy for the carriers. Yet due to slight differences in their network architectures, there are some differences in the features that they offer. Some of the features that are offered by VNs are outlined here, and not all the features work the same way between carriers.

11.5.1 Network Management Related Features

Network management and control systems: Management is a very crucial aspect of VN offerings. It allows the customer to hand over the networking problems to the carrier, but yet gives the customer control over it. Managers can access the data for their network via a terminal or a PC to monitor traffic, track alarms, do adds-moves-and-changes for individuals, and reroute traffic as it becomes necessary.

Reporting capabilities: Private network managers are accustomed to having CDR (Call Detail Recording) available from their PBXs on a regular basis. The IXCs provide the same types of reports for easy migration to a hybrid or a pure virtual network. Included in these reports are who called from what group, what access method or line was used, etc. Also traffic reports are provided showing statistics about the average length of calls, number of calls blocked, and so on.

Accounting codes: After dialing the telephone number, the user hears another dial tone or an announcement, then the user dials a 2 or 3 digit account code for the call to go through. This identification helps the call detail recording statement to be categorized by account codes and departments or individuals. This limits the abuse of the network, and is a feature that is duplicated from WATS service.

Authorization codes: This is like a password for identifying the caller and is also entered after the calling digits are entered. This can be changed or cancelled and new ones can be added by the telecom manager by accessing the carrier's database through a terminal or a PC. This is used with the call screening feature. These two features and the accounting codes feature are some of the most widely used features of virtual networks.

Call screening: This is also called class of service restriction. As mentioned in Chapter 8, class of service is assigned to the terminal and either provides or limits calling privileges based on area codes, and/or exchanges. This powerful feature can also be supported by the carrier. As a call enters a VN, the carrier's database can compare the customer number, the account code, the authorization code and/or the ANI (Automatic Number Identification) to either allow the call to go through or to block it. Through the use of network management systems, the telecom manager can provide broader calling privileges or cancel a lost calling card.

11.5.2 Call Processing Features

Direct termination overflow: When an incoming 7-digit on-net call is blocked, either because all the capacity of the DALs is used up or they have failed, the POP can reroute the call through the CO over the public switched network. This of course, requires a private 7-digit to a public 10-digit number conversion.

Forced on-net routing: If a person dials a public 10-digit number without knowing that the location is on that customer's VN, the carrier will do a 10-digit to 7-digit number conversion and place the call on the VN which in effect lowers the call's cost.

This also may be used by previous private network callers who don't want to learn the new 7-digit equivalents of the older 10-digit numbers. For users who tend to oppose changes, this makes the transition easy to bring the remote outlying off-net locations into the corporate dialing plan. The VN accepts either form and routes the call accordingly.

Virtual ringdown: This is like a hot-line. A user picks up the phone and without dialing any digits, a call is placed to a predefined number.

Virtual FX (Foreign eXchange) circuits: If Kansas City has many customers in San Francisco, then virtual circuits between the two cities allow Kansas City employees to dial a San Francisco local number. And likewise, San Francisco customers can dial a local number and reach their Kansas City reps.

Network intercept announcements: Recorded messages are played back giving reasons why a call can not be completed. The messages may be defined either by the VN provider or by the customer.

11.5.3 Integrating VN features

Many calls over a VN require the services of more than one feature. Here is an example of a call that requires three features. We have two customer support centers, one located on the west coast and one in the east. A residential customer who is not part of the VN calls the east coast support center by dialing an 800 number. The carrier, realizing this 800 number belongs to a virtual network, connects this call into that VN.

As just described, Phone 1 dials a public 10-digit number to access the east coast support center. This is shown as step 1 in Figure 11.7.

The SSP (Service Switching Point) realizes this VN call and sends the calling data to the SCP (Service Control Point) via the STP (Signal Transfer Point) to find out its POTS number. This is step 2.

Step 3 in the figure shows the SCP realizes this is an on-net location and converts the 10-digit number to an on-net 7-digit number. This is forced on-net routing. However, the SCP realizes that this 7-digit private number is on the east coast and the database says to route it to the west coast, because currently it is after 4 PM EST. This is called time-of-day routing.

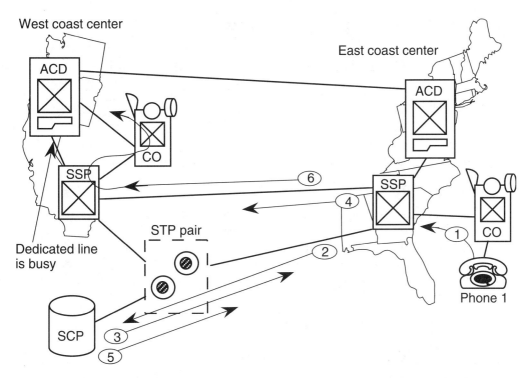

Figure 11.7 The sequence of steps a call may take in being completed through a virtual network.

In step 4 the east coast SSP tries to establish a connection with the west coast SSP through the STP, but the west coast SSP signals back to the east coast SSP that the dedicated circuits are all busy on the DALs to the west coast center.

The east coast SSP asks the STP what to do since the DAL is blocked on the west coast. The STP looks in the SCP database, in step 5, to see if a recorded message, such as "all circuits are busy" should be played back to the caller or not. It finds out that the customer has alternate routing available on its network called direct termination overflow. So it converts the 7-digit number to a public 10-digit number.

Finally, step 6 shows that the call is completed by the east coast SSP through the west coast CO instead of the dedicated facility. Without any one of these features, the call would have been blocked.

11.5.4 Global VNs

Using a virtual network, one can call internationally with reduced rates. But the idea of a global VN encompasses more than that. With global virtual networking, virtual network offerings from various countries can be interconnected into one seamless network, worldwide. Of course, the feature set provided by the international VNs may not coincide with each other, yet the ability to do 7-digit dialing between international sites of the same organization is quite attractive.

11.5.5 Conclusion on VN Features

Many other features are available on virtual networks, but these are not necessarily provided by all the carriers. Most features are not needed by VN users, but just as there is a price war waging between the carriers, there's also a feature war. Each one is trying to provide more features with lower costs than their competitors. This allows their per-minute prices to be lower than any of their other long-distance services.

11.6 CARRIER PROFILES

11.6.1 AT&T

AT&T's SDN (Software Defined Network) started in November of 1985. SDN has two service versions. One is called basic SDN which includes account codes, uniform dialing plan, class of service, and a few other popular features. But it lacks authorization codes, direct termination overflow, forced on-net routing, and many other advanced features. It is targeted for the customers who don't need advanced features. For customers who do, AT&T offers the custom SDN option with at least 15 more features available than the basic option.

The basic architecture of SDN is shown in Figure 11.8. Here, the ACP (Action Control Point) is the 4ESS switch in the AT&T network. NCP, as mentioned in Chapter 7, stores the customer's description of the virtual network. This description is stored redundantly, with 4 copies existing in two different locations for increased reliability. SMS (Service Management System) is accessed through a CPE terminal; it can do deletions with adds-moves-and-changes requiring a service order. NSC (Network Service Complex) stores and plays announcements for the caller. SDNCC (SDN

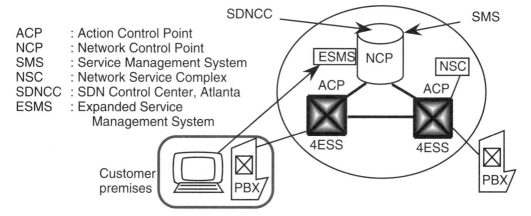

ACP   : Action Control Point
NCP   : Network Control Point
SMS   : Service Management System
NSC   : Network Service Complex
SDNCC : SDN Control Center, Atlanta
ESMS   : Expanded Service
                Management System

Figure 11.8 AT&T's SDN network architecture.

Control Center) is located in Atlanta. Customers have maintenance technicians located at the SDNCC to serve them around the clock.

AT&T provides SDN customers with end-to-end control of their networks through a blueprint called UNMA (Unified Network Management Architecture). UNMA helps customers to manage their networks by supporting the interconnection of management hardware and software from various vendors.

Using ASW (ACCUMASTER Services Workstation) and the SDN Network Manager software, managers can proactively control their network from a single vantage point. With it, one can schedule tests of access trunks, generate routine traffic reports, analyze calling patterns, detect security violations, monitor network performance, reconfigure the network, and perform other tasks.

The SDN Network Manager is divided into functional systems called EMSs (Element Management Systems). CNAR (Customer Network Administration Reports), RTNM (Real-Time Network Management), OCDD (On-line Call Detail Data), and NRAMS (Network Remote Access Monitoring System) are some of the EMSs provided.

The management elements provided through UNMA are SMS (Service Management System), DATTS (Direct Access Trunk Test System), CNAR (Customer Network Administration Report), CTDR (Customer Traffic Data Report system), and NRA (Network Remote Access monitoring system).

CNAR provides information on calling patterns to help weigh costs to performance issues, such as when to add a new location to the network, the amount of total costs, usage cost per minute, number of calls made after hours, and other reports. RTNM provides near real-time status on the dedicated access lines. It provides average holding times, blocking factors, half-hour and daily traffic reports.

OCDD enables the customer to retrieve complete call detail recording for calls two minutes after they are terminated. Call records can be searched by authorization codes, dialed or dialing numbers, and other items. NRAMS helps to identify unauthorized use of 800 number access by flagging individuals who exceeded the acceptable number of calls in a day, and by other reports.

Virtual Networks   **205**

11.6.2 MCI

MCI's virtual network called Vnet doesn't offer two plans as AT&T does, but a customer can pick and choose features on an individual basis.

NETCAP (NETwork CAPabilities manager) is the global manager for the entire network as shown in Figure 11.9. It acts as the interface to the network for both MCI and VN customers.

NMS (Network Management Services) provides the customer interface to its database stored in the network. Depending on the level of management that is needed, a customer can choose between CM (Configuration Management), NIMS (Network Information Management Systems), or INMS (Integrated Network Management Systems). INMS allows customers to access and change much more data in the database than either CM or NIMS. INMS reports and alarms are available on an SNA host through MCIView.

MCI manages its network through two NNMCs (National Network Management Centers) to monitor and reconfigure the network, install new customers, and provide customer services and billing reports.

MCI is providing extensive remote network management capabilities, making Vnet very competitive and appealing in the marketplace.

11.6.3 Sprint

In May 1985, Sprint was the first carrier to offer a VN. Its VPN (Virtual Private Network) was inherited from ISACOMM which had been providing virtual network services since 1982 through SBS (Satellite Business Systems). The first three letters of the name Sprint are an acronym for Southern Pacific Railroad. Today, Sprint is 100% owned by United Telecom.

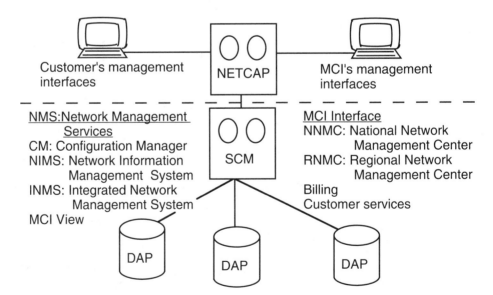

Figure 11.9 MCI's Vnet management systems for Vnet users and for MCI.

It has two VPN offerings called option I and option II. At the time of this writing, it is the only carrier that offers a speed dialing feature, whereas MCI is the only carrier that offers routing of calls based on the point of origination and AT&T is the only carrier that offers routing of calls based on the time of day or day of week. However, one should keep in mind that feature offerings are continuously changing.

For management purposes, it provides a customer with an INSITE (Integrated Network System Interface and Terminal Equipment) terminal. It is being deployed in four phases.

11.7 SWITCHED DIGITAL SERVICES

11.7.1 What Is Switched Digital Services?

The reason why this topic is placed in the virtual network section is that these switched digital services are provided by all three major carriers as a feature of their virtual networks. Since voice is digitized for transmission, data can just as well be digitized (and video for that matter) and made to go over the voice network.

In fact, Sprint does precisely that. (Unlike Sprint, both AT&T and MCI use separate digital networks to carry their data services.) Whenever a voice call is made over the Sprint network, it is transmitted over a 64 kbps channel. Now the user can use that channel anyway she or he prefers. 64 kbps of data can be sent just as easily as sending 64 kbps of voice.

Furthermore, to increase the efficiency of transmission, manufacturers are selling CPE (Customer Premises Equipment) that takes several voice, data, and fax circuits and compresses them into one 64 kbps voice call. So for the price of one voice call, for example, an additional 3 voice and one 9600 bps circuit can be obtained for free. This is done, of course, by using voice compression techniques that bring the bandwidth of one voice channel below 16 kbps. The equipment uses proprietary protocols so only one vendor's product may be used at the end points of the network. However, for the price of one voice call, so many circuits can be compressed and switched that it provides an impressive cost savings in networking.

11.7.2 Carrier Offerings

In 1985, AT&T introduced switched 56 kbps data services and called it "Accunet Switched 56 kbps." It allowed a customer to dial a 56 kbps channel to whichever point that was required. However, at that time, the service wasn't available to all POPs and the price was 85 cents per minute. This service was essentially used to backup dedicated lines.

Currently, prices are down to 6 cents per call-minute. Furthermore, availability of the services has expanded, the local exchanges are providing better access to such services, and more CPE is being introduced to interface with switched data services.

AT&T has two services. One is called Accunet Switched Digital Service which allows a customer to dial a contiguous 384 kbps channel using ISDN's H0 channel. Accunet also offers 1.536 Mbps using the H11 channel.

The other service is called SDDN (Software Defined Data Network) which is a feature provided under SDN. SDDN provides a complete set of ISDN features.

However, Accunet provides better international connectivity and the capability to simultaneously broadcast one-way transmissions to several locations.

MCI provides switched data services at rates of up to T3 and calls it VPDS (Virtual Private Data Service). Sprint currently does not provide contiguous blocks of data above 64 kbps, but the user must dial the number of channels that is necessary to equal the bandwidth that is being transmitted.

11.7.3 Digital Dial-Up Bandwidth on Demand

Digital dial-up bandwidth on demand is very similar to switched digital services, except the former implies that the amount of bandwidth is adjustable as the customer's requirements change in real time. Just as one can call up anyone on an ordinary phone to have a voice conversation, digital dial-up services provide the same capabilities for digital transmissions. However, unlike a voice call where only one 4 kHz voice channel is provided between the end points, bandwidth on demand allows the user not only to set up a connection but also to specify its bandwidth. So the customer is billed according to the distance and duration as well as the bandwidth of a call.

A user no longer has to fine tune a digital tie-line with T1s or FT1s. When a T1 circuit lies idle or underutilized during the night or otherwise, the user is still paying for that line. However, with digital dial-up bandwidth on demand, a user creates a call only when there is data to transmit, and terminates it when done.

To give an example, once a credit card company used a large digital tie-line network to provide credit card authorization nationwide. It was critical that the network provided no blocking whatsoever. Therefore, the network was optimized for large volume days such as the Monday after Thanksgiving, etc. Now for the few busiest days during the year, the network had the necessary capacity, but for the remainder of the year, the network was very underutilized.

After replacing the network with bandwidth on demand services, the company only paid for the bandwidth that it needed. This provided no blocking of traffic even on busy days, which was a major concern, and yet the costs during other days was dramatically reduced. In conclusion, these services provide maximum flexibility at minimum costs.

Videoconferencing among several locations is another popular application for such services. With a T1 network, one has to schedule a conference at a certain time. If an executive at one of the locations decides to postpone it, because something else came up, then the bandwidth that was scheduled for the videoconference becomes unused. With on-demand services, the dialing for the videoconference can be done at the last minute, with no scheduling necessary. Also, the bandwidth can be selected at the time of the conference depending on what quality of video is desired.

Of course, there is a cut-off point, where changing to a tie-line network becomes more cost efficient. If the amount of traffic is consistently high, say for example over 5 hours per day, then using a T1 or an FT1 would become the better choice. One has to be current with the existing tariffs to make the proper choice between tie-lines and switched services. However, when tie-lines are converted to switched digital services over international boundaries, then the savings become much more pronounced than the savings gained with domestic services.

11.7.4 Implementing Digital Dial-Up Services

Initially, SW56 (SWitched 56) services were provided by an SW56 access line, and the two terms were used interchangeably. Now access to SW56 network services can be gained by a SW56 line, BRI, T1, or PRI. These services are provided by either the LEC or the IXC. If a T1 is used by the CPE to access the LEC, then up to 24 SW56 circuits can be set up through the carriers' networks. In this case, the customer only has to pay a fixed amount for the T1 between the CPE and the CO. However, now he/she has the flexibility to call up to 24 individual circuits, because he/she has the necessary access for that many circuits to the carriers' networks.

If a PRI is used for accessing the network, then the customer has the greatest flexibility in that he can access SW56, SW64, SW384, SW1536, or multirate services. On the other extreme, SW56 access can't access SW64 or higher rate services.

Multirate services are a multiple of 64 kbps ISDN channels, such as 64 kbps, 128 kbps, 192 kbps, etc. The type of service that the customer is calling up is given in the D channel of ISDN. The SW384 and SW1536 are called the H0 and the H11 ISDN circuits, respectively. The bandwidth of an H channel has to stay together within the network as one unit, and may only be subdivided at the CPE. Currently, SW56 service is the most widely available service, and with it, one can communicate between any access types, whether it be SW56, SW64, BRI, or PRI.

When bandwidth is requested to the carrier using ISDN H0, H11, or multirate channels, the network manages the allocation of bandwidth and the customer need only specify how much bandwidth is needed. This is called network-based bandwidth on-demand services. On the contrary, a customer's I-Mux (Inverse Multiplexer) allows him to automatically dial as many circuits as are needed by the application (videoconferencing, file transfer, etc.). Here, the customer's equipment manages the allocation of bandwidth and not the carriers' networks.

An I-Mux splits the customer's data over several individual circuits and sends it to the destination I-Mux. There the units of data arrive in different order, because of the diverse routing paths. So the remote I-Mux will adjust for delay, order these arriving units, and present the data to the receiving application as if it were sent over one channel.

Figure 11.10 shows the differences between network-based services and the inverse multiplexing technology using the currently available SW56 services. The application depicted is an x-ray machine transferring a 12 Mbit file from a Seattle hospital to a specialist in radiology in Boston. In Figure 11.10(a), a 3x64 kbps ISDN multirate channel is used and all the data arrives at the image display over one large pipe.

In Figure 11.10(b), the I-Mux dials up 3 individual SW56 circuits, and the remote I-Mux combines the data into one stream. The applications on both ends don't know or care if the data traveled over separate routes or if they came over one circuit as in Figure (a). Neither do the carrier switches need to know in Figure 11.10(b) that these circuits are related to the setting up of one call.

Until ISDN services become widely available, inverse multiplexing will have an upper hand, because it provides the most efficient utilization of access lines and network services. It provides many methods of accessing the network. However, with

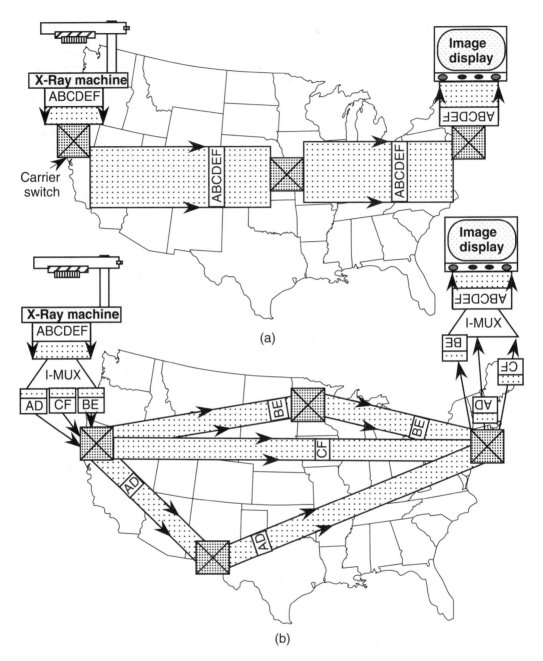

Figure 11.10 (a) Using network-based bandwidth on-demand services, the carrier transports 168 kbps of user traffic on one 192 kbps ISDN multirate channel. (b) The same capacity can be transported by inverse multiplexers, using three SW56 circuits.

ISDN services on the horizon, the carriers would be able to offer pricing discounts for large volume customers, but with I-muxes, the customer may have to pay more, because the carriers would still have to manage multiple low-speed circuits.

Exercises

1. Which of the following is NOT an advantage of virtual networks?
   a. They require a substantial amount of capital investment in networking products, which can be regained if the products are resold on the secondary market.
   b. They drastically reduce the amount of traffic engineering that has to be done on a private network.
   c. Network configuration changes can be done within a reasonable amount of time.
   d. They provide better reliability over traditional tie-line networks.

2. Which type of feature group is the least commonly used in virtual networks?
   a. Feature group A
   b. Feature group B
   c. Feature group C
   d. Feature group D

3. Which type of feature group is used for providing high quality access to non-AT&T POPs? Choose from the choices in exercise 2.

4. Which type of a call can be made with WALs?
   a. Inbound local calls
   b. Inbound inter-LATA calls
   c. Outbound local calls
   d. Outbound inter-LATA calls

5. MCI calls its virtual network by what name?
   a. VPN
   b. SBS
   c. Vnet
   d. SDN

6. Sprint defines how many types of calls for billing purposes?
   a. 3
   b. 4
   c. 8
   d. 9

7. Name the virtual network feature which will place the call on the network even if the caller doesn't realize that he/she could have used a 7-digit virtual number.
   a. call screening
   b. virtual ringdown
   c. direct termination overflow
   d. forced on-net routing

8. Which IXC provides the INSITE management terminal?
   a. AT&T
   b. MCI
   c. Sprint
   d. none of the above

9. In a traditional tie-line network, typically what percent of the traffic goes through the DDD network?

10. Where is the customer's data stored for a virtual network? What do the three major carriers call this database?

11. Name the four elements of a virtual network.

12. A private network dialing plan usually has how many dialing digits?

13. Which feature groups use trunk-side terminations for the POPs?

14. Typically, what type of access allows a person in transit to use the virtual network?

15. What are the two broad categories of switched data services provided by AT&T?

16. What type of device allows a high speed data stream to be sent on many low speed channels?

17. Discuss the virtual network advantages that are management related.

18. Discuss the virtual network advantages that pertain to a uniform dialing plan.

19. Discuss equal access, its characteristics, and the two methods of acquiring it.

20. Discuss the types of calls defined by Sprint for billing purposes.

21. How are the features, authorization codes, and call screening similar and different?

22. Explain in your own words how and what the three features are that are being utilized in Figure 11.7.

23. Explain the various management components of the MCI network.

24. What is gained by using switched data services over digital tie-lines?

Chapter 12

SNA

12.1 THE SNA ENVIRONMENT

SNA was introduced in 1974 by IBM as a proprietary solution to eliminate the chaos of many types of networking protocols which existed in that era. Today it is the most dominant network architecture with well over 40,000 networks installed world-wide. The number of stations attached to these networks, of course, far exceed that number. Before detailing the SNA architecture, protocols, and how it is implemented, let us take a simplistic view of SNA and its purpose.

12.1.1 How SNA Was Initially Used

Figure 12.1 shows a number of terminals that are geographically dispersed and are connected via the network to a host, which in IBM's terminology is a mainframe. The mainframe is located at the corporate data center and for the sake of an example, let us say it is used to provide data base access for agents of an airliner.

A database is a sophisticated collection of data records that are organized so that access to those records is done efficiently. Two popular database management systems by IBM are called IMS (Information Management System) and DB2 (DataBase/2). IMS, a traditional approach, uses a hierarchical method of organizing data. This method uses parent-to-children or inverted tree structures. Alternatively, DB2 uses a relational database structure where data is logically organized in tables.

As an example, staffing these remote terminals might be travel agents who have authorization to access the database. The agents issue requests, called transactions, for the database. These requests may be asking for availability of seats for a particular flight on a given date, or may be asking to cancel a reservation, or any number of such queries. These requests which are made to the database by the many travel agents nationwide, are processed by programs called transaction applications. After accessing

Diane Pozefsky of IBM made me go through rigorous work to make this chapter informative and accurate. Many thanks go to her for her patience. Additionally, I am greatful to Atul Kapoor of Kaptronix, Inc. of Haworth, N.J. for his vast contributions.

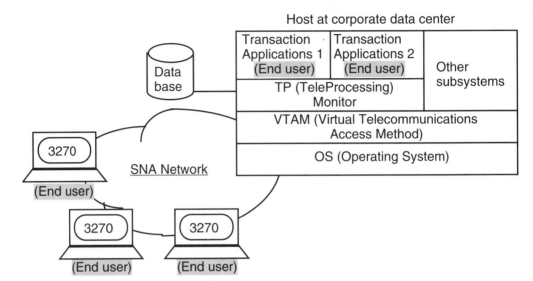

Figure 12.1 A high level view of the SNA Network, with the end users of the network highlighted.

the database these applications send responses back to the agents, stating whether the requests were satisfied or not. The applications which interact with the agents, as well as the agents themselves, are users of the SNA network and are hence called end users.

Although this scenerio of how SNA was originally implemented is quite trivial, today SNA has evolved into a more mature networking architecture. It can support sophisticated services such as file transfers, distributed processing, distributed databases, electronic mail, and so forth.

12.1.2 Teleprocessing at the Host

Now let us briefly describe the major software components of the host, which are needed to process these transaction applications from remote sites. As shown in Figure 12.1, they are called the operating system, VTAM (Virtual Telecommunications Access Method), and TP (TeleProcessing) monitor.

The host itself is managed and controlled by the operating system. It schedules all jobs and manages all resources. MVS (Multiple Virtual Systems) is an example of a popular operating system that is used on IBM mainframes. Unlike AT&T's UNIX, MVS was not designed to handle communications over a network. This was partly due to its complexity and size. Hence, MVS needs VTAM to perform communications related tasks. VTAM then interfaces with a TP monitor under whose control the transactions are processed. Now each type of TP monitor doesn't have to deal with communications procedures, because they are provided in this module—VTAM.

Two common types of TP monitors are CICS (Customer Information Control System) and IMS/TM (Information Management System/Transaction Manager), which was formerly called IMS/DC. If the applications ran under the supervision of the operating system directly instead of the TP monitor, then each application would require a single memory partition or region of address. This would load down the operating system. However, a TP monitor relieves the operating system of much of the burden by managing all transactions in one partition. This makes the host run efficiently and also streamlines the development of software applications.

Just as the operating system controls the operation of the entire host and its resources, the TP monitor controls the transaction applications which process the transactions. The TP monitor does this by running several applications in one memory partition so that the operating system thinks it is running one job. Yet in fact, the TP monitor is actually running many processes simultaneously. From the applications' perspective, they think the TP monitor is the operating system and from VTAM's or operating system's perspective, it thinks that the TP monitor is the application so VTAM must first connect itself to the remote user and then the user may establish a connection with the TP monitor of its choice.

TP monitors are examples of subsystems; other examples of subsystems include TSO (Time Sharing Option) and JES (Job Entry Subsystem). TSO and JES are subsystems which don't run under TP monitors, but must run under telecommunications access methods, such as VTAM.

Currently, the term "TP monitor" is also being used for Unix-based OLTP (On-Line Transaction Processing) systems. These TP monitors are integrated with client/server systems which originally provided relational databases for a small number of client workstations. In contrast with the traditional TP monitors, such as CICS, these systems provide a better price to performance ratio and a GUI (Graphical User Interface). Comparing against client/server-based database systems, TP monitors support a large number of concurrent transactions, access to traditional data, and better security.

12.2 SNA HARDWARE

So far we've been primarily discussing the host, and have said very little about the SNA network cloud which connects the terminals to the host. Traditionally, SNA has had just that orientation, a hierarchical network where devices are controlled by other devices which in turn are ultimately subject to the host.

Today SNA is becoming what is called a "flat" network, where terminals are becoming less dependent on the host. This new rapidly changing architecture is called APPN (Advanced Peer to Peer Networking). Nonetheless, we'll present SNA here as a hierarchical network and discuss these current trends towards the end of the chapter. Let us now "open up" the SNA cloud of Figure 12.1 and look at the many hardware components as shown in Figure 12.2, which are typically used with SNA.

12.2.1 The Host and Its I/O Channel

At the top-left corner of the figure, a mainframe, or a host in SNA terms, is shown. In a purely distributed environment, any intelligent workstation is also called a host. The family of hosts based on system 370 are the 30xx, 43xx, and the 93xx series. The letter "x" is used in product nomenclature to indicate there are other related models with numbers substituted in place of the "x"s. So for example, the 30xx designation encompasses models 3090, 3080, and the 3030.

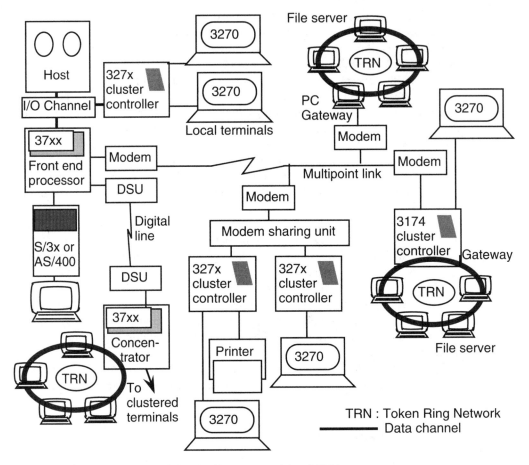

Figure 12.2 A hardware overview of SNA components.

Connected to the host there is a processor responsible for all input and output operations of the host. It is called the I/O (Input/Output) channel and it exchanges information between the host and other devices connected to it locally, such as disk and tape drives, cluster controllers, communications controllers, etc.

12.2.2 The FEP

The communications controller can either be used as an FEP (Front End Processor) connected to a host or as a concentrator remotely located from a host. We will simply refer to it as an FEP. All network transmission lines are connected to the FEP, which is a communications processor to assist the host. For example, it does error detection and recovery, assembly and disassembling of packets, buffering of data from low speed lines to the high speed data channel for the host, etc. SNA's designation for it are 3705, 3720, 3725, and 3745.

If many transmission lines exist from one geographical area to the FEP, then the cost of these lines could become prohibitive. In such a case, a communications controller could be located in the area where these lines originate. This communications controller would then collect the data from these points and send it over just one high speed link. Here the communications controller would be called a concentrator. Figure 12.2 shows one using a digital link.

12.2.3 The Cluster Controller

Attached to the FEP, traditionally, has been the cluster controller. It comes in models 3174, 3274, and 3276. In Figure 12.2, three of them are shown to be sharing a multipoint link and one is shown to be channel attached. Typically, it communicates with the FEP using the SDLC (Synchronous Data Link Control) protocol and with the terminals using BSC (Binary Synchronous Communication). SDLC is defined by SNA, but BSC predates it. The FEP polls the cluster controller and the cluster controller polls its terminals.

The 327x terminals, usually connected to the cluster controller, are called dumb devices. This is because they are unable to do any local processing. It is the most widely used synchronous terminal and it operates on the BSC protocol using a coax cable. However, PCs networked in LANs are quickly replacing these 3270 family of products.

The 3172 deserves an extra word here. Introduced in 1989 to connect various kinds of LANs to SNA, it has become a low-cost box for all purposes. It supports not only SNA protocol, but also TCP/IP (Transmission Control Protocol/Internet Protocol), APPN (Advanced Peer to Peer Networking), and OSI protocol stacks. It reduces the number of instruction cycles required by the host by off-loading the TCP/IP stack. It can not only attach LANs but also interconnect hosts and their peripherals using channel-to-channel connections with T1s. It can also perform many of the 3745 FEP routing functions.

12.2.4 Connecting LANs

Practically any kind of LAN can be used in SNA, though we've only shown TRNs (Token Ring Networks) in the figure. An intermediate router, sometimes called a gateway, is used to connect a LAN to the SNA network. Typically, in a LAN, the file server, and the gateway would be two different stations, so that the workload would be distributed between them.

The word "gateway" has many meanings. In OSI terminology, a gateway can be the most sophisticated kind of device, performing protocol translations for all seven layers. On the other hand, IP (Internet Protocol) routers are also called gateways. Here protocol conversion is only done for the lower three layers of the OSI model. They are called gateways because the network addresses are different on both sides. Finally, the same term used in much SNA marketing literature refers to a device which does protocol conversion for only the lower two layers. In this chapter, we'll refer to gateway as meaning an SNA gateway.

The functions of a gateway in an SNA network can be provided by a PC, 3745, 3174 cluster controller, and a few other devices. Figure 12.2 shows three of these methods. A gateway is connected to the SNA network with an SDLC interface and to the LAN with a NIC (LAN Network Interface Card) or a TIC (TRN Interface Card).

The gateway, upon receiving an SDLC frame from the SNA network, strips off the SDLC header and the trailer, then appends the MAC (Media Access Control) header, the LLC (Logical Link Control) header, and the MAC trailer to the data portion of the frame, before sending the frame to its proper destination on the LAN. When stations on the LANs send data to the host, this process is then reversed. In other words, only the headers and trailers of the second layer are replaced, while the headers and data from the upper layers are kept intact.

The PCs on the LAN would be emulating the 3270 terminal so that the host thinks it is talking to 3270 terminals. Also, the FEP would be normally polling the 3174 or the PC gateway on behalf of the stations on the ring. (This is called group polling.) Otherwise, the FEP would have to poll each individual station on the rings.

12.2.5 The AS/400 and Local and Remote Devices

The AS/400 (Application System/400) is a minicomputer which is also called a midrange computer or a distributed processor. Running the OS/400 operating system, it provides intense multiuser processing for business environments. Predecessors to the AS/400 were Systems 36 and 38.

Lastly, any device that is attached to the I/O channel is considered a local device, whereas devices connected to an FEP are called remote devices. For instance, in Figure 12.2, even if the AS/400 were physically close to the FEP, it would be thought of as being remote, since it is connected to the FEP.

12.3 NAUs AND SESSIONS

12.3.1 NAU Defined

Back in Figure 12.1, an end user was said to be an application or the person using the program via a terminal. Either of these end users create and transmit data using RUs (Request/response Units). In order to deliver the RUs to their proper destinations, SNA defines NAUs (Network Addressable Units). NAUs are logical communication ports to the SNA network through which end users and SNA devices can gain access to the network. Terminals, cluster controllers, applications, VTAM, and TP monitors are all examples of NAUs. Any device or application that must transmit and receive data in the network must have an NAU. LU (Logical Unit), PU (Physical Unit), and SSCP (System Services Control Point) are the three types of NAUs.

12.3.2 LUs

LU is an NAU type that is required by the end users to gain access to the network. Figure 12.3 shows where LUs may be found in an SNA network, and their types. The LU itself is defined in the software supporting the particular device. This software provides a wide range of functions and intelligence which are categorized as LU types.

LU type 0 supports pre-SNA protocols such as the BSC 3270 terminal. LU type 1 is used for terminals using batch transfers of data while LU type 3 is used for printers.

LU type 2 is used by an application program communicating with an interactive device such as the 3270 using the SNA data stream. Initially, the LU function for the 3270 was actually located in the software running at the cluster controller. However, on a PC, this software may be in the PC itself.

LU type 6.2 is a general-purpose program-to-program LU which enables two terminals to communicate with each other using minimum resources from the host. This is a deviation from the traditional hierarchical networking concept. Another name for it is APPC (Advanced Program to Program Communication) and is covered later on. The CICS TP monitor can act as any of these LU types simultaneously depending on which LU type it is communicating with. Therefore, an LU type is an NAU that is determined by the capabilities of both partners of a session.

12.3.3 PUs

A PU is not a physical device but rather a set of functions and routines that are provided in the device's software which require network access. It is a resource manager for SNA devices providing configuration services, requesting software downloads, generating diagnostic information, and the sort. PUs manage and control LUs which are connected to them.

As with LUs, PUs are also divided into categories called PU types. PU types are also called SNA node types. Currently, the important node types are 2, 2.1, 4 and 5. These are illustrated in Figure 12.4. PU type 5 is implemented in VTAM, while type 4 is implemented in NCP (Network Control Program) running in the FEP. PU type 2 is associated with cluster controllers and PU type 2.1 is needed to support APPN and is the most advanced type of all PUs. It can communicate directly with peer or adjacent PU2.1s without requiring the facilities of the host.

In Figure 12.4, the functions of a PU are shown to be provided either in the gateway or in the PCs of the TRN. If the PU functions are provided in the PCs then the gateway only has to do MAC/LLC to SDLC conversions. However, then the host has to maintain tables and manage sessions with the individual PCs.

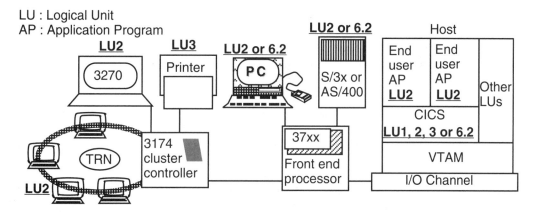

Figure 12.3 Examples of where various types of LUs may be found.

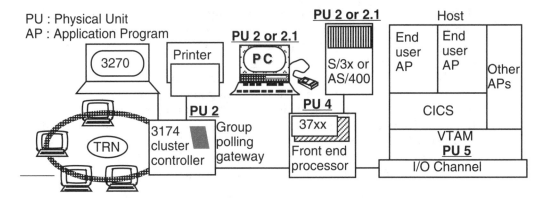

Figure 12.4 Examples of where various types of PUs may be found.

On the contrary, placing a single PU definition in the gateway and providing only the LU definitions in the workstations can lighten the load on the host processor and also reduce the memory requirements for the workstations.

12.3.4 SSCP, Domains, and Addressing

Just as a PU controls and manages all LUs attached to it, the SSCP controls and manages all PUs and LUs logically attached to it, except in APPN. SSCP is a subset of VTAM and hence exists only in the host. It is responsible for initializing the network and deactivating it. All devices that are under such control of the SSCP are said to be in its domain. The PUs assist the SSCP to manage the resources of the network. For example, the SSCP or VTAM must activate the PUs in the NCP and the cluster controller before it can activate the LUs for the end user at the terminal.

Figure 12.5 shows a multidomain network. This is a network with more than one domain. A domain consists of one type 5 node (host) and its associated network, including the type 4 nodes (FEPs). Each domain is further divided into subareas, where a subarea consists of one type 4 or type 5 node and its associated network. The host and the FEP themselves are called subarea nodes. Any SNA node that is not a subarea node is called a peripheral node.

In a multidomain network, all subareas are assigned unique identifiers called subarea numbers. Figure 12.5 shows four subareas. Furthermore, within each subarea, every NAU is assigned an element number. So to identify an NAU, one must provide the subarea number as well as the element number. Peripheral nodes do not use these subarea-element number pairs in addressing the devices connected to them. Instead they use local forms of addressing which are called local addresses and link station addresses. For the sake of simplicity, we'll abbreviate them as LOA and LSA, respectively.

These LSA and LOA pairs are unique within each subarea. For instance, in Figure 12.5 an LSA of 4 and LOA of 4 addresses the 3270 terminal in subarea 3. The LSA identifies the controller and the LOA identifies the terminal. This LSA and LOA pair may not be assigned to any other device in this subarea, although it may appear in other subareas.

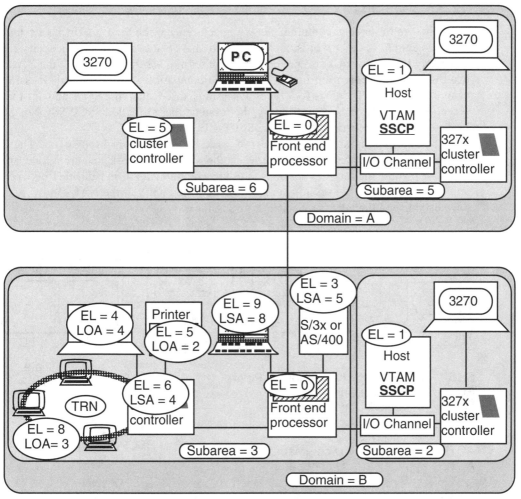

LSA : Link Station Address   EL   : ELement address
LOA : LOcal Address   SSCP : System Services Control Point

Figure 12.5 Traffic within a subarea uses LOA-LSA form of addressing and between subareas uses the subarea-element form of addressing.

Now, when the application in the host sends a message to the 3270, it knows and uses only the subarea and element address pair. This address pair is then translated into the local identifiers by the NCP, residing in the FEP, before being sent to its destination.

Consequently, the FEP is also called a boundary function node, since it does this type of address conversion. A host may also serve as a boundary function node for the peripherals attached to it via the I/O channel. In conclusion, the subarea-element pair is used to address devices residing in subareas, while the local addressing form is used by the subarea node to address the peripheral nodes from the boundary function out.

12.3.5 Sessions

Two end users can communicate with each other when their NAUs have established a session. In other words, an SNA session between two NAUs is necessary for an orderly flow of traffic between them. When a session is being initialized, the NAUs determine if protocols used between them are compatible. If not, then the session cannot be initiated. There are four types of sessions, three involving SSCP and one that is set up between two LUs. Specifically, the session types are called SSCP-SSCP (used in a multidomain network), SSCP-PU, SSCP-LU, and LU-LU.

SSCP sessions are typically set up when the network is brought up. These sessions provide network control between the various network resources that are available, while the LU-LU sessions provide communication capabilities between applications. An LU-LU session cannot be established until all the NAUs in the path have established the necessary SSCP type sessions.

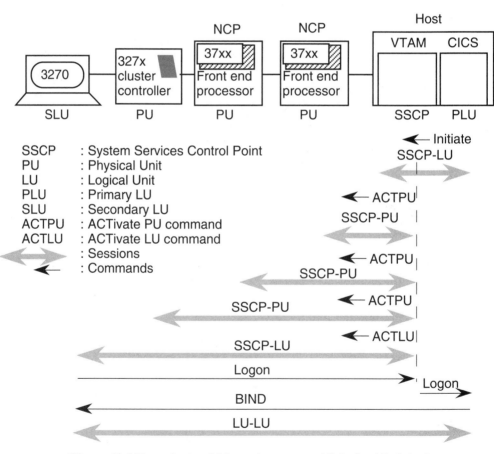

Figure 12.6 The order in which sessions are established, while bringing up a network.

Figure 12.6 illustrates the steps involved in setting up sessions in a single-domain network, in order that a network terminal may access CICS. Here the host LU is called the PLU (Primary LU) while the network LU is called the SLU (Secondary LU). PLUs may participate in many LU-LU sessions, but SLUs may only participate in one. This basically applies for dependent LUs but not for the independent LU 6.2. CICS first initiates a session with VTAM to establish a SSCP-LU session, making itself available for other LUs to log on to itself. Then, VTAM (or SSCP) initiates sessions with all the PUs in the order that they are physically connected to the LU. This is done by issuing ACTPU commands: first to the first FEP, then to the next, then to the cluster controller. Lastly, it initiates a session with the LU associated with the 3270 terminal.

So now the user logs onto CICS, the host LU. SSCP sends the log on message to the host LU, providing a profile of the SLU. Using this information, the host LU can determine whether or not it can support a session with that network LU. If it can, it will issue a BIND command and the LU-LU session will be established. This process of establishing an LU-LU session is called binding.

12.4 SNA ARCHITECTURE

12.4.1 SNA Layers

Figure 12.7 shows the seven layers of SNA. Layer 1 or the physical layer may be implemented by a modem or a DSU using the RS-232 protocol as usual. The second layer is typically implemented by the SDLC (Synchronous Data Link Control) protocol. Both of these layers parallel the functions of the first two layers of the OSI reference model. SDLC is part of the SNA definition, but RS-232 is not.

As OSI's network layer (X.25) performs routing and congestion control over the transport network, so does the path control layer in SNA. However, unlike X.25, SNA doesn't have permanent and switched virtual circuits. The path control layer also provides segmentation, which divides large messages into smaller segments.

A connection-oriented service sends all message units along one physical path for a session, and this path is determined before traffic is transmitted. SNA provides such a connection-oriented service. The transmission control layer checks for session sequence numbers, pacing, and encryption. Pacing prevents one NAU from sending data at a rate that is faster than what the receiving one can accept. This feature is called data flow control and, interestingly, it is provided by other layers but not the data flow control layer.

The data flow control layer, layer number 5, provides chaining, session responses, assignment of session sequence numbers, etc. Layer 6 is called the NAU services layer and its functions approximately correspond to OSI's presentation control layer. The NAU services layer includes the transaction and presentation services sublayers. The presentation services provide programming interfacing and data formatting and transaction services and are covered in Section 12.8.3. The last layer, the applications or transaction services layer is the user at the terminal or the application running at the host.

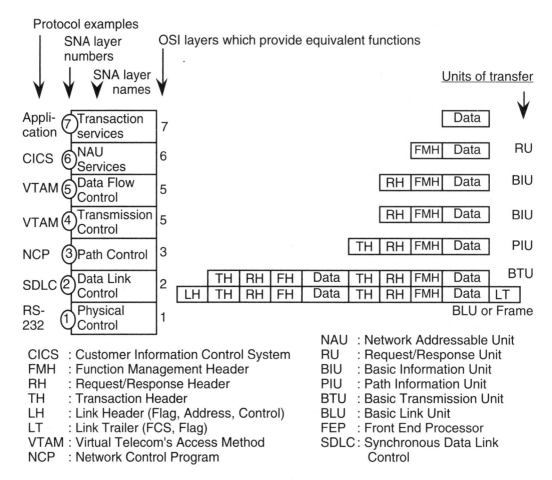

Figure 12.7 SNA Architecture. Typically, a host supports all layers, whereas an FEP supports layers 1 through 3.

12.4.2 SNA Units of Exchange

As data is sent by the application layer, the 6th layer adds a FMH (Function Management Header), which then together are called an RU (Request/response Unit). An RU could be a request RU, a response RU, or a control RU, which is also a request and is used for network management. The fifth layer adds an RH (Request/response Header) to the RU which then becomes a BIU (Basic Information Unit).

The path control layer adds a TH (Transmission Header) which specifies the routing information and whether the BIU associated with it is a complete message or one of several segments which make up a larger message. Depending on how much data the second layer is able to buffer, it may then combine multiple PIUs into a BTU (Basic Transmission Unit) for the SDLC protocol to process. SDLC processes frames or BLUs (Basic Link Units). Let us next look at the second, third, and upper layer protocols in more detail.

SNA

12.4.3 LU Profiles

The presentation services (part of NAU services), data flow control, and transmission control layers each support a range of possible protocols. For each of these three layers, SNA selects sets of protocols and categorizes them into profiles so that a specific PS (Presentation Services) profile represents a given set of protocols supported by the PS layer. Depending on what set of functions is needed, the appropriate profile number is selected when setting up a session. Similarly, the sets of protocols supported by the data flow control and transmission control layers are called FM (Function Management) and TS (Transmission Services) profiles, respectively.

These profile numbers are then used to identify LUs and their capabilities so that each LU is defined in terms of the profile number for each of these three layers. For example, LU type 2 uses a PS profile of 2, a FM profile of 3, and a TS profile of 3; LU type 6.2 uses a PS profile of 6.2, a FM profile of 7, and a TS profile of 19.

12.5 SDLC

SNA supports a number of data link control protocols, out of which we'll discuss one, SDLC. SDLC is used to build upon topics in Chapters 13 through 16.

Figure 12.8 shows the format of 3 types of BLUs used in SDLC. They are called information, supervisory, and unnumbered frames. This figure should be continuously referenced while studying this section. Unlike BSC (Binary Synchronous Communication), SDLC is a bit oriented and a full-duplex protocol. Hence, SDLC makes a more efficient use of the transmission facilities than BSC. Additionally, it can combine data, acknowledgments, and poll all in one frame.

12.5.1 The Flag and the Address Fields

An SDLC frame always begins and ends with a flag with a fixed bit pattern of "01111110." The same flag can be used to end the previous frame as well as begin a new one. So that this pattern may not appear anywhere else in the frame, a technique called "bit stuffing" is used. This requires that the sending station transmit an extra 0 after every 5 consecutive 1s and that the receiver remove one 0 after every 5 consecutive 1s. If the receiver doesn't detect a zero after 5 consecutive 1s, but a zero after 6 consecutive 1s, then it assumes that it is the terminating flag. See the graphical explanation given in Figure 12.9 on page 227.

After the flag, the next field is an 8-bit address providing the LSA (Link Station Address) or typically the cluster controller ID. This is an example of an individual address. An example of a group address is when a 3174, being used as a gateway, polls all PCs on a TRN. The FCS is a 16-bit CRC character that is used for error detection on the preceding fields.

12.5.2 The Control Field

The control field has a number of purposes. If its last bit is zero, it identifies the frame as carrying information. The information field encapsulates information that is passed down from the upper frames. The other two types of frames don't carry information from the upper layers. The length of this field is a multiple of 8 bits, except for the stuffed bits.

The Ns is a 3-bit field, and it identifies the frame number of the frame being transmitted. This is also called a frame sequence number. With 3 bits allocated for Ns, frame numbers can range from 0 (binary 000) to 7 (binary 111) or it can have 8 possible values. The Nr specifies the next frame number that the transmitter is expecting from the distant end. If station A transmits a frame with its Ns equal to 2, then when station B transmits its frame, it will set its Nr to 3, indicating that 3 is the next frame it is expecting from A.

Because there are only 3 bits allocated for Ns and Nr, the maximum number of frames that can be transmitted without requiring a response from the receiving end is 7. This figure is called the window size. Imagine, if a transmitter did send 8 frames in a row from Ns = 0 to Ns = 7 and then waited for an acknowledgment from the opposite end. Now if the opposite end responds with an Nr of 0, then the transmitter wouldn't know whether it is asking to retransmit the first frame number 0 or if it is acknowledging the seventh frame and is requesting the transmission of a new frame numbered 0. To avoid this ambiguity, the window size is kept to 7 for SDLC frames. SDLC also has facilities to provide window sizes of 127, where the Ns and Nr fields are extended.

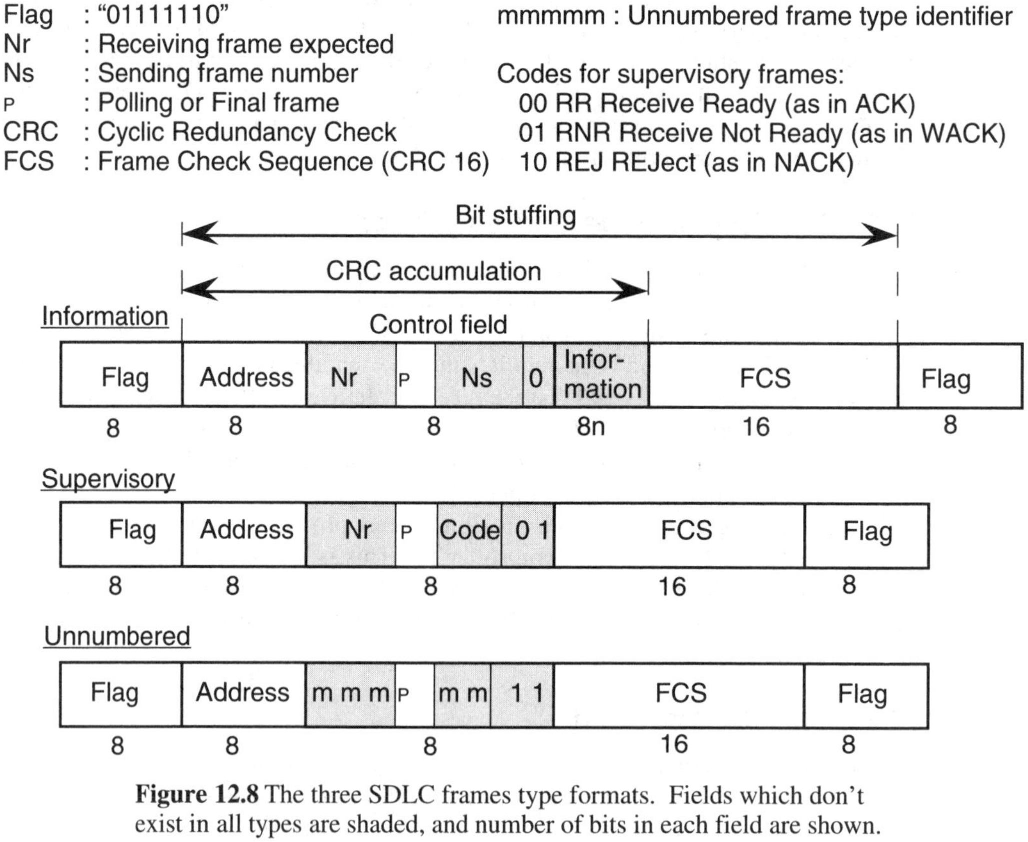
Flag : "01111110"
Nr : Receiving frame expected
Ns : Sending frame number
P : Polling or Final frame
CRC : Cyclic Redundancy Check
FCS : Frame Check Sequence (CRC 16)
mmmmm : Unnumbered frame type identifier
Codes for supervisory frames:
00 RR Receive Ready (as in ACK)
01 RNR Receive Not Ready (as in WACK)
10 REJ REJect (as in NACK)
Bit stuffing
CRC accumulation
Information
Control field
Flag
Address
Nr
P
Ns
0
Infor-
mation
FCS
Flag
8
8
8
8n
16
8
Supervisory
Flag
Address
Nr
P
Code
0 1
FCS
Flag
8
8
8
16
8
Unnumbered
Flag
Address
m m m
P
m m
1 1
FCS
Flag
8
8
8
16
8

Figure 12.8 The three SDLC frames type formats. Fields which don't exist in all types are shaded, and number of bits in each field are shown.

Data to be transmitted.

. . . 0 1 1 1 1 1 0 0 1 1 1 1 1 1 1 1 0 0 1 1 1 0 . . .

Data actually transmitted after stuffing a zero after every 5 consecutive 1s.

. . . 0 1 1 1 1 1 0 0 0 1 1 1 1 1 0 1 1 0 0 1 1 1 0 . . .

Data received is the same.

. . . 0 1 1 1 1 1 0 0 0 1 1 1 1 1 0 1 1 0 0 1 1 1 0 . . .

Data interpreted after removing one zero after every 5 consecutive 1s.

. . . 0 1 1 1 1 1 0 0 1 1 1 1 1 1 1 1 0 0 1 1 1 0 . . .

Figure 12.9 Bit stuffing prevents the flag (01111110) from appearing anywhere inside a frame.

The poll/final bit may be used over master-slave connections. In these types of connections, the primary device controls a secondary one. For example, an FEP acts as the primary device to a cluster controller and a cluster controller acts as the primary device to an end terminal. The poll/final bit is used as a poll bit for frames originating at the primary and is used as a final bit for frames originating at a secondary. That is, it is set to 1 by the primary if it is polling a secondary; otherwise it is set to 0. For frames originating at a secondary, this bit is set to 0 if it is not the last frame in a sequence of frames; otherwise it is set to 1.

Figure 12.10 summarizes the purposes of the control and address fields by showing an exchange of two frames sent by the FEP and one frame as it is sent by the controller. First the controller sends its frame number 0 then its frame number 1. This is shown in the Ns field. The first frame has the P/F field set to 0, since it is not the last frame, and the second frame has this field set to 1, signaling the controller that this is a poll. Then the controller sends its frame number 0 and acknowledges the FEP's frame number 1 by setting its Nr to 2.

Now let us turn our attention to the other two types of frames as shown in Figure 12.8. In the control field, if its last bit is a 1, then no information is being sent. In other words, it is either a supervisory or an unnumbered frame. The control field of the supervisory frame ends with a "01" and the control field of the unnumbered frame ends with a "11."

In BSC terminology, supervisory frames are used to send ACKs, NACKs and WACKs. The supervisory code for an acknowledgment is RR (Receive Ready), for a negative acknowledgment it is REJ (REJect), and for a wait with an acknowledgment it is RNR (Receive Not Ready). An RNR indicates to the sending station to temporarily stop the transmission maybe because the receiver's buffer is full.

Finally, SDLC has 14 types of unnumbered frames which are used for initializing a connection, removing a connection, and other functions. These type of frames also appear in X.25 and ISDN, and their discussion will be left for Chapters 13 and 15.

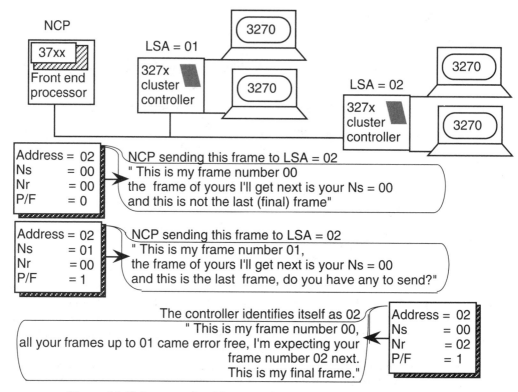

Figure 12.10 An example of frame exchanges on a multipoint line.

12.5.3 An Example of an SDLC Transmission Exchange

Figure 12.11 shows an FEP (Front End Processor) being connected to two cluster controllers via modems and a CO, which is providing a multipoint link. Here, the FEP and the cluster controller serve as examples of primary and secondary stations, respectively. There is a protocol analyzer inserted between the FEP and its modem to monitor the traffic on the link. The left side of the display shows the frames sent by the FEP and the right side shows the frames as they are sent by the cluster controllers. The address field specifies to which cluster controller frames are being sent or from which one they are being received.

To begin with, the FEP sends a supervisory frame to the cluster controller C2 with a code of RR, because the FEP has no errors unresolved. The P/F bit is 1, and since it is the FEP setting it, this bit indicates that C2 is being polled. Supervisory frames have no Ns field, but do have an Nr field. The 0 bit for Nr indicates to C2 that the FEP is expecting its frame number 0 next. The good CRC indicates that the frame has no errors at this point.

In the figure, C2 sends the next frame, since it has just been polled. It has an option to send information frames, but apparently, it doesn't have any information, so it also sends an RR type of supervisory frame. It is expecting frame number 1 from the FEP next; hence the Nr is 1. Also, there are no more frames that will follow this one, so the P/F is 1, and the frame is good coming through the analyzer.

Next, the FEP polls the C3. It is expecting frame number 5 from C3 next. Unlike C2, C3 does have data to send, so it sends information frames starting at frame number (or Ns of) 5. It sends four frames, and since the Ns field is only 3 bits long, the Ns rolls back to zero after frame number 7. All frames have been received without error, and all of their P/F bits are set to 0 except for the final one. When the cluster controller sets the P/F bit, it takes on the meaning of whether or not it is the final frame. Polling is only done by the primary (the FEP in this case).

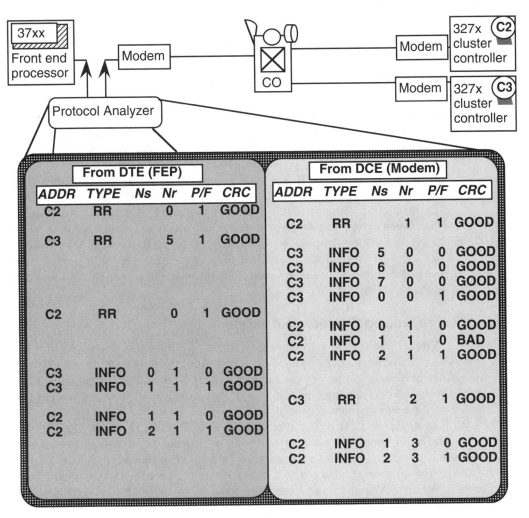

Figure 12.11 A snap-shot of SDLC frame exchange between an FEP and its two cluster controllers, as seen on the screen of a protocol analyzer.

After this, the FEP polls C2 again to see if it now has any data to send. This time C2 does have data. It sends frame numbers 0, 1, and 2. Notice that frame number 1 has an error, but before the FEP notifies C2 about this error, it first sends information to C3 and polls it. Notice that the FEP has acknowledged C3's four frames (5, 6, 7, and 0) by sending an Nr of 1, since C3's frame number 1 is what the FEP is expecting next.

C3 has no information, so it sends an RR frame; however, it acknowledges the FEP's frames 0 and 1 by setting the Nr to 2.

Now, the FEP gets back to C2. It signals that it received frame number 1 with an error, by setting the Nr to 1. While the FEP notifies C2 about this error, it sends two information frames. Then C2 retransmits all the frames starting with the problem frame, which was frame number 1, and at the same time it acknowledges the FEP's frames 1 and 2 by setting the Nr to 3. The exchange then continues.

12.6 THE PATH CONTROL LAYER

Moving up the SNA architecture stack from the data link control layer, we come up to the path control layer. It routes traffic between the various nodes within the SNA network. These nodes include the peripheral nodes as well as the subarea nodes. Based on the path of a session, subarea nodes are further categorized into boundary function nodes and intermediate nodes. A boundary function node is the subarea node which is closest to the end node of a session that is in progress, whereas intermediate nodes are the subarea nodes that lie in the path of a boundary function node and the host. For example, in Figure 12.12, if CICS is in session with LUa via SA7 (Sub-Area node 7), then SA6 is the boundary function node while SA4 and SA7 are the intermediate nodes.

In this section, let us at first consider the terms and the issues dealing with the routing between subareas and then do the same by extending the discussion to include the routing within the subareas. Typically, FID 4 (Format ID 4) is the TH (Transmission Header) used between subarea nodes and carry subarea-element forms of addressing, and FID 2 is the TH used between a subarea node and its peripherals. FID 2 TH carries the local form of addressing.

12.6.1 Routing Between Subareas

Virtual Routes: A TG (Transmission Group) is a collection of parallel links between two subarea nodes. For added reliability or to provide different classes of service, multiple TGs can be placed between them. Various TGs are shown in Figure 12.12. As PIUs (Path Information Units) travel over TGs, they are assigned TG sequence numbers, which appear in the TH field.

As a PIU travels from one subarea node to another, its TH carries the address of the destination subarea or boundary function node which helps the intermediate node properly route the PIU. So for instance, in the figure, SA3 knows that all PIUs going to SA6 should be directed to go to SA4 and it doesn't know where SA4 will direct those PIUs. All that SA3 cares about is that the next node is SA4. In SNA, this complete end-to-end path determined by each SA (Subarea Node) forwarding the PIU to the next SA node is called a virtual route. This differs from X.25's virtual circuit, as we'll see in Chapter 13.

In Figure 12.12 notice that there are three virtual routes available for traffic between CICS and LUa. These are VR1: SA3-SA4-SA6; VR2: SA3-SA4-(over TG1)-SA7-SA6; and VR3: SA3-SA4-(over TG2)-SA7-SA6. These virtual route paths are then defined in the routing tables of all pertinent SA nodes. Also, the entire virtual routes are not defined in any one of the SA nodes, but each SA node only has the forwarding address for the virtual routes which pass through it.

During session setup, one virtual route will be defined as the primary route and the others as alternate routes. All traffic in both directions for the session will follow the selected virtual route. If the virtual route in use fails during a session, then the session fails and while the session is being reestablished, another virtual route will be selected.

Virtual routes are two-way routes and they are comprised of two one-way routes called explicit routes. In other words, a virtual route is defined in terms of an outbound explicit route and an inbound explicit route. These routes are defined in what are called path tables, which reside in VTAM and NCP.

Class of Service: To provide prioritization of traffic, SNA nodes also contain COS (Class Of Service) tables. These tables specify the priority of traffic originating or terminating at nodes in the network. So in Figure 12.12, if LUa is to be given a higher priority than LUb, then the primary route for LUa could be VR1 (Virtual Route 1) and the alternate routes could be VR2 and VR3. Likewise, the primary route for LUb could be VR2 and the alternate routes could be VR1 and VR3.

Now if VR1 failed, perhaps due to a break in TG1 between SA6 and SA4, then the traffic for LUa would be routed over VR2, or if necessary over VR3. But in either case, it would have a higher priority than the traffic for LUb. This type of "bumping" of traffic, or who can bump whom, is spelled out in the COS tables. Each COS is given a COS name, which is selected during log-on procedures.

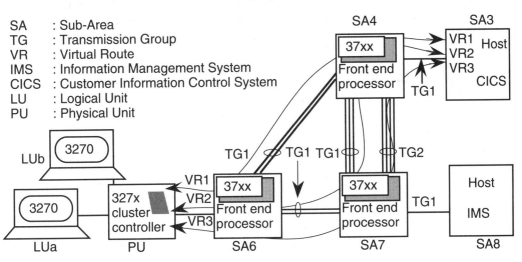

Figure 12.12 The transmission groups between subareas and the three possible virtual routes between SA3 and the PU are shown.

Virtual Route Pacing: When a subarea node cannot temporarily accept more data maybe because its buffer is getting full, it can stop the transmitter from sending more PIUs by not sending pacing responses. When the buffer is getting empty and it can receive more data, it can then send a pacing response. This signals the subarea node to send another group of PIUs.

What has just been described is called path control pacing or virtual route pacing. This technique allows subarea nodes to signal transmitting nodes whether to send more PIUs. The number of PIUs which can be sent by a transmitting node without requiring a response from the receiver is called the window size. This can be increased or decreased depending on the amount of congestion and activity occurring at the receiving node.

Virtual route pacing affects the data flow for the PIUs of all sessions between two adjacent subareas. Likewise, SNA also has what is called session pacing (covered in Section 12.7), which controls the data flow between two end users and only affects the particular session between them. It is necessary to provide both types of pacing. Virtual route pacing is required when all affected sessions are running fine, but the resources to support them are being strained. Session pacing allows the shutting down of a specific session if that application is in trouble.

12.6.2 End-to-End Path Control Routing

So far we've been considering the issues of routing traffic between SAs. Now let us see how traffic is routed from the boundary function nodes to their peripheral nodes, but first let us review SNA address types.

The subarea-element form of addressing is only used between SAs which are provided in the TH of FID4 type of PIU. The peripheral nodes do not use this type of addressing. Instead, they understand LSA (Link Station Address) and LOA (LOcal Address) forms of addressing. The subarea nodes do not use this local form of addressing, but the boundary function nodes provide the conversion between these two forms of addressing.

Consider Figure 12.13. Here IMS is sending a message to LUa. VTAM doesn't know the local address pair (LSA and LOA) of LUa, but it does know its subarea-element pair (SA = 6, EL = 2), which it provides in the FID 4 TH. The data link protocol between the host and the FEP is not shown in the figure.

The NCP at SA7 notices the destination subarea address of the PIU to be 6 and not its own. After searching its tables, it adds an SDLC address of 4, since SA6 is on the other end of this link.

SA6's NCP notices its own address of 6 in the TH and it strips off the SDLC header, trailer, and the FID 4 transmission header. Then it adds a new TH of type FID 2, with an LOA of 2, which corresponds to subarea 6 and element 2. It also adds a new SDLC header and trailer, giving the address (LSA) of 2. Notice that this boundary function node has done an address type conversion and, in so doing, has also done a TH type conversion, although there are other differences, besides the address forms, that are different in the two types of THs.

The controller at LSA of 2 then detects this frame as being its own and using the LOA of 2, given in the TH, directs the information to LUa.

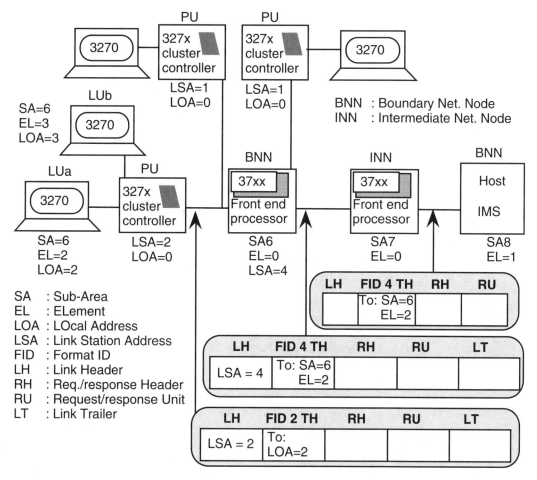

Figure 12.13 The conversion of subarea-element form of addressing to the local forms of addressing as it is done in the transmission header by the front-end.

12.7 CHAINING, PACING, AND SEGMENTING

This section concentrates on the functions which are provided by the upper layers of SNA, namely NAU services, data flow control, and transmission control.

12.7.1 Chaining

In many transaction processing systems, it becomes necessary to identify a number of requests as one unit of work, so as to maintain the integrity of the database (or databases). If all of the requests are successful then the database can be committed, or else, using the saved records of all changes, it can be rolled back to its initial state. The mechanism used to treat such logical data or RUs as one entity is called chaining. The PIUs belonging to a chain are called elements.

When an LU-LU session is first established, the PLU (Primary LU) finds out the buffer size of the SLU (Secondary LU). The PLU determines in what amounts to divide a message or in what sizes to send the PIUs, so that the SLU's buffer may not overflow.

In Figure 12.14, an application has a 4800 byte message to send to the SLU. Since its buffer size is only 1600 bytes, during session activation, the PLU or CICS has agreed to send elements that are not greater than 1600 bytes. This will allow the SLU to receive the message in three parts, each of which can fit in its buffer. (The figure also shows how each element may be divided into four segments to accommodate the cluster controller's buffer size, but we'll get to that later.) Each of the three elements of the chain is given a sequence number in the TH. It is called the SNF (Segment Number Field) and they are labeled as SNF = 1 through SNF = 3. In the RH, there are two fields which are called BC (Begin Chain) and EC (End Chain) which let the SLU know which elements are the first, last, and the intermediate elements. The BC bit is 1 for the first element, the EC bit is 1 for the last element, and the rest of the bits for all elements are set to 0.

12.7.2 Session Pacing

Sometimes the transmitted PIU size is made smaller than the receiver's buffer size. In such cases, the PLU may send several PIUs consecutively, without requiring a response from the SLU, as long as the SLU has room for that many units in its buffer. After the SLU has completed processing these PIUs, it would then send a response to the PLU to transmit the next set of PIUs. This procedure enables the SLU to control the rate at which the PIUs are sent and is called session pacing, contrary to virtual route pacing described in Section 12.6.1. The number of PIUs that are sent consecutively is called the size of the pacing window. Furthermore, it is important to note that SNA uses a pacing mechanism that permits smooth flow of traffic when no congestion exists between the end points.

Therefore, chaining divides up messages into smaller units, so that these units may fit in the SLU's buffer, while session pacing allows the receiver enough time to process the data that is in its buffer before another load of data is transferred to it.

12.7.3 Segmentation

As the chain is being sent to the SLU, the elements are sent through the boundary function node (or FEP2 in Figure 12.14) to the PU. At the FEP2, the PIUs or the chain elements may have to be divided further, because of the PU's small buffer size. The dividing up of PIUs into smaller PIUs by a boundary function node is called segmentation. However, bits for segmentation are coded in all FID types, so it is possible that segmentation can occur anywhere in the network. With APPN, it may occur between hosts.

In our example, the PU's buffer is only 400 bytes, while the PIUs arriving at FEP2 are 1600 bytes long. So FEP2 has to divide each PIU into 4 segments or a total of 12 segments to send the entire 4800 byte message. In the figure, the first chain element is shown to be segmented into four smaller size PIUs.

The RH, being the same as the chain element's RH, is transmitted only in the first segment and not in the rest of them. However, the TH appears in all of the segments.

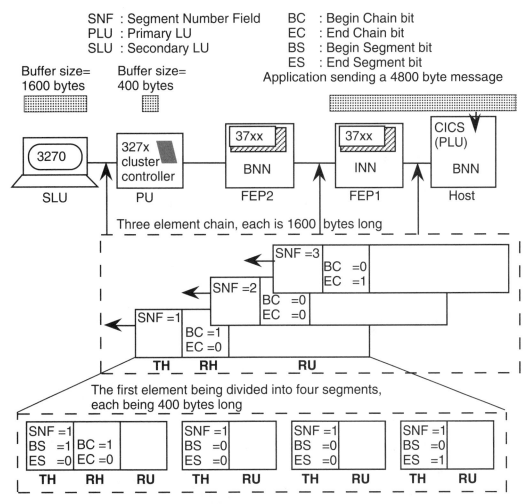

Figure 12.14 A 4800 byte long message having to be divided into a 3-element chain, because the buffer of the SLU is only 1600 bytes. Likewise, FEP2 has to divide each of these PIUs into 4 segments, since the PU's buffer size is only 400 bytes.

Here, the SNF portion is copied in every segment, identifying that these segments all belong to the same chain element. Furthermore, a BS (Begin Segment bit) and ES (End Segment bit) fields of the TH are set, similar to the BC and EC fields of the RH field, identifying the first, last, and the intermediate segments.

12.8 APPC OR LU 6.2

12.8.1 Introduction

Since its inception in 1974, SNA has been a host driven network. All resources and users were totally dependent on the host, and if the host ever failed, the network came to a grinding halt. In 1984, IBM introduced APPC (Advanced Program to Program Communications) which was the beginning of turning SNA into a network that was not totally oriented to a host. In SNA terminology, this means a mainframe. In 1991, APPN (Advanced Peer to Peer Networking) was introduced which didn't require an SNA network to have a host at all. In this section, we will outline APPC and in the next section outline APPN.

To facilitate APPC, a new LU type called LU 6.2 was introduced. These two terms are now interchangeable. Also, about the same time, LEN (Low Entry Networking) was introduced so that two peripheral LUs could communicate with each other and establish a session between them. This was a drastic deviation from the established SNA environment where all LU-LU sessions required a host LU. See Figure 12.15. However, LEN required a creation of a new PU type which is called PU 2.1. Without LEN, each peripheral LU could only maintain one session at a time with a host LU and would have to be the SLU in such a session. With the advent of LEN, network LUs could maintain several sessions at a time and also act as PLUs.

APPC allows for distributed transaction processing in real time. This means that when a request is initiated by a terminal operator with a transaction application running on host, that transaction may initiate another transaction to yet another host. Upon receiving its response, the original host may either satisfy the operator's request, fail the request or perhaps follow through with another transaction before providing the response to the operator. Here the term host is used to mean mainframes, minis, or micros.

Let us revert back to the example of the travel agent that was introduced at the beginning of this chapter. Let us say that the agent's customer has a reservation with Airline-A from Miami to Rio de Janeiro on a particular date. Because of a change of

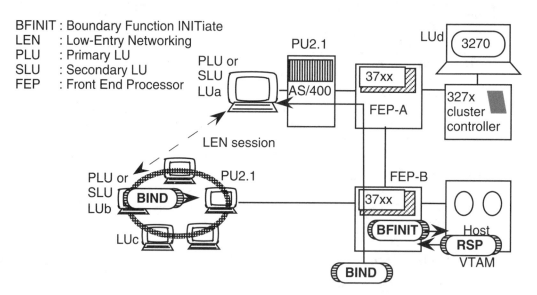

Figure 12.15 The steps taken in setting up an LEN session.

plans, the customer wants to fly to Brasilia and then using a domestic carrier called Airline-B wants to reach Rio de Janeiro. However, the agent cannot determine if the connection is good between these two airlines without interrogating both airlines' databases. Airline-C also flies from Miami to Brasilia and the reservations should be changed to this airline if it provides a better connection. The agent initiates a distributed transaction which interfaces with the data bases of all three airlines, canceling and making reservations as they become necessary.

APPC allows the travel agent to provide these types of real time services to her customers, regardless of the hardware and their vendors, the programs or the operating systems that are running at the various nodes, as long as they are LU 6.2 nodes. In other words, APPC begins to provide an open architecture interface which is becoming less vendor dependent.

12.8.2 LEN

At first, LEN was only provided between directly connected nodes, such as LUb and LUc as shown in Figure 12.15. However, starting with NCP version 5.2 and VTAM version 3.2, the host and FEP began supporting LEN. These new releases of the subarea node software allow LUa and LUb to communicate with each other, even though they are not directly connected. The LEN session between them is shown with a dashed line.

In order to establish a LEN session that crosses subarea boundaries, VTAM has to know or find out where these LUs are located, and provide this information to the NCP that needs it to create a session.

When creating a LEN session, first VTAM must establish SSCP-PU sessions with each of the pertinent FEPs. The type 2.0 boxes need VTAM to set up a LEN session, while the 2.1 boxes don't require the services of VTAM at all.

Using this addressing information, VTAM establishes an SSCP-PU and an SSCP-LU session with the controller and its terminal. However, it only adds the independent LUs' names and addresses to its Resource Definition table, and doesn't establish sessions with the type 2.1 nodes or their associated LUs.

Now, if LUb wants to establish a session with LUa, it sends a BIND request to FEP-B. FEP-B will then send a BFINIT (Boundary Function INITiate) message to VTAM, expecting LUa's network address from it. VTAM responds with this address and then the BIND is forwarded to LUa by FEP-B. This establishes a LEN session between LUa and LUb, and VTAM is then no longer needed even to terminate the session. Notice that VTAM only provided the mapping of addresses.

APPC allows us to have an intelligent entity on both sides of a session. Without it, an LU 2.0, typically a 3270 terminal, could only participate in one session at a time, but LU 6.2 allows participation in multiple sessions simultaneously. When an LU 6.2 has multiple sessions with another remote LU 6.2, these sessions are said to be in parallel.

12.8.3 APPC Architecture

If Figure 12.15 didn't provide LEN, then only connectivity would have existed between LUa and LUb. However by introducing LEN, we were able to communicate between these LUs. APPC takes networking between these nodes a level higher by allowing the transaction application programs at these nodes to communicate using LEN sessions. The communication between two LUs is called an LU-LU session, and the communication between two TPs (Transaction Programs) is called a conversation. Because of this concept of a conversation, the term "program to program communication" is used.

To allocate a conversation, a session is first automatically established, if one is not already available. A conversation must use a session and a session may only support one conversation at a time. A conversation may also be called a thread, and if a TP requires several conversations with other TPs, then the TP is called a multithreading TP.

Figure 12.16 illustrates many APPC concepts. Let us for now notice that there are two sites communicating with each other using all 7 layers of SNA. At the top of the stack, TPs are shown as ATPs (Application TPs) which participate in conversations with each other. Also, to support these conversations, two parallel sessions are made available by the LUs.

The session establishes a path for a conversation between the peer presentation services layers. The NAU services layer (layer 6) is subdivided into two layers called the transaction services and the presentation services layers.

The presentation services provide the interface between the transaction program and LU 6.2. This is called the LU 6.2 API (Application Program Interface). This layer makes sure that the calls which are made by the TP are of the proper format and are converted to the proper data streams.

The transaction services provide management of sessions between LU 6.2s and the services of STP (Service Transaction Program). STPs are similar to TPs; however, they are written as part of the LU 6.2 package to provide it with enhancements. When a service is needed by many TPs, then it is prepackaged as one unit as an added feature to APPC. This allows writing of TPs to be done easily, since the bulk of the coding is implemented in the STPs. The interface between an ATP and an STP is called an STP defined API.

Some examples of STPs are DIA (Document Interchange Architecture), SNADS (SNA Distributed Services), and CNOS (Change Number Of Services). DIA provides a centralized library of documents and the services necessary to manage and distribute them in an office environment. However, it doesn't actually use LU 6.2 protocols. SNADS is a distribution service between DIA sites, and the user doesn't have to log on to SNADS as he/she must log on to DIA services. CNOS allows one to increase or decrease the number of parallel sessions between LUs.

Figure 12.16 also shows that there are two kinds of conversations. If the conversation uses STPs, it is called a basic conversation, whereas if it interfaces directly to an ATP, then it is called a mapped conversation. STPs use basic conversations. Basic conversations are more flexible and powerful because they use harder to program low-level programming calls. Mapped conversations, on the other hand, are easier to use, but are not as efficient. TPs which are commonly used have already been designed and are made available so that they are compatible. Before LU 6.2, application design teams would have to write TPs which could not communicate with TPs written by other design teams. With APPC, much of the work is already done for the programmer. All that he/she needs to know is the names of the remote LU and the remote TP.

Without getting into the details of the data streams between the various interfaces, let us only identify them as depicted in Figure 12.16. At the lowest level for both mapped and basic conversation, the data stream is called the GDS (for Generalized Data Stream). It contains a GDS header and data. Several GDSs can be combined into one RU.

Mapped conversations use what is called data records which are converted into MCR (Mapped Conversation Record) before being transformed into a GDS. TPs with basic conversations use the data stream called logical records.

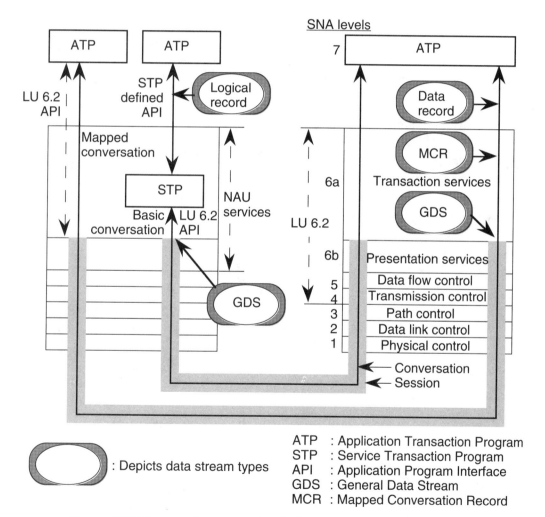

Figure 12.16 Conversation types and their data stream types at key points.

12.8.4 An APPC Conversation Example

Let us now look at an example of how data is transferred over an APPC conversation. In Figure 12.17, the TP at site A has a file which needs to be transferred to the TP at site B. TPa requires a confirmation from TPb after every 8 records.

To initiate a conversation, TPa sends an ALLOCATE verb or a command to its LU, giving the names of the destination LU and the destination TP as parameters for this verb. To do this, the TP must first be in the reset state, after which it enters the send state. To create a conversation, a session must be available between the two LUs. If not, LUa will create a session. Then TPa sends its 8 data records to its LU by sending them with 8 SEND_DATA verbs. Because it wants a confirmation after 8 records, TPa sends a CONFIRM verb to its LU and waits.

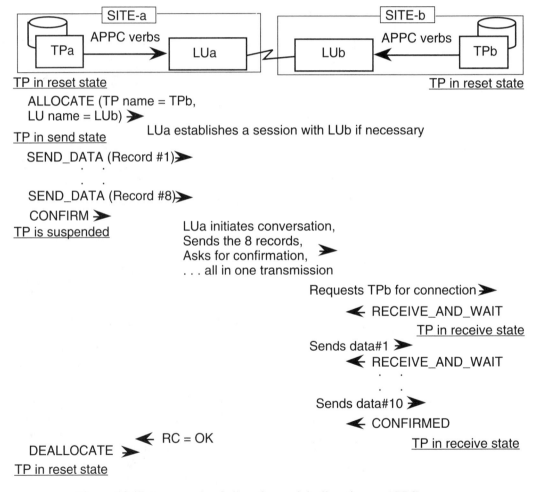

Figure 12.17 An example of allocating and deallocating an APPC conversation with transmission of data.

All this time, no information from TPa is sent to TPb but is buffered by LUa. The RU can be sent automatically when it becomes full or it can be explicitly sent by the user. LUa now flushes its buffer and transfers this information to LUb. LUb then starts up TPb. Upon receiving the conversation allocation request, TPb sends a RECEIVE_AND_WAIT verb to its LU and changes its state from reset to receive.

LUb then deblocks the data in sizes which fit the TPb's buffer. Notice that here the TP's buffer size is smaller than the record size so more units of data (10 in our example) are transferred to TPb than the original number of records (which was 8). After each unit of data, TPb sends a RECEIVE_AND_WAIT and goes into the receive state by sending a CONFIRMED verb.

This CONFIRMED verb is translated into a RC (Return Code) of "OK" by LUa to mean that all the data was received correctly by TPb. At this point, TPa may send another 8 records by sending SEND_DATA verbs until the data is confirmed by the remote TP, or else TPa may terminate the conversation by sending a DEALLOCATE verb to LUa. After this, both TPs will enter the reset state.

Notice in the sending state, a TP may only send data, ask for a confirmation, send error messages, or deallocate a conversation. Likewise, a TP may only receive data when it is in the receive state. Conversations are half-duplex transfers which conform with most business related transactions, which are inherently half-duplex as well.

12.9 APPN

APPN (Advanced Peer to Peer Networking) introduces distributed processing in SNA networks which orients network devices away from a central host completely. This architecture is more compatible with the LAN and router environment that is spawning most businesses today. Hence, APPN is also called the new SNA architecture. It doesn't use architectural concepts such as PUs, SSCPs, or subareas. Old SNA architecture, especially relating to type 4 and 5 nodes, was implemented on specific devices, making SNA to appear as being device dependent. APPN, on the contrary, doesn't bind itself to specific devices per se, but makes itself open to be implemented over any intelligent devices. APPN is the next logical derivation of SNA from APPC. APPC still required VTAM to store and provide routing information between subareas while setting up a session, while APPN allows the absence of VTAM altogether.

APPN may be implemented using only PCs and AS/400s, without using any expensive hosts or front ends. (However, typically users would have an old SNA network which they would want it to migrate to a LAN based transport.) This will give them added reliability, better utilization of links, and less demand for FEP ports. This allows users to expand their networks without replacing their existing equipment. Figure 12.18 outlines such an integration of an old SNA network with APPN.

APPN defines two types of nodes. The EN (End Node) resides at the end points of the network and requires a connection to an NN (Network Node) to gain full access to the network. An NN and all the ENs connected to it is called a domain. The NN acts as a network server for the ENs in its domain.

When an EN requires an address of a remote LU, it can obtain it from the NN dynamically and store it in its own network address directory for future use. There are several types of devices which can act as NNs or ENs or both.

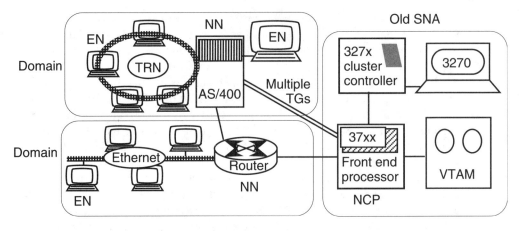

Figure 12.18 An exanple of integrating new SNA with the old.

The figure shows an AS/400 and a router acting as NNs while the PCs are shown as ENs. One physical link between two NNs is called a transmission group, and several transmission groups may exist between them.

Every APPN node contains two kinds of NAUs. LU 6.2 is one type and the other is called a CP (Control Point). A CP roughly replaces the PU and only one CP exists per node. This introduction of a new NAU type brings with it a new session type called the CP-CP session, or simply the CP session. CP sessions are full duplex and require the use of two parallel LU 6.2 sessions, each of which is half-duplex. CP sessions are necessary for nodes to pass addressing and routing information.

An NN maintains two types of directories. One is called the local directory which contains information about the ENs and LUs in its domain and the other is called the distributed directory which contains information about other domains and their respective LUs. An NN can also determine the best route between two nodes in the APPN.

The integration of an old and new SNA is shown in Figure 12.18. Both NNs may act as SNA gateways to VTAM and its resources. An EN may communicate with a host LU using this gateway feature and a 3270 terminal emulation, or else it may communicate with another EN using the NN as a network server. No one can predict how this evolution of multi-vendor SNA into a LAN and router based network will lead into many viable alternatives.

Exercises

1. What is an end user?
   a. only a host application
   b. only a person using a terminal which accesses the SNA
   c. only a terminal
   d. host application and a person using the SNA

2. What is a remotely connected device?
   a. a device which is connected to the I/O channel

b. a device which is connected to an FEP

c. a device which is at least 1 mile from the host

d. a device which is at least 10 miles from the host

3. Which of the following is a communications controller?
   a. an FEP   b. a modem
   c. a DSU   d. a cluster controller

4. What is the logical network address called which is required to access SNA?
   a. LU   b. PU
   c. NAU   d. SSCP

5. What type of session is created when binding occurs?
   a. SSCP-SSCP   b. SSCP-PU
   c. SSCP-LU   d. LU-LU

6. Specific characteristics of LU types are given by what item?
   a. session sequence numbers   b. virtual routes
   c. explicit routes   d. profiles

7. In SDLC, which field determines what type of frame it is?
   a. address   b. information
   c. control   d. code

8. Which of the following is NOT a path control layer function?
   a. segmentation
   b. virtual route pacing
   c. conversion between FID 4 TH and FID 2 TH
   d. class of service

9. Which software component aids the host's operating system, such as MVS, to communicate with remote terminals?

10. What is the nomenclature of the most flexible kind of cluster controller?

11. What is a network called which has more than one host running?

12. What is a collection of parallel links between two subarea nodes called?

13. A virtual route is defined using what two other types of routes?

14. APPC introduced what new type of session?

15. APPN introduced what new type of session?

16. How many conversations are possible between two TPs using one session?

17. Discuss the various methods of using an FEP.

18. What are some basic differences between LUs and PUs?

19. What are some basic similarities between PUs and SSCPs?

20. How is a domain defined both in the old SNA and in the new SNA?

21. What is a virtual route and how is it defined?

22. Discuss the steps in how an LEN session is initiated.

23. Explain the items in Figure 12.16 in your own words.

24. Compare and contrast segmenting versus chaining. Which are based on LU's buffer size? Which are based on PU's buffer size? Which is done by PU? By LU? Which one determines SNF numbers? Pacing window?

Chapter 13

X.25
and Packet Switched Networks

13.1 DEVELOPMENT

13.1.1 Origins

In the early 1960s, Paul Baran of the Rand Corporation had first conceptualized a packet switched network. Afterwards, the DoD (Department of Defense) worked with Rand Corp. to develop this type of network for the transmission of both voice and data. The security of transmission and the fault tolerance of the network were very attractive to the DoD.

The network consisted of many switches or nodes that were connected with each other over a wide area by leased lines. Packet switched networks can be placed in two broad categories, each of which will be introduced here.

13.1.2 The Datagram Concept

DTE, or the Data Terminal Equipment, was the terminal device, such as a remote terminal or a computer. When the DTE sent a message to another DTE connected to the network, it would break up the message into small parts called datagrams. As shown in Figure 13.1, these datagrams would have a header added to the front of it, providing the destination address, source address, datagram number, and other such information. The datagrams would be sent into the network using various links. The nodes, by looking at the header and their own routing tables, could determine which link to forward the datagrams to or else to keep them, depending on the destination addresses.

Security was enhanced in this type of network, because if anyone tapped onto a line, they would only get fragments of the transmission. The network also didn't have a single point of failure, because if one link or node failed or was sabotaged, traffic could be routed using alternate paths. The control for this network was distributed with many nodes, and this was in sharp contrast with the hierarchical networks that were used in the AT&T PSTN (Public Switched Telephone Network) as well as the forthcoming SNA data network of IBM. In the SNA network, if the host failed, the entire network crashed, but the packet networks were less susceptible to failure.

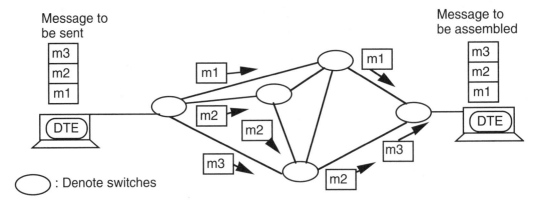

Figure 13.1 The datagram approach to packet switched networking.

In 1967, DoD started ARPANET (Advanced Research Projects Agency NETwork), connecting many universities and government agencies across the country. This was the first test bed for packet switched networks. It used the datagram type of protocol. It was fast and performed as well as it did in theory. The value of such networks was realized, and soon many research projects sprung up to improve on this basic concept.

13.1.3 Packetization Concept

Many protocols were introduced to connect a DTE with a packet switched network. CCITT (Consultative Committee for International Telegraphy and Telephony) standardized this interface in 1974 and called it X.25. CCITT falls under the umbrella of ITU (International Telecommunications Union), which is part of the UN (United Nations). ISO (International Standards Organization) has adopted X.25 to be the protocol used in the first three layers of their OSI (Open System Interconnect) reference model.

X.25 differs from Paul Baran's original concept of datagrams in many ways. Datagrams are still used in the TCP/IP protocol suite, but even ARPANET now runs on X.25. X.25 uses packets instead, which utilize a call connect phase to establish a link with the distant DTE. During the call connect phase, on most X.25 implementations, a path is selected through the nodes and links, and all the data during the data transfer phase travels on this given route. The fixed route is called a virtual circuit which we'll discuss later. Unlike X.25, datagrams formed out of one message use different routes depending on which links are available. Of course, since all packets use one route, it does not provide the best possible security. However, the billing for a connection is more like what customers expect from PSTN, since the path and the duration of the call is known. In this chapter, we will use X.25, packet switched networks, and packet networks interchangeably.

13.2 PURPOSE

Ever since 1880, the PSTN (public switched telephone network) has been developing into a network where any phone can call any other phone within the network. Over the years, cost effectiveness, reliability, fast connection time, and quality has been improving. Packet switched networks have the same basic objectives but instead of providing a network designed to pass voice and make phone calls, it is designed to pass data and make interactive data connections. Packet switched networks also provide high quality, reliability, low cost connection, and fast connect time.

The PSTN was originally designed to handle only voice, but in the 1950s people started using this infrastructure to transmit data as well by using modems. However, the transmission of data was limited by the analog equipment of the phone system, and so packet networks were introduced specifically for networking data terminals and hosts. These data terminals and hosts are called DTEs or data terminal equipments. In just a few decades, they have become very popular and have evolved into a billion dollar per year market.

The telephone network and the packet network both use a mesh topology, which provides a terminal, with access to any other terminal, whether it be a phone or a DTE. The mesh type of topology also provides high reliability in the network, in that if one link or point fails, then the traffic can be rerouted easily using alternate links and points.

In the PSTN, once the connection is made, any protocol can be used during the conversation. It could be spoken English or another language, or it could be modulated data using ASCII, EBCDIC, or any other protocol. Similarly, a packet network also provides connectivity, and the two end points using the same protocol can have a dialogue. Sometimes, a packet network is misunderstood and is thought to do a protocol conversion, such as an IBM host talking to a DEC host, but all that a packet network provides is connectivity. Services such as protocol conversions are provided by the upper layers of the OSI model.

Let us now switch our attention to the differences between PSTN and packet switched networks. The telephone network is inherently a circuit switched network. This means that once a connection is made between the end points, there is one circuit dedicated to carry their conversation, and no other conversation can be transmitted on that same circuit. In a packet network, the link between two end points is shared by other connections. Data is typically transfered in packets of 128 bytes, and these packets are statistically multiplexed on each link that a connection is made across, while over the PSTN, digitized voice is time division multiplexed on the intermachine trunks. Statistical multiplexing will be reviewed shortly. The units of information that are conveyed over the X.25 network are octets or bytes, while the PSTN primarily supports 4 kHz voice. Another main difference between the PSTN and packet networks is that it may take around ten seconds to make a long distance connection and in a packet network it usually takes less than one second.

13.3 DIAL-UP LINES , LEASED LINES , AND PACKET NETWORKS

The advantages posed by packet networks will become evident once we compare dial-up lines and leased lines with packet switched networks. Dial-up lines which use the telephone network are easily available, and they provide access to many points readily. See Figure 13.2. The user is charged only for the time that the connection is made. However, accessing the switches using analog lines degrades the quality of the

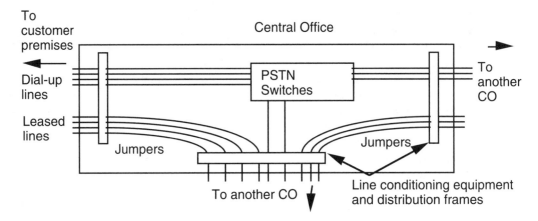

Figure 13.2 The difference between installing dial-up and leased lines inside a CO.

connection and data speeds are normally restricted to 9.6 kbps. They also have problems with security which can be overcome by the host calling back to the caller to verify its address (or phone number), However, that takes time and is costly.

Leased lines, on the other hand, provide better security and data speeds can be up to 19.2 kbps for voice grade lines. They don't go through switches.

Payment is on a 24 hour basis, so these lines are used for high volumes of traffic. However, they are expensive and time consuming to install, and don't come with redundant paths for added reliability.

Packet switched networks, as depicted in Figure 13.3, try to capitalize on the strengths of both the dial-up network and the leased lines. Packet networks are said to a have a reliability of better than 99.9%. That is just a few hours of outage during a year. If a node or a link within the network dies, the network is automatically "healed" by alternate routing. This is done without any loss of data and without the end users being aware of the failure. They provide data speeds of up to 64 kbps with an error rate of 10^{-9}. This means

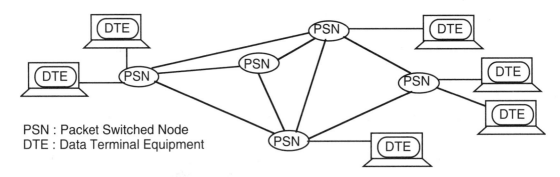

Figure 13.3 A packet switched network allows terminals at various locations to communicate with each other.

X.25 and Packet Switched Networks

that there is one error in one billion bits! This makes a typical packet network a highly accurate network.

Many users can share the same link. If one user has stopped transmitting momentarily, data packets belonging to other dialogues can be sent on the same link. Of course, the protocols used by the various users on the same link don't have to be the same.

Packet networks also provide speed conversions through the buffers that are available in the nodes. This means that a host running at 64 kbps can be talking to a terminal running at 1200 bps.

13.4 PUBLIC DATA NETWORKS (PDNs)

There are basically two varieties of packet switched networks. A private packet switched network belongs to a private company which leases lines connecting the various nodes to each other. The private network, as the name implies, is accessed and used by one company, whereas a PDN or public data network is generally made available to any company or individual, just as the PSTN is made available to the public for voice calls.

In either case, these are considered to be either MANs (Metropolitan Area Network) or WANs (Wide Area Networks). A MAN has all its network access points restricted to one metropolitan area, whereas a WAN may span many cities, states, or nations. For example, Infopath is owned by NY Telephone and is available to all users in the New York city area. Also SprintNet, formerly Telenet, owned by US Sprint, is available to the users and subscribers in the US. Infopath then is termed to be a MAN where SprintNet is considered to be a WAN.

PDNs are refered to many times as VANs or Value Added Networks, because PDNs may not only provide connectivity between many sites, but also may provide computing or database services.

The two most widely used PDNs in the United States are BT Tymnet by British Telecom and SprintNet. There are many others, and they all provide X.25 connectivity. Transpac is famous for going into most homes that have a phone in France. It provides a small data terminal which can be used to get on-line directory service, which eliminates the problem of printing and distributing telephone directories, discarding old ones, and keeping the data up to date. Transpac is also used for educational purposes. Networks, such as First Data Resource, provide a means of clearing credit card charges. With a dedicated line going to one of their packet network points, companies can get a credit card charge authorized using their clearing house in 5 to 6 seconds.

Many countries have at least one PDN. In Europe, the PDNs are owned by the PTTs (Post Telephone and Telegraph), a government agency similar to our US Postal Service. TELPAC in Mexico, and EASTNET in the Philippines are other examples of PDNs.

The PDNs are not used for transferring large volumes of data, but are cost effective for low and medium volume traffic. They don't charge by the distance of the call but by the amount of traffic that is sent and also according to the connect time. PDNs have all the advantages of a typical packet switched network, and many times they are used in conjunction with a private network in case the private network fails or if it carries too much traffic that needs to be diverted elsewhere.

Basically, there are two ways to access a PDN and the method chosen depends upon how much usage the PDN gets. If the PDN is used a lot then a leased line is installed to a dedicated port of the PDN. If the usage is occasional, then a dial-up line is used to access the PDN. Dial-up ports of a PDN must have enough modems to accommodate the number of callers that may be calling in, or else callers will be blocked.

13.5 THE OPERATION OF A PACKET SWITCHED NETWORK

13.5.1 What Is Packet Switching?

To best understand the operation of a packet network, it is good to review the workings of statistical multiplexers or stat-muxes for short.

With stat-muxes, it is possible to have the link speed be less than the sum of the terminal speeds. When a network like this is designed, it is assumed that not all terminals are constantly typing simultaneously. In Figure 13.4 (a), x1 can only talk to y1 on the other end, so that each terminal communicates with its respective terminal on the remote end.

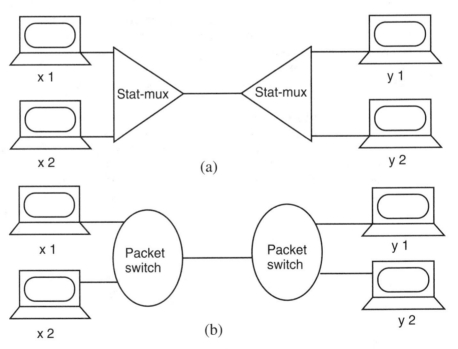

Figure 13.4 (a) In this statistical multiplexing connection, x1 may only link up with y1. (b) In this packet switched connection, x1 may connect with any of the other terminals.

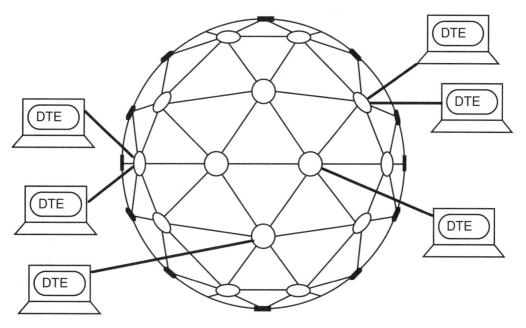

Figure 13.5 A packet switched network typically provides many alternate paths.

Figure 13.4 (b) is a very simple X.25 network, where we have replaced the stat-muxes with packet switches, also called nodes. The terminals are X.25 compatible. With this network, x1 can talk not only to y1 but to any other terminal because a packet switch not only provides statistical multiplexing but also switching. However, x1 must know the address of the terminal it wants to talk to. The link between the nodes, again, are statistically multiplexed, so the aggregate speed of the link can be less than the sum of the terminal speeds.

In Figure 13.5 we have a more usable X.25 network with many links and switches connected in a mesh topology to provide alternate routing and greater reliability. Again, any terminal can connect itself with any other terminal on the network, as long as the addresses are known.

A terminal is designated as a DTE (Data Terminal Equipment) in X.25 terminology. DTEs could be data terminals, mainframes, or anything else where data can terminate or originate. The component of the switch which interfaces with a DTE is called a DCE or Data Communications Equipment (sometimes, Data Circuit terminating Equipment). Many times, a switch or a node serves as a switch as well as a set of DCEs, depending on how many ports it may have. The packet network consists of the nodes, links and the DCEs, but not the DTEs. Many refer to a packet switched network as the "cloud," for short

The X.25 standard is defined between the DCE and the DTE. No standard is defined between the nodes, so usually in such a network, one vendor's equipment is used and a proprietary protocol is used inside the cloud.

X.25 and Packet Switched Networks   **251**

13.5.2 Protocols Relating to X.25

Many times a DTE is not X.25 compatible, in which case, a PAD (packet assembler/disassembler) must be used to get connectivity with the network. A PAD can come with a number of ports, which are synchronous or asynchronous depending on the type of terminals a user wants to connect to the network. The PAD may be located near the terminals if they are located in one place, or if the terminals are not in one location, the PAD may be placed with the DCE.

The services of an asynchronous PAD are specified in X.3, and the interaction between the PAD and the non-X.25 terminal are specified by X.28 by CCITT. See Figure 13.6. Packet networks can be interconnected or internetworked. In that case, X.25 level gateways are needed in each network to communicate with each other. Another name for this gateway is an STE, or a Signaling Terminal Equipment. The CCITT protocol that is used between STEs is X.75. X.121 is the protocol that provides the proper way of addressing networks that are interconnected. It specifies the country code, network code, and the terminal number.

The international address can be up to 14 digits long plus an optional prefix of a "0" or a "1." For international calls, the prefix of 1 is used. After the optional prefix, the next four digits specify the country and then the PDN within that country. This four digit field is called the DNIC (Data Network Identification Code). Finally, the last 10 digits identify the DTE that is attached to that network. This way, DTEs can call other DTEs around the world that are not part of the same PDN.

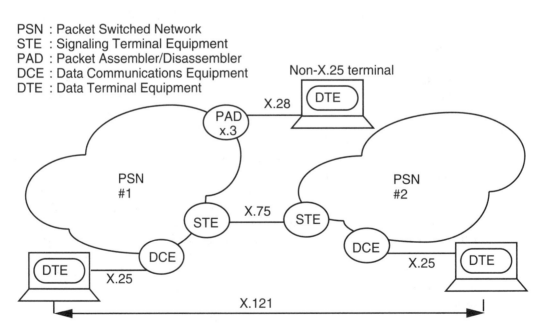

PSN : Packet Switched Network
STE : Signaling Terminal Equipment
PAD : Packet Assembler/Disassembler
DCE : Data Communications Equipment
DTE : Data Terminal Equipment

Figure 13.6 CCITT's X.25 related protocols.

In the international address of "31101234567890," for example, the "31" specifies the United States, the "10" specifies the SprintNet PDN, and "1234567890" identifies the terminal number in SprintNet.

13.6 LAP/B: THE DATA LINK LAYER OF X.25

In the physical layer of X.25, CCITT recommends using X.21. This has a 15 pin connector with 7 pins that are actually used. The X.21 standard, though part of X.25, is not really implemented widely. Most installations use EIA's RS-232 or V.35 standards at the physical level.

For the data link control layer, CCITT recommends LAP/B or Link Access Procedure/Balanced, which is similar to SDLC or HDLC. SDLC has already been covered in detail, and as it was then noted, there are three types of frames, namely, information, supervisory, and unnumbered. Information and supervisory types of frames were covered at length. Unnumbered frames will be covered now, because they are used in establishing and disconnecting communications links.

At the data link layer three basic modes of operation exist. First is SNRM (Set Normal Response Mode), where a multipoint protocol is used to perform polling and selecting. Then there is SARM (Set Asynchronous Response Mode) which is used for a half duplex, point to point operation. Lastly, SABM (Set Asynchronous Balance Mode) is used for a full duplex and point to point operation. X.25's LAP/B uses this last mode of operation to connect and disconnect a link. When a link is said to be balanced it means that either end can initiate the connection; in LAP/B, this means either the DTE or the DCE.

LAP/B has 5 types of unnumbered frames; they are SABM, UA (Unnumbered Acknowledge), DISC (DISConnect), FRMR (FRaMe Reject), and DM (Disconnect Mode). UA frame is sent to acknowledge SABM or DISC frames. The SABM frame is used to get a DTE or a DCE in a connect mode and the DISC is sent to put them in a disconnect mode. If information is sent to either a DTE or a DCE that is in a disconnect mode, it will reply with a DM indicating that the recipient isn't connected. Only an SABM frame can get the DCE or the DTE in a connect mode.

A FRMR frame is sent if an illegal frame was received. This is contrary to the REJ type of supervisory frame, which indicates that there was an error in the data itself. A FRMR frame is sent if an invalid control field was received, an incorrect length frame was received, an invalid Nr was received, or an unexpected ACK was received. FRMR also retransmits the rejected frame's control field to let the receiver know the reason for the rejection.

To summarize these points, an example of transmission exchanges is shown in Figure 13.7. The DTE sends an information frame and the DCE replies with a DM frame, notifying the DTE that it is in the disconnect mode. The DTE then brings the DCE in a connect mode by issuing a SABM. The DCE then completes the connection by sending a UA. Then the link goes into a data transfer mode. Here, the DTE sends two frames numbered 0 and 1. The DCE acknowledges that by sending a Nr of 2, indicating that it is expecting to receive DTE's frame number 2. Finally the link is disconnected. The disconnect can be requested by either the DTE or the DCE.

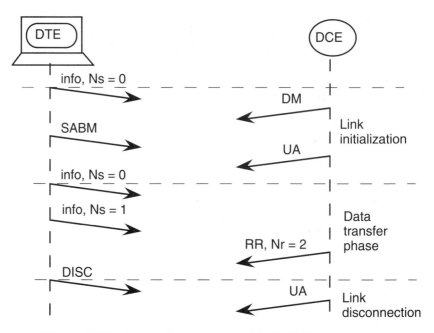

Figure 13.7 Exchange of frames over a DTE-DCE link.

13.7 THE X.25 PACKET LAYER

13.7.1 The Mechanism of Communications Through Layers

When data is sent through a network, first it arrives at the network layer as shown in Figure 13.8. It encapsulates the data into a packet by adding a header to it. The network layer then hands over the packet to the data link layer which then forms an information field out of the packet itself. The packet in the data link layer is called the information field. The information field is then encapsulated into a frame by adding the fields as shown in the diagram. Lastly, the physical layer will transmit the actual bits

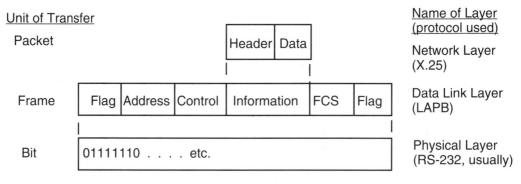

Figure 13.8 The three layers of X.25.

at the appropriate rate, using correct voltages and so on. The receiving end does this process in reverse.

In Figure 13.9, DTE1 is transmitting to DTE2. The physical layer of DCE1 will receive the raw bits and the data link layer of DCE1 will check and correct the errors on the link with DTE1. The network control layer then receives error-free packets from the data link layer. It then decides from its header how to route the packet so that it is sent in the direction of its destination. When the link is chosen, this same process occurs from the DCE/switch to the next switch. As the packet is sent through the network, this layering process is repeated over each link until the packet reaches the intended DTE. Over each link between devices or packet switches, the physical layer transmits and receives bits, the data link layer controls the errors over the links, and the network layer does the routing of the packets.

13.7.2 Permanent and Switched Virtual Circuits

When a DTE establishes a call, it has to provide the X.121 address of the remote DTE. The switches will find a path through the network using the various links that are available. This bidirectional association between two DTEs across a PSN (Packet Switched Network) is called a virtual circuit.

The physical links between the switches are statistically multiplexed, so that the links are shared by many connections. Each link has about 4096 logical channels available and these logical channels can be assigned to that many data conversations. A logical channel is designated by the LCI (Logical Channel Identifier) and is provided in the packet header. When a switch receives a packet, it will route that packet to the appropriate link depending on its LCI, changing the LCI over the next link.

For example, in Figure 13.10, a packet switching node is receiving three packets. It routes packets with LCIs of 1500 to PSN-A changing the LCIs to 600, and routes the packets with LCIs of 1000 to PSN-B, changing their LCIs to 1100. The PSNs which

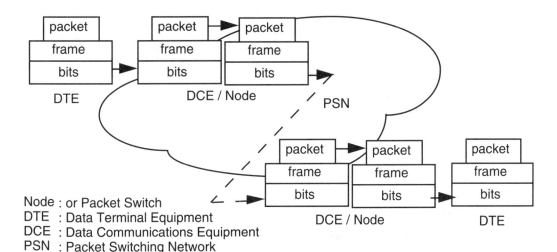

Node : or Packet Switch
DTE : Data Terminal Equipment
DCE : Data Communications Equipment
PSN : Packet Switching Network

Figure 13.9 The transfer of data through a packet network.

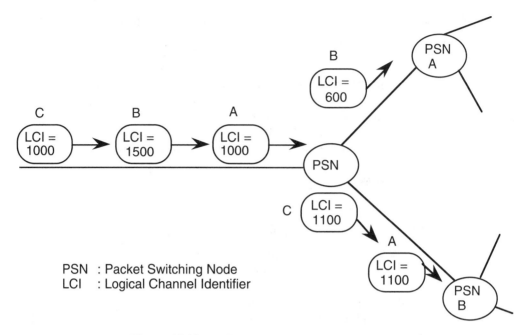

Figure 13.10 Routing of packets through a switch.

PSN : Packet Switching Node
LCI : Logical Channel Identifier

receive these packets similarly continue this routing procedure, so virtual circuits are not only defined by the physical links which they use, but also by which LCIs they occupy over the respective links.

Each node maintains a table specifying which LCIs on which links are routed to which new LCIs and links. New entries are made to these tables during the call establishment phase of calls. This example assumes a virtual circuit implementation of internodal links, but this may not always be true.

There are two types of virtual circuits and they are called PVC for permanent virtual circuit, and SVC for switched virtual circuit. Out of the possible 4096 channels that are possible, channel 0 is used for network diagnostic purposes. The rest of the channels are assigned in groups of the following: PVCs, incoming SVCs, two-way SVCs, and outgoing SVCs. The LCIs are assigned as calls are being made and are freed as calls become disconnected.

PVCs provide a dedicated channel between two users, and no call set-up phase is required. PVCs oppose X.25's philosophy of bandwidth on demand, so they are not that popular. Switched virtual circuits provide a temporary logical connection between two DTEs and are established when making the call.

13.8 PACKET TYPES

13.8.1 Packet Headers

Data, flow control, and supervisory are three types of packets. The basic header for data packets will be studied first. Figure 13.11 shows a header that is typically 6

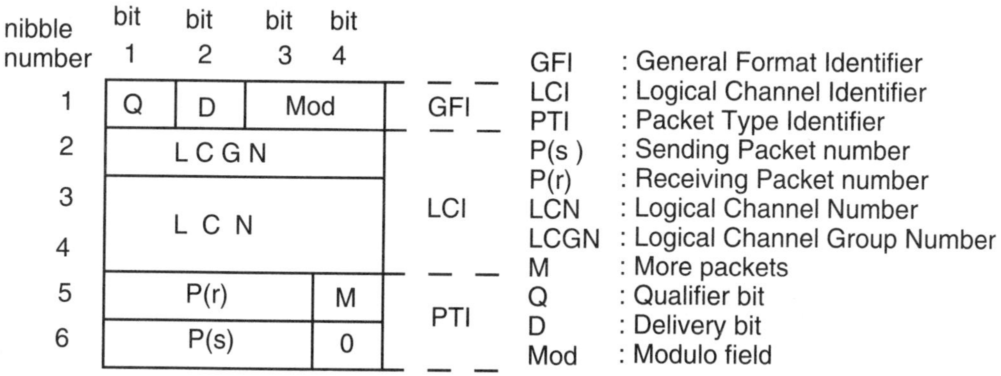

Figure 13.11 The three-octet packet header.

nibbles or 3 octets long. The first nibble is the GFI for General Format Identifier, the next three nibbles are the LCI (Logical Channel Identifier) which actually consists of the LCGN (Logical Channel Group Number) and the LCN (Logical Channel Number). To make life interesting, many refer to the LCI as the LCN. The last two nibbles are the packet type identifier.

The Q or the Qualifier bit in the GFI determines whether the packet is intended for the remote DTE or simply the remote PAD. The D or the Delivery bit specifies whether the acknowledgment is either local or end-end.

In Figure 13.12, the difference between these two types of acknowledgments is illustrated. In the local acknowledgment, the ACK or RR (Receiver Ready) is supplied by the local DCE. It confirms that the packet reached the network, but not necessarily the destination. This is similar to when a child drops a letter in a mailbox and comes back to say that the letter was mailed, but cannot confirm that it actually reached its destination. Likewise, local acknowledgment confirms that the packet reached the network, but not the destination.

End-end acknowledgment is similar to "return receipt requested" offered by the postal service. As in the postal service, this type of confirmation takes longer to receive and is more costly.

P(s) and P(r) fields of the PTI are similar to the N(s) and the N(r) fields in SDLC frames. Except here, P(s) and P(r) are referring to the packet numbers and not frame numbers. P(s) is the sending packet number and P(r) is the next packet the sender is expecting from the receiver. For example, if a DTE is sending a packet with P(s) of 3 and P(r) of 2, that indicates the DTE is sending its packet number 3 and has received all the packets up to and including packet number 1 from the remote end.

The modulo field of the GFI determines if the transmission mode is normal control or extended. In the normal control mode, the P(s) and P(r) fields are represented using 3 bits each, as shown in Figure 13.11. In the extended mode, 7 bits are used to represent these two fields. In that case, the packet header, unlike that shown in Figure 13.11, would be 4 octets long. The window size, which determines the number of consecutive packets that can be transmitted without requiring a response, is 7 for the normal mode and 127 for the extended mode. The extended mode is more suitable for transmissions with a long delay, such as satellite transmissions.

LCGN, being 4 bits long, allows for 2^4 or 16 numbers of LCGNs. LCN, being 8 bits long, allows for 2^8 or 256 numbers of LCNs. Since every group (or LCGN) out of a possible 16 can each have 256 channels, a total of 4096 channels (LCIs) exist.

Finally, the "more" field simply signals the remote end if additional packets are to be expected or not. This field is used by the upper layers for information unit segmentation (or breaking up of information units into smaller units) and assembly.

13.8.2 Supervisory Packets

Data packets are indicated with a 0 in the 8th bit of the PTI, as shown in Figure 13.11. If the 7th and the 8th bits of the PTI are "01" then the packet type is flow control. Flow control packets are used to positively or negatively acknowlege transmissions.

If the 7th and 8th bits of the PTI are "11," then it is a supervisory type of packet. These packets are used to establish and disconnect connections, and also to bring up circuits in case of problems .

Figure 13.13 not only shows how a connection is made and broken in layer 3, but also summarizes the same for the first two layers. Let us now concentrate on the third layer.

When a DTE needs to establish a call, it provides the address of the DTEs in a CALL REQUEST packet to its DCE. As this packet finds its destination DTE, the address is converted to LCIs on the corresponding links. Once the call is set up the

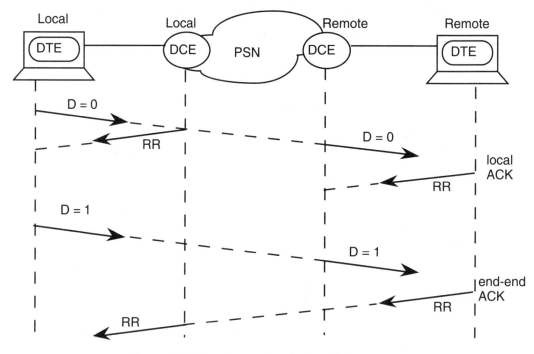

Figure 13.12 Local vs. end-end acknowledgments.

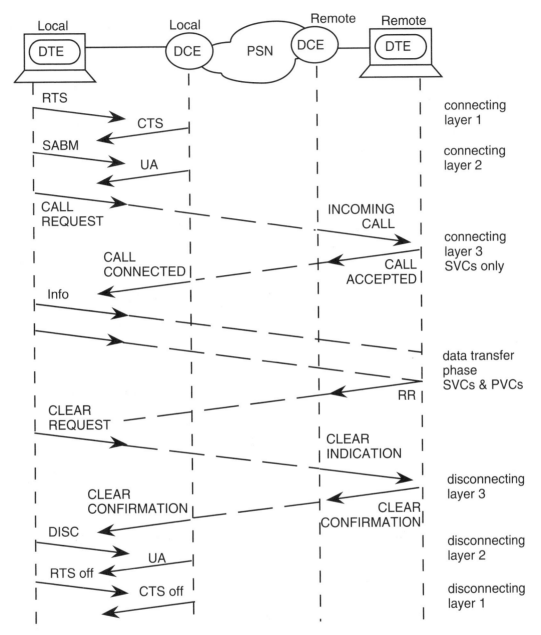

Figure 13.13 Establishing a connection using the 3 layers of X.25.

addresses are not needed, only the LCIs. When the packet arrives at the called DCE, it will send an INCOMING CALL packet to its DTE. The called DTE then may send a CALL ACCEPTED packet to its DCE and the calling DTE would receive a CALL CONNECTED packet from its DCE. Now that the call is established, data transfer can occur.

After the data transfer phase, either DTE may disconnect the virtual circuit. This is done by issuing a CLEAR REQUEST. On the opposite end the DTE would receive a CLEAR INDICATION and transmit a CLEAR CONFIRMATION packet. The CLEAR CONFIRMATION packet is also received by the call clearing DTE.

In establishing a call, if the network doesn't want to accept the call, the calling DCE will send a CLEAR INDICATION back to the calling DTE. If the called DTE doesn't want to accept the call, it would send a CLEAR REQUEST packet instead of the CALL ACCEPTED packet.

When abnormal conditions exist during the data transfer phase, there is an ordered set of procedures to follow to bring the circuit up. First a RR is sent to request the remote DTE to respond. If that doesn't work, then an INTERRUPT, then a RESET, then a CLEAR, then as a final resort a RESTART is issued by the DTE. Let us consider them in order.

An INTERRUPT packet is sent during the data transfer phase to obtain an immediate response from the distant DTE. The distant DTE must then send an INTERRUPT CONFIRMATION. This process will synchronize the $P(s)$s and the $P(r)$s.

If the INTERRUPT CONFIRMATION is not received, then the DTE knows that there's a problem with the virtual circuit, and it may then issue a RESET. This type of supervisory packet will reset the $P(s)$ and the $P(r)$ counters to zero.

If the RESET CONFIRMATION is not received from the remote end, the DTE may send a CLEAR REQUEST if the circuit is a switched virtual circuit. This request disconnects the virtual circuit and the LCI associated with it is freed.

If the clear is not confirmed, then as a last resort a RESTART packet may be transmitted. This packet will clear all SVCs and PVCs associated by the requesting DTE. All transient data will be lost, so this is primarily done after a power failure. The RESET, CLEAR, and the RESTART packets contain a code to indicate the reason for issuing them.

13.9 X.25 FEATURES AND FACILITIES

Just as PBXs provide features in a voice environment, X.25 also provides a wide range of features for packet networks. A few examples of such features are described here.

Outgoing Calls Barred: This facility can restrict the DTE from making calls.

Incoming Calls Barred: This restricts the DTE from receiving any calls.

Closed User Groups: This facility creates a virtual network within a larger public network, and DTEs can only talk to one another that belong to the same group. However, one DTE can belong to a number of such groups.

Fast Select: This facility is used for credit card authorization. Data is sent in the CALL REQUEST packet to a host, providing the credit card number, amount of purchase, etc. The host will immediately send a CLEAR REQUEST packet instead of the CALL ACCEPTED packet authorizing or not authorizing the purchase. No data transfer phase is used here.

Call Redirection: Similar to the call forwarding feature in PBXs, this allows one DTE to redirect the calls it receives to other DTEs.

Reverse Charging: Similar to a call collect, here a DTE can reverse the charges in a packet network. Dial-up ports on PDNs use this feature extensively.

13.10 INTERCONNECTING X.25 WITH IBM'S NETWORKS

It's common knowledge that IBM is a major vendor of computer equipment and that SNA (System Network Architecture) is IBM's proprietary protocol used to network its computers. SNA networks are most widely used in the business world. The traditional method of connecting SNA networks is by using leased lines for primary links and dial-up lines for backup. However, packet switched networks, public or private, provide an enhanced method of connecting SNA network links. Packet networks are more resilient to failure, provide excellent transmission quality and also are inexpensive, since the cost of the connections are shared among many users. Therefore, many organizations prefer an X.25 network backbone to run their SNA networks.

Let us consider three methods of doing this.

13.10.1 The Software Approach
for Implementing SNA over X.25

Figure 13.14 shows one alternative to interconnecting SNA to an X.25 network This involves using a software package called NPSI (NCP Packet Switched Interface).

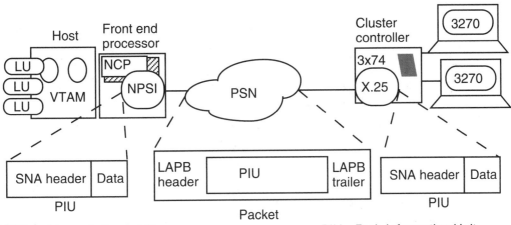

NCP : Network Control Program
NPSI : NCP Packet Switching Interface
VTAM : Virtual Telecommunications Access Method

PIU : Path Information Unit
LU : Logical Unit

Figure 13.14 Using NPSI to run SNA over X.25.

X.25 and Packet Switched Networks

NPSI runs under NCP (Network Control Program) in the front end processors, namely the 3725 or the 3745. NPSI does encapsulation of SNA units into X.25 packets. NCP sends a PIU (Path Information Unit) containing the RU (Request/response Unit) and the SNA headers to NPSI, which in turn adds the packet header and trailers to the PIU. This then makes the data ready for the packet network. Encapsulating the data or the RU into a PIU and then again into a packet is called double encapsulation. Packets arriving from the network do this same process, but in reverse.

Now that a packet contains not only X.25 headers but also SNA headers, the maximum size of the data that can be sent becomes smaller. This requires the need for more packets to be sent and received. The performance of the 3725 is reduced by about 30% and of the 3745 by about 15% because of this overload. Performance can be improved by increasing the packet size from 128 to 256 bytes.

Similarly, in the tail circuit, an X.25 interface package can be incorporated in the cluster controller. This package is functionally the same as the NPSI, but it is designed for the type 2 node.

Simply by adding the appropriate software on both ends, packet networks can be used to transport SNA data streams. This allows the user to preserve his investment in the SNA equipment and still get the benefits of packet networks. Although LU switching is generally done by SNA, PU switching is possible with this software approach. You may recall that PU switching allows everyone on a cluster controller to have access to only one application on one host, whereas LU switching allows everyone on the cluster controller to access any application on any host.

13.10.2 The Hardware Approach

A hardware approach to solve the SNA-X.25 connectivity problem is shown in Figure 13.15. On the host's side, a host PAD or HPAD is connected between the FEP and the network. Also, a terminal PAD or TPAD is connected on the other end.

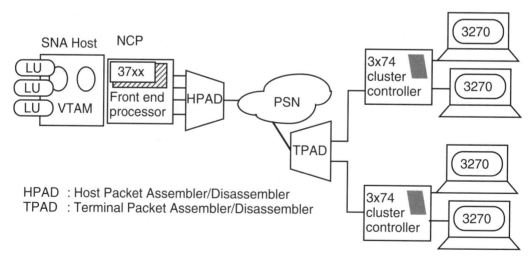

HPAD : Host Packet Assembler/Disassembler
TPAD : Terminal Packet Assembler/Disassembler

Figure 13.15 Using PADS to run SNA over X.25.

Although this requires extra boxes and cabling, it is less costly than using the NPSI method, and is more popular. One of the key advantages of this method is that it doesn't load down the FEP. Just as the front end relieves the host from doing communications related processing, the HPAD relieves the FEP from having to assemble and disassemble packets, allowing the FEP to concentrate on the SNA protocol. With NPSI, if the line quality to the network becomes poor, the front end's performance drastically goes down, instead an HPAD takes care of error correction and frees the front end from having to do it.

HPADs also improve the host's processing time. They provide better network management type of capabilities and also LU switching. Network changes, such as adding or removing PUs or cluster controllers, are done easily if properly planned in advance.

TPADs are functionally complementary to HPADs, but they are designed for the tail end circuits. TPADS provide local polling, so that only the payload goes across the network. TPADs can be used with NPSI residing on the host's end.

Using QLLC (Qualified Logical Link Control), both the software and physical approaches can be combined on one network. This protocol may exist along with NPSI and also in the PADs. QLLC packets convey SDLC commands and responses over the X.25 network, which are converted to SDLC equivalent frames at the end points.

13.10.3 The XI Approach

Another approach introduced by IBM in 1988 in the US to interconnect X.25 over SNA is called XI (X.25 to SNA Interconnection). Previously we mentioned that X.25 protocol is simply defined between the DTE and DCE and that the protocol used between the DCEs and switches is sometimes proprietary. As shown in Figure 13.16, this proprietary protocol used with XI is SNA's SDLC, and the interfaces between the DTEs and FEPs are still X.25. Using XI involves using a packet network connected by FEPs and SDLC links. All DTEs must be connected to FEPs. XI resides under the

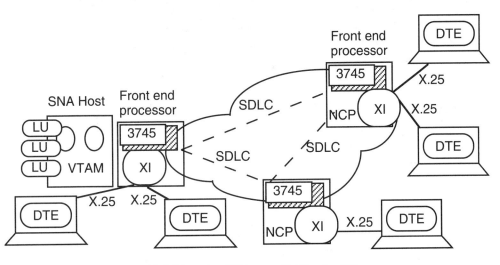

Figure 13.16 Running SNA over X.25 using XI.

X.25 and Packet Switched Networks

FEP's NCP, and all packets must come and go through XI. One copy of XI can provide up to 256 DTE interfaces.

A single LU-LU session exists between the various FEPs or XI nodes, and X.25 virtual circuits are multiplexed on these single LU-LU sessions. This improves performance, because sessions don't have to be created and terminated dynamically. Virtual circuits are transported through the already available sessions. Packet sizes can be as large as 1024 bytes, which also improves on performance of the FEPs. XI also supports NetView, IBM's network management product.

Recently, third party vendors are introducing communications processors to be used in place of the 37x5 FEPs, which look like a type 4 node to the host. These processors are designed with X.25 in mind, so duplication of SNA/SDLC and X.25 functions are minimized and provide a non-hierarchical structure to SNA.

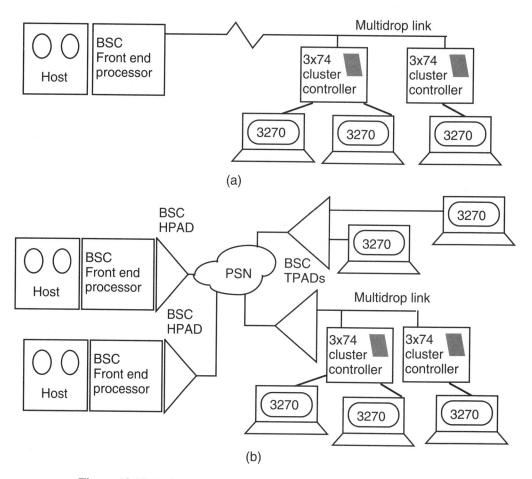

Figure 13.17 (a) A typical BSC network. (b) Implementing a BSC network over a packet switched network introduces many new benefits.

13.10.4 Advantages of Using X.25 for BSC Networks

Other advantages of X.25 are made apparent when studying a pre-SNA Bisync or BSC network. In Figure 13.17 (a), a BSC host is connected with half duplex multipoint terminals. The highest speed on typical analog lines would be 14.4kbps. Polling is done from the FEP making such delays significant. The host is also under utilized, because it can only support one device at a time.

By inserting BSC PADs on either end of a packet network as shown in Figure 13.17 (b), the transmission becomes full duplex. Transmission is half duplex only from the FEP to the HPAD and from the TPAD to the terminals, which are the insignificant parts of the link. Speeds through the packet network can go up as high as 64kbps from 14.4kbps. Polling delays are minimized, because polling is done locally from the TPADs and not over the entire network. The terminals are now not restricted to one application on one host, but because of the LU switching provided by the TPADs, they can access any application on any host simultaneously. Similar advantages can be gained for SDLC backbones as well.

Exercises

1. A PDN is also referred to as what?
   - a. LAN
   - b. MAN
   - c. VAN
   - d. WAN

2. Packet switching networks do not provide
   - a. reliability
   - b. security
   - c. low cost
   - d. high transfer rate

3. LAPB uses which type of transmission mode?
   - a. SNRM
   - b. SARM
   - c. SABM
   - d. SNBM

4. Which fields determines the type of acknowledgment requested?
   - a. P(r) and P(s)
   - b. mod
   - c. Q bit
   - d. D bit

5. A call request packet becomes what type of a packet on the receiver end?
   - a. call accepted
   - b. call connected
   - c. call acknowledgment
   - d. incoming call

6. Which type of X.25 and SNA interconnection method requires SDLC to be used as the internode link protocol in the network?
   - a. NPSI
   - b. HPAD-TPAD
   - c. XI
   - d. BSC method

7. Which protocol defines the interface between two different packet networks?
   - a. X.25
   - b. X.3
   - c. X.75
   - d. X.121

8. Which X.25 feature doesn't allow a user to make any calls?
   a. outgoing calls barred
   b. incoming calls barred
   c. reverse charging
   d. call redirection

9. The X.25 standard is specified by which organization?

10. What type of lines incur a flat monthly charge?

11. In LAPB, which frame acknowledges a DISC frame?

12. When a call is being connected between two end points through a packet network, the destination address is converted to _____s between each link in the network.

13. Which packet is transmitted to initiate a disconnection between two points?

14. Which packet header field determines the window size?

15. NPSI operates in which device and under which protocol?

16. On a BSC network running over a packet network, polling of terminals is done from which device?

17. Discuss the differences between using datagrams and packets.

18. Discuss the differences between dial-up lines and leased lines. Which of these benefits exist in packet networks?

19. How is packet switching and statistical multiplexing similar and how different?

20. List the protocols which are related to X.25 and give their purpose.

21. Explain how packets traverse through a network. Give the function of the layers.

22. Draw a four-octet packet header for the extended mode of transmission, giving the reason why the window size is 127 and the number of packet numbers is 128 (0 through 127).

23. Describe the sequence of events that take place when no response is received from the far end in X.25.

24. What are the pros and cons for running SNA traffic using NPSI? Using HPADs and TPADs?

Chapter 14

Signaling System 7

14.1 INTRODUCTION

Back in Chapter 5, the various methods of signaling were introduced, including the differences between per-trunk and common channel interoffice signaling. This chapter is merely a continuation of CCIS, specifically that of SS7. The reader should have obtained an operational overview of SS7 in Chapter 7. The version which is widely used in North America is called CCS7 (Common Channel Signaling number 7), and differs slightly from that of the CCITT's version, which is called SS7. Japan also has its own varient. (These varients differ from each other primarily by their point code sizes and MTPs. CCITT uses a point code size of 14, USA uses a size of 24 and Japan 16. These terms will be explained later.) Though the discussion will be more based on CCS7, we will simply refer to it as SS7. However, when crossing international boundaries the CCITT version is used. Hopefully, all these versions will converge sometime in the future.

14.1.1 Advantages

SS7 is a voice network application of packet switched networks, and brings with it many of the advantages of packet switching discussed in Chapter 13. Aside from those advantages and those of CCIS pointed out in Chapter 5, let me point out a few more here.

Probably the most beneficial advantage of SS7 is its flexibility. Since the signaling is software driven, instead of being electro-mechanical in nature, new features can be readily implemented in the network by modifying the software and distributing copies of it at all points in the network. This is easier than having to remanufacture new signaling interfaces for all locations every time someone wants to introduce a new signaling function. However, the downside of SS7 is that the program-

---

Over from Scotland, Peter Locke of Hewlett Packard, Queensferry Telecommunications Division, has been very kind in greatly enhancing this chapter. Because of him, the section on digital wireless systems (Section 7.4) was included.

ming code for it is quite complex and one bug in it can cripple all communications in one part of the country.

SS7 allows the IXCs, LECs, the international carriers, and soon even equipment for large private networks to talk to one another using one standard language. This allows customers using one 800 number to route calls over different IXCs' networks depending on the time of day, amount of traffic, or tariff structures. Customers will be able to manage their own databases which interact directly with the carrier's signaling network. In short, SS7 opens up a wide variety of creative options to the user.

SS7 predates ISDN and OSI and has been chosen as the interface between switches of carrier networks. SS7 provides many capabilities which ISDN doesn't have to implement, and so SS7 is considered necessary for ISDN to become a reality. ISDN then becomes a user application of SS7. Finally, SS7 provides management signals, through which it becomes easy to maintain, monitor, and administer the network.

Figure 14.1 shows how the various signaling systems co-exist in a modern digital environment. Between the end-subscriber and the local CO, ISDN or DTMF may be used for signaling. Q.931 is the standard which specifies ISDN signaling with the subscriber. These protocols are then translated into SS7 at the CO. One should remember throughout this chapter that SS7 has no direct interface with the subscriber. Additionally, "subscriber" is the term used for the person at the phone and "user" is the term used for SS7 nodes, such as the digital switch at the CO.

14.1.2 History

Prior to SS7, CCITT had specified other signaling systems which were more common in Europe than in North America. SS1 was specified for manually operated ringdown circuits, where one phone is connected to only one other, so that when a phone rings it is always the same phone calling it. SS2 used 600 Hz and 750 Hz tones for supervisory and address signaling. SS3 specified a 2280 Hz signal similar in function to our 2600 Hz SF tone. SS4 (using 2040 Hz and 2400 Hz) and SS5 (using 2400 Hz and 2600 Hz) were variations of SS3.

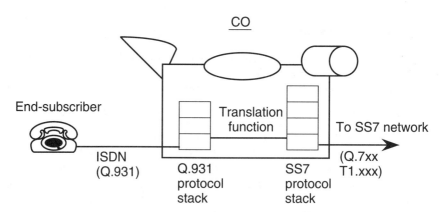

Figure 14.1 ISDN is used for signaling by the end-subscriber. The digital switch at the CO is the user of the SS7 signaling network.

These first five signaling systems used CAS (Channel Associated Signaling). CAS is the formal term for what we have so far called per-trunk signaling. Then in 1976 SS6 was introduced in the North American network. It used 2.4 kbps data links in the signaling network, which was later doubled to 4.8 kbps. It provided 800 number services and was designed for analog voice networks.

SS7, on the other hand, was being deployed by the IXCs in the late 1980s. It used 56/64 kbps signaling links and required that stored program control digital switches be used in the voice network.

14.2 TOPOLOGY

14.2.1 Types of Nodes

Figure 14.2 shows the types of nodes existing in an SS7 network. They fall into two categories called SPs (Signaling Points) and STPs (Signal Transfer Points). SPs can be thought of as the end nodes in the network where packets, called messages, originate and terminate, whereas the STPs are the packet switches which route the messages to their proper destinations.

Furthermore, there are three kinds of SPs (Signaling Points) which are called switching points, SSPs (Service Switching Points), and SCPs (Service Control Points). Switching points are the hardware and the software associated in the digital switches which convert the external signaling protocol such as ISDN or DTMF into SS7 format messages so that they could be deciphered by the STPs. The switching points are part of the 4ESS, DMS-250, or any such digital switch that is part of the SS7 network. The switches that are not SS7 compliant can have access to the intelligent network through an SSP.

Lastly, the SCP is a database system which is used for credit card authorization, subscriber records for virtual networks, billing information, 800 number conversion tables, and other special services functions. An SCP service can either be provided via a separate switch, via an intelligent peripheral connected to an STP or as an adjunct processor on an SSP/STP.

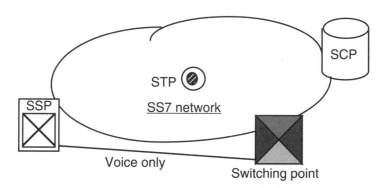

Figure 14.2 Types of SS7 nodes

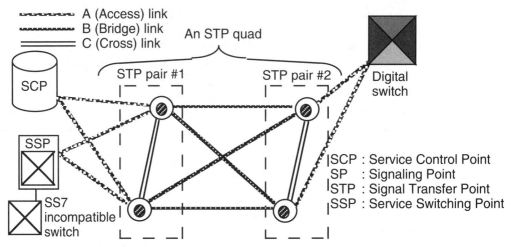

Figure 14.3 An STP quad configuration, showing the three types of SPs and the signaling links which connect them.

14.2.2 Types of Links

Figure 14.3 shows these three types of SPs being connected to STPs. STPs are deployed in what are called mated pairs and they each share the traffic load between them. Two such mated pairs which are interconnected are called an STP quad.

From each SP there are two links to a mated STP pair to which the SP is "homed." These links are called A or access links. The STPs in a pair are connected to each other by C or cross links. Since the traffic between the two STPs is shared, if one fails, the other has enough capacity to accept all of the traffic.

Each STP in a pair is connected to every other pair using B (bridge) links. The redundancy in all of the components of the signaling network make it less susceptible to failure. Half of the components and links may fail and the network could still remain operational.

Figure 14.4 shows a more general network where the signaling links are fully integrated between an IXC and an LEC network. Notice that the LEC network is shown with a regional STP pair which is a level higher than the local STP pairs. The local and the regional STPs are also called secondary and primary STPs, respectively. The links between such STP pairs are called D or diagonal links.

14.2.3 AIN

Figure 14.5 shows a functional diagram of an AIN (Advanced Intelligent Network). An intelligent network provides an array of data, service logic, and assistance, in service functions in a distributed enviornment, using SS7. The components of such a network are briefly outlined.

The adjunct is like an SCP that provides geographically localized services to the AIN digital switch. While the SCP provides a centralized source of data to many switches, the adjunct primarily serves only one switch.

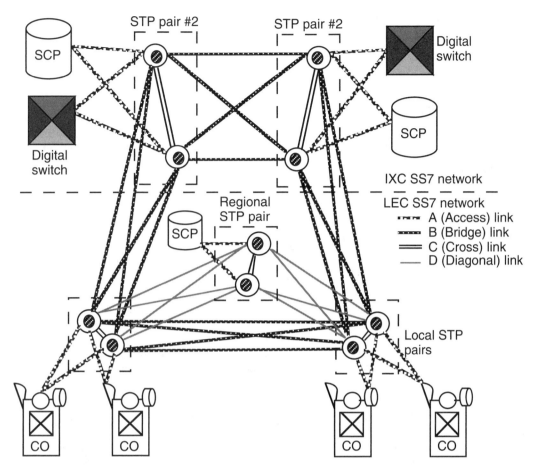

Figure 14.4 A fully interconnected SS7 network between an LEC and an IXC.

Among other services, the IP/SN (Intelligent Peripheral/Service-circuit Node) provides announcements, voice synthesis and recognition, store and forward services for fax transmissions. These services are provided to both the adjunct and the SCP. The IP/SN can be connected to the AIN switch using ISDN.

ABS (Alternate Billing Service) permits customers to charge for calls using collect calling, third number billing, and credit card charging. Information about these details are stored in the LIDB (Line Information Data Base). CLASS (Custom Local Area Signaling Services) provides customers with the following seven services: Return Call, Priority Call, Repeat Call, Select Forwarding, Call Block, Caller ID, and Call Trace.

Triggering allows a switch to query an SCP while processing a call. Examples of triggers are when a caller answers the phone or when a virtual network number is dialed. One can readily see that the simple signaling protocol which was originally set up only to route 800 calls will soon be used to perform much more complex services.

Signaling System 7　　　　　　　　　　　　　　　　　　　　　　　**271**

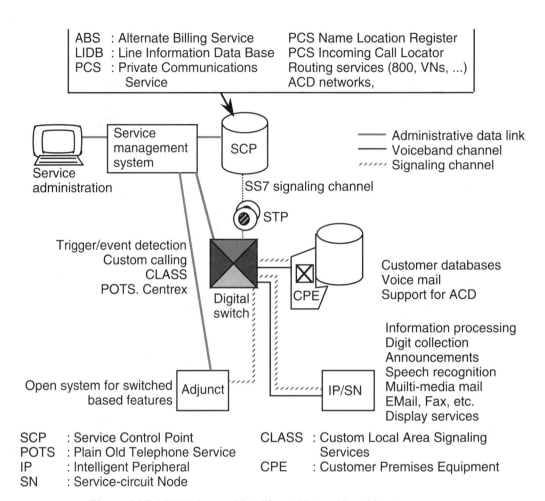

Figure 14.5 AIN (Advanced Intelligent Network) architecture.

14.3 SS7 PROTOCOL ARCHITECTURE

14.3.1 Comparison with X.25

In X.25 a customer interfaces a DTE with a DCE of the PDN (Public Data Network). Similarly in SS7, a customers telephone or a PBX interfaces with a switching point. In X.25 a virtual circuit is established prior to sending data between two end DCEs. Similarly, in SS7 a virtual connection, called an SCCP (Signaling Connection Control Part) connection, can be provided between the two end SPs. Think of the SPs as being similar to X.25's DCEs, which provide entry points into the SS7 network. Additionally, the STPs are similar to the packet switches or the transit switches of X.25.

Each network node in an SS7 network has a unique PC (Point Code) associated with it, providing the address of the node. These PCs are implemented by the SCCP layer of SS7, similar to that of the X.25's layer 3 address.

14.3.2 The Layers of the Architecture

Figure 14.6, page 274, shows the four layers of SS7 and its various sub-layers. Alongside these layers the units of transfer and their headings are shown. Items in this figure will be explained through the remainder of the chapter, so it is not necessary to understand it fully at this time. The figure shows how the four SS7 layers map onto the seven OSI layers. The first layer of SS7 is called MTP-L1 (Message Transfer Part, Level 1) or signaling data link. This is similar to OSI's physical layer, which specifies the electrical and physical properties of the signaling links.

The second layer is simply called the signaling link layer or MTP-L2. It provides error detection and correction across the signaling links. MTP-L3, also known as the signaling network layer, receives messages from the signaling links and, after examining their point codes, determines if the messages should be routed to another link or be handed over to level 4, locally.

SCCP which is the lower portion of layer 4 provides flow control and sequence control for the messages on an optional basis. Together with MTP, SCCP provides complete network services as the OSI model's first three layers do.

The rest of layer 4 falls into two vertical categories. One category is called ISUP (ISDN User Part) which is used to make an end to end call, such as a simple telephone call. It provides the transfer of signaling information between two end users. The other vertical layer is called TCAP (Transaction Capabilities Application Part), and it usually requires a call made to an SCP so that routing information may be obtained for an ISUP call. An example of a TCAP call is when an 800 number is converted to a POTS number. Therefore, it is said that circuit-related functions are needed for an ISUP call while non-circuit related functions are needed for a TCAP call.

ISUP and TCAP layers are further divided into yet other functions. ISUP can exchange messages with MTP-L3 by using the LBL (Link-By-Link) signaling method, or by transferring PAM (Pass-Along Message) messages, or by using SCCP messages. Since SCCP is not always used by ISUP, it is shown to be "chopped off" and not occupying the entire lower layer of ISUP.

TCAP is divided into two sublayers called CSL (Component Sub-Layer) and TSL (Transaction Sub-Layer) layers. TCAP is actually a sublayer of TC (Transaction Capabilities) along with ISP (Intermediate Signaling Part). However, since ISP is not currently defined, the scope of TC and TCAP are identical. More on all this later.

14.4 SIGNALING UNITS

Frames in SS7 are called SUs (Signaling Units). There are three types of SUs as there are 3 types of frames in HDLC. However, their functions do not correspond. The SU types are shown in Figure 14.7.

An MSU (Message SU) encapsulates or carries information from the upper layers. It also sets up and terminates links and provides status for managing the network. The LSSU (Link Status SU) also provides status about the link, whether it is getting congested, or if the link has to be aligned, etc., but doesn't contain any information from the upper layers. The FISU (Fill-In SU) is transmitted when the link is idle and not carrying any traffic, so that the receiving end knows that the other end is only idle and not out of service.

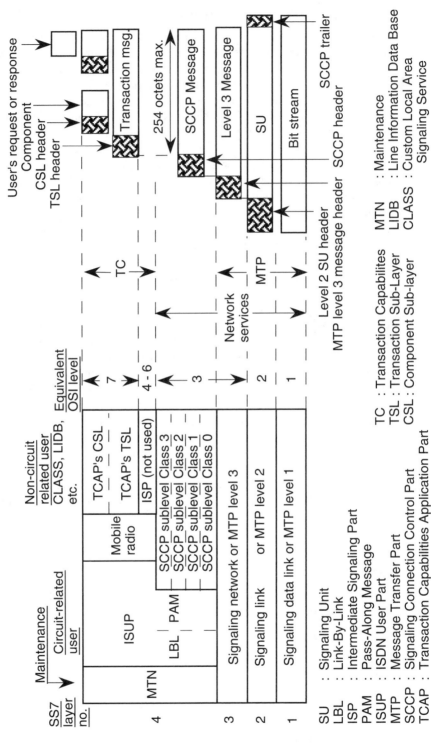

Figure 14.6 The layered architecture of SS7 and the units of transfer .

SU   : Signaling Unit
LBL   : Link-By-Link
ISP   : Intermediate Signaling Part
PAM   : Pass-Along Message
ISUP : ISDN User Part
MTP   : Message Transfer Part
SCCP : Signaling Connection Control Part
TCAP : Transaction Capabilities Application Part

TC   : Transaction Capabilites
TSL   : Transaction Sub-Layer
CSL   : Component Sub-layer

MTN   : Maintenance
LIDB : Line Information Data Base
CLASS : Custom Local Area
         Signaling Service

14.4.1 SU Fields

The first and the last fields of an SU are the '01111110' flag, which requires that the rest of the fields must be bit-stuffed, so that the flag doesn't appear anywhere in between. But the activity at this layer is very high and frames are sent one after the othere with only one flag between successive frames.

LI (Length Indicator) specifies the length in octets of the SIF (Signal Information Field) for MSUs or the SF (Status Field) for LSSUs. It is set to 0 for FISUs, 1 or 2 for LSSUs and 3 through 63 for MSUs. If the MSU length is less than or equal to 63 octets, then the LI field is set to the actual length. For higher lengths up to 272 octets, this field is still set to 63. This field value is limited to 63, because its length is only 6 bits. The SIF contains information that is being sent by the application user and the SIO (Service Information Octet) specifies which user this information belongs to. The SF field provides the status of the link.

The 16 bit CRC field provides error detection for the SU. FSN (Forward Sequence Number) is the identification number of the MSU being sent while the BSN (Backward Sequence Number) provides the last number of the MSU that was received correctly. FIB (Forward Indicator Bit) indicates that this MSU is being retransmitted if its value is different than the previous FIB that was sent. If the values of the previous and current FIBs are the same, then that is an indication that this MSU is being sent for the first time.

If the BIB (Backward Indicator Bit) is opposite in value from the previous one then an error is indicated and a request for retransmission is signaled. However, if they are the same then no error is indicated.

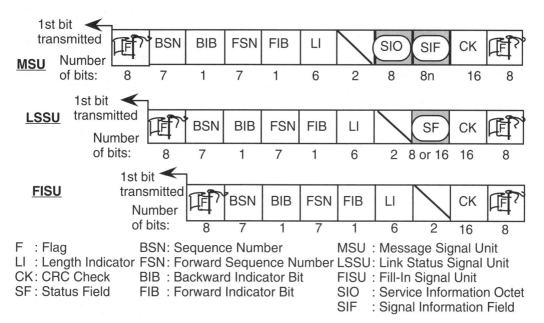

F   : Flag   BSN: Sequence Number   MSU : Message Signal Unit
LI : Length Indicator FSN: Forward Sequence Number LSSU: Link Status Signal Unit
CK: CRC Check   BIB : Backward Indicator Bit   FISU : Fill-In Signal Unit
SF : Status Field   FIB : Forward Indicator Bit   SIO   : Service Information Octet
                                                                              SIF   : Signal Information Field

Figure 14.7 The three kinds of signal units are shown. Fields which are unique to one kind of a signal unit are shaded.

14.4.2 An Example of SU Transmission Exchange

Let us look at an example of how these fields are used, and hopefully their functions will become clearer. In Figure 14.8, we have two nodes exchanging a sequence of SUs with each other. An SP and an STP are shown at each end of the link, but they could be any pair of valid SS7 nodes. The types of SUs are shown to be MSU and FISU, but the actual type only depends on whether information is being transmitted or not. Time progresses from top to bottom and for the most part, we'll start the discussion of every SU with a new paragraph.

First, the SP sends a MSU whose number is 1, which is specified in its FSN.

Then a MSU with a number of 2 is sent by the SP.

The STP, which is on the opposite end of this link, sends its MSU number 1. So its FSN is set to 1. At this time, the STP acknowledges the SP's MSU number 2. This is shown by a 2 in its BSN, meaning that the STP received the SP's MSU number 2.

The SP sends its MSU number 3 and acknowledges the STPs MSU number 1 by setting the BSN to 1. Here the FIB is 0 which is the same as the FIB for the previous MSU. Since these FIBs are the same, it further confirms to the STP that MSU number 3 is being sent for the first time. Similarly, since the BIB is 0 for both of these MSUs sent by the SP, it signals no request for retransmission from the STP.

Now the STP sends a FISU to tell the SP that there was an error in its transmission of MSU number 3. A FISU is sent instead of a MSU since it has no signaling information to convey at this time. Let us compare the fields of this FISU with the fields of the MSU sent by the STP. The FSN is still one, since only MSUs increment this field. The BSN is still two, even though the SP transmitted its MSU-3, meaning MSU-3 was received incorrectly. The BIB has changed, so this indicates to the SP that the STP wants this SU retransmitted.

The SP retransmits MSU-3. The FIB has been changed from 0 to 1, indicating that this SU is being retransmitted. The BSN is still 1, since the last error-free SU received from the STP is 1.

The STP now receives the SP's MSU-3 correctly which is shown by the 3 in the BSN field. No request for retransmission is given since the BIBs are kept the same as the previous FISU.

The SP sends its MSU-4 and indicates that this is a new MSU by maintaining it's FIB at 1.

However, the STP receives this one incorrectly and reverses the BIB bit, requesting a retransmission and maintaining the BSN at 3.

The SP retransmits with the FIB reversed from before and the STP receives it correctly, but now since it has signaling information to send from one of its users, it assembles its MSU number 2. The last MSU sent by the SP in this sequence is 5 and it acknowledges the STP's MSU-2 by setting its BSN to 2.

What we have just shown is a half duplex communication exchange, but SS7 calls for full duplex links, either running at 56 kbps or 64 kbps. In this method, all MSUs are retransmitted beginning from the MSU which caused an error. For satellite links, this would create additional delays and a different error control method called preventive cyclic retransmission is used.

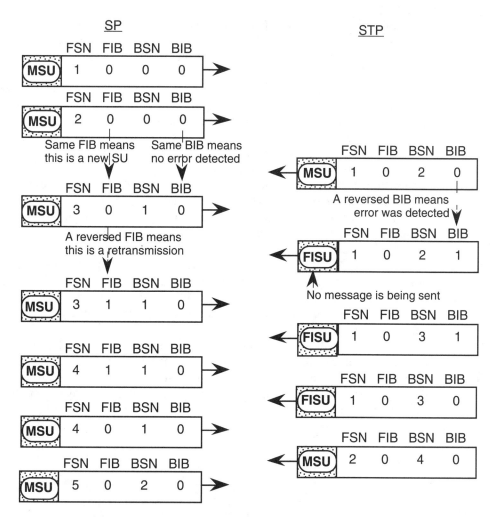

Figure 14.8. An example of exchanges of signaling units.

14.5 MTP LEVEL-3

The purpose of the third layer of SS7 is to provide routing, so that a node which receives a message knows whether the message is being handed over to level 4 locally or whether it is being forwarded to another node, and if so on which link.

The header for this level is 64 bits long for the ANSI standard and 32 bits long for the CCITT standard. It contains the SLS (Signaling Link Selection), OPC (Origination Point Code), and the DPC (Destination Point Code) fields. Each node in the network, whether SPs or STPs, has a unique point code assigned to it, and it corresponds to the address of the node. However, gateways connecting multiple SS7 networks may have more than one point code associated with them, one for each network.

Between any switching point and an adjacent STP there can be a maximum of 16 links. Since every switching point is connected to two STPs, there are 32 possible links terminating a switching point, 16 per set. For the sake of clarity, Figure 14.9 shows only 3 such links per set.

When a message is to be sent out to an STP, the third layer randomly selects an SLS out of 32 possible values. Each of these values correspond to one of the possible links. This ensures that the traffic between the two STPs is shared and balanced.

In the figure, messages initiating at the switching point with an SLS of 1, 4, 6, etc., will traverse to the STP which has a point code of 3, and the messages with SLSs of 0, 2, 3, etc., will traverse to the STP which has a point code of 2. In the same fashion, the traffic is balanced as the messages go from one STP pair to the next.

Note that when an application requires that multiple messages arrive in the same order in which they were transmitted, then this layer would assign the same SLS for those messages. This will ensure that the messages follow the same path and so are forced to arrive in order.

For instance, all messages with an SLS of 6 will go to point code 3 and then to point code 4. In conclusion, the assignment of SLSs ensure that the load is balanced in the network and that a fixed path can be provided for messages when needed. This fixed path then can be provided without requiring a sequence number field in the level 3 header, as it is done in X.25.

Realize that the FSN of layer 2 is used for error control only between two point codes, whereas the SLS remains the same until the message arrives at the DPC (Destination Point Code). Furthermore, layer 3 doesn't provide a virtual connection or datagram service by assigning the same or different SLSs, as it appears to do. This is a function provided by SCCP.

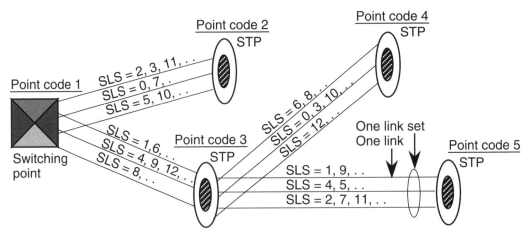

Figure 14.9 The SLS (Signaling Link Selection) field of the MTP level-3 header provides a means of balancing the load in the network and provides a fixed path if necessary.

14.6 SCCP

14.6.1 The Sublayering of SCCP

Back in Figure 14.6, SCCP is shown to be the lower portion of layer 4 in the SS7 architecture. It is always required by TCAP, the non-circuit related protocol and is sometimes required by ISUP, the circuit related protocol. SCCP segments tranmitting messages into 279 octet units (MSUs) for the lower layer protocols and reassembles them into messages at the receiving end.

SCCP is further divided up into 4 sublayers called class 0 through class 3. Classes 0 and 1 are for connectionless transmission of messages. This means that the receiving protocol cannot associate which messages logically belong with the same transmission. With these classes, higher layer protocols contain fields to identify the transaction in a query-response connection service. However, a class 2 or 3 level protocol is able to group such units, but not classes 0 and 1.

Classes 0 and 1 both provide connectionless services, but class 1 ensures that the sequence in which the messages were transmitted is maintained.

Class 2 service provides a virtual connection by using a local reference number in the SCCP header. This is similar to X.25's LCI, and similar to X.25; a connection has to be set up between the end points before transmission of data can take place. Lastly, class 3 provides control over data flow and provides data recovery by implementing additional fields.

14.6.2 An Example of a Class 0 Service

Figure 14.10 shows an example of class 0 service provided by this SCCP sublayer. Although this setup is most common in the US, other setups are possible. Let us say that the phone calls 800-123-4567 and the message unit is assembled at the switching point whose point code is 07. The switching point needs to send this message to the SCP which can translate this 800 number into a POTS number. The information about which 800 numbers can be translated by which SCPs is stored at all STPs. Therefore, the switching point sends this message to one of its STPs. The person dialing the number is called an end subscriber, while the applications executing at the SP and the STP are called users.

First at point code 7, the application layer provides the 800 number and the SCCP also provides the 800 number in its header. The OPC here is 7. The network layer at point code 7 copies the OPC in its header and inserts a DPC of 5. The DPC is inserted after selecting an SLS randomly.

The message unit arrives at point code 5, and here the SCCP layer is invoked since the end point code is equal to 5. After retrieving the 800 number, the STP knows where the SCP is located for this number and selects its DPC (4). The OPC in the SCCP layer stays at 7 since on the return trip, the STP must be able to send the message to the correct SP. However, the OPC in the MTP layer is set to 5, since point code 5 is generating this message.

The message unit may go through another STP such as point code 8, as depicted in the diagram, but doesn't get processed by the SCCP layer. The network layer is utilized, though, in order to select the proper link to the SCP.

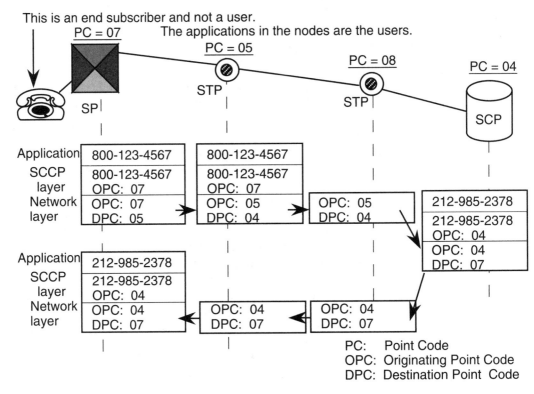

Figure 14.10 An 800 number is sent by the SP to its STP, which then finds the point code of the SCP which has its POTS number and sends the 800 number to be converted. The entire message is sent through each point, but where only the network layer functions are implemented, the network layer headings are outlined. The users are the applications which are running at PC numbers 7, 5, and 4.

At the SCP the message is processed by all of the layers, and the application will convert the 800 number to the POTS number, which is then copied in the SCCP header. Also, the point code of 7 is copied from the OPC from the old SCCP header to the DPC of the new network layer header. On the return trip, the SCCP function is not invoked until it reaches point code 7, since now the end point (DPC = 7) is not any intermediate STPs but the SP. Once the POTS number is obtained, the user at the SP must use the ISUP layer to actually connect the circuit for the end subscriber. But first let us take a look into the TCAP layer.

14.7 TCAP

This section outlines the first of the two vertical layers of SS7 as shown in Figure 14.6, namely TCAP (Transaction Capabilities Application Part). The database query example which we looked at in the last section is an example of a non-circuit related user function. Non-circuit related functions place a call to a SCP so that routing information can be retrieved from it, which is the general purpose of this layer. Usually, after the TCAP is utilized, the ISUP is needed to complete the call.

14.7.1 Classes of User Requests

Turning our attention back to Figure 14.6, we see that the TCAP layer is divided into what is called the CSL (Component Sub-Layer) and the TSL (Transaction Sub-Layer). A TCAP user, or the network application which is executing at a SS7 node, can either send a request or a response to a peer user at another node in the network. The types of requests fall into four classes of operation and they are based on the kinds of responses that are expected.

A class 1 type of request requires that the remote user perform the requested operation and respond whether the operation was successful or not. A class 2 type of request requires the remote node to respond only if the operation failed, whereas a class 3 requires it to respond only if the operation was successful. Finally, class 4 requires no response from the receiving node.

An example of a class 1 request is to convert an 800 number to a POTS number which always requires a response. An example of a class 2 request is to perform a routine test and respond only if there was some kind of a problem, whereas a class 3 request may broadcast a message to many nodes and only the node for which the message pertains replies. Finally, a class 4 request may simply be a warning that is broadcast to many nodes.

14.7.2 The Two Sublayers of TCAP

Figure 14.6 shows that as a request or a response is being sent down through the layers, it is first processed by the CSL of TCAP. Here the unit of message is called a component. Then it is sent through the TSL at which time one or more components are assembled into a transaction message. One component may contain only one request or only one response. However, a transaction message may contain several components.

A component may contain a request that is of one of the four class types mentioned, a response stating that the operation was successful or not, or a response stating that the received request (or the response) was not understandable.

The TSL provides a connection-oriented dialogue for the CSL peers to communicate with each other using components. This is done through the connectionless functions provided by the class 0 and 1 layers of SCCP. In other words, using the connectionless services of SCCP, TSL provides a connection for the CSL sublayer.

14.7.3 The CSL Sublayer

There are five kinds of CSL components. The INVOKE component contains one request and only one. The RETURN RESULT-NOT LAST component contains a report of a successful operation and signals that more components are to follow, which belong with this report. The RETURN RESULT-LAST component is the final component in a report containing such multiple components. A report may have to be divided into multiple components because a SCCP message is limited to a maximum of 254 octets.

If a requested operation was unsuccessful, then a RETURN ERROR component will be sent and if the received message was not understandable, then a REJECT component will be issued.

Each component is identified by a CID (Component IDentifier), so that the returning responses can be associated (or matched) with the requests which were transmitted, even if they were sent by two different applications to the same destination point.

Figure 14.11 shows an example of components being exchanged by the peer users. Initially, the switch wants to translate an 800 number to a POTS number, so it sends an INVOKE component and gives it a CID of 3. A CID is also called an invoke ID.

The SCP upon receiving this request can't provide a response because it needs more information from the switch, let's say, since this 800 number is converted to different POTS numbers depending on what service the customer wants. So the SCP in turn issues another request, stating to dial a 1 to talk to the sales department, and so on. This request, created because of the original request, also becomes an invoke component at the CSL layer, and receives its own ID of 8. An invoke generated as a result of another is called a linked invoke. Also, a request generated as a result of another request is called a linked operation, as in this case.

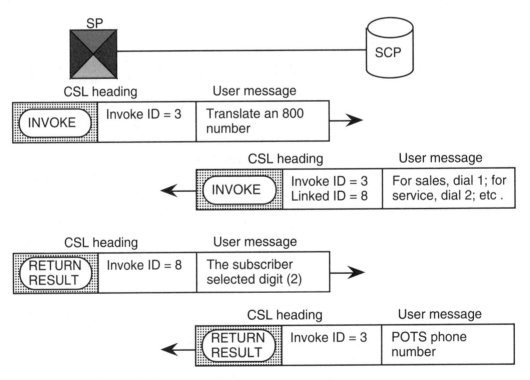

Figure 14.11 An example of component sequence of exchanges.

The user or the application at the switch receives the correct digit, let us say "2," from it's end-subscriber. This selection is returned in a RETURN RESULT component with a CID of 8. The SCP user matching the CID of 8 with the linked ID of 8 is now able to provide a RETURN RESULT component (CID = 3) with the correct POTS number. Now the switch is able to complete the call for the process which was initiated with an invoke identifier of 3.

14.7.4 The TSL Sublayer

As noted before, TSL provides an end-to-end connection for the CSL layer using the connectionless services of SCCP. This end-to-end connection is called a dialogue or a transaction. To provide a connection, the TSL message header contains a field, similar to X.25's LCI, called the TID (Transaction IDentifier). Using this TID, users can initiate, maintain, and terminate a dialogue with other users. The CIDs allow the end points to match the receiving responses with those requests which were sent out.

There are five types of TSL messages: BEGIN, END, CONTINUE, UNIDIREC-TIONAL, and ABORT. If the BEGIN and CONTINUE messages don't contain any components or upper layer messages, then they are akin to X.25's CALL REQUEST and CALL ACCEPTED packets, respectively.

The END message is similar to CLEAR REQUEST of X.25, and may be issued by either of the TSL peers. However, unlike X.25, the END message does not get confirmed.

If the BEGIN contains an INVOKE component (that is, of any of the 4 class types) and is replied by an END, then the dialogue as shown in Figure 14.12(a) is similar to X.25's fast select feature. In this case, the END message may be empty, or may contain a class 4 INVOKE, which doesn't require a response, or it may contain a RETURN RESULT, RETURN ERROR, or REJECT component. If a problem occurs and the TSL layer can't maintain the dialogue, then an ABORT is issued with diagnostic information.

Figure 14.12(b) depicts an UNIDIRECTIONAL message which is used to provide a class 4 type of operation. No response is needed here.

As a last example of a simple TSL dialogue, let us look at Figure 14.12(c), where a node may request to have a credit card call authorized. The user may create the request giving the items as shown in the figure, such as the calling party number. The CSL will then encode its header for a class 1 INVOKE, since this operation requires a response. The TSL creates a fast select message out of it and sends a BEGIN. The SCP upon receiving this message validates the call, and may send a class 4 INVOKE requiring the call be limited to 3 minutes.

14.8 ISUP

ISUP (ISDN User Part) is a protocol providing circuit-related functions between switches. It is the protocol used between ISDN end subscribers supporting voice, data, video, and other applications in a digital environment. TUP (Telephone User Part) which is the predecessor of ISUP primarily supports voice connections only using analog subscriber lines.

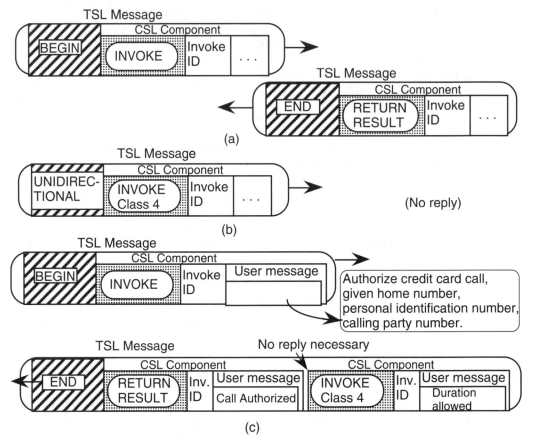

Figure 14.12 Three examples of TSL message exchanges.

14.8.1 Bearer and Supplementary Services

ISUP services are divided into basic bearer services and supplementary services. Bearer services are for the switches which allow them to set up a 64 kbps circuit-switched connection between the end subscribers. They also specify the supervision and the release of such connections. The discussion surrounding Figure 5.1 showed how these functions were provided using CAS (Channel Associated Signaling or per-trunk signaling) in an analog world. These same functions are provided with SS7 in a digital network by the basic bearer services.

Supplementary services are advanced services, provided directly for the end subscriber, which were not available with the CAS signaling methods. They bring a rich variety of services to the ordinary ISDN end subscriber, similar to the kinds of features available with a PBX. Let us outline a few of them here.

Calling Line Identification: Commonly known as caller-ID, this service is provided to the called party which gives the calling party's phone number, and the extension or the subaddress if it has one.

Calling Line Identification Restriction: This service is provided to the calling party so that his or her phone number may not be presented to the person being called.

Call Transfer: This service enables either end of a connection to establish a connection with a third party and then drop off. If the person doesn't drop off then it becomes a conference call.

Call Forward Busy: While a connection is established between two subscribers, a new call comes in for one of them, then the call is forwarded to a different predefined number.

Direct Dialing In: Without having to coordinate a call with an attendant, an end subscriber can dial into a PBX and then its extension or subaddress directly through the ISDN.

Closed User Group: Similar to the X.25 feature, subscribers can form a sub-network and users who are not in the group may be restricted to call any one in the group, and/or vice versa. Designated members of a group may have added privileges or restrictions and may belong to a number of such groups.

14.8.2 ISUP Messages

The protocol data unit for ISUP is simply called an ISUP message. The message consists of parameters and information about them. The first two parameters are each an octet and are always needed. They are the CIC (Circuit Identification Code) and the MT (Message Type) parameters. The CIC specifies the 64 kbps physical circuit between two switches that this message pertains to and the MT identifies the type of message or the format for the rest of the message. In the previous analog systems, one trunk carried one voice circuit. Here, the CIC, analogous to one trunk, is not only restricted to voice, but may carry any information the bearer may want to send over a 64 kbps channel.

Other parameters of ISUP messages are categorized into mandatory and fixed length, mandatory and variable length, and optional parameters. The combination of these parameters used in a message define the type of the message. Panel 14.1 summarizes the categories and the types of ISUP messages. We will look at a sampling of these shortly.

14.8.3 The ISUP Signaling Connection

Figure 14.13 shows the CIC links between three switches. These are the links over which no signaling is sent but only user information at 64 kbps. From one switch to another a given CIC appears only once. From PC3 to PC4, there is only one circuit with a CIC of 5; however, a CIC of 5 may also exist going to PC2. So the combination of CIC and the DPC (Destination Point Code) uniquely specifies a circuit leaving a switch. The number of CICs between a given pair of switches depend on the demand for traffic.

Figure 14.13 further shows how a circuit-switched connection is being initiated between two end offices, PC2 and PC4. PC3 is an intermediate office through which a connection has to be switched. First the subscriber calls 212-012-3456 and PC2 decides to make the connection through PC3, maybe because no direct CICs (trunks) are available to PC4. PC4 is the only switch which can complete the connection to the called subscriber.

So PC2 finds a free circuit which has a CIC of 5 connecting to PC3. It generates an IAM (Initial Address Message), listed in Panel 14.1, and sends it through the signaling network, via PC5 and PC6 to PC3. The IAM message contains the called party's number and all the required routing information. Layer 3, the network layer, assigns an SLS of 5 and sets the OPC to 2 and the DPC to 3 in its header.

PC3 opens up the ISUP message and realizes that the connection should be made next to PC4. It then finds an idle circuit (CIC = 3) and assembles and sends its own ISUP message to PC4. Layer three chooses an SLS of 4 and sends a new IAM message as shown in the figure.

Now, as long as the call is still active, all messages arriving into PC3 from PC2 that have a CIC of 5 and an SLS of 5 are regenerated there and are sent to PC-4 with a CIC of 3 and an SLS of 4. This establishes a one-way signaling path. Having always the same SLS between two switches ensures that the messages arrive in the same order that they were sent for that call, while the CIC identifies the circuit that is being used for that call.

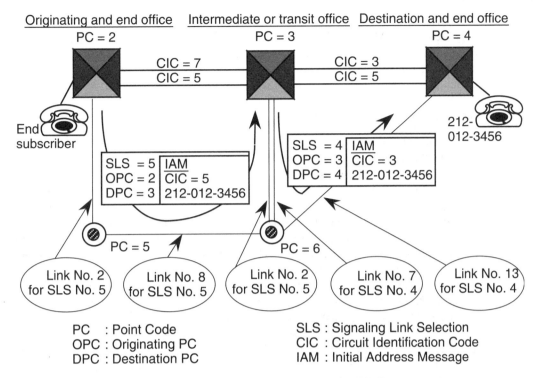

Figure 14.13 Initiating a connection using ISUP.

The figure only shows the signaling path that is established in the forward direction, but one is also established in the reverse direction, using the same set of CICs over the links, but not necessarily the same set of SLSs as were used in the forward direction. Notice that the destination doesn't receive the originating office's PC, but the set of CIC-SLS pairs through intermediate points are used to send messages back to the originating office. An ISUP signaling connection is made up of one such forward and one such reverse signaling path.

14.8.4 ISUP Signaling Methods

What we have just finished describing is the LBL (link-by-link) signaling method. Here all the ISUP messages are interpreted and modified by the transit switches. Alternatively, when messages are not interpreted by the transit switches but only by the end offices then it is called end-to-end signaling. End-to-end signaling is achieved either by sending PAM (Pass-Along Messages) or by utilizing the SCCP connection-oriented or connectionless layers. Figure 14.6 depicts these options, while Panel 14.1 lists PAM.

An example of where end-to-end signaling may be needed is when a destination switch, after receiving an IAM, requests and receives more information from the call originating office, in order to complete the call. Here the transit switches don't need to know the contents of this information exchange.

When a PAM message, a kind of an ISUP message, arrives at a transit switch, it only looks at the MT and CIC parameters. The MT is examined to see that it is a PAM message and the CIC is examined to send the message over the next proper link. But the rest of the contents of the message are not interpreted or regenerated by such switches.

14.8.5 Call Set-Up and Release

In conclusion let us outline how a circuit-switched call may be connected and disconnected using these ISUP messages and the signaling messages sent over the D channel between the subscriber's phone and the switch.

As it will be pointed out in Chapter 15, a residential customer's line multiplexes two B channels used for sending voice and data simultaneously and one D channel for signaling the switch at the CO. An ISDN phone sends a SETUP message to the switch on the D channel when it goes off-hook, instead of closing the local loop and setting up a DC current as it is done with a POTS line. Look at the first three steps as shown in Figure 14.14. It then receives a SETUP ACK message from the switch instead of receiving a dial tone. Similarly, when a telephone number is dialed, an ISDN phone sends an INFO message, and when the phone at the distant end is ringing, it receives an ALERTING message instead of a ringback.

All these signaling messages are sent over the D channel between the subscriber and the switch and are specified in CCITT's Q.931 protocol. The conversations are carried over the B channels. Although digital messages are being transferred over the subscriber's line, the user still hears the analog signals that were heard with a POTS line. To accomplish this, the dial tone, ringback, and other analog signals are now provided by the subscriber's terminal and not by the local switch. Keeping this user interface consistent on an ISDN phone as it was with a POTS phone allows a smoother transition to ISDN for telephone customers.

Figure 14.14 shows an example of a set-up and a release of a connection over the ISDN. The messages between a switch and a phone are ISDN's layer 3 messages sent over the D channel, while the messages between the switches (via the STPs) are ISUP or Q.931 messages as listed in Panel 14.1. Each step is numbered in sequence.

As just mentioned, the telephone and the switch exchange SETUP, SETUP ACK, and INFO messages over the D channel. Then an ISUP message (IAM) is generated and sent to the intermediate switch, which regenerates another IAM which is sent to the destination switch. If more information is to be sent than can be contained in an IAM message, then the originating switch will follow the IAM with a SAM (Subsequent Address Message). A SAM is not shown here. (It appears that the standards committee may have just finished an intense discussion of Dr. Seuss's Green Eggs and Ham when these acronyms were chosen. Apparently, the ham was mistakenly named PAM.)

Figure 14.14 shows that the destination switch needs more information to complete the connection and it sends an INR (INformation Request) message enveloped inside of a PAM (Pass-Along Message) back to the call originating switch. The INR may be required to obtain the phone number of the caller, to accomplish proper billing, or for other reasons. Step 8 shows that the originating switch replies with an INF (INFormation) message, and the destination sends a SETUP message to the distant

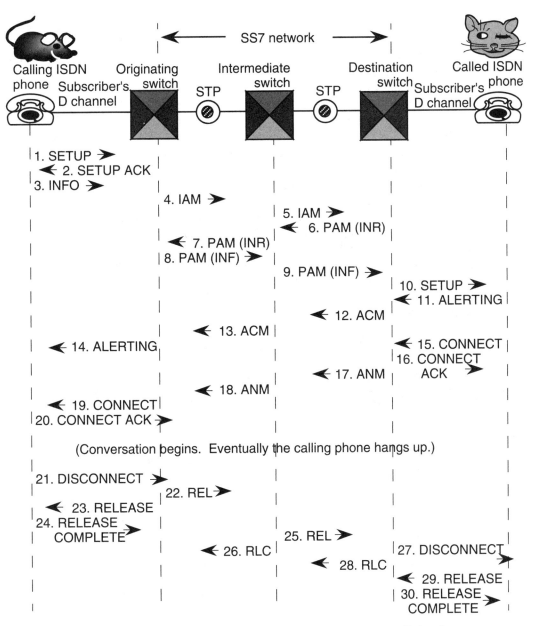

Figure 14.14 A scenario of connecting and disconnecting a call showing the Q.931 messages at the subscriber phones and ISUP messages between the switches.

phone. The phone begins to ring and it sends an ALERTING message over the D channel. Then the switch generates an ACM (Address Complete Message) which then translates into an ALERTING message to the caller.

When the called subscriber picks up the phone, a CONNECT message is sent and the switch sends a CONNECT ACK to the subscriber and an ANM (ANswer Message) through the network. After an exchange of CONNECT and CONNECT ACK at the calling end, conversation can then begin.

The figure shows that the ACM (Address Complete Message) was sent by the switch after it received an ALTERING from the phone. However, it is possible for the switch to send the ACM first before it receives the ALTERTING signal. In that case, it will send a CPG (Call ProGress) message upon receiving the ALERTING from the phone. It is also possible that the called party may pick up the phone immediately and send a CONNECT without sending an ALERTING message at all.

Finally, either party may hang up first, which generates a DISCONNECT. Here the calling party sends a DISCONNECT which maps into a REL (RELease) to the intermediate switch. At the same time, a RELEASE is sent from the originating switch to the telephone and a RELEASE COMPLETE is received back. The intermediate switch then sends a REL to the destination and an RLC (ReLease Complete) in the reverse direction. Similarly, an exchange of DISCONNECT, RELEASE, and RELEASE COMPLETE occurs on the called party's D channel. Notice that some Q.931 messages such as SETUP, CONNECT, and DISCONNECT can be sent either from the telephone or from the switch.

Exercises

1. Why is SS7 more flexible than CAS signaling methods?
   a. It is software driven.
   b. It uses digital switches.
   c. It uses high speed data links.
   d. It uses electromechanical technology.

2. STP pairs are connected to other STP pairs using what type of links?
   a. A-access links
   b. B-bridge links
   c. C-cross links
   d. D-diagonal links

3. SS7's layer 4 is divided into which major sublayers?
   a. CSL, TSL, and MTP
   b. CSL, SCCP, and ISUP
   c. TCAP, SCCP, and MTP
   d. TCAP, SCCP, and ISUP

4. Which SU (Signaling Unit) has only the fields that exist in the other two types of SUs?
   a. MSU
   b. LSSU
   c. FISU
   d. not any

5. Which class of operation responds only if the requested operation failed?
   a. Class 1
   b. Class 2
   c. Class 3
   d. Class 4

6. Which of the following Q.931 messages are only sent from a calling phone?
   a. DISCONNECT
   b. SETUP
   c. CONNECT
   d. INFO

7. Which CCITT's signaling system corresponded closely with our SF signaling?

8. SCCP and MTP layers are compositely called by what name?

9. In Figure 14.6, if the STP didn't have any information to convey to the SP in the last SU, what type of an SU would that have been?

10. If the number of links between two point codes were reduced, the number of SLSs on each of those links would increase, decrease, or stay the same?

11. In Figure 14.8, users (applications) at which PCs provide their services on the "sending trip" and which ones on the "return trip"?

12. An ISUP signaling path is specified by which pair of items between each pair of switches in the path?

13. Describe the SP and its three types.

14. If the second MSU sent by the STP were received incorrectly by the SP, show the contents of the SUs that would follow in order to resolve that error.

15. What are the three sublayers of TC, and what are their functions?

16. In Figure 14.9, if the SCP could not find the 800 number in its data base to convert, what type of a CSL component would it send back? Suppose that component had an error in its heading; what type of a component would the SP send? How would then the SCP reply? Draw a diagram outlining this scenario.

17. Which ISUP supplementary service not listed in the text would you like to see implemented? In other words what would you like to be able to do with your home phone that you think you can't do now?

18. Describe the three methods by which the ISUP can gain services of the MTP layer. What is end-to-end signaling and does that relate to these methods?

Chapter 15

ISDN and SONET

15.1 INTRODUCTION AND BENEFITS

Imagine if in our homes, refrigerators, radios, toasters, etc., all required different voltage sources, each had to have their own wiring, and that the plugs for the appliances were all incompatible. Then we would not be able to move the appliances around the house as freely as we do today, because they would not be able to plug into any AC outlet in a house. Though this sounds outlandish, currently we are doing just this sort of connecting with our telecommunications services. Customers are required to channel voice, switched digital data, packetized data, etc., on separate networks, because all operate on different standards.

ISDN (Integrated Services Digital Network) brings with it integration of such services. One common outlet (RJ-45) can now provide integrated access to a variety of services, similar to the common AC jack. Currently, many buildings have separate networks wired for voice, video, data, security alarm systems, and so on. Each network type is independent from others as shown in Figure 15.1(a). With ISDN, the same wire (and jack) can be used for any of these services, and as shown in Figure 15.1(b), they become integrated. In fact, each device doesn't need a separate wire as it did before, but multiple devices may share the same line. Consequently, ISDN provides flexibility, in that terminals are now portable, and provides efficiency, in that one line can be shared by multiple terminals.

ISDN is a natural evolution of the PSTN. The PSTN originally was designed to carry only voice over analog lines, but then in the 1950s, modems were introduced to carry data. However, due to the limitations of transmission rates and quality with modems, carriers had to create separate digital transmission systems to support data at higher speeds and with better quality. Something had to be done to eliminate incompatibilities in network services, and so ISDN was conceptualized.

Though presently the cost to convert to ISDN is rather high, over time, it should prove to be more economical than carrying voice and data over the present POTS

Graciously, this chapter has been enriched by Robert Fishel of AT&T.

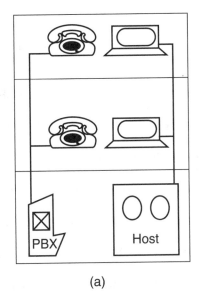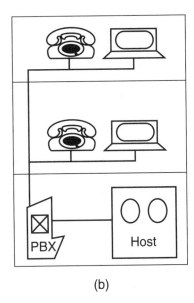

(a) (b)

Figure 15.1 (a) WIthout ISDN, voice and data terminals need separate wiring. (b) With ISDN, the same wiring is shared by all terminals and all plug into the same jack.

services. Residences can continue using the same 2-wire pair for the local loop. Since the network will be all digital, the components will cost less and consume less power. Competition among equipment vendors will drive down the prices of ISDN devices, and because there is a limited set of standard interfaces, the production of these devices will become less costly. However, the chances of ISDN replacing POTS for providing only one voice circuit to the home are quite small.

ISDN should then be beneficial to manufacturers, carriers, and the end-users. Services that are currently available only to large corporations will be available to small businesses and individuals as well. Many voice mail systems instead of being connected by tie-lines at various branch locations would only be needed at one location, which could then be accessed by any location, even from the remotest sites and still provide the same functionality. A residential customer could dial a catalog sales office, view an item on a TV screen, place an order using a PC and make the payment from his bank all on one ISDN basic service wire line. Other applications will be created, once the capabilities of ISDN are fully realized.

15.2 DEFINITIONS

ISDN, though first proposed in 1968 by CCITT, didn't become a standard until 1984 when CCITT published the Red Books. Since then new recommendations are published every four years. Like SS7, the North American version of ISDN is driven by ANSI, and is slightly different from that of CCITT.

15.2.1 Access Interfaces

There are two methods of accessing the ISDN. The BRI (Basic Rate Interface) access is designed for the residential and small business customers, as well as individuals within a large business. The PRI (Primary Rate Interface) access is primarily for large businesses. BRI is comprised of two B channels, each rated at 64 kbps and one D channel rated at 16 kbps. The upper layer protocols for the B channel or the bearer channel are flexible, so that the subscriber may transmit any information in any format that is needed. Using one pair of metallic wires from the CO, an individual can talk on one B channel using PCM encoding and also have a data connection to a different location at 64 kbps on the other B channel.

If voice is compressed at 16 kbps at both end points, then over one B channel 4 separate conversations are made possible between them. It will be left up to the end points to multiplex, demultiplex, and switch these 4 channels. It is also possible to send slow motion video, fax, and any other information on the B channel; however, the terminals on the receive end must be compatible with the information that is transmitted. Additionally, a 128 kbps data stream can be fed into an inverse multiplexer and sent over both B channels, where the signal is then recomposed at the distant end back to 128 kbps.

The D, or the delta channel, provides the necessary signaling to setup and disconnect the B channels as required. The messages conveyed over the D channel are defined by CCITT's Q.931 and Q.932, or I.451 and I.452, respectively. (When two CCITT groups agree on the same set of recommendations, the protocol ends up having two different nomenclatures.) Though the primary purpose of the D channel is to control signaling, it is also used for low-speed packet switching and telemetry, such as having utility metering be done automatically. BRI may be configured as 2B + D, B + D, or simply as D.

The PRI access in North America and Japan runs at T1 rate and in Europe at E1 rate. PRI's D channel operates at 64 kbps and not at 16 kbps as in BRI. At the T1 rate, it is either specified as 23B + D or as 24B. Unlike T1, the bearer channels are clear with no bits being robbed for signaling purposes. With E1, the PRI can be configured as 30B + D or 31B. Typically, the business customer of PRI will have a PBX or a host connected to its trunk.

Besides the B and D channels, there are H or higher-rate channels as well. H0, H11, H12 channels operate at 384, 1536, 1920 kbps, respectively. These are multiples of 64 kbps. The H4 channel operates at 135.168 Mbps and is capable of carrying standard PCM based color television signals.

15.2.2 Functional Devices and Reference Points

In order to fully identify the purpose and function of each device, ISDN describes a limited set of devices and the interfaces between them, as shown in Figure 15.2. If these interfaces are implemented correctly, then one vendor's equipment could easily be replaced by another's.

Devices which are not ISDN compatible are categorized as TE2 (Terminal Equipment 2) devices. These could be analog phones, PCs, 3270 terminals, and so on.

To connect a TE2 to the ISDN, a TA (Terminal Adapter) must be used. The TA will allow the TE2 to appear as an ISDN terminal to the rest of the network; conversely, it will allow the rest of the network to interact with the TE2 as if it were an ISDN terminal. The interface between them is called the R reference point, and it will depend on the kind of TE2 that is being connected.

TE1 (Terminal Equipment 1) is a device which is fully ISDN compatible and is connected to the ISDN using the S interface. It could be a digital telephone, an IVDT, a workstation, or a number of other devices.

NT2 (Network Termination 2) provides switching, multiplexing, concentrating, or distribution of information for the customer's premises. For example, it could be a LAN server, multiplexer, FEP, or a PBX. Typically, a PRI connection would require an NT2, and a BRI connection would not.

NT1 (Network Termination 1) provides proper line termination at the customer's premises. It can provide line monitoring, power feeding, error statistics, and proper timing. Think of it as a DSU/CSU device.

The function of the NT1 can easily be done on a single card which could then become part of the PBX or a PC. In such a case, the device which functions both as an NT1 and as an NT2 is dubbed as an NT12 device. The reference point between these devices is called the T interface. With BRI, without the NT2, the point between the NT1 and the TE is called the S/T interface. In the remainder of this chapter, we'll refer to both the TE1 and the TA-TE2 combination simply as TE. Furthermore, the term NT will be used to mean either the NT1 or the NT2, depending on which one is connected to the TE.

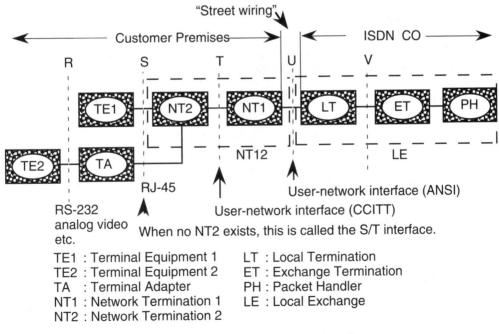

Figure 15.2 Functional groupings and their interfaces.

Unlike ANSI, CCITT considers NT1 to be part of the local network and doesn't mention the U reference point. However, the FCC designates the NT1 as belonging to the customer, and so the ANSI defines the U interface as the line going to the CO. In ISDN terminology, the CO is called an LE (Local Exchange). The LE itself is comprised of LT (Local Termination), ET (Exchange Termination), and PH (Packet Handler).

The LT complements the functions of the NT1 on the LE side, and is similar to the OCU (Office Channel Unit) described in Chapter 10. The ET is the ISDN circuit switch and the PH is like a gateway to PDNs.

15.3 TELECOMMUNICATIONS SERVICES

Since ISDN integrates many kinds of services, we need to define what constitutes a service. ISDN does that well by defining services using a limited set of attributes (or distinctive features). By specifying these sets of attributes, what is expected from the ISDN is clearly stated, and all the "pieces" of the ISDN can fit better with fewer misunderstandings among equipment manufacturers, carriers, and users. These attributes then are transmitted on the D channel when requesting a service, such as a telephone connection.

15.3.1 Types of Services and Their Attributes

Telecommunications services are classified as bearer services, teleservices, and supplementary services, and they are defined in terms of their attributes. Teleservices include bearer services, and supplementary services are provided to both the bearer services and teleservices.

As seen in Figure 15.3 bearer services are network services in that they are characterized by the first three layers of the OSI Reference Model, whereas teleservices provide terminal equipment functions for communications between the end users. These services require the interaction of all 7 layers of the OSI model. The bearer services are categorized into access, information and supplementary attributes.

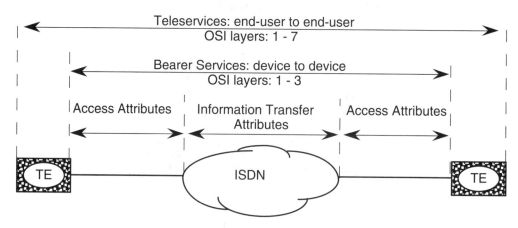

Figure 15.3 Classifications and scopes of telecommunication services.

Table 15.1 Bearer Services Attributes	
Attribute	Attribute Description
Information Transfer Attributes	
1. Information Transfer Mode	Circuit Switched Packet Switched
2. Information Transfer Rate	Bit Rate in kbps: 64, 2x64, 384, 1536, 1920, Throughput in PPS
3. Information Transfer Capability	Unrestricted Digital Audio in khz: 3.1, 7, 15 Speech, Video
4. Structure	Service Data Unit Integrity Unstructured 8 khz Integrity TSSI, RDTD
5. Establishment of Communication	Demand Reserved Permanent
6. Symmetry	Unidirectional Bidirectional Symmetric Bidirectional Asymmetric
7. Communication Configuration	Point-to-Point Multipoint Broadcast

Table 15.1 (Cont)	
Attribute	Attribute Description
Access Attributes	
8. Access Channel and Rate	D (16kbps) D (64 kbps) B, H0, H11, H12
9. Signaling Access and Information Access	I.430/431 I.451, I.461/462 HDLC, LAPB LAPD, and others
General Attributes	
10. Supplementary Services	Calling Line ID Call Transfer and others
11. Quality of Service	To be defined
12. Interworking	To be defined
13. Operational and commercial	To be defined

Supplementary services have already been outlined in section 14.8.1, in the discussion of the ISUP, and are not discussed any further here.

Table 15.1 shows the three categories of bearer services attributes: access attributes (which provide methods of accessing network functions), information attributes (which specify the capabilities for transmission of information through the ISDN), and general attributes. General attributes are listed as items 10 through 13 in Table 15.1. They include supplementary services, and specify how much delay or what error rate is acceptable and how to interwork ISDN with other ISDN and non-ISDN networks.

15.3.2 Information Transfer Attributes

In this section we will describe the seven information transfer attributes in the order they are listed in Table 15.1.

The first attribute is called the information transfer mode. It identifies one of two mode types: circuit switched or packet switched. The information transfer rate attribute is given in kbps for circuit switched mode and in PPS (Packets Per Second) for the packet mode. The 2 x 64 kbps is provided if a user needs to connect both B channels when establishing a call. In this case, the user has to send both channels over the network separately.

The information transfer capability attribute can be specified as speech for normal voice conversations where data compression can be used. When using a modem, no compression can be requested by specifying this attribute as 3.1 kHz audio instead. 7 kHz is used for transmitting mono radio broadcasts and 15 kHz for transmitting stereo. The default setting for circuit mode transfer is speech whereas for packet switched mode, it is unrestricted. Unrestricted digital information allows any bit pattern to appear anywhere in the data stream. For instance, the service doesn't care if the bits are stuffed or not, as long as they are within SDLC frames.

An unstructured value for the structure attribute means that the boundaries of the octets don't have to be preserved on delivery of the data stream, whereas 8 kHz integrity (the default for circuit mode) requires that the boundaries be preserved so that the 8 bits for each voice sample are kept together.

RDTD (Restricted Differential Time Delay) specifies that the delay through the ISDN be no more than 50 msec, which is necessary with speech. TSSI (Time Slot Sequence Integrity) requires that information be conveyed to the distant end in the same order as it is delivered to the network for multiple access channels which are sent together, such as the 2 x 64 kbps channels.

Communication can be established on demand, where one receives a connection when requested and terminates it when no longer needed, as in dialing a telephone number. A communication can be established in advance using the reserve attribute. Here, the setup and release of a connection is initiated automatically by the network and not by the end user. Lastly, this attribute could be specified as permanent, where a connection is provided, analogous to a leased line, between two points for the duration of time that the service is being subscribed.

If the symmetry attribute is specified as unidirectional, then data flows in only one direction, as when a studio is sending a broadcast to a radio transmitter. If it is specified as bidirectional symmetric, then the transmission occurs in both directions and at the same rate. A bidirectional asymmetric service transfers information in both directions, but the rates are not the same. This type of symmetry is used when one end is transferring data while the other end replies with an occasional ACK or NACK.

Finally, the communication configuration attribute specifies whether the service involves only two users, (as in point to point), if it involves two-way communication among several users (multipoint), or if only one point is transmitting to several at once (broadcast).

Table 15.2 Teleservices Attributes	
Attribute	Attribute Description
Low-Layer Attributes	
Information Transfer, Access Attributes, and Supplementary Services	Identical to bearer services
High-Layer Attributes	
Type of User Information Layer 4 Protocol Layer 5 Protocol Layer 6 Protocol Resolution (if applicable) Graphic Mode (if applicable) Layer 7 Protocol	Speech (3.1 khz), Sound (15 khz), Text, etc. x.224, T.70 x.225, T.62 T.73, T.61, T.6, T.100 in ppi: 200, 240, 300, 400 Alphamosaic, Geometric, Photographic T.60, T.500

15.3.3 Access Attributes

The information transfer attributes specify how the information is transferred across the ISDN, and the access attributes, on the other hand, specify how the user accesses the network: with which channels, what rates, and which protocols. Table 15.1 lists several of the values for these attributes. Signaling access protocols describe what signaling methods are used between the user and the network, and information access protocol describes how the information is exchanged from end-user to end-user.

15.3.4 Teleservices Attributes

These services not only include the bearer services, but also the OSI's higher layer attributes. These are outlined in Table 15.2, and are not discussed at any length here.

15.4 PHYSICAL LAYER OF BRI

15.4.1 Introduction

As we have said, multiple devices can share the same ISDN interface; that is, many devices can be connected to the same 2B + D interface. In order to accomplish this, ISDN defines three layers similar to OSI's lower three layers: physical, data link, and network layers.

As depicted in Figure 15.4, ISDN recommendations specify the three layers for only the D channel. However, ISDN issues concerning the B channel are limited to only the physical layer. The protocols for layers 2 through 7 for the B channel are the responsibilities of the TEs. ISDN simply transfers the bit stream for the B channel over the network. The figure seems to imply that the B and the D channels are physically separated over the line to the LE; however, they are time division multiplexed over the same physical link.

This figure also shows that CCITT defines the network boundary to include the NT1, while ANSI excludes it. In either case, NT1 is part of the customer's premises. In this section, we will look at each boundary individually.

The physical layer, besides providing transmission capabilities for the B and D channels, also provides timing and synchronization. The layer also describes the signaling capabilities for activation and deactivation of terminals, and to gain an orderly access of the D channel.

BRI access can be provided for residential, centrex, or PBX customers, and with 2B + D configuration (typically, over one pair) each B channel can be assigned its own phone number. Though the local loop would still be the same as before, residential customers would need a sophisticated NT1, the inside wiring may have to be changed to 2 or three pairs, and the modular jacks may have to be converted to 8-pin jacks, not to mention the cost of the TEs would be higher than today's simple POTS phones.

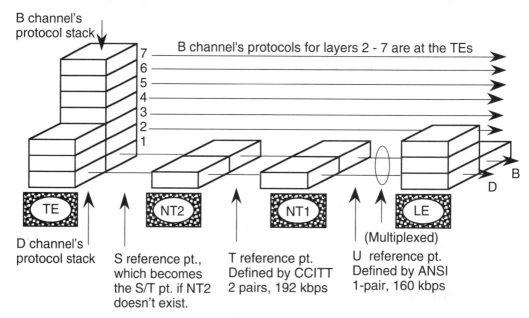

Figure 15.4 CCITT's ISDN protocols are specified only at the S and T reference points. Only the D channel is specified for the lower three layers. The B and D channels are simply multiplexed at the physical layer over the same link. ANSI specifies the U reference point, but the difference between it and the S/T points is only at the physical layer.

15.4.2 ANSI's U Reference Point

At this reference point, the NT1 terminates a local loop by providing an 8-pin modular plug called the RJ-45. Out of these 8 pins, only the middle two are used. Since the S/T interface uses 4 wires, NT1 must provide a means of converting the in-house 4 wires to the 2 wires that are used with the LE. To accomplish transmitting and receiving on the same pair without a loss of available bandwidth, echo cancelling is used here.

Echo Cancelling: In Figure 15.5, the S/T interface is shown to be transmitting a positive pulse toward the LE. Part of this positive pulse is fed to the delay circuit and part of it to the hybrid circuit. The hybrid transmits the pulse, but since the impedance of the local loop is not perfectly matched, some of this transmitted signal is reflected or echoed back. At the same time, the NT1 is receiving a negative pulse from the LE, and these two signals superimpose on the same line. In this example, let us say that these two signals are of equal amplitude, but since they are of opposite polarity, they cancel each other. Hence, a straight line or 0 V is received.

The hybrid circuit forwards this 0 V signal to the echo canceler, which subtracts the transmitted positive pulse from the delaying circuit which enables the echo canceler to recover the negative pulse that was intended for the NT1. The amount of power that is echoed and the changes in the delays which occur in the echoed signal are automatically detected and compensated for or adapted by the echo canceler.

To summarize, echo cancelling allows full duplex transmission over a one-pair line by using this equalizing network. This is done by cancelling the effect of the

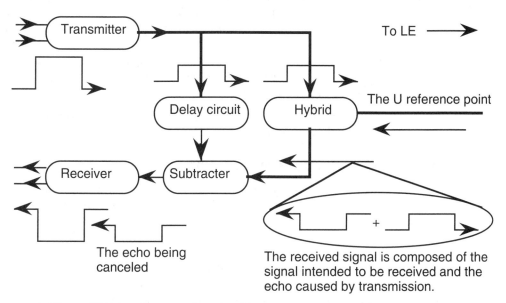

Figure 15.5 An echo canceling circuit, which is part of the NT1, provides full duplex operation over one pair of wires.

transmission from the composite received signal to extract the intended received signal. Of course, echo cancelling must be done on both ends of the local loop.

2B1Q Line Coding: The line code used over the U reference point is called 2B1Q (2 Binary 1 Quaternary) and an example of it is shown in Figure 15.6. The data stream is divided into groups of two bits called quats. There are four possible values for quats, and their voltage levels are given in the accompanying chart. In the data stream shown, notice that the "00" quat is transmitted by sending – 3 V and the "11" quat by +1 V, and so on.

However, the problem with this coding is that the line is not balanced for DC voltage. That is, unlike the bipolar format used with T1s, there is not an equal number of positive pulses as there are negative pulses. Consequently, a scrambling algorithm is used in the transmitting side and a descrambling algorithm is used in the receive side to achieve DC voltage balancing. By providing DC voltage balancing, the range of the line is extended.

Framing: The bits across the U reference point are sent by using 2B1Q transmission frames. Eight of these frames are combined, as shown in Figure 15.7, to form one superframe. We see that each frame begins with a SW (Synchronizing Word) which has a fixed bit pattern. However, the first frame of a superframe begins with an ISW (Inverted SW) field, which merely complements the SW bits; 1s are set to 0s and 0s to 1s. This field is then followed by 12 groups of 2B + D bits. One 2B + D group contains 8 bits for each B channel and 2 bits for the D channel. The frame then ends with 6 overhead bits called the M field. This field is used to initiate loop backs, get error statistics, and to perform other maintenance procedures over the line. The 18 bits for the SW, 216 for the 2B + D groups, and 6 for the M field make the frame 240 bits long.

We can see that this number of bits per frame agrees with those rates which exist at the U reference point by solving this question: If out of a possible 240 bits, only 216 are used for the B and D channels, then what is the aggregate rate required to transmit these channels? By setting up the ratios as follows and by solving for the unknown, we get the proper bandwidth of 160 kbps at the U interface.

$$\frac{216 \text{ bits per frame for B and D bits}}{\text{Total of 240 bits needed per frame}} = \frac{144 \text{ kbps for the B and D channels}}{\text{Total rate at the U interface}}$$

15.4.3 CCITT's S/T Reference Point

Configurations: Directing our attention now to the other side of the NT, we look at the interface between it and the TEs. Figure 15.8 shows four possible ways of configuring TEs with an NT. The first one is simply called a point-to-point configuration. It allows a maximum length of 1 km between the NT and the TE. In this configuration as well as the others, the propagation delay of the D channel's echo bits (discussed later) constrain the maximum distance and the spacing between terminals.

The next three types are variations of the point-to-multipoint configuration. In each case, up to 8 TEs may be connected. And to determine which terminal can transmit on the bus is decided by the D channel protocol. The S/T interface uses two pairs of wires which are connected in parallel with the multipoint TEs.

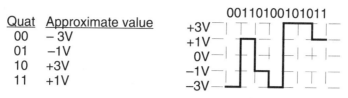

Quat	Approximate value
00	− 3V
01	−1V
10	+3V
11	+1V

Figure 15.6 2B1Q (2 Binary, 1 Quaternary) signaling scheme used in ANSI T1.601's U reference point.

Figure 15.8(b) uses a short passive bus. Aside from the maximum distance between the bus and the terminal being 10 meters, there are no restrictions in how these terminals are placed. However, for a cable with an impedance of 150 ohms, the maximum distance is limited to 200 meters, and for a 75 ohm cable, this distance is 100 meters.

Figure 15.8(d) shows an extended passive bus which increases the distance limitation to 1 km; however, all the terminals must be clustered at the far end of the bus. Here, the distance between them must be kept between 25 and 50 meters. The last wiring configuration shows a star topology that is composed of up to 8 point-to-point connections terminating at one card in the NT.

The Connector: Regardless of which configuration is used, the plug is standardized and is called the I.430 connector or the RJ-45. This connector is shown in Figure 15.9. It has 8 pins and is similar to the common RJ-11 jack. A 6-pin connector, when

Number of bits:	18	8 +8+2	8+8+2		8+8+2	6
2B1Q frame #1	ISW	B1+B2+D	B1+B2+D	. . .	B1+B2+D	M
2B1Q frame #2	SW	B1+B2+D	B1+B2+D	. . .	B1+B2+D	M
2B1Q frame #3	SW	B1+B2+D	B1+B2+D	. . .	B1+B2+D	M
2B1Q frame #4	SW	B1+B2+D	B1+B2+D	. . .	B1+B2+D	M
2B1Q frame #5	SW	B1+B2+D	B1+B2+D	. . .	B1+B2+D	M
2B1Q frame #6	SW	B1+B2+D	B1+B2+D	. . .	B1+B2+D	M
2B1Q frame #7	SW	B1+B2+D	B1+B2+D	. . .	B1+B2+D	M
2B1Q frame #8	SW	B1+B2+D	B1+B2+D	. . .	B1+B2+D	M
	Synchronization word	Group 1	Group 2	. . .	Group 12	Overhead

Figure 15.7 The format for the 2B1Q superframe. One frame contains 240 bits (18 + 18x12 + 6), while one superframe contains 1920 bits (240 x 8).

ISDN and SONET

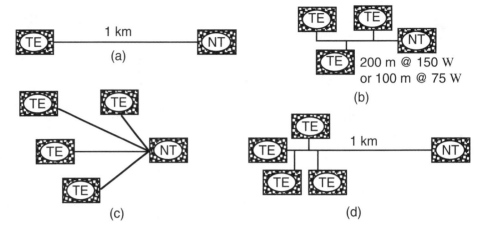

Figure 15.8 Four possible configurations for the wiring on the S/T interface. (a) Point to point, (b) Short passive bus, (c) Star, (d) Extended passive bus.

plugged into an 8-pin jack, doesn't make contact with pins 1 and 8. Likewise, a 4-pin connector would not make contact with pins 1, 2, 7, and 8. The chart in the figure shows the pin functions with respect to the TE. These are reversed for functions with respect to the NT. That is, pins 3 and 6 are used for the TE to transmit while for the NT, they are used to receive, and so on.

The RJ-45 is used for PRI as well as BRI. However, over the local loop, the PRI uses two pairs while the BRI uses only one. The assignment of the pin functions, shown in Figure 15.9, are for the S/T interface. This interface only appears with the BRI access and not with PRI. The use of the middle 4 pins is mandatory with both access types.

Figure 15.10 shows how a point-to-multipoint configuration may be set up using these 8 pins. Notice here, that the NT's transmission on pins 4 and 5 is received by all of the TEs on the bus. Similarly, all the TEs transmit on pins 3 and 6 while the NT receives over these pins. The D channel bits and its echo bits determine which TE may

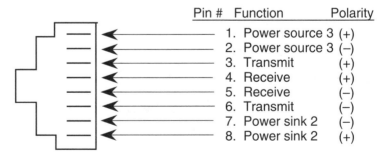

Pin #	Function	Polarity
1.	Power source 3	(+)
2.	Power source 3	(−)
3.	Transmit	(+)
4.	Receive	(+)
5.	Receive	(−)
6.	Transmit	(−)
7.	Power sink 2	(−)
8.	Power sink 2	(+)

Figure 15.9 The function assignments for the pins of an RJ-45 or the I.430 connector in reference to TEs. Power 1 is phantomed over pins 3,4,5, and 6.

transmit on the bus at any given time. Now let us look at the complicated yet flexible power distribution scheme that is available at this interface.

Power Distribution: With POTS, the network (that is the CO) provides the power to operate the telephones. This is advantageous for the user in the event that there is a local power failure, because a CO is better equipped to handle power outages. However, with ISDN, the power may be available from various sources. It could come from the network, NT1, NT2, or the TE. Since the power to drive devices may come from various sources, a portable terminal should not expect power to be available from any jack that it is plugged into.

As seen in Figure 15.10, there are three power sources (and sinks) available. All power is provided at 40 VDC. The NT may provide the power by phantoming it over the 4 required pins (3 to 6). This is called power source 1. Here, the transmitted and received digital signals share the same metallic path as the DC voltage. This power is rated at 1 watt and may be used to drive all of the TEs associated with it. The NT may obtain this power either from the network or from a local AC outlet or a battery.

Power source 2 which is available from an NT on pins 7 and 8 may provide power of up to 7 watts for the TEs. Instead of each device having its own power source it is advantageous to drive them from fewer devices (NT and TEs). This way, fewer power backup systems would become necessary.

The figure further shows that one TE may provide power to other TEs as well as the NT by using power source 3. This source is not part of the CCITT recommendations, and its implementation will vary from site to site.

15.4.4 Framing over the S/T Reference Point

For BRI, the signaling over the S/T interface uses what is called pseudoternary coding, which is depicted in Figure 15.11. A logical 1 is transmitted by 0 V and a logical 0 by either +1 V or −1 V. The polarity of the voltage alternates with every 0 bit and if two consecutive 0s are transmitted with the same polarity, then it is called a code violation. Code violations are used on purpose to maintain synchronization.

Figure 15.12 shows the format of the I.430 transmission frame which is used over the S/T interface. It consists of 48 bits being sent in 250 microseconds. The frame format is different from the NT to TE direction as it is from the TE to NT direction. The TE derives its synchronization from the NT, so the TE's transmission is delayed by two bits.

The figure shows all possible pseudoternary values for each bit. Within the 48 bits of each frame, two groups of 8 bits of the B1 channel, and two groups of 8 bits of the B2 channel exist. There are 4 D channel bits per frame. This accounts for 36 bits. Out of the 48 bits per frame, this leaves 12 bits for overhead. Doing the same calculations as were done for confirming the line rate at the U interface, we see that the rate at the S/T interface also corresponds with 192 kbps.

$$\frac{\text{B and D channels' 36 bits}}{\text{Total of 48 bits per frame}} = \frac{\text{144 kbps for the B and D channels}}{\text{Rate for the S/T interface}}$$

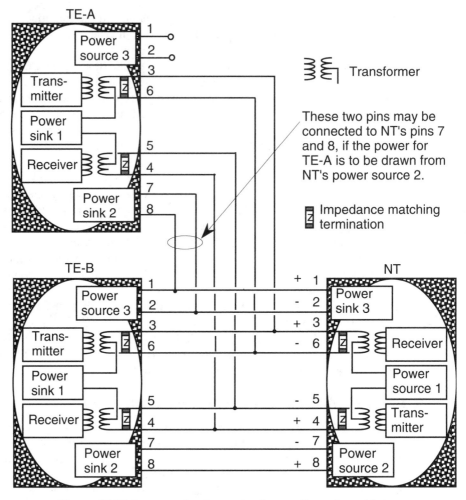

Figure 15.10 An example of a passive bus configuration with its power distribution.

Let us now look at the purpose of the overhead bits, except for the D and E bits, which we'll leave for the next section.

The polarity of the F (Framing) bit is always positive and it marks the beginning of the frame. It is followed by the L (baLancing) bit which is always negative to provide

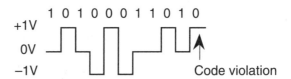

Figure 15.11 Pseudoternary line coding example.

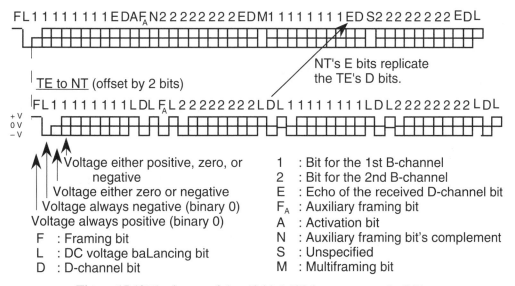

Figure 15.12 The format of the 48-bit I.430 frames across the S/T interface.

DC voltage balancing for the F bit. Likewise, the rest of the balancing bits are set to either +1, 0 or – 1 V depending on the settings of the previous bits.

In the NT to TE direction, the Fa (Auxiliary Framing) bit is set to 1 in every fifth frame and M (Multiframing) bit is set to 1 in every 20th frame. These bits are set to 0 in all of the other frames. Together these bits help to group multiple frames and keep the line synchronized. The N bit is always set to be the opposite of Fa, so if the Fa bit is 0 then the N bit would be 1.

In the TE to NT direction, the Fa bits are all set to 0 except for every fifth frame. These Fa bits in every fifth frame create a subchannel called Q, whose purpose is not defined yet. Similarly, the purpose of the S bit is also undefined.

The A (Activation) bit is used by the NT to convey to the TE that the interface is active and operational. Figure 15.13 outlines this activation procedure. An INFO 0 signal is shown as being sent by the TE, but it could be sent by the NT as well. This is an absence of any signal and all it indicates is that the line is deactivated. Recall that 0 V corresponds to a binary 1 and a binary 0 is transmitted by either a positive or negative voltage.

The TE's power is then turned on and it sends an INFO 1 signal which is a continuous transmission of "+−111111." This signals the NT that the TE wants to activate the line and so the NT sends an INFO 2 signal with B, D, E, and A bits set to 0. The density of 0s on the line rapidly alter the polarity of the signal, which enables the receiver to synchronize quickly. Now the TE may send operational data using INFO 3 signals and so may the NT using INFO 4 signals. Here the A bit would be set to 1 indicating that the line is active.

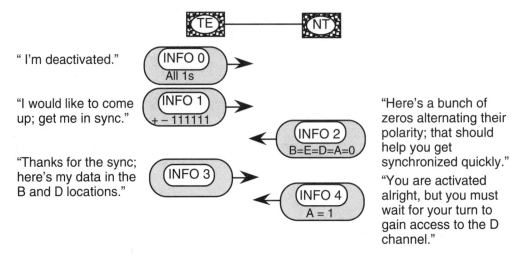

Figure 15.13 An exchange of INFO signals meant to get the TE activated, at which time the A bit is set to 1.

15.4.5 D-Channel Access Control

Recall that the D channel is used for signaling and ISDN defines the three layers for its operation. As far as ISDN is concerned, the B channel is a layer 1 issue and it only transports its bits.

With BRI, TEs may be connected in a point-to-multipoint configuration. We saw this in Figures 15.8 and 15.10. The terminals will transmit the B channels on the bus only when they are given the access through the D channel so there is no problem with contention on the B channels. However, this is not the case with the D channel. Problems with contention among the TEs for the D channel have to be resolved. That is, how do we determine which TE may transmit over the D channel at any given time, since the TEs must share the bus to the NT?

The D bits are sent by the TEs as well as by the NT. However, the E bits are echoed back by the NT from the TEs' last D bits. These E bits help the TEs to know whose transmission the NT is getting. If one terminal sends a 0 for a D bit, while another terminal sends 1 for that bit-time, whose bit will the NT receive?

The answer to that question is the TE that sent the zero. Since pseudoternary line coding is used, regardless of what the rest of the terminals are transmitting, if one terminal is transmitting a binary zero then the NT will receive a zero. Remember, a binary 1 provides no voltage on the line while a binary 0 does.

The use of the D channel falls into two priority classes as shown in Table 15.3. Priority class 1 is used for ISDN layer 2 frames which carry signaling information, and priority class 2 is used for frames which carry other information, such as low speed packet switching, telemetry, etc.

Within each priority class there are two levels specified as normal and lower. The priority class is set to the kind of information that the terminal needs to send to the NT. If a terminal has not sent any level 2 frames yet, then it will have its priority level set to normal. And according to the number corresponding to the class and level in the table, the TE will have to count that many successive 1s (or 0V levels) in the E channel it receives from the NT before being allowed to transmit.

After the transmission is complete, the TE will lower its priority level in order to give other TEs a chance to transmit. Once it is able to count as high up as the lower level priority number, then it will know that others who had wanted to transmit have done so. Consequently, it will raise its level back to normal and begin another transmission, if necessary.

Notice that the number of 1s that must be received by a TE which is wanting to transmit is greater than 6. This is because if some other TE is transmitting on the line, it will at most have 6 consecutive 1s in its second layer frames. Recall from the discussion of SDLC from Chapter 12 that due to bit stuffing, frames are allowed to have at most 6 consecutive 1s and that too in the flag field. In the next section, we'll discuss ISDN's second layer which is similar to SDLC. For now, let's look at an example.

Only two terminals, A and B, are shown in Figure 15.14 as sharing the line. Their terminal numbers are called TEIs (Terminal End-point Identifiers) and are shown in the figure. This is part of the second layer's address field which comes after the flag ("01111110") field. The TEIs are 16 ("0010000") and 0, respectively. They have both been activated and have set their priorities to 8, since they both have signaling information to send. Both of them transmit logical 1s (0 V) over the D channel and since no one else is on the line, the NT echoes back these 1s with its E bits.

They both count 8 successive 1s and begin transmission of their level 2 frames. Both of their flag fields are the same, so they both receive the same pattern back on the E channel. Right after these flags, they simultaneously transmit their TEIs and since they differ at the third address bit, B's binary 0 forces a voltage on the line, despite A's binary 1 (0 V). The NT "sees" a binary 0 and echoes it back, but terminal A doesn't get its 1 echoed and so terminates its transmission. However, B doesn't have to restart transmission but continues until it is done, at which time it lowers its priority to 9.

All this time, A has been trying to consecutively count up to 8, but has failed. A can only count up to a maximum of 6 consecutive 1s, due to the number of 1s in B's flags. Actually, 7 consecutive 1s are possible in a frame, which occurs when a frame is being cancelled.

Now that B is done and has to be quiet (no voltage), A is able to count up to 8 and start its transmission. B is unable to transmit now, since it must count up to 9. Finally, when B's transmission is complete, it sets its priority to

Table 15.3 D Channel Access Priorities		
	Priority Class = 1 Signaling information	Priority Class = 2 Non-signaling information
Normal Lower	8 9	10 11

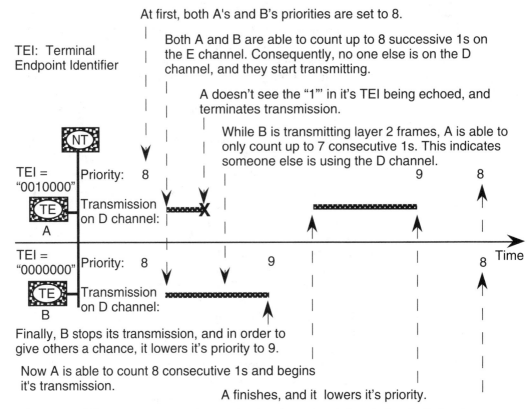

At first, both A's and B's priorities are set to 8.

TEI: Terminal Endpoint Identifier

Both A and B are able to count up to 8 successive 1s on the E channel. Consequently, no one else is on the D channel, and they start transmitting.

A doesn't see the "1"' in it's TEI being echoed, and terminates transmission.

While B is transmitting layer 2 frames, A is able to only count up to 7 consecutive 1s. This indicates someone else is using the D channel.

NT

TEI = "0010000" Priority: 8   9   8

TE Transmission on D channel:
A

TEI = "0000000" Priority: 8   9   8   Time

TE Transmission on D channel:
B

Finally, B stops its transmission, and in order to give others a chance, it lowers it's priority to 9.

Now A is able to count 8 consecutive 1s and begins it's transmission.

A finishes, and it lowers it's priority.

Both A and B can count up to 9 consecutive 1s and so bring their priority back up to 8. Now either or both may start transmitting again.

Figure 15.14 CSMA/CR (Carrier Sense Multiple Access with Collision Resolution) allows, as shown in this example, for B to continue transmission, even while A detected a collision at point x.

9. And if no one else is transmitting, then they both can count up to 9 and reset their priorities to 8. This method of gaining control over the D channel is called CSMA/CR (Carrier Sense Multiple Access with Collision Resolution).

15.5 THE PHYSICAL LAYER OF PRI

PRI typically stops at the NT2, so there is no S/T interface defined to the TEs. In other words, PRI provides a trunk connection between say a PBX at the customer's site and the local exchange. There are two variations possible at this interface. They are called the 1.544 Mbps and 2.048 Mbps interfaces or CCITT's G.703 and G.704 recommendations respectively.

The 1.544 Mbps interface based on T1, uses the ESF format with clear channel signaling. That is, all of the signaling for the 23 B channels is done over the one D channel operating at 64 kbps. This allows for call-by-call service selection in real-time.

That is, each channel can be set up for a different service and can be connected to separate destinations. Although this is possible with T1s, it has to be provisioned beforehand, and cannot be configured dynamically, as with PRI. Therefore, the D channel is what gives PRI its appeal. Without the D channel, this interface would be not much different from T1s as described in chapter 10.

Not directly related to PRI is a technology specified by Bellcore called HDSL (High-bit-rate Digital Subscriber Line). This new technology using 2B1Q encoding method allows a customer to access T1 rates over the local loop. Typically, T1 access is expensive over the local loop, because it requires repeaters every mile or so. HDSL, on the other hand, provides access over 24 gauge copper wires to a CO or POP 12,000 feet away without requiring any repeaters. This allows a customer inexpensive access to long-haul carrier services which they themselves are offered at reasonable prices.

15.6 THE DATA LINK LAYER

15.6.1 Why LAPD?

The second and third layers of ISDN concern only the D channel, as has been said before. The protocol used over the second or the data link layer is called LAPD (Link Access Procedures over the D channel) which is similar to SDLC and LAP/B covered in Chapters 12 and 13, respectively. Please refer back to these chapters when necessary, since this section builds upon that material.

Unlike LAPD, LAP/B is only a point-to-point protocol which is used over the DTE-DCE link. LAPD, on the other hand, can be used between an NT and multiple TEs. It is a full-duplex point-to-multipoint protocol, but so is SDLC. One reason why SDLC wasn't chosen for ISDN, which can operate on multipoint configurations, is that it uses polling, which makes an inefficient use of the available bandwidth. As we have seen in the previous section, CSMA/CR allows multipoint transmission to occur with less overhead and minimum delay. Now only the LAPD issues which differ from those of LAP/B and SDLC will be covered.

15.6.2 Basic Frame Formatting

Figure 15.15 shows the format of the three types of frames which exist: information, supervisory, and unnumbered. After the first flag is transmitted, the EA (Addresses Extension) bit, whose value is 0, is transmitted indicating that there is another octet in this address field. Eight bits later, an EA bit of 1 is transmitted indicating that this is the last octet of the address field.

The C/R (Command or Response) bit is set by the user to 0 and is set by the LE to 1, if the transmitting frame is a command. This bit is reversed if the frame is a response to a command frame. All information frames are commands, all supervisory frame types (RR, RNR, and REJ) can be either, and out of the unnumbered frames, SABME, DISC, UI are commands; UA, DM, FRMR are responses; and XID can be either.

SABME (Set Asynchronous Balanced Mode Extended), UI (Unnumbered Information), and XID (eXchange IDentification) are the frame types that are new for us. SABME is used for establishing a link which can transfer 127 consecutive frames without requiring a response. UI, as we'll soon see, sends information that doesn't require an acknowledgment and XID is used to automatically set up a data link.

The two S bits give the supervisory frame type and the five M bits give the unnumbered frame type. The P/F bits are used for error control as in SDLC.

15.6.3 The DLCI Field

The DLCI (Data Link Control Identifier) is the combination of SAPI (Service Access Point Identifier) and TEI (Terminal Endpoint Identifier) fields. The TEI identifies the terminal on the interface while the SAPI identifies the access point for the LAPD network layer process in the terminal which is logically connected to its peer process in the LE. Figure 15.16 shows an example of how various terminals and their service-access points may establish logical links with their corresponding entities with the LE. Thus the frame doesn't only have to specify to which terminal it is going, but also to which service-access point of that terminal.

A SAPI of 0 is used to specify the service access point which controls circuit switching procedures, a SAPI of 1 is used for transmission in the packet switching mode, a SAPI of 16 for x.25 communications, and a SAPI of 63 for OAM (Operations, Administrations, and Maintenance) procedures.

There are three types of TEI assignments: broadcast, automatic, and nonautomatic. A TEI of 127, which is all 1s, is the broadcast address, and frames sent with this address

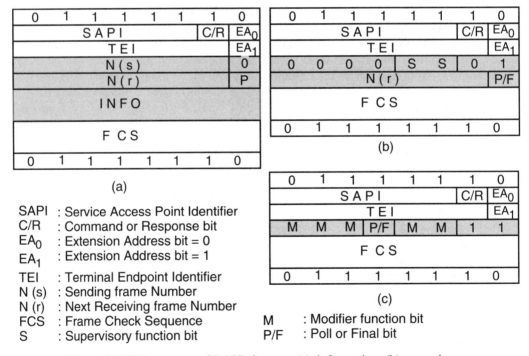

Figure 15.15 Three types of LAPD frames: (a) information, (b) supervisory, (c) unnumbered. The fields which are shaded are characteristic of those particular frame types.

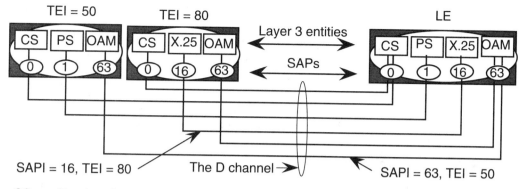

Figure 15.16 The DLCI (Data Link Control Identifier) consisting of the SAPI and the TEI provide the address of frames, specifying not only the terminal, but also the SAP, which provides access to the desired layer 3 process.

are directed to every terminal on the line. Nonautomatic TEIs are hardwired in the terminals, either by encoding the address in ROM (Read Only Memory), by setting switches, or by some other physical method. Before a nonautomatic TEI can be used, the network side, that is the LE or the NT2, has to approve its use. These TEIs fall in the range from 0 to 63 whereas automatic TEIs range from 64 to 126.

Automatic assignment of TEIs is done by the terminal asking the network for a TEI via the LAPD protocol. Referring to the example in Figure 15.17, we see that this is accomplished by the terminal first sending a UI frame to the LE. The information in

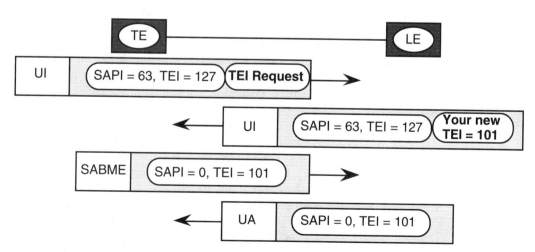

Figure 15.17 Requesting a TEI from an LE, and establishing a link.

ISDN and SONET

this frame indicates to the LE that the terminal is requesting a TEI. Since such an operation is an administrative detail, it uses a SAPI of 63 and since the terminal doesn't have a TEI yet, it uses the general TEI of 127.

The LE also replies with a UI frame with the same SAPI and TEI values that it received. However, in the information part of this frame, the LE grants a TEI of 101. Now the TE may exchange data after establishing a logical link by transmitting a SABME and receiving a UA. Note that the SAPI of 0 corresponds to a circuit switched connection, whereas a TEI of 101 corresponds to the TEI assigned by the LE.

15.7 THE NETWORK LAYER

Because the scope of the D channel network layer is quite complex, we won't study it in much detail. We have already introduced its function in a circuit switched mode while discussing Figure 14.14. There the establishment and the release of a call connection were shown as the D channel network layer interfaced with the SS7's ISUP layer. Table 15.4 summarizes the network layer messages.

The network layer establishes, maintains, and terminates ISDN connections between application processes or entities. It provides a user-to-network layer interface. Addresses to ISDN destinations are composed of three variable length parts. They are the country code (up to 3 digits), the national significant number (up to 17 digits), and the subaddress (up to 40 digits).

This ends our discussion on ISDN; now let us turn our attention to another important standard called SONET (Synchronous Optical NETwork), which is necessary for building a BISDN (Broadband ISDN).

15.8 SONET

15.8.1 Sonnet, Isn't That a Kind of Poem?

T1 was designed by the Bell Telephone Laboratories back in the 1960s to transmit 24 voice channels digitally over metallic wires. T3 technology, which was an extension of T1, was then introduced to support transmission of 672 voice channels, over microwave systems. Since T1 and T3 were both based on the transmission of electrical signals, a new technology which was more appropriate for transmission of optical signals was needed. This technology should be designed so that the problems which were inherent with the T-carrier systems would be minimized, and thus be easier to network.

It was 1985, when Bellcore provided a solution for these issues in a specification called SONET (Synchronous Optical NETwork). Since then, SONET has become standardized by ANSI and as SDH (Synchronous Digital Hierarchy) by CCITT. The term "optical" was dropped by CCITT, because by that time SONET was being transported by other media, such as digital microwave.

SONET is a multiple level protocol used to transport high speed signals using circuit switched synchronous multiplexing. It is the only standard for high speed fiber systems which can become the vehicle for making future-generation services such as broadband ISDN, ATM (Asynchronous Transfer Mode), and others a reality.

The left two columns specify whether corresponding ACK and REJ message types exist. The right two columns specify if this message is sent by the user, by the network, or both.

ACK	REJ	Message Type	Brief Description and Purpose	user	netw.
		Call Establishment Messages			
a		SETUP	Request for call establishment	a	a
a		CONNect	Call party answered the call	a	a
		ALERTing	Called phone is "ringing"	a	a
		CALL PROC	Call proceeding, received all info.		a
		Call Information Phase Messages			
		USER INFO	For sending info. to another user	a	a
a	a	SUSPend	Call on hold, but channel connected	a	
a	a	RESume	For resuming a suspended call	a	
		Call Clearing Messages			
a		DETach	Call info. saved, channel disconnected	a	a
		DISConnect	Info. saved until REL COM is received	a	a
		RELease	Channel and call info are released	a	a
		REL COM	Release complete, channel free again	a	a
		Miscellabneous Messages			
a	a	CANcel	Request to cancel a facility	a	
a	a	FACility	Request for facility, i.e., call forwarding	a	a
a	a	REGister	For facility registration in a data base	a	a
		STATUS	To report conditions of a call	a	a
		CON CON	For congestion control or flow control	a	a
		INFOrmation	To establish a call, and other reasons	a	a

15.8.2 Benefits of SONET as Compared with T3

When a M13 multiplexer receives DS1 signals at its input ports, the DS1s are not necessarily synchronized to a common clock. DS1 signals, instead of being exactly 1.544 Mbps, can have a tolerance so that they may be off by plus or minus 75 bps.

Hence, a M13 multiplexer must add extra bits here and there to compensate for these differences in bit rates. This is necessary to properly frame the DS1s into a DS3 frame. The technique of adding these extra bits is called "bit stuffing," which unfortunately uses the same phrase as stuffing a 0 after every 5 consecutive 1s, as it is done in SDLC. Because bit stuffing is used in T3, it is said to be asynchronously multiplexed or asynchronously formatted. Note that the use of the asynchronous term here has nothing to do with start and stop bits.

One of the problems with asynchronous multiplexing is that when two points are sending a multiplexed signal to each other, a third location in between them cannot select one channel without first demultiplexing the entire set of channels. This is because with an asynchronous bit stream, bits belonging to a particular channel do not occur at regular intervals, there are extra bits stuffed depending on the timing of the input sources. So an intermediate node which must drop channels (or add channels for that matter) from a signal stream, must have a M13 multiplexer to demultiplex, a patch panel to cross connect, and another M13 multiplexer to re-multiplex the new signal stream. This is difficult to operate and manage, and it requires expensive equipment.

On the other hand, SONET equipment performs synchronous multiplexing, so that no bit stuffing is required. The bytes belonging to each channel are easily identified, which allows SONET to use ADMs (Add and Drop Multiplexer). This device "plucks" (or drops) out only the bits for the channels which are needed and allows the rest of the data stream to pass undisturbed. SONET's synchronous multiplexing also allows channels to be switched or routed from one link to another within milliseconds. Compare this with up to 30 minutes to cross-connect with a T1 DCS (or DACS). Photonic switching, when it becomes available, will allow signals to be switched at optical speeds rather than having to first convert them to electrical signals.

This almost instantaneous switching capability of SONET provides it with what is called APS (Automatic Protection Switching) which can reroute traffic from a link that has failed to another active link without losing any data. With asynchronous networking, as with T1s, APS is possible, but there is a glitch and one loses some data. When bandwidth is required without much notice, as in disaster recovery, networks can be automatically reconfigured.

Such management capabilities are some of the most exciting benefits of SONET. But then again these capabilities become even more necessary than for previous methods, since a substantial amount of traffic is depending on these fiber links. Nearly 5% of SONET's bandwidth is used to monitor, control, reconfigure, test, and provision the digital network, compared to 0.5% used in ESF formatting. Furthermore, as we'll see in Figure 15.18, the network management capabilities are provided in layers of hierarchy, allowing the carriers as well as the customers to manage their part of the network. This is done through SONET's OSS (Operation Support System).

With SONET, end-users and carriers don't have to become "hostages" to their vendors as becomes the case when dealing with T3 equipment. This is because T3 formatting is proprietary. On the contrary, SONET is an international standard interface for end-users as well as for carriers and equipment manufacturers. This allows customers to switch vendors and interconnect equipment made by different vendors. This capability is called "mid-span meet." While proprietary T3 equipment will have

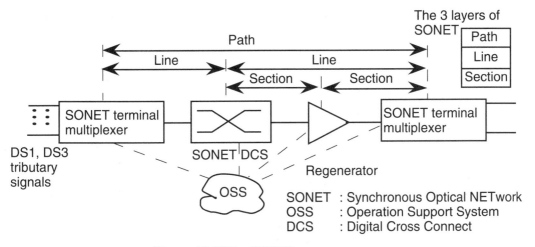

Figure 15.18 The SONET transport.

to keep its prices up, SONET prices should eventually drop below that of T3, because there will be more vendors providing standardized SONET-based equipment.

Incidently, SONET rates are standardized to 2,488 Mbps, which is much higher than DS3 rates, and has provisions to go up to 13 Gbps. Yet, SONET has the capability to transport existing signal formats such as DS3, DS1, and E1.

15.8.3 SONET Rates And Devices

Table 15.5 shows the popular physical interfaces for SONET. An STS (Synchronous Transport Signal) frame carries data in electrical form while its corresponding signal in optical form is called an OC (Optical Carrier). To produce an OC signal from its STS derivative, the STS signal is scrambled. Notice, because of synchronous multiplexing, STS levels are exact multiples of each other, unlike for example, the DS3 level (44.736 Mbps) which is not exactly 28 times that of a DS1 signal level (1.544 Mbps).

Table 15.5 Popular SONET interfaces		
Synchronous Transport Signal	Line Rates in Mbps	Optical Carrier Designations
STS-1	51.84	OC-1
STS-3	155.52	OC-3
STS-12	622.08	OC-12
STS-48	2488.32	OC-48

Figure 15.18 shows three types of SONET devices: the terminal multiplexer, the DCS (Digital Cross-connect System), and the regenerator. The terminal multiplexer serves as a local as well as a long-haul access point to the SONET network. If it is used by the local loop provider, it would be called a DLC (Digital Loop Carrier system). In that case, it would be used as a concentrator of DS-0 signals, which would be connected to the CO switch either locally or remotely.

The DCS provides direct synchronous switching at DS1 and DS3 and other rates. In the figure it could be replaced with an ADM to add or drop channels as necessary. Regenerators are needed every 35 miles for fiber; however, besides for reconstructing the signal, these devices provide error checking, maintenance facilities and other sophisticated services.

Based on the links between these devices, three types of network spans are defined. Corresponding to these spans three layers are defined, the lowest of which is the section layer. It is used for framing, scrambling, and locating faults.

A line exists between two nodes and it is used for multiplexing, synchronization, switching, and cross-connecting SONET signals. It is used for gathering data for network management. Lastly, the end to end logical links between customer users is called a path. It is the circuit between two entry points of the SONET cloud. It provides a high degree of maintenance service to the customer. ADM is a path layer device, so that if it replaced the DCS in the figure, then there would be two paths present instead of one.

15.8.4 SONET Transport Structure

In an STS-1 frame, as shown in Figure 15.19, there are 90 columns and 9 rows, totaling 810 bytes. This frame is divided into a transport overhead and an SPE (Synchronous Payload Envelope), which consists of 3 columns and 87 columns, respectively. The order of transmission is such that the first 3 bytes of the transport overhead is sent, then 87 bytes of the SPE, after which the next row of 3 plus 87 bytes are sent, and so on. The transport overhead is further divided into a section overhead and a line overhead, while the SPE is divided into a path overhead and the payload where the tributary data is carried. The DC (Data communication Channel) fields in the transport overhead are used for network management information.

The payload of the SPE is divided into seven VT (Virtual Tributary) groups and 18 packing bytes. Each VT group is 12 columns wide and may contain one or more VTs of the same type. A VT type is a given block of data which can carry a fixed amount of bandwidth for the user. VT1.5 is used to transport one DS1 signal, VT2 is used to carry one E1 signal, etc., as shown in Figure 15.19. If the one entire SPE is used to carry a DS3 signal, then no VTs are needed. So VTs are subdivisions of the SPE and the type of VTs that is used is determined by what the tributary has to send. There are two extra columns of "padding" bytes available to accommodate for multiplexing asynchronous signals.

The SPE is assembled at a terminal node and its path overhead contains the end to end management information. For example, the signal label indicates if the payload contains one DS3 or a combination of lower rate signals, that is, the type and the number of VTs used. The path overhead stays with the SPE until it arrives at the

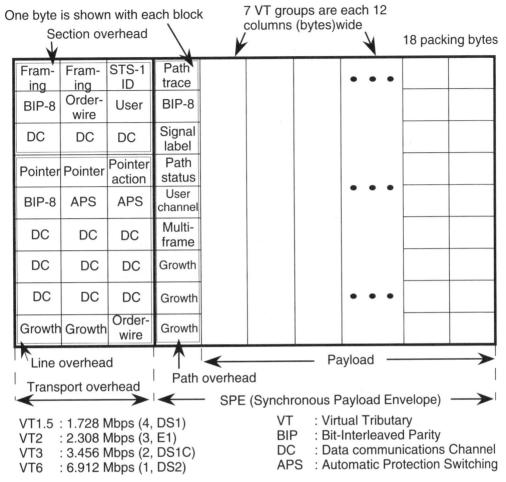

One byte is shown with each block

Section overhead

7 VT groups are each 12 columns (bytes)wide

18 packing bytes

Fram-ing	Fram-ing	STS-1 ID	Path trace
BIP-8	Order-wire	User	BIP-8
DC	DC	DC	Signal label
Pointer	Pointer	Pointer action	Path status
BIP-8	APS	APS	User channel
DC	DC	DC	Multi-frame
DC	DC	DC	Growth
DC	DC	DC	Growth
Growth	Growth	Order-wire	Growth

Line overhead

Transport overhead

Path overhead

Payload

SPE (Synchronous Payload Envelope)

VT1.5 : 1.728 Mbps (4, DS1)
VT2 : 2.308 Mbps (3, E1)
VT3 : 3.456 Mbps (2, DS1C)
VT6 : 6.912 Mbps (1, DS2)

VT : Virtual Tributary
BIP : Bit-Interleaved Parity
DC : Data communications Channel
APS : Automatic Protection Switching

Figure 15.19 The format of the STS-1 frame is shown as being 90 columns by 9 rows. It is 810 bytes long and takes 125 microseconds to transmit; that is, 8000 frames are sent in every second. The payload capacity is 49.54 Mbps. Next to the rates of the VTs, the number of VTs that can fit in one group and the digital signal levels that can be accommodated by the VTs are shown in parentheses.

destination node, hence the term "path." Likewise, the line overhead is processed at all nodes and the section overhead is processed at all nodes as well as at the regenerators.

One of the advantages of SONET is that an entire SONET signal can be handed off in bulk between carriers (LECs or IXCs), without requiring it to be demultiplexed into DS0 levels. However, many carriers use their own stratum one clocks to keep their networks in sync and very small differences do exist between these clocks. They are said to be plesiochronous. Instead of using bit stuffing, SONET allows for these clocking differences by permitting the SPE to start anywhere in the STS frame. So

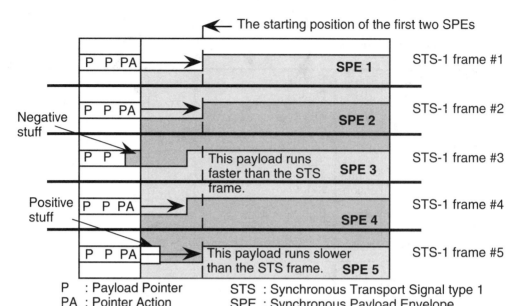

P : Payload Pointer   STS : Synchronous Transport Signal type 1
PA : Pointer Action   SPE : Synchronous Payload Envelope

Figure 15.20 The SPEs are floated in the STS frames, to compensate for slight timing differences. The starting position of the next SPE may differ by only one octet.

SPEs usually start in one frame and end in the next one as shown in Figure 15.20. This is called "floating the payload."

To notify the receiving node where an SPE starts, pointers are used in the line overhead. A pointer is simply the byte address in the STS frame indicating at which byte the payload begins. As shown in the figure, none of the SPEs start at the beginning of an STS frame so the pointers contain the byte addresses of where they do begin. SPE3 was loaded into the STS frame too soon, so the pointer action byte is used to contain the data for SPE2, so as to allow SPE3 to start earlier. This is called a "negative stuff." SPE5, on the contrary, came in a little late, so a "positive stuff" byte is inserted in SPE4 to allow for the timing difference in SPE5.

Besides indicating for these STS pointers where each SPE begins within the STS frames, VTs may also have pointers indicating where each VT begins within the SPE. Hence the VTs are also allowed to float.

Mappings: The method of how VTs are loaded into the frames is called a mapping. The types of mappings depend on whether the VTs are floated or not, whether the tributary signals are synchronized with the SONET clock or not, etc. If VTs are floated within an SPE, then additional pointers are required indicating where the VTs begin. Let us look at four popular mappings in the order that they are illustrated in Figures 15.21(a) through (d).

The simplest and inflexible type of mapping is the asynchronous DS3 mapping. It allows the popular DS3 signals to be loaded in the SPE as one "block." Here, the DS3 bits aren't necessarily synchronized with the SONET clock and the DS3 signal can't be synchronously switched, yet it does allow the transport of existing DS3 signals. Notice that the SPE rate of 51 Mbps is less than the DS3 rate. Additional bits have to be added to make up the difference.

Unchannelized floating mode DS1 mapping will allow the VTs to float and the tributary bits may or may not be synchronized with the SONET clock. Here, more set of pointers have to be processed by the equipment, but it allows for synchronous switching of the VTs. This means, for example, that a DS1 signal may be addressed and added or dropped "on the fly," but not a DS0 signal.

Channelized or byte-synchronous floating mode DS1 mapping requires the DS1 signal's bytes be synchronized with that of SONET. Here, not only DS1s, but also DS0 signals can be identified and switched.

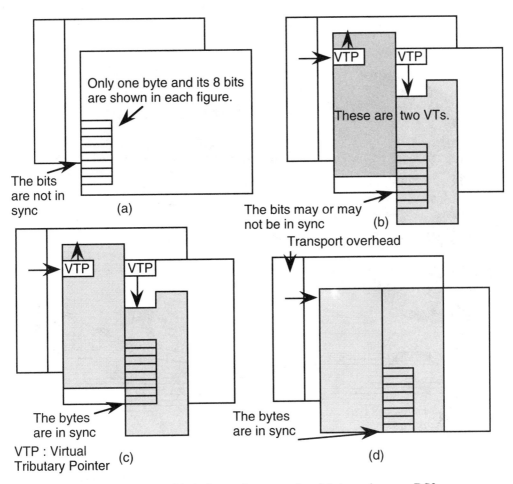

Figure 15.21 Four kind of mapping examples: (a) Asynchronous DS3 mapping. (b) Unchannelized floating VTs. (c) Channelized floating VTs. (d) Channelized locked VTs .

Lastly, the channelized or byte-synchronous locked mode DS1 mapping doesn't allow the VTs to float and so requires less pointer processing. However, phase and frequencies have to be maintained in order to benefit from easier cross-connection and switching of DS0 channels. On the down side, the locked mode introduces more delay than the floating mode.

15.8.5 Summary

To conclude this section on SONET, let us review its concepts by comparing it with the canal system of the 1800s, even before trains or cars became popular. This is illustrated in Figure 15.22.

The canal waterway is like the fiber "lightway" of SONET. The barge, along with the mule team and the hoggee driving it, are akin to one STS frame. Consider the barge itself as the SPE and the mule team with its hoggee as the transport overhead. The transport overhead is further divided into a segment overhead (the mule team) and a

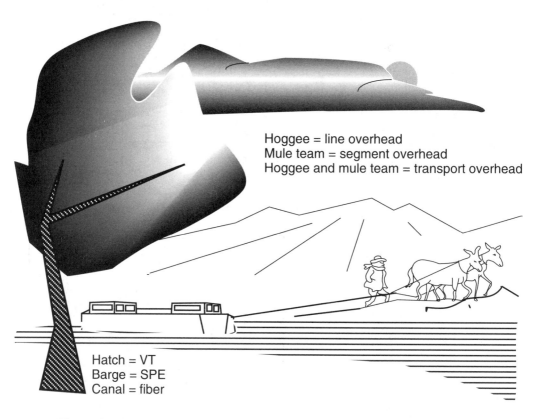

Hoggee = line overhead
Mule team = segment overhead
Hoggee and mule team = transport overhead

Hatch = VT
Barge = SPE
Canal = fiber

Figure 15.22 In the 1800s, hauling a barge from Albany to Buffalo took only 9 days at $6 per ton, instead of taking 20 days at $100 per ton using horse wagons. Now, SONET can haul digital traffic in even less time.

line overhead (the hoggee). A shipment of goods may be loaded in one barge and continue into the next one just as one SPE may float from one STS frame to another.

The captain who stays in the barge until it reaches its destination, let us say, is the path overhead. He/she knows the barge's contents and their locations within the barge. However, for the sake of our analogy let us assume that the hoggee who is driving the mule team is only going to the next canal intersection. There the barge will get a new transport overhead (mule team and the hoggee) and continue on its journey to the next intersection or its terminal destination.

Between two intersections, the mule team which is our segment overhead may need "regeneration" by requiring food and water or rest by being replaced with another team which is riding in the barge.

We can think of the three big hatches in the barge as analogous to the VT groups. Let us say that each hatch is designated for a specific purpose, such as one hatch is designated for only food while the others are only used for carrying coal and lumber exclusively. Similarly, the VT groups may carry only one kind of VT. The VTs themselves could be considered as the sacks which carry grain or other containers that carry products depending on what the user wants to ship. So in many ways, transporting information over SONET is analogous to transporting goods over a canal system.

Exercises

1. Which ISDN functional device is used to make non-ISDN devices become part of the ISDN?
   a. TE1
   b. TE2
   c. TA
   d. NT12

2. A CO's ISDN compatible DMS100 switch corresponds to which functional device?
   a. NT1
   b. LT
   c. ET
   d. PH

3. Which telecommunications service is provided to both the bearer services and teleservices?
   a. supplementary
   b. information transfer
   c. general
   d. access

4. What is the bit rate at BRI's U interface?
   a. 144 kbps
   b. 160 kbps
   c. 196 kbps
   d. 1.544 Mbps

5. The U interface is defined by what standards group?
   a. IEEE
   b. ANSI
   c. CCITT
   d. ISO

6. Which line coding is used at the U reference point?
   a. Pseudoternary
   b. AMI
   c. 2B1Q
   d. unipolar

ISDN and SONET

7. Which station will transmit first, if A has a TEI of 12 and a priority level of 9, B has a TEI of 14 and a priority level of 10, C has a TEI of 10 and a priority level of 9, and D has a TEI of 8 and a priority level of 10?
   a. station A
   b. station B
   c. station C
   d. station D

8. What is SONET's management scheme called?
   a. ADM
   b. OSS
   c. APS
   d. mid-span-meet

9. Name the bearer service attribute which identifies whether the connection is circuit switched or packet switched.

10. What technique is used to provide full duplex transmission on a 2-wire line to the CO?

11. What pin numbers are used by the NT to transmit data? What pins are used by the NT to provide power to the TEs?

12. How many E bits are sent from the TE to the NT in one frame?

13. Which INFO signal is sent by the NT to the TE to provide it with synchronization?

14. Which fields in the LAPD information frame do not exist in the LAPB information frame?

15. A TEI of 10 tells what about the way the terminal was assigned the TEI?

16. The payload and the path overhead together are called what in SONET?

17. List some advantages and disadvantages of ISDN over traditional POTS service.

18. List as many default attributes as possible for an ordinary telephone call.

19. Discuss the various methods and their advantages of how power source 3 could be used to distribute power.

20. What is the difference between activation and access to the D channel?

21. Explain access to the D channel as briefly as possible.

22. What is the advantage of LAPD over LAPB?

23. Explain the parts of the DLCI field and their uses.

24. What are the advantages and disadvantages of SONET over T3?

Chapter 16

LANs

16.1 INTRODUCTION

In the early 1980s, when PCs (Personal Computers) began to proliferate businesses, office workers were relieved that they were becoming less dependent on a central host. Many of the tasks were done right on the PCs which were sitting on their desks. They were able to accomplish tasks themselves, rather than having to wait for the data processing department to get around to doing them.

However, it soon became evident that these processors would have to be networked, since workers typically have to work with each other. Initially, "sneaker-netting" (hand-carrying files on diskettes from PCs to PCs) proved sufficient, but soon, as the volume of such data transfers increased, networking became essential.

Basically, LANs allow sharing of resources. These resources could be information, such as data files, multimedia files, electronic mail, voice mail, or software. They could be peripherals, such as special purpose printers, plotters, scanners, or storage devices. LANs also provide workstations to share each other's processing capabilities or to access a central host. Of course, with these advantages LANs also bear some disadvantages: concern for security of files and accounts being a major one.

A LAN is a private network that allows computer related devices to communicate with each other within a range of a few miles, typically within the boundary of a building. It connects computers and their peripherals with each other under decentralized control.

A LAN can be thought of as being similar to a telephone network. A telephone network uses a phone wire installed in a star topology. Similarly, a LAN must also use a transmission media installed using a selected topology. The phone itself is analogous to the NIC (Network Interface Card) of a PC, and dialing a number on a telephone corresponds to the access protocol of a LAN.

Ted Haller of Hewlett Packard was very kind to provide his invaluable assistance in creating this chapter.

Finally, once the distant end is connected with the calling telephone, a communication protocol has to be established, such as English, Spanish, etc., so that the two parties may be able to understand each other after they have gained the access. Examples of communications protocols for LANs include NetBIOS, NetWare, and so on, which I will cover in this chapter.

16.2 TOPOLOGIES

Before a LAN is installed, careful planning must be done on how to wire up or physically lay out the network. Once the network is installed, it becomes very difficult and expensive to alter the layout, or the topology as it is called. Hence, LANs connected using wireless technologies are gaining acceptance. Let us now look at three basic types of topologies and their derivatives.

16.2.1 The Star

The star topology [Figure 16.1(a)] may be implemented when using existing telephone wiring to set up a LAN, since that is how in-house wiring is installed. In such a case, the installation of a LAN is simple, especially if there are wire-pairs that are not used.

The star topology has a central node or hub to which the workstations are separately connected. Even though the reliability of the network depends on the reliability of the central node, monitoring, controlling, and troubleshooting of the LAN becomes easy because of it. Every station requires two interfaces, one at the station and one at the central node; a separate circuit or line from the hub is also required.

When a star network is cascaded, as shown in Figure 16.1(b), it is called a tree. Because of its exceptional managing characteristics, many LANs are physically wired using the star configuration. However, since it introduces a common point of failure (the central node), the communication methods are not centrally controlled, but instead are distributed.

16.2.2 The Bus

The most popular topology is still the bus, but that may change any day. See Figure 16.1(c). Network components are connected to one common wire, called the bus, over which they communicate. They can listen to all the traffic on the bus, which is broadcast by the transmitting device. However, only the device to which the traffic is addressed listens to this data.

Sometimes, the main cable (the bus) is connected to the NIC using a drop wire and sometimes it is connected directly to the NIC. If the main cable is "cut" and the two cables are separately connected to the NIC as shown in Figure 16.1(d), then the topology is called a "daisy chain." There is no common bus over which communication occurs, but instead signals are received and retransmitted as they travel through intermediate nodes.

The bus provides a simple topology that is fairly easy to install. Separate connections for each station from a central hub is not required. Even though the bus

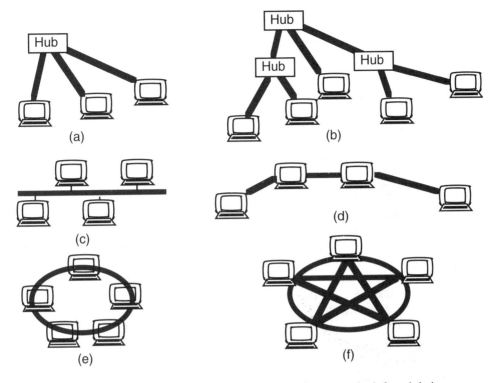

Figure 16.1 The three primary topologies are shown on the left and their derivitives are on the right. (a) star, (b) tree, (c) bus, (d) daisy chain, (e) ring, (f) mesh.

doesn't have a hub that is a common point of failure, bus topologies are more susceptible to failure.

Another reason why the bus is reliable is because its NICs are typically passive devices, allowing the network to stay up even when one station fails. However, some of its disadvantages include strict constraints on the placing of the stations as well as their number. Also, it is difficult to isolate a failure when determining a fault.

16.2.3 The Ring

The ring topology is like the daisy-chain topology, but with all nodes connected in a circle. See Figure 16.1(e). When additional paths are placed in between the nodes of a ring as shown in Figure 16.1(f), then the network becomes much more resilient to failure. This topology is called a mesh and it commonly appears in WANS. The figure shows a fully-connected mesh network.

The ring connects each node with a point-to-point link until all nodes are connected in a circle. This makes the ring more suitable for fiber-based LANs, since fiber-link transmission requires a transmitter and a receiver. Traffic travels in only one direction. All node interfaces are active; they retransmit the received signal. This allows the distance between adjacent nodes to be longer than those used with a bus.

Theoretically, the ring provides a relatively simple design with circuit costs being lower than those for the star. The ratio of throughput to the rate of the transmitted signal speed is higher than that for the bus. However, since the ring nodes are active, providing store and forward switching, they become more vulnerable to failure. Furthermore, if one node is slow or error-prone in relaying the ring signals, then the performance of the entire network is degraded.

16.3 ACCESS METHODS

16.3.1 CSMA/CD

Once the LAN is laid out with the chosen topology, we need an access method so that one node can get the attention of another, and so that data can be transferred. The first and most popular access method is called CSMA/CD (Carrier Sense Multiple Access with Collision Detection). The rules of this protocol are relatively simple.

The station which wants to use the transmission media for sending data must first listen to the media to hear if anyone else is transmitting. If not, then the station may transmit immediately. However, while the transmission is still taking place, the transmitter must also listen to hear if anyone else has begun transmitting on the line or not. If there is someone else transmitting, then the station must abort the transmission and after waiting a random amount of time, may start the process over. This process is done until all the data has been transmitted without it being destroyed by another transmission.

Let's consider an example. In Figure 16.2, three network nodes are shown on a bus topology, with nodes X and Y being close to each other while node Z is a distance away from them. First node X listens to the line to make sure that no one else is using it. Then it begins its transmission. After a short time, node Y is prevented from transmission, because X's signal has had time to reach Y. However, node Z, which is much further away from X than is Y, hasn't heard X's signal on the line yet, and so has begun its transmission.

Eventually, node Z hears X's signal and stops its transmission, and likewise, X hears Z's transmission and also stops. They then both wait an arbitrary amount of time and attempt again to transmit their data.

Notice that once a collision is detected, the data which was sent up to that time, can't be used, and the entire block of data must be retransmitted. In other words, the throughput of the data is always less than the bandwidth of the medium. For this reason, in Ethernet, which uses CSMA/CD, the throughput may be as low as 30% of the total bandwidth available on the media. Of course, this figure depends on how the network is configured and used.

Anyway, the performance of this access method is good for low to medium traffic loads and only becomes poor once there are many stations attempting to transmit simultaneously, at which time one has to install bridges and routers to divide up the network into several LANs.

If you remember from Chapter 15 on ISDN, we introduced CSMA/CR (CSMA with Collision Resolution) which provided better throughput than CSMA/CD. There,

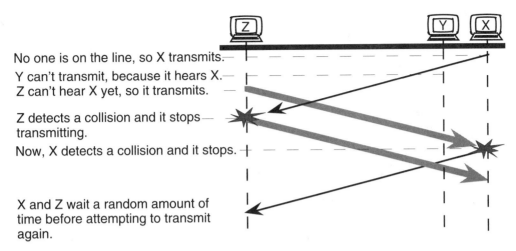

No one is on the line, so X transmits.

Y can't transmit, because it hears X.

Z can't hear X yet, so it transmits.

Z detects a collision and it stops transmitting.

Now, X detects a collision and it stops.

X and Z wait a random amount of time before attempting to transmit again.

Figure 16.2 A CSMA/CD access method scenario.

no data had to be retransmitted, even after a collision had occurred on the line. However, in CSMA/CD, the entire block of data has to be retransmitted after a collision.

16.3.2 Token Passing

CSMA/CD is a contention or non-deterministic type of access method. This means that several nodes may try to access the entire bandwidth of the media all at the same time. It is also said to be a probabilistic access method, because how long a node has to wait to gain access to the network depends on the amount of traffic at that time.

Contrary to CSMA/CD, token passing is a non-contention based access method, where every network node is guaranteed some amount of the available bandwidth. Also, instead of being probabilistic, it is considered to be deterministic, because the access to the network is predictable.

Token passing is primarily used on ring and bus networks, where all nodes are logically placed in order. Data signals are passed from node to node until it comes back to the transmitting node. While the data is circulating, the receiving node copies the data into its buffers. If a node wants to transmit, it must wait to receive a certain bit pattern called the token. Once the token is received, instead of placing it back on the ring, data is sent in a frame by the transmitting node. Then when the receiver identifies its own address in the frame, it receives the frame and checks for errors.

If the frame is received error-free, a copy bit is set at the end of the frame by the receiving node and the frame arrives back at the sender. Here, the sender can check the copy bit to see if the frame was received or not. If it was, then the token can be sent to the next station down the ring, or else the frame can be retransmitted. Figure 16.3 illustrates such a sequence of events as node C sends data to node E. In (a), node A has sent a token to B which doesn't have any data to transmit. So node B passes the token on down to C which does have data to send (b).

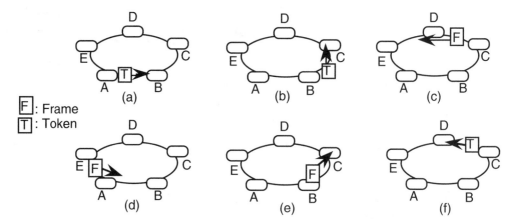

Figure 16.3 (a) A token passes through B, since it has nothing to send. (b) C has data to send, so it removes the token. (c) C sends a frame of data for E. (d) Data is received by E and it sets the copy bit, acknowledging it. (e) C gets the acknowledgment. (f) C places the token back on the ring to give others a chance to transmit.

In (c), node C removes the token from the ring and sends a data frame to node E. Node D realizing that the frame is for someone else, simply passes the frame down the ring. In (d), the frame is read by node E without any errors, and the frame is sent back to node C with the copy bit set. This is shown in (e). Finally, in (f), node C, realizing from the copy bit that the frame was received, removes the frame and places the token back on the ring to give someone else a chance to transmit.

16.4 SOFTWARE BASICS

In this section we'll turn our attention to software components which are needed to build a LAN. We'll assume the IBM PC is used as a network node, discuss its networking components, and give a brief overview of the PC LAN program. Finally, we will extend our discussion to include the IEEE 802 and proprietary protocols, and show how they relate to each other and the OSI reference model.

16.4.1 NetBIOS

Before we talk about the networking capabilities of the IBM PC, let us briefly look at the roles that BIOS (Basic Input Output System) and DOS (Disk Operating System) have within a PC.

BIOS and DOS: BIOS is a set of machine language routines of which many are part of a ROM (Read-Only Memory) chip. It physically comes inside the computer. Unlike BIOS, DOS comes on a floppy diskette and is loaded in the RAM (Random Access Memory) of the computer when it is turned on. DOS uses higher level instructions than does BIOS.

The primary function of BIOS is to provide software-based control for video displays, keyboards, disk drives, etc., that are connected to the PC. Anytime a person types a character on the keyboard, the BIOS receives it and presents it to the application. Similarly, whenever an application needs to display anything on the screen, it must go through the BIOS, and so on.

DOS provides a higher level interface for the user or the application. Therefore, it is easier for a user to execute a DOS command rather than perform a BIOS call. As shown in Figure 16.4, software applications can either perform BIOS calls or DOS calls. However, BIOS calls are executed faster, since they don't have to go through DOS. Applications which make DOS calls are more portable; that is, they can run over a variety of machines which are emulating the BIOS and using the designated version of DOS.

NetBIOS and NOS: To our stand-alone PC, let us now add a NIC to make it a part of a LAN. Here, we don't care whether it is a TRN, ethernet, or whatever other kind of NIC it is. In any case, the machine language code for NetBIOS (Network BIOS) routines resides in a ROM chip on the NIC. NetBIOS handles all OSI model's session layer functions, while the NIC itself supports all the layers below and including that layer. See Figure 16.5.

NetBIOS receives data frames from the local system and transmits them to the network. To interface with NetBIOS, we need an operating system for the LAN called a NOS (Network Operating System). One example of a NOS is IBM's PC LAN Program. The NOS interacts with the NetBIOS in the same manner as DOS interacts with BIOS. One inconsistency in this analogy is that the PC LAN program is itself running under DOS.

If the application requires access to the local disk, DOS will gain this access via the BIOS and if the application requires access to a network disk or a resource, the request is directed through the PC LAN program which goes through NetBIOS.

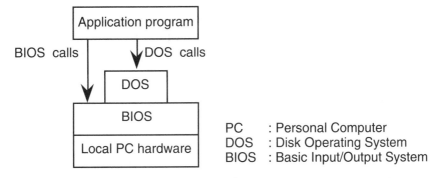

Figure 16.4 An application which makes BIOS calls is more efficient, but the application which makes DOS calls is portable.

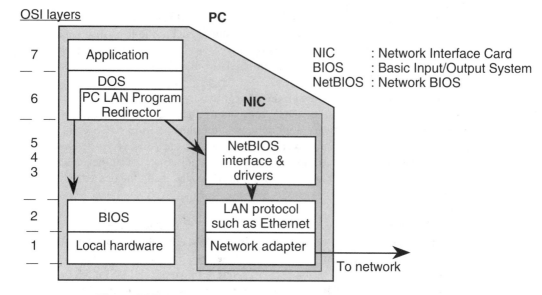

Figure 16.5 DOS can access the local hardware through BIOS or the network devices via NetBIOS.

16.4.2 The PC LAN program

There are two types of NOSs. The PC LAN program is an example of a peer-to-peer NOS or simply a peer NOS. These NOSs are usually DOS based and are slower than their server-based NOS counterparts. Server-based NOSs are also called centralized NOSs or client-server based NOSs.

A server-based NOS runs on one machine which is dedicated to be a server, and the network stations or clients access its files. Server-based NOSs are more powerful, because they don't run under DOS, but the NOS takes over the entire server. They are not limited by DOS and can handle many more clients than do peer NOSs.

Nonetheless, a peer NOS allows a low-cost connectivity between the network nodes. Any PC which has a hard drive can be a file server. The network is less dependent on one machine. Anyone can be in anyone else's programs, if it is so desired. However, these small-scale networks do not integrate well with larger, enterprise-wide networks. This makes them difficult to expand.

To get an idea of how peer-to-peer networks work, let us briefly look at how IBM's PC LAN program may be used.

In Figure 16.6, we have a redirector called Donnie and a server called Daisy. A redirector is the most elementary type of a network node, while a server is the most sophisticated. After these stations boot up under DOS, the LAN software with its drivers (software components) is loaded in. On the server, this is typically done off the hard drive and on the redirector it may be done using floppies.

Attached to the server, there is a printer and a hard drive labeled C. In the C drive there is a directory called APPS. Daisy doesn't mind sharing the printer or the files that are under APPS, but doesn't want anyone else to have access to her personal files in subdirectory X. See the Figure 16.6. Let us next look at the steps involved in letting Donnie access Daisy's resources.

After the network is loaded in, Daisy executes the NET START command as shown. The SRV designates the machine as a server and DAISY then becomes the network name of this PC, by which other PCs can access it. Donnie's PC executes a NET START command configuring itself as a redirector (RDR) and naming itself as DONALD.

Next Daisy executes the NET SHARE command, making the path "C:\APPS" available to others using the shortname of APPLICAT. She doesn't want anyone to write or modify the files in this directory, so she only grants read access by using a "/R" on the command line.

Now this directory is available to everyone on the network, and Donnie wants to use it, so he executes the NET USE command. This command line as shown, assigns the APPLICAT subdirectory of server Daisy (specified by "\\DAISY") available to him on his E drive (given by "E:").

Now Donnie can change his drive to E and execute the DIR (DIRectory) command in DOS. This command goes over the network and gets executed on Daisy's machine, which then responds with the two subdirectories under APPS, as shown. At the E: prompt, Donnie now has all the capabilities he would have had if he were to be at Daisy's PC under the APPS directory. The only difference is that Daisy has restricted him to only read.

The example continues by Daisy making her printer available to others by executing the NET SHARE command and Donnie, after executing the NET USE

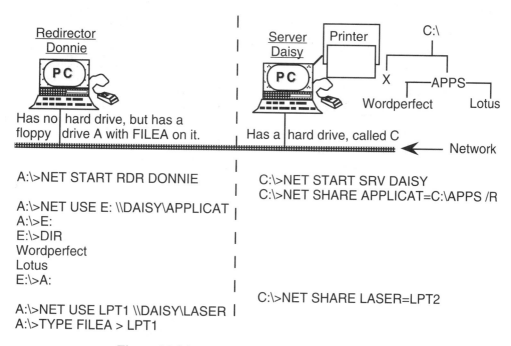

Figure 16.6 An example of peer to peer networking.

command, makes Daisy's printer available to himself. Now, if Donnie prints his file A from drive A using the TYPE command of DOS, it is then printed on Daisy's PC.

Notice how this software runs under DOS. When Donnie changes his drive from A to E, the services of NetBIOS are invoked by DOS, and when the drive is changed back to A, DOS invokes the BIOS services instead.

16.4.3 IEEE 802 Standards

In February of 1980, IEEE decided to standardize LANs and using this year and month number, the 802 project was started. The intention of this project was to standardize the many existing LAN protocols under one "umbrella," called the 802 standards.

For now disregarding the upper half of Figure 16.7, let us only look at layers 1 and 2 as they are defined by the IEEE 802 family of protocols. 802.1 is a standard specifying network control and management, which effects all the other "802-dot" protocols.

Toward the top of the 802 stack are the 802.2 specifications, which define the LLC (Logical Link Control) layer. Under it, are the MAC (Medium Access Control) and physical layers. The LLC layer and the MAC layer together provide the functions of the data link control layer of the OSI model, while the MAC layer and the physical

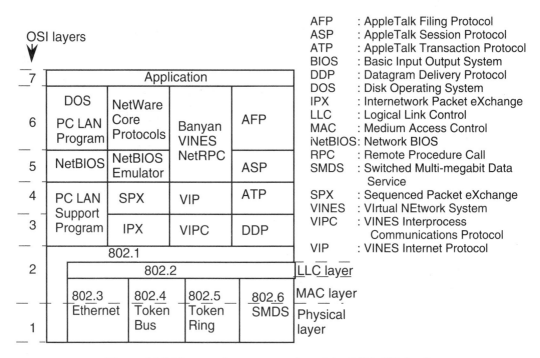

Figure 16.7 The proprietary protocols and the IEEE 802 family of protocols as they stack against the OSI reference model.

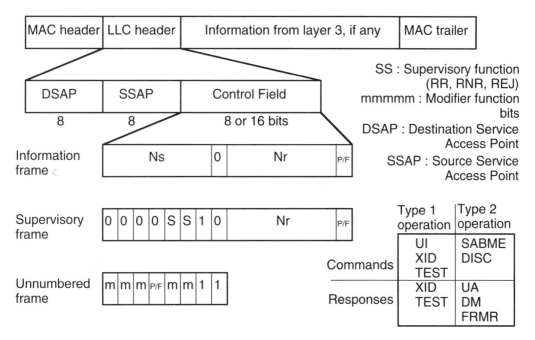

Figure 16.8 The LLC headers for each of the three types of frames, with modifier functions shown in the table.

layers are combined in outlining the details of specific types of LANs. For instance, 802.3 specifies an Ethernet standard, and so on.

Since no routing is required on a LAN, in that an intermediate node doesn't have to redirect a received frame over a different link (because there is only one link in a LAN), no network layer is specified by the 802 protocols. As a frame is received by a node, it contains a MAC address and an LLC address called a SAP (Service Access Point). The MAC address specifies the physical node on the network which is physically coded in the NIC.

The SAP address provides the network layer protocol which is being used in the communication. In other words, the SAP provides a logical address to a protocol being addressed in the third or network layer, whereas the network node is specified by the MAC or physical address. For example, E0h is the SAP address for NetWare and F0h is for IBM's NetBIOS. The "h" next to the address indicates a hexadecimal address. The LLC layer provides an interface between the network layer and the MAC layer.

Figure 16.8 details the functions of the LLC layer further and shows how it fits in the MAC frame. The MAC header and trailer are determined by the specific LAN protocol, such as, Ethernet or TRN. The MAC layer treats both the data from the upper layers and the LLC header as information.

The LLC layer manages the LLC header with its 3 fields: the DSAP (Destination SAP), SSAP (Source SAP), and the control field. There are three types of control fields,

LANs   335 each determined by the type of LLC frame it is handling. These are information, supervisory, and unnumbered frames. The control field for an unnumbered frame is only 8 bits, while for the other two, it is 16 bits long.

All of the fields shown have already been discussed in sections 12.5 and 13.6. Lastly, there are two types of LLC services. Type 1 is used for unacknowledged, connectionless, or datagram delivery type of services, and type 2 is used for connection-oriented type of services between the communicating SAPs. The chart depicts the types of unnumbered frames and labels them as either commands or responses.

16.4.4 Proprietary Protocols

Directing our attention to the upper half of Figure 16.7, we see a sampling of various proprietary LAN protocols and how they fit in the overall LAN protocol picture. Each of these upper layer (3 to 6) stacks can be implemented over any of the 802.3 through 802.6 layers. Otherwise, they may be implemented over some other proprietary lower-layer protocols. For example, AppleTalk, which is shown in the right most column, can run over layers 1 and 2 protocols, collectively called LocalTalk, or it can run over one other lower-layer protocol shown in the figure. Notice how IBM's PC LAN Program and NetBIOS fit in the protocol stack.

Moving across the figure, we have Novell's NetWare protocol stack. NetWare, as well as 3Com's NOS, is based on Xerox's XNS (Xerox Network System). XNS was very influential in defining the OSI model.

Applications can interface with NetWare at various layers. When a network node accesses files on a server using DOS requests, it is using the application layer interface called the Workstation Shell Interface. At the session layer, applications can make NetBIOS-compatible calls, since NetWare's NetBIOS is an emulation of IBM's NetBIOS. A virtual-connection interface is provided at the transport layer for applications which require connection oriented delivery of packets. This is accomplished by the use of sequence numbers in the SPX (Sequenced Packet eXchange) header. Finally, applications can interface at the network layer for connectionless communications of datagrams. This is provided through the IPX (Internetwork Packet eXchange) protocol.

Banyan Systems Inc.'s VINES (VIrtual NEtwork System) is a NOS which is based on the Unix operating system. It can be incorporated over various types of networks and platforms. On a DOS platform, the workstation is DOS based, but on a server, it runs under a Unix kernel. Many of these protocols which are primarily Unix based, will be covered in later chapters.

Apple Computer's AppleTalk is primarily used with the Macintosh computers. These computers already come with a LocalTalk network interface. At the bottom of the AppleTalk stack is DDP (Datagram Delivery Protocol) which provides communication interface with the appropriate process within the network node.

Although there are several protocols which could be implemented at the upper layers, only the primary ones are shown in the diagram. At the transport layer ATP (AppleTalk Transaction Protocol) provides a sequential and reliable delivery of packets, while ASP (AppleTalk Session Protocol) manages and maintains sessions between sockets (or processes). Lastly, AFP (AppleTalk Filing Protocol) supports file transfers between remote locations.

16.5 ETHERNET

16.5.1 Ethernet Frame Formats

Ethernet was originally created by Xerox, DEC, and Intel corporations. In 1985, IEEE standardized it as 802.3, which is slightly different from the original de facto standard. In the previous section, specifically in Figure 16.8, we have seen how a header is added to the information received by the LLC layer and forwarded to the MAC layer. Now let us look at the headers and trailers as they are added by the MAC layer in Ethernet. Then when we go over TRNs, we will do the same for that standard.

Figure 16.9 shows both Ethernet and IEEE 802.3 frame formats. Both frames have a maximum length of 1526 and a minimum length of 72. The preamble field in Ethernet is 8 bytes long which has a string of "10"s terminating with a "11." The IEEE frame defines a 7-byte preamble and a one-byte SFD (Start Frame Delimiter) field which together define the same bit pattern as the 8-byte preamble for Ethernet. Due to its many 1-0 transitions, this 8-byte string pattern is used for synchronizing the receiver.

The next two fields specify the MAC or physical address of the destination and source nodes. This address field is usually 6 bytes long. The first 3 bytes are administered by IEEE (previously by Xerox) and are assigned to NIC manufacturers. The address bits for the last 3 bytes are assigned and maintained by each manufacturer. So, globally, this physical address for all Ethernet cards are kept unique.

Usually, this address is burned in the ROM of the NIC, but can also be assigned using a diagnostic diskette. If the physical address needs to be kept the same, then when changing the boards, the ROM chip should also be swapped along with it.

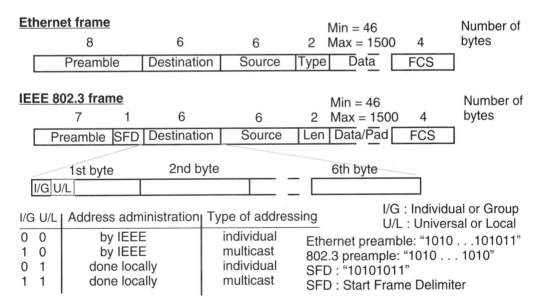

Figure 16.9 The formats of the two types of Ethernet. In source routing, the I/G bit in the source address is set to 1; otherwise it is 0.

In both frame types, if the I/G (Individual/Group) address bit is set to 0 by the sender, then the frame is sent to only one station, or else it is sent to a group of stations, which is called a multicast transmission. If all 48 bits are set to 1, then it is a broadcast and all stations receive that frame. IEEE frames use the U/L (Universal or Local) address bit to indicate if the address field conforms to IEEE addressing standards or if it uses some other local scheme of addressing.

The type field gives the type of Ethernet protocol used in the data field. For example, 0800H is used for IP and 0805H is used for X.25, etc. Notice that the type field doesn't exist in the IEEE frame because the LLC's SAP address provides its function.

The length field in the 802.3 frame gives the length of the data. If this length needs to be conveyed to the receiver in Ethernet, then the upper layers must handle that process. Also, in Ethernet the upper layer must make sure that the data field is at least 46 bytes, while in the IEEE frame, the MAC layer pads additional bytes if necessary. From this point on, we'll refer to both the IEEE 802.3 and Ethernet standards simply as Ethernet.

16.5.2 10BASE5

Different variations of Ethernet are dubbed as 10BASE5, 10BASE2, 10BROAD36, 10BASET, etc. The first number (10) designates the transmission speed in Mbps over the media and the last number designates the maximum segment length in 100's of meters. The BASE or the BROAD indicates whether the media uses baseband signaling or broadband signaling. For now, let us look at standard Ethernet which is called 10BASE5. This is the original standard which runs at 10 Mbps using 500 meters as the maximum length of segments. It uses a baseband cabling system.

The components of this Ethernet are shown in Figure 16.10. The main cable, or the bus, uses a RG-4 (Radio Grade 4) coax. The impedance of this cable is 50 ohms.

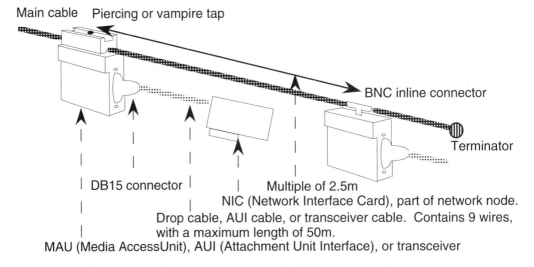

Figure 16.10 The components of a 10BASE5 (standard) Ethernet.

On this main cable, there are AUIs (Attachment Unit Interfaces) connected at intervals of 2.5 meters or multiples thereof. They are also called MAUs (Media Access Units) and transceivers. The maximum number of taps on a segment is 100. These AUIs are attached using either a piercing vampire or an in-line BNC type connector.

From the AUI, the station is connected using an AUI cable, which is also called a drop cable. It is not a coaxial cable but a cable with 9 wires. Its maximum length is 50 meters. It is connected to the transceiver using a DB15 connector and the other end of it is connected to the NIC which is inside the workstation. The main coaxial cable must be terminated at both ends with 50 ohm terminators and one of them should be grounded.

The transceiver provides several functions. It can detect if signals are present on the cable and whether or not the cable is available for transmission. If it is, the AUI transmits the signal and backs off if it detects a collision. In the event that the terminal is continuously transmitting (or jabbering), the transceiver will prevent it from transmitting over the line, giving other nodes a chance to communicate. Finally, the AUI provides a heartbeat signal to the terminal, indicating that it is up and operational.

When the performance begins to degrade, due to too many stations on the cable, or because the main cable is exceeding the 500-meter length limitation, then the network can be expanded by adding other segments. This is done by connecting repeaters between segments. Repeaters do not eliminate collisions between stations on two different segments; they merely enable the extension of the range of the LAN. In a later chapter we'll see how bridges and routers are able to isolate traffic over individual segments.

The maximum number of repeaters between any two nodes of a network is 4. On the right side of Figure 16.11, a multi-story building is shown which has a backbone

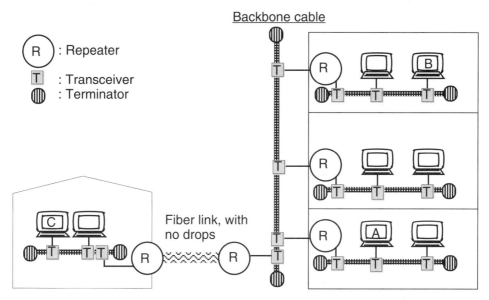

Figure 16.11 The range of an Ethernet network can be extended from 500 meters to 2500 meters using repeaters.

cable running vertically. Using repeaters, network segments from each floor are connected to this backbone segment. Notice that here nodes from any two floors may communicate with each other using only two repeaters. On the left side of the figure, we have another location on campus that is also connected to this LAN. Typically, a fiber link is preferred over such distances for better quality signals. Here, any station in one building can communicate with another station in the other building using no more than 3 repeaters.

16.5.3 10BASE2

In 1985, a less costly version of Ethernet was standardized as 10BASE2. Since it uses thin coax which is easy to install, it is also called ThinNet and CheaperNet. This version still uses the baseband signaling technique with many of the same characteristics of that of 10BASE5. However, it has more distance and node placement requirements.

Figure 16.12 shows how typically the NIC is attached directly to the main coax, without the use of the AUI cable. The NIC comes with a BNC connector and the circuitry for the transceiver. Attaching the NIC to the main coax is done easily without needing to pierce the coax. The cost per node is also significantly lower than that of 10BASE5. Furthermore, the cable designated as RG-58 is only 0.25 inches thick, which makes it not only inexpensive, but also easy to work with.

Unfortunately, it has some limitations. The maximum segment length is only 185 meters. The nodes are attached at 0.5 meter intervals with up to 30 taps per segment. The maximum number of nodes per network, including repeaters, is 1024. This figure is the same as that for 10BASE5 and 10BASET. However, the maximum length of the network is only 925 meters, versus the 2500 meters for 10BASE5.

16.5.4 10BASET

Introduction: ThinNet, due to its low cost and ease of installation, became more popular than standard Ethernet very quickly. Because of this immediate success, another type of Ethernet was introduced that would drive the cost even lower and make installation even easier than before. It is called 10BASET.

10BASET uses standard 24 AWG telephone wire instead of coax. This wiring, in many instances, is already in place in existing buildings. Therefore, it needs a

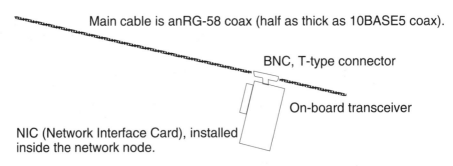

Figure 16.12 10BASE2 hardware.

minimum amount of installation. Furthermore, 10BASET can coexist with other types of Ethernets, making it suitable to expand existing networks without having to replace the older technologies.

Initially, 10BASET was introduced by Syncoptics (an offshoot of Xerox Palo Alto Research Center), as Ethernet over UTP (Unshielded Twisted Pair). In 1990, IEEE adopted it as a standard.

A Hub-Centered LAN: At the heart of the network is a hub. It is also called a concentrator when it is residing in a chassis to which expansion modules can be added. Coming out of the hub (see Figure 16.13) is a standard 50-wire telephone cable which is attached to an M-66 type punch-down block. This may be done using the standard 50-pin RJ-21 connector. From the punch-down block, the wiring distribution is laid out in the same manner as that for telephone circuits.

Each of these circuits from the block would typically go to a wall jack. From there, using a standard RJ-45 connector and a telephone wire, a connection is made to the NIC. Out of the 8 pins available on the RJ-45, 2 are used to transmit, 2 are used to receive, and 4 are not used at all. Since each station uses only 4 wires, a 50-wire cable from the hub can support up to 12 stations.

Many times the hub itself may have twelve RJ-45 jacks directly on it, or else, using a harmonica block, the RJ-21 can simply be converted to a set of RJ-45 jacks. In any case, notice that this topology, being a star-wired bus, is drastically different from the topologies of the other Ethernets. Yet, it still uses the same type of frame and the CSMA/CD access method as used on the other Ethernets. Collisions occur on the bus which is inside the hub. When a station transmits, the signal arrives at the hub and after being repeated, it is retransmitted over all the other ports. This is why the hub is also called a multiport repeater.

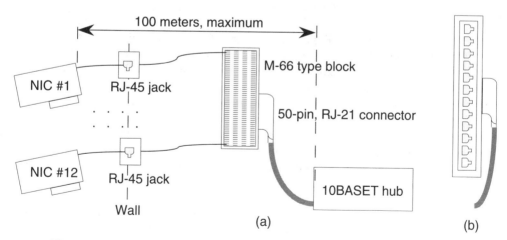

Figure 16.13 (a) As an example, the 10BASET hub can be connected to a punch-down block using 48 wires of a 50-wire telco cable. From here, connections can be provided for up to 12 network nodes. Each node requires 4 wires. (b) Alternatively, using a harmonica block connected to the 50-wire cable, 12 RJ-45 plugs can be provided directly.

The hub constantly monitors the stations on each of its branches by sending test signals to them. The branches which respond to this signal are allowed to communicate with the other branches, while those that don't are shut off by the hub. Status lights over each port on the hub indicate which branches are active and which are not. When an older Ethernet adapter which doesn't respond to this link test signal is connected to a port, its link test can be turned off manually. This allows existing Ethernet segments to be connected to the hub.

Sometimes with 10BASE2, a user may move his workstation by unplugging the T-connector from its back. Since the bus goes through this connector, this operation inadvertently brings down the network. That is because the tap becomes improperly terminated.

On the contrary, with 10BASET if something does happen to one station or its link, the rest of the network is unaffected. This is because the hub would shut down the defective node since it would fail the link test. This is called partitioning a port. After a hub partitions a defective port, it continues to test this branch to see if it is fixed. When someone does fix the link or its node, the hub notices it due to the continuous testing of the link and will bring that port up, automatically.

Jabbering is transmission of excessively long frames. If this occurs over the network, the hub can easily detect which node is doing that and can partition it. This is not as easy on other Ethernets. The hub can also act as a network monitoring device, providing error and collision statistics around the clock for each of its ports. This data can be obtained from a remote location, and using a software package, easy to understand reports can be generated.

Even though the hub is very attractive in that it provides a means for better management and control of the network, it becomes a crucial element of the network. Care must be taken in selecting and purchasing it, because the reliability of the network becomes very much dependent on it.

First Phase of Expansion: Figure 16.14(a) shows how the standard Ethernet LAN of Figure 16.11 can be expanded to include 10BASET and Figure 16.14(b) shows the second phase of expanding this network. In Figure 16.14(a), a new LAN with 20 stations is being added to one of the floors and it is being connected using an AUI cable to the 10BASE5 backbone. First, let us look at the 20 station LAN.

Suppose we have decided to use 12 port hubs for the 10BASET LAN, then we would need at least two hubs to accommodate the 20 stations. These two hubs can be cascaded by connecting together a port from each of the two hubs. However, the send-pair and the receive-pair of these two ports must be crossed, either by using a cable that does that or by flipping a switch on the hub. This would leave us with 22 ports to add stations to.

We have said that the hub acts like a repeater, because it retransmits the signal which it receives from one port to the rest of the ports. So IEEE specifies that between any two nodes on a network, the signal may only go through 4 hubs. One can easily see that when hubs are connected in series, as in a daisy-chain topology, the number of ports available is much less than if they were connected in a tree configuration.

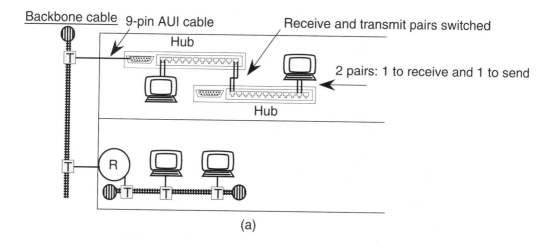

(a)

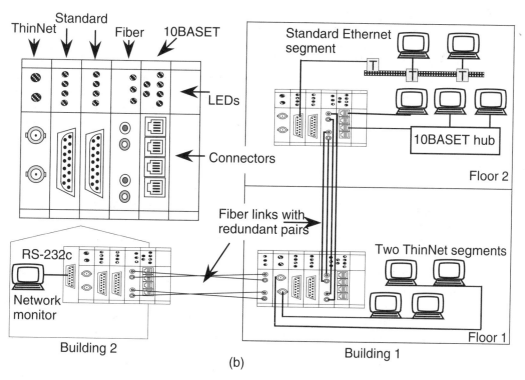

(b)

Figure 16.14 (a) Expanding the network of Figure 16.11 to accommodate up to 22 10BASET stations. (b) Installing a fiber backbone with concentrators on each floor. Ethernet concentrator is shown in the inset. Modules of various types of Ehternet can be inserted in the chasis as needed. Typically, fiber is used between floors and buildings. Their transmit and receive pairs are shown to be crossed, since that is necessary.

LANs

343

To connect our 20-node 10BASET LAN to the existing 10BASE5 backbone, we simply connect one of the hubs to the backbone. This is done by using an AUI cable from a hub to the transceiver on the backbone.

Second Phase of Expansion: As more new and existing LANs are integrated in the network, concentrators (also called hubs) can be added to every floor. This is shown in Figure 16.14(b) as the second phase of the network expansion project. Here, the old coax backbone is removed and concentrators are interconnected using fiber instead. This is installed in redundant pairs, hopefully, routed over different paths.

The chassis of the concentrators are then fitted with the appropriate modules depending on the types of networks existing on each floor. Although the diagram shows all concentrators being configured the same way, they don't have to be. The concentrators allow one to plug and play as requirements change. Lastly, we've added a monitor to perform management functions over the network. As requirements continue to grow, the chassis may be fitted with bridges and routers.

16.6 TOKEN-RING NETWORKS

16.6.1 Basic Configuration

TRNs (Token-Ring Networks) use a token passing access method over a ring topology. Just as the hub provides greater management capabilities in 10BASET networks, TRNs use a wiring concentrator to achieve the same purpose. A wiring concentrator is also called a MAU (Multistation Access Unit). This acronym should not be confused with 10BASE5's transceiver which is also called a MAU, which stands for Media Access Unit.

TRN's MAUs typically provide connections for 8 stations as seen in Figure 16.15(a). The figure shows a type 1, data-grade cable. This cable is a STP (Shielded Twisted Pair), since it contains two 22-AWG twisted pairs enclosed in a shield. The shield helps to fend off electromagnetic interference. The connector for this cable is genderless and can be directly connected with another one. The cable is connected to the workstation using a DB9 plug.

Many times, standard telephone UTP (Unshielded Twisted Pair) cabling is also used to connect the workstations with an MAU. This is called type 3 cabling. It uses RJ-45 connectors on both the MAU and the NIC. Since this cable is graded for voice, it has more stringent distance limitations than type 1 cable does.

Physically, the TRN looks like a star, but logically it is a ring. As shown in Figure 16.15(b), when data travels from one node to another, it must first go through the MAU. Therefore, the TRN is called a star-wired ring. Similarly, 10BASET is called a star-wired bus. The connection from a NIC to the MAU is called a lobe. TRNs operate at either 4 Mbps or 16 Mbps, but to operate at the higher speed, all NICs must be rated for 16 Mbps.

When a station is connected to the MAU and is powered up, it provides a phantom voltage of 5 VDC on the cable. This voltage pulls back a relay at the connector in the MAU, making the node become part of the ring. This is shown for ports 3, 4, and 7 in the figure. If for some reason, a NIC from a station can't provide this voltage to the

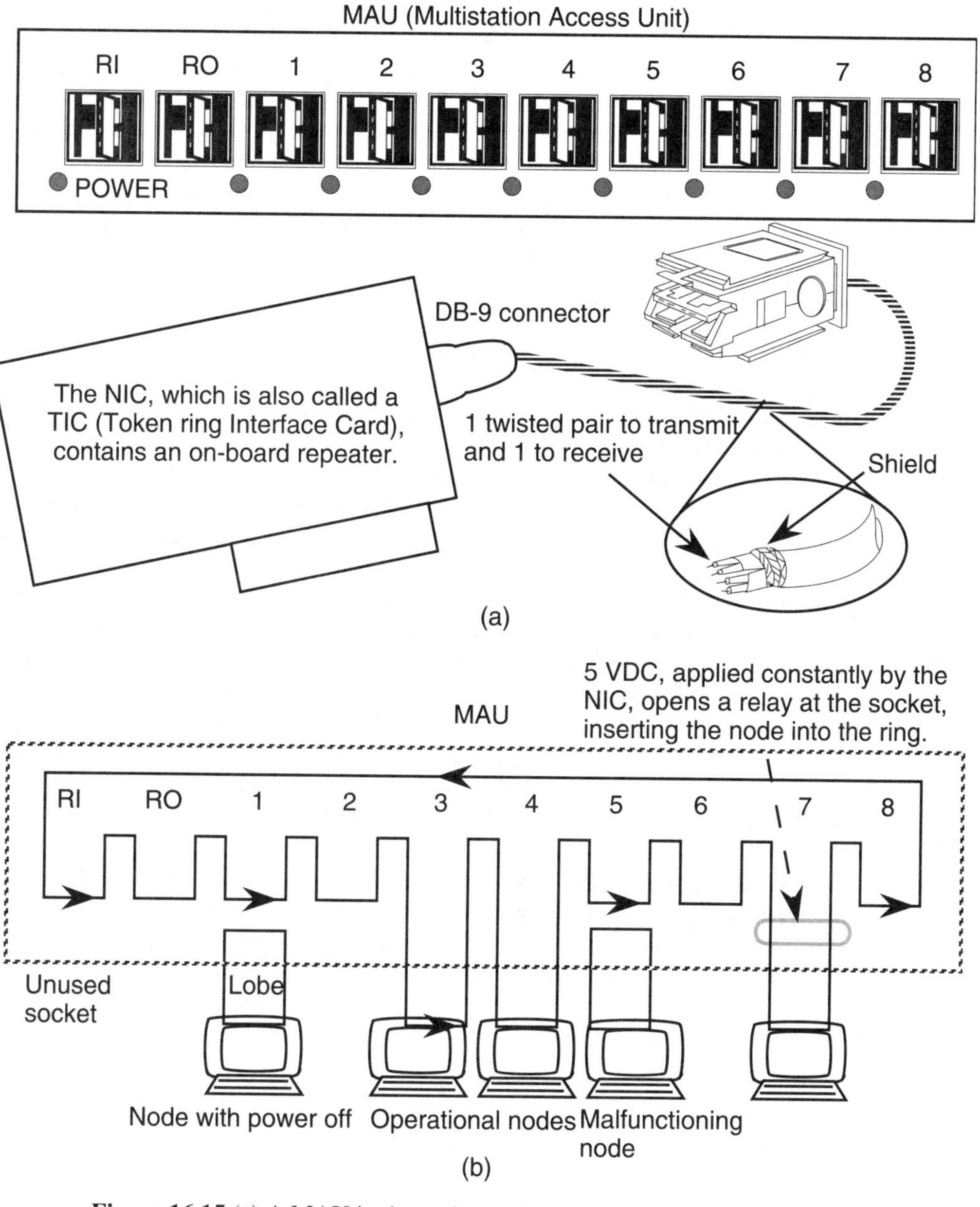

MAU (Multistation Access Unit)

| RI | RO | 1 | 2 | 3 | 4 | 5 | 6 | 7 | 8 |

POWER

DB-9 connector

The NIC, which is also called a TIC (Token ring Interface Card), contains an on-board repeater.

1 twisted pair to transmit and 1 to receive

Shield

(a)

5 VDC, applied constantly by the NIC, opens a relay at the socket, inserting the node into the ring.

MAU

| RI | RO | 1 | 2 | 3 | 4 | 5 | 6 | 7 | 8 |

Unused socket

Lobe

Node with power off   Operational nodes Malfunctioning node

(b)

Figure 16.15 (a) A MAU is shown here with the type 1 connector and the STP (Shielded Twisted Pair). (b) The MAU and its stations become a star-wired ring network.

MAU's port, then the MAU will keep that node off the ring. This could be because a station is turned off (such as port 1 in the figure), because it is malfunctioning (port 5), or due to a break in the cable.

LANs   **345**

16.6.2 Extending the Size of the TRN

Figure 16.16(a) shows how a TRN can be easily expanded to more than 8 stations. This is simply done by placing several MAUs in a ring of their own and then connecting the stations to these MAUs. The ring which is created by connecting the MAUs is called the main ring. The MAUs are connected in a ring by placing a cable from one MAU's RI (Ring In) port to another's RO (Ring Out) port. All the MAUs in the main ring may be placed in one rack or they could be placed in different wiring closets. The figure shows the bottom two as being in one closet and the top one being in another.

Notice that all nodes now become part of the ring. Each node serves as a repeater; therefore, the maximum length of the lobe for a 4 mbps network is specified at 300 meters, while for Ethernet, the maximum length of an entire segment is 500 meters. The maximum distance between wiring closets is 200 meters, which can be extended to 730 meters using a pair of repeaters, placed at each end of their connecting link. If fiber is used, this range can be extended even further to 3000 meters.

Sometimes only one lobe needs to be extended. In that case, only one repeater is used to increase its range from 300 meters to 610 meters. The maximum number of MAUs and workstations is 33 and 260, respectively. When networks begin to get much larger, they have to be divided into smaller networks which are interconnected using bridges. All the specifications cited above are maximum figures for 4 Mbps networks using type 1 cabling. These limitations become more stringent as the network becomes large or if 16 Mbps speeds are used or if UTP cabling is used.

Notice in Figure 16.16(a) that as the signal travels from node to node only the outside path is used and the inside path is not. It is there as a backup. Every station has NAUN (Nearest Active Upstream Neighbor), which is the node from where it receives its signals. In the figure, for example, B is a NAUN to A, since A receives its signal from B.

If the cable breaks between the two MAUs as shown in Figure 16.16(b), then a person can remove the connecting cable at both ends and the ring heals itself, using the backup path. On some intelligent MAUs, this healing is done automatically. Here, even if the signal travels through all of the other nodes, B remains as the NAUN for A.

16.6.3 The Active Monitor

When the network is first turned on, the nodes send MAC frames to one another to determine their NAUNs. During this time, they also assign the NIC, typically with the highest address as the active monitor. This special "network overseer" provides synchronization for all the stations. It also buffers up to 24 bits in its shift registers, in order that an entire token, which is 24 bits long, may fit on the ring. This buffering is needed when the ring is too small.

Once the active monitor has been selected, it initializes the ring by purging the ring and generating a new token. This is also done if it doesn't see any activity over the ring at every 10 millisecond interval or if it sees the same high-priority token or frame circulating around the ring more than once. It is able to detect such tokens or frames by setting their monitor bits to 1 every time they come around. The station sending the

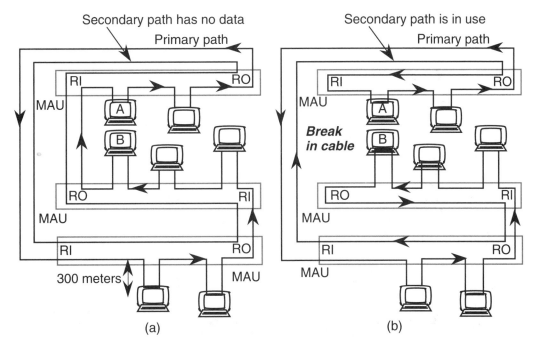

Figure 16.16 (a) Two MAUs in the lower portion are in one closet and the top one is in another. They are all interconnected using the RI and RO ports. (b) If one cable between the closets is faulty, then the ring can be restored again by utilizing the backup path.

tokens or frames resets the monitor bit to 0 and if the active monitor notices that this bit is already set, it will restart the ring. Furthermore, the active monitor broadcasts to all nodes that it is still in control, or else a standby monitor will take over the control of the network.

16.6.4 Signal Encoding

Ethernet uses Manchester encoding to transmit its digital signals. The advantage of this is that it provides a high-to-low or low-to-high level transition with every bit, helping the receiver to stay synchronized. Figure 16.17(a) shows this encoding method. A binary 1 is always a low-to-high level transition and binary 0 is just the opposite.

TRNs, on the other hand, use what is called a differential Manchester encoding. It requires that a binary 1 start at the same level as the previous bit ended. In other words, at the beginning of a 1, there should not be a level transition and at the beginning of a 0, a transition should occur. See Figure 16.16(b).

Besides providing a method of encoding data bits 1 and 0, TRNs also use two non-data bits call J and K. These bits are differential Manchester code violations, in that they do not have a mid-point level transition. The signal level for J is the same as the previous bit and that for K is not, as seen in Figure 16.16(c).

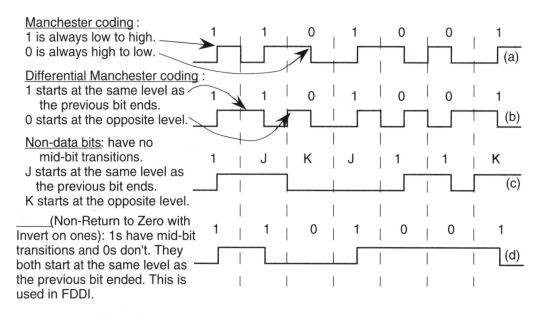

Figure 16.17 Manchester coding, differential Manchester coding, and the non-data bits as used with token-ring networks.

While we are looking at signal encoding methods, let us look at how FDDI handles it. FDDI uses NRZI (Non-Return to Zero with Invert on 1s) encoding method. Here, both a 0 and a 1 begin at the same level as the end of the previous bit. However, a binary 0 doesn't contain a level transition whereas a binary 1 does. Because of this, FDDI restricts a maximum number of consecutive 0s in its data stream. More on that later.

16.6.5 TRN Frame Format

MAC Frames: The frame for the TRN is more complex than that for Ethernet, as can be seen in Figure 16.18. Yet, it has more features. TRN frames are divided into two broad categories called LLC (Logical Link Control) frames and MAC (Medium Access Control) frames. LLC frames are used to send user data and have the same heading as shown back in Figure 16.8. MAC frames, on the other hand, are used to send management and control frames.

The FF (Frame Format) bits in the FC (Frame Control) field indicate whether the frame is an LLC or a MAC frame. The Z bits are primarily used to code various types of MAC frames. For instance, this could be a signal to all the stations to purge the ring or to notify them that the monitor is still present. Beaconing is also coded in here. A beacon MAC frame is sent by a node which hasn't received any signals from its NAUN for a while, maybe because of a break in cable. When this frame arrives at the NAUN it will take itself off the ring to perform lobe tests. If the tests fail, it will stay off, or else the station which transmitted the beacon will perform self-tests.

The format of the MAC frame is given in Figure 16.18, depicting that it has its own header called the LLID (mac Length ID) followed by a set of fields called subvectors. The reader will be spared from having to learn the details about these fields.

General Frame Formatting: All frames begin with an SD (Starting Delimiter) which is encoded, as shown in Figure 16.18, as "JK0JK000." This field merely marks the beginning of a frame. Similarly, the next to the last byte is called an ED (Ending Delimiter) and is encoded as "JK1JK1" plus an I (Intermediate frame) bit and an E (Error detected) bit.

The I bit, although rarely used, is set to 1 if more frames are being sent after the present one. Its E bit is set by any node on the ring, if an error is detected as the frame is passing through a node. Hence, error detection is performed on every NIC as the frames traverse around the ring. Each node keeps a record about how often it has set the E bit, making it easy to detect error-prone links.

After the SD field, comes the AC (Access Control) field, which contains the M (Monitor count) bit. As we have seen, it is used by the active monitor to detect high-priority frames and tokens which go around the ring more than once. It also contains

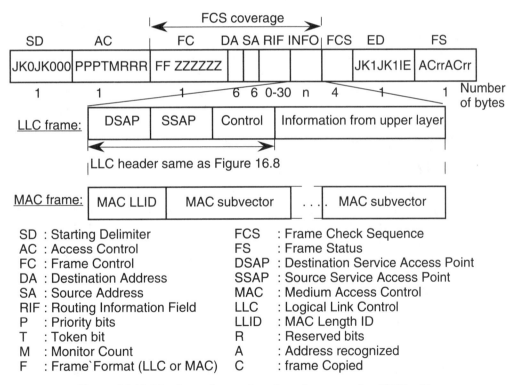

Figure 16.18 The frame format for token-ring networks. If FF = 01, it is an LLC frame and if FF = 00, it is a MAC frame.

the token bit which is set to 1 for frames and is set to 0 for tokens. A token consists of only the SD, AC, and the ED fields which add up to 24 bits.

Within the AC field, there are also the PPP (Priority) bits and the RRR (Reservation) bits. A token may contain a priority from 0 to 7 and when a token reaches a node that has data to transmit, it will take off the token and transmit the data. It will be allowed to do this, only if the priority of the data that is to be transmitted is greater than or equal to the priority given in the token. If this is not the case, the node will set the reservation bits to reserve the token next time it becomes available, as long as the reservation bits already in the token or frame are not greater than the level of the priority being requested. We will have an example later on to further clarify these fields.

The SA and DA (Source and Destination Address) fields are similar to the address fields of 802.3 Ethernet. However, it is common to interconnect TRNs using source routing bridges. In such cases, the RIF (Routing Information Field) is used to encode the addresses of the bridges. To use the RIF field in a frame, the least significant bit of the SA has to be set to 1. Remember, this is the I/G bit. The RIF contains bridge addresses in the order in which the frame should go in the event the DA is on a different ring than the SA. Source routing is efficient, since the bridges interconnecting the rings don't have to decide on the route. However, the sending node must first investigate the route before it can encode the RIF.

The FCS (Frame Check Sequence) field is used to detect errors. The FS (Frame Status) field contains the C (Copy) and A (Address recognized) bits. These bits are duplicated, since they are not accumulated into the FCS. Both the C and the A bits are set to 0 by the transmitter. The r bits are currently not in use.

The A bits are set by the receiver and the E bit is set by any node except the transmitter. The receiving node acknowledges that it understood that the frame was meant for it by setting the A bits to 1. If the receiver notices that the E bit is 0 and that the FCS checks out, then it will copy the data into its buffer and set the C bits to 1.

16.6.6 Example of Operation

Let us next run through Figure 16.19, which illustrates a few concepts of a TRN. We have four stations in the ring, with station 40 being the active monitor. Frames and tokens are moving to the right and then on down to the next row. They are shown as they are leaving the respective node and are not shown at all if they remain unchanged. As new concepts are introduced, only the necessary fields are shown, so that they stand out better. The smaller boxes are the tokens (T = 0) and the larger ones are frames (T = 1). Notice that the DA, A, and C fields are not part of the token.

The E, A, and C Bits: At first, node 40 sends a token to node 10. Node 10 doesn't need to transmit, so it sends the token down the ring. Station 20 grabs the token, and sends a frame to station 10, setting the E, A, and C bits to 0. It goes around the ring until it arrives at 10. It copies the frame and sets the A and C bits to 1, indicating that it understood the frame was meant for itself and that the frame was copied with no errors. Node 20 then receives this frame back and generates a new token so that others may have a chance to transmit.

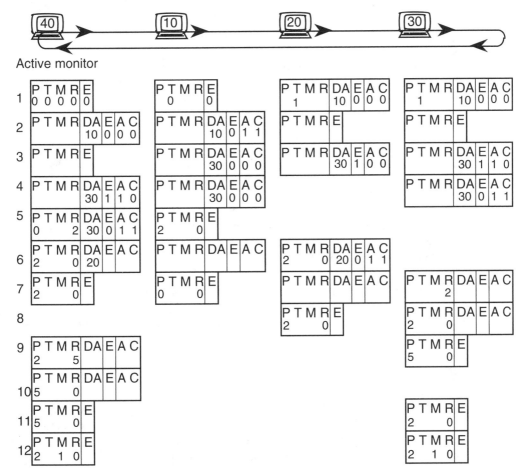

13 Ring purged, token restarted, because node 20 goes off the ring and M is still 1.

Figure 16.19 Frames (larger size) and tokens (smaller size) are shown to be circulating to the right around the ring. If they are not being changed by a node, then they are not drawn here. Also, only the values necessary to understand the concept being explained are shown to keep the figure from being cluttered with unnecessary information.

At line 3 of the diagram, node 10 then sends a frame to node 30, but while the frame was going through node 20, it detected an error in the FCS field and set the E bit to 1. So node 30 acknowledged that it understood the frame was meant for it, but indicated an error by leaving the C bit to 0. This frame circulates back to node 10 in line 4, which retransmits that frame. Node 30 gets it error free and it arrives at station 10 at line 5.

The P and R Bits: While this frame was coming back to node 10, node 40 reserved a token to level 2 by setting the R bit to 2. Node 2 now sends a token at P of 2 which prevents other lower priority stations from grabbing the token before node 40 does. At line 6, node 40 sends its urgent data frame to node 20 which then comes back to node 40, at which time it puts out a token with a priority of 2 at line 7 and node 10 receives this priority token.

The station which raises the priority of a token must bring the priority down to the previous level again. So node 10, upon receiving this priority token, sends out a token with the original priority of 0. Node 20 then transmits a frame while node 30 reserves a token for a priority of 2 at the end of line 7.

Bumping Up the Priority Further: At line 8, node 20 sends a token at a P of 2, because it received an R of 2. This allows node 30 to transmit at the higher priority. While node 30 is sending data, node 40 reserves a token for a level of 5 (start of line 9). Node 30 issues a token at a P of 5, which allows node 40 to transmit a frame at P = 5. At line 11, node 40 issues a token with P = 5, which node 30 receives. Node 30 remembers that it raised the priority from 2 to 5 so it now lowers the priority to 2. Eventually, the token of level 2 would arrive at node 20 which should lower the priority to 0, but node 20 shuts itself off.

The M Bit: The active monitor in line 12 sets the M bit to 1 for this priority token and since node 20 isn't around to lower the priority, this token comes back to the active monitor. It sees that the M bit is still 1 at line 13, purges the ring, and reinitializes the ring.

16.7 FDDI

16.7.1 A Layer-Based Standard

FDDI (Fiber Distributed Data Interface) is a high capacity LAN standard initially defined by ANSI's X3T9.5 Task Group. This standard operates at 100 Mbps which complements and coexists with Ethernet and other LAN standards. Although copper-based technologies which use FDDI concepts are also being defined, we will concentrate only on the fiber based standards.

Figure 16.20 shows how FDDI fits neatly in IEEE's 802 family of standards. At the lowest level, PMD (Physical Medium Dependent) is responsible for cables, connectors, and their related equipment.

The PHY (PHYsical layer protocol) defines clocking, encoding, generating signals called symbols, and other functions. Together the PMD and the PHY layers comprise OSI's first layer. Above the PHY is the MAC (Media Access Control) layer responsible for ring initialization, token handling, framing, and addressing. Finally, serving all of the above mentioned layers, SMT (Station ManagemenT) standard provides managing and monitoring of connections and the ring. SMT is further broken down into components as shown in Figure 16.20.

16.7.2 The PMD Layer

There are four types of PMDs. The first one is simply called PMD which uses LEDs over a multimode fiber. SMF-PMD uses single-mode fiber and lasers. LCF-PMD uses LEDs over a low-cost multimode fiber and lastly, TP-PMD standardizes STP and some categories of UTP.

FDDI uses two counter-rotating rings, which help it to provide high reliability. The devices which attach to both rings are called dual attached and the ones which attach to only the primary ring are called single attached devices. Furthermore, devices which allow other devices to attach to the primary ring are called concentrators, while those which are actually using the network are called stations, such as hosts. By making combinations of these categories, FDDI devices are defined as SAS (Single Attached Station), DAS (Dual Attached Station), SAC (Single Attached Concentrator), and DAC (Dual Attached Concentrator). For example, a DAS is attached to both rings and doesn't provide direct FDDI ring connections to other devices, while a SAC is attached only to the primary ring of FDDI and does provide ring connections to other devices.

Figure 16.21 shows a dual-ring of trees configuration of an FDDI network. Notice that the dual attached devices are part of both rings, except for the DAS in building 1 which is being used as a SAS. Stations, either SASs or DASs, don't provide ports for other devices to attach, whereas concentrators do: both single and dual attached.

Just as in TRNs, if a cable connecting two MAUs breaks, the ring can heal itself. FDDI allows the rings to wrap around, if necessary. It is also possible to install an optical bypass relay at the fiber and device connection. If the device fails, the ring is still intact, because the optical signal would then bypass that device. However, since the signal does not get regenerated through a relay, the new distance between the neighboring stations may exceed the maximum allowable limit.

Since dual-attached devices are connected to both rings, they are not usually turned off. Turning such a device off would force the rings to wrap around and turning two such devices off could bring down the network. A dual-attached adapter in a server, bridge, or a router can provide the device with a hot-link to a concentrator and a standby link to a different concentrator so if one concentrator goes down, the standby link would become connected. This feature is called dual-homing.

A MIC (Media Interface Connector) is used to connect multimode fiber with a station or a concentrator. There are four kinds of these connectors and they are shown in Figure 16.21. They are keyed in such a way that the network can't be configured improperly.

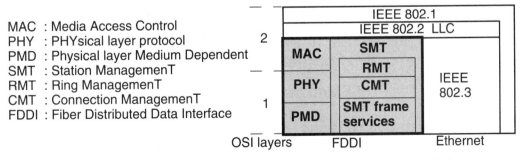

MAC : Media Access Control
PHY : PHYsical layer protocol
PMD : Physical layer Medium Dependent
SMT : Station ManagemenT
RMT : Ring ManagemenT
CMT : Connection ManagemenT
FDDI : Fiber Distributed Data Interface

Figure 16.20 FDDI standards fit nicely within IEEE family of LAN standards.

LANs

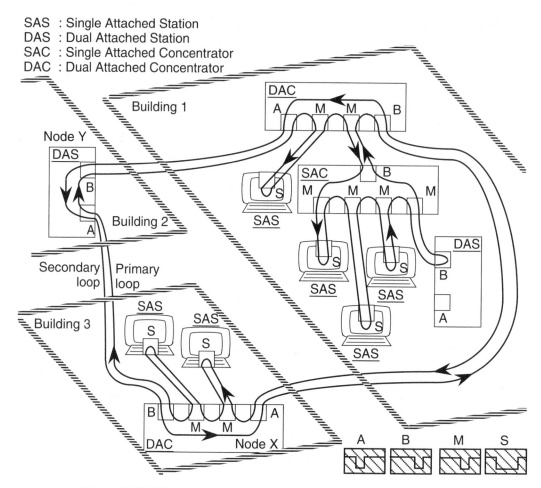

SAS : Single Attached Station
DAS : Dual Attached Station
SAC : Single Attached Concentrator
DAC : Dual Attached Concentrator

Figure 16.21 FDDI 's secondary ring doesn't go through single attached devices. A DAS could be a minicomputer. Below the diagram, the four types of MICs (Media Interface Connectors) are depicted. The SAC and its stations could be in another building off of building 1.

MIC A (or port A) is used to connect the primary ring in and the secondary ring out ports of a DAS or a DAC. Locate a MIC of type A in the figure and notice that. Port B (or MIC B) complements it. Port M connects a concentrator to another concentrator or a station over the primary ring only. Port S connects a SAS to a concentrator.

16.7.3 The PHY Standard

With FDDI running at high speeds, it is necessary to keep the clocks synchronized. As shown in Figure 16.17, FDDI uses NRZI (Non-Return to Zero with Invert on ones) encoding. This encoding provides level transitions for only binary 1s. Level transitions are necessary for clocks to stay in sync. To keep the receiver's clock synchronized and happy, FDDI doesn't allow more than three consecutive 0s when transmitting information. To ensure that this rule is satisfied, the PHY standard converts every group of 4 data bits (called a symbol) into a 5-bit code group which contains at least two ones.

For example, when a data symbol of "0000" is transmitted, it is first converted to a "11110" code group. Table 16.1 shows how 4-bit groups of data are converted into 5-bit code groups. Notice that there are never more than 3 consecutive 0s for any pair of valid symbols. Codes which generate more than 3 consecutive zeros are not implemented and are invalid. Now that we are throwing in extra 1s to help keep the receiver in sync, we must increase the clock speed of FDDI devices to 125 Mbps so that data can be sent at 100 Mbps.

Doing this 4-bit to 5-bit conversion not only helps the clocks to stay in sync, but also provides 8 extra valid combinations that are used to send control signals between devices. They are J, K, T, R, S, Q, I, and H. For example, if a station receives more than 15 consecutive Q symbols, it assumes that the connection is dead, or else a device is being initialized when it receives 8 pairs of HQ symbols, etc.

16.7.4 The MAC Layer

Frame Format: FDDI defines a frame format as shown in Figure 16.22, that is similar to IEEE's 802.5. The maximum length of a frame is 4500 bytes. It begins with a PA (PreAmble) field, which contains 16 consecutive I symbols. This steady stream of 1s gets the receiver in sync quickly. The J and K symbols follow the PA field.

The FC (Frame Control) field contains 8 bits as shown, first of which is a class bit indicating whether the class of service is synchronous or asynchronous. An asynchronous class of service means that the data is not delay sensitive, as the transmission of voice would be. In synchronous transmission of services, a station is guaranteed a prespecified fraction of the 100 Mbps of bandwidth for delay sensitive applications.

The L or the address length bit indicates either a 6 byte or a 2 byte address field. Typically, the address is 6 bytes long. The FF and ZZZZ bits define tokens, SMT, MAC, or LLC frames. SMT frames are used for such functions as passing station

Table 16.1 CODE GROUP ASSIGNMENTS FOR SYMBOLS							
Code Group	Symbol	Code Group	Symbol	Code Group	Symbol	Code Group	Symbol
00000	Q(Quiet)	01000	invalid	10000	invalid	11000	J
00001	invalid	01001	1(0001)	10001	K	11001	S(set)
00010	invalid	01010	4(0100)	10010	8(1000)	11010	C(1100)
00011	invalid	01011	5(0101)	10011	9(1001)	11011	D(1101)
00100	H(Halt)	01100	invalid	10100	2(0010)	11100	E(1110)
00101	invalid	01101	T	10101	3(0011)	11101	F(1111)
00110	invalid	01110	6(0110)	10110	A(1010)	11110	0(0000)
00111	R(reset)	01111	7(0111)	10111	B(1011)	11111	I(Idle)

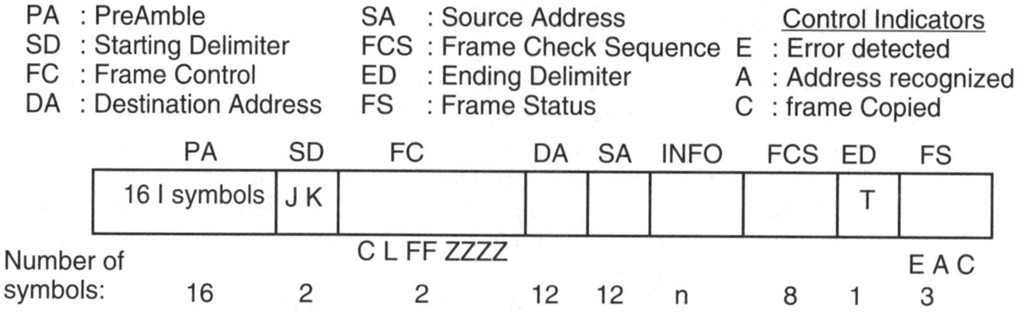

PA : PreAmble   SA   : Source Address   Control Indicators
SD : Starting Delimiter   FCS : Frame Check Sequence E : Error detected
FC : Frame Control   ED   : Ending Delimiter   A : Address recognized
DA : Destination Address FS   : Frame Status   C : frame Copied

PA	SD	FC	DA	SA	INFO	FCS	ED	FS
16 I symbols	J K						T	

                               C L FF ZZZZ   E A C

Number of symbols: 16   2   2   12   12   n   8   1   3

Figure 16.22 FDDI frame format. The token contains only PA, SD, FC, and ED fields, with ED containing two T symbols.

addresses and port statuses to create the topology (or the map) of the physical ring. SMT and MAC frames do not cross over bridges and routers to other LANs as LLC frames may.

The ED field contains two T symbols for tokens and one for frames. Finally, the frame status may use R and S symbols to code control indicators. These are the E (Error detected), A (Address recognition), and C (frame Copied) control indicators.

Ring Initialization: Before a ring can be initialized, the SMT components exchange information on port types and addresses over all links between adjacent nodes. Then they run link confidence tests which determine their links' qualities. Once these operations are performed then one by one all stations join the ring. This procedure is called establishing a connection with adjacent neighbors and is primarily a function of SMT.

Once this connection is established for all stations on the ring, then the stations bid to determine who is going to send the first token. This is called ring initializing and it is done by a procedure called the claiming process.

Here, all stations issue claim frames giving their SAs and TTRT values. TTRT (Target Token Rotation Time) is equal to one-half the time it takes for a token to arrive back at a station, once it has been released. Unlike an auction, where the highest bidder wins, here the station with the lowest value of TTRT wins the right to send the first token.

At first, many claim frames from all stations flood the ring simultaneously. During this time, if a station receives a claim frame whose TTRT is lower than its own, then it will pass that claim frame through and stop sending its own claim frames. Eventually, only one station's claim frame makes it all around the ring, at which time the winning station issues a token. While this first token goes around the ring, each station copies the TTRT value in its own buffer. On the second pass of the token, stations may send synchronous data and thereafter may send asynchronous data.

Steady-State Operation: FDDI uses the timed-token protocol which differs from 4 Mbps TRN's protocol, in that in a 4 Mbps TRN only one frame can exist on the ring at a time. Also, the token is not released until the station transmitting a frame gets it back. However, in FDDI, a station is only allowed to hold on to the token a certain amount of time determined by the THT (Token Holding Timer). So even if a station isn't finished transmitting, it must stop transmitting and release the token for the next user. Notice that the token is released as soon as the frame is sent and doesn't wait until the frame comes back around the ring. This is known as early token release, which allows many frames to exist on the ring at one time. 16 Mbps TRN allows multiple frames to exist on the ring at one time, but both types of TRNs send only one frame per token access, whereas FDDI may send multiple 4500 byte frames per access.

Unlike IEEE's 802.5, where an active monitor maintains the ring, in FDDI, this function is distributed and all stations are responsible for ring maintenance. Each station maintains a TVX (Valid Xmission Timer). The "X" is short for "trans." TVX is used to determine if the no transmission is occurring on a link. If this timer exceeds, because of noise or a loss of token, it will first start the claim process. Let us go through the steps node X, an uplink station, and node Y, a downlink station, may take if the link connecting them degrades for some reason. Figure 16.21 shows nodes X and Y.

First Y's TVX will exceed, because it didn't receive any information from X. It will start sending claim frames. Since X can't forward these frames to Y, due to a bad cable, the claim process fails and no token is generated. Now X begins the beacon process. Just as a beacon from a lighthouse warns ships of danger, a beacon frame notifies all nodes that the ring may be broken.

Again, X can't forward the beacon frames to Y. After about 10 seconds, a directed beacon is sent informing the nodes that the beacon is stuck. If this fails, then a trace function is initiated using PHY signaling or line states. The trace message is sent over the secondary ring from Y to X, which forces them to perform self-tests. If the tests are successful, then the nodes will join the ring, or else the ring will wrap itself around, healing itself.

Exercises

1. Which type of topology is primarily used in WANs?
   a. Star
   b. Ring
   c. Mesh
   d. Bus

2. Which of the following is NOT a rule used in CSMA/CD?
   a. Listen before you transmit
   b. Listen after you transmit
   c. Listen while you transmit
   d. If someone is on the line, do not transmit

3. What software component in a PC is directly responsible for sending data to the network?
   a. NetBIOS
   b. BIOS
   c. DOS
   d. Application

4. Which of the following terms is NOT associated with a server-based NOS?
   a. Client-server based NOS
   b. centralized NOS
   c. peer NOS
   d. NetWare

5. Which of the following protocol stacks are most closely related to Unix?
   a. NetWare
   b. Vines
   c. AppleTalk
   d. DOS

LANs

6. Which field name isn't used in both types of Ethernets?
   a. Type
   b. FCS
   c. Preamble
   d. SA

7. Which of the following types of Ethernets allows the longest network segment over a bus topology?
   a. IEEE 802.3
   b. 10BASET
   c. 10BASE2
   d. 10BASE5

8. Which of the following devices is used to connect TRN stations in a physical star topology?
   a. Repeater
   b. bridge
   c. MAU
   d. NIC

9. In 10BASE5, what is the device that does collision detection?

10. What type of cabling is used with 10BASET?

11. How does a MAU know to place a node in its ring or not?

12. What is the station from which all transmissions are received called in a TRN?

13. What type of a TRN frame sends data?

14. What are the two special code violations called in TRN?

15. Name the four types of FDDI devices and four types of FDDI connectors.

16. In FDDI, the station with the lowest ___ value gains the right to send the first token.

17. What is the difference between an access protocol and a communications protocol, how do they relate to the OSI model?

18. Using only 10BASET, what is the maximum number of nodes that can be attached to a network. Sketch the network.

19. What is the purpose of the RIF field in TRN and how is it used?

20. Describe how NetBIOS, BIOS, and DOS interact with each other.

21. Give the advantages and disadvantages of the six topologies discussed.

22. Give the functions of the active monitor.

23. Draw the Manchester, differential Manchester, and NRZI waveforms for sending 00101110. Assume the bit before the first one ended with a zero in each case.

24. What are the reasons for converting every 4-bit group of data into 5-bit group codes in FDDI?

Chapter 17

NetWare

In Chapter 16 we saw the various methods of connecting LANs. We introduced their software components and even looked at how a peer-to-peer NOS (Network Operating System) is utilized. Now let us look at an example of a server-based NOS. Here, only Novell's NetWare v3.11 is selected so as to allow the discussion more depth than would have been possible if several NOSs were presented. If at all possible, you should try the commands on a network as they are presented. It will make this chapter much more meaningful. Let us hope we still remember some of the basic DOS concepts as we come across them.

17.1 SESSION MANAGEMENT

17.1.1 Directories

The name of the server we will refer to in this chapter is called S1. There may be other servers on the network as well. This server is divided into two volumes called MFG and SYS. As a drive is referred with a colon in DOS, so is a volume referred with a colon in NetWare. See Figure 17.1.

When NetWare is first installed, by default it creates four directories and some files which it needs for normal operation. These directories are called LOGIN, SYSTEM, PUBLIC, MAIL. Along with these system generated directories, we may also have other directories that suit the needs of our site. In the figure these are shown as APPS and USERS. Under each of these directories, there may be yet other subdirectories and files.

One can relate this structure to a file cabinet. In our figure, the cabinet may be thought of as a server, with each drawer representing a volume. The hanging folder is like a directory, while manila folders and pieces of paper inside it are like subdirectories and files, respectively.

Special thanks go to Annabelle Soper of DeVry Technical Institue of Woodbridge, N.J. and Steve Silva of DeVry Institute of Technology, Phoenix, for their help in reviewing this document.

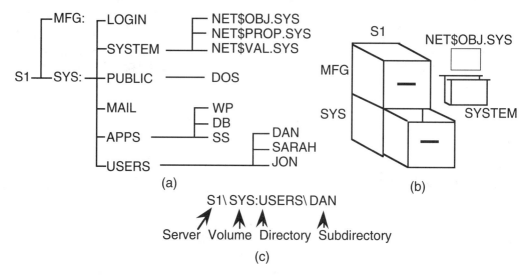

Figure 17.1 (a) A simple NetWare directory structure. (b) An analogy to a file cabinet. (c) NetWare naming convention.

The LOGIN directory contains the commands that are necessary for users to get on the network. The SYSTEM directory contains command line utilities which are only available to the supervisor or supervisor equivalent. The PUBLIC directory contains information and NetWare commands for all users. And finally, MAIL contains subdirectories for each user where login scripts are stored. Our APPS directory may hold user applications such as wordprocessing, spreadsheets, and data bases. Users may be restricted to store their own files here, not in their own subdirectories under USERS.

To reference any part of this directory structure, one may provide the entire path name, starting at the file server's name, for example, S1\SYS:USERS\DAN. Or else, depending on which point the user is in, only the relative path name may be given. As an example, if the user is on server S1, then to reference the DAN directory, only SYS:USERS\DAN is necessary. This is as it is in DOS.

17.1.2 Drive Mappings

Drive mappings (or pointers) are used in NetWare to reference directories which are commonly used without having to specify the full path name. There are two types of drive mappings. A regular or a network drive mapping is used to point to directories where data is stored, and a search drive mapping is used to point to directories where executable files are stored. Drives A through E are used by DOS to point to local disk drives. Starting from drive F and going up to drive Z are used for network drive mappings, while starting from drive Z and coming back down to the last network drive defined, are used for search drives. One may have up to 16 search drive pointers. Let us show how the MAP command is used in NetWare.

```
G:\>map
Drive A:  maps to local disk
Drive F: = S1\SYS: \USERS\SARAH
Drive G: = S1\SYS:USERS\BETH \
____
SEARCH1: = Z:. [S1\SYS: \PUBLIC]
SEARCH2: = Y:. [S1\SYS: \PUBLIC\DOS]
SEARCH3: = X:. [S1\SYS: \APPS\WP]
G:\>f:
F:\USERS\SARAH>g:
G:\>
```

Here, from the output of the MAP command, we can see that only drive A is locally available to the user. Drive F maps to the subdirectory of SARAH under USERS and drive G maps to the root directory under the SYS volume. Both F and G are network drives. Notice that these drives are assigned starting from F and the search drives are assigned in reverse order, starting from Z. Now the user can directly go to the SARAH subdirectory by typing F, a network drive and not having to type the full path name. There the prompt shows the user's default path in the directory structure. This way defining network drives allows us to hop around the directory structure just by typing a letter.

Notice, also, that at the F drive the directory path is shown, but at the G drive, it isn't. This is because from the output of the MAP command, we see that the definition for drive G ends with a " \". This indicates that this is an imaginary root. However, the display for drive F is different. For applications which require themselves to be in the root drive, defining imaginary roots becomes handy. Furthermore, we can change our directory by one level up the directory tree in F, but not in G. Consider:

```
G:\>cd..
G:\>f:
F:\USERS\SARAH>cd..
F:\USERS>
```

That is, doing a "cd.." at the G drive still keeps us at the G drive, but doing the same at the F drive will bring us up to the USERS directory. Now if a MAP is done, we will see that drive G still points to BETH, but F points to USERS instead of SARAH.

Search drives are used to specify the order in which a executable file should be searched for, when an executing such a file. In DOS, this function is provided with the PATH command. Let us say that at the F drive, a word processing package is invoked by typing WP.

```
F:\USERS\SARAH>wp
```

Since the executable file called WP is not in the SARAH directory, the system will first search drive Z. WP is not in PUBLIC, so it will look in the second search drive, which is drive Y. Drive Y, however, has all the DOS files so it will then search drive X. Since WP exists here, that file will be executed and we would be in our word processing application. Notice, though, that our default drive would still be F.

17.1.3 Introduction To Menu Maps

Now let us look at a menu driven utility called SESSION. At the command line, type:

```
G:\>session
```

The screen will look something like that shown in Figure 17.2. In all menu driven utilities, we will call the information given at the top of the screen the banner. It contains the name of the utility, such as Session Manager. On the right side, the date and the time are given and in the center, the names of the user and the file server are given. On other utilities, instead of the user name, the current path may be given and one can see it change as the path is changed in the utility.

On all of these windows, the arrow keys on the keyboard highlight a choice and pressing the Enter key selects that choice. If Change Current Server is selected, then the File Server and User window will be displayed. Figure 17.3(a) shows how this window is brought up. It shows the name of the current server and the user. To change the file server, the insert key is pressed, which shows a list of available file servers, S2 and S3 in our case. If one of these is selected then the user would be prompted for his name, after which if he presses the Enter key, he would be prompted for a password, after the Enter key is pressed one more time, the new server and the user name should appear in the File Server and User window and also in the menu banner.

Figure 17.3(a) introduces the use of menu maps. It saves a lot of dull verbal explanations, because the necessary keystrokes are summarized in the map. An arrow

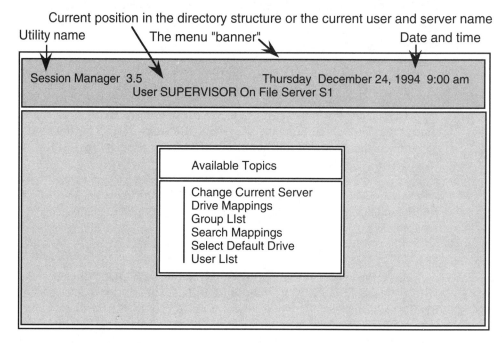

Figure 17.2 The first window of the menu driven utility of SESSION.

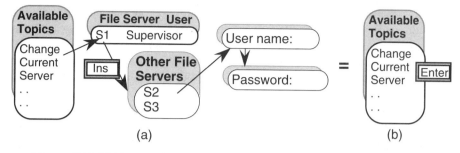

Figure 17.3 (a) How to change the current server. (b) The Enter key will abbreviate the keystrokes for changing an object, such as the server.

always means to press Enter to go forward and to press Esc to go backwards between the windows. An "Ins" with an arrow means to press the Ins (Insert) key to add or change an entry, as we just did. This set of keystrokes is summarized by an "Enter" by a window selection. This is shown in Figure 17.3(b) and will be used in future menu maps.

17.1.4 The Session Utility

Figure 17.4 shows a more thorough map for the session utility. We have already seen how to change the current server. Next, if Drive Mappings is selected, then the Current Drive Mappings is displayed. Here, the enter key will show the effective rights of the selected drive; soon their meaning will be covered. The Del (Delete) key will

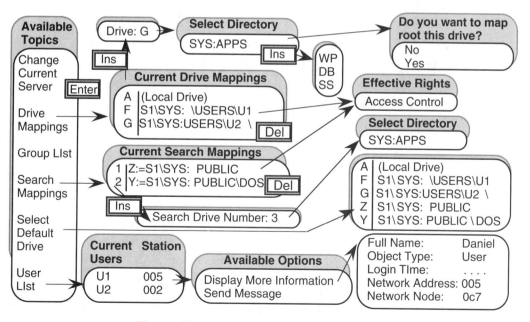

Figure 17.4 The menu map for SESSION.

remove the selected drive from the mappings and the Ins (Insert) key will allow a new drive mapping to be defined. It will pick the next available drive to assign the mapping; however, it can be changed by using the Backspace key.

While the path is being typed, the Ins key may be used. It will prompt the user with available options that exist at that point. So if no server is given yet and the Ins key is pressed, then all available server names will be shown from which the desired one would be selected. However, if the server name is typed, then all the available volumes will be shown. Finally, once the directory path is entered, the utility will prompt the user and ask if this drive should be an imaginary root or not, as drive G was in our last example.

Search mappings are handled the same way and they are outlined in the figure. To change the default drive, go to the appropriate one. Here, the utility banner will not indicate a change, whereas other utilities may. However, after escaping out of session, one can see that the default drive is indeed changed.

Lastly, let us look at the User List option. Here, the users which are logged on are displayed. From there, we can get more information about a particular user. This shows the user's full name, when he was logged in, his network address, and the node and address which he is logged on. One can also send a message to the selected user. A message sent to a user will lock his station until a Ctl-Enter is pressed. To prevent others from sending messages and possibly stopping a process at a station, type CASTOFF at the command line. The command CASTON complements it.

17.2 SECURITY

17.2.1 Types of Users and Groups

During installation, NetWare creates users called supervisors and guest and a group called everyone. A supervisor has unlimited privileges, while guest and everyone have the most restrictions. All users are included in the everyone group and this group should not be deleted. Besides for these users and groups, the supervisor may create additional users and groups, which include administrative type users. These administrative types allow the supervisor to delegate network responsibilities to others.

The supervisor equivalent is given all of the privileges of the supervisor himself or herself. Under him or her, are workgroup managers who can be either users or groups. They can manage disk space and also create users and groups. Generally, they may only delete the users/groups which they have created. They may also create print queues and print servers.

A user account manager has primarily the same level of authority as the workgroup managers, except that they cannot create new users and groups or delete them. They are also allowed to grant rights and privileges which have been assigned to them.

The last two kinds of administrative types of users, which any user may become, are called the print server operators and the print queue operator. The print server operator can manage, configure, enable and disable print servers, but they cannot delete them. The print queue operators can manage, enable and disable print queues. However, they can't create print queues.

17.2.2 Security Rights

While these administrative object types provide management support for the network, rights security allows directories and files to be managed by the appropriate users/groups. These could be the right to read a file in a subdirectory, or to create one, etc. In order to determine if a user or a group can perform an operation to a file, one must consider three types of rights. They are called trustee rights, IRM (Inherited Rights Mask) or directory rights, and file attributes.

Trustee rights are privileges given to a user/group in a directory. The IRM are rights allowed for any user/group in a directory and together with the trustee rights determine the effective rights for that user/group. Attributes specify what functions are allowed with a file or a directory.

IRM supersedes trustee rights and file attributes supersede the IRM. For example, let us say that a given directory's IRM allows one to read, write, or create a file. This is depicted by the large oval of Figure 17.5. and in this directory there is a file which only has the read attribute assigned to it. It is depicted by the narrow oval in the figure. If User2 has the trustee rights to read, write, or erase any files in this directory, his effective rights will only be read and write. Even though the trustee rights allow the user/group to erase files in this directory, the IRM prevents it, for everyone, in general. Hence, the effective rights are read and write for User2. Furthermore, even if the effective rights did allow this user/group to write a file, the attribute for this file would not have allowed it.

Notice that this figure has another user with a different set of trustee rights for this directory. They are create and write. The effective rights stay the same, but the file attributes prevent the use of either of these rights, so that the user can do nothing with this file. Table 17.1 lists the types of security rights with brief definitions while Table 17.2 does the same for file attributes. One should remember that an IRM applies only to the directory to which it is assigned, but trustee rights apply to the assigned directory as well as all the subdirectories under it.

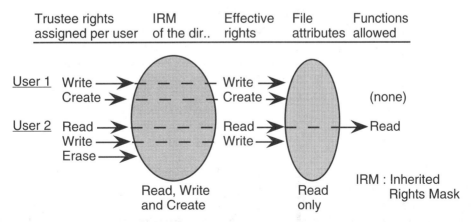

Figure 17.5 Different kinds of rights and how they relate to each other.

	Table 17.1 Security Rights	
Symbol	**Name**	**Description**
S	Supervisory	All rights to directory, their subdirectories and their files.
R	Read	May see the contents and make use of the file.
W	Write	May change an existing file.
C	Create	May create new files and subdirectories.
E	Erase	May delete existing files and subdirectories.
M	Modify	May change attributes of files and subdirectories
F	File Scan	May see if files/subdirectories exist, as in a DIR command.
A	Access Control	Other users may be given the privilege for the above rights.

Consider Figure 17.6. Here a user, Beth, is the trustee of the directory labeled as DIR_1. Under DIR_1, SUB_1 directory exists and under it SUB_2 exists. Finally, in SUB_2 directory, a file exists. The IRMs for the directories and the attributes for the file are shown. Beth has the supervisory rights at DIR_1. This is an unusual right since the other seven rights are also automatically assigned with it and the S right cannot be taken away by any of the IRMs under DIR_1. So although other lower level IRMs limit what others can do there, Beth has full privileges right down to the file. However, if

	Table 17.2 Attributes	
Symbol	**Name**	**Description**
A	Archive needed	File has been changed since its last backup.
C	Copy inhibit	Doesn't allow files to be copied.
D*	Delete inhibit	Doesn't allow files to be deleted.
H *	Hidden	Files aren't listed through DIR, unless File Scan is granted.
P*	Purge	These files are not recoverable, if deleted.
R*	Rename inhibit	Renaming of files isn't allowed.
Ra	Read audit	(not used)
Ro	Read only	Files may only be read or used.Can't rename or delete them.
Rw	Read write	Data files are usually read from and written to.
S	Sharable	Several users may read this file simultaneously.
Sy*	System	DIR doesn't list these files; they cannot be copied or deleted.
T	Transactional	Database files which are tracked for incomplete transactions.
Wa	Write audit	(not used)
X	eXecute only	COM and EXE files that are executable. First, back them up!!

* Denotes attributes which may also be applied to directories.

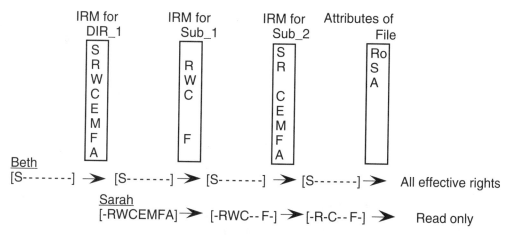

Figure 17.6 How IRM (Inherited Rights Mask) and file attributes change effective rights for two sample users.

she wants to write to this file, she must first assign this attribute first. She can change attributes because she has the M (Modify attributes) rights.

Sarah, on the other hand, is made a trustee of SUB_1, but she lacks the supervisory rights. So the IRMs in subsequent subdirectories revoke her rights. In SUB_1, the IRM has the E, M, and A rights missing, so they are taken away from her and in SUB_2, the W right is taken away. Finally, she ends up with R, C, and F rights in SUB_2. This allows her to read the file, see if it exists using a DIR command, but doesn't allow her to change the file attributes or write to it.

17.2.3 The FILER Utility

Let us next see how these IRMs and attributes are set through the menu driven utility caller FILER. It is entered simply by typing FILER at the command line. The banner of the screen shows the current directory path. This can be changed by selecting the Select Current Directory of the Available Topics menu. This uses keystrokes which are similar to those used in changing the Current File Server in the SESSION utility, as shown in Figure 17.3. Hence, only the Enter key is shown in Figure 17.7.

Selecting Current Directory Information gives the information for the directory shown in the menu banner. Typically the one who created the directory is the owner of it. This can be changed by pressing Enter on the Owner and then selecting a user from the Known Users window. At this time, we are prompted to specify if this new owner is going to own only the directory or the directory and all of the subdirectories under it.

Selecting Directory Attributes shows the current attributes for this directory. In this window the I/D symbol in a circle represents the following set of keystrokes, which are shown in Figure 17.8(b). By pressing the Insert key, other available attributes will be shown from where a new attribute could be chosen. Here, the F5 function key allows multiple attributes to be selected together and then pressing Enter will add them to the

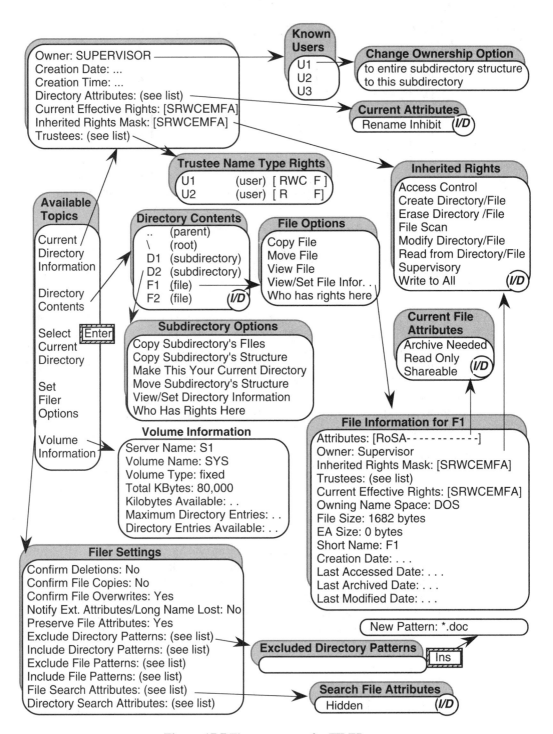

Known Users
U1
U2
U3

Owner: SUPERVISOR
Creation Date: ...
Creation Time: ...
Directory Attributes: (see list)
Current Effective Rights: [SRWCEMFA]
Inherited Rights Mask: [SRWCEMFA]
Trustees: (see list)

Change Ownership Option
to entire subdirectory structure
to this subdirectory

Current Attributes
Rename Inhibit (I/D)

Trustee Name Type Rights
U1   (user) [RWC F]
U2   (user) [R   F]

Inherited Rights
Access Control
Create Directory/File
Erase Directory /File
File Scan
Modify Directory/File
Read from Directory/File
Supervisory
Write to All (I/D)

Available Topics
Current
Directory
Information

Directory
Contents

Select [Enter]
Current
Directory

Set
Filer
Options

Volume
Information

Directory Contents
..   (parent)
\   (root)
D1   (subdirectory)
D2   (subdirectory)
F1   (file)
F2   (file) (I/D)

File Options
Copy File
Move File
View File
View/Set File Infor. .
Who has rights here

Current File Attributes
Archive Needed
Read Only (I/D)
Shareable

Subdirectory Options
Copy Subdirectory's FIles
Copy Subdirectory's Structure
Make This Your Current Directory
Move Subdirectory's Structure
View/Set Directory Information
Who Has Rights Here

Volume Information
Server Name: S1
Volume Name: SYS
Volume Type: fixed
Total KBytes: 80,000
Kilobytes Available: . .
Maximum Directory Entries: . .
Directory Entries Available: . .

File Information for F1
Attributes: [RoSA- - - - - - - - - - - -]
Owner: Supervisor
Inherited Rights Mask: [SRWCEMFA]
Trustees: (see list)
Current Effective Rights: [SRWCEMFA]
Owning Name Space: DOS
File Size: 1682 bytes
EA Size: 0 bytes
Short Name: F1
Creation Date: . . .
Last Accessed Date: . . .
Last Archived Date: . . .
Last Modified Date: . . .

Filer Settings
Confirm Deletions: No
Confirm File Copies: No
Confirm File Overwrites: Yes
Notify Ext. Attributes/Long Name Lost: No
Preserve File Attributes: Yes
Exclude Directory Patterns: (see list)
Include Directory Patterns: (see list)
Exclude File Patterns: (see list)
Include File Patterns: (see list)
File Search Attributes: (see list)
Directory Search Attributes: (see list)

New Pattern: *.doc

Excluded Directory Patterns
[Ins]

Search File Attributes
Hidden (I/D)

Figure 17.7 The menu map for FILER.

list in the Current File Attribute window. The Delete key will enable one to delete attributes. This is summarized in Figure 17.8(a).

Going back to Figure 17.7, the Current Effective Rights under Current Directory Information shows the inherited rights at this directory. These can be changed using the same set of keystrokes as are shown in Figure 17.8 (which is denoted by the I/D in a circle). Selecting Trustees shows the user/groups that are trustees of the current directory.

From the main menu, Directory Contents shows the directories and files in the current directory. The I/D symbol indicates that new directories can be inserted or old ones may be deleted. From this menu if a directory is selected, the Subdirectory Options window is given. And if a file is selected, then the File Options window is displayed. Here, the View/Set File Information gives the file information for the chosen file. From this window, the IRM or the attributes of the file can be displayed and from these windows, their entries can be changed (inserted or deleted).

From Available Topics, the Set Filer Options displays the FILER settings. These are the parameters that are enabled when using FILER. For example, the first parameter is Confirm Deletions. This is set to No, so that while deleting a file, it will not provide a prompt asking if we really want to delete it or not. However, if we try to copy one file over an existing one, the system will give us a chance to change our mind. This is because the overwrite parameter is set to Yes.

The Figure also shows that certain patterns can be selected in the Exclude Directory Patterns option. This means that while copying directories, these types of files will not be copied. The Include Directory Patterns gives the patterns of files which should be copied. The default is "*" or all files. The File Search Attribute gives the files with these attributes that will be displayed when doing a Dir. If the Hidden attribute is selected, then hidden files will also be displayed.

To help clean up directories and manage disk space the Volume Information window is helpful. This window has no shadow shown in the figure, which corresponds to having single borders on an actual screen. A double border around a NetWare window (or the presence of a shadow in our menu maps) means that information displayed in the window may be changed. Since this is a single border screen, it is a view-only screen.

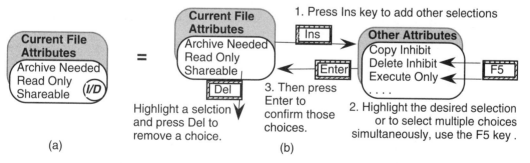

(a)   (b)

Figure 17.8 (a) The I/D symbol abbreviates all possible keystrokes, shown in (b), to insert or delete selections from the given window.

17.3 THE SYSCON UTILITY

The SYSCON (SYStem CONfiguration) utility is probably the most widely used of all utilities. It allows one to control security on the network, namely to create users/ groups and also provide rights or impose restrictions for them.

We will need two maps shown on pages 372 and 373 to outline this utility. The first one is displayed in Figure 17.9. Starting at the Available Topics window, the User Information selection shows the names of the users on the current server. Once a user is selected, a User Information window is displayed. This window and all its related subwindows are shown in Figure 17.10. So both Figures 17.9 and 17.10 outline the functions available in SYSCON. Let us start with Figure 17.9. As before, the current file server can be changed, which would then appear in the SYSCON menu banner.

17.3.1 Accounting

From the accounting menu, we can charge users/groups for using network services. The Blocks Read Charge Rates window shows the rates for all the time increments during a week. In the figure from Sunday to Tuesday and from 8 AM to 9 AM, the charge rate is 1. On the left side of the window, the meaning of this rate is given as "no charge." However, using the arrow and the F5 keys, a set of time slots can be blocked off or marked. Pressing the enter key, another charge rate can be selected for this period or else a new one can be defined.

The figure shows a second charge rate of 1/20 as being defined. Now the selected block of four 1s will be changed to 2s and a new rate of 2 being 1/20 will appear on the left side of the window. This means that the network can charge one unit for every 20 blocks of data that are read from the server during this time period. It is up to the networking department to define what is meant by one unit of service. Similarly, other services can be charged for writing blocks of data to the server, for being logged on the server, and so on.

17.3.2 File Server Group Information

File Server Information can be seen with a view-only screen for the selected file server. It provides information about how it is configured for someone who might be servicing it. SFT (System Fault Tolerance) gives the level of reliability features provided in the server and TTS (Transaction Tracking System) prevents data from being corrupted due to an aborted transaction.

Starting at the Group Information, selecting a Group Name and arriving at the Group Information window shows a list of options. The first choice is Full Name, which shows the longer, more descriptive name of the group.

The Managed User And Groups shows the users/groups which the selected group manages, whereas the Managers option shows the users/groups which manage the selected group. In the figure, G2 manages U1 and U2 and the Managers option would show who manages G2. It is important to note that the term manager here means a user account manager and not a workgroup manager, as defined earlier in Section 17.2.1.

The Member List shows the members belonging to this group. Remember, the I/D symbol means that this list can be changed using the Insert and Delete keys. Trustee

Directory and File Assignments options are also given in Figure 17.10, under User Information. We will cover them in Section 17.3.4.

17.3.3 Supervisor Options

The Default Account Balance/Restriction and the Default Time Restrictions windows are similar to the corresponding windows under User Information. Both are shown in Figure 17.10. The options which are set under Supervisor Options only affect the new users which are created and not the existing ones.

The Default Account Balance/Restriction window in Figure 17.9 shows that the account has no expiration date. Therefore, Date Account Expiration has no value. If the former were set to yes, then the latter would have to be given a value. The setting in the figure shows that all new users that are created will have no expiration date. Also, a person could log on the network concurrently from many stations and no password would be required. A home directory would not be created by default. The remainder of the menu items will be covered in Figure 17.10.

NetWare is capable of detecting network intruders by preventing them from attempting to log in a specified number of times. In Figure 17.9, this number is 7, after which the intruder is locked out from logging in for two days. These numbers can be changed. A supervisor, who is unable to log in because of this mechanism, can log in at the file server console by typing:

```
:enable login
```

The File Server Error Log can be looked at from this option, and from this display it can also be cleared. The Workgroup Managers show who are the workgroup managers, which can be changed

17.3.4 User Information

The User Information menu is shown in Figure 17.10 for the user which was selected in Figure 17.9. For this selected user, the Account Balance shows the user's balance to be 100,000 units with a credit of another 2,000 units.

The Account Restrictions window was already partially discussed. Here, we can force this user to have minimum length passwords and to change passwords every so many days. Login and Grace Logins Allowed determine how many times a person with an expired password can log in without changing his password. If required, Unique Passwords is set to Yes; then a user may not use the same password for the next 7 new passwords.

The Groups Belonged To option shows of which groups this user is a member. Login Scripts will be covered later. The Managed Users And Groups and Managers are the same as groups. The Other Information window shows who is using how much disk space and it also shows which directory in SYS:MAIL (given by User ID) corresponds to the user's directory.

Users and groups specified by the Security Equivalences window shows which other users and groups have the same privileges as the current user. This is good when users/groups are working together on the same project.

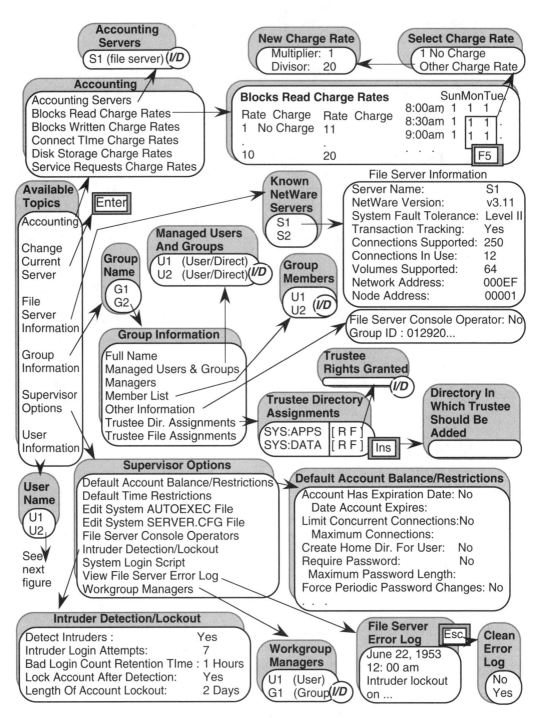

Figure 17.9 Menu Map for SYSCON, continued in Figure 17.10.

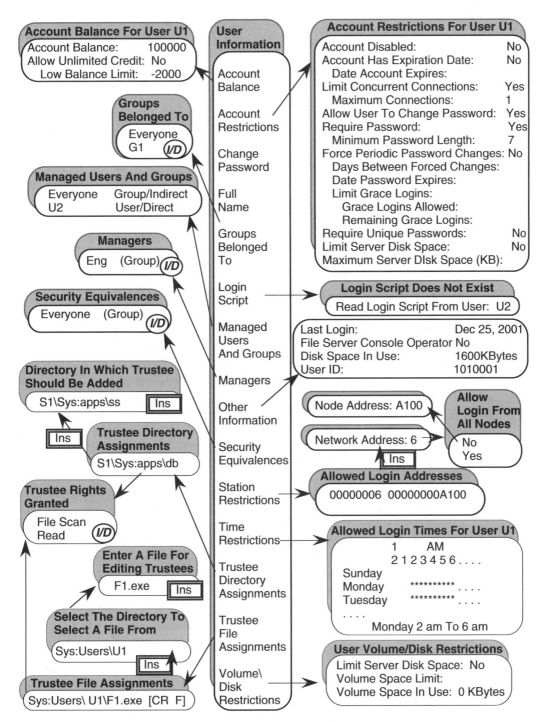

Figure 17.10 SYSCON menu map (continued).

NetWare, by default, allows users to log in on any network and at any terminal. However, this can be restricted through Station Restrictions. Figure 17.10 shows how a restriction can be imposed on the current user. Here, this user may log in only at node A100 on network number 6. Figure 17.4 shows how through the SESSION utility these addresses can be obtained.

We can also restrict the times this user is allowed to log on. In the figure, an asterisk means that a person is allowed on the network. By pressing the space bar over them, the asterisks can be removed. They may also be removed by using the F5 and the arrow keys and then pressing the Delete key.

To see which directories and files this user is made a trustee for, the corresponding option can be selected. Here, pressing Enter will show the Trustee Rights Granted, pressing Delete will remove an entry, and pressing Insert will allow an addition of an entry. The second Insert key in these menu paths will display a list of available directories or files.

17.4 PRINTING ISSUES

17.4.1 Print Servers and Remote Printers

Figure 17.11 shows the basic components for supporting printing on a NetWare network. We have a file server in the top right corner to which all print jobs are first sent. The file server will place these jobs in subdirectories under SYS:SYSTEM. Here they are waiting in queues for printers to become free so that they can get redirected to a printer. Print servers act as "crossing guards," directing jobs from queues to printers which are under their control. (A queue is a place in storage where usually the files which arrive first are given service first, just as bank customers in a queue are waited upon by the next available teller.)

Both a file server and a dedicated network station may act as a print server. For a file server to function as a print server it must have an NLM (NetWare Load Module) called PSERVER.NLM loaded. Alternatively, a DOS-based workstation may also act as a print server (shown at the lower right of the figure) by executing the PSERVER.EXE file. This method helps to relieve the processing load off the file server.

Both the file server based and the DOS-workstation based print servers can print to printers which are directly attached to themselves. The maximum number of directly attached printers is five. NetWare also allows print servers to send jobs to printers which are attached to user stations. Such printers are called remote printers. However, to be able to use a printer attached to a user workstation, that workstation must first run the RPRINTER.EXE program. The maximum number of printers a print server may support, including self-attached printers, is 16.

Figure 17.11 shows the file server acting also as a print server. A print server is shown under it. Each may have up to 5 directly attached printers (or local printers) and, including its remotely controlled printers, it can have a total of 16. The files which this PSERVER must have in SYS:LOGIN are shown in the figure. Also, the minimum required commands of its autoexec.bat file are shown. According to this file, PS1 is the name of this print server.

The workstation which is providing the remote printers for the print servers, must run the RPRINTER.EXE file. This is the station on the lower left hand side. It must also

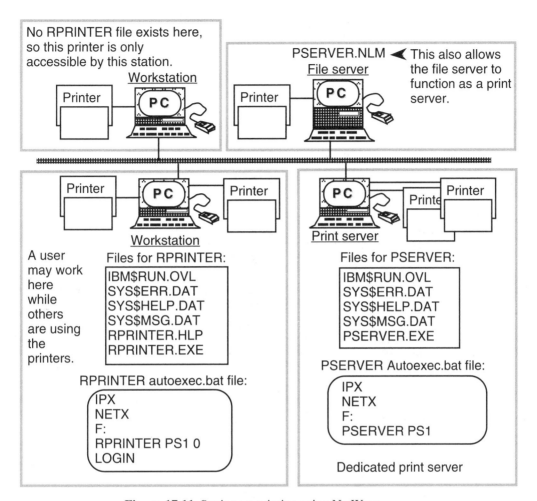

Figure 17.11 Setting up printing using NetWare.

have the files as shown in its LOGIN directory, which can be copied from the SYS:PUBLIC directory. From its autoexec.bat file, we can see that it is making available its printers to the print server, PS1. The workstation on the top left corner isn't running RPRINTER, so no one else but that station may print on its printer.

17.4.2 Setting Up a Print Server

Let us now outline how to set up a new print server, called PS1, using the utility called PCONSOLE shown in Figure 17.12. We have to tell PS1 which printers it can print on and which queues it must serve. Under Available Options, select Print Server Information to get to the Print Servers screen. Here, using the Insert key insert the print server called PS1. Pressing Enter there and then again at Print Server Configuration, we get to the Print Server Configuration Menu. File Server To Be Serviced is shown to be the first option. Here, we can choose up to 8 file servers from where printing jobs

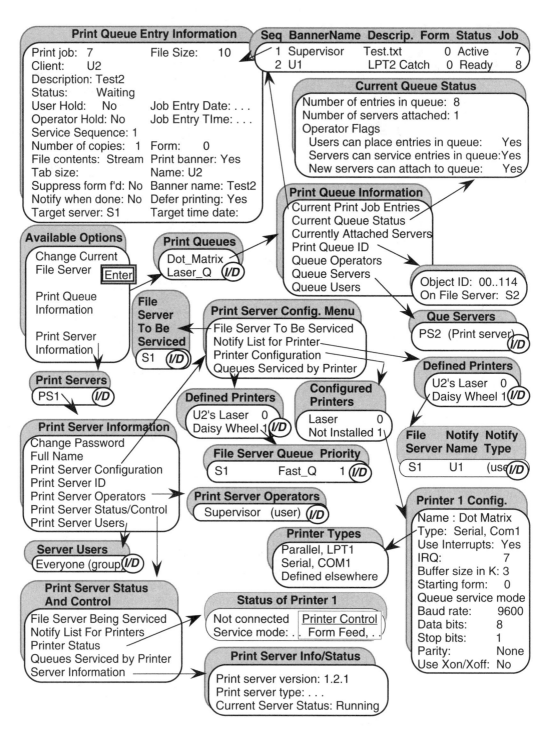

Figure 17.12 The menu map for PCONSOLE.

will be printed, but if this print server is also a file server, then it will only be able to print its own jobs.

The Notify List for Printer selection may show up to 16 defined printers. Selecting a printer here will show the users/groups that will be notified if there is problem with this printer. If another user/group is going to be added to this list, the utility will ask how often they should be notified of the problems.

The Printer Configuration selection from the Print Server Configuration Menu shows a list of configured printers. Selecting one of these printers shows the configuration of that printer. Pressing Enter on the Type field, will show 7 possible types of local printers and 7 possible types of remote printers. For each of these 7 types, there are three that are "parallel LPT" and four that are "serial COM" types.

The Queues Serviced by Printer in the Print Server Configuration Menu window will show which printers are defined as being used by this print server and, in the next window, which queues are being served.

Moving backwards to Print Server Information window, the Print Server Operators will show that information and then other operators can be added or removed. The Print Server Users show the users who can use the print server. By default, it contains the group Everyone.

In the Print Server Status and Control window, the Printer Status for the chosen printer is shown. It may note that the printer is "not connected," meaning that the RPRINTER.EXE file has not been executed yet. Here, if the Printer Control is selected, then another menu is given, from which we can abort a job, do a form feed, stop the printer, etc. The Print Server Info/Status window shows the print server is still "Running." If Enter is pressed there, and the "Down" option is selected, then it would bring down the print server.

17.4.3 Controlling Print Queues

Turning our attention from print servers to print queues, let us again follow Figure 17.12 in outlining how queues are handled using PCONSOLE. Under Available Options, the Print Queue Information shows a list of current queues. Here, we may add or delete them. Selecting a particular queue brings us to the Print Queue Information window, from where we will consider several selections.

The Current Print Job Entries selection shows the jobs that are currently in this queue. The job with a sequence number of 1 will get printed out first.

A job may have one of five statuses. If it is currently being printed, then it is said to be active. A job may be placed on hold. If a job is still in the process of being sent by the user, its status is adding. If a job has a status of waiting that means that the job is set for "deferred" printing, with a target time and date when it will get printed. Lastly, any job that has no constraints placed on it for printing is labeled as being ready. Pressing Enter on any entry in the queue will display the Print Queue Entry Information window.

Choosing the Current Queue Status selection gives a screen with information about the queue. If a printer is being serviced temporarily and we don't want to shout or send messages to everyone to stop printing, then the Server Can Service Entries In Queue flag can be first set to No. When the printer is up, it can be reset to Yes. This way the jobs are received in the queue and only printed when the printer becomes available.

17.5 ESTABLISHING THE USER ENVIRONMENT

17.5.1 Login Scripts

Login scripts are files similar to the autoexec.bat files in DOS. They are executed when users log in. For each user, the system login script is executed first; then the user login script is executed, if it exists. Otherwise, a default login script is executed.

The system login script is actually a file called NET$LOG.DAT, which is stored in the SYS:PUBLIC directory. It can be edited by the supervisor using the SYSCON utility by choosing the Supervisor option. The file which holds the user login script is called LOGIN, which is found in the user directory under SYS:MAIL. It can also be edited in SYSCON under User Information. A user can edit his own login script, but care should be taken when mapping to the same drives as the mapped drives in the system login script, or else they may be inadvertently redefined.

Figure 17.13 shows an example of a system login script. It begins with a comment. Comments start with an asterisk in the first column. The first command is like the ECHO OFF command in DOS. It doesn't show each command line of the script while it gets executed. Similarly, the ERRORS OFF command doesn't show trivial errors and warnings on the screen, which may make users uneasy as they are logging in. Then the script defines three search drives similar to what we did in the Session utility. However, here it is done as if it were done on the command line. The MAP ROOT command defines U as a network drive that makes U a false root.

%LOGIN_NAME is a parameter available for script files, which stores the user's login ID at log-in time. Parameters always begin with the "%" sign and others are available besides for the user's ID. If a user logs in as "LOGIN JON SS," then "JON" can be accessed by either %LOGIN_NAME or %1. %1 stands for parameter number 1. Likewise, %2 would provide parameter number 2 or "SS." Looking further down the script, notice that another parameter called %GREETING_TIME is used in a WRITE statement. This parameter provides the time of day, such as morning, evening, etc.

Next, the COMSPEC (COMmand SPECifier) command identifies the search drive where the command.com file is found. This is needed to run basic DOS commands. The IF statement makes the control exit this login script and gives the user a DOS prompt if the user is the supervisor. In this case, it will not execute the user login script. When a DOS executable file name is placed after the EXIT statement, then that file gets executed upon exiting the script.

To execute a DOS command while being in the script file, #COMMAND /C is used before the DOS command. As shown in this example, #COMMAND /C CLS will execute the CLS (CLear Screen) command of DOS and return back to the script file. The DRIVE U: command changes the default drive to U and FIRE PHASERS 9 makes a sound on the terminal to draw the user's attention.

Finally, when an IF statement has more than one command to be executed, then those statements must be placed in a BEGIN-END block. The first IF statement didn't need this, because only one statement, namely EXIT, needed to be executed if the IF condition were satisfied. The MEMBER OF LABCLASS condition checks to see if the

```
*THIS IS THE SYSTEM LOGIN SCRIPT          #COMMAND /C CLS
MAP DISPLAY OFF                           DRIVE U:
MAP ERRORS OFF                            FIRE PHASERS 9
MAP S1:=SYS:PUBLIC                        IF MEMBER OF LABCLASS THEN BEGIN
MAP S2:=SYS:PUBLIC\DOS                      WRITE "GOOD %GREETING_TIME"
MAP S3:=SYS:APPS                            DISPLAY SYS:PUBLIC\PICTURE1:TXT
MAP ROOT U:=SYS:USERS\%LOGIN_NAME          PAUSE
COMSPEC = S2:COMMAND.COM                    MAP S16:=SYS:APPS\WP
IF %LOGIN_NAME=SUPERVISOR THEN EXIT       END
```

Figure 17.13 An example of a system login script.

user belongs to the LABCLASS group or not. If this is the case, then all of the statements in the BEGIN-END block get executed; otherwise, none of them will.

The WRITE statement is similar to DOS's ECHO command, which simply displays the message on the line. Here it would be GOOD AFTERNOON, for example, if the current time of day is the afternoon. The DISPLAY command is similar to DOS's TYPE command, which simply types the PICTURE1.TXT file on the screen. PAUSE displays the message: "Strike any key when ready . . . ," giving the user a chance to look at the screen, and the MAP S16 command maps the next available search drive to point to the WP directory under APPS. In this example, although not all of the script commands are used, it gives an idea of what they are capable of doing.

17.5.2 Custom Menus

When a user is logging in, we may want to display a menu of options that he may want to use. In NetWare it is typically done by executing a menu script. For the sake of an example, let us say that we have such a file called STARTUP.MNU. A menu script ends with an extension of .MNU and can be executed directly from the login script by calling a DOS batch file, say CALLMENU.BAT. This batch file should then execute the menu file using this MENU command: MENU STARTUP. In summary, the login script file executes a batch file by executing EXIT "STARTUP.BAT" and STARTUP then calls the menu script by executing "MENU STARTUP." An example of a menu file is shown in Figure 17.14(a) and its result in Figure 17.14(b). Let us first see what is expected of the file.

In Figure 17.14(b), when the user first enters the menu script, he/she only sees the Sample Menu window. If Applications is selected, then the Application Menu window In the top left corner will come up. Here, the user may enter in any application that is in the menu by selecting it. If the Escape is pressed, that will bring us back to the Sample Menu window.

Here, if the System Menu item is selected, then that window will come up in the upper right hand corner of the screen. If Syscon is selected, then the SYSCON utility is entered into and if the Printer Settings is selected, then the lower windows will come up. They will prompt the user to give the printer queue and the number of copies expected, when printing a job. Let us see the menu file in Figure 17.14(a) that creates this user-work environment.

NetWare   379

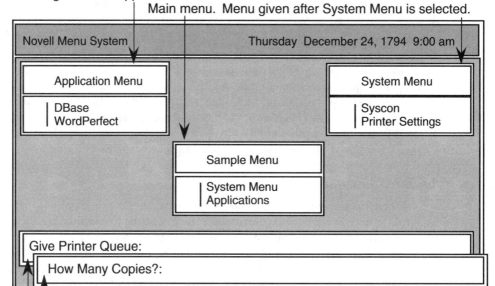

```
%Sample Menu                          %Application Menu,1,1,1
System Menu                           DBase
  %System Menu                          map g:=data
Applications                            g:
  %Application Menu                      db
%System Menu,1,80,4                     u:
Syscon                                  map del g:
  syscon                               WordPerfect
Printer Settings                        wp
  capture q=@1"Give Printer Queue"
          c=@2"How many copies?"
```

(a)

Menu given after Applications is selected.

Main menu. Menu given after System Menu is selected.

```
Novell Menu System                    Thursday  December 24, 1794  9:00 am

   Application Menu                          System Menu

   | DBase                                   | Syscon
   | WordPerfect                             | Printer Settings


                    Sample Menu

                    | System Menu
                    | Applications


 Give Printer Queue:

 How Many Copies?:
```

Capture parameters are inputted after Printer Settings is selected in System Menu.

(b)

Figure 17.14 (a) An example of a .MNU file to create custom menus.
(b) The result of executing this file.

All menu windows begin with a percent sign in the first column of the file. %Sample Menu starts in the first column and so the menu with the heading of Sample Menu is displayed first. The other two menus, System Menu and Application Menu, also begin with the percent sign at column 1. These three menus are placed after each other. The %Sample Menu line has no numbers as the %System Menu and %Application Menu do. The first number is the line number and the second number is the column number where the menu will be displayed on the screen. Typically, a screen has 24 lines and 80 columns. The third number specifies the choice of color for the window. If these numbers are left out, as with the Sample Menu, then the default settings are chosen.

In Figure 17.4(a), we see that the menu choices are placed starting at column 1 of the file, using no percent signs. For Sample Menu, these choices are System Menu and Applications. If the System Menu is selected, then the System Menu is called. This is seen by a percent sign before the System Menu. Likewise, if Applications is selected then the Application Menu is executed.

If System Menu is selected, then Syscon and Printer Settings choices will be displayed. If Syscon is selected, then the SYSCON utility will get executed, otherwise the CAPTURE command will get executed. This is used to set the printer environment. If the user types in Laser_Q for the printer queue and 2 for the number of copies, then the CAPTURE command will effectively be:

```
CAPTURE Q=LASER_Q C=2
```

This will send all printouts from this user to the LASER_Q queue and each time will provide two copies of the same document. There are many other flags which can be set with the CAPTURE command.

If the Application Menu is selected, then DBase and WordPerfect choices are presented. Here, if WordPerfect is selected, then the "wp" file is executed and the user will go in that application. If DBase is selected, then a new drive mapping for G will be defined, the default drive will be changed to G, and then the "db" application will get executed. Once the user exits out of DBase, then he/she will be placed back on the U drive and the G drive mapping used for data will be deleted.

Using menu files, the users' working environment can be made seamless, without them having to learn NetWare and DOS commands.

Exercises

1. Which of the following directories are not created by default when installing NetWare?
   - a. USERS
   - b. LOGIN
   - c. PUBLIC
   - d. SYSTEM

2. Which utility allows one to find the network address and the node address of a user who is logged on the network?
   - a. FILER
   - b. SESSION
   - c. SYSCON
   - d. PCONSOLE

3. Which rights cannot be revoked by an IRM?
   - a. R (Read)
   - b. A (Access Control)
   - c. S (Supervisory)
   - d. F (File Scan)

4. Which selection under SYSCON's Available Topics will let us start assigning charge rates for users who are logged on the network?
   - a. Supervisory Options
   - b. File Server Information
   - c. User Information
   - d. Accounting

5. Which selection under SYSCON will help us in restricting certain individuals from using the network during certain times?
   a. Supervisory Options
   b. File Server Information
   c. User Information
   d. Accounting

6. What file needs to be executed on a workstation to make its printers available to print servers?
   a. RPRINTER.EXE
   b. PSERVER.EXE
   c. ENABLE.EXE
   d. PSERVER.NLM

7. How many file servers can a print server running PSERVER.EXE service?
   a. 5
   b. 8
   c. 16
   d. 24

8. Which utility allows a user to edit his own login script?
   a. SESSION
   b. FILER
   c. SYSCON
   d. PCONSOLE

9. How does one reference a file called FILE_A, which is in the USERS directory, under the SYS volume and in the server called CLASSERV?

10. What command shows the current drive mappings?

11. Which option under which utility allows one to see who is logged in?

12. Which kind of rights take away rights from a user?

13. Which kind of a NetWare window is used for viewing only? (Single border or double border?)

14. Which option under which utility allows one to lock out network intruders?

15. Which file allows a file server to act also as a print server? In this case, can it serve other file servers?

16. Which NetWare script command is similar to DOS's ECHO OFF command?

17. Name the two kinds of drive mappings and give their purpose.

18. What is the difference between trustee rights and effective rights? How do they affect each other and what other factors affect them?

19. What is the difference between workgroup managers and user group managers? If you have NetWare where you work or study, who are these object types at your installation? (If they exist.)

20. Which trustee right is the most powerful and for what reasons?

21. Briefly describe how a PSERVER.EXE can print to printers on other workstations?

22. What are the set of script commands that will greet the user as "Welcome Larry!!," then execute a DOS file called GETSTART.BAT if the user's group name is EVERYONE and the user's login ID is Larry?

23. When writing a custom menu, how can we tell the difference between the calling of a submenu and the heading (or start) of the submenu?

24. Have the GETSTART.BAT call a menu file and have the menu simply display two choices, Choice 1 and Choice 2. Nothing should happen if the user selects one of these choices. Write the batch file and the menu file.

Chapter 18

Interconnecting LANs

18.1 INTERNETWORKING DEVICES

As soon as personal computers were being connected into LANs, there became a need for connecting LANs and WANs into complex internetworks. Internetworks, or internets for short, are networks made up of many networks. Many times, internets use a set of protocols based on TCP/IP (Transmission Control Protocol/ Internet Protocol) to "glue" different networks together. The largest of these internets is called the Internet, spelled with a capital "I." The Internet is funded by DARPA (Defense Advanced Research Project Agency) and with over 1,500,000 computers connected, it is the world's largest network. This chapter will outline the devices, protocols, and services relating to internetworking.

18.1.1 Adding Bridges to a Network

Back in Figure 16.11, we saw how a LAN could be extended over many floors of a building or even to other buildings in a campus setting by using repeaters. Repeaters boost the signal over the cable so that a LAN is not restricted from being confined to a certain area. With Ethernet, the range of a LAN can be extended from 500 meters to 2500 meters by placing up to four repeaters.

When we wanted to use a less expensive LAN technology than 10Base5, we incorporated hubs at various points in the network as was shown in Figure 16.14. This allowed us to mix the various kinds of LAN technologies. The hubs also provided a point from where signals could be repeated as well as provide better management and troubleshooting capabilities.

Repeaters, however, only repeat the signals and if we keep adding more stations to the LAN, and add more traffic to it by using it more than before, then eventually our throughput will degrade. This is because the number of collisions will increase. If

---

We had the honor of having Radia Perlman of Digital Equipment Corporation make enhancements on this chapter. Tony Eldridge of Rutgers University was my patient teacher on router configuration. Thanks also go to Rory Pope of Bellcore for sharing his expertise on Sections 18.5 to 18.8.

nodes on both sides of a repeater are simultaneously trying to communicate with each other, then they wouldn't be able to, because repeaters cannot isolate traffic, but simply transfer the signals between each LAN segment.

For example, in Figure 18.1(a), A can't communicate with B at the same time as E is communicating with F. One way to solve this problem is to isolate the segments as shown in Figure 18.1(b). Now A and E may send data simultaneously; unfortunately they can't communicate with each other. So in order to have both capabilities, we add a bridge between these networks. A bridge is capable of filtering, that is, if A is talking to B, it won't pass that frame towards E and G. However, frames sent by A to E will be transferred over. See Figure 18.1(c). In Figure 18.1(a) only one pair of nodes may communicate with each other, since only one communication path exists between all nodes. In Figure 18.1(c), the network is divided into two segments and communication can occur over each segment simultaneously.

However, the decision of where to place a bridge should be done carefully, so that the network is segmented into existing logical groups. That is, the stations on a given side of the bridge should primarily communicate among themselves and communicate between each other only occasionally. A general rule of thumb is that 80% of the traffic should be localized within segments with only 20% of it crossing the bridges. Once these percentages begin to equal each other, then maybe more bridges should be added, segmenting the network further. Bridges also allow one to exceed a LAN's distance limitations.

On the other hand, if we are not using our network heavily, repeaters provide a good solution. They are protocol independent. This means that they don't care about the meaning of the fields in the frames, since they only copy the bits from one side of the bridge to the other. They present only a one or two bit delay in the network and, sometimes, they may gain or lose bits. They don't check for errors, because they

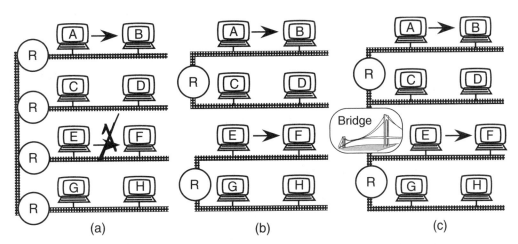

Figure 18.1 (a) E cannot talk to F at the same time that A is talking to B, using repeaters. (b) This is possible by dividing the network, but now A cannot talk to E - H at all. (c) Using a bridge, both things are possible.

operate at the OSI's physical layer. The end nodes in a network don't know about their existence and since repeaters aren't configured, they can always be swapped with other models.

18.1.2 Adding Routers to a Network

Bridges are easy to install and can provide a rudimentary level of security at the hardware level. For example, certain users may not be allowed to go out of their own segment. Bridges are easily managed and don't require technical expertise when the network is operating normally. However, in a bridged network with loops, a small problem in one segment can bring the entire network to its knees. Then troubleshooting can become difficult.

Also bridges do not isolate broadcasts (transmission to all nodes) and multicasts (transmission to a group of nodes). There are two types of broadcasts: normal and abnormal. Normal broadcasts are periodic transmissions sent to all nodes in a network by each node, stating their presence on the network. This can take much of the bandwidth on a large network. Abnormal broadcasts are also called broadcast storms; they are due to a failure in a network component. A network with bridges looks like and behaves as one single network.

Once we start adding other networking sites to our internet, especially using WAN links, we would want to form loops in the topology to provide alternate routing. This is shown in Figure 18.2(a). Here, once we start using the network for mission critical applications, where we want high reliability, then a better alternative would be to replace the bridges with routers.

At one time, separate routers and WAN links had to be installed for every type of protocol that needed to be routed. Today, multiprotocol routers handle several protocols simultaneously. They can isolate broadcast and multicast traffic. The type of traffic which exists in different parts of the network can be controlled. Network security and management is much more robust than with bridges, and if the network goes down, the problem can be easily isolated to one port of a router, making it possible to restore the network quickly.

Bridges may not use WAN links efficiently. They are better to use with small distances and typically have only two ports, whereas routers will look at the network layer's header and decide from its internal tables which route seems to be the best. If there is congestion, delay, or extra expense to use one route over another, it will make the desirable choice. Therefore, routers are more intelligent than bridges.

Bridges are protocol independent. They operate at the data link layer unlike routers which operate at the network layer of the OSI model. Protocols which don't have a third layer, such as DEC's LAT (Local Area Transport) and NetBIOS, can't be routed and must be bridged.

With multiprotocol bridge/routers, one can install them as a bridge, and after seeing how the network performs and grows, they can be configured as routers. They can also be configured to bridge some protocols and route others.

Using Figure 18.2, let us illustrate what is meant by a device operating at the data link layer and the network layer. Suppose we have three networks (numbered 1000, 4000, and 7000) connected to each other. The nodes have three digit IDs, so a

Interconnecting LANs

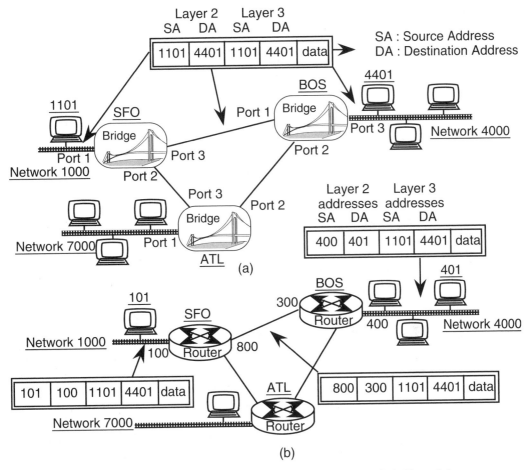

Figure 18.2 (a) The frame remains the same as it goes via bridges. It is one large network. (b) The bridges are replaced with routers. Here, the data link addresses change, as the frame goes through them.

combination of the network ID and the node ID uniquely identifies any node in the network.

Let us say node 1101 (node 101 on network 1000) is sending a packet to node 4401. In Figure 18.2(a), the node will code the second layer SA (Source Address) and DA (Destination Address) to be the same as the third layer SA and DA. In this case, SA and DA are 1101 and 4401, respectively. The SFO bridge, the bridge in San Francisco, will determine from the DA in the second layer that this frame should go over its port 3. Similarly, the BOS (or Boston) bridge will determine that 4401 is on its own network and forward the frame to node 401, using the DA from the second layer.

But, as shown in Figure 18.2(b), in a router-based network, a packet is routed from link to link. First, when node 101 assembles a packet, it sets the SA to 1101 and the DA to 4401 in the third layer header. Using the second layer, it then encloses this packet in a frame with an SA of 101 and a DA of 100, the address of the router's port for network 1000.

The frame reaches the SFO router, which discards the second layer header and trailer after checking for errors. If an error occurs, it would request a retransmission. This router then, only reading the DA in the packet header, decides to send this packet over the direct link to the BOS router. It does this by enclosing the same packet in a new frame which now has an SA and DA of 800 and 300, respectively. This gets the packet to the BOS router.

This router then checks for errors and discards the frame header and trailer. It then decides that this packet can be directly delivered to the recipient. So it encodes the SA as 400 (its own second layer address) and the DA as 401. Finally, node 401 accepts and interprets the data that it receives.

This way, bridges read and process only the data link control information, while routers process the network layer information as well. Because they have less information to process, bridges can send more frames per second than the number of packets routers can send per second. Also, since the frame doesn't get changed as it passes through the bridges, the layout of Figure 18.2(a) is considered to be one large network, while the layout of Figure 18.2(b) is considered as six separate networks.

18.1.3 Collapsing the Backbone

Back in Figure 16.14, we saw by adding hubs and concentrators on each floor how the network was made easy to expand. To allow the network to grow further, we can now add bridge or router cards in these hubs.

However that configuration, with the backbone stretching several floors and buildings, has several problems. If a card fails in one of these hubs, first, a technician may have to carry a LAN analyzer to those various locations, looking for the fault. In the closets where other types of wiring and equipment exist, access to these hubs may be poor. And even if a card is detected to be faulty, the technician may have to come back to the office for a replacement. Having these hubs scattered over various sites prevents a network from coming up in a timely fashion. Furthermore, even during normal operation, file servers on each floor may not be as easy to secure as if they were all located in one room designated solely for such a purpose.

A third generation hub, or a network with a collapsed backbone, places all components which are critical to the network's operation in one secure room. Let us call it the NOC (Network Operations Center). See Figure 18.3. The backbone, instead of spanning large distances, is totally located in one place and all important network components as well as the segments themselves are connected here. Logically, the hub in the NOC can be thought of as a superhub. The same advantages gained by tying all components on one floor to a "closet" hub can be achieved for the networks themselves by tying them all to one central hub in the NOC.

A LAN analyzer incorporated in a management console gives the network manager full control of the network from one vantage point. At night, to keep the file server data secure, the manager can make sure that all file servers are properly brought down. There is only one room to be kept secure, rather than multiple wiring closets which have to be shared among other facility services.

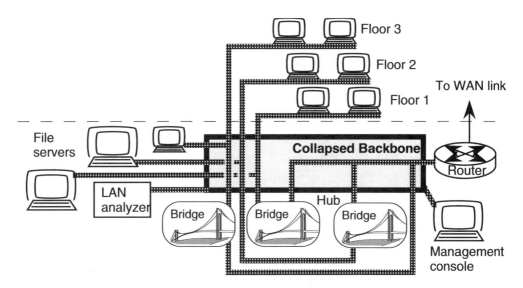

Figure 18.3 An integrated hub with all networking equipment located in the network operations center, shown below the dashed line.

If a segment goes down, the manager can isolate the fault quickly from the console. All equipment, including spare devices, are already plugged in the hub, making changes in the configuration possible through the hub's software. If a server or a bridge needs to be swapped temporarily, it can be done using the console instead of physically plugging and unplugging the equipment. Therefore, third generation hubs can greatly improve the manageability, availability, and control of an extended LAN, but much caution should be taken so that the hub system itself is quite fault tolerant.

18.2 BRIDGES

18.2.1 Translating and Encapsulating Bridges

Figure 18.4 shows two types of bridges which are not the most commonly found. Figure 18.4(a) shows the operation of what is called a translating bridge. It is used to connect two networks that differ at the first and second layers. A frame on the token ring, if addressed to reach an Ethernet node, is translated by the bridge. It does this by discarding the TRN header and trailer and adding the Ethernet header and trailer. This process is reversed for data traveling in the opposite direction.

Any frame which is addressed to a node on the same network is not forwarded by the bridge. Lastly, the bridge cannot perform fragmentation. Fragmentation is a process which divides large frames into fragments, because the data transporting network cannot handle large sized frames. Therefore, nodes connected to a translating bridge must be configured so that they do not transmit large frames.

The encapsulation bridge, depicted in Figure 18.4(b), is used over a backbone network, such as the FDDI ring. Here, the protocols of the first two layers of the end systems must be the same and the backbone network encapsulates frames which it

Interconnecting LANs   **389**

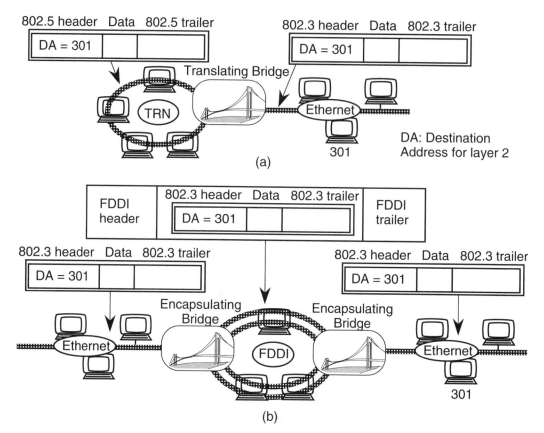

Figure 18.4 (a) A translating bridge converts the layer 2 header and trailer from one format to another. (b) An encapsulating bridge installs one layer 2 frame into another one.

receives from the branch or access networks. The figure shows the left Ethernet LAN transmitting an 802.3 frame which is destined for the Ethernet LAN on the right hand side. The first bridge encapsulates this frame in an FDDI frame and then the bridge on the right hand side removes the FDDI header and trailer, sending the original Ethernet frame on to its destination.

18.2.2 Transparent Bridges

A translational bridge, as described in the last section, is a special kind of a transparent bridge. Transparency here means that the end systems (or hosts) don't need to know the existence of the bridges in the network. That is, the bridges operate transparently, relative to the nodes. A transparent bridge only passes frames which should be forwarded to another port of the bridge and drops the others. The method by which a transparent bridge finds out the addresses of the nodes connected to its ports is called learning. Figure 18.5 illustrates how this works.

In this figure, there is a cascaded network with two bridges. Units of time are shown on the far left. Under each bridge, its forwarding table is shown as it gets created. As a bridge learns about the existences of the nodes in each segment, these tables become bigger. Each entry in the table specifies on which port which nodes exist and at what time they were last seen there. The bridges use the source addresses in the frames being sent to learn where nodes are located.

At first, when the network is powered up, the bridges don't have anything in their tables. At time = 1, node A sends a frame to G, so bridge X makes an entry in its table noting that A was seen on its port 1 at time = 1. X doesn't know where G is or if it is powered up, so it simply forwards the frame to Y which processes the frame the same way. This frame is said to flood the network, since no one knows where the destination is located.

Next, F sends a frame to D and just as before, the two tables get updated, but this time, the time is equal to 2. Next, I sends a frame to F. X and Y both receive this frame and filter it. They treat the frame differently from each other. X knows that F is on its port 1, so it forwards the frame to that port. As it does this, it adds I to its table as being on port 2. Y, on the other hand, knows that F is on its port 1 side and drops the frame from going over on its port 2 segment.

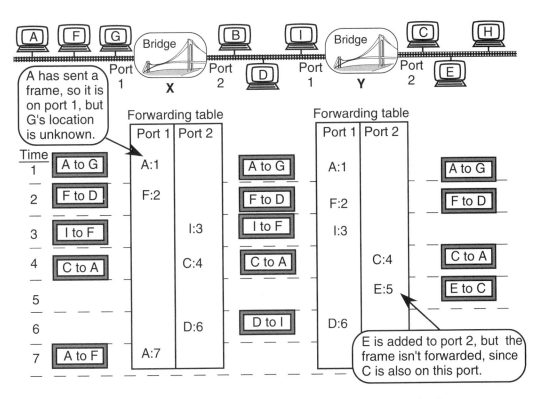

Figure 18.5 How bridges learn the addresses on their ports. The times that the frames were observed are given after the colons.

Then C sends a frame to A, which makes each bridge add C to its forwarding tables. Now both bridges have 4 entries each. Notice that, relative to X, I and C are on the same segment or on the same port. X doesn't know about the existence of Y in this process. If X and Y were routers they would have. Similarly, Y doesn't know on which segment A, F, and I exist; hence X is transparent to Y.

At time = 5, E sends a frame to C. Y has C in its table stating that C is also on port 2, so this frame is dropped and not forwarded. Also, when D sends a frame to I, both bridges drop the frame, because now they know where I is. Lastly, when A sends a frame to F, X updates the time it saw A on port, which is now 7. If the broadcast and the mutlicast modes were enabled on the bridges, then those messages would be forwarded as well, or else they would be dropped.

18.2.3 Spanning Tree Algorithm

To provide alternate routing and reliability in a network, we know we have to add loops in our network. This way if one link fails, we can use other available links. However, with bridges that introduces a problem.

Consider bridges W, X, Y, and Z being connected as shown in Figure 18.7 on page 395. For now let us only look at the topology shown at the top of this figure and disregard the rest of it. Let us say that a node (call it A) on port 1 of bridge X sends a frame to a node on some other segment. So X notes that A is on its port 1 and forwards the frame to Y, which forwards it to W and Z. Now all four bridges have noted that A is on their port 1 side of the network. What happens when W's copy of the frame arrives on port 3 of Z? Z will note that A has moved from port 1 to port 3 and passes this information to Y. Y will make a note of this change and pass the frame to both X and W. This way, from one frame, many more copies are created and they keep bouncing off of each other, keeping the bridges needlessly busy. Hence, the tables never become stabilized.

Therefore, bridges couldn't be placed in loops until Radia Perlman of DEC introduced the spanning tree algorithm. For the sake of reliability, loops are preferred in networks. This method makes bridges pass special configuration messages among themselves to determine the topology of the network. Links are removed, until they are needed again. The bridges place themselves in a logical tree, where only one bridge is the root and the others form the branches of a hierarchical structure. This way, the problem of looping in a bridged network is eliminated.

A configuration message, among other fields, contains a root bridge ID, a cost, and a sending bridge ID. All bridges have a unique, 48-bit address. When a bridge sends a configuration message, the bridge which it thinks is the root and the number of hops it is away from that root are encoded in it. Periodically, bridges pass these messages among themselves to eliminate any loops which may have been introduced in the network. If a link goes down where alternate paths are available, then those paths or links will be reactivated by this algorithm.

When a bridge receives a configuration message on its ports, it will determine the best message out of these and from the one that it can send. The best message is the message which has the smallest root ID. If root IDs are the same, then the cost field is used as the tie breaker. If these are also the same, then the sending bridge ID is used to determine the best configuration message.

If the best configuration message is received on one of the ports then that port is considered the root port and if the bridge in question can send the best message, then it considers itself as the root bridge. If there are any ports to which the bridge cannot send a better message than what was received on it, then those ports are blocked. But if there are ports to which the bridge can send better messages, then those ports are included in the spanning tree. When a port is included then data is received and forwarded over that port and when it is blocked it isn't. In either case, configuration messages are received and forwarded.

For example, Figure 18.6(a) shows a bridge, with an ID = 70, having six ports. The best configuration messages arriving at each port are also shown. The bridge then determines that port 4 has the best message, since 40-2-80 (representing the root ID, cost, and the sending bridge ID) is less than any other message. Messages from ports 1, 5, and 6 are worse, because their root IDs are greater than 40. Port 3 is also worse, because even though the root is 40, its cost is higher than 2. And port 2 is also worse than port 4, because its sender ID is larger. Port 4 is then referenced as the root port, because cost wise it is closest to the bridge which it thinks is the root.

This bridge then determines that the best message it can send is 40-3-70. This has a hop count of one more than what it received on port 4. Since this message is better than what it received on ports 1, 5, and 6, it will send 40-3-70 on these ports. See Figure 18.6(b). However, 40-3-30 and 40-2-90 from ports 2 and 3 are better than what this bridge can send, so those ports are pruned or blocked. Although it will continue to read the configuration messages from these ports, no data will be read from them or forwarded to them.

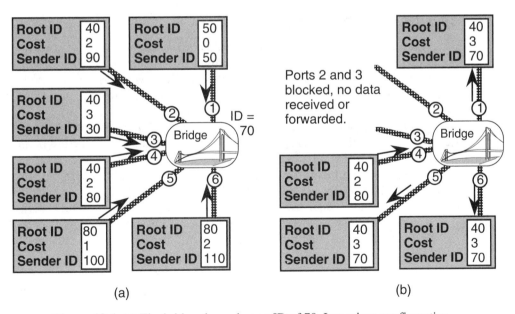

(a)   (b)

Figure 18.6 (a) The bridge shown has an ID of 70. It receives configuration messages from other bridges on its six ports. (b) After it applies the spanning tree algorithm, it decides that port 4 is closest to the root and that ports 2 and 3 would form loops.

Figure 18.7 illustrates how a bridged network removes its loops by the use of this algorithm. Let us say at first that X thinks it is the root and sends the 20-0-20 message over both of its ports. Y realizes that its own ID of 40 is worse than 20. So it sends a message of 20-1-40 over its other two ports. This message indicates that bridge 40 is 1 hop count away from the bridge it thinks is the root. Y also labels port 1 as the root port, because it learned that X is the root from its port 1. Likewise, Z also sends a similar message over its ports 1 and 3.

W, upon receiving these messages from Y and Z, considers itself better than either of them, because its own ID is 10. W then sends 10-0-10 to Y and Z. They make a note that the root is changed to 10 and also the root is 1 hop count away from them. X receives 10-1-40 from Y and 10-1-30 from Z. X picks Z as being closest to the root and determines that the best message it can send is 10-2-20. This is worse than what it receives from 40 (10-1-40), so it blocks port 2 and considers port 1 as the root.

Y also blocks its port 2, since the message which it can send (10-1-40) is worse than what it receives on that port (10-1-30), but continues to send its 10-1-40 on its port 1. Z can send a better message 10-1-30 than what it receives on either ports 1 and 2, so it does.

Now the map of the network is redrawn in Figure 18.7(b). The final root is 10 and all of the loops are removed. In the event W goes down, it will stop sending messages and the other bridges will determine that too much time has passed since W made its presence known. They will then time out W and the entire process will be repeated without W in the new configuration. But if W comes back up, then the configuration will be restored as shown, automatically without any human intervention.

18.2.4 Source Routing Bridges

Unlike transparent bridges which maintain forwarding tables, source routing bridges rely on the source of the frame to provide the path over the bridges. When an end system (host) sends a frame which must travel over several bridges, it encodes the bridge addresses in the proper order in this field to specify the route it must take. This way, each bridge knows which port to forward the frame to.

Source routing bridges are primarily used with TRNs (Token Ring Networks). Referring back to Figure 16.18, notice that the 802.5 frame allows the use of an RIF field. Recall that if the I/G bit (Figure 16.9) of the source address is set to 1, an RIF (Routing Information Field) is used and if it is 0, it is not used in the frame. This bit is available to indicate the presence of the RIF field, because even if a frame could have a multicast destination address, it can't have a source address of several stations.

If a device doesn't know the route to the desired destination point, then it must first find out that route. This is done by the device sending an explorer frame, which is also called a route discovery frame. This frame is flooded in the network as each bridge forwards it to all the others. Before a bridge forwards a frame over its ports, it copies its own address in the frame's RIF field. Eventually, a number of these explorer frames appear at the destination, which then decides which is the best path between the two end points. Usually this is determined by the explorer frame which arrives first. The receiver then sends only one frame back to the sender, who then copies the addresses which define the path to that destination for future reference. Then it sends

Interconnecting LANs

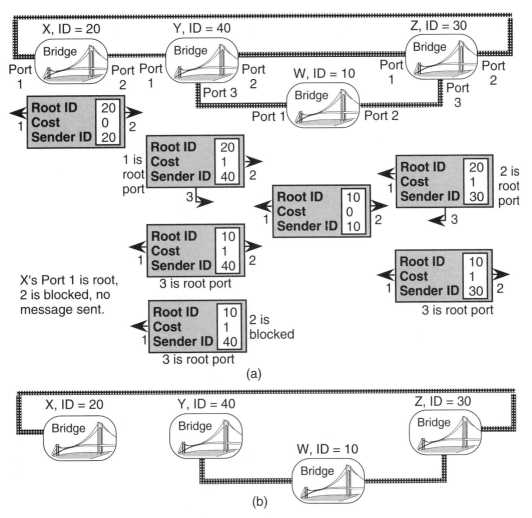

Figure 18.7 (a) The process of sending configuration messages in the spanning tree algorithm. (b) The final network after trimming out all of the loops.

its message. If this machine is turned off and comes back on line, it has to go through this process again. One can see that route exploration performed by each station on every network can generate excessive traffic over large extended LANs.

There are two types of explorer frames. One type sends these frames in all directions and is called the All paths explorer. The Spanning tree explorer frame, on the other hand, sends out these frames only along the branches of a spanning tree. Hence, it is necessary to define three types of RIF fields. One type is where the route is known and is explicitly specified to its destination. The other two types correspond to the two types of explorer frames, where the addresses of the bridges are collected in this field.

Some of the differences between transparent bridges and source routing bridges are that, with transparent bridges, the network appears as one single network to the end nodes. That is, the bridges are transparent to the end nodes. However, source routing bridges are not transparent to the end nodes. The end nodes have to know about their existence and must be able to handle source routing. Even if source routing bridges may cost less, the cost of the more intelligent end nodes outweighs the savings. Transparent bridges can typically be swapped, but source routing bridges must be configured by assigning every segment and bridge a unique number. The problem of finding a route is calculated by the end systems in source routing bridges and is done by the bridges, when using transparent bridges.

Lastly, an SRT (Source Route Transparent) bridge is a bridge which can function as either type. According to IEEE, all bridges must be transparent and they can add source routing as an added feature. The SRT bridge merely observes the multicast bit in the source address of a frame to determine whether this frame should be bridged transparently or be bridged using the source routing method.

18.2.5 Ethernet Switching

Now, let us step back to Figure 18.1(a). Here, due to the high number of devices and traffic generated by them, we had to segment the network by adding a bridge in Figure 18.1(c). This configuration created two paths over which transmission could take place, as long as these transmissions were isolated on either side of the bridge. In other words, while C was transmitting to E over the bridge, no other transmission could take place.

This limitation of only one channel per LAN in Ethernet is lifted by a device called an Ethernet switch. This switch incorporates fast packet switching and circuit switching all in one unit to allow multiple paths over a LAN.

Consider Figure 18.8(a), where the bridge in Figure 18.1(a) is replaced by an Ethernet switch. Similar to the transparent bridge, the switch learns the addresses of the nodes on each port. Now if node A is communicating with B, A's frames are dropped by the switch, but if A is sending a frame to C, then that frame is forwarded over port 2 only. See Figure 18.8(b). While this connection is made between ports 1 and 2, another connection between ports 3 and 4 can also be provided, if necessary.

However, if while ports 1 and 2 are in use, the switch receives a frame, from let's say port 3 for port 1, then the switch will place that frame in its buffer and send it to port 1 as soon as it becomes available. As shown in Figures 18.8(c) and (d), the switch provides two paths of communication between the two segments of the LAN at any given time, whereas the bridge provides only one. With more than four ports on the switch, more simultaneous paths are possible.

Ethernet switches can have a latency delay of about only 30 microseconds, because while a switch is reading the addresses in the header, it is already forwarding the frame to the correct output port. Fast bridges operate at about 1000 microseconds, because they must read the entire frame before deciding what to do with it. This way, the Ethernet switch performs both packet switching and circuit switching on-the-fly. The blockage in these switches is minimized, yet they can buffer more than 100 full sized frames. Because of these features, these switches can be cascaded in a tree structure with more than 10 hops between the end devices.

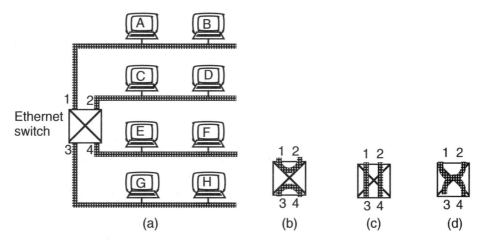

Figure 18.8 (a) A four-port Ethernet switch. (b) through (d) show the concurrent possible paths through the cross-point switch.

18.3 ROUTING PROTOCOLS

18.3.1 Routing, Routing Protocols, and Routed Protocols

In this section we will discuss routing protocols and methods in which they operate. Routing protocols, routed protocols, and routing itself are all dissimilar terms. Routers are the type of packet switches which are used in internetworking LANs. They contain routing tables which determine how incoming datagrams (or packets) will be forwarded to their next destination. This is called routing. Routing is simply the act of looking through the routing table to direct the datagram to the next router or end system.

The procedure used for routing is trivial compared to the procedures used to create the tables in the first place. The method in which these routing tables are created and updated is called a routing algorithm and the specific implementation of it is called a routing protocol. Routing protocols exist and operate only in routing devices whereas network protocols such as IP (Internet Protocol), NetWare, or DECnet, which are routable through routers, are called routed protocols. Now, let us discuss the details of RIP, OSPF, and BGP, which are routing protocols.

18.3.2 Distance Vector Routing and RIP

Basic Algorithm: The first routing protocol which became widely used is called RIP (Routing Information Protocol). Originally, it was used in XNS in 1980 and currently it is available in most implementations of Unix as "routed," pronounced as "route Dee." RIP falls in a class of routing algorithms called distance vector routing. The best path to a destination is determined by the least number of hops. However, the best path may be determined by some other metric than the number of hops. Since RIP is a routing protocol which specifies how routing tables are built, let us consider how RIP handles that process.

The basic idea behind RIP is that each router first determines who its neighbors are. Then they transmit an update message to only their neighbors every 30 seconds. Every time a router receives an update message from one of its neighbors, it looks at the addresses and their respective distances which its neighbors can reach. If the neighboring router can reach a destination which is currently unreachable, it will add that destination as being reachable. In this table, it will also maintain the distances to reach the various nodes. The distances to the destinations are measured in the number of hops.

If another neighbor can reach a destination with fewer hops, it will enter that route in the table instead. If the distance necessary to reach a destination is more than 15 hops, it will not enter that destination in its table and assumes that it is unreachable. Therefore, RIP is only good for networks where the number of routers between any two nodes is 15 or less. After the "diameter" of the network exceeds this amount, one must resort to other protocols. Let us look at an example of how RIP works and then make refinements to this basic description as we encounter problems.

An Example: Figure 18.9(a) shows four networks, A through D, internetworked by three routers (R1 through R3). This example illustrates how RIP builds the routing tables in each of the routers by having the routers pass update messages to each other. The tables are shown as having four columns under the routers and the update messages are shown under the networks which they travel.

Initially, the routing tables are empty, except for the networks which are directly connected to them. For example, R1 has entered a distance or a cost of 0 to reach networks A and B, since they are directly connected to its ports. R1 doesn't yet know that C and D exist.

After 30 seconds, all routers send update messages to their neighbors. R1 tells R2 that it can reach A and B at a cost of 0 hops each. R2 after analyzing this message disregards the fact that R1 can reach B directly, because R2 can also. However, R2 learns that R1 can reach A at a cost of 0. So it adds A to its table and enters the cost to be one more than the cost from R1, since R2 is one hop away from R1. Now R2 can also reach A at a cost of 1. Hence, after the transmission of the first round of update messages, R2 can get to all four networks, but R1 and R3 can only get to three of them.

Not until another 30 seconds have passed and until R2 sends another set of update messages, do R1 and R2 find out that they can reach the networks on the far ends. In other words, R1 learns from R2 that R2 can reach network D at a cost of 1, so it adds D to its table, making the cost equal to 2. Similarly, R3 adds A to its table at a cost of 2. Now the network is said to be converged. That is, all routers have the proper information about how to reach all reachable destinations in the network.

Counting to Infinity: Now what if R3 fails? How will R1 be notified? If R1 is not notified, it will send datagrams to R3, unnecessarily using the network bandwidth. To avoid this problem, RIP requires that the update messages are sent every 30 seconds, even if the sender's data base hasn't been changed. This way, all routers keep their tables current and keep a timer for each entry.

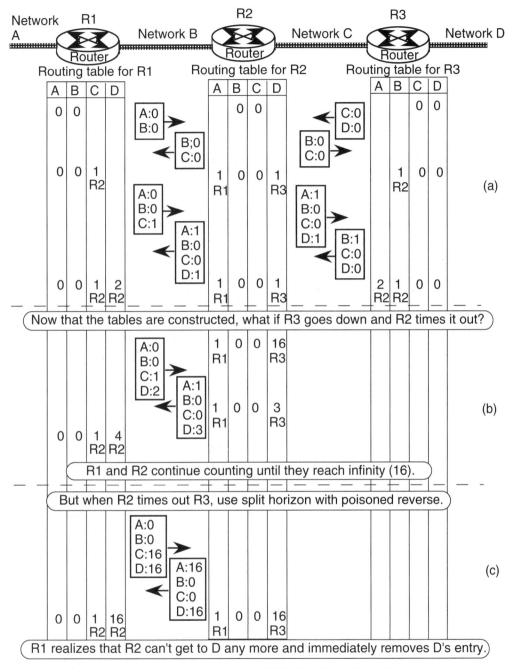

Figure 18.9 (a) The basic operation of RIP (Routing Information Protocol). (b) The problem of counting to infinity. (c) Convergence occurs quickly using split horizon with poisoned reverse.

If a router fails to receive a confirmation from a network that is already in its table for 180 seconds, it will set the hop count to 16, indicating that this network is unreachable. After another 120 seconds, if it still doesn't receive a message, it will remove that entry from the table altogether. This is called garbage collection. Garbage collection prevents "I can't reach this network" messages from taking up network bandwidth, which becomes unnecessary after awhile.

Referring to Figure 18.9(b), let us see another problem which arises if R3 goes down. Let us say if R3 goes down, R2 will not receive any entries from R3. After 180 seconds it will set the cost of D to 16, or unreachable. Next time R2 sends a message to R1, it indicates its cost to D as 16, also considered to be infinity in RIP. However, R2 learns that R1 can get to D with a cost of 2. So R2, not realizing that R1 considers reachability through R2, merely updates its own database, entering a route to D with a cost of 3. This is one more than the assumed cost from R1.

Then R1 learns from R2 that R2's cost to D has gone up to 3. Therefore, R1 updates its cost to D to become 4. Then R2 ups its cost to 5 until the entries for D at both routers reach 16 and they time out. This is called "counting to infinity" and is caused by a routing loop. Here, the network has converged or stabilized slowly, because R1 thought it could get to D via R2 and R2 thought it could get to D via R1. Therefore, RIP has purposely set the infinity count to a low 16.

Split Horizon: To avoid routing loops, a technique called split horizon is used. This prevents a router from sending update information to a neighbor from whom it received that information to begin with. For instance, R1 should never send reachability information for D to R2, since R1 received that information from R2 in the first place. So if R3 goes down as it did at the beginning of Figure 18.9(b), instead of sending a cost of 16, R2 will not send an entry for network D at all and let R1 time out D. Hence, unreachability for a node is determined at every router.

RIP actually uses a mechanism called split horizon with poisoned reverse. This is illustrated in Figure 18.9(c). Here, instead of R2 not sending an entry for D at all, it will send an entry with a cost of 16. R1, upon noticing that R2's cost to D has gone to infinity, and that its route was learned from R2, will consider 16 as "poison" and delete that entry for D immediately. This way, convergence is achieved quickly and prevents R1 from transmitting wrong information to other nodes. Also, note that R2 sends a cost of 16 for A to R1 since R2 learned that information from R1 to begin with.

However, routing loops do exist in RIP for other configurations as when R1 thinks it can get to D via R2 and R2 thinks it can get to D via R3 and R3 thinks it can get to D through R1. Here, a mechanism called triggered updates will send new information learned about the topology almost immediately, reducing the looping problem. When even this technique doesn't work, then unreachability can still be achieved by counting to infinity.

18.3.3 Link State Routing and OSPF

Link State Protocols: There are two types of link state protocols. They are OSPF (Open Shortest Path First) and IS-IS (Intermediate System to Intermediate System). Although each has its benefits and drawbacks, we will primarily concentrate on OSPF.

Again, giving details of one and not the other does in no way imply that one is better than the other. It only allows us to study the pertinent concepts in more depth.

In the distance vector algorithm, we saw how each node transmits its entire routing table to only its neighbors. This makes the network converge slowly because two routers that are many hops away from each other will not know about their existence until the intermediate routers have updated and forwarded their tables, one router at a time.

With link state routing protocols, this is not the case. Each router, instead of transmitting its entire data base to only its neighbors, transmits the information about its neighbors to all of the other nodes in the internet. While the intermediate routers between two distant end routers are creating their tables, the information for the end routers to create their tables is already in transit. This causes the network to converge rapidly. Furthermore, if a change occurs, only that change, rather than the entire data base, is transmitted to all nodes. OSPF is a routing protocol which implements this link state routing algorithm.

Unlike in RIP, where the cost between two routers is the number of hops, OSPF allows one to choose a preferred route based on a number of link characteristics, called metrics. These metrics can be specified in terms of reliability, delay, bandwidth, cost of the link, load of the link, and other such items. Many of these metrics are dependent on one another, depending on the configuration of the network. And while for one instance reliability may be the most important metric, for others it may be cost or some other factor. With OSPF one can choose the cost between two points based on these metrics rather than just on the number of hops.

OSPF Routing Tables: In Figure 18.10, we have a mesh network of routers, using point-to-point links. It is important for the routers to know who their neighbors are. This is accomplished using the Hello protocol. At the beginning, each router will send a Hello Packet to each of its neighbors giving its own router address. These Hello Packets are sent periodically to detect changes in their adjacent links and they are not forwarded by the receiving routers. For example, R1 will send Hello Packets over each of its interfaces to R2 and R3. When they in turn send their Hello Packets back with R1's address, R1 will have established two-way communications with them. At this time, the cost of the links will be established.

Once each router has determined its neighbors, the adjacent pairs synchronize their databases. LSAs (Link State Advertisements) are then flooded throughout the network. These are packets of information sent by each router specifying its link state at that time.

In the figure, four LSAs are shown as they are sent by each router after the links are initialized. R1, for instance, broadcasts its data base (which specifies that R2 and R3 are 4 and 1 units away, respectively) to all nodes. Therefore, even though R4 is not directly connected to R1, soon it will also receive that LSA. These LSAs are flooded in all directions simultaneously. However, for the sake of explanation, let us assume each LSA arrives at each of the other routers one at a time. This will help us see how the "shortest path" routing tables are built.

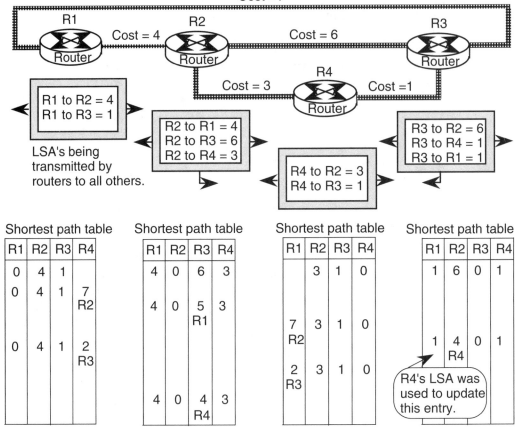

Figure 18.10 As the LSAs (Link State Advertisements) from the various sources reach their multiple destinations, the shortest path tables for each of the routers are built . The router number under table entries denote that the path is not direct and that this is the next hop router designation. In this example, it also indicates the router whose LSA was used to update that particular table entry.

Initially, R1 doesn't know about R4's existence, but when it receives R2's LSA, it computes the cost to R4 to be 7, 4 to R2, and then 3 to R4. R2, upon receiving R1's LSA, notes that the cost from R1 to R3 is only 1, so it chooses the shortest path to R3 as being through R1, since 5 (or 4 + 1) is less than the cost to R3 directly (which is 6).

Let us say that R4 receives R2's LSA first and notes that R1 is now also accessible at a cost of 7. Then R3, upon receiving R4's LSA, updates its cost to R2 to be 4 (or 3 + 1) via R4, which is less than the cost to R2 directly. Similarly, R1, using R3's LSA, adjusts its cost to R4 to be 2 and R4 does likewise. Finally R2 adjusts its cost to R3 to be 4, via R4.

What has happened here is that every router has created an identical link state data base, which describes the topology of the network. Using this data base, each router, relative to itself, has created a routing table that is based on the shortest path tree. Each router's path tree is derived with it as being the root of the tree.

Multi-Access Networks: In the last section, over every network or link only one pair of routers could communicate with each other. Consider Figure 18.11. Over the Ethernet, R4, R5, and R6 can communicate with each other and using the PSN (Packet Switched Network), they can communicate with the rest of the routers. Both the Ethernet and the switched network are considered to be multi-access networks. Note that these are not the same as a multi-drop networks, where each point only has direct access to one controller. In a multi-access network, every router can communicate directly with any other. Switched networks are typically non-broadcast and Ethernets are broadcast types of multi-access networks.

In multi-access networks, instead of each router establishing adjacency with every other router, based on their IDs, they elect what is called a DR (Designated Router). They also elect a BDR (Backup DR) to take over in case the DR fails. Next, each router establishes adjacency with only the DR. This eliminates one-to-many combinations with each router, which reduces the amount of unnecessary protocol traffic over the network. The DR then assigns a name to its network that includes its own name. In the figure, R4 has been elected the DR for both networks and it has assigned the switched network the address of R4.1 and the Ethernet the address of R4.2. The DR now sends LSAs on behalf of the network as well as for itself. So each router that is not a DR advertises that it only has a link to its network, rather than all the other routers in its network.

The chart in Figure 18.11 shows that a link to the R4.1 network is advertised by R1 through R4 and a link to R4.2 is advertised by R4 through R6. R4.1 advertises that it has links to R1 through R4 and hosts, H1 and H2. Similarly, R4.2 advertises a list of its routers and hosts. The transmission of LSAs for R4, R4.1, and R4.2 are all handled by R4.

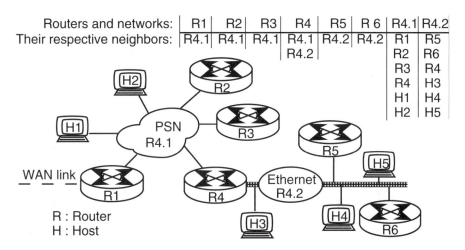

Routers and networks:	R1	R2	R3	R4	R5	R 6	R4.1	R4.2
Their respective neighbors:	R4.1	R4.1	R4.1	R4.1 R4.2	R4.2	R4.2	R1 R2 R3 R4 H1 H2	R5 R6 R4 H3 H4 H5

WAN link

R : Router
H : Host

Figure 18.11 Establishing neighbors in a multi-access network.

Interconnecting LANs

Now, if R1 receives an LSA from its WAN link, which must be forwarded to all the routers in the switched network, then the R1 will multicast this LSA to the DR and the BDR. The DR will then multicast it for R1 to R1 through R3 and wait for an explicit acknowledgment of that LSA. For a router which doesn't provide an acknowledgment, R4 will retransmit the LSA, using the data link layer.

OSPF Areas: When more and more routers are added to an internet, routing traffic between routers can increase sharply, consuming a large amount of bandwidth on the network. Regardless of the algorithm chosen, it eventually becomes necessary to divide up the internet into smaller internets, called areas. Then a copy of the routing protocol can run independently in all areas and much of the routing traffic can be localized within the areas.

All routers in one given area maintain their own database. If a change occurs, that change is propagated to all routers only in that area. This restricts the flooding of LSAs only to the area of concern, reducing the interarea traffic. This is the description of level 1 areas.

However, to provide access to routers outside of level 1 areas, a level 2 area is used to interconnect them. Figure 18.12 shows a level 2 area (actually, called a backbone area) that is used to interconnect two level 1 areas, hierarchically. Although each of these routers may run the OSPF protocol, they can be classified into 4 types of routers. The figure shows the kinds of routers each router is.

An internal router has no direct connection to any other area, except for its own area (R2, R5, R6, R8, R9, and R10). A backbone router is a router with an interface to the backbone (R1 through R4, and R7). An area border router is a type of a backbone

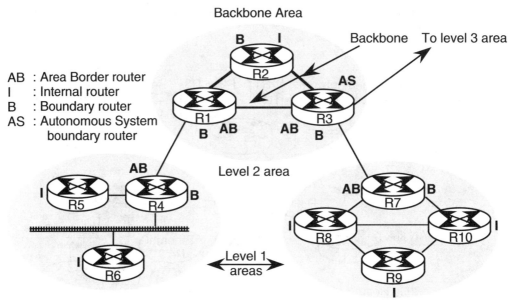

Figure 18.12 Types of OSPF routers.

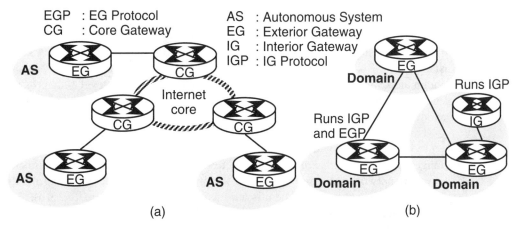

Figure 18.13 (a) Traditionally, when the ASs were connected to the core, the Internet was structured hierarchically. (b) Currently, the ASs are also called domains, which access each other directly.

router which is connected to at least two areas (R1, R3, R4, and R7). And finally, an AS (Autonomous System) boundary router is one which attaches to other higher level areas called ASs. ASs will be covered shortly.

IS-IS: OSPF was actually derived from IS-IS and so the two are very similar to each other. An IS is OSI's cool way of referring to a router whereas an ES (End System) refers to an end host node. While OSPF only routes the IP protocol, because it is encapsulated in IP datagrams, IS-IS routes all routable protocols. It was designed by researchers at DEC headed by Radia Perlman for OSI's CLNP (ConnectionLess Network Protocol).

If an area is partitioned, say because of a loss of a critical link, IS-IS can automatically repair it using a virtual link, whereas with OSPF, a virtual link must be manually configured. With IS-IS, every link has separate passwords to transmit and receive for authenticating packets, but with OSPF only one password is used. Because OSPF routes only IP datagrams, it is optimized for routing, while IS-IS is optimized on minimizing storage and processing requirements. In any case, choosing a routing protocol involves making tradeoffs on such issues. Lastly, IS-IS can be used for inter-AS and intra-AS routing, but OSPF can only be used for intra-AS routing.

18.3.4 Autonomous Systems and BGP

Back in the early days of the Internet, ARPANET served as the backbone network over which long-haul traffic was transported. The backbone network was called the Internet core and its routers were called the core gateways. Hierarchically attached to these core gateways were other routers called external gateways. External gateways were the entry points into other network areas called ASs (Autonomous Systems). See Figure 18.13(a).

Since an AS is a large collection of networks and routers which is administered by a single authority, such as a university, it is typically maintained and paid for by one entity. It tries to shield itself from routing problems which may occur in other ASs. One must apply to the NIC (Network Information Center) of DDN (Defense Data Network) to obtain an AS number. Within an AS, there may be level 2 and level 1 areas as were discussed in the section on OSPF. In that case, the routing between ASs can be thought of as level 3 routing.

Traditionally, inter-AS routing was done via the core. But as the Internet grew, the core became too crowded and hard to manage. Now, the core as we once knew it no longer exists. The ASs are being connected directly to each other making this high layer of the network topology flat, rather than hierarchical. Although the term AS is still used, the correct term for them is a domain, as shown in Figure 18.13(b).

The routers used to exchange traffic between domains are called inter-domain routers (or gateways). They use a family of routing protocols called inter-domain routing protocols or EGPs (Exterior Gateway Protocols) for short. The protocols used within a domain are called intra-domain routing protocols or IGPs (Interior Gateway Protocols). RIP and OSPF are examples of IGPs.

Examples of EGPs include BGP (Border Gateway Protocol) and a protocol which is itself called EGP. EGP, therefore, may either refer to a set of inter-domain protocols or it may refer to a protocol named EGP.

BGP is a distance vector algorithm. With it, all the exterior gateways between two adjacent domains are joined using a fully connected mesh topology. They use TCP (Transmission Control Protocol) to send reliable messages between each other. BGP provides a more powerful method of authentication of packets than does OSPF. This in fact is better, since the method of maintaining security on each network can be kept confidential.

BGP uses source routing in a sense that the routing information block, when being transmitted, lists the AS numbers in its routing path. All messages have a 16 byte field called the marker in its header. It is reserved for authentication, possibly employing a mechanism for digitizing signatures. BGP uses the OPEN, UPDATE, NOTIFICATION, and KEEPALIVE messages.

The OPEN message is used when two routers are first connected. Besides for the header's marker used for authentication, this message itself has another 13 bytes reserved for future implementation of an authentication scheme. It also provides the AS number and specifies the hold time. This is the time interval in which the receiver should be expecting to get messages from its neighboring gateway. When a router has no messages to send, it will send a KEEPALIVE message which only contains a 19 byte BGP message header. This will prevent the connecting router from timing out the transmitting router.

The UPDATE message is used to transfer routing information. It specifies whether this information comes from the interior gateway protocol or if it was learned from BGP or by some other means. Along with other attributes, it also specifies the AS_Path and the address of the next router in the path. Finally, when one router wants to terminate a connection with its neighbor, it will send a NOTIFICATION message providing the reason for it.

18.4 ROUTER CONFIGURATION

Let us now change our emphasis from algorithms and protocols to setting up a router in real life. Let us outline the configuration of a Cisco M-Chassis type router with two ports. This is by no means a training tutorial, but only an overview of some of the tasks that are done in configuring a typical router. Again, we will discuss one specific product to make the explanation meaningful. The reader should be warned that using a Cisco router doesn't imply that other routers are inferior. In fact, each vendor has its own unique set of features and services that one must carefully evaluate before forming an opinion. Here it is assumed that illustrating how one specific product operates makes learning products from other vendors much easier.

This router with its two ports will connect an existing, isolated Ethernet LAN to the Internet. So, for its installation, we need two Internet addresses (one for each port) from our network administrator. First, we will configure it on the bench connecting an ASCII terminal to its terminal port and nothing connected to its Ethernet ports. Then we will take it to the site and install the two Ethernet connections and power it up, after which it will run Cisco's proprietary IGRP routing protocol and if everything goes well, we won't need to do anything else to it.

This router has two Ethernet interfaces on its back panel, which are connected to the Ethernet board inside it. The router has to also come with a processor board. The processor board will typically have a jumper at pin pair 9 and if the router is going to be booted up locally, there should also be a jumper on pin pair 1. If the booting is done off the network, then pin pair 3 should be jumped instead (for a CSC3 processor card). There are dip switches on the Ethernet board, which have to be set according to the slot position the board will go in the chassis. Let's turn on the box!

The connected terminal will display:

```
CSC3 (68020) processor with 4096k bytes of memory.
1 MCI controller (2 Ethernet, 0 Serial)
2 Ethernet/IEEE 802.3 interface
32k Bytes of non-volatile configuration memory
4096k bytes of flash memory on MC+ card (via MCI)
```

This information shows that the box (or the router) uses the Motorola 68020 microprocessor with 4 kbytes of RAM. It supports two Ethernet interfaces. It also has 32 kbytes of non-volatile memory and 4 kbytes of flash EPROM memory. Flash EPROMs can be programmed while they are in the box, without having to be removed.

Then it will ask:

```
Would you like to enter the initial configuration dialogue?
[yes]:no
```

The default setting is shown in brackets; we chose "no" at this time. Then a prompt with the router's name for user access appears. User access is shown by ">." And typing "enable" gives us a privileged access, shown by "#." This can be password protected at a later time. Then we type "setup" and we can go through the configuration dialogue as shown below.

Interconnecting LANs   **407**

```
Router>enable
Router#setup

Configuring global parameters:

Enter host name: matchbox
Enter enable password: matchhead
Enter virtual terminal password: matchstick
Configure SNMP Network Management? [yes]: no
Configure IP? [yes]:
    Configure IGRP routing? [yes]:
        Your IGRP autonomous system number [1]:
Configure DECnet? [no]:
Configure XNS? [no]:
Configure Novell? [no]: yes
Configure AppleTalk? [no]: yes
  Multizone network? [yes]:
Configure CLNS? [no]:
Configure Vines? [no]:
Configure bridging? [no]:

Configuring interface parameters:

Configuring interface Ethernet0:
    Is this interface in use? [yes]:
    Configure IP at this interface? [yes]:
        IP address for this interface: 128.6.1.1
        Number of bits in subnet field [0]: 8
        Class B network is 128.6.0.0, 8 subnet bits;
            mask is 255.255.255.0
    Configure Novell on this interface? [yes]:
        Novell network number [1]:
    Configure AppleTalk on this interface? [yes]:
        Extended AppleTalk network? [yes]:
```

The setting of global parameters determines which protocols we will be prompted for as we set up each interface. For example, since Novell was set to "yes" in the global settings, we were asked about it while setting up Ethernet interface 0. The meaning of IP addresses and masks will be covered in Chapter 19. In the same fashion as this interface is set up, Ethernet interface 1 will also be set up. At the end of the dialogue session, we will be asked the following:

```
Use this configuration? [yes/no]: yes
```

Now this image is stored in the non-volatile EPROM. It is stored as a command script, which will be used every time the box boots up. Of course, it can be changed. These parameter names and their settings as they were generated in the setup dialogue are stored in a file called the command script file. This script can be viewed by simply typing:

```
matchbox#write terminal
```

Notice that the prompt shows the router's name as it was given during the setup dialogue. If we type the following, we will be shown information about what has transpired on that particular interface:

```
matchbox#show interface ethernet 0
Ethernet 0 is administratively down, line protocol is down
    Hardware is MCI Ethernet, address is 0000.0c03.e1f8
    MTU 1500 bytes, BW 10000 kbit, DLY 1000 usec, rely 255/255,
      load 1/255
    Encapsulation ARPA, loopback not set, keepalive set (10sec)
    ARP type: ARPA, ARP timeout 4:00:00
    Last input never, output 0:27:17, output hang never
    Last clearing of "show interface" counters never
    Output queue 0/40, 0 drops, input queue 0/75, 0 drops
    Five minute input rate 0 bits/sec, 0 packets/sec
    Five minute output rate 0 bits/sec,
        0 packets/sec 0 packets input, 0 bytes, 0 no buffer
        Received 0 broadcasts, 0 runts, 0 giants
        0 input errors, 0 CRC, 0 frame, 0 overrun, 0 ignored,
          0 abort
        26 packets output, 5193 bytes, 0 underruns
        0 output errors, 0 collisions, 1 interface reset,
          0 restarts
```

Notice that this interface is down. Its MAC address is 0000.0c03.e1f8. This hardware address can be stored on a network server which can map its MAC address with the IP address using ARP (Address Resolution Protocol). The last input field indicates the time when data was last received into this interface and the last output indicates when data was last transmitted. These are useful when debugging a problem. Other fields provide other data pertaining to the activity over this interface.

If we type configure, we can bring up this interface as shown here.

```
matchbox#configure
Configure from terminal, memory, or network? [terminal]:
Enter configuration commands, one per line.
Edit with DELETE, CTRL/W, and CTRL/U; end with CTRL/Z
interface ethernet 0
no shutdown^Z

matchbox#
```

Now, if we type "show interface ethernet 0," we will see that Ethernet 0 is not administratively down and that the line protocol is up. This is because we did a "no shutdown." The configure command changes settings in the RAM, but not for booting up purposes. If booting up is to be done from the non-volatile memory, then typing "write memory" will save those changes there.

Basically, we are finished. Now we can connect the box at the site and hope it flies. If problems occur, then from our shop we can telnet to the box and log onto it as if we were there physically and perform the tasks similar to the ones we have just described.

18.5 FAST PACKET TECHNOLOGIES

At the time of this writing, there is a high demand for services which interconnect LANs over wide areas. This demand is currently being met by FR (Frame Relay) and SMDS (Switched Multi-megabit Data Services), and soon it is expected to be met by ATM (Asynchronous Transfer Mode). ATM will not only provide LAN interconnection, but also provide transmission of isochronous traffic. Isochronous traffic, such as voice or multimedia, requires the digitized packets to arrive at the destination with minimum latency (or delay). We don't mind if the next packet of data comes a little late, but we can't afford the next syllable in a voice conversation to arrive late. Since the market for these technologies is currently being driven by users needing to interconnect LANs, these topics are covered here.

Typically, these technologies are called fast packet technologies, because they are designed more for transmitting data fast, rather than for transmitting data with error correction or any other feature. FR uses frames while SMDS and ATM use 53-octet cells to transmit data. Generally speaking, frames are variable length PDUs (Protocol Data Units) while cells' sizes are fixed.

Furthermore, FR and ATM are connection-oriented technologies that are suited for PVCs (Permanent Virtual Circuits). With a PVC, the connection is available at all times and with an SVC (Switched Virtual Circuit) it has to be established. An SVC can be set up using ISDN's D signaling channel, before data can be transmitted.

SMDS is a connectionless service that is more suitable for SVCs. It defines a complete set of services such as quality, billing, operations, and management. It can operate at DS-3 speeds and higher and requires new and sophisticated equipment for its implementation. To convert a network to FR, very often one only has to load a new release of software on the existing equipment. This is a drastic savings in cost to upgrade a network to handle LAN traffic. Maybe it is for that reason that FR was introduced one year and became widely implemented the next, unlike ISDN.

Initially, FR was perceived to be implemented in private networks, but later, it became a public network offering. SMDS, developed by Bellcore, has always been a service offered by the BOCs and unlike FR it has only one set of standards defined by Bellcore. Currently, public FR is a WAN service while SMDS is a MAN service limited to a LATA. Soon they should both be WAN offerings. SMDS is based on cell switching which makes it a preferred candidate to migrate to ATM with.

FR is based on HDLC which originally ran on low-speed networks. Although it could run at DS-3 speeds, no proposals have currently been made for that. Yet it suffices most of the existing network needs which operate at DS-1 speeds. Let us now turn our attention to each of the individual technologies.

18.6 FRAME RELAY

18.6.1 Advantages of FR over T1s

A network which is used to interconnect LANs must be able to handle very bursty traffic. This is because LAN traffic is usually sent at irregular intervals and runs at speeds from 4 Mbps to 100 Mbps. This is not suited for traditional T1 technology which was originally designed to carry voice, which is more predictable. Additionally, T1 networks are too difficult to reconfigure if certain applications require a sudden increase in bandwidth.

For instance, in Figure 18.14(a), we have three sites which are interconnected by a T1 network. If a router needs to be able to communicate with three other routers on the network, then we would need three connections between it and its mux. If the router is not local to the mux, then the cost of these connections would increase. In any case, we would need three ports on the mux dedicated for the router.

The bandwidth allocated for each port of a mux would then be preset. If a router had a burst of traffic to fire into the network, while the channels for the front ends and the PDNs were idle, it could not, since each port had its bandwidth already preallocated.

Figure 18.14(b) shows the private T1 network being converted into a private FR network. Here, the bandwidth can be reassigned instantaneously (or dynamically allocated) depending on which system demands it. Also, each device may communicate with any other, requiring only one port. In Figure 18.14(c), we go to public FR networks. Maybe we would have to install FRADs (FR Assembler/Disassembler), which are similar to PADs used in X.25 networks. They allow equipment (currently, that includes most of it) that is not FR compatible to be used in such networks.

Here, the added benefits are such that we don't have to pay for the dedicated T1 leased lines. We just pay for the service as we use it, as in virtual networks. Additionally, installing a new site with a T1 network requires that the network be redesigned, whereas using public FR, one simply needs to install a new access link. As with PDNs, the pricing for FR networks are not milage sensitive.

18.6.2 Advantages over X.25

FR technology originally was developed through CCITT's ISDN and X.25 standards. Although these standards were designed for 64 kbps circuits using SVC networks, a group of four equipment manufacturers (Cisco, DEC, NT, and StrataCom), so to speak, increased the speed dial to DS-1 rates and simplified the protocol to handle only PVCs. This protocol was named LMI (Local Management Interface). Currently, FR is both an ANSI and CCITT standard.

Back in the days when X.25 was introduced, many analog lines had an error rate of 10^{-2} (1/100) or 1 error in every 100 bits that were transmitted. Then it was appropriate to check for errors at layers 2 and 3 on links between every node pair along the transmission path. It was better to detect and correct errors as soon as they occurred, rather than forwarding them to the next node.

Today, with more fiber being installed in our networks, this amount of error checking becomes an overkill, where error rates of 10^{-15} are achievable. Why check for errors every second when the possibility for one to occur exists only once a week! There is no need to burden the network and make it less efficient by requiring it to check for nonexisting errors.

FR, therefore, was conceived as a stripped down version of X.25, without its overhead. The network layer has been eliminated and error checking is left up to the end nodes and not to this transmission protocol. The lack of error control in FR is what gives it its advantage—efficient and faster transmission. An FR switch is up to ten times as fast as a packet switch. This savings in time is multiplied by the number of switches along a path. Furthermore, a packet switch uses store and forward methods

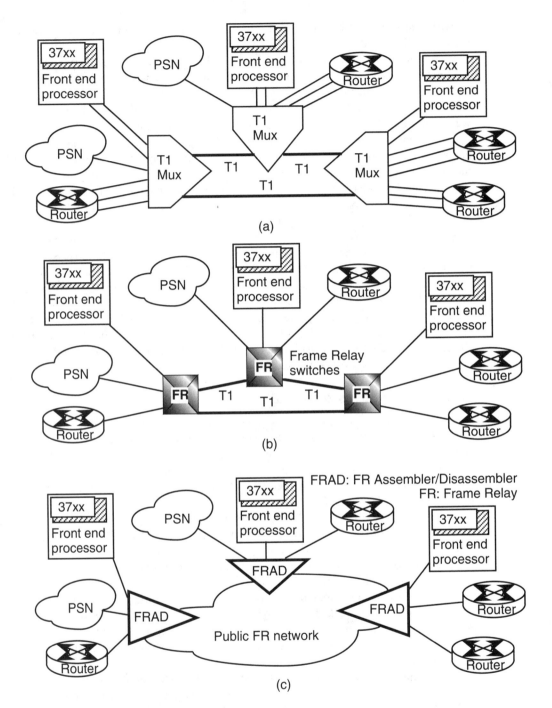

Figure 18.14 (a) A T1 based network. (b) Converting to a private FR network. (c) Or converting to a public FR network.

Interconnecting LANs

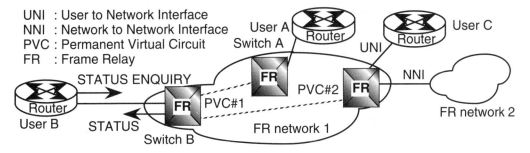

Figure 18.15 An FR network can establish multiple PVCs simultaneously.

which typically are configured with small frame-window sizes. This requires it not to send the next set of packets until the current ones are acknowledged. This type of bottleneck doesn't exist in FR, although, as we will see later, it introduces problems in controlling congestion.

18.6.3 PVCs

When a user subscribes to PVCs in a public FR network, there are access lines to each of the user's end nodes. See Figure 18.15. Notice, the connections to multiple destinations can be achieved over a single access line. The maximum burst rate cannot exceed the rate of the access lines, although, typically, the rate of transfer is less than the access line rate. PVCs are like "nailed up" circuits, similar to leased lines, but cost less, since the traffic from all users is statistically multiplexed over the network.

The interface between the user and the network is called the UNI (User to Network Interface) and between two FR networks is called the NNI (Network to Network Interface).

Over the access line, the end user node polls the network every 30 seconds by sending STATUS ENQUIRY messages. This is called a heartbeat poll. The network responds by sending STATUS messages back to the user. These messages specify which virtual circuits are new or being disconnected, and so on. The absence of receiving either of these messages means that the link is down.

18.6.4 Frame Format

Figure 18.16 outlines the format for an FR frame. FR does not use the third layer, but only the first two. The nice thing about this frame is that virtually any kind of protocol can be encapsulated in it, such as SNA, DECNET, X.25, etc. Like SDLC (and HDLC), the frame begins and ends with a flag and contains an FCS field. The FCS could be used by FR switches to discard, without notification, any frames that come damaged. The fields in the second and third octet are similar to the fields used in ISDN; see Figure 15.15.

The DLCI is like an LCI used in the third layer of X.25, which allows for routing of frames. It is only 10 bits, giving a total of 1,024 channels. There are other variants

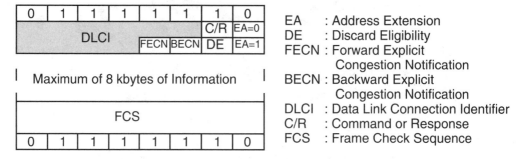

Figure 18.16 The frame format for FR using a 2-octet header.

of this frame which allow for more DLCIs. The FECN (Forward Explicit Congestion Notification), BECN (Backward Explicit Congestion Notification), and DE (Discard Eligibility) bits are the topic of the next section.

18.6.5 Congestion Control

Previously, we said that since FR was not limited by window sizes used in X.25, it allowed for faster relaying of frames through the network. However, removing the windowing mechanism also removes a network's ability to have data flow control. That is, FR switches cannot signal the transmitter to throttle back or slow down its transmission, because the network is getting congested. This is a major concern in FR networks. Let us now consider methods of controlling congestion.

One way this is done is by using the FECN and BECN bits. If, for example, the network in Figure 18.15 experiences congestion, partly due to user B transmitting a lot of data to user A, then the network switch B will set the BECN bit for frames going to B, hoping that user B will slow down its transmission. Likewise, the network switch A will set the FECN bit for the frames going to user A, hoping that it will request less data from B. Notice, here, that the end devices are not obligated to respond to these bits, and if the network cannot handle the traffic load it will simply start discarding some frames.

Ironically, if the routers at the end points do want to help the public FR network from getting congested, it has no method of notifying the LAN applications to stop transmitting momentarily. Additionally, when frames are discarded due to congestion, LAN applications typically retransmit more frames, adding to the problem.

On the other hand, when the network discards data, the intelligent end devices may assume that the data is being lost due to congestion and may stop transmitting momentarily. This is called implicit congestion detection, since the end nodes are not directly notified of the problem.

If an end node transmits frames which it doesn't mind losing, such as routing updates, then it can set the DE bit for such frames. The frames with their DE bits set will be transmitted if possible; otherwise, they will be the first ones to be discarded.

CIR: To deal with this problem, carriers are selling their services to users by amounts of CIR (Committed Information Rate). CIR is the amount of bandwidth the carrier guarantees to the user. As long as the user does not exceed this rate over a PVC, it will send the data. If the user exceeds that rate temporarily, the carrier will send the data if it can; otherwise, it will first discard the frames which have their DE bits set, and if congestion persists, it will then start discarding other frames as well. A carrier may buffer the frames and delay the transmission instead of discarding them.

To prevent one user from abusing the public FR network and thus forcing "good" customers to lose data, a mechanism called the CMB (Credit Manager Bandwidth) can be used in the switches. This algorithm assigns a buffer at the switch to each PVC and users can fill those buffers at any rate they wish. However, the carrier will transmit data from those buffers over the network depending on their CIRs and the availability of network bandwidth. Now, if a customer sends much more data than what he/she paid for the CIR, only his/her data will be lost and not the data of others. This congestion avoidance system introduces fairness to the public network.

18.7 SMDS

18.7.1 Network Interfaces

Unlike FR, SMDS is connectionless. This allows anyone to instantaneously send a burst of data to anyone else on the SMDS network, without first setting up a connection. However, the interconnection and troubleshooting of SMDS networks between the LECs and the IXCs can be difficult.

Specifications for SMDS were derived from ATM and IEEE's 802.6 MAN standards. 802.6 basically defines four items: segmentation and reassembly of frames, DQDB (Distributed Queue Dual Bus), connection-oriented mode, and guaranteeing cell delivery times for isochronous traffic. Although 802.6 allows for transmission of voice and video, as its name implies, SMDS is inherently designed for the transmission of data. However, as mentioned earlier, SMDS defines a full set of services, not only a data transport protocol.

DQDB originally was developed by an Australian firm called QPSX Communications. It uses a much more robust algorithm than FDDI, which allows a fair access of the network by all network nodes. It is also designed for isochronous traffic. SMDS uses DQDB over the interface between the CPE (Customer Premises Equipment) and the SS (SMDS Switching System). This interface is called SNI (Subscriber Network Interface). See Figure 18.17.

Additionally, the interface between SSs within a LATA is called ISSI (Inter-Switching System Interface) and between an LEC and IXC is called ICI (Inter-Carrier Interface). Typically, the CPE in the figure would be an SMDS compatible unit which interfaces with the existing equipment, such as routers. This interface is called DXI (Data eXchange Interface). Due to the high amount of overhead used in SMDS, if the access link to the SS is a T1, the data rate over the DXI is limited to 1.179 Mbps instead of 1.536 Mbps.

18.7.2 PDU Structures

SMDS uses three levels called SIP 1, 2, and 3. SIP is the acronym for SMDS Interface Protocol. The format of the frame over the DXI interface is shown toward the

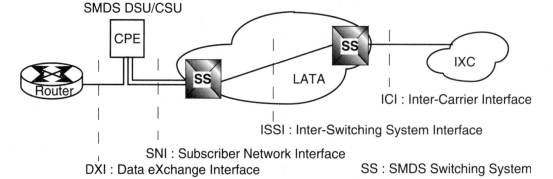

Figure 18.17 The various interfaces defined in an SMDS network.

top of Figure 18.18. The user may send up to 9,188 bytes of data, which is sufficient for LAN frames. The CPE, upon receiving a DXI frame, would extract the data and enclose it in an SIP level 3 PDU (Protocol Data Unit). The header for this PDU is 36 bytes and the trailer is 4 bytes. The CPE would then segment this level 3 PDU into 53-octet level 2 PDUs, before sending them over the access link. The level 2 PDUs are compatible with the 53-octet ATM cells.

In the figure, not all fields are shown. For a given SIP level 3 PDU, the Btag (Beginning Tag) and the Etag (End tag) values are made the same. The address fields are 8 bytes long and their format, similar to the format of telephone numbers, is shown in the figure. After the multicast and country code nibbles (4 bits), there are 10 nibbles used for the address. Each nibble encodes a decimal number using the BCD (Binary Coded Decimal) method. The last four nibbles are always set to 1s.

Notice, SMDS is just like LANs, which are connectionless and carry all the addressing information in their frames. And just like LANs, it allows a frame to be sent to multiple locations using the multicast field.

The level 2 protocol segments the level 3 PDUs into 44 byte chunks and adds its own 7-byte header and a 2-byte trailer. 5 bytes of the header correspond to the ATM header. Four of these bytes are set to a hex "FFFFF022," which corresponds to connectionlessness in an ATM header. Multiple level 3 PDUs can be segmented simultaneously, so each of them is assigned an MID (Message IDentifier). Therefore, all the level 2 PDUs segmented from the same level 3 PDU have the same MID and the segment type field specifies whether it is the first segment (BOM), the last segment (EOM), or an in-between segment (COM). These terms stand for Beginning, End, and Continuation of Message, respectively.

The sequence number field numbers these segments in order. If a level 2 PDU has less than 44 bytes of information, the length field is used to specify how much. Lastly, the CRC field is used to check for errors in the SMDS switches. If an error occurs in one of the cells, it will simply be discarded it and leave it to the upper layer protocols at the end nodes to detect and resolve the problem.

Cells are continuously transmitted whether data is present or not. In the cell's header's first byte, there is a bit that is called the busy bit. If the cell has data, then that

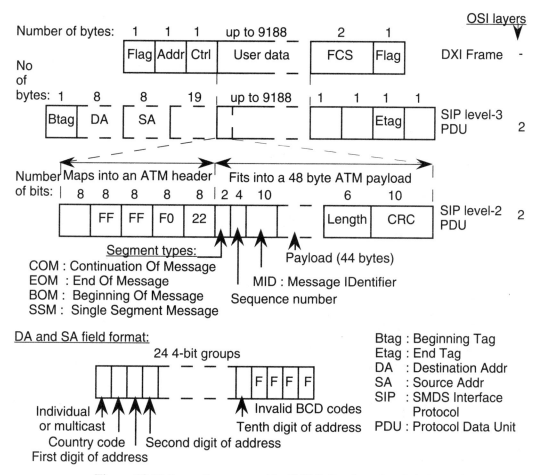

Figure 18.18 Frame formats used in SMDS. For the sake of clarity, only certain fields are shown.

bit is set and if it is idle, it is not. Let us next look at an example of these various fields as they are used.

18.7.3 Example of Segmentation

Figure 18.19 has two level 3 PDUs of length 60 and 40 bytes to be fired into the SMDS network. First, each of them is assigned a Btag and an Etag as shown in the top of the figure.

In level 2, let us say that the first level 3 PDU is assigned an MID of 41 and the second one is assigned an MID of 22. The first message is segmented into 3 cells and they all have a MID of 41. Their sequence numbers are 0, 1, and 2. Also, note that the first cell is set to BOM, second to COM, and the last one to EOM.

The first cell's payload contains 36 bytes of level 3 header and the first 8 bytes of data. The second cell's payload only carries 44 bytes of data and the remaining 8

Interconnecting LANs

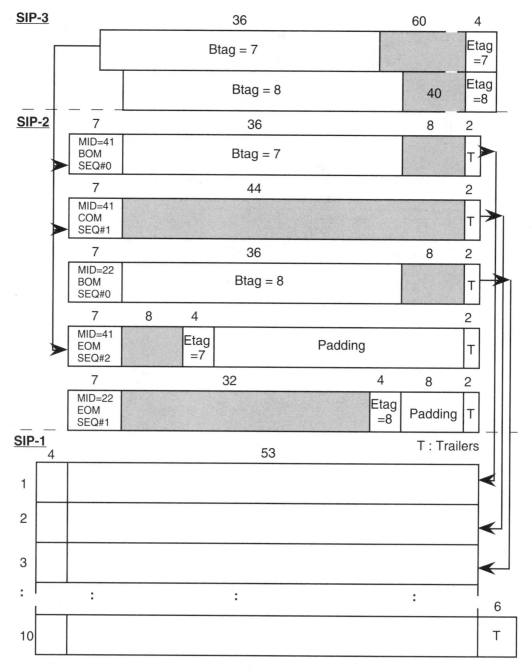

Figure 18.19 Two SIP level 3 PDUs are segmented into octets, which are leaved in an SIP level 1 frame. Information fields are shaded and the diagram is drawn to scale. Field lengths are shown in octets.

bytes of data and 4 bytes of level 3 trailer are loaded in the last cell. 32 bytes of this last cell are unused and the length field in that cell will denote it.

18.7.4 PLCP

Depending on how segmentation occurs for the two level 3 PDUs, the cells from each one could be interleaved as shown in Figure 18.19. When they are sent over a physical medium, they are processed by the PLCP (Physical Layer Convergence Protocol) for that medium. The figure shows how this protocol places 10 cells in an ESF frame for transmission over a T1 link.

From Chapter 10, you may recall that an ESF frame is 24 by 193 bits long. With the first bit of every 193rd bit used for framing, we are left with 24 by 192 bits or 4608 bits for data.

SMDS's PLCP frame for DS1 carries ten 53-octet cells, each with a 4 octet overhead. Among other things, these octets are used for framing and path overhead. In a PLCP frame, each cell requires 57 octets for its transmission. The frame also contains a 6 octet trailer. Together, they amount to 576 (or 57 times 10, plus 6) octets or 4608 bits (576 times 8).

This fits nicely in an ESF frame. In a PLCP frame, if all 10 cells contain 44 octets of data (this amounts to 44 times 8 or 352 bits per cell), then it can carry a total of 3520 (or 352 times 10) bits of data. 3520 bits of data capacity divided by 4608 bits needed total, including overhead, gives the ratio of 0.76. That is, 76.4% of T1 bits can be used to transport actual data. If we multiply this ratio by T1's data rate of 1.536 Mbps, we get the 1.179 Mbps rate specified over the DXI interface. This is the maximum data rate one can transmit over a T1 access link. Other PLCPs are also defined for DS-3 and higher rates.

18.8 ATM

18.8.1 Why Yet Another Protocol?

Let us now turn our attention to ATM (Asynchronous Transfer Mode), by first contrasting it with existing technologies. In Figure 18.20, let us suppose that we have a voice source and a data source, which are contesting for a fixed amount of bandwidth on the transmission link. At t = 0, or time frame 0, we have voice traffic that needs to be transmitted. This amount of traffic is labeled as V1, but at the same time, we have a burst of data coming in that is three times the amount as V1. Hence, each of these data units are labeled D1 through D3.

The height of these units represent the rate of transfer, say, in bits per second and the width represents time. Hence, multiplying the rate times the time (or height times the length) represents the amount of data (bits) that has to be sent over the communication channel. This example shows voice being transmitted at t = 0, 2, and 5, while data is being transmitted at t = 0, 1, and 4. The amount of data sent at t = 4 is twice that of what is sent by voice at t = 0, 2, or 5.

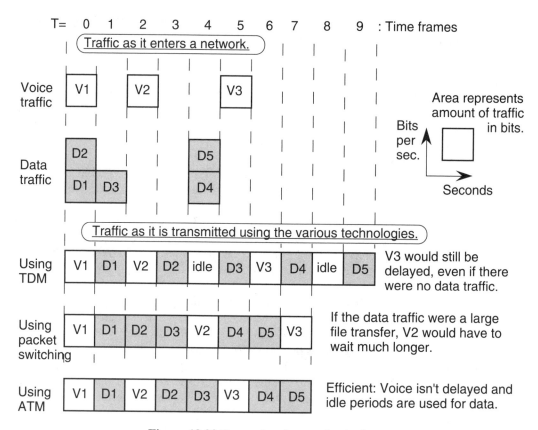

Figure 18.20 Comparing three technologies.

If we were using TDM (Time Division Multiplexing) technology to transmit this mix of traffic as is done in T1 multiplexers, then each source would have to occupy its assigned time slot in the frames that are transmitted. In this example, the voice channel is assigned the even time slots and the data channel is assigned the odd time slots.

If we follow this example to t = 4, where we don't have voice traffic, but have data traffic, we cannot place the data traffic at that slot. That slot belongs to the voice channel and so it gets wasted. The receiver is synchronized to interpret all even time slots as belonging to the voice channel and the odd ones to the data channel, so we can't use a time slot for the wrong channel.

Now, when voice is being sent at t = 5, we cannot send it, because that channel belongs to data. Instead, that voice traffic has to be delayed to t = 6. For the rest of the time frames, we see that the data also has to be delayed to t = 9, even though there was bandwidth capacity at t = 8.

Here, there are two time frames wasted. If the voice channel were idle, then all 5 time frames for it would be wasted. This is not only an inefficient use of bandwidth, but it delays the transmission of data, although delaying of data is not as crucial as delaying isochronous traffic.

Let us see the advantages of packet switching over TDM. Here, instead of alternating between the two sources, we send each transmission as one unit rather than break them up into time frames. V1 is sent first, then D1 through D3 as one unit. Because of this data packet, V2 doesn't get out until t = 4. Similarly, V3 is delayed two time frames for the same reason.

Packet switching technologies, such as X.25 and FR, make an efficient use of bandwidth. In the example, all data is transmitted 3 time frames earlier than it was with TDM. However, the voice traffic was delayed by 4 time frames (2 for V2 and 2 for V3), while with TDM, the voice was delayed by only 1 time frame. If the data transmission at t = 0 were a long file transfer, then V2 would have to wait a substantial amount. We can't afford to delay voice as we can data. Hence, TDM favors voice and packet switching favors transmission of data. So if only data needs to be transmitted, FR offers a good solution.

With ATM, all traffic is broken into 53 octet cells; 5 for the header and 48 for information. At t = 2, although data has been waiting longer to be transmitted, this voice cell gets transmitted first. The same advantage of packet switching over TDM is achieved with ATM. It makes an efficient use of the bandwidth. They both finish transmitting before t = 8, with no wasted time frames. However, the advantage of ATM over packet switching is that the delay for voice is zero (versus 4). In fact, ATM proved to be even better than TDM here, because the delay for voice with TDM was one time frame. Notice, that although ATM transmits data at a constant rate, it adapts to applications which are transmitting at varying rates.

With TDM, we know the destination of information by its time frame position. But with ATM, we need a header or label which gives the cell's destination. Hence, ATM is said to be a form of label multiplexing.

What is asynchronous about ATM? In Figure 18.20, the delay between D1 and D2 is one time frame, but between D2 and D3 there is no delay. The rate at which information is fed into the ATM network is not necessarily the same as the rate at which it comes out of the network. Hence it is called asynchronous. One can not determine when the next data cell is going to arrive. Likewise, with start and stop bits used in asynchronous transmission, the receiver doesn't know when the next character is going to arrive, or rather, the next start bit.

Contrast this with TDM, which really should be thought of as STM (Synchronous Transmission Mode). There the interval between each transmission of data is known. It is fixed.

Terminology gets confusing though, when we think that STM is transmitted using asynchronous multiplexing and ATM is transmitted using synchronous multiplexing (or SONET). STM requires bit stuffing due to the input signals being timed from different sources. Each input channel is not synchronized to a common clock, while SONET requires all inputs to be synchronized to a common clock.

18.8.2 Other Benefits

Conforms to Application: Probably the most important benefit of ATM is that one network can serve all applications. As we have seen, isochronous traffic can be transmitted quickly at the same as time large file transfers can be made without wasting any bandwidth. However, ATM goes beyond that. It can transmit channels at any rate effectively and not force the application to conform to the network's constraints.

For example, to transmit a 50 kbps channel over a T1 facility, one normally has to dedicate a full DS0 channel, wasting 14 kbps. Similarly, if one has to transmit at 10 Mbps, one has to play with inverse multiplexers and use 7 T1s and still have 0.7 Mbps of bandwidth left over. Additionally, these networks have to provisioned before hand.

On the contrary, ATM gives the amount of bandwidth that is required during connect time. ATM doesn't force the application to accept BW in given increments. It doesn't force the application to conform to the network as previous technologies did. Instead, ATM conforms to the needs of the network applications.

Freedom to choose the amount of bandwidth is only part of the ATM advantage. It also provides the freedom to switch traffic between different end points as required, without requiring provisioning, such as with DCS switches. Additionally, the user only pays for what is used.

Hardware-based Switching: The fixed cell size enables switching to be performed by simple hardware circuitry, rather than through software. This permits switching to be performed at speeds of gigabits-per-second. The hardware switching capability will allow a smoother migration to optical switches when it becomes available. This almost instantaneous switching capability allows ATM to remove the boundaries of LANs and WANs and make them appear seamless.

Consider a virtual LAN which is defined by software rather than by the stations' hardware addresses. If a worker who is on one LAN is part of a department, and now gets promoted to another department which has its own LAN, then he can be part of that LAN without having to move his office or having to bring the physical LAN cabling into his office. Such managerial changes as moves, adds, and deletes can be done via a console, if physical LANs are part of an ATM switch (or switches).

When additional bandwidth is needed by a LAN one simply adds a new module to the switch or adds another switch, without degrading the performance of the existing LAN. With ATM, one IP (Internet Protocol) subnetwork can be physically located in two or more areas without being restricted by distance.

18.8.3 Cell Format

Originally, the European community, which was primarily interested in moving voice through the ATM network, required that the cell size be not less than 64 bytes. At the same time, the North Americans who were primarily interested in transporting LAN traffic, required that the cell size not be greater than 32 bytes. This is because voice traffic adopts better to larger cells while data adopts better to smaller sized cells.

The final decision was to compromise and make the information portion of the cell 48 bytes. Adding 5 bytes for a header, the final size became 53 bytes. There is no trailer. See Figure 18.21.

The first field is 4 bits long and is called GFC (Generic Flow Control). It is only used between the user and the network over the UNI (User to Network Interface). Once the cell is in the network, the VPI can be extended to include these 4 bits to gain additional virtual channels.

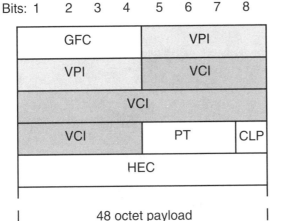

Figure 18.21 The ATM cell format.

The GFC allows for fair access into the public network. When CADs (Computer Aided Devices), multimedia, or medical imaging terminals which require greater amount of bandwidth must share the same access as low-speed data terminals, this field allows all devices to gain an equitable share of the access facility.

ATM is a connection-oriented service like X.25. The connection can be either a PVC (Permanent Virtual Channel) or an SVC (Switched Virtual Channel). The virtual channel is defined by two fields: VPI (Virtual Path Identifier) and VCI (Virtual Channel Identifier). One VPI can bundle up to 2^{16} VCIs. This way, up to 2^{16} channels can be manipulated together as one unit through the network.

Suppose, if a user wants to create a subchannel between the two end points with the carrier, the PT (Payload Type) field makes that possible. Among other services, this field allows a user to verify the quality of service provided by the carrier by creating a management channel.

Similar to the DE (Discard Eligibility) field of FR, the CLP (Cell Loss Priority) field is set by the user for cells which should be discarded first, in the event that there is network congestion.

Notice that the cell has no flag but has an HEC (Header Error Control) field which not only provides a means to establish logical synchronization, but also provides an error check in the header. This field allows ATM to determine the start of a cell. This is done by the receiving ATM device continuously checking sequences of 5 octets to determine which sequence checks out error-free. Once one cell is correctly identified, the rest of the cells must come next to each other without any gaps. If the transmitter has no data to send, then an empty cell is transmitted. Once the beginning of one cell is detected, the start of the remaining cells is easily achieved.

Notice that the cells are not given sequence numbers as is done with level 2 protocols, such as SDLC and LAP/B. This is because cells are transferred through only one physical path and hence must arrive in the same sequence as they were transmitted.

Another reason why ATM can switch cells faster than a packet switch is that its layer 2 protocol has to process the data to check for errors, whereas an ATM switch only checks the first 5 octets and doesn't process the other 48. We should remind ourselves that all these advances in technology are partly due to the large installed base of fiber networks.

18.8.4 Cell Routing

ATM is a connection-oriented network service. Figure 18.22 reviews the terms associated with the various forms of communication. X.25, FR, and ATM are connection-oriented while SMDS, LANs, and datagrams are connectionless. With connectionless service, every PDU being fired into the network contains its destination address.

There are two kinds of connection-oriented network services: physical and virtual. When we make a phone call, the digital switches in the PSTN assign us with certain time slots which are used by the conversation. Using leased lines and physical distribution frames, we can have a wire pair assigned to us for communication.

A virtual connection, on the other hand, is provided to us when channel identifiers assigned from node to node provide us with a physical path. This was covered in Chapter 13. If a logical channel is permanently assigned, then it is called a PVC; if it is assigned as needed, then it is called an SVC.

To illustrate how virtual circuits are handled in ATM, consider Figure 18.23. User A has established a virtual path, specified by a set of VPIs, from Switch 1 to Switch 3. It doesn't matter for the sake of this illustration whether it is a PVC or an SVC being described here. If it is a PVC, the connection is permanently available; otherwise, it will be disconnected shortly. The virtual path is defined in the lookup tables at those three switches. This definition is as follows:

Switch 1 transfers all cells with VPI of 100 from User A to Switch 2 with a VPI of 120.

Switch 2 transfers all cells with VPI of 120 from Switch 1 to Switch 3 with a VPI of 110.

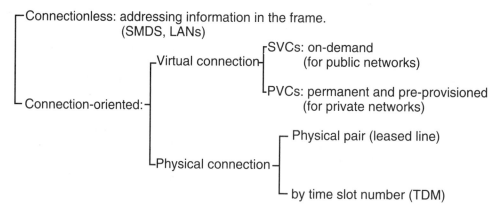

Figure 18.22 Methods of communication.

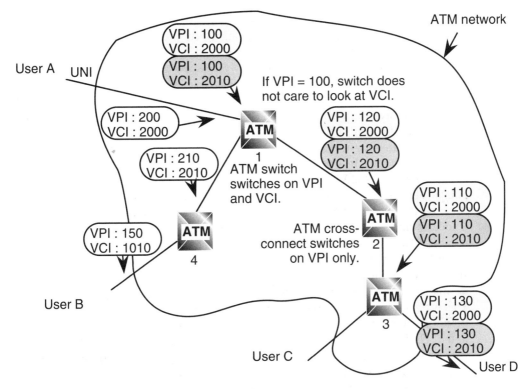

Figure 18.23 All shaded cells belong to one virtual path, which is defined through switches 1, 2, and 3.

Switch 3 transfers all cells with VPI of 110 from Switch 2 to User D with a VPI of 130.

Users A and D, and not the switch, worry about the differences between VCIs. The use of virtual paths are convenient between two locations, if there are many applications running between them. The user's equipment sorts out which cell belongs to which application, while the ATM network only has to process the VPIs. This further increases the speed at which the switches operate. Notice that through a virtual path, the VCI remains unchanged. In the figure, the virtual path shown by the cells which are shaded contain the same VCIs, i.e., VCIs of 2000 and 2010.

For users who require only one channel rather than a group of channels, the ATM switches must also process the VCIs as well. In Figure 18.23, a virtual channel is shown by the unshaded cells going from user A to user B. Switches which can only process on VPIs are called ATM DCSs (Digital Cross-connect Systems) and those which can switch on both VPIs and VCIs are called ATM switches.

18.8.5 A Layered Architecture

ATM's network architecture is shown in Figure 18.24(a). Basically, the architecture is divided into 4 layers which correspond to the first 2 layers of the OSI model.

The physical layer of ATM is concerned about the transmission protocols used over the physical medium. Typically using fiber, these protocols would be either SONET/SDH or DS3. Although ATM has been defined to operate at DS1 rates now, because of DS1's delay in asynchronously multiplexing and 10 to 15% overhead associated with ATM, it is not the recommended choice. FR would be a better choice at that speed. The overhead for ATM is high because in its 53-octet cell, only 48 octets or less can be transferred. At much higher speeds such as those offered by SONET, the high overhead doesn't become an issue.

Above the physical layer, the ATM layer manages the transmission over a link between two nodes. It is not concerned about the end-to-end transmission. The routing of cells using VPI and VCI is a node-to-node issue and doesn't concern the end network points. This layer adds and manages the 5-octet header of the cell.

Next comes the AAL (ATM Adaptation layer). This layer is not a link-to-link (or a node-to-node) process, but unlike the ATM layer, concerns itself with only the end points. ATM provides services to different kinds of applications, whether it be images, video, etc. As its name implies, AAL adapts these varying kinds of applications to the single type of transmission mode provided by ATM. AAL provides the same functions as a PAD (Packet Assembler/Disassembler) does in X.25, but with more flexibility. This is the layer which allows ATM to mix different types of information as shown in Figure 18.20. Since AAL is only implemented at the end points or at the CPEs and not in the ATM network switches, the network switches only have to concern themselves with routing of cells and not have to worry about the type of data carried in its payload.

AAL is divided into CS (Convergence Sublayer) and SAR (Segmentation And Reassembly) sublayers. The SAR sublayer divides the application data stream into cells while transmitting and, while receiving, it reassembles them into a data stream compatible to the application.

To address the different problems associated with various types of applications running over ATM, the CS sublayer specifies the requirements for those applications. These requirements are divided into Class A, B, C, and D as shown in Figure 18.24(b). These classes correspond to 1, 2, 3, and 4 service types.

For example, in an application requiring a connection-oriented service, a variable bit rate transfer and low latency would be classified as a Class B application. Packet video is an example that requires Class B service. In other words, the AAL on the transmitting side would break up the video into cells and require the network to provide Class B service. And when the cells appear at the receiving end, this layer would reassemble them back into video.

SMDS is a Class D application. If we go back to the format of SMDS PDUs shown in Figure 18.18, the SIP level-2 PDU corresponds to a SAR PDU and the SIP level-3 PDU corresponds to the CS PDU.

A fifth class has also been defined which is called SEAL (Simple and Efficient Adaptation Layer). SEAL does not use the headers and trailers used in Class D, but loads all 48 bytes of the cells with information. This class allows many applications to send their information in the order in which they arrive. This allows ATM to operate as if it were an FR network.

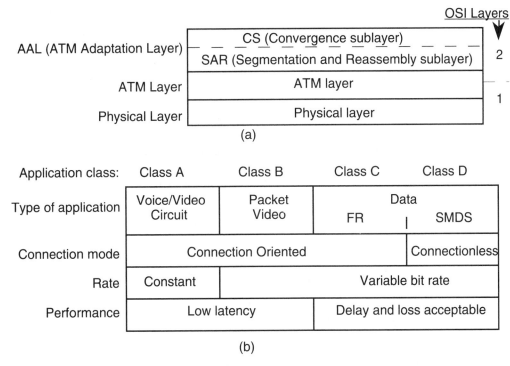

Figure 18.24 (a) Layers of ATM. (b) Classes of services for AAL.

Exercises

1. Which device operates at the physical layer of the OSI model?
   - a. Repeater
   - b. Bridge
   - c. Router
   - d. Gateway

2. Which device doesn't isolate traffic from two segments?
   - a. Repeater
   - b. Bridge
   - c. Router
   - d. Gateway

3. When a frame passes through which device, does the second layer header change?
   - a. Repeater
   - b. Bridge
   - c. Ethernet switch
   - d. Router

4. What disadvantage does collapsing the backbone present?
   - a. poor security
   - b. poor maintenance
   - c. single device dependance
   - d. poor management

5. Which type of a bridged network requires the transmitting node to know the addresses of the bridges along the path?
   a. learning bridge
   b. encapsulating bridge
   c. source routing bridge
   d. translating bridge

6. Which intra-domain routing protocol requires each node to transmit its information about the network to its neighbor?
   a. RIP
   b. OSPF
   c. IS-IS
   d. BGP

7. Which intra-domain routing protocol requires a node to transmit the information about its neighbors to all nodes?
   a. RIP
   b. IS-IS
   c. EGP
   d. BGP

8. Which of the following technologies is connectionless?
   a. FR
   b. SMDS
   c. SONET
   d. ATM

9. Which of the following technologies uses frames instead of cells for transmitting information?
   a. FR
   b. SMDS
   c. SONET
   d. ATM

10. Which of the following technologies was derived from ISDN and X.25?
    a. FR
    b. SMDS
    c. SONET
    d. ATM

11. Which type of a second layered device will convert one frame format to another one?

12. Which type of a second layered device will perform both circuit switching and packet switching?

13. The act of looking through the tables and routing a packet to the correct router is called what?

14. How often does RIP send update messages and in number of hops, what is the largest network diameter possible?

15. In RIP, what is it called when two nodes keep adding the number of hops to a failed destination until they reach 16?

16. Give two examples of link state routing protocols.

17. Which routing protocol uses source routing, in a sense?

18. Before configuring a router, one must obtain which addresses?

19. Name the device which allows non-compatible devices to use an FR network.

20. What type of error detection is done with ATM?

21. What are some advantages of bridges over routers?

22. What are some advantages of routers over bridges?

23. Name the types of bridges covered and describe each using one or two sentences.

24. List the advantages of collapsing the backbone.

25. Describe how the spanning tree algorithm removes loops in a bridged network.

26. What is split horizon?

27. What is the purpose of creating OSPF areas?

28. What are some advantages of FR over SMDS?

29. What are some advantages of SMDS over FR?

30. What are some reasons that ATM has become popular?

Chapter 19

TCP/IP

19.1 TCP/IP ARCHITECTURE

19.1.1 The Beginnings

In 1974, Vinton G. Cerf and Robert E. Kahn proposed a design for a set of protocols in an article published in *IEEE Transactions of Communications*. This set of protocols would be able to internetwork many types of networks, regardless of the network protocols or the vendors of their equipment. The DoD (Department of Defense) had a need to interconnect networks belonging to various organizations, such as NSF (National Science Foundation), NASA, and research and educational institutes. So the DoD through DARPA (Defense Advanced Research Projects Agency) provided funds to BBN (Bolt, Beranek, and Newman) to implement a set of protocols based on the article.

There are many protocols which were developed, out of which TCP (Transmission Control Protocol) and IP (Internet Protocol) are the most popular. The collection of these protocols, therefore, is called the TCP/IP protocol suite. These protocols were first implemented in BSD (Berkeley Software Distribution) Unix and so the Unix operating system still plays an important role with TCP/IP. Although these protocols are implemented in many operating systems, this chapter is primarily based on Unix. Unlike other operating systems, Unix is written in a high level language, which makes it portable to various types of hardware platforms. Furthermore, Unix lends itself to networking more than any other operating system.

19.1.2 The First Layer

The architecture of TCP/IP protocols is shown in Figure 19.1(b) on page 432. Unlike OSI, TCP/IP defines only 4 layers, with the lowest layer being called the network access layer. TCP/IP, through this layer, provides the interconnection to various kinds of networks. If an Ethernet LAN is to be interconnected, it provides the

---

Thomas P. Brisco of Rutgers University provided invaluable assistance in preparing this chapter. Little did he know that he would write large portions of it!

functions of OSI layers 1 and 2. If an X.25 network is to be interconnected, it provides the functions of OSI layers 1, 2, and 3. The protocol implemented at this layer is determined by the underlying physical network and here, the unit of exchange is typically called a frame.

As the network access layer receives a frame from the connecting physical network, it removes the frame's header and trailer, uncovering the data structure which beomes the data portion of the datagram.

19.1.3 The Second Layer's IP

If the media frame type is indicated as IP, as specified by the Ethernet frame type or by LLC's SAP (Service Access Point), the datagram is then passed to the internet layer. From Figures 19.1(a) and (b), we can see that there are choices of protocols above and below this layer. However, at this layer, only IP must be used and so it is probably the most important protocol in this architecture.

As we saw in Chapter 13, X.25 is a connection-oriented protocol, because it establishes a connection with the receiving end before transferring data. All the packets are then sent over the established virtual circuit, after which it removes that connection.

On the contrary, IP is a connectionless protocol. Datagrams belonging to one message are sent independently of each other and may travel separate routes to their destination. No initial connection is necessary because each datagram header contains the address of the final destination. If a connection is necessary, then the upper layers must provide it.

In OSI errors may be checked and corrected at various layers, but in TCP/IP error control is provided in the upper layers. IP doesn't provide it and so IP is said to be unreliable. It will deliver the datagram to its proper destination, but will not check for transmission errors.

19.1.4 The Second Layer's ICMP

At the internet layer, ICMP (Internet Control Message Protocol) is used to signal and solve problems with routing and other factors such as flow control by sending special messages. These messages are placed inside an IP datagram so in that sense, it can be thought of as a sublayer of IP. Examples of these messages are as follows.

An ICMP Source Quench message is sent by a router to provide data flow control. The router signals the sender to stop sending datagrams because its host cannot accept any more datagrams at this time.

Additionally, a router may receive a datagram from one network which has to be routed to another network. If it decides that another router on that network would be more suited to do the routing, then it would send an ICMP Redirect message to the host. This would signal to that host, "here, send this to that router instead." Lastly, an ICMP Echo message is used to see if a host is up and running and an ICMP Destination Unreachable message is used to notify the sender that a host is unreachable.

19.1.5 The Third Layer

Above the internet layer, the applications have a choice of either using TCP or UDP (User Datagram Protocol) as the protocol for the transport layer. When data is

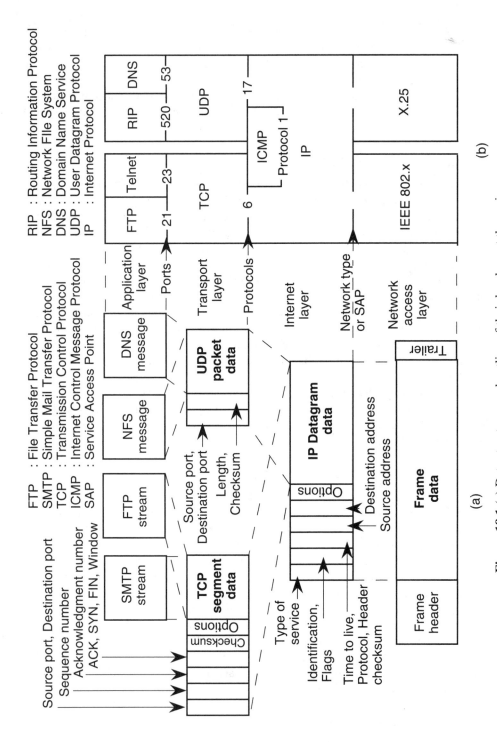

Figure 19.1 (a) Data structures and outline of their headers at the various layers. Each vertical box in the headers represents 32-bit words. (b) Examples of protocols used at each of the TCP/IP layers.

432

received from the lower layers, the internet layer can direct it to the proper protocol, because the protocol number is encoded in the datagram header. See Figure 19.1. If the protocol number is 1, then the data portion of the datagram is sent to ICMP for processing. If it is 6, then the data portion, called a segment, is sent to TCP. If the protocol number in the header is 17, then the data portion, called a packet, is sent to the UDP protocol for processing.

It should be noted that with the TCP/IP protocol suite, the term reliable means that the delivery is reliable. In other words, the data is guaranteed to arrive at the correct destination. However, it does not mean data reliability where the data is checked for errors and corrected. Although UDP does provide a checksum to ensure the correctness of data.

Since UDP is similar to IP, in that they both are unreliable connections, why would an application want to use UDP instead of using IP directly? Examples of applications are services such as RIP and TFTP (Trivial File Transfer Protocol). The primary purpose of using UDP is that its header provides the port numbers of the source and destination applications. The port numbers in the UDP header facilitate UDP to direct the message to the correct application out of many other possible ones available. However, since the UDP header is small, two 32-bit words compared with TCP's six, the processing at this protocol is faster than what is required with TCP. In summary, the facilities UDP provides over IP are data integrity and port addressing, while over TCP it provides for faster processing.

If an application is reliable, that is, it provides its own error control, then UDP provides a less costly alternative to TCP. UDP is also preferred when an application doesn't require a connection, either because it creates its own connection, or it doesn't need one at all. However, when an application needs a transport protocol to provide reliability, a connection, or data ordering, then TCP is used. Data ordering is ensuring that the data arrives in the same order in which it was sent. The specific application which the transport layer is using to send data is specified in the destination port field. For example, data being sent to telnet must have its protocol set to 6 (for TCP) in the datagram header and have the port set to 23 (for telnet) in the segment header.

19.1.6 An Example of TCP Exchange of Segments

The data structure at the TCP layer is called a segment. Using only selected fields of the TCP segments header, Figure 19.2 shows how TCP establishes a connection, transfers data by maintaining a reliable data stream, and then removes the connection. Instead of numbering segments as other protocols number frames, TCP numbers the individual bytes. The sequence number of a segment identifies the number of the first byte in the segment being transmitted. The acknowledgment number identifies the byte number of the sender that the receiver is expecting next. The ACK, SYN, FIN fields are one-bit flags that are part of the TCP header.

The first segment sent by host A has set the SYN (SYNchronize sequence number) bit flag to 1 and the sequence number to 0. This tells the TCP module in host B that A is numbering its segments starting at 0. Then host B, using a sequence number of 10, will set both SYN and ACK bits to 1, acknowledging that it is willing to provide a connection to A. It has also set the window size to 1000, signaling A that it can only accept up to that many octets in its buffer during this transmission. This enables B to control the amount of transmission from A so it isn't sent too fast for B. Host A then acknowledges B's acceptance of the connection (ACK bit is 1) and sends the first stream of data (starting at sequence number 1). This completes the connection using a three-way handshake.

A chooses to send 100 octets of data in the first segment, so its sequence number for the second segment would be 101. After receiving A's segment, B sends its second segment with a sequence number of 10. B isn't sending any data. In this segment, it has set the ACK bit to 1, indicating that the next octet it expects to receive is given in the acknowledgment number field. Specifically, B is acknowledging A's octet number 220 by setting the acknowledgment number to 221. Notice that by acknowledging A's octet number 220, B has acknowledged all the octets which A has sent in its last two segments.

A can then send another 1000 octets after its octet 220 without requiring an acknowledgment from B, because of the window size dictated by B. However, B sends an acknowledgment for A's octet number 500 by stating that it expects to get A's octet number 501 next. This moves A's transmission window to octet number 1500 (500 +

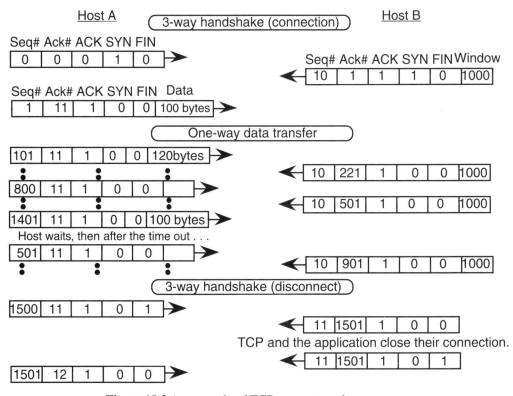

Figure 19.2 An example of TCP segment exchange.

1000). During this time, A doesn't receive any acknowledgments for any of its segments. After an appropriate time-out, it sends the unacknowledged octets over again starting at segment number 501. Notice that if B gets an error, then it doesn't send a NAK (Negative AcKnowledge), but instead just waits for the retransmission.

B acknowledges A's octet number 900 and A then proceeds to close the connection by setting the FIN (FINished) bit flag to 1. B acknowledges A's request to terminate the connection by ACK'ing A's segment number 1500. After TCP and the application close the connection, B notifies A about this, by sending another segment, and setting its own FIN bit to 1. A then concludes this three-way handshake by sending an ACK for B's last segment.

19.1.7 Connections

Being able to transfer data between two hosts as we have just seen is not sufficient. The host must also know what data belongs to which process. For example, in Figure 19.3, there are two users which are telnet'ing to a single remote host. Telnet allows users to log on to remote hosts and access their services. The internetwork must know which transmission belongs to which user.

As was shown in Figure 19.1(b), IP accesses TCP by setting the protocol to 6 and TCP accesses telnet by setting the port number to 23. The protocol and port numbers are specified in datagram and segment headers.

When a user wants to telnet to a host, a copy of telnet is provided to the user which first initiates a connection. The connection is provided by assigning the user a

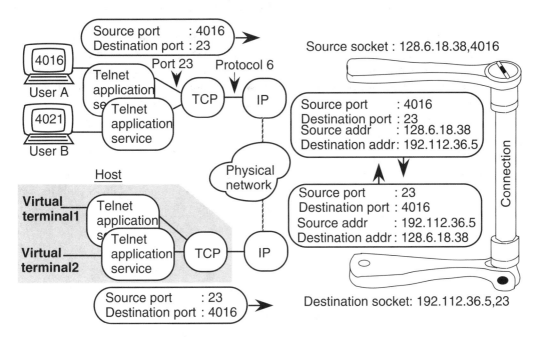

Figure 19.3 A connection between a user and a host is specified by their pair of sockets.

port number (4016 for user A) by the operating system of the originating host. The remote host is continuously running a program called intelnet.d which listens for connection requests on port 23. Once the connection is established between the user and the remote host, the two telnets communicate using the TELNET protocol.

In Figure 19.3, A is given the port number of 4016 and B is given the number of 4021. These port numbers help TCP to distinguish between the data streams for the two users. Figure 19.3 shows how data is exchanged between the remote host and user A. When A sends a data stream, its source port is 4016 and the destination port is 23. Upon its arrival at the host, TCP knows to direct this transmission to telnet from the port number of 23. In the reverse direction, when data is received by TCP at the user's end, TCP knows the user by noting the destination port number.

IP addresses uniquely identify hosts in the Internet. The combination of the source port number and the source IP address is called the source socket. In Figure 19.3, the source IP address is 128.6.18.38 and the source port number is 4016. The combination of these two numbers is called the source socket. Similarly, the combination of the destination IP and port addresses is called the destination socket. Lastly, the communication (or in OSI terminology, the session) between these two sockets is called a connection. This pair of sockets uniquely defines a connection in the entire Internet.

19.2 UNIX

Now that we have a broad understanding of TCP/IP, let us look at some Unix commands, which will then lead us into familiarizing ourselves with TCP/IP services. Let us do this by illustrating a dialogue with a Unix based system, which is attached to the Internet. The commands which we will use are only for the purpose of getting a feel for Unix and not to explore all of its features. You should execute the commands illustrated in this chapter on your own network. It will make the concepts clear as they are presented. Although the dialogues given are presented from my network's viewpoint, you should be able to perform the same tasks relative to your network with minor modifications.

19.2.1 Logging In

Remotely, we first dial into a terminal server. A terminal server provides us with a connection into a network, which provides access to a number of hosts. This terminal server is called Waller and we get its prompt. I have an account on a host called pilot so let us type pilot.

```
waller>pilot
```

Then we log on:

```
login: ramteke
password: . .
```

Now we've logged onto pilot. From here on let us go through the dialogue as shown in Figure 19.4. The commands which we will type are shown in bold. From the first line in the dialogue, we see that we are placed in the directory called u4 under root. The root directory is shown by the slash (/). U4 is called the home directory, because at login time the system places us at that point.

19.2.2 Directories and Files

Here, we make two subdirectories called d1 and d2. Then, using the echo command, we display what is on the echo line; specifically, "another test?" After that, we use the same echo command, but instead of letting this line be displayed on the screen, we redirect it (>) to a file called f1. Now, the "ls –l" command lists the files and directories we have at the current working directory. From the last items of the three entries displayed here, we see that the just created d1, d2, and f1 are in this directory. We can also see that d1 and d2 are directories from this listing, because the very first character of their entries start with a "d." The entry for f1, though, starts with a dash (–), so it is a file.

Now, let us look at the contents of f1 by typing "cat f1." The "pg" command allows us to do the same thing, except it stops at every screenful of text. We try to use this command, but it is not found. By using the "whereis" command, we find that it is found in two places. The first location is where the actual executable command exists

```
/u4%mkdir d1
/u4%mkdir d2
/u4%echo another test?
another test?
/u4%echo another test? > f1
/u4%ls -l
drwx------ 2 ramteke 512 June 1 20:10 d1
drwx------ 2 ramteke 512 June 1 20:10 d2
-rwx------ 1 ramteke   13 June 1 20:11 f1


/u4%cat f1
another test?
/u4%pg f1
pg: Command not found.
/u4%whereis pg
pg: /usr/5bin/pg /usr/man/man1/pg.1v
/u4%/usr/5bin/pg f1
another test?


/u4%cd d1
/u4/d1%mkdir sub1
/u4/d1%cd sub1
/u4/d1/sub1%cd ..
/u4/d1%cd ../..
/%cd
```

```
/u4%ln -s d1/sub1 .
/u4%ls -l
drwx------ 2 ramteke   512 June 1 20:10 d1
drwx------ 2 ramteke   512 June 1 20:10 d2
 -rwx------ 1 ramteke 1200 June 1 20:11 f1
lrwxrwx-- 1 ramteke  7 June 1 sub1 -> d1/sub1
/u4%cp f1 sub1
/u4%ls -l d1/sub1
 -rwx------ 1 ramteke 13 June 1 20:11 f1


/u4%df
Filesystem kbytes used avail capacity Mounted on
/dev/sd0a 24223 19478   2322 89%   /
/dev/sd2d 408223 356974 10426 97%   /usr
/u4%cd /rutgers/font
/a/font.rutgers.edu/rutgers/font%df
Filesystem kbytes used avail capacity Mounted on
/dev/sd0a 24223 19478   2322 89%   /
/dev/sd2d 408223 356974 10426 97%   /usr
rutgers.edu:/rutgers/font
            358035 209043 113188 65%
                /a/font.rutgers.edu/rutgers/font
```

Figure 19.4 A simple UNIX session.

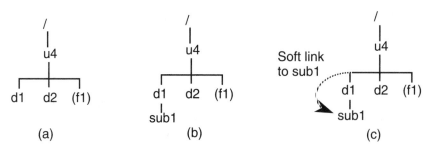

Figure 19.5 (a) Creating two directories and a file. (b) Adding a (sub)directory. (c) Establishing a soft link to sub1.

and the second location is where the manual page of how to use that command exists. Executing "pg" from the directory of where it is stored gives us the contents of f1.

So far, our directory tree looks like that shown in Figure 19.5(a). Let us change our working directory to d1 and there make a new directory called sub1. See Figure 19.5(b). Then let us change directory ("cd") again, this time to sub1. Doing a "cd ..," brings us up by one level and doing a "cd ../.." brings us up two additional levels in the directory tree. Then doing a simple "cd," with no arguments following it, places us back in the home directory.

Here, using the "ln –s" command, we soft-link "d1/sub1" to the home directory. Doing a "ls –l" confirms that. Looking at the fourth entry of that display, we see that it starts with an "l" instead of a "d" or a dash. The "l" indicates that this file or directory is a soft link. It shows that sub1 is actually pointed (->) to "d1/sub1." Graphically, this is pictured in Figure 19.5(c). Now we can refer to "sub1" directly, without mentioning "d1" as being in its path. For example, the copy (cp) command shown, copies file f1 into the linked directory called sub1 without mentioning "d1." This is confirmed by listing ("ls –l") the files in the "d1/sub1" directory. Notice that doing a "ls –l sub1" would have given the same display.

19.2.3 Mounting Filesystems and NFS

Next we type "df." This command shows all the filesystems which are mounted on our directory tree. Mounting makes physical disk devices appear as files to the user in his directory tree. A filesystem is a directory tree which actually resides on a physical device. For example, "sd0a" is a physical SCSI (pronounced "scuzzy") drive which is directly attached and mounted on root ("/"). Likewise, "sd2d" is another drive which is mounted on "/usr." From Figure 19.6(a), we see that although "sd0a" and "sd2d" are two different pieces of hardware devices, to the user they appear as if they are all part of one single directory tree. On the contrary, DOS forces users to maintain a separate directory tree for each drive, such as "A:" or "B:". On pilot, as with many networked systems, some of the mounting is done via NFS (Network File System) which was introduced by Sun Microsystems.

NFS enables the mounting of file systems between two machines on a network. For just "mounting" (not over the network), Unix uses a different means—though the terms are very similar ("network mounting" vs. "mounting"). The "look and feel" of

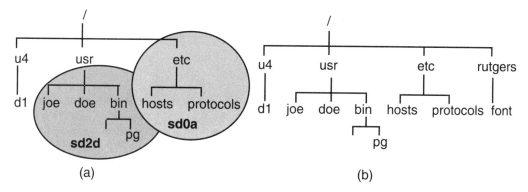

Figure 19.6 (a) The mounting of the sd0a and sd2d local drives. (b) The result after mounting /rutgers/font.

the Unix file hierarchy is a property of how Unix interprets the mounted file systems, and not of NFS per se., e.g., one can mount file systems from either (1) SCSI disks (or other disk controller types), (2) the network, (3) a tape drive, (4) from memory (a RAM disk), or from various other :"media." Once the disk is mounted, the operating system interprets the disk in the familiar "/" notation. NFS provides a means of talkling about file systems over the network; the operating system presents it in the "/" notation.

Now we want to access the /rutgers/font directory which is stored on a host whose address is rutgers.edu. So, we type "cd /rutgers/font." Unix, realizing that this directory is stored on rutgers.edu, automatically mounts it on pilot for us. Our directory tree now looks like that shown in Figure 19.6(b), and the working directory is changed to: "/a/rutgers/font."

Notice, from the display of the "df" command, that the filesystem /rutgers/font is stored on the host called font.rutgers.edu. Also, note that the host name and its directory is separated by a colon (:). The "/a" means that this filesystem is mounted automatically and will be dismounted automatically if no one uses it for a certain time-out period. Automounting of filesystems prevents users from tying up resources over the network for long periods of time.

In the preceding example of NFS-(auto)-mounting of filesystems, our host, pilot, is considered the client and the host from where the filesystems were exported, rutgers.edu, is considered the server. In order to be able to mount filesystems across a network, the client and the server hosts must run what are called daemons. Daemons are processes (or programs) which run continuously on hosts and their names usually end with a "d." For example, "nfsd," "rpc.mountd," "biod," "rpc.lockd," and "rpc.statd" are all daemons which run on servers, while "biod" runs on clients.

If we want to know which directories can be exported from a server to be mounted on clients, we can use the "showmount" command:

```
%showmount -e hardees
export list for hardees:
/foo     rootmounters
/usr/man  everyone
```

Here we see what directories are exportable by whom from the host called "hardees." If we are given the privilege by the system administrator to mount filesystems manually, we could enter:

```
%mount hardees:/usr/man /u4/d2
```

This will mount the "/usr/man" directory from hardees on to our "/u4/d2" directory. The mounting can be confirmed again by using the "df" command. Now if we access anything under "/u4/d2" directory, we are actually accessing the "/usr/man" directory in the host called "hardees." However, we view that remote directory as if it were part of our local host. "Umount /u4/d2" will unmount the filesystem.

19.3 APPLICATION SERVICES

The "who" command in Figure 19.7 shows who is logged on to pilot, the host to which we are logged on.

19.3.1 Using Telnet

If we type "telnet nic.ddn.mil," we are actually logging on this computer and so it shows that it is trying to connect to that computer. Once we are connected, then that computer provides us with its prompt. In this case, it is the "@" sign.

Telnet allows us to log onto a remote computer. Many times, the computer will ask for the login ID and password, but in this case, the host allows guest logins. Unix also provides a remote login facility called "rlogin," but it can be configured so as not to ask for a password. rlogin is a remote virtual terminal protocol developed under Unix, similar to telnet. So many installations prefer not to use it, because if not properly implemented, it can play havoc on network security. Once you are logged in one computer, you can get into others. Furthermore, while "rlogin" allows remote login to only Unix machines, telnet allows remote logins to any kind of host.

At "nic.ddn.mil," we connect to a lesser used database of persons on the Internet by typing "whois." At the "whois" prompt, we type "binde" and it will show some information about that person. Quitting from "whois" provides us with the higher level "@" prompt. A question mark (?) here lists the commands which are available to us. And, finally, doing an "exit" terminates our telnet session.

19.3.2 Using FTP

Now we invoke the services of FTP (File Transfer Protocol) by doing an anonymous FTP to a host called athos. (Unix's counterpart to FTP is called "rcp" on BSD systems.) We don't have an account on this machine either, so for "name," we type "anonymous." For the password, we identify ourself as a courtesy to "athos" by providing our internet address. Then we get the "ftp>" prompt.

Here, if we enter a question mark, it will give us a list of commands which we have access to. We want to read an RFC-1058 (Request For Comment), but athos will not allow us to read it. (RFCs are a set of documents which specify TCP/IP procedures.) We will have to transfer that file in our directory at pilot and then we can read it there.

```
/u4%who                                      Password: ramteke@pilot.njin.net
towey    ttyp1 Jun 1 20:00 (mingus.rutgers.e) ftp>ls -l
ramteke ttyp2 Jun 1 20:05 (waller.rutgers.e)  200 port command successful
                                              drwxr-s--- 2 0  512  Dec 16  3bin
/u4%telnet nic.ddn.mil                        drwxr-sr-x 2 0  17408 Feb 28 rfc
Trying 192.112.36.5 . . .                     226 Transfer complete.
Connected to nic.ddn.mil.                     ftp>cd rfc
@whois                                        250 CWD command successful.
Connecting to id Database . . . . . .         ftp>ls -l
Whois: binde
Binde, Beth E. (BEB5) BINDE@RUTGERS.EDU       . . .
  Rutgers University ...                      ftp>get rfc1058.txt
                                              200 port command successful.
  . . .                                       150 opening ASCII mode data connection
Whois: quit                                   226 Transfer complete.
@?                                            ftp>quit
BLANK    DAYTIME   FINGER  HELP  HOST         221 Goodbye.
KERMIT   LOGIN     LOGOUT  NIC   QUERY        /u4%ls -l rfc*
SYSTAT   TACNEWS   WHOIS                      -rwx------1 ramteke 91435 June 1 rfc1058.txt
@exit                                         /u4%gopher
Connection closed by foreign host            1. Information About Gopher /
                                             2. Computer Information /
u4%ftp athos                                  . . .
Connected to athos.rutgers.edu.              type ? for help, q to Quit, u to go up
Name (athos:ramteke): anonymous              q
331 Guest login ok                           /u4%
```

Figure 19.7 Using Telnet, FTP, and Gopher.

We enter "ls –l," find the "rfc" directory, and go to that directory. Again, doing an "ls –l" at the "rfc" directory, we find the file called rfc1058.txt. The "get" command then actually copies or transfers that file to our working directory in pilot. Finally, doing a "quit" brings us back to pilot. At pilot, we do a "ls –l rfc*" to confirm that we indeed transferred the file into our account and now can read it at our convenience.

Lastly, a higher level user interface to FTP and Telnet are programs like "gopher" and "archie." By typing "gopher," a menu is presented with available options for the user. By exploring the various menu paths, one can automatically Telnet or FTP to various hosts in the Internet community. This is like traveling free of charge around the world, but be careful! Like traveling to foreign lands, just because you can hear the language, doesn't mean you can understand it. You could very well wind up getting the Japanese language in the Kanji character set! (That is, if your terminal can handle it.)

19.3.3 SMTP

The Basic Protocol: Electronic mail is probably the most popular application of TCP/IP networks, and it is essentially a special type of memoranda forwarding protocol. The protocol used on top of TCP/IP for mail transfers is SMTP (Simple Mail Transfer Protocol), and is essentially a "chat" protocol for establishing certain information about the mail message. Chat protocols use 7-bit ASCII codes to exchange communication control messages, unlike protocols which use binary numbers. ASCII based messages, such as, "message number 220" or "MAIL FROM: . . ," make these protocols easy to write and debug. On the other hand, FTP is written in binary codes. One must know how to work with the hexadecimal numbering system in order to interpret its commands.

There are essentially two primary parts to a mail message: (1) The "envelope" and (2) the "body." The "envelope" contains the "To:" and "from:" fields, which indicate the obvious. The "body" portion is passed as data, and is never inspected as part of the protocol. SMTP uses TCP as substrate for having the SMTP session. The SMTP session, after the TCP session is established, would look something like this:

```
%mail -v ramteke@pilot.njin.net
220 pilot.njin.net, Sendmail 5.59/SMI4.0/RU1.5/3.08
HELO hercules.rutgers.edu
250 pilot.njin.net Hello hercules.rutgers.edu, nice to meet you
MAIL FROM: <brisco@hercules.rutgers.edu>
250 postmaster... Sender ok
RCPT TO: <ramteke@pilot.njin.net>
250 <ramteke@pilot.njin.net>... Recipient ok
DATA
354 Enter mail, end with a "." on a line by itself
[data is transferred]
.
250 ok
QUIT
221 pilot.njin.net closing connection
```

Here mail is the command used to send mail. The "–v" asks the mailer to let us see the SMTP conversation. All lines starting with a number are from the remote or receiving host; all lines starting with characters are from the local or sending host. Note that the entire protocol is 7 bit ASCII characters, and the protocol elements correspond nicely to English words. The "HELO" statement identifies the local machine to the remote machine. The "MAIL FROM:" specifies the sender of the mail. The "RCPT TO:" specifies to whom delivery should ultimately occur (it need not be local). The "DATA" statement puts the remote system into data collection mode, and it will continue to collect the body of the mail message until a "." is seen as the only character on a line. The "QUIT" statement terminates the SMTP session.

Interpreting Responses: The lines with leading numbers make it easy for the sending program to understand the returned statements, and the English comments following it make it easy for humans to read. The SMTP response codes are in five different classes:

100 series messages are positive preliminary replies. The command has been accepted, but the requested action is being held in abeyance pending confirmation.

200 series messages are positive completion replies. The requested action has been successfully completed.

300 series messages indicate a state of change. The command has been accepted, but is being held in abeyance, pending receipt of further information.

400 series messages indicate a temporary error. The command was not accepted, and the requested action did not occur. Try again later.

500 series messages indicate a permanent error. The command was not accepted, and the requested action did not occur. Do not try again.

Considering some examples of these message types should give a better idea of how they are classified. 100 series messages are uncommon. One may encounter this message type when sending mail through another network other than the internet. This would indicate that the mail was sent but whether it reached its destination can't be guaranteed.

The purpose of 200 and 300 series messages are evident from the SMTP output provided above. In that output, "250 Recipient OK" could be replaced by a 400 series message which says, "420 File system is full." This would indicate that the recipient doesn't have room in his file system to receive mail and that the sender should try later. In that same location "520 No such user" could be substituted, if the address or the name of the user were incorrect. This 500 series message tells the sender not to try this same user again.

Depending upon the first digit, the sending program can decide whether to supply additional information (i.e., proceed with sending the message), save the message for later re-transmission (as if for temporary errors), or return the message to the user (for permanent errors). The other digits also have similar significance, but are not discussed here. The reader is referred to RFC 821 for complete discussion of SMTP.

Parts of the Protocol: Fortunately, users of electronic mail need not memorize the entire SMTP protocol (there are more than those mentioned above). Most mailer systems can conceptually be broken into three different parts: (1) The MUA (Mail User Agent), (2) The MTA (Mail Transfer Agent and (3) the MDA (Mail Delivery Agent). These three programs can model any type of electronic message passing system.

Typically the MUA worries about things like collecting particular information from the user, such as for whom the message is intended, what the subject is (which is passed as data), and any CCs, BCCs (Blind Carbon Copies), and FCCs (File Carbon Copies), and (of course) the body of the message. With the CC, BCC, TO, and FROM fields one can really tell that the electronic mail was modeled after memos. Often MUAs will provide features other than those listed above, but it need not necessarily do so.

The MTA is the element that typically takes a file (which contains the electronic mail), and parses enough of it to determine the originator and recipient of the message; it then has the SMTP session with the remote system. The MDA takes care of delivering the mail message to the appropriate user (it accounts for things like quotas, available disk space, etc.) on the system once it is received from the MTA.

Usually, there is a program for each of these three agents, but it need not necessarily be the case. In some cases, particularly with Unix systems, the MTA and MDA are often the same—this is the case with sendmail. Sendmail also has the ability to discern the different methods for delivering mail—used over networks other than the Internet—instead of the Internet.

Other electronic mail protocols—such as MIME (Multipurpose Internet Mail Extensions)—are being developed in order to support 8-bit binary information, and multimedia information as well as plain 7 bit ASCII text.

19.4 IP ADDRESSING

19.4.1 Assignment of Addresses

In this section, we will discuss IP addresses, which are assigned to hosts and networks. Recall from Figure 19.1(a), that the datagram header allows 32-bit fields to specify source and destination addresses. If an internet is connected to the Internet, then this IP address must be unique in the entire Internet. Otherwise, a datagram sent to one address may end up at two hosts.

DDN's (Defense Data Network's) NIC (Network Information Center) located in Chantilly, VA, is in charge of assigning these IP addresses. Since to keep tabs on each and every address would be a formidable task, they assign a group of addresses to each organization that wants to be part of the Internet. Then those organizations, in turn, manage the individual assignment of those addresses. An organization's range of available addresses is called its address space.

Hence, Rutgers University is given a range of addresses and its local administrator has assigned a unique 32-bit IP address to pilot's two network interfaces. See Figure 19.8 for the address of one of them. The 32-bit binary number is cumbersome to specify, so it is converted to what is called a dotted-decimal representation. Let us convert the last 8 bits to the decimal format, as a review.

Every bit position starting at the right is given a decimal weight in powers of 2. The right most bit has a weight of 2^0 or 1, the next one has a weight of 2^1 or 2, and so on until the 8th bit winds up having a weight of 2^7 or 128. To find the value in decimal, we simply add up all the weights for the positions which are binary "1"s. In this case, it is 38 (or 32 + 4 + 2). Likewise, the other three groups of 8 bits are converted to a decimal number in the same manner, giving the final IP address of 128.6.7.38.

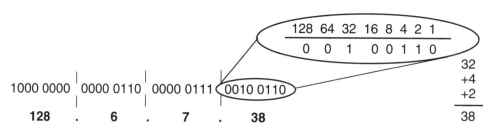

Figure 19.8 The IP address of a port in binary being converted to the dotted-decimal format. Simply add up the positional weights for each bit that is a "1."

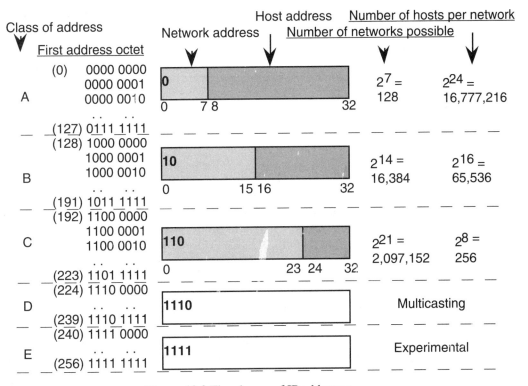

Figure 19.9 The classes of IP addresses.

19.4.2 Address Classes

If we enumerate all the binary numbers of the first 8 bits of an IP address, we'll end up with a list which is summarized on the left side of Figure 19.9. This will be from "0000 0000" to "1111 1111." What NIC has done is to block this set of addresses (a total of 2^{32}) into five address classes.

If the first bit of the first octet of the IP address is a 0, then the address is classified as a class A address. From the figure, we see that a class A address' first decimal number must fall in the range from 0 to 127. Similarly, as we go down the list, we see that class B addresses begin with a binary "10" and are in the range from 128 to 191. Class C addresses begin with a "110" and fall in the range of 192 to 223. Likewise, class D and class E addresses are shown, which are used for multicasting and experimental purposes only.

Class A, B, and C addresses are further broken down into two parts. One part provides the network address and the second part provides the host on that network. As seen in the figure, a class A address has only 7 bits allocated to specify the network number and 24 bits allocated to specify the host number. This means that there are 2^7 or only 128 networks which have a class A address, but each of those networks may have up to 2^{24} or 16,777,216 hosts on them.

As seen in the figure, class B address uses 14 bits to specify the network number and 16 bits to specify the host number. Likewise, class C uses 21 bits for the network ID and 8 bits for the host ID.

Many of Rutgers' hosts and networks use a class B address, because they start with a 128. Notice that there are 256 class B networks which start with a decimal 128, but only one class A network which starts with a decimal 26. This is because a class B network is specified by the first 16 bits (or two dotted-decimal places) and a class A network is specified by only the first 8 bits. Hence, the addresses for Rutgers' hosts begin with the same two dotted decimal numbers; namely, 128.6.

19.4.3 Subnetting

Just as the NIC assigns a range of addresses to each organization and lets them individually manage their address space, the network administrator for an organization can further subdivide the address space, allocating smaller chunks of addresses to the various departments within that organization. This allows address management to be distributed and easier to control. A technique called subnet addressing is used to accomplish this.

As the network administrator is responsible for all the host addresses for a given network, he or she can divide all these available addresses into subnet addresses and their hosts. For example, as we said before, Rutgers uses a class B address starting with 128.6. According to Figure 19.9, class B address allocates 16 bits for the host address. These host address bits can be further subdivided into a subnetwork address and a host

Class B addressing without subnetting		Network address		Host number	
Class B addressing with subnetting on the octet boundary		Network address		Subnet address	Host number
IP address	(128.6.7.38)	1000 0000	0000 0110	0000 0111	0010 0110
Subnet mask	(255.255.255.0)	1111 1111	1111 1111	1111 1111	0000 0000
Address of the subnet	(128.6.7.0)	1000 0000	0000 0110	0000 0111	0000 0000
Host number within that subnet	38	0000 0000	0000 0000	0000 0000	0010 0110
Broadcast address for this subnet	(128.6.7.255)	1000 0000	0000 0110	0000 0111	1111 1111

Figure 19.10 AND'ing the IP address and the mask bits yields the subnet address. The IP address bits for which the mask bits are 0 yields the host number and the IP address with the host bits set to 1 yields the broadcast address.

address. At Rutgers, as with many other locations, this division is done on an octet boundary. Although, it doesn't have to be, it makes interpretation of numeric addresses easier. Exactly how subnetting is used, if its at all used, is a local issue and doesn't involve the rest of the Internet.

In order to facilitate routing, a bit mask called a subnet mask is defined to quickly separate the subnet address and the host number from an IP address. At the top of Figure 19.10, a class B addressing scheme is redrawn and under it is our class B address scheme using one octet for subnetting. Here, the third octet is used to represent the subnet address and the fourth octet is used to represent the host number. In this case, the subnet mask of 255.255.255.0 is used.

Using an IP address and the subnet mask, let us see how the subnet and host addresses are derived. The IP address of 128.6.7.38 gives a subnet address of 128.6.7.0. This is found by AND'ing the mask and address bits. The result of AND'ing is a logical 1, only if the AND'ed bits are both 1s, the result is a logical 0. The host number, on the other hand, is found by masking out the IP address using only the 0 bits of the mask. From the illustrated mask, the IP address of 128.6.7.38 identifies host 38 on the subnet 128.6.7.0.

A broadcast address for a subnet is specified by setting all host bits to 1 on a subnet address. So, for our example, if pilot wants to broadcast a message to all the nodes on its subnet, it will set the address as 128.6.7.255.

19.4.4 ARP

So far, we've been discussing IP addressing, which pertains to the addressing used at the internet layer. Since the internet layer is stacked on top of the network access layer, we need a method to convert (or map) an IP address to its physical network address (or the MAC address). This is done in Ethernet using a protocol called ARP (Address Resolution Protocol).

This protocol requires each host to maintain an ARP entry for every host that is on its subnet. The ARP table maps the IP addresses to their Ethernet addresses, so that when it has to send a frame to an IP address (128.6.18.2), it encodes its corresponding Ethernet address (08:0:20:9:43:dd) from this table. If an IP address is not found in the table, then it will broadcast an "ARP REQUEST" message to all the hosts on its subnet asking, "who has this particular IP address?" The target host will then reply with an "ARP REPLY" message, stating its own IP and Ethernet addresses. This will then allow the inquiring host to update its ARP table, for future references.

The table can be viewed by entering:

```
% arp -a
plinius (128.6.18.45) at 08:0:20:9:3e:be
hardees (128.6.18.2) at 08:0:20:9:43:dd
lil-gw (128.6.7.5)  at aa:0:04:0:98:f4
waller (128.6.7.41) at 00:0:0c:1:08:38
```

In this display, the host names are given along with their IP addresses and their corresponding 6-byte Ethernet addresses in hex. The first three bytes of an Ethernet address identifies the manufacturer of the Ethernet card. The first three bytes of plinius and hardees are 8:0:20, which identify their manufacturer to be Sun Microsystems. lil-gw is running DECnet which requires it to have a DEC Ethernet address and waller, our terminal server, is manufactured by Cisco.

We at pilot can now construct a partial network map as shown in Figure 19.11. However, we are told (which we will soon verify) that the host pilot is also acting as a gateway between the 128.6.18.0 and 128.6.7.0 subnets. When a host is connected between two or more subnets it is then also acting as a gateway. Hence, all gateways are hosts, but all hosts are not necessarily gateways. In this chapter, we will be using the term gateway instead of router.

In case of problems on the network, this information about manufacturers should agree with what we physically know about the systems, i.e., that waller is indeed a Cisco host. If, for example, waller's address started with 0:0:c, then we could suspect that the ARP table has become corrupt.

It is also possible, when someone configures a host, that they give it an incorrect IP address used by someone else. For example, if plinius is configured with an incorrect IP address of 128.6.18.2, which is also hardees' address, then hardees may log an error message that 8:0:20:9:3e:be (plinius) was sending a duplicate IP address. Such messages may be found in /usr/adm/messages, at hardees.

Also, using the arp –a command on pilot, we could verify that plinius was indeed advertising the wrong IP address. It is, of course, best to reconfigure plinius with its correct IP address and then let the ARP tables be automatically updated. However, we could also manually delete the wrong ARP entry for hardees and add the correct one by entering the following at pilot:

```
#arp -d hardees
hardees (128.6.18.2) deleted
#arp -s hardees 8:0:20:9:43:dd
```

The pound sign (#), also called the tic-tac-toe or the musical sharp sign, indicates that this command should be done from the superuser's account. The command with the –d option deletes hardees from the table and the command with the –s option adds

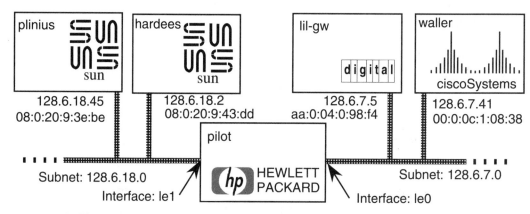

Figure 19.11 Drawing a partial network map using some of the entries from pilot's ARP tables.

hardees back to the ARP table with the correct ARP address. Manually adding an entry to the ARP table prevents it from being updated automatically. In other words, plinius won't be able to make pilot think that it has hardees' IP address anymore. Hardees would never see packets from plinius, because plinius has the wrong MAC address for hardees. Therefore, the problem with plinius should be corrected anyway.

19.4.5 Proxy ARP

Proxy ARP is a fairly simple, but subtle, means of determining the network gateway between the local host and the requested remote host, a host not on the same subnet as the local host, i.e., a way of avoiding a lot of static routes.

"Proxy" ARP is a method (not a protocol) for responding to ARP requests. It is currently defined as correct and appropriate behavior.

In proxy arp, if a gateway sees an ARP request for an IP address that is not on the local cable, *and* it knows how to get to that IP network, it will respond with an ARP response. But instead of the remote host's ethernet address, it will put its own in there, on behalf of the remote host. Hence the term "proxy" is used. Essentially, the gateway tricks the querying host into thinking that it (the gateway) is the remote host.

This is done on the hosts by what is now a standard routing entry:

```
route add default <my_own_ip_address> 0
```

implying that the entire world is attached to the local ethernet, and that everything is 0 hops away. The "route add" command will be covered in more depth, in Section 19.6.2.

Now what happens is that whenever an ARP request for a remote address is issued, a gateway will respond with (essentially) "send it over here" and will forward the packet correspondingly. For all intents and purposes, the host believes that the gateway is the remote system.

Consider the following terminal dialogue executed from our host, pilot: The ping command merely checks to see if a host is active or not.

```
%arp -a
. .
(no entry for foghat or vax003.stockton.edu systems)
%ping foghat
foghat.rutgers.edu is alive
%ping vax003.stockton.edu
vax003.stockton.edu is alive
%arp -a
. .
foghat.rutgers.edu (128.6.13.13) at aa:0:4:0:98:f4
vax003.stockton.edu (134.210.1.6) at aa:0:4:0:98:f4
```

Notice according to their IP addresses, foghat is on subnet 128.6.13.0 and vax003.stockton.edu is on subnet 134.210.1.0. However, pilot is on neither of these subnets. It is on 128.6.18.0 and 128.6.7.0. See Figure 19.11. Yet, by observing foghat's and vax003's Ethernet addresses, to pilot they both appear as having lil-gw's Ethernet address.

Of course, this results in a larger ARP table, but ARP entries are supposed to time out (be expired) after three hours. This avoids having to have lots of route entries in the routing table.

A route tells the host to which gateway a packet should be sent in order to access a remote system. At Rutgers, we have 150 active subnets—obviously static routes for all networks would produce a huge routing table. The average size of the ARP tables tends to be about 20 entries—since hosts always tend to talk to a "closed set" of other hosts.

Also, note an odd side effect. If you have a route entry for a specific gateway, and that gateway goes down, you're out of luck. All your packets will fall on deaf ears.

If you're using proxy ARP, you'll timeout waiting for a response, purge that ARP entry in your table, and re-ARP again. If there is more than one gateway on the local ethernet, then the other gateway will answer (if it knows how to get to the intended remote network), and the IP session will recover. This allows you to dynamically switch between gateways, while never losing connectivity.

Generally ARP tables provide the addresses of hosts and routers on the local subnet, that is, the systems which are directly connected on the same LAN. On the other hand, routing tables provide the addresses for systems which are not connected to the local subnet. So, what is the purpose of proxy ARP?

Suppose a host uses routing tables to access a remote host which goes down. By the time the routing tables are updated by the routing protocol, the TCP sessions with that host will become disconnected. However, using proxy ARP, the ARP tables are updated fast enough before TCP sessions have a chance to become disconnected.

There are some other, more subtle, oddities to the ARP mechanism, but they are outside the scope of this book. For example, there are some troubles with regard to the delay of ARP responses from heavily loaded routers, etc. See RFCs 826 and 1126 for a more complete discussion. They are available from various sources on the Internet.

19.5 EXPLORING THE EXISTING NETWORK

19.5.1 The Network Interfaces

Let us take a look at our existing network from pilot. As shown in Figure 19.11, we can verify that we have two network interfaces available on pilot by using this netstat command:

```
pilot%netstat -ain
Name  Mtu    Net/Dest      Address     Ierrs Opkts Collis Queue
le0   1500   128.6.7.0     128.6.7.38   .  ..    ...
le1   1500   128.6.18.0    128.6.18.38  .  ..      ...
lo0   1536   127.0.0.0     127.0.0.1      .    ..       ...
```

The –i option in this command asks for the displays of the interfaces which are configured. The –a option requires that all of these interfaces are displayed. And the –n option makes the addresses be displayed using the numeric format. If we left out the –n option, then our display would be:

```
pilot%netstat -ai
Name  Mtu    Net/Dest                Address  Ipkts  Ierrs Opkts
le0   1500   BROAD-7-0.RUTGERS.EDU   pilot    .  ..    ...
le1   1500   broad-18-0.rutgers.edu  pilot    .  ..    ...
lo0   1536   loopback                localhost .      ..
```

The order of the entries in both of these displays is the same, the only difference being whether numeric addresses or names are given. Let us disregard the fields shown with dots. Their understanding is not necessary to understand basic interface configurations. From these two displays we see that the names of the configured interfaces are le0, le1 and lo0. "Le" is used to denote Ethernet interfaces, of which we have two: le0 and le1.

The lo0 interface exists on all hosts and is called the local interface or the loopback interface. The le interfaces are on our network map of Figure 19.11, but the loopback interface is internal and doesn't appear on such maps. A loopback interface is used to do loopback tests by the local host to see whether or not it is fit to be connected to the external networks. By default, the loopback address for all hosts is 127.0.0.1.

The address field of these two displays specifies the IP address assigned to each interface, which corresponds to its 6-byte Ethernet address. The Network/Destination field displays the network or the host which is accessible from this interface. Since these addresses end with a ".0," for both Ethernet interfaces, we can say that these are subnet addresses and not host addresses. If, for example, an le2 was added to pilot whose Net/Dest address were configured to be 128.6.10.1, then we could say that this interface is connected to only one host whose address is 128.6.10.1. In this case, this would be a point-to-point link with access to only one computer, unlike le0 and le1, which have access to entire subnets.

19.5.2 Subnet Masking

Now that we have verified that we have two network access interfaces on pilot, let us verify that the subnetting is done, using the last octet of the IP address. Consider the following three commands which show the information about each of the three interfaces:

```
%ifconfig le0
le0: flags=63<UP,BROADCAST,NOTRAILERS,RUNNING>
     inet 128.6.7.38 netmask ffffff00 broadcast 128.6.7.255

%ifconfig le1
le1: flags=63<UP,BROADCAST,NOTRAILERS,RUNNING>
     inet 128.6.18.38 netmask ffffff00 broadcast 128.6.18.255

%ifconfig lo0
le0: flags=49<UP,LOOPBACK,RUNNING>
     inet 127.0.0.1 netmask ff000000
```

Here, again, we see the IP addresses assigned for each interface, but now we can also make sure that the masking is properly set. Notice that the netmasks are given in hex. Also, notice for le0 and le1, the first 3 octets are masked for the subnet and the last octet for the host number. The broadcast address matches correctly with how the subnet mask is set up, as was explained using Figure 19.10.

If the subnet mask is set incorrectly, then a host may be able to communicate with hosts on its own subnet and with remote hosts, but not with hosts on other local subnets. Shortly, we'll see how to configure a subnet mask.

19.5.3 Routing Tables

The next thing we want to see is pilot's current routing tables. This is done using the netstat command with the –r option for routing. Again, let us see the display using both the host and network names and their numeric addresses.

```
%netstat -r
Routing tables
Destination              Gateway               Flags      Inter
localhost                localhost             UH         lo0
igor.rutgers.edu         nb-gw.rutgers.edu     UGHD       le0
okapi.rutgers.edu        lil-gw.rutgers.edu    UGHD       le0
default                  pilot                 U          le0
broad-18-0.rutgers.      pilot                 U          le1
BROAD-7-0-RUTGERS.E      pilot                 U          le0

%netstat -nr
Routing tables
Destination              Gateway               Flags      Inter
127.0.0.1                127.0.0.1             UH         lo0
128.6.13.26              128.6.7.1             UGHD       le0
128.6.11.3               128.6.7.5             UGHD       le0
default                  128.6.7.38            U          le0
128.6.18.0               128.6.18.38           U          le1
128.6.7.0                128.6.7.38            U          le0
```

Again, the order of the entries in these two displays is the same. From their last columns, we recognize our three familiar interfaces: lo0, le0, and le1. The destinations for the last two routes are 128.6.18.0 and 128.6.7.0. They both end with a ".0," so these are routes to subnets and not to individual hosts. If a destination ends with a non-zero number, then it typically specifies a route to a host. This can also be seen by noticing that the H(Host) flag is set for host routes and not for subnet routes.

As we have seen before, the last two entries are the routes to two subnets to which pilot is directly connected. These entries state that the gateway to either of these subnets is pilot. In one case it is the le1 interface (128.6.18.38) and in the other case, it is the le0 interface (128.6.7.38). Apparently, all routes are up and running, since the U(Up) flag is set for them all.

The loopback interface provides a route to the local host and it is always in the routing table. The default route specifies to which gateway packets must be sent if the route is not found in the table. This entry helps the table from becoming too long. So, for instance, if we want to send data to NIC.DDN.MIL (192.112.36.5), which is not listed in the table, then the data packet is sent to the default gateway to route the packets.

Lastly, we come across two routes, one to igor and one to okapi. Both of these routes use remote gateways, that is, gateways connected to other subnets. This is indicated by the G flag being set for them. In the first case, the remote gateway which provides access to igor is called nb-gw and in the second case, the remote gateway which provides access to okapi is called lil-gw. These routes also have their D flags set, meaning that these routes were added due to ICMP redirects. See Section 19.1.4.

From the display of netstat –nr, we see that the address for nb-gw is 128.6.7.1 and that for lil-gw is 128.6.7.5. This means that both of these gateways are on the 128.6.7.0 subnet, which is connected to le0 of pilot. Now our updated network map looks like that shown in Figure 19.12.

19.5.4 Tracing Routes

How do we know if igor and okapi are directly on the other sides of nb-gw and lil-gw or if there are other gateways in between them? This can be easily answered by using the traceroute command as shown. Let's first do a traceroute to igor.

```
%traceroute igor
traceroute to igor.rutgers.edu (128.6.13.26), 30 hops max,
    40 byte packets
1. nb-gw.rutgers.edu (128.6.7.1) 4ms 2ms 2ms
2. monster.rutgers.edu (128.6.4.3) 2ms 2ms 2ms
3. igor.rutgers.edu (128.6.13.26) 3ms 2ms 2ms
```

What is happening here is that pilot is sending 40 byte UDP packets to the destination specified in traceroute. The packets are sent with an illegal port number of 33434. The first UDP packet is sent with the TTL (Time To Live) field set to 1. The TTL field is part of the IP datagram header as seen in Figure 19.1. When the first gateway along the route to igor gets this packet, it decrements the TTL by 1 and cannot forward the packet to its destination. See Figure 19.13(a). It sends an ICMP message back to the source, stating that the time to live for that UDP packet has exceeded.

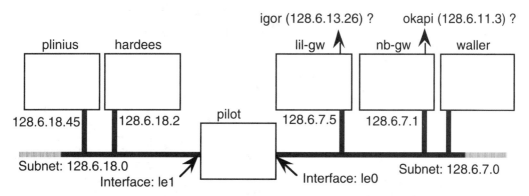

Figure 19.12 Discovering the existence of igor and okapi. We would like to know how many hops they are away from pilot.

Pilot will notice who sent the ICMP message from its IP datagram source address. In this case, it is nb-gw. Pilot will also measure the time it took for this round trip transmission of packets to occur. This procedure with the TTL set to 1 is repeated three times and the time is measured each time. In our display, these times were 4ms, 2ms, and 2ms.

Now in Figure 19.13(b), pilot will perform the same procedure, but this time with the TTL field set to 2. nb-gw decrements TTL by 1 and routes the packet to monster. monster, however, decrements the TTL to 0 and can't forward the packets any further. So it sends an ICMP time-exceeded message back to pilot. Now pilot knows the gateway for the second hop and its round trip delay.

Finally, in Figure 19.13(c), pilot sends out UDP packets with a TTL of 3 and this time doesn't receive a time-exceeded message, because it reaches its destination address. However, instead, it sends a port-unreachable message. Pilot knows it has reached the final destination. The port number in the UDP packet was set on purpose to an illegal number so as to induce this ICMP message. Notice, that each of the three UDP packets sent with a TTL of 2 took 2ms each and the ones sent with a TTL of 3 took 3ms, 2ms, and 2ms.

Now we know that to get to igor, there exists one other gateway called monster. Similarly, when we do a traceroute to okapi, we come across another gateway called

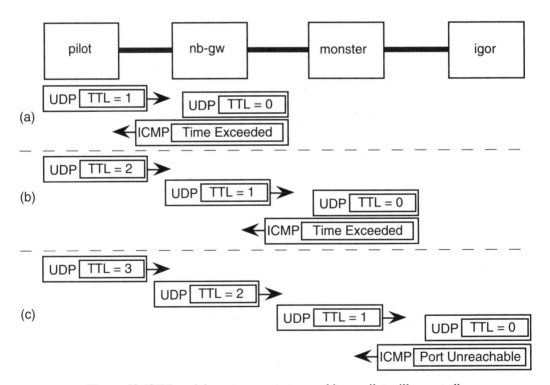

Figure 19.13 When doing a traceroute to an address, pilot will repeatedly send UDP packets, increasing the TTL (Time To Live) by one, until it receives a port unreachable message back.

waks-gw, which is a gateway between lil-gw and okapi. This time, let us use the numeric address of okapi to do the following traceroute:

```
%traceroute 128.6.11.3
traceroute to 128.6.11.3 (128.6.11.3), 30 hops max,
    40 byte packets
1 lil-gw.rutgers.edu  (128.6.7.5)  9ms 2ms 2ms
2 waks-gw.rutgers.edu (128.6.12.3) 5ms 3ms 3ms
3 okapi.rutgers.edu   (128.6.11.3  3ms 3ms 4ms
```

Datagrams travel different routes and independently from each other, so the times shown in the traceroute displays may not always seem consistent. Now, compiling all the information from our traceroutes, our new network map is as seen in Figure 19.14.

Figure 19.15(a) shows a more interesting traceroute to rins.st.ryukoku.ac.jp, a host located in Japan. The .jp designates the address as being in Japan. Many of the gateways along the route are named using the cities where they are located. It is easy to see, for instance, that the route goes through Chicago, San Francisco and Hawaii, before reaching the last three gateways in Japan. Also, notice the significant jumps in times when reaching the first gateway in Hawaii or in Japan. Depending on the delays associated with links, these measured times can vary.

Figure 19.15(b) shows an unsuccessful traceroute. Here, a set of three asterisks is shown after ru-alternet-gw, indicating that the problem lies between that point and the next. The asterisks are repeated up to 30 times.

A better way to check to see if a host is up and running is to simply do a ping. It does not use up network bandwidth as much as traceroute does. Here's an example, where a ping is done two times to a host in Australia, using 56 bytes of data:

```
%ping -s csuvax1.murdoch.edu.au 56 2
PING csuvax1.murdoch.edu.au
64 bytes from csuvax1.murdoch.edu.au (134.115.4.1):
    icmp_seq=0. time = 3299 ms
64 bytes from csuvax1.murdoch.edu.au (134.115.4.1):
    icmp_seq=1. time = 2975 ms
2 packets transmitted, 2 packets received, 0% packet loss
```

Obviously, if pings are done for all possible addresses on subnet 128.6.12.0, then we could find out all the hosts connected on the other side of lil-gw and could extend the network map beyond what is shown in Figure 19.14. Similarly, other subnets could be explored, but your network administrator could just as easily provide you with a network map for your installation and prevent you from using up network bandwidth.

19.6 INSTALLING A NEW SUBNET

19.6.1 Configuring the Interfaces

Let us now expand our network by adding a new subnet labeled 128.6.101.0. On this subnet, we need to add a workstation called pascal (128.6.101.2) and interconnect

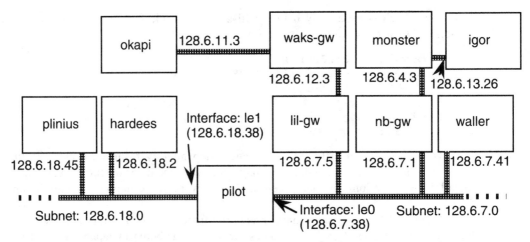

Figure 19.14 Adding more gateways and interfaces to our network.

```
%traceroute rins.st.ryukoku.ac.jp
traceroute to rins.st.ryukoku.ac.jp (133.83.1.1), 30hops max, 40byte packets
 1  lil-gw (128.6.18.30)  3 ms  2 ms  2 ms
 2  ru-alternet-gw (128.6.21.8)  2 ms  3 ms  2 ms
 3  Washington.DC.ALTER.NET (137.39.18.1)  11 ms  9 ms  10 ms
 4  ENSS136.t3.NSF.NET (192.41.177.253)  14 ms  12 ms  12 ms
 5  t3-1.Washington-DC-cnss58.t3.ans.net  (140.222.58.2)  14 ms  13 ms  16 ms
 6  t3-3.Washington-DC-cnss56.t3.ans.net  (140.222.56.4)  17 ms  13 ms  16 ms
 7  t3-0.New-York-cnss32.t3.ans.net  (140.222.32.1)  18 ms  20 ms  19 ms
 8  t3-1.Cleveland-cnss40.t3.ans.net  (140.222.40.2)  34 ms  34 ms  41 ms
 9  t3-2.Chicago-cnss24.t3.ans.net  (140.222.24.3)  44 ms  46 ms  40 ms
10  t3-1.San-Francisco-cnss8.t3.ans.net  (140.222.8.2)  83 ms  83 ms  80 ms
11  t3-0.San-Francisco-cnss9.t3.ans.net  (140.222.9.1)  81 ms  85 ms  84 ms
12  t3-0.enss144.t3.ans.net  (140.222.144.1)  83 ms  83 ms  84 ms
13  ARC2.NSN.NASA.GOV  (192.52.195.11)  93 ms  96 ms  87 ms
14  imp.Hawaii.Net (132.160.249.1)  141 ms  141 ms  148 ms
15  menehune.Hawaii.Net (132.160.1.1)  138 ms  146 ms  144 ms
16  132.160.251.2 (132.160.251.2)  257 ms  409 ms  392 ms
17  jp-gate.wide.ad.jp (133.4.1.1)  392 ms  341 ms  251 ms
18  wnoc-kyo.wide.ad.jp (133.4.7.2)  336 ms  351 ms  331 ms
19  rins.st.ryukoku.ac.jp (133.83.1.1)  355 ms  373 ms  484 ms
```

(a)

```
%traceroute rins.st.ryukoku.ac.jp
traceroute to rins.st.ryukoku.ac.jp (133.83.1.1), 30hops max, 40byte packets
 1  lil-gw (128.6.18.30)  3 ms  2 ms  2 ms
 2  ru-alternet-gw (128.6.21.8)  2 ms  3 ms  2 ms
 3  * * *
 4  * * *
   .    .
30  * * *
```
(b)

Figure 19.15 (a) Doing a traceroute to a host in Japan. (b) An unsuccessful traceroute.

it to subnet 128.6.18.0 using the gateway called ada. See Figure 19.16 for these addresses given to us by our network administrator. First, let us configure the interfaces for pascal, then for ada.

On pascal's /etc/rc.boot file used for booting up purposes, we add these lines: (The slash is the continuation character for extending a command over multiple lines.)

```
ifconfig    lo0 127.0.0.1
ifconfig    le0 128.6.101.2 netmask 255.255.255.0 \
                    broadcast 128.6.101.255
```

This way, every time pascal is booted up, the loopback interface and the le0 interface is properly configured. Subnetting is done on the last octet boundary, as before, as seen by the subnet mask and the broadcast address. Notice that for all interfaces on a subnet, the netmask and broadcast addresses must be the same.

If for some reason we need to disable the le0 interface from the network, we could enter:

#ifconfig le0 down

And to bring it back up, we would enter:

#ifconfig le0 128.6.101.2 up

Likewise, for ada's bootup file, we would add these lines:

```
ifconfig lo0 127.0.0.1
ifconfig le0 128.6.101.3 netmask 255.255.255.0 broadcast \
                128.6.101.255
ifconfig le1 128.6.18.30 netmask 255.255.255.0 broadcast \
                128.6.18.255
```

19.6.2 Configuring Static Routing

After executing these ifconfig statements, our routing tables on pascal look like:

```
%netstat -nr
Routing tables
Destination          Gateway          Flags  ...    Interface
127.0.0.1            127.0.01         UH            lo0
128.6.101.0          128.6.101.2      U             le0
```

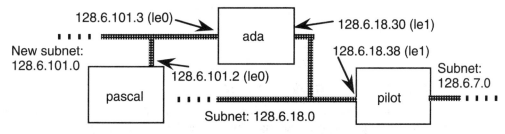

Figure 19.16 Adding a new subnet (128.6.101.0).

Notice, since only the router to its own subnet is given, pascal can't get to pilot yet.

```
%ping pilot
Sendto: Network is unreachable
```

To add an explicit route to pilot from pascal, we could do the following:

```
#route add 128.6.18.38 128.6.101.3 1
```

This would add 128.6.18.38 to pascal's routing table, making 128.6.101.3 the le0 interface on ada as the gateway. The 128.6.101.3 must be a gateway on the same subnet that pascal is on. Such a gateway must be one hop away. The 1 at the end of the line states that the metric for the number of hops is 1, since the gateway is one hop away.

However, why only add a host route? Let us, instead, add a subnet route of 128.6.18.0. This will give pascal access to not only pilot but also to all the hosts on that subnet.

```
#route delete 128.6.18.38
#route add    128.6.18.0  128.6.101.3  1
```

The route delete command will delete the route to pilot and the route add will add a route to subnet 128.6.18.0. Now, let us go even a step further and make ada the default gateway for all other routes. This is done by entering:

```
#route -n add default   128.6.101.3 1
add net default: gateway 128.6.101.3
```

So now pascal's routing tables should look like:

```
#netstat -rn
127.0.0.1              127.0.0.1          UH        lo0
default               128.6.101.3         UG        le0
128.6.101.0           128.6.101.2         U         le0
```

The following command will make pilot the default gateway for ada:

```
#route -n add default 128.6.18.38 1
```

So ada's routing tables will be:

```
#netstat -rn
127.0.0.1              127.0.0.1          UH        lo0
default               128.6.18.38         UG        le1
128.6.101.0           128.6.101.3         U         le0
128.6.18.0            128.6.18.30         U         le1
```

19.6.3 Configuring Dynamic Routing

Instead of configuring ada for static routing, a better choice would be to configure it for dynamic routing. This means having the gateway run a routing protocol. In our case, since we are only connecting two subnets, RIP would be sufficient. If on the other hand, we were interconnecting to a different domain, then we might want to run EGP or BGP, as well. The routing daemon used to run RIP is called routed and a daemon used to run RIP, Hello, EGP, and BGP is called gated (Gateway Routing Daemon).

To run routed, simply enter:

```
#routed
```

When starting routed from the setup file, routed will look in the /etc/gateways file to see if any routes are predefined. On ada, we may want to specify the default route in this file as follow:

```
net 0.0.0.0 gateway 128.6.18.38 metric 1 active
```

Here, the net identifies this address as a network address. If it were an address to a host, then the line would begin with the keyword host. A network address of 0.0.0.0 denotes the default route. The address following the keyword gateway specifies 128.6.18.38 as the gateway for that route. The metric of 1 indicates the number of hops to the destination and active means that RIP may update this route if necessary. If update messages are not received for the allotted time frame, then RIP may delete it, as well. It also means that this gateway may send update messages to others. A passive route, on the other hand, makes the designated route a static route which can't be updated or deleted by RIP.

19.7 DOMAIN NAME SERVICE

19.7.1 Purpose and Operation

So far we have been using host names and addresses interchangeably. However, we have not mentioned how a name is converted to its IP address, which must be done in order to generate a datagram. For example, in Figure 19.15 when we asked pilot to do a traceroute to rins.st.ryukoku.ac.jp, how did it find its IP address to be 133.83.1.1? This is done by a service called DNS (Domain Name Service). It allows people to use host names which are easier to remember than IP addresses. It is the responsibility of DNS to convert a name into its correct IP address.

The way DNS handles this is by using a distributed database containing host names and addresses information, organized hierarchically. See Figure 19.17. At the top of the hierarchy is one root domain. This domain is served by a set of name servers which store information only for the top level domain servers. Examples of top level domains are net, mil, etc. The servers in the top level domains, in turn, only have information about the servers in the second level domains and so on. Each server stores information about the servers that are in the domain below it. This makes it unnecessary to maintain one large file that contains the names and addresses of all the million or so hosts on the Internet.

Now, if a local server, for example pilot.njin.net, wants to find the address of the host, rins.st.ryukoku.ac.jp, it will first look in its cache (or memory). If it isn't there, then it will search for the address of a server of one of the subdomains in the given host name. If none of these addresses is found in the cache, it will query a root domain server, which will give the address of a server in the jp domain. This server will do the

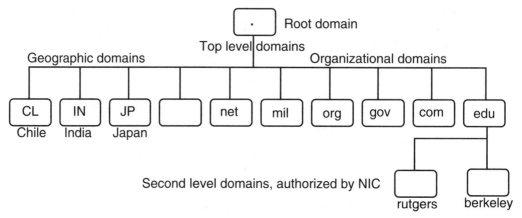

Figure 19.17 The domain hierarchy.

same and provide a server address for the ac.jp domain to pilot. This is done repetitiously until pilot receives the IP address of rins.st.ryukoku.ac.jp.

The local server will then store the address of the host as well as the addresses of all the domain servers it had to encounter. This is done for future reference. Then if it needs to find the address of another host in the st.ryukoku.ac.jp subdomain, it knows the server who would have that. Notice that the dots separate each subdomain in a name. For example, ac is a subdomain in jp and ryukoku is a subdomain in ac, etc. Also, notice that subdomains and subnetworks are not necessarily related.

19.7.2 DNS Servers

To run DNS, most Unix systems use the BIND (Berkeley Internet Name Domain) software. This basically uses a client and server model. Figure 19.18 shows that all computers can act as a client, which can direct queries to servers. A server can provide the answer to a client's question. If it can't, it can at least provide the address of another server which can, or the nameserver can forward the request to a nameserver who can answer the query. This is how caching nameservers learn new addresses. In BIND, a client is actually called a resolver and a server is actually a name server.

As shown in Figure 19.18, there are three types of servers. A primary server loads the information for the domain from a local disk. This information is called the zone file. Here, the word "zone" is being used for domain. This zone file is maintained by the domain administrator and contains the most up to date information about the domain. From the primary server, other servers receive their information. There is only one primary server per domain.

Secondary servers act as a backup to the primary and they receive their information by performing zone file transfers, periodically, from the primary server. Both the primary and the secondary servers are considered to be authoritative or master servers.

Then there are caching-only servers, which are not authoritative. The only way they inherit domain information is when a resolver queries them for information which

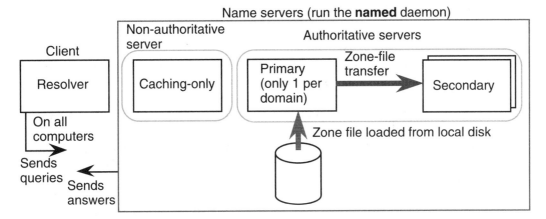

Figure 19.18 The client-server model used by the DNS service.

they don't have. Then they ask other servers who may have the answer or knows who does. Upon acquiring the information, they cache it and that information is then available for future reference.

To configure a resolver, one only needs the /etc/resolv.conf file. This file is used as necessary, by the BIND library of routines. However, servers use a daemon called named, which is configured by configuring the following five files: named.boot specifies where domain information is available; named.ca specifies where the root domain servers are; named.local specifies the local loopback domain; and named.hosts and named.rev are the zone files which convert host names to IP address and vice versa.

The named.boot file contains configuration commands, while the other four files store information using resource records. Resource records are written in a standard format and each record is categorized by its records type. Some of these record types are shown in Table 19.1.

Table 19.1 Resource record types used in DNS		
Type	Type meaning	Function
A	Address	Maps a host name to an IP address
CNAME	Canonical Name	Host nick-name or alias
HINFO	Host Information	CPU and operating system name
MINFO	Mailbox Information	Mail list or mailbox information
MX	Mail Exchanger	Domain's mail exchnager host name
NS	Name Server	Domain's authoritative name server
PTR	Pointer	Maps an IP address to a host name
SOA	Start of Authority	Parameters which specify zone implementation

19.7.3 Nslookup

Next, let us use a tool called nslookup to get better acquainted with DNS. Let us follow the dialogue as shown in Figure 19.19.

We start off by typing nslookup. This command is not found in the current path. We ask the system where it is and it finds it in the /usr/etc directory. Using that path, we execute nslookup again and we are in that program.

The first thing it does is list the default server as being pilot. This is the name server which will handle all our quries, until we change it. Then we query it for the IP address of a host (hardees), and it finds it. This is because the record type is set to A by default in nslookup and this type of record maps a host name to its address. See Table 19.1.

We can change the record type by using the set command, as is done next. Here we change the record type of NS (Name Server) and it will stay as such until we change it again.

Now we enter the root domain by simply typing a dot. And because the type was set to NS, we will be given the servers for the root domain. You may want to refer to Figure 19.17. In these displays we will not show all the servers. Using the server command, we now change our default name server from pilot to terp.umd.edu, a root domain server found in the previous list.

Next, we come down the hierarchy of domains by listing the servers for the domain named nasa.gov. Then we do the same for berkeley.edu. Here, we change the default server to one of the berkeley.edu domain servers and then find the servers for the subdomain cs.berkeley.edu.

Now, we reset the record type to A and use the ls command as shown. This transfers the information (or resource records) for the cs.berkeley.edu domain into a file called ourfile into our account at pilot. Using the view command, we can see the contents of that file. This file shows the entire list of host names and their addresses in the cs.berkeley.edu subdomain; this may be necessary if we can't remember the correct spelling of the host in that subdomain.

Of course, if all we needed was the address of a particular host in the cs.berkeley.edu domain, then we could have simply queried the cs.berkeley.edu server, without having to transfer the entire list. This is done next. The query could have also been answered by pilot itself. Lastly, we set the query to host information and find the kind of CPU and the operating system used by al.cs.berkeley.edu.

19.7.4 Walking Through a DNS Lookup

For a final illustration, let us sit in DNS's "driver seat" and look up information as DNS would. This will show how each domain delegates control and authority to its subdomains' nameservers, without requiring any nameserver to maintain full knowledge of the entire network. If we ask DNS to give the IP address of al.cs.berkeley.edu, it will give it to us directly. However, let us walk through the steps which DNS would to obtain its IP address.

At the top of Figure 19.20, we set the record type to NS (NameServer). This will display only such records for all queries which are made. As in Figure 19.19, we enter the root (".") domain and we are given its nameservers.

```
%nslookup
nslookup: command not found
%whereis nslookup
/usr/etc/nslookup
%/usr/etc/nslookup

Default Server: pilot.njin.net
Address:        128.6.7.38

>hardees.rutgers.edu
non-authoritative answer:
Name:   hardees.rutgers.edu
Address: 128.6.18.2

>set type=NS
>.
Default Server: pilot.njin.net
Address:        128.6.7.38

non-authoritative answers:
(root) nameserver = NS.NIC.DDN.MIL
(root) nameserver = Terp.UMD.EDU
(root) nameserver = NS.NASA.GOV
   :        :        :
authoritative answers can be found from:
NS.NIC.DDN.MIL inet addr. 192.112.36.4
Terp.UMD.EDU   inet addr. 128.8.10.90
NS.NASA.GOV    inet addr. 128.102.16.10
   :        :        :
>server terp.umd.edu
Default server: terp.umd.edu
Address:        128.8.10.90

>nasa.gov
Default server: terp.umd.edu
Address:        128.8.10.90
non-authoritative answers:
nasa.gov nameserver = NS.NASA.GOV
   :        :        :
authoritative servers can be found from:
NS.NASA.GOV inet addr. 128.102.16.10
NS.NASA.GOV inet addr. 192.52.195.10
   :        :        :
```

```
>berkeley.edu
   :        :        :
authoritative servers can be found from:
Vangogh.cs.Berkeley.edu  addr = 128.32.130.2
VIOLET.Berkeley.EDU inet addr =
128.32.136.22
UCBVAX.Berkeley.EDU inet addr =
128.32.133.1

>server vangogh.cs.berkeley.edu
Default Server: vangogh.cs.berkeley.edu
Address:        128.32.130.2

>cs.berkeley.edu
   :        :        :
ucbvax.berkeley.edu inet addr. = 128.32.130.12
ucbvax.berkeley.edu inet addr. = 128.32.149.36
vangogh.cs.berkeley.edu addr. = 128.32.130.2

>set type=A
>ls cs.berkeley.edu > ourfile
>view ourfile
CS      128.32.131.12
CS      server = ucbvax.Berkeley.edu
CS      server = vangogh.cs.berkeley.edu
acacia  128.32.131.120
adder   128.32.130.64
al      128.32.131.144
   :        :        :
>al.cs.berkeley.edu
Default server: cs.berkeley.edu
Address:        128.32.131.12

Name:           al.cs.berkeley.edu
address:        128.32.131.144

>set query=HINFO
>al.cs.berkeley.edu
Default server: cs.berkeley.edu
Address:        128.32.131.12

al.cs.berkeley.edu  CPU= ti/explorer, OS=lisp
```

Figure 19.19 An example of a session with **nslookup**.

Then we enter "edu." which provides us with the nameservers for the "edu" domain. These nameservers are the same as they are for the root domain. Note the dot (".") after the "edu." Out of the list provided for us, we choose ns.nic.ddn.mil as our nameserver for the edu domain by using the "server" command.

To this nameserver, we ask for the nameservers for the berkeley.edu domain. Out of the handful, we choose vangogh.cs.berkeley.edu as our server for the berkeley.edu domain. Then we query vangogh.cs.berkeley.edu for the nameservers for the

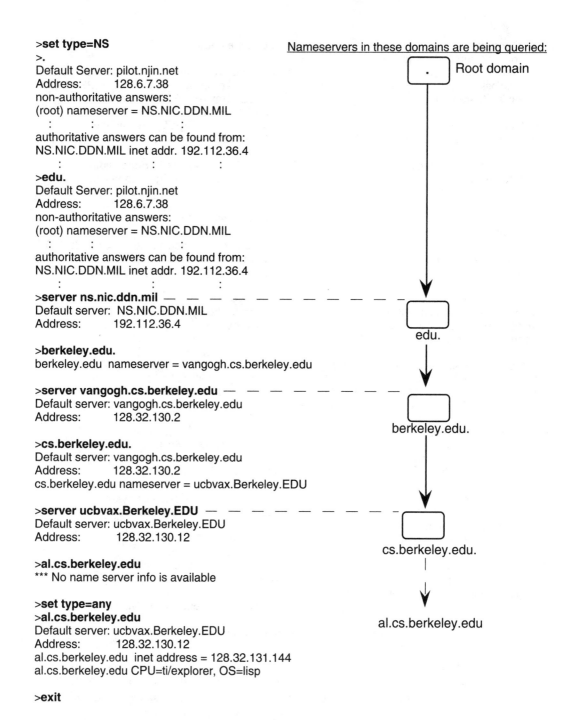

```
>set type=NS                                    Nameservers in these domains are being queried:
>.
Default Server: pilot.njin.net
Address:       128.6.7.38
non-authoritative answers:
(root) nameserver = NS.NIC.DDN.MIL
    :          :        :
authoritative answers can be found from:
NS.NIC.DDN.MIL inet addr. 192.112.36.4
    :          :        :
>edu.
Default Server: pilot.njin.net
Address:       128.6.7.38
non-authoritative answers:
(root) nameserver = NS.NIC.DDN.MIL
    :          :        :
authoritative answers can be found from:
NS.NIC.DDN.MIL inet addr. 192.112.36.4
    :          :        :
>server ns.nic.ddn.mil — — — — — — — — — —
Default server:  NS.NIC.DDN.MIL
Address:       192.112.36.4

>berkeley.edu.
berkeley.edu  nameserver = vangogh.cs.berkeley.edu

>server vangogh.cs.berkeley.edu — — — — — — —
Default server: vangogh.cs.berkeley.edu
Address:       128.32.130.2

>cs.berkeley.edu.
Default server: vangogh.cs.berkeley.edu
Address:       128.32.130.2
cs.berkeley.edu nameserver = ucbvax.Berkeley.EDU

>server ucbvax.Berkeley.EDU — — — — — — — —
Default server: ucbvax.Berkeley.EDU
Address:       128.32.130.12

>al.cs.berkeley.edu
*** No name server info is available

>set type=any
>al.cs.berkeley.edu
Default server: ucbvax.Berkeley.EDU
Address:       128.32.130.12
al.cs.berkeley.edu  inet address = 128.32.131.144
al.cs.berkeley.edu CPU=ti/explorer, OS=lisp

>exit
```

Figure 19.20 Doing a lookup for al.cs.berkeley.edu. Only one nameserver is shown per query.

cs.berkeley.edu domain and we are given ucbvax.berkeley.edu as one of the choices. Now we make it our nameserver to be queried and ask for the information about al.cs.berkeley.edu.

Here, we get an error message, because the record type is still set to NS from before and al.cs.berkeley.edu is not a domain, so it doesn't have nameservers. It is a host. Changing the record type to "any" we are then given the IP address among other information for that host. To end, we exit nslookup.

19.7.5 Reverse Lookups

Looking up a host's name based upon its IP address is a function very similar to normal host name lookups. In figure 19.21 we are looking for the host name which has an IP address of 134.115.4.1, a host in Australia. To find the name associated with the address 134.115.4.1, the nameserver library would form the name "1.4.115.134.IN-ADDR.ARPA." Note that the address is reversed, and is looked up under the domain IN-ADDR.ARPA—the "IN-ADDR" is "Internet Address."

When looking up the "IN-ADDR" name, a nameserver checks its cache for an address for the IN-ADDR.ARPA nameserver. If it's not there, it would contact the root nameserver. In the session with the IN-ADDR.ARPA nameserver, the local nameserver would request the nameserver for the 134.IN-ADDR.ARPA nameserver. When the local nameserver requests the nameserver for 115.134.IN-ADDR.ARPA, it would

```
>set type=any
>.
Default Server: pilot.njin.net
Address:       128.6.7.38
authoritative answers can be found from:
NSINTERNIC.NET inet addr.  198.41.0.4
   :        :                 :
>server 192.112.36.4
Default server: [198.41.0.4]
Address:       198.41.0.4
                       (Don't forget this dot.)
>in-addr.arpa.
Default server: [198.41.0.4]
Address:       198.41.0.4
*** No any type information is available . . .

>134.in-addr.arpa.
Default server: [198.41.0.4]
Address:       198.41.0.4

>115.134.in-addr.arpa.
Default server: [198.41.0.4]
Address:       198.41.0.4
115.134.in-addr.arpa
   nameserver=ns.adelaide.edu.au
```

```
>server ns.adelaide.edu.au
Default server: ns.adelaide.edu.au
served by:
   MUNNARI.OZ.AU
   128.250.1.21

>4.115.134.in-addr.arpa.
Default server: ns.adelaide.edu.au
served by:
   MUNNARI.OZ.AU
   128.250.1.21
4.115.134.in-addr.arpa
   nameserver=csuvax2.csu.murdoch.edu.au

>1.4.115.134.in-addr.arpa.
Default server: ns.adelaide.edu.au
served by:
   MUNNARI.OZ.AU
   128.250.1.21
1.4.115.134.in-addr.arpa.
   hostname=csuvax1.murdoch.edu.au

>exit
```

Figure 19.21 Doing a reverse lookup for 134.115.4.1

receive an "edu.au" address, since authority for the network 134.115 belongs to "edu.au." The local nameserver would continue on down to the 4.115.134.IN-ADDR.ARPA nameserver. When it asked for the namerserver for 1.4.115.134.IN-ADDR.ARPA nameserver, it would get an error—since there is no nameserver for it. It would then ask for the "PTR" record, and receive the information that 1.4.115.134.IN-ADDR.ARPA (the 134.115.4.1 address) has the name "csuvax1.murdoch.edu.au."

Just as there is a defined hierarchy for finding the addresses of machines given the names, there is a mirror hierarchy for finding the names of machines when the address is known.

Exercises

1. Which of the following is NOT a layer defined in the TCP/IP protocol architecture?
   a. data link   b. application
   c. internet   d. transport

2. What field in the datagram header specifies whether the data portion of the datagram goes to TCP or UDP?
   a. type of service   b. destination port
   c. protocol   d. destination address

3. If the TCP layer in a host receives an error in a segment, what does it do?
   a. It sends a NAK.
   b. It requests the transmitting process to reduce the window size.
   c. It simply waits until the segment is resent.
   d. It sets the ACK flag to 0.

4. What Unix command shows the files which are mounted?
   a. df   b. ls –l
   c. ln –s   d. cd

5. Which of the following is NOT a kind of a file transfer?
   a. telnet   b. Email
   c. NFS's rcopy   d. FTP

6. Which of the following classes of addresses do NOT use a host address field?
   a. class A   b. class B
   c. class C   d. class D

7. Which of the following commands show the state of the routing tables?
   a. netstat –ai   b. ifconfig le0
   c. netstat –r   d. route add

8. Which of the following items is NOT a server type used in the BIND software?
   a. resolver   b. caching-only
   c. primary   d. secondary

9. All data being processed through TCP/IP protocols must be processed by which layer?

10. Name the most important transport layer protocol which is unreliable.

11. A source socket is a combination of which two fields?

12. Which Unix command gives all directories which are NFS exportable?

13. Which character in Unix typically lists all commands available to the user?

14. Convert "c0.a0.d3.49" from hex to an IP dotted-decimal address.

15. For the address given in question 14, give its address class, the subnet address, and   the host address, if subnetting is done using the last 4 bits of the address.

16. Which command lists the gateways to a distant host?

17. What are some differences between the OSI reference model and the TCP/IP architecture?

18. Which commands use ICMP messages?

19. What is the purpose of the ARP protocol?

20. If you were given the choice, how would you increase the number of IP addresses available?

21. What are some flags which may be given when displaying a routing table and what do they mean?

22. What are some similarities and some differences between subnetworks and subdomains?

23. Explain what the loopback address is.

24. What set of commands allows one to see the address records at vangogh.cs.berkeley.edu?

Appendix A

Last Call for Soup

2B1Q	2 Binary, 1 Quaternary		ARS	Automatic Route Selection
4WTS	4-Wire Terminal Set		AS	Autonomous System
AAL	ATM Adaptation Layer		ASCII	American Standard Code for Information Interchange
AAR	Automatic Alternate Routing			
AA	Automated Attendant		ASR	Automated Speech Recognition
AC	Alternating Current		AT&T	American Telephone & Telegraph Co.
ACD	Automatic Call Distributor			
UCD	Uniform Call Distributor		ATM	Asynchronous Transfer Mode
ACP	Action Control Point		ATP	Application Transaction Program
ADM	Add and Drop Mux		AUI	Attachment Unit Interface
ADPCM	Adaptive Differential PCM		AWG	American Wire Guage
AFT	Analog Facility Terminal		B8ZS	Binary 8-Zero Suppression
AIN	Advanced Intelligent Network		BBN	Bolt, Beranek, and Newman
AMI	Alternate Mark Inversion		BCM	Bit Compression Mux
AMPS	Advanced Mobile Phone Service		BECN	Backward Explicit Congestion Notification
ANI	Automatic Number Identification			
ANSI	American National Standards Institute		Bellcore	BELL COmmunications REsearch
			BGP	Border Gateway Protocol
AP	Adjunct Processor (MCI)		BIND	Berkeley Internet Name Domain
AP	Action Point (SDN)		BIOS	Basic Input/Output System
API	Application Program Interface		BIU	Basic Information Unit
APPC	Advanced Program to Program Communications		BLU	Basic Link Unit
			BOC	Bell Operatin Company
APPN	Advanced Peer to Peer Networking		BPV	BiPolar Violation
APS	Automatic Protection Switching		BRI	Basic Rate Interface (2B + D)
ARP	Address Resolution Protocol		BSC	Binary Synchronous Communications
ARPANET	Advanced Research Projects Agency NETwork			
			BT	British Telecom

BTU	Basic Transmission Unit	CRC	Cyclic Redundancy Check
C/I	Carrier to Interference ratio	CS	Convergence Sublayer
CAD	Computer Aided Design	CSL	Component Sub-Layer
CAP	Competitive Access Providers	CSMA/CD	Carrier Sense Multiple Access with Collision Detection
CAS	Centralized Attendant Service (PBX)		
CAS	Channel Associated Signaling	CSMA/CR	CSMA with Collision Resolution
CCIR	International Radio Consultative Committee	CSS	Center-Stage Switch
		CSU	Channel Service Unit
CCIS	Common Channel Interoffice Signaling	CTDR	Customer Traffic Data Report
		DA	Destination Address
CCITT	Comité Consultatif Internationale de Telegraphiqué et Telephoniqué	DAC	Dual Attached Concentrator
		DACS	Digital Access and Cross-connect System
CCR	Customer Controlled Reconfiguration		
		DAL	Dedicated Access Line
CCS7	Common Channel Signaling 7	DAP	Data Access Point
CDMA	Code Division Multiple Access	DARPA	Defense Advanced Research Projects Agency
CDR	Call Detail Recording		
CD	Compact Disc	DAS	Dual Attached Station
CEPT	Conference on European Posts & Telecommunications	DATTS	Direct Access Trunk Test System
		Db	Decibel
CICS	Customer Information Control System	DC	Direct Current
		DCE	Data Communications Equipment
CID	Component IDentifier	DCP	Data Communications Protocol
CIR	Committed Information Rate	DCS	Distributed Communications System
CLASS	Custom Local Area Signaling Services	DDD	Direct Distance Dialing
		DDN	Digital Data Network
CLNS	ConnectionLess Network Service	DDN	Defense Data Network
CM	Configuration Management	DDS	Digital Data Service
CMA	Communications Managers Association	DDS	Dataphone Digital Services (AT&T's Digital Data Service)
CMB	Credit Manager Bandwidth	DE	Data Eligibility bit
CMC	Communications Management Center	DEC	Digital Equipment Corporation
		DECT	Digital European Cordless Telecommunications
CNAR	Customer Network Administration Report		
		DIA	Document Interchange Architecture
CNI	Common Network Interface	DID	Direct Inward Dialing
CNOS	Change Number Of Services	DIP	Dual In-line Package switch
CO	Central Office	DOD	Direct outward dialing
Codec	Coder-Decoder	DISA	Direct Inward System Access
COS	Class Of Service	DISC	DISConnect
CP	Cable Pair number	DLC	Digital Line Carrier
CPE	Customer Premises Equipment	DLCI	Data Link Control Identifier
CPU	Central Processor Unit	DM	Disconnect Mode
CPI	Computer-PBX Interface	DMI	Digital Multiplexed Interface
CPI	Common Programming Interface	DNHR	Dynamic Non-Hierarchical Routing

DNIC	Data Network Identification Code	FT1	Fractional T1
DNS	Domain Name Service	FTP	File Transfer Protocol
DoD	Department of Defense	FX	Foreign eXchange
DOS	Disk Operating System	FXO	Foreign eXchange, Office
DOV	Data Over voice	FXS	Foreign eXchange, Subscriber
DPC	Destination Point Code	GDS	Generalized Data Stream
DQDB	Distributed Queue Dual Bus	GFI	General Format Identifier
DR	Designated Router	GSM	Global System for Mobile communications
DS-0	Digital Signal, level 0	HDLC	High-level Data Link Control
DS-1	Digital Signal, level 1	HDSL	High-bit-rate Digital Subscriber Line
DSP	Digital Signal Processing	HEHO	Head-End Hop Off
DSU	Digital Service Unit	HIVR	Host Interactive Voice Response
DSX-1	Digital System cross-connect 1	HMDF	Horizontal Main Distribution Frame
DTE	Data Terminal Equipment	HMM	Hidden Markov Modeling
DTMF	Dual Tone Multi-Frequency	HPAD	Host Packet Assembler/Disassembler
DTW	Dynamic Time Warping	I/G	Individual/Group bit
DVCC	Digital Verification Color Code	I/O	Input/Output
EIA	Electronics Industries Association	IBM	International Business Machines Corp.
EGP	Exterior Gateway Protocol	ICMP	Internet Control Message Protocol
EKS	Electronic Key System	IDDD	International DDD
EMS	Element Management System	IDF	Intermediate Distribution Frame
EPN	Expansion Port Network	IEC	Inter Exchange Carrier
ES	End System	IEEE	Institute of Electrical and Electronics Engineers
ESF	Extende Super Frame		
ESN	Electronic Serial Number	IGP	Interior Gateway Protocol
ESS	Electronic Switching System	IMS	Information Management System
ETN	Electronic Tandem Network	IMT	Inter-Machine Trunk
FACCH	Fast Associated Control CHannel	IMTS	Improved Mobile Telephone Service
FCC	Federal Communications Commission	INMS	Integrated Network Management Systems
FCS	Frame Check Sequnce	INSITE	Integrated Network System Interface and Terminal Equipment
FDDI	Fiber Distributed Data Interface		
FDL	Facility Data Link	IP	Internet Protocol
FDM	Frequency Division Multiplex	IRM	Inherited Rights Mask
FDMA	Frquency Division Multiple Access	IS	Intermediate System
FDX	Full DupleX	IS-IS	IS to IS protocol
FECN	Forward Explicit Congestion Notification	ISDN	Integrated Services Digital Network
		ISO	International Organization for Standardization
FEP	Front End Processor		
FID	Format ID	ISSI	Inter-Switching System Interface
FISU	Fill-In Signal Unit	ISUP	ISdn User Part
FMH	Function Management Header	ITU	International Telecommunications Union
FOT	Fiber Optic Terminal		
FR	Frame Relay		
FRL	Facility Restriction Level		
FRMR	FRaMe Reject	IVDT	Integrated Voice/Data Terminal

IVR	Interactive Voice Response	MUA	Mail User Agent
IXC	IEC	MUX	MUltipleXer
JES	Job Entry Subsystem	MVS	Multiple Virtual Systems
KSU	Key System Unit	NANPA	North American Numbering Plan Administration
LAN	Local Area Network		
LAP/B	Link Access Procedure/Balanced	NAU	Network Addressable Unit
LAPD	Link Access Procedures over the D Channel	NAUN	Nearest Active Upstream Neighbor
		NCP	Network Control Program (SNA)
LAT	Local Area Transport	NCP	Network Control Point (PSTN)
LATA	Local Access and Transport Area	NEMOS	NEtwork Management Operation support System
LCI	Logical Channel Identifier		
LCR	Least Cost Routing	NetBIOS	Network BIOS
LED	Light Emitting Diode	NETCAP	NETwork CAPabilities manager
LEN	Low Entry Networking	NFS	Network File System
LESA	Local Exchange Switched Access	NIC	Network Interface Card
LLC	Logical Link Control	NID	Network Interface Device
LMU	Line Monitor Unit	NIMS	Network Information Management Systems
LOA	LOcal Address		
LORAN-C	LOng RAng Navigation-C	NIU	Network Interface Unit
LPC-RPE	Linear Predictive Encoding with Regular Pulse Excitation	NNI	Network-Network Interface
		NNMC	National Network Management Center
LSA	Link State Advertisement		
LSSU	Link Status Signaling Unit	NOC	Network Operations Center
LU	Logical Unit	NOS	Network Operating System
MAC	Media Access Control	NPSI	NCP(oint) Packet Switching Interface
MAN	Metropolitan Area Network		
MAU	Media Access Unit (Ethernet)	NRA	Network Remote Access
MAU	Multiple Access Unit (TRN)	NRAMS	NRA Monitoring System
MCI	Microwave Communications Inc.	NRZI	Non-Return to Zero Inverted
MCR	Mapped Conversation Record	NSC	Network Service Complex
MDA	Mail Delivery Agent	NSF	National Science Foundation
MDF	Main Distribution Frame	NT	Northern Telecom
MF	MultiFrequency	NT1/2	Network Termination 1 and 2
MFJ	Modified Final Judgment	NTI	Northern Telecom Inc.
MFS	Metropolitan Fiber Systems	OAI	Open architecture interface
MFT	Metallic Facility Terminal	OC-1	Optical Carrier, level 1
MIC	Media Interface Connector	OCU	Office Channel Unit
MID	Message ID	OE	Office Equipment designation
MSU	Message Signal Unit	OLTP	On-Line Transaction Processing
MTA	Mail Transfer Agent	OPC	Origination Point Code
MTP	Message Transfer Part	OPX	Off-Premise Extension
MTS	Message Telecommunications Service	OSI	Open Systems Interconnection
		OSPF	Open Shortest Path First
MTSO	Mobile Telecommunications Switching Office	OSS	Operation Support System
		PAD	Packet Assembler/Disassembler
MTTR	Mean Time To Repair	PBX	Private Branch eXchange

PC	Personal Computer	SDLC	Synchronous Data Link Control
PCM	Pulse Code Modulation	SEAL	Simple and Efficient Adaptation Layer
PCS	Personal Communications System		
PDN	Public Data Network	SF	Single Frequency
PDU	Protocol Data Unit	SIP	SMDS Interface Protocol
PIU	Path Information Unit	SIVR	Speech Independent Voice Recognition
PLCP	Physical Unit Control Point		
PLU	Primary Logical Unit	SLC-96	Subscriber Line Carrier
PMD	Physical Medium Dependent	SLS	Signaling Link Selection
POP	Point of Presence	SLU	Secondary LU
POTS	Plain Old Telephone Service	SMDR	Station Message Detail Recording
PPN	Processor Port Network	SMDS	Switched Multi-megabit Digital Service
PRI	Primary Rate Interface (23B or 30B + D)		
		SMS	Service Management System
PSTN	Public Switched Telephone Network	SMTP	Simple Mail Transfer Protocol
PTT	Postal, Telephone, and Telegraph	SNA	Systems Network Architecture
PU	Physical Unit	SNADS	SNA Distributed Services
PUC	Public Utility Commission	SNF	Segment Number Field
PVC	Private Virtual Circuit	SNI	Subscriber Network Interface
QLLC	Qualified Logical Link Control	SNID	Smart NID
RBOC	Regional BOC	SONET	Synchronous Optical NETwork
RDPS	Reverse Direction Protection Switching	SP	Signaling Point
		SPARC	Scalable Processor ARChitecture
RFC	Request For Comments	SPC	Stored Program Control
RH	Request/response Header	SPE	Synchronous Payload Envelope
RIF	Routing Information Field	SRDM	Sub-Rate Data Multiplexing
RIP	Routing Information Protocol	SS	SMDS Switching system
RTNR	Real Time Network Routing	SS7	Signaling System 7
RU	Request/response Unit	SSCP	System Services Control Point
SABM	Set Asynchronous Balanced Mode	SSP	Signal Service Point
SAC	Serving Area Concept (PSTN)	STE	Signaling Terminal Equipment
SAC	Single Attached Concentrator (FDDI)	STP	Signal Transfer Point (PSTN)
SACCH	Slow Associated Control CHannel	STP	Shielded Twisted Pair (LANs)
SAP	Service Access Point	STS	Synchronous Transport Signal
SAPI	SAP Identifier	SU	Signaling Unit
SAR	Segmentation And Reassembly	TA	Terminal Adapter
SAS	Single Attached Station	TCAP	Transaction Capabilities Application Part
SBS	Satellite Business Systems		
SCCP	Signaling Connection Control Part	TCP	Transmission Control Protocol
SCM	Service Control Manager	TDM	Time Division Multiplex
SCP	Service Control Point	TDMA	Time Division Multiple Access
SCPMS	SCP Management System	TE	Terminal Equipment (1 or 2)
SDDN	Software Defined Data Network	TEHO	Tail-End Hop Off
SDN	Software Defined Network	TEI	Terminal Endpoint Identifier
SDNCC	SDN Control Center	Telco	TELephone COmpany

TFTP	Trivial File Transfer Protocol	UNMA	Unified Network Management Architecture
TG	Transmission Group	UTP	Unshielded Twisted Pair
TH	Transmission Header	VAN	Value Added Network
THT	Token Holding Timer	VCI	Virtual Channel Identifier
TIC	Token Ring Interface Card	VINES	VIrtual NEtwork System
TN	Terminal Number	VLSI	Very Large Scale Integration
TP	Transaction Program	VMDF	Vertical MDF
TP	TeleProcessing	VPDS	Virtual Private Data Service
TPAD	Terminal PAD	VPI	Virtual Path Identifier
TRN	Token Ring Network	VPN	Virtual Private Network
TSL	Transaction Sub-Layer	VR	Voice Recognition
TSO	Time Sharing Option	VSAT	Very Small Aperture Terminal
TTL	Time To Live	VSELP	Vector Sum Excited Linear Prediction
TTRT	Target Token Rotation Time	VT	Virtual Tributary
TTS	Text-To-Speech	VTAM	Virtual Telecommunications Access Method
TVX	Valid Transmission Timer		
U/L	Universal or Local	WAL	WATS Access Link
UA	Unnumbered Acknowledge	WAN	Wide Area Network
UCD	Uniform Call Distributor	WATS	Wide Area Telecommunications Service
UDP	User Datagram Protocol		
UN	United Nations		
UNI	User to Network Interface		

Below, Table A shows many of the metric prefixes. To use them, simply substitute their correct value. For example, 700 kHz is the same as 700 times 10^{+3} Hz or 700,000 Hz and 200 msec is 200 times 10^{-3} seconds or 0.200 seconds

Table A: Metric Prefixes		
Prefix	Meaning	Value (in powers of 10)
T	Tera	+12
G	Giga	+9
M	Mega	+6
k	kilo	+3
–	–	0
m	milli	−3
μ	micro	−6
n	nano	−9
p	pico	−12

Index